D1599023

Judaism and the Gentiles

Judaism and the Gentiles

Jewish Patterns of Universalism (to 135 CE)

Terence L. Donaldson

Baylor University Press

Waco, Texas 76798

Cover Design by Joan Osth
Composition by Scribe, Inc.

Library of Congress Cataloging-in-Publication Data

Donaldson, Terence L.
Judaism and the Gentiles : Jewish patterns of universalism (to 135 CE) / Terence L. Donaldson.
p. cm.
Includes bibliographical references and index.
ISBN 978-1-60258-025-1 (pbk. : alk. paper)
1. Gentiles. 2. Judaism—Relations. 3. Universalism. 4. Judaism—History—Post-exilic period, 586 B.C.-210 A.D. 5. Jews—History—168 B.C.-135 A.D. 6. Greek literature, Hellenistic—History and criticism. 7. Latin literature—History and criticism. I. Title.

BM720.N6D66 2007
296.3'909014—dc22

2007034702

Printed in the United States of America on acid-free paper with a minimum of 30% pcw recycled content.

To Chester and Marion Donaldson
my parents and first teachers

CONTENTS

Preface

For a long time now—indeed, for much of my scholarly life—I have been interested in the kinds of texts discussed in this book and the phenomena they reflect. In conjunction with various projects over the years I have worked on different subsets of them and in so doing began to build up a substantial database of texts dealing with what I have come to call Jewish patterns of universalism. This book, then, is the product—or perhaps by-product—of a long process of study and reflection.

The book itself is both more and less than I had envisioned it at various stages in the process. Initially, after I had completed my *Paul and the Gentiles*, I thought I might prepare a kind of sourcebook in which I would present the texts in translation (and perhaps in their original languages), with bibliographic and other reference information, but with only a brief introduction. On reflection, however, I came to the conclusion that more was needed. For one thing, many of the texts present significant interpretive problems that require discussion; for another, in the scholarly discussion of these problems, the texts are often treated as isolated entities, with inadequate attention to the larger contexts in which they are properly to be seen. Consequently, I conceived of a work that would assemble all the primary evidence into a single collection, provide a detailed analysis of each piece of evidence in its larger literary or (in the case of the few pertinent inscriptions) archaeological context, and conclude with a synthesis of the various Jewish patterns of universalism.

This is essentially the book that emerged, but in order to keep it to a (somewhat!) reasonable length it became necessary to contract its scope. I settled on a *terminus ad quem* of 135 CE (i.e., the end of the Bar Cochba revolt), which left some sets of pertinent texts out of consideration (rabbinic, Christian, inscriptional). I also decided to exclude texts that pertained to the topic of universalism in a secondary way—specifically those that assigned to Israel or to the Torah some positive role with respect to the other nations (light, priesthood, etc.) but did not deal directly with the nations themselves—and those that categorically excluded Gentiles from any positive relationship with Israel's God.

Further, the decision to concentrate on texts that dealt more or less directly with the religious status of Gentiles means that other pertinent evidence (e.g., having to do with the social realities of life in the Diaspora or with the structure and functions of the synagogue) or issues (how to move from texts to social realities) could not receive detailed focal attention. In other words, this is not an exhaustive study of "Judaism and the Gentiles" or of "Jewish patterns of universalism." Nevertheless, I believe that it makes a needed contribution to such a study and hope that others will find it useful.

While scholars often work in solitude, scholarly work is not a solitary enterprise; we are necessarily dependent on the work and support of others. I am acutely aware of my own dependence and would like to acknowledge this by expressing my thanks to a number of people and institutions.

A glance at the author index will provide some measure of the debt that I owe to a large company of scholars from whom I have learned much and whose work has undergirded or intersected with my own. In particular, I would like to thank a number of colleagues who at various points along the way have provided particular encouragement for this project (sometimes without realizing it); I think especially of Shaye Cohen, Paula Fredriksen, Lloyd Gaston (may he rest in peace), Lester Grabbe, Robert Jewett, Mark Nanos, Steve Notley, Anders Runesson, Peter Richardson, Alan Segal, and Steve Wilson. I am also appreciative of the students over the past eight years who have taken my graduate seminar "Readings in Jewish Literature" and whose engagements with some of these texts has helped me to sharpen my own thinking.

Over the same period several students have provided valuable assistance with the project. Murray Baker entered many texts into the database and carried out very helpful research into some of them. Ryan Wettlaufer painstakingly checked all quotations of and references to the ancient source material, catching many errors and saving me from several embarrassments in the process. (If any errors remain, they are to be charged to my account.) More recently, Graeme Donaldson helped me meet a deadline by checking the whole manuscript against the first draft of the bibliography. A research grant from the Social Sciences and Humanities Research Council of Canada (2001–2005) provided very welcome funding that allowed me to hire student assistants (as well as supporting my research in other ways).

I am also very appreciative of the support provided by the institutional context in which I work. Wycliffe College granted me a sabbatical in the fall of 2002—a period of concentration in which I was able to decide on the shape of the project as a whole and to make significant advances in several parts of it. Wycliffe is part of a larger consortium of theological schools (the Toronto School of Theology), which in turn is affiliated with and located on the campus of the University of Toronto. One could not ask for a richer scholarly environment—bright students, stimulating colleagues, supportive institutional infrastructure, and a superb library system. With respect to the latter, despite the size and arcane character of my bibliography, I could count on my thumbs the number of times I have had to acquire books through interlibrary loan.

In addition, I am very grateful to Carey Newman and Baylor University Press—for the alacrity with which he responded to my initial overture, for the enthusiasm he conveyed for the project from the beginning, and for the efficiency with which he and his team have worked with a long and complex manuscript and readied it for publication. It has been a real pleasure to work with him, with the BUP staff (Laura Barth, Stacy Buford, Diane Smith, Laura Stewart, and Myles Werntz), and with the team at Scribe (Mark Fretz and Henry Whitney).

Finally, I want to thank my family for their continued love and support: Graeme, Meredith and David, who also know the pleasures and challenges of scholarly endeavor and who add joy to my life; and Lois, who brings wisdom, integrity, and optimism to all that she does. In addition, I would like to thank my parents, who in their own way instilled in me an interest in Judaism and the Gentiles. This book is dedicated to them.

ACKNOWLEDGMENTS

Some portions of chapters 2 and 3 have appeared in another form in my article "Royal Sympathizers in Jewish Narrative," *Journal for the Study of the Pseudepigrapha* 16 (2006), 41–59 (copyright 2006 by Sage Publications, Inc.). The material is reprinted here by permission of Sage Publications.

A portion of chapter 9 appeared in my chapter "Jerusalem Ossuary Inscriptions and the Status of Jewish Proselytes," pages 372–88 in *Text and Artifact in the Religions of Mediterranean Antiquity: Essays in Honour of Peter Richardson*, edited by Stephen G. Wilson and Michel Desjardins (ESCJ 9; Waterloo, Ont.: Wilfrid Laurier University Press, 2000). It is reprinted here by permission of Wilfrid Laurier University Press.

Abbreviations

In matters of style, including abbreviations, I have followed *The SBL Handbook of Style* (Peabody, Mass.: Hendrickson, 1999). Since I have chosen an author-date format for citations, abbreviations have been kept to a minimum. Where texts or translations have been drawn from standard multi-author reference works and other resources, I have used an abbreviation in addition to the author-date reference. These abbreviations, together with one or two not included in the handbook, are listed below.

APOT	*The Apocrypha and Pseudepigrapha of the Old Testament.* Edited by R. H. Charles. 2 vols. Oxford: Clarendon Press, 1913.
BDB	F. Brown, S. R. Driver and C. A. Briggs. *A Hebrew and English Lexicon of the Old Testament.* Oxford: Clarendon Press, 1953.
BHS	*Biblia Hebraica Stuttgartensia.* Edited by K. Elliger and W. Rudolph. Stuttgart: Deutsche Bibelstiftung, 1977.
CIG	*Corpus Inscriptionum Graecarum.* Edited by A. Boeckh. 4 vols. Berlin: G. Reimarus, 1828–1877.
CIJ	*Corpus Inscriptionum Judaicarum.* Edited by J.-B. Frey. 2 vols. Rome: Pontificio Istituto di Archeologia Cristiana, 1936, 1952.
CIRB	*Corpus Inscriptionum Regni Bosporani.* Edited by Vasili Vasilevich Struve et al. Leningrad: Akademia nauk SSSR, Institut istorii, 1965.
DJD	*Discoveries in the Judaean Desert.* 39 vols. Oxford: Oxford University Press, 1951–2002.

ESCJ	Studies in Christianity and Judaism/Études sur le christianisme et le judaïsme.
JIWE	*Jewish Inscriptions of Western Europe.* Edited by David Noy. 2 vols. Cambridge: Cambridge University Press, 1993, 1995.
LCL	Loeb Classical Library.
LXX	*Septuaginta.* Edited by A. Rahlfs. 2 vols. Stuttgart: Deutsche Bibelgesellschaft, 1979.
MAMA	*Monumenta Asiae Minoris Antiqua.* Edited by W. M. Calder. 10 vols. Manchester: Manchester University Press, 1928–1988.
Nestle-Aland 27th ed.	Eberhard Nestle, Barbara Aland, et al. *Novum Testamentum Graece.* 27th ed. Stuttgart: Deutsche Bibelgesellschaft, 1979.
NRSV	New Revised Standard Version
OTP	*Old Testament Pseudepigrapha.* Edited by James H. Charlesworth. 2 vols. Garden City, N.Y.: Doubleday, 1983, 1985.
Pauly-Wissowa	*Paulys Realencyclopädie der classischen Altertumswissenschaft.* Edited by A. F. Pauly and G. Wissowa.
SEG	*Supplementum epigraphicum graecum.* Edited by H. W. Pleket, R. S. Stroud et al. Alphen aan den Rijn: Sijthoff & Noordhoff, 1923–.
SGDI	*Sammlung der griechischen Dialekt-Inschriften.* Edited by Hermann Collitz et al. Göttingen: Vandenhoeck & Ruprecht, 1884–1915.
TDNT	*Theological Dictionary of the New Testament.* Edited by G. Kittel et al. 10 vols. Grand Rapids: Eerdmans, 1964–1976.

CHAPTER 1

INTRODUCTION

In an older form of (largely Christian) scholarship, Judaism in the Second Temple period and beyond was routinely characterized as particularistic, a term defined and given pejorative force by means of a contrast drawn with Christianity. In this definition of terms, Christianity was universalistic precisely by virtue of its ability to break through the ethnic and religious restrictions of Judaism and thus to become an inclusive, worldwide religion. Such a characterization of Judaism, however, is unfair and tendentious and is increasingly being seen as such.[1] During this period Judaism was in its own ways just as "universalistic" as was Christianity—indeed, in some ways even more so. The purpose of this book, to be described more precisely as we proceed, is to demonstrate this aspect of Judaism by documenting and exploring the various Jewish "patterns of universalism" that can be identified in this period.

To begin by putting the issue into its broader context, questions concerning the religious status of non-Jewish nations and people were unavoidable for Jews in the Greco-Roman world. For one thing, their own self-defining story tended to provoke such questions. Despite significant differences in interpretation and outlook, Jews everywhere identified themselves with reference to the biblical narrative, a narrative in which the cosmic and universal is oddly intertwined with the national and particular. On one hand, Jews understood their God to be the one, universal deity, a God who had created the whole world and

1. For descriptions and criticism of this older approach, see, e.g., Balch (1998, 24); Boccaccini (1991, 251); Feldman (1992, 24); Runesson (1999).

who continued to exercise sovereignty over the created order and all the nations within it. On the other, Jews believed that this God had chosen them out of all the nations of the world to be a special people, that the will and the ways of this God had been revealed uniquely in Israel's scripture, that the God who had created the cosmos was nevertheless uniquely present in the Jerusalem temple, and that despite the Jews' temporal misfortunes, eventually Israel would be vindicated and exalted to a position of preeminence over all other nations. Jews could not tell their own national story without reference to the other nations, and if perhaps it was possible to narrate the story in such a way that the nations functioned simply as a foil for Israel, the story itself contained at least latent questions about the relationship between these other nations and the God who had created them.

In addition to this intrinsic factor, several other factors of a more extrinsic character tended to force these latent questions out into the open. One of them was Israel's actual experience, which in various ways forced them to negotiate emergent tensions between their self-identifying story, in which the nations played their assigned roles, and their ongoing encounters with non-Jewish people and nations. This was especially the case in the Diaspora, where Jews interacted daily with their non-Jewish neighbors and where Jewish communities in many cases had achieved a comfortable *modus vivendi* in the midst of Gentile cities. To the extent that these interactions were positive, as they often were, Jews were prompted to ask whether and on what terms Gentiles might come into a positive relationship with Israel's God. And even when their actual experiences with Gentile nations were more painful and distressing, many Jews could not help but dream of an ideal or future world in which Gentiles might recognize the truth and, in one way or another, come to worship the God of Israel.

But the factors forcing the questions were not restricted to Jewish circles. Various attitudes and actions on the part of Gentiles themselves also compelled Jews to consider the matter. Most important here is the phenomenon of Gentile attraction to Judaism. Many Gentiles found Jewish belief, practice, and communal life to be very appealing; and not a few of them were prepared, to greater or lesser extents, to adopt Jewish ways and to attach themselves to the Jewish community. Evidence for such attraction is widespread, from Seneca's lament[2] to Josephus's boast[3] and many points in between. In such circumstances, the religious status of the "other" could scarcely be disregarded, especially for a people whose self-identity was so bound up with their own sense of religious otherness.

2. "Meanwhile the customs of this accursed race have gained such influence that they are now received throughout all the world; the vanquished have given laws to the victors" (Seneca *On Superstition*, preserved in Augustine *City of God* 6.11).

3. "The masses have long since shown a keen desire to adopt our religious observances; and there is not one city, Greek or barbarian, nor a single nation to which our custom[s] . . . ha[ve] not spread" (Josephus *Ag. Ap.* 2.282).

But a similar result could also be generated by the opposite impetus, that is, by Gentile criticism of Jewish religion. It was not coincidental that Josephus's most emphatic statements about Jewish willingness to include Gentiles are to be found in the treatise *Against Apion*, his response to Apion and other Hellenistic critics who wrote disparagingly of what they perceived to be Jewish exclusivity and misanthropy. For several reasons, then, Jews in the Second Temple period found it necessary to give thought to the religious status and ultimate fate of the Gentiles.

To be sure, while the issue could not be avoided, it tended not to be a defining issue, in the sense that it raised fundamental and divisive questions about Jewish identity and self-understanding. By way of contrast, the question of the extent to which Jews could adopt Gentile ways or accommodate their common life to the wider non-Jewish world *was* such a defining issue; one thinks of the Maccabean revolt and its aftermath or of the two wars with Rome. But the question of whether and in what way Gentiles could have a positive share in the religious dimensions of Jewish existence was not. One indication of this is that, while there is considerable evidence for a range of Jewish opinion on the issue, evidence for actual debate is much more limited. Explicit clashes of opinion are rare, and those that do appear in the literature—such as that between R. Joshua and R. Eliezer in *t. Sanh.* 13.2 or between Ananias and Eleazar in *Ant.* 20.41–47—are restricted in their scope.[4] Related to this is the fact that the differences of opinion on the issue do not tend to line up with any of the more fundamental debates and divisions within the Judaism of the later Second Temple period. Although some patterns are discernible, the various opinions cannot be correlated exclusively or distinctively with identifiable groups (Pharisees, Sadducees, Essenes, etc.), geographical regions (Diaspora, Judea), degrees of Hellenization, literary genres (e.g., apocalyptic, wisdom), or the like.

Even if it was not a defining issue, however, the sheer volume of pertinent extant material indicates that it was of widespread interest and concern. But while the question could not be avoided, the answer was by no means readily apparent. Although Israel's self-defining story could not be told without manifold reference to the nations, the story itself provided no normative indication of their religious status and, more specifically, no indication of how they might enter into a positive relationship with Israel's God. Indeed, some aspects of the question could not even be posed in the same way in the biblical period. As we will see in more detail later in this chapter, it was not until the Hellenistic period that it was even possible to think of ethnic identity as a culture that an outsider could adopt or as a citizenship that a foreigner could assume. For the biblical writers in the period prior to this, religion and ethnic identity tended

4. Evidence of debate and conflict over the terms on which to include Gentiles is much more forthcoming from early Jewish Christianity than from Judaism itself; further, in passages such as Acts 15 and Galatians 2 a greater range of opinions and positions is on display.

to be coterminous. Israel's religion was restricted to members of the *ethnos* Israel; the only way in which a person could become part of Israel was by birth. The idea of conversion or proselytism, which became such a significant factor in the Greco-Roman period, was simply not a conceivable option.

Still, the idea of proselytism when it did develop was significantly influenced by a biblical model, that of the resident alien (גר), who was incorporated into the social and religious life of Israel in significant ways.[5] This is one instance of several ways in which Israel's scripture provided raw material for attempts to deal with the question of the Gentiles and their religious status. Indeed, each of the positions that will be documented in this study could—and in many cases did—appeal to scripture for support. Thus while Israel's tradition did not provide a normative answer to the question, it certainly opened up a number of possibilities, ranging along a spectrum from the harsh exclusion of *Jub.* 15:25–26 to the generous quasi-pluralism of *Let. Aris.* 16. That portion of the spectrum in which we encounter a positive attitude toward Gentiles—that is, in which the Gentiles are able, in one way or another, to relate positively to the God of Israel and to share somehow in Israel's ultimate destiny—I am describing as "universalistic." Within this portion of the spectrum, we can identify several different construals of the relationship between Gentiles and the God of Israel; these I am calling "patterns of universalism." The goal of this work, then, is to identify and document these various Jewish patterns of universalism.

In modern religious dialogue and scholarship, of course, "universalism" tends to refer to approaches that ascribe legitimacy to the religious "other" without requiring conversion. A religion in which conversion is the only option is particularistic rather than universalistic. Since one of the patterns of universalism that will be examined here is conversion or proselytism, my choice of the term requires some justification. One reason for speaking of Jewish "universalism" is that, as already has been noted, the term has been used in the past to compare Judaism unfavorably with Christianity. In other words, this work is a contribution to a discussion in which the term is already well established. Another reason is that in three of the four main patterns that will be identified Gentiles are accorded a positive place in the divine scheme of things without having to convert to Judaism. In these instances, at least, "universalism" is being used in a manner similar to its use in contemporary study of religion.[6] Further, while conversion is not generally seen as a form of universalism in contemporary discourse, our interest here is the world of late

5. See ch. 11.

6. If we subdivide universalistic religions into those that ascribe full legitimacy to other religions as independent entities (pluralistic) and those that somehow see other religions as included within a single construction of religious reality in which their own is primary or central (inclusivistic), then within Judaism we can find examples of both inclusivism (chs. 11 and 14) and, to some degree at least, pluralism (ch. 13).

antiquity, a world in which proselytism represented a striking step in a universalistic direction. As has already been mentioned, in a world where religion had traditionally been embedded in the constitutive domains of a tribe or a people, the idea that religious identity was something that could be adopted was a significant innovation. Thus while the limitations of the term are not to be overlooked, "universalism" nevertheless is an appropriate way to describe our subject of interest.

While we are on the topic of terminology, a word is in order about "Gentiles." The term derives from the Latin *gens*, nation, and receives its sense of "non-Jew" from the fact that in biblical tradition "nations" (גוים, ἔθνη) was commonly used to refer to the nations other than Israel. In time the term came to apply not only to non-Jewish nations but also to individuals. The term is thus one that has meaning only in a Jewish frame of reference. Non-Jews would not ordinarily think of themselves as "Gentiles," unless they were associated in some way with the Jewish world. Further, as will become readily apparent before we have proceeded very far into our study, this was by no means the only term that was used in Jewish discourse.[7] Thus "Gentile" is to be seen as a term of convenience. It is not inappropriate, in that it derives from Jewish usage. But this sense of the term was restricted to the linguistic world of the Jews and, even there, existed alongside other terms. As we carry out our purpose in this study, we will need to guard against the possibility that convenience will engender an artificial sense of uniformity.

Our purpose is further complicated by a number of related issues that emerge from the material under discussion and that have received significant scholarly attention. Although it lies beyond the scope of this work to carry out any thorough and free-standing examination of these issues, in order to accomplish the primary goal it will be necessary to give second-level attention to each of them along the way. Here I will simply identify and describe the most important of them, leaving any discussion of the primary and secondary material until the appropriate points in the chapters to follow.

Was Judaism a missionary religion? Jewish communities may have attracted a penumbra of admirers, sympathizers, and adherents, some of whom even became full converts, but to what extent was this the result of deliberate initiative by Jews to search out and encourage such sympathetic Gentiles? A range of positions have been taken on the issue: some have perceived Judaism as engaging in a vigorous mission;[8] others have denied it just as emphatically;[9] others

7. See the discussion of vocabulary and terminology in ch. 10.

8. Bamberger (1968); Braude (1940); Boccaccini (1991, 252); Feldman (1992; 1993, 106, 289–93); Georgi (1986); Harnack (1908, 9); G. Moore (1927–1930, 1.323–24); Schürer (1986, 3:160).

9. Goodman (1992; 1994); Kraabel (1982); McKnight (1991); Munck (1959, 264–71); Will and Orrieux (1992).

have emphasized Gentile initiative, thinking in terms of centripetal attraction rather than centrifugal mission;[10] others have portrayed the Jewish attitude as passive acceptance at best; and still others have emphasized diversity, the answer varying with different groups and different geographical locations.[11] The discussion of the question has been inextricably linked with Christian origins, both because scholars tend to assume that Christianity provides the model of a missionary religion *par excellence* and because the emergence of a universal Christian mission is often accounted for on the basis of, or in contrast to, patterns presumed to have already been present within Judaism. But partly because of this the question is often bedeviled by extraneous issues and assumptions. For one thing, common depictions of the early Christian "mission" (as centrally organized, concerted, carried out by designated missionaries) require significant re-examination.[12] What is assumed when the question of a "missionary religion" is posed may have more to do with models of Christian mission in the modern period than with anything that might have happened in the early decades or centuries of the church. For another, answers to the question have been affected by cultural assumptions. In an era when mission was seen as a positive thing and an indication of a "universalistic" outlook, Christian and Jewish scholars tended to emphasize the missionary credentials of their own forebears. In our own pluralistic environment, when aggressive proselytism is seen by many as distasteful[13] and when partisan historiography is frowned upon, there is a disinclination either to claim the label "mission" for one's own tradition or to attach it to that of someone else. Recent attempts to provide a more scientific typology of different types of mission will help move the discussion forward,[14] but much work remains to be done.

Was Jewish apologetic literature really addressed to a Gentile readership, or was it primarily intended for internal consumption? This question overlaps considerably with the previous one. There is a considerable body of Jewish literature written in Greek that seeks to present Jewish tradition in Hellenistic forms and terms (e.g., *Sibylline Oracles*) or that otherwise attempts to engage the wider

10. In addition to those cited in the previous note, see Barclay (1996); Dickson (2003, 11–85); Cohen (1987b, 56–58; 1992); Hengel and Schwemer (1997, 61–62); Wander (1998).

11. Barclay (1996, 317, n. 89); Cohen (1987b, 56–57; 1992); J. J. Collins (2000, 262–63); Mason (1996, 187).

12. On this point see MacMullen (1984, 33–35).

13. For an intriguing discussion of how the activity denoted by "proselytism" has shifted from that of the convert (who "comes to" [πρός + ἔρχομαι] the new religion) to that of those who aggressively seek out converts, see Will and Orrieux (1992, 25–49).

14. Cohen (1992, 14–15); Dickson (2003, 11–85); Goodman (1994, 3–5); Wander (1998, 221–23).

Greco-Roman world (e.g., Philo). Some of it even addresses a non-Jewish readership explicitly—for example, Josephus's *Against Apion*, addressed to Epaphroditus and, reading over his shoulder, "all who desire to know the truth concerning the antiquity of our race" (*Ag. Ap.* 1:3); or the *Letter of Aristeas*, purportedly written by a Gentile sympathizer (Aristeas) to his brother Philocrates. Taken at face value, this literature could readily be understood as part of a concerted Jewish attempt to enlarge the penumbra of adherents and converts, or at least to cultivate a more sympathetic disposition among literate outsiders. But form and function do not necessarily line up so neatly. Such literature could just as easily have been written to allay the anxieties and confirm the identity of Jewish readers who, existing in a bi-cultural environment and being pulled in different directions by loyalty to Jewish tradition on the one hand and the blandishments of the surrounding culture on the other, were in need of just such reassurance.[15] While the question is not easily answered, how we answer it will have a significant impact on our interpretation of the literature, just as a failure to take it into account will run the risk of allowing unexamined assumptions to skew the interpretive process.

Was there a class of Gentile sympathizers (known, for example, as "God-fearers") who adopted some aspects of Judaism without becoming full converts and who were granted some form of official recognition by the Jewish community? There can be little doubt that Gentile sympathizers did exist, though legitimate questions can be raised about the size and extent of the group. But this question goes beyond mere existence to ask about Jewish attitudes and policies toward such people.[16] The question actually can be subdivided into two. First, we can ask about the existence of a recognized class. From the Jewish perspective, was this just an amorphous group of curious and sympathetic outsiders, or did they form a recognized group with some established status within or in relationship to the Jewish community? If the latter, what did it take to become a member of this group? How much of the Jewish way of life and set of beliefs did a Gentile need to take on board? How much of their native culture and religion would such Gentiles need to leave behind? Further, what was the religious status of

15. Those who see Jews as engaged in a concerted mission to Gentiles understand this literature as having been written to support this venture. Tcherikover (1959) has argued strongly for an internal intended audience; see also Gruen (1998; 2002).

16. Even to pose this question, however, is to raise another that should be kept in view. Jewish attitudes were not the only ones in play. Any inquiry into the status and identity of Gentile sympathizers needs to recognize a multiplicity of perspectives. The phenomenon was open to view by various interested parties—the Jewish community, the Gentile sympathizers themselves, their families and friends, the wider non-Jewish world—each of whom may well have had their own differing perceptions of the situation. Gentile outsiders, for example, may have seen a single class where Jews saw several; or they may have had different perceptions of the point at which someone had "become a Jew." See Cohen (1999, 13).

such a group, if indeed it did exist? To what extent were they allowed to participate in the life of the Jewish community? Were they perceived as just potential converts, or was the perception that in their present situation they enjoyed some positive religious status or stood in some positive relationship with Israel's God? The second subdivision of the primary question has to do with nomenclature. Were there specific terms to designate such a group? Or, turning the question around, were such terms as do exist—for example, "God-fearers" (φοβούμενοι τὸν θεόν, *metuens*) or "God-worshippers" (σεβόμενοι τὸν θεόν, θεοσεβεῖς)—used as technical or quasi-technical terms to refer to such a recognized class of people? The questions, which have been hotly debated, have a direct bearing on our investigation and thus will need to be considered in detail.[17]

What connections are there between textual image and social reality? This, of course, is a perennial question, one encountered by anyone who attempts to use literary documents as a source of raw material for historical reconstruction. When the fictional Gentile sympathizer Aristeas tells the king that Zeus is just another name for the same God who is worshipped by the Jews (*Let. Aris.* 16), are we to imagine that there were Jews who believed this or who would have applauded Gentiles who did? When the author of Judith tells us that Achior the Ammonite "believed firmly in God, was circumcised and joined the house of Israel, remaining so to this day" (Jdt 14:10), are we to understand this as a common occurrence in the experience of the intended readers, as something that the author wanted to encourage, or simply as a narrative device to heighten the vindication of Israel through the clever piety of Judith? What is the relationship between the world projected by such narratives and other literary works, and the social realities of the world inhabited by their authors and intended readers? The questions are as difficult as they are important, and there certainly are no global and ready-made answers that we can import into our investigation. But such questions need to be recognized and incorporated into the examination of each piece of textual evidence.

Finally, *should we conceive of Judaism as a single organic whole despite its variations, or as a set of distinct socio-religious entities despite its common history and traditions?* Can we talk of "Judaism" or, as is increasingly the case, is it necessary to speak instead of "Judaisms"? To a certain extent, the answer is a matter of perspective and definition. On the one hand, it is not without significance that Greek and Roman writers tend to view "the Jews" as a single entity; only rarely do we encounter finer distinctions, such as Pliny's recognition of the Essenes as a distinct group, which in any case does not affect his overall perception of the Jewish people as a whole (Feldman 1993, 45). On the other hand, one cannot help but think that Philo and the author of *Jubilees* occupied symbolic worlds

17. See the section on Luke-Acts in ch. 8 and also ch. 10.

that were quite distinct and hardly compatible. Given the nature of this study, which will consist largely of a case-by-case study of the evidence (on which more presently), it will be both appropriate and prudent to leave the issue open until all the evidence is examined. Our procedure will be to take each passage, document, or inscription as evidence for its own time and place, to be open to the possibility of sociological, temporal, and geographical variation, and not to assume that what was true in one instance is necessarily valid in another. At the end it will be possible to make some observations about the matter of unity and diversity,[18] though this will not be a major goal.

Thus the primary question that will concern us in these pages is part of a larger nexus of questions that have to do with central aspects of Judaism in the period of the Second Temple and beyond. Consequently any additional light that can be shed on this question will contribute to a better understanding of Judaism as a whole. Further, since earliest Christianity needs to be seen as one aspect of Second Temple Judaism broadly considered, a better understanding of these Jewish patterns of universalism will contribute to a better understanding of how and why early Jewish Christianity began to attract Gentiles and of the debates and conflicts that ensued. While the precise nature of the relationship needs to be carefully explored and is not to be assumed in advance, any proper understanding of the Gentile mission in the early church needs to recognize that the early Christian movement came to birth in an environment that was already universalistic. Early Christian debates about whether and on what terms Gentiles could be included in the movement are to be seen not as *sui generis* but as variations of debates that were already well established within Judaism.

Of course, as will be amply illustrated in the discussion to follow, there has been no lack of scholarly interest in this aspect of Judaism. Substantial work has been done on specific aspects of the question[19] and on individual authors or bodies of material.[20] In addition, quite a few detailed surveys of primary material have appeared,[21] usually as part of some larger discussion or particular thesis. But there is still the need for a study that will accomplish two things. One

18. See ch. 14.

19. E.g., sympathizers (Wander 1998); proselytes (Carleton Paget 1996; Cohen 1999, 107–238; Will and Orrieux 1992); the question of a Jewish mission (Cohen 1992; Dickson 2003; McKnight 1991; Goodman 1994).

20. E.g., Josephus (Cohen 1987; Mason 1996; 1998); Philo (Birnbaum 1996); Qumran (Deines 1994; Schiffman 1997).

21. Boccaccini (1991, 251–65); Bockmuehl (2000, 87–111); Cohen (1999, 140–74); J. J. Collins (2000, 261–72); Dickson (2003); Donaldson (1997, 51–78); Georgi (1986, 81–153); Feldman (1993, 288–382); Hengel and Schwemer (1997, 61–76); Kraus (1996, 45–107); Levinskaya (1996); McKnight (1991); Murray (2004, 11–27); Schnabel (2004, 92–172); Schürer (1986, 3:150–76); Segal (1993); Siegert (1973); Wander (1998); Will and Orrieux (1992, 81–137).

is a thoroughgoing attempt to place each piece of primary material in its full literary (or inscriptional) context. All too often a passage from Philo or a text from Horace is cited in isolation, without sufficient attention to the place and function of the material in its larger context.[22] There is a need for something akin to the form of presentation in Menahem Stern's *Greek and Latin Authors on Jews and Judaism* (1974), where each pertinent text receives its own full discussion, containing a literary and historical introduction to the larger work in which the text is found, a description of its place in this larger setting, and a detailed commentary.

A second area of need is comprehensiveness. While there are a number of studies that deal with both sympathizers and full converts (e.g., Feldman 1993; Cohen 1999, 140–74), it is rare to find a study that extends the range so as to include expectations concerning Gentiles in the end times or conceptions about natural law and ethical monotheism. Since these various conceptions are related, each attempting to deal with a similar set of questions and experiences, there is a need for a work that will include all of the Jewish patterns of universalism within its scope.

The *purpose* of this work, then, is to provide a thorough collection, with full introduction and commentary, of texts (including inscriptions) that provide evidence (direct or indirect) for these various patterns of universalism. While our ultimate goal is to identify and document these patterns, which means that our primary concern will have to do with Jewish perceptions and conceptions, we will need to cast our net more widely. For example, we will need to look at every passage that describes Gentile worship at the Temple in Jerusalem, even those that do not provide any direct indication about what Jews thought about such worship.

By the end of the study, we will be able to recognize four main patterns of universalism, connected with four broad textual categories.

1. *A Spectrum of Sympathizers*: texts dealing with Gentiles who demonstrate some degree of sympathization—that is, who engage in activity that seems to imply a measure of sympathy for Jews and Judaism (worshipping at the Jerusalem temple; adopting some aspects of Jewish custom and belief; associating with the Jewish community; and so on).
2. *Converts*: texts that deal with proselytes specifically or that refer in other terms to Gentiles who fully adopt a Jewish way of life and are incorporated into the Jewish community.

22. This criticism is more true of literary material than of inscriptions. Still, since inscriptional evidence accounts for just a small proportion of the pertinent material, the qualification does not weaken the criticism significantly.

3. *Ethical Monotheists*: texts in which an attempt is made to align Torah religion and Greek philosophy by construing the Torah as a particular expression of a natural law accessible to everyone through reason and by seeing Torah religion and Greek philosophy as parallel paths to the same goal—namely, a vision of one universal deity and a life of virtue (ethical monotheism).
4. *Participants in Eschatological Redemption*: texts that describe Gentiles as beneficiaries of the end-time redemption of Israel—that is, as coming in pilgrimage to worship God in Jerusalem, as abandoning their idols and turning to Israel's God or, more generally, as having a share in the blessings of the age to come.

Given the comprehensive character of our purpose, it is necessary to give careful consideration to the *parameters* within which it will be pursued. Temporally, our period of interest will begin with the start of the Hellenistic era and will end with the second Jewish revolt under Bar Cochba (132–35 C.E.). Some comments are in order about the decision to define the period in this way.

First, while this choice of *terminus a quo* has the effect of excluding the Hebrew canon from our body of evidence for the most part[23] and thus is partially a matter of convenience, the primary reason for the choice is the change in the social location of religion that was effected with the arrival of Hellenism. As North (1992) has observed, in an earlier era religion was not a separate entity within a culture but was embedded in the structures of kinship and politics (cf. Hanson and Oakman 1998, 8–10, 20). Religion did not exist in the form of a distinct group or institution to which one could choose to give one's allegiance; instead, one was automatically involved in specific religious activities by virtue of one's membership in a family, clan, or nation. But this began to change in the Hellenistic era. In part it was the result of factors that were already present in the Persian empire: toleration of the customs and traditions of conquered peoples, travel and mobility, migration, and the development of ethnic diasporas. But as Cohen (1999, 109–39) has observed, the Greeks added a further significant factor with their idea that "Greek-ness" was not restricted to those born into this particular *ethnos* but instead was a culture that others could assimilate and a political entity in which others could gain citizenship. Taken together, these factors served to create an environment of religious pluralism, one in which religion was no longer embedded completely in other cultural structures and in which the possibility existed for one's religious identity and association to be a matter of choice.[24] The transition from the Greek empires to that of the Romans only served to extend and accentuate these trends.

23. On Daniel, see §§4–9. But biblical material will be significant in a secondary way.

24. See also Barclay (1996, 403). On religious conversion more generally, see Rambo (1993); Segal (1990).

Along with the rest of the Mediterranean world, the Jewish *ethnos* was swept up into this new pluralistic environment. Given its distinctive features—for example, its exclusiveness—it was affected by this environment in unique ways. Nevertheless, the arrival of the Greeks marked the beginning of a new era in the relationship between Judaism as a religious entity and its non-Jewish neighbors. This, therefore, provides us with a decisive temporal starting point.

My choice of the Bar Cochba revolt as the *terminus ad quem* is also partly a matter of convenience in that it enables me to keep this project within manageable proportions by leaving to one side substantial bodies of later material—especially rabbinic, but also Christian and inscriptional. This is regrettable at the same time, of course, in that the second and third centuries were important for the development of Judaism vis-à-vis its Gentile environment. Still, the choice is not arbitrary, in that the defeat of Bar Cochba marked a decisive turning point. It brought a definitive end to the kind of zealous nationalism that had marked Judean society for a century and more, while at the same time extinguishing any hope that the Jewish temple-state would be restored any time soon. The impact was felt more immediately in Judea and environs than in the Diaspora, of course. But even in the Diaspora it was not without effect. For one thing, now that Judaism was no longer intrinsically connected to a foreign political entity, it became easier for Gentiles to associate with the Jewish community and to adopt Jewish ways, and the issues raised by such association and adoption existed in a different socio-political framework. The Bar Cochba era also coincided with the emergence of Gentile Christianity as a distinct and aggressive player in the religious marketplace. Because the Jewish roots of Christianity were well known to thoughtful Greeks and Romans in the second century (e.g., Celsus), what in an earlier period was a bilateral relationship (Jews and Gentiles) now became increasingly three-cornered. Thus the Bar Cochba period marks the end of a distinct phase of Jewish existence in the Greco-Roman world.

The primary material for our study, then, will consist of all pertinent texts (including inscriptions) that were produced from the third century B.C.E. through the first third of the second century C.E. More specifically, this will include the book of Daniel; the Septuagint, especially where it seems to reflect interpretive tradition that departs from the Hebrew textual tradition; the assortment of Jewish literature conventionally referred to as the Apocrypha and Pseudepigrapha; the writings of Josephus; those of Philo; Qumran literature; Greek and Roman authors; early Christian authors; and inscriptions.

Two bodies of literature that fall outside our temporal framework require comment. First, while the Hebrew canon for the most part will be excluded from direct study, as we have already noted, it functioned as a seedbed for the development of later patterns of universalism. Thus we will pay some attention to this material at appropriate points. Second, given the emphasis on tradition in the rabbinic movement and the resultant fact that rabbinic literature certainly contains traditions stemming from our period of interest, an argument could be made for including the early layers of rabbinic material within our purview. How to determine these layers, however, gets us into tricky methodological issues that would sidetrack our discussion considerably and extend the project unduly. In view of the fact that several important treatments of Gentiles in rabbinic literature have been produced in recent years by scholars whose expertise far surpasses my own,[25] I am content at this point to defer to their work. Still, the rabbinic witness to the earlier period is significant; at appropriate points I will summarize what I take to be its evidential value for our project.

This leads, finally, to a few comments about *procedure*. The work will fall into two parts. Part I (Texts and Commentary), by far the longer of the two, will deal with the pertinent texts in eight chapters arranged according to source or corpus. Each chapter will contain an introduction, followed by a seriatim listing and discussion of individual texts (English translation; information concerning provenance and bibliography; categorization; introduction to the literary work; full commentary on the text) and, in two chapters (those dealing with Philo and Josephus), a conclusion. For the most part the texts are discussed in each chapter in chronological order. Part II (Patterns of Universalism) will synthesize the findings from Part I by identifying four distinct patterns of universalism arising out of the four broad textual categories described earlier (sympathization, conversion, ethical monotheism, eschatological participation). While it is more convenient and economical to arrange the texts according to source or corpus, one consequence is that each chapter in Part I will contain material dealing with more than one of the patterns identified in Part II. To facilitate cross-referencing, each text in Part I will be assigned to one (or more) of the four categories described earlier. This categorization should be seen as a matter of convenience, a way of indicating the chapter (or chapters) in Part II to which the text is most pertinent. While in most instances the assigning of a category means that in my opinion the text provides direct evidence for the corresponding pattern of universalism, this is not necessarily the case. For definitive judgments about passages readers are referred to the commentary itself.

25. Cohen (1999), especially chs. 7–10; Hayes (2002); Novak (1984); Porton (1988). Some earlier studies are still significant: Bamberger (1968 [1939]); Braude (1940); G. Moore (1927–1930, 1.323–53).

Part I

Texts and Commentary

CHAPTER 2

SCRIPTURE, SEPTUAGINT, AND APOCRYPHA

Introduction

This chapter will survey passages from the book of Daniel, the Septuagint, and the Apocrypha. Most of the passages come from the Apocrypha, about which nothing more needs to be said here. A word of introduction is in order, however, concerning the others.

Daniel is the only biblical book from our period containing passages of interest. For convenience we will consider both the Hebrew-Aramaic and the Greek versions of the book in a single section.

Most Septuagint texts that refer in positive terms to Gentiles simply reproduce the sense of the Hebrew and thus fall outside the scope of our study. We are interested here only in those texts that vary from the Hebrew in ways that might reflect the influence of later perspectives.[1] Of course, we need to leave

1. In addition to the passages discussed, Overman (1988, 20–21) has suggested that the references to οἱ φοβούμενοι [τὸν κύριον] in several passages (LXX 2 Chron 5:6; Ps 113:19[115:11]; 117[118]:4; 134[135]:20; Mal 3:16) might have had Gentiles in view. But except for 2 Chron 5:6, these "fearers of the Lord" are clearly Jewish. The situation is a little less clear in 2 Chron 5:6, where οἱ φοβούμενοι [without τὸν κύριον], which has no Hebrew counterpart in the MT, appears in a list with πᾶσα συναγωγὴ Ισραηλ and οἱ ἐπισυνηγμένοι αὐτῶν. Since the next chapter (2 Chron 6) contains the famous prayer of dedication in

open the possibility in each case that the differences between the LXX and the MT originated not from the process of translation but from the use of a Hebrew *Vorlage* that differed from the MT. In such cases, LXX readings that differ substantially from the MT would not be as significant for our purposes. But even so, they would not be totally irrelevant, in that they would provide evidence for attitudes and ideas that were in circulation during our period. In most of the texts that will come up for discussion in this work, however, there is little reason to believe that the underlying Hebrew differed from the MT.

Texts and Commentary

LXX Prophets

§1 LXX 4 Kingdoms 17:34, 40

> *To this day they were doing according to their judgment; they fear* [i.e., the Lord] *and they do according to their regulations and according to their judgment, and according to the law and according to the commandment which the Lord commanded the sons of Jacob, the name of whom he made to be Israel.. . .* [40]*And you shall not listen to their judgment, which they do.*

Text: LXX (Rahlfs, 1979)
Translation: Author's own
Date: Second century B.C.E.
Provenance: Greek-speaking Diaspora
Category: SYMPATHIZATION

The Hebrew version of 2 Kings 17 recounts the fall of Samaria and Israel to the Assyrians, who then "brought people from Babylon, Cuthah, Avva, Hamath, and Sepharvaim, and placed them in the cities of Samaria in place of the people of Israel" (v. 24). As the story unfolds, in order to appease the "god of the land" (v. 26), the king of Assyria sent an Israelite priest to teach them "how they should worship the LORD" (v. 28). The result is a religious amalgam; the nations continued to worship their own gods (v. 29), but "they also feared the LORD" (v. 32). Verse 41 says that this situation of syncretistic worship has continued "to this day." Verse 34b, however, paints a different picture. "To this day"

which Solomon calls on God to hear the prayer of foreigners who come to pray in the temple, a reference to Gentile "God-fearers" cannot be ruled out here (Strack-Billerbeck; see the discussion in Barrett 1994, 630). But no Gentiles are actually present in 2 Chron 6, and in ch. 5 the list of those present is completely Jewish (e.g., 5:2). Thus there is no compelling reason to see a reference to Gentiles here.

they worship only their own gods and "do not fear the LORD." It is possible that verses 34b–40 have been added by a later Deuteronomistic editor who looked with less favor on such mixed worship.[2]

The Septuagint differs from the Hebrew, however, in verses 34 and 40. The elimination of the negative in v. 34 serves to bring this statement in line with vv. 29–33 and 41: "To this day" these nations continue both to fear the Lord and to follow their own customs. In v. 40, the Septuagint shifts from the third person, "they would not listen," to the second, "you shall not listen." The effect of this shift is to change the statement from a flat-out condemnation of the nations—they quickly abandoned any worship of the Lord and reverted to their original worship practices—to a warning directed at the Jews not to follow them in their mixed worship of the God of Israel and the gods of the nations.

The end result is that the Septuagint speaks more uniformly than does the MT of Gentiles who continue to worship their own gods but who also fear the Lord. It is doubtful, however, that this Greek rendering should be taken as evidence that the translators were interested in this phenomenon for its own sake, even less that they wanted to encourage it. Their Hebrew *Vorlage* contained a rough transition in v. 34—perhaps a seam resulting from the later addition of vv. 34b–40—and they simply attempted to smooth it out.

§2 LXX Isaiah 54:15

> *Behold, proselytes shall come to you through me*[3] *and shall flee to you for refuge.*

Text: LXX (Rahlfs, 1979)
Translation: Author's own
Date: Third or second century B.C.E.
Provenance: Greek-speaking Diaspora
Original Language: Greek (translation of Hebrew original)
Category: ESCHATOLOGICAL PARTICIPATION

Of course, the passages in the Hebrew scriptures that deal with the eschatological pilgrimage tradition appear also in the Greek translation. But while these texts would repay study,[4] they do not contribute enough to our investigation to

2. See Gray (1963, 597); Montgomery (1951, 477). For an attempt to read 17:24–41 in a more unified way, see Hobbs (1985, 219–41). His reading of v. 34b, however—"There were no people who feared Yahweh exclusively" (p. 222)—introduces a qualification ("exclusively") that is not justified by the Hebrew and is at odds with the use of the same clause (יראים את־יהוה) in vv. 32, 33, and 41.

3. Several later recensions, including Vaticanus and Lucian's version, add "and will sojourn among you" (καὶ παροικήσουσίν σοι).

4. For example, there is a tendency in the LXX for πάντα τὰ ἔθνη to become a standard term for the non-Jewish world, rendering not only גוים but also עמים where it refers to

justify dealing with each in turn. There are two texts, however, in which the Septuagint contains eschatological pilgrimage themes that are not present in the Hebrew MT and that therefore represent either interpretations of the Hebrew *Vorlage* or the preservation of a variant tradition. Since in each case the Greek can be understood as an attempt to make sense of something in the MT, they are probably to be seen as instances of the former.

The first such text is found in a chapter of Isaiah that looks ahead to the future consolation of Israel. It appears near the beginning of the final section of the chapter (vv. 14–17) in which Israel is assured that any threat to its security will inevitably come to naught. The central difficulty of the verse—also the occasion for the Septuagint rendering—is the threefold use of the verb גור. The most common meaning of this verb—to live as a resident alien—is scarcely possible in this context. Most commentators have taken it to be a homonym, with the meaning "to stir up strife, to attack."[5] The Hebrew verse would then read: "See, anyone who makes an attack [גור יגור]—I have not prompted it. Anyone who attacks [מי־גר] you will fall before you" (Baltzer 2001, 456).

The Greek translators, however, understood גור in its most usual sense, rendering גור יגור as προσήλυτοι προσελεύσονται. This is perhaps their only recognizable translational move, as the rest of the verse is a very free rendering. They seem to have first decided, on the basis of גור, that the verse had to do with proselytes coming to Israel, and then to have constructed the rest of the verse accordingly. The resultant reading is certainly not out of place in the chapter as a whole. Verses 1–14a deal with Israel's vindication and restoration, precisely the context in which eschatological pilgrimage texts are to be found.[6] So one can readily understand how the presence of גור, together with an awareness of eschatological pilgrimage traditions, would have led the translators to render the verse as they did.

This rendering provides evidence, then, that eschatological pilgrimage ideas were present among Greek-speaking Diaspora Jews in the second or third century B.C.E. The translators evidently were aware of the expectation that Gentiles in the end time would turn to God, and allowed this awareness to shape their translation. Further, if we take the translation literally, they expected these Gentiles to become proselytes. One should not put a great deal of stress on this point; the choice of προσήλυτοι was determined by the presence of גור in the Hebrew *Vorlage* and does not indicate in and of itself that these end-time

---

non-Jewish nations (e.g., Lev 20:24, 26; Deut 2:25; 4:6; 7:14) and πάντα being added in places where there is no corresponding כל in the Hebrew (e.g., Isa 14:12; 36:20; 40:15; Ezek 38:16; 39:21, 23; Joel 3:12; Zech 14:16, 18).

5. Perhaps related to the noun גור, meaning "young lion." See BDB (158); Baltzer (2001, 458); Blenkinsopp (2002, 359, 365–66).

6. Except for the absence of the temple; see Blenkinsopp (2002, 364).

pilgrims were expected to be circumcised and to become full converts. Still, the choice is not without significance; the translators did not think it out of the question that such Gentiles could be described as proselytes.

§3 LXX Amos 9:11–12

> *On that day I will raise up the tabernacle of David, which has fallen, and I will rebuild its ruins and I will raise up what has been torn to the ground and I will rebuild it as in the days of old, [12]so that the remnant of humankind, even all the nations upon whom my name has been called, might seek me, says God the Lord who is doing these things.*

Text: LXX (Rahlfs, 1979)
Translation: Author's own
Date: Third or second century B.C.E.
Provenance: Greek-speaking Diaspora
Original Language: Greek (translation of Hebrew original)
Bibliography: Bruce (1979)
Category: ESCHATOLOGICAL PARTICIPATION

In the Hebrew version of Amos 9:12, the restoration of the Davidic line will make it possible for Israel to "possess [יירשו; "inherit"] the remnant of Edom [אדום] and all the nations [כל־הגוים] who are called by my name." The phrase "called by my name" (literally "upon whom my name is called" [אשר נקרא שמי עליהם]) is somewhat unexpected in this context, since it is usually used in a positive sense to refer to Israel as chosen by God.[7] For this reason Andersen and Freedman (1989, 912–18) interpret the term in a positive sense here as well, as referring to nations "that are converted to the true faith." They also take these nations to be the real subject of v. 12, which then reads: "So that they [i.e., the nations, as specified in the second part of the verse] may dispossess the remnant of Edom, even all the nations over whom my name was pronounced." But such a reading strains the syntax of the sentence and has not found a following.[8] It is much more likely that the text anticipates a future situation in which Gentile nations will be made subservient to a restored Israel. The phrase "called by my name" in its most basic sense indicates possession (e.g., 2 Sam 12:28; Isa 4:1), with the nature of the possession to be determined from the context. While the phrase is unusual here, it probably refers to the subservience of the nations to God.

Perhaps it was precisely the positive connotations surrounding the phrase "upon whom my name is called" that triggered the Septuagint rendering. This

7. E.g., Deut 28:10; 2 Chron 7:14; Isa 63:19. It is also used of the temple (Jer 7:10) and of the prophet Jeremiah (Jer 15:16).

8. Since כל־הגוים is preceded by ו (and), it is much more likely that "all the nations" is to be paired with "the remnant of Edom." See Paul (1991, 291–92).

rendering presupposes a Hebrew original that had ידרשו (will seek) instead of יירשו (will inherit), אדם (humankind) in place of אדום (Edom), and no direct object marker (את) before שארית (remnant). Rather than postulating the existence of a variant Hebrew text, it is simpler to imagine that the translators read the phrase in question as a predication of a positive relationship between the God of Israel and the nations, and reconstrued the rest of the sentence accordingly.

Nevertheless, however it came about, the resultant Greek version anticipates a time when "the remnant of humankind [οἱ κατάλοιποι τῶν ἀνθρώπων], even[9] all the nations [πάντα τὰ ἔθνη] upon whom [God's] name has been called," witness the restoration of Israel and are moved by it (ὅπως) to seek Israel's God.[10] In other words, the translators have understood this verse as anticipating an end-time event in which a certain portion of the Gentile world turns to worship the God of Israel.[11] But nothing in the translation indicates what the translators thought of the status of these Gentiles with respect to native-born Israelites or whether or to what extent they embraced the Torah.

Daniel

There are passages of interest in both the original Hebrew-Aramaic book of Daniel and the Greek version. We begin with the former.

§4 Daniel 2:47

The king said to Daniel, "Truly, your God is a God of gods and Lord of kings and a revealer of mysteries, for you have been able to reveal this mystery."

§5 Daniel 3:28–29

Nebuchadnezzar said, "Blessed be the God of Shadrach, Meshach, and Abednego, who has sent his angel and delivered his servants who trusted in him. They disobeyed the king's command and yielded up their bodies rather than serve and worship any god except their own God. Therefore I make a decree: Any people, nation, or language that utters blasphemy against the God of Shadrach, Meshach, and Abednego shall be torn limb from limb, and their houses laid in ruins; for there is no other god who is able to deliver in this way."

9. It is likely that καί is to be taken in an epexegetic sense; "the nations over whom my name is called" is the equivalent of "the remnant of humankind."

10. The object of ἐκζητήσωσιν remains unexpressed, but με is no doubt to be supplied; cf. Acts 15:17.

11. On LXX Amos 9:11–12 as an example of theologically influenced translation, see Bruce (1979, 17).

§6 Daniel 4:34–37

> *When that period was over, I, Nebuchadnezzar, lifted my eyes to heaven, and my reason returned to me. I blessed the Most High, and praised and honored the one who lives forever. For his sovereignty is an everlasting sovereignty, and his kingdom endures from generation to generation.. . .* [37]*Now I, Nebuchadnezzar, praise and extol and honor the King of heaven, for all his works are truth, and his ways are justice; and he is able to bring low those who walk in pride.*

§7 Daniel 6:25–27

> *Then King Darius wrote to all peoples and nations of every language throughout the whole world: "May you have abundant prosperity! I make a decree, that in all my royal dominion people should tremble and fear before the God of Daniel: For he is the living God, enduring for ever. His kingdom shall never be destroyed, and his dominion has no end. He delivers and rescues, he works signs and wonders in heaven and on earth; for he has saved Daniel from the power of the lions."*

Text: *BHS*
Translation: NRSV
Date: 167–164 B.C.E.
Provenance: Judea
Original Language: Aramaic
Bibliography: J. J. Collins (1993); Goldingay (1989); Wills (1990)
Category: SYMPATHIZATION

While in its final canonical form the book of Daniel dates from the Maccabean period, the court tales found in the first six chapters stem from an earlier period, perhaps even as early as the Persian era. Four of the tales culminate in scenes in which the king of Babylon, having come to recognize the power and sovereignty of Israel's God, acknowledges God with a formal speech or declaration. In each case the recognition scene coincides with a reversal of fortune. In three of the tales the reversal involves pious Israelites, as a threat against their lives is lifted and they are exalted to high positions in the royal court. In the other case, it is the king himself who experiences a reversal of fortune.

The stories are well known and thus require little elaboration. In the first story (ch. 2) King Nebuchadnezzar has had a dream that he wants his wise men to interpret, a task that he makes doubly difficult by refusing to tell them the dream itself. In this story the threat falls on Daniel and his friends simply because they belong to the company of Babylonian wise men; they are not singled out for their own beliefs. When Daniel is able to tell him both the dream and the interpretation, the king responds by praising Daniel's God (2:47) and promoting Daniel and his three friends to positions of influence. In the second story (ch. 3), the threat falls on Shadrach, Meshach, and Abednego specifically because they refuse to worship a golden statue erected by the king. When they are delivered unharmed from the "furnace of blazing fire," the king issues a decree prohibiting anyone from "utter[ing] blasphemy against the God of Shadrach, Meshach and Abednego" (3:29).

In the first two stories the king appears simply as a comic figure, a royal buffoon who is forced to change his tune. The other two stories, however, present us with more sympathetic royal figures, kings with whom Daniel enjoys privileged and trusted relationships and who themselves are brought to a point of sincere veneration. The third story (ch. 4) involves a direct confrontation between the king of Babylon and the "king of heaven" (4:37). In rebuke for his pride (4:30), God afflicts Nebuchadnezzar with madness until he comes to learn that before God "all inhabitants of the earth are accounted as nothing" (4:35). Daniel again plays the role of an interpreter of dreams, but this time as a trusted and sympathetic confidant (4:8, 19–20). In the final story (ch. 6), the threat to Daniel comes not from the king (now Darius) but from other members of the court and royal officials who are jealous of Daniel's relationship with the king. Constrained by the irrevocability of "the law of the Medes and Persians" (6:8, 12, 15), Darius has to stand helplessly by as Daniel is thrown into the lions' den. Daniel's deliverance leads the king to acknowledge the God of Daniel as "the living God, enduring forever" (6:26).

These tales have to do primarily with the pressures and problems of Diaspora existence and not with the spiritual condition of foreign kings. Still, the stories are striking not only for the optimism with which they view the possibility of living faithfully as Jews in the Diaspora but also for their sympathetic portrayal of the king. Especially in chapters 4 and 6, the transformation experienced by the king goes beyond what would be required in a story of simple vindication. In each case the king's veneration of Israel's God seems to be valued for its own sake.

§8 OG Daniel 4:34

> *From now on I will serve him. . . . Every day of my reign I will offer sacrifices to the Most High for my life, for a pleasing odor to the Lord, and I will do what is pleasing before him, I and my people, my nation and the countries that are under my authority. . . . King Nebuchadnezzar wrote a circular letter to all the nations in their individual places, and to countries and people of all languages which live in all the countries in generation after generation: "Praise the Lord, the God of heaven, and offer sacrifice and oblation to him in public.*

§9 OG Daniel 6:26–27

> *All the people in my kingdom should adore and worship the God of Daniel, for he is a living God who endures for generations after generations, forever. I, Darius, will adore and serve him all my days, for the idols made by hand are not able to save as the God of Daniel redeemed Daniel.*

Text: Ziegler (1999)
Translation: J. J. Collins (1993)
Date: Late second century B.C.E.
Provenance: Egypt
Original Language: Greek (translation of Aramaic original)
Bibliography: J. J. Collins (1993)
Category: SYMPATHIZATION

The Old Greek of Daniel was supplanted in Christian editions of the LXX by Theodotion's translation but is still extant. It differs significantly from the extant Aramaic version in chapters 4–6, including several places where the piety of the Gentile kings is more elaborate and more specific than in the canonical version. While it is probable that the OG in general reflects a different Aramaic *Vorlage*, it is difficult to determine in specific instances whether differences are due to a different Aramaic original or to the translators themselves. In either case, however, the texts are pertinent.

Two passages are of particular interest here. In chapter 4, after his seven-year bout with madness, Nebuchadnezzar finally acknowledges "the Most High." In the Aramaic version he is described as blessing, praising, extolling, and honoring God (4:34, 37). In the OG, he also says that he will "serve" (λατρεύσω) God, that he will "offer sacrifices to the Most High" and will "do what is pleasing" to God. In addition, in a letter[12] to "all the nations" (πᾶσι τοῖς ἔθνεσι) he enjoins his subjects to do likewise, including the offering of "sacrifice and oblation [θυσίαν καὶ προσφοράν] to him in public." Since there is no suggestion that either the king or his subjects would make a pilgrimage to the Jerusalem temple, the assumption seems to be that sacrifices offered in their own localities would be acceptable to God.

The king's veneration is also made more explicit in chapter 6, though here the emphasis is on monotheism. After Daniel's deliverance from the den of lions, the Aramaic version ends simply with Darius's decree that the whole kingdom should fear Daniel's God. In the OG version, however, the king enjoins his subjects to "worship and serve" (προσκυνοῦντες καὶ λατρεύοντες) the God of Daniel and then goes on to make his own affirmation. He says that he, too, will worship and serve Daniel's God, for "idols made by hand" (τὰ εἴδωλα τὰ χειροποίητα) are not able to save. In this case, the king seems to be committing himself to exclusive veneration of Daniel's God.

12. In the Aramaic version, the whole of chapter 4 is in the form of a letter "to all peoples, nations and languages" (4:1). The OG presents Nebuchadnezzar's experience as a straight third-person narrative, leaving the sending of the letter to the end of the account.

§10 Bel and the Serpent 28

> *All the people of the country rallied against the king and said, "The king has become a Jew; he has destroyed Bel, and killed the serpent."*

Text: Greek: Ziegler (1999)
Translation: OG: J. J. Collins (1993) Theodotion: Wills (1990, 140–42)
Date: Second century B.C.E.
Provenance: The eastern Diaspora, or perhaps Judea
Original Language: Semitic
Bibliography: J. J. Collins (1992); C. Moore (1977); Schürer (1987, 3:722–30); Wills (1990).
Category: SYMPATHIZATION, CONVERSION

Bel and the Serpent is one of three segments that are present in the Greek versions of Daniel (both OG and Theodotion) but not in the canonical, Hebrew/Aramaic version. On the basis of stylistic considerations scholars have long suspected a Hebrew or Aramaic original. Such a possibility has been strengthened by the discovery of other non-canonical Daniel narratives at Qumran, discoveries that have also lent support to the idea of a Judean provenance.[13] The OG version probably is closer to the original form of the story, though the existence of a Theodotion-type text prior to the (second century C.E.) translation of Theodotion himself means that this version may be almost as early.[14] The *terminus ad quem* for the composition of the additions is c. 100 C.E., when the Greek version of Daniel was first produced. Since the additions probably circulated independently before being incorporated into Daniel,[15] they may well have originated before the final compilation of canonical Daniel in the 160s B.C.E. The reference in Bel and the Serpent to the king becoming a Jew, however, probably indicates a date no earlier than the second century.[16]

13. 4Q242–246, 4Q551–553. Babylonia or Egypt has also been suggested (the latter on the assumption of a Greek original). For thorough discussions of introductory issues, see C. Moore (1977, 117–29).

14. C. Moore argues that the LXX is a translation of an Aramaic original, while Theodotion is based on a Hebrew rendering of the Aramaic (Moore 1977, 119–20). Wills suggests, more simply, that Theodotion is a reworking of the LXX (Wills 1990, 129–30).

15. The LXX version of Bel and the Dragon begins with an introduction of Daniel, which hardly would have been necessary if it had been produced as a supplement to the canonical book.

16. See J. J. Collins (1992, 343), who observes that "the idea that a Gentile could 'become a Jew' is not attested before the second century." The statement appears in both OG and Theodotion.

The story recounted in Bel and the Serpent unfolds in three main episodes, which may have originated as independent units but which now have been integrated into a single story. Central to the narrative is the relationship between Daniel and the king of Babylon (identified as Cyrus the Persian in Theodotion; v. 1). On the one hand, the relationship is close; Daniel is a trusted advisor, "a companion of the king and . . . more distinguished than all his friends" (v. 2). On the other hand, they differ—at least at the outset—on the matter of the Babylonian gods. The purpose of the narrative is to effect a transformation in the attitude of the king, from "You are great, O Bel, and there is no deception with you at all" (v. 18) to "You are great, O God of Daniel, and there is no other except you" (v. 41).

The first two episodes of the story have a somewhat parallel structure: the king draws Daniel's attention to a Babylonian god, thus raising the issue of idolatry; Daniel affirms his faith in the living God; Daniel then cleverly demonstrates the impotence of the Babylonian god. In the first episode this is followed by the reaction of the king, which brings the episode to an end. In the second episode it is the people who react, which precipitates the final episode and the conclusion of the story.

The first episode has to do with a god named Bel, whom the Babylonians provided each day with "twelve bushels of choice flour and forty sheep and six measures of wine" (v. 3). When Daniel asserts that this god of clay and bronze has never consumed anything (v. 7), the king sets up a contest. If the priests of Bel can prove that the food is consumed by the god, Daniel will die; otherwise, the priests will die. Both sides cheerfully accept the contest—the priests because they have a secret entrance by which they and their families come into the temple at night to consume the food; Daniel, because he knows about this scheme (but how?) and has a plan to expose it by sprinkling ashes on the floor without the knowledge of the priests. The next morning the king's initial exultation at the disappearance of the food ("You are great, O Bel, and in you there is no deceit at all" [v. 18]) quickly turns to anger when Daniel points to the telltale footprints in the ashes. He puts the priests to death and gives Daniel permission to destroy the temple. However, his basic attitude toward the gods has not really changed.

In the second part of the story, the king believes that he is on firmer ground in that the god in question—a snake or dragon—is very clearly alive. This time Daniel takes the initiative, claiming that he can kill this god "without sword or rod" (v. 26). This he proceeds to do (after receiving permission from the king) by feeding the snake with cakes that he has prepared out of pitch, fat, and hair. Unlike Bel, this god was quite able to eat. But eating was as disastrous for the snake as was the inability to eat in the case of Bel: once the snake had gobbled up the cakes, it promptly burst open and died. This time it is the Babylonians who respond with anger. Accusing the king of having become a Jew himself, they force him to throw Daniel into a den of lions. This third episode of the story, clearly a variant of the narrative found in Daniel 6, concludes with Daniel's miraculous deliverance, the king's acknowledgment of Daniel's God, and the destruction of Daniel's opponents.

Bel and the Serpent is thus similar in form to the narratives in Daniel 1–6. In each, faithful Jews face threats to their well-being because of their monotheistic beliefs; in each their steadfastness is vindicated; in each their vindication results in a change of heart on the part of the king. However, Bel and the Serpent differs from the other narratives in several ways: its focal concern with the folly of idolatry; the active initiative taken by Daniel, in contrast to the more passive role in the canonical narratives; the emphasis on human cleverness in contrast to divine intervention.[17] Wills has made a significant contribution to the formal analysis of the narrative in his study of what he calls Jewish court legends, a genre that includes Esther, in addition to the Daniel cycle. For our purposes, however, what is of interest is a feature of the narrative that is neither typical of such court narratives nor found in the vindication tales in Daniel 1–6. Not only does the king come to the point where he can declare that Daniel's God is great and that "there is no other except you" (v. 41), but his subjects take his change of heart as evidence that he has "become a Jew" (v. 28).

What are we to make of this statement, especially as it relates to the function of the narrative as a whole? John Collins (1992, 345) seems to place considerable weight on this aspect of the story. In his view, Bel and the Serpent "expresses the hope for the triumph of monotheism even within the domain of Gentile sovereignty. The hope was that the destruction of idols might be accomplished if the king, even in a loose sense, were to become a Jew." While Collins's study is full of insight, this statement concerning the functional "hope" of the narrative seems to overstate the matter. The purpose of the narrative, it seems to me, is more to give Jews the confidence to live as monotheists in a polytheistic world than it is to foster the hope that if only Gentile monarchs would become Jews, then polytheism would disappear.

Let us look more closely at the question of intended function. Clearly, the narrative is directed at a Jewish readership. Prior to v. 28 there is no explicit reference to Daniel's Jewishness. The author simply takes it for granted that well before they have reached this point in the story his readers will have recognized Daniel as a Jewish hero and the "living God" whom he worships as the God of Israel. The highlight of the narrative is not the destruction of the idols but the change in the king's outlook. The destruction of the idols—which is accomplished by Daniel, not the king—has the narrative function of bringing about the king's change of heart. It is not the case that the king "becomes a Jew" and so destroys the idols; rather, it is Daniel's demonstration of the impotence of idols that convinces the king that there is no other God than Daniel's God.

17. On the differences see Wills (1990, 129–34); J. J. Collins (1992, 132–33).

Thus, as is the case with other narratives of this type, the heart of the story is the vindication of Daniel and the acknowledgment of Daniel's God on the part of the Gentile king; these, in turn, are meant to reaffirm for Jewish readers the inherent value of Jewish identity and to reinforce their commitment to Jewish distinctives. This effect is enhanced by the comedic parody of idol worship, parody that is underlined by Daniel's derisory laughter (vv. 7, 19). Nothing enhances group solidarity like shared humor at the expense of the "other." Also important is the contrast between the king, who is presented in very sympathetic terms, and Daniel's opponents, who are drawn from the priests and idolaters. The message seems to be that despite the inevitability of opposition, faithfulness to God and loyalty to the king will make it possible for Jews to live confidently as Jews in a Gentile world.[18]

But what of the fact that the king not only comes to acknowledge the God of Israel but is also described as having become a Jew in the process? From one perspective—that of the narrative and its structure—this statement is not all that significant. It is uttered by Daniel's opponents, the Babylonian idolaters, who are indignant at the king's willingness to be dissuaded about the validity of their gods. The statement is isolated and disconnected from the narrative as a whole. Nothing to this point suggests that the interaction between Daniel and the king had anything to do with becoming a Jew. Nor is the idea even acknowledged, let alone affirmed, by anyone else in the narrative, whether the king, Daniel, or the narrator himself. In particular, at the climax of the story, when the king finds Daniel alive and finally comes to a full recognition of Daniel's God (v. 41), there is no indication that readers are to see the king as having become a Jew, "even in a loose sense." In other words, the statement functions simply as an insult, rather than as an indication of how anyone in the narrative—the narrator included—would perceive the king's status.

This means that we should not draw any rash conclusions from the absence of any reference to circumcision, law observance, or incorporation into the Jewish people. Bel and the Serpent does not provide any evidence that there were Jews in antiquity who believed that Gentiles could become Jews simply by rejecting idolatry and worshipping the God of Israel. Even if readers are to see the Babylonians as holding this view,[19] the idea certainly is not endorsed by the author of the work. But it is more likely that the absence of any reaction in the narrative to the statement in v. 28 suggests that we are to read it simply as an insult. At most one could suggest that the author intended it to be read ironically: unlike the Babylonian idolaters, the author and his readers know that

18. This aspect of the text seems to suggest a Diaspora provenance.

19. Of course, as Cohen (1999, 153) has observed, there is evidence that Gentiles were ready to consider someone as having become a Jew whom the Jews themselves still viewed as a Gentile.

more is involved in becoming a Jew than simply destroying some idols. At the same time, we should not simply assume that we know what that "more" might be. The purpose of these comments is not to smuggle into the narrative some particular understanding of what is involved in "becoming a Jew," but simply to argue against any attempt to carry away from the narrative any illegitimate understanding.

But even if the idea of becoming a Jew is not developed thematically in the narrative, the reference is still quite significant. The terminology is striking: in place of the more common but also more vague Ἰουδαΐζειν (to Judaize, to live as a Jew),[20] we find Ἰουδαῖος γέγονεν ([he] became a Jew). The phrase itself refers to a full transformation from one ethnic identity to another. Even if such a transformation is not depicted in the narrative itself, the possibility of such a transformation was part of the author's set of beliefs. Although the author did not expect his readers to see the king as having become a Jew, he nevertheless expected his readers to know what was meant by the phrase that he put on the lips of his characters. While we cannot say precisely what was involved in the transformation as author and intended readers understood it, we can say that abandonment of idolatry and exclusive worship of Israel's God was an essential first step.

LXX Esther

The version of Esther that appears in the Septuagint is the end result of a process that has gone through several stages. The result is a narrative that differs from the Hebrew version in several respects, including the presence of substantial additions. We are interested here in two passages: first, the Greek rendering of a verse in the Hebrew original and second, one of the additions.

§11 LXX Esther 8:16–17

> *And the Jews had light and gladness in every city and province wherever the decree was published; wherever the proclamation was made, the Jews had joy and gladness, a banquet and a holiday. And many of the Gentiles were circumcised and became Jews out of fear of the Jews.*

Text: Greek: LXX (Rahlfs, 1979)
Translation: NRSV
Date: Late-second or early first-century B.C.E.
Provenance: Greek-speaking Diaspora
Original Language: Greek (translation of Hebrew)
Bibliography: C. Moore (1977); Cohen (1999, 181–82); Gruen (1998, 177–86)
Category: CONVERSION

20. On Ἰουδαΐζειν, see the next entry (§11).

We begin with the Hebrew version. The verse appears at the climax of the story. Haman has just been hung on his own gallows, Mordecai has been vindicated and a counter-edict, giving Jews the right to take vengeance on their enemies, has been proclaimed throughout the land. This gives rise to joy and merrymaking in every Jewish community, with the result that "many of the peoples of the country [מעמי הארץ] professed to be Jews [מתיהדים], because the fear of the Jews had fallen upon them" (8:17). The verb—the hithpael participle of a hypothetical qal form יהד—appears nowhere else in the Hebrew Bible. The hithpael construction generally has a direct or indirect reflexive sense, so that the formation with יהד has the general sense of making a Jew of oneself, or acting as a Jew. Some commentators, taking note of the fact that the Gentiles were motivated by fear, take the term in the sense of pretense: they "pretended to be Jews" (C. Moore 1971, 82; Cohen 1999, 181–82). We will return to this suggestion in a moment.

The Greek translators rendered מתיהדים with the verb Ἰουδαΐζειν; but to clarify the sense in which they understood the term, they added a reference to circumcision: "many of the Gentiles [πολλοὶ τῶν ἐθνων] were circumcised [περιετέμοντο]."[21] In an article devoted to the term Ἰουδαΐζειν, Cohen (1999, 175–97) has demonstrated that in normal Greek usage, verbs of this pattern—that is, an ethnic indicator plus the ending -ιζειν—denote three types of accommodation to or sympathy with the ways of a different ethnic group: giving political support, adopting their customs, and speaking their language. In addition to its use in Christian material,[22] Ἰουδαΐζειν appears once in the Septuagint (the passage under discussion here), twice in Josephus (*J.W.* 2.454, 463), and once in Plutarch (*Cicero* 7.5). Nowhere is the term used to refer to the adoption of a foreign language, but the other two elements of the pattern are present—namely, the political (identification with or support of Judea as a state or Jews as a political entity in the Diaspora) and the cultural (adopting observances or beliefs of the Jews).

In LXX Esth 8:17, the translators have apparently understood the term in the second sense, with perhaps an aspect of the first: by being circumcised, the Gentiles identified themselves with the Jews and against their opponents who

21. Assuming that the Hebrew *Vorlage* of the LXX resembled the MT at this point. There is another Greek text of Esther, the A text, which renders the passage thus: "And many of the Jews circumcised themselves, and no one opposed them; for they feared them" (see Clines 1984, 245). The translation is absurd; while the A text at many points bears witness to an early variant version of the Hebrew (Clines 1984, 71–92), the garbled rendering of 8:17 has nothing to add to our discussion here.

22. The earliest such usage is in Gal 2:14, also the only appearance of the term in the New Testament. It also appears in Eusebius's citation of Alexander Polyhistor's paraphrase of Theodotus *On the Jews* (see §37 below). Since there is little reason to attribute the term to Eusebius (he tends to quote, not paraphrase), this would represent an additional Jewish (if it originated with Theodotus) or Gentile (if Polyhistor) use of the term.

had planned to do them harm. But what, more specifically, can we say about the attitude of the text to these "Judaizers"? What does it tell us about the phenomenon of proselytism in the context of LXX Esther?

Cohen's reading of the passage represents perhaps the most restrictive view: "The Jews had been given carte blanche by the king to kill their enemies, and therefore many gentiles pretended to be Jews in order to protect themselves."[23] This reading is grounded not in Ἰουδαΐζειν itself—verbs of this form have no inherent sense of pretense—but in the reference to fear. Against this reading, however, stands the fact that pretending to be Jews would not have afforded these Gentiles any protection at all. In the context of the story, the conflict between the Jews and their "enemies" is localized ("in every city and province" [8:17]). Disguise is not a plausible option in such circumstances. The Jews knew full well who belonged to their community and who to the company of their enemies. If there was pretense involved, it had to do with proselytism; that is, in order to protect themselves, the Gentiles pretended to be converts, even going so far as to have themselves circumcised. This is the only sort of pretense or insincerity that would be plausible, given the logic of the story.

The world reflected in LXX Esther, then, is one in which the possibility of proselytism can be taken for granted,[24] even if the role of the proselytes in the story is just to underline the reversal of fortune that the Jews experienced. But is this the extent of their role in the story? There is additional evidence a little further on that suggests a more positive attitude toward proselytes and their significance for Israel. The outcome of the story, of course, is the establishment of the feast of Purim. When the vindication of the Jews has taken place, Mordecai and Esther decree that "these days of Purim should be a memorial and kept from generation to generation, in every city, family and country" (9:27). The result is that "the Jews took upon themselves, upon their descendants [ἐπὶ τῷ σπέρματι αὐτῶν], and upon all who would join them [ἐπὶ τοῖς προστεθειμένοις ἐπ᾽ αὐτῶν], to observe it without fail." Clearly, "those who have joined them" are proselytes.[25] The connection with 8:17 is equally clear; just as many Gentiles joined the Jewish community during the climactic events themselves, so it is expected that "those who have joined" the community will take a regular part in the commemoration of those events. While fear may have been the motivation for their conversion, fear is not a negative thing in LXX Esther (1:22; 2:20; 15:13). The "Judaizers" of 8:17 are to be seen as full converts, those "who have joined" the community of Israel.[26]

23. (Cohen 1999, 181). C. Moore (1971, 82) interprets the Hebrew account in a similar way.

24. Cf. Berg (1979, 115, n. 8) on the Hebrew version of 8:17.

25. προστίθημι is proselyte language; see LXX Isa 14:1; Jdt 14:10.

26. Fox (1991, 121–22) makes a similar observation about the Hebrew version.

Thus LXX Esther is positive in its attitude toward proselytes, taking it as a matter of course that Gentiles will be drawn by Israel's success and seek to convert. This positive attitude is taken over from the Hebrew version;[27] what is added in the Septuagint is the identification of circumcision as the decisive element in "becoming a Jew" (Ἰουδαΐζειν). Once again, however, the action is centripetal; Gentiles are attracted to Judaism, rather than coming as a result of any deliberate activity on the part of the Jews.

§12 LXX Esther 16:15–16

> *But we find that the Jews, who were consigned to annihilation by this thrice-accursed man, are not evildoers, but are governed by most righteous laws and are children of the living God, most high, most mighty, who has directed the kingdom both for us and for our ancestors in the most excellent order.*

Text: Greek: LXX (Rahlfs, 1979)
Translation: NRSV
Date: First-century B.C.E.
Provenance: Alexandria
Original Language: Greek
Bibliography: Balch (1998); Bickerman (1944); J. J. Collins (2000, 110–12); Day (1995); Gruen (1998, 177–86); C. Moore (1977); Schürer (1987 3:718–22); Wills (1995, 93–131)
Category: SYMPATHIZATION, ETHICAL MONOTHEISM

The speaker is the Persian king Artaxerxes, who here is addressing "the governors of the [Persian] provinces from India to Ethiopia" (16:1) in an edict written after the vindication of Mordecai and the collapse of Haman's plot against the Jews. Before we can examine the king's statement directly, we need to set it in the context of the Greek version of Esther.

The edict is one of six substantial segments present in the Septuagint but not in the canonical Hebrew text.[28] These additions, usually designated A to F,[29]

27. The date of the Hebrew version is a matter of some dispute (C. Moore 1971, lvii-lx), complicated by the probability that the text developed through several forms. Still, the final version is probably pre-Maccabean, which means that the text provides evidence of a positive attitude toward proselytes at least by the early second-century C.E.

28. In addition to the LXX version, there is another Greek version (the A text), that differs considerably from MT and the LXX where the latter two overlap; possibly it has been based on a different Hebrew original (see Clines 1984, 71–92). The six additions, however, agree with the LXX and most probably have been taken over from it. Thus for our purposes we do not need to take the A text into account here.

29. The chapter-and-verse references in what follows derive from the Vulgate, in which the additions are grouped together at the end of the canonical text. In an alternative system of citation, verse numbers are simply appended to the capital-letter designations, e.g., A

are as follows: A (11:2–12:6), located at the beginning of the narrative, containing accounts of a dream experienced by Mordecai and of his discovery of a plot against the king; B (13:1–7), appearing between 3:13 and 14 and giving the text of the edict mentioned in 3:13, in which the king commands the destruction of the Jewish people; C (13:8–14:19), appearing at the end of chapter 4 and containing prayers offered by Mordecai and Esther; D (15:1–16), an expansion of the account of Esther's approach to the king in 5:1–2; E (16:1–24), appearing between 8:12 and 13 and giving the text of the king's edict mentioned in 8:9–12 and containing the material under discussion here; and F (10:4–13), found at the end of the narrative, in which Mordecai recognizes that the events of the story had been presaged in the dream experienced at the outset. This is followed by a colophon (11:1), which identifies the "preceding letter about Purim" as having been translated "by Lysimachus son of Ptolemy, one of the residents of Jerusalem," and subsequently brought (presumably) to Egypt[30] "in the fourth year of the reign of Ptolemy and Cleopatra."

The six additions are not uniform in style and character. In particular, B and E stand apart from the rest. For one thing, they differ in theological and cultural outlook. To be sure, all of the additions, together with other alterations in the Greek version, are concerned to introduce the kind of overt piety that is so strikingly absent in Hebrew Esther. However, as we will presently see in more detail, B and E are much less marked by Jewish particularism than are the other additions. Another difference is linguistic: while the others seem to have been based on Semitic originals, Additions B and E are Greek compositions of high literary quality. These two additions, then, though probably written by the same person, almost certainly originated in different circumstances than the rest of Greek Esther. Most scholars are prepared to see the colophon as authentic and thus to envisage the existence of a Hebrew version, containing Additions A, C, D, and F, that was translated into Greek in Judea and subsequently brought in its translated form to Egypt. Additions B and E, which would fit very nicely into an Egyptian context, were probably produced in Alexandria and inserted into the narrative at a later point. The two main possibilities for "the fourth year of the reign of Ptolemy and Cleopatra" are 114 and 77 B.C.E. There is no scholarly consensus on which of these two dates is more likely.[31] For

1–16 = 11:1–12:6. In yet another system of citation (found, e.g., in Rahlfs' edition of the LXX), lowercase letters are added to the canonical versification; so: 1:1a-s = A 1–16 = 11:1–12:6.

30. The text simply reads εἰσήνεγκεν: "they brought it in." The reference to Ptolemy and Cleopatra, however, implies that they brought it into Egypt.

31. Bickerman (1944) has argued strongly for the later date (followed by J. J. Collins 2000, 110–11); Schürer (1986, 3:506) prefers the earlier. A date of 48 is also possible but is generally considered to be unlikely given the political unrest in the Roman world at that time (see Gruen 1998, 178).

our purposes it is probably not necessary to force a decision. Since the version containing Additions B and E was well enough established by the end of the first century C.E. to have been used by Josephus, it is probable that these additions were produced sometime before the middle of the first century B.C.E.

Thus our primary interest here is not with the Greek version of Esther as a whole but with the particular interpretation that is put on this narrative by the specific account of the king's transformation as reflected in the two edicts represented by Additions B and E. If we look at the narrative as it presumably appeared before these final additions were made—that is, if we bracket Additions B and E and just read the narrative that remains—Artaxerxes emerges as an erratic figure, at times ineffectual, absent-minded, and oblivious to things that are happening around him, and at other times impulsive, authoritarian, and even terrifying. Apparently unaware of Haman's sympathies for the eunuchs who had plotted against him (12:6), he nevertheless appointed Haman to a position of high honor and power in the kingdom (3:1). When Haman came to him with his plan to annihilate a whole ethnic group "scattered among the other nations in your kingdom" (3:8), the king gave him carte blanche to proceed without even pausing to ask about the identity of the group and oblivious to the animosity toward Mordecai that was fueling Haman's plan. The king even waved off Haman's offer of money for the royal treasury (ten thousand talents!), airily telling him to "keep the money and do whatever you want with that nation" (3:11).

To Esther, however, the king is a figure to be feared. When Mordecai urged her to appeal to the king on behalf of her threatened people, she replied that "all nations of the empire know that if any man or woman goes to the king inside the inner court without being called, there is no escape for that person" (4:11). Consequently, when she decided that she must act regardless, she was "seized with deadly anxiety" (14:1) and approached the king outwardly radiant but with a heart "frozen with fear" (15:5). Her fears were well founded, for the king responded to her arrival with "fierce anger" (15:7), which caused her to faint dead away. God came to the rescue at this point—the only direct action of God in the narrative—"chang[ing] the spirit of the king to gentleness" (15:8). His change of heart, however, involves only his attitude toward his wife. Although he became tender toward her, "[taking] her in his arms . . . [and comforting] her with soothing words" (15:8), he had no inkling of the source of her distress. Even when she finally revealed her plight and her petition—two banquets later!—the king still was not able to make the connection with Haman and his machinations (7:5). His ultimate condemnation of Haman was prompted more by his mistaken perception that Haman was trying to assault Esther in his own house than by Haman's murderous intentions against Esther's people (7:7–8). Further, his willingness to issue a new edict was based more on the elevation of the individuals Esther and Mordecai to positions of higher honor in the kingdom than on any new appreciation of the Jews as a people.

Thus, while in this penultimate version of Greek Esther Artaxerxes does experience a change of heart, this change is minimal, going no further than what is required for the outworking of the plot. The king remains a comic figure, with no greater insight into the nature or virtue of Judaism at the end of the narrative than he had at the outset.[32] This portrait of the king is in keeping with another aspect of the Greek version apart from Additions B and E—namely, a heightened emphasis on Jewish particularism. Such particularism is readily apparent in the account of Mordecai's dream and its interpretation, (11:2–12 [A] and 10:4–13 [F]). In the dream, the human world is sharply divided into two groups: the "righteous nation" of Israel (11:9) and all the other nations that "gathered to destroy the name of the Jews" (10:8). At the end of the story, as Mordecai reflects on the dream and its meaning, he concludes that God "made two lots, one for the people of God and one for all the nations, and these two lots came to the hour and moment and day of decision" (10:10–11). In other words, the struggle between Haman and Mordecai (10:7) is the focal point of a more fundamental conflict between Israel and the Gentiles. The either-or character of this conflict is reflected in Esther's attitude toward her marriage to the Gentile king: while praying for divine assistance just before she approaches the king with her crucial request, she declares: "I hate the splendor of the wicked and abhor the bed of the uncircumcised and of any alien" (14:15).[33] (Perhaps this explains why the king could let a month go by without summoning her [4:11]!) Likewise Mordecai prays: "O Lord God and King, God of Abraham, spare your people; for . . . [our foes] desire to destroy the inheritance that has been yours from the beginning" (13:15). There is thus a categorical chasm between the Jews and the rest of humankind, a chasm that can be bridged only by proselytism (8:17). And even here, conversion is seen as a measure of how much Gentiles fear the Jews rather than of how much they admire the law or the God who gave it. Since the king, who had no particular reason to fear the Jews, thus remains firmly on the other side of the divide, the narrative has no interest in attributing to him any degree of virtue or religious insight.

A strikingly different portrait, however, emerges from Additions B and E. According to the original narrative, both edicts, while promulgated in the king's name, were actually written by others—Haman in the first instance (3:12–13) and Esther in the second (8:8–12). The edicts that were inserted later (Additions B and E), however, display such a uniformity in style and such a compelling first-person voice that readers naturally—and rightly—encounter

32. On the comic aspects of Greek Esther, see Gruen (1998, 177–86). His argument that Additions B and E continue to see the king simply as a figure of ridicule, however, is much less convincing (see Gruen 1998, 181).

33. Gruen (1998, 183–84) argues convincingly that there is an element of self-justification, and thus of a "bad conscience," in the prayers of Mordecai (ch. 13) and Esther (ch. 14).

them as the words of the king himself. What emerges from the two edicts, taken together in the context of the narrative in which they are embedded, is the portrait of a well-meaning, righteous, and God-fearing monarch who was duped for a while by a scheming courtier but who in the end comes to his senses and recognizes the value of the Jews to his own kingdom and the place of his kingdom within the universal sovereignty of the Jewish God.

In the first edict, the king emerges as noble in both his demeanor and his intentions. He has not allowed his position as "ruler of many nations and master of the whole world" (13:2) to make him haughty or arrogant; instead he was "not elated with presumption of authority" and was "always acting reasonably and with kindness." His goal for the kingdom was the kind of cosmopolitan utopia that had been a Hellenistic ideal since the time of Alexander: "I have determined to settle the lives of my subjects in lasting tranquility and, in order to make my kingdom peaceable and open to travel throughout all its extent, to restore the peace desired by all people" (13:2). There is nothing ironic about this portrait. Although his subsequent description of Haman—"who excels among us in sound judgment, and is distinguished for his unchanging goodwill and steadfast fidelity" (13:3)—will lead readers to question the soundness of the king's own judgment, the values that the king espouses, and mistakenly believes to be exhibited also by Haman, are values that readers are expected to share. Haman's duplicity is measured by his success in convincing the king that the only thing standing in the way of his noble intentions was the existence in the kingdom of "a certain hostile people," whose lack of loyalty and perverse adherence to "a strange manner of life and laws" is preventing "the unifying of the kingdom that we honorably intend" (13:4–5). The king, then, emerges as a sympathetic figure—noble in his ideals and intentions, but unwittingly opening the door to disaster because of a mistaken belief that Haman was equally noble.

The nobility of the king remains intact in the second edict. Again he appears as a kind and generous benefactor (16:2), one who values "goodness" (16:4) and is concerned "to render our kingdom quiet and peaceable for all" (16:8). But he now recognizes the extent of Haman's treachery and the way in which he himself had been deceived. As a result, not only has he reversed his opinion on the nature of Judaism and the effect of the Jewish community on the stability of the kingdom; he has also come to recognize the Jewish God as the true universal sovereign to whom his own kingdom is subject.

The edict begins in a roundabout way, with a general denunciation of certain "people" who "know nothing of goodness" and who thus respond to goodness and benefaction by becoming proud and power-hungry, going so far as "to scheme against their own benefactors" (16:2–3). Moving closer to the topic at hand, the edict goes on to say that such persons, when "entrusted with the administration of public affairs," have often "by the false trickery of their evil natures beguile[d] the sincere goodwill of their sovereigns," with the result that innocent rulers "have been made in part responsible for the shedding of innocent blood" (16:2–6). At this point the edict moves from the general to the particular: Haman, who enjoyed the king's "goodwill" "so fully" that he was elevated to a position "second to the royal throne," was nevertheless full of "intricate craft and deceit" and so conspired against the king and sought "to deprive us of our kingdom and our life." In fact, the origin and extent of Haman's conspiracy is "revealed" here for the first time: Haman, the king informs his subjects, was really a Macedonian.[34] This explained both his lack of virtue—he was naturally lacking the "kindliness" that comes with "Persian blood"—and his ultimate intentions: his goal was to "transfer the kingdom of the Persians to the Macedonians" (16:10–14).

This reversal in the king's perception of Haman's character has evidently precipitated a corresponding reversal in his estimation of Jews and Judaism. Not only does he acknowledge Mordecai as "our savior and perpetual benefactor" and Esther as "the blameless partner of our kingdom" (16:13), but he recognizes that they belonged to the "nation" targeted by Haman, a nation that he explicitly identifies as that of the Jews (16:13, 15). Further, far from being a threat to the nation, the Jews "are not evildoers, but are governed by most righteous laws" (16:15). Central to the king's decree is that Jews are to have the freedom to live in accordance with these laws throughout the whole kingdom.

But the king does more than simply recognize the loyalty of the Jews and the virtues of their laws, thus establishing the Jewish community as a legitimate and important component of his kingdom. He adds to the virtues that he has displayed from the beginning by acknowledging the God of the Jews as well. There are four references to God in the edict. The first appears in the introductory section, where the king is engaging in his general denunciation of the "many people" who repay kindness with injury and deceit. The climax of this denunciation is that such people "even assume that they will escape the evil-hating justice of God [θεοῦ μισοπόνηρον δίκην], who always sees everything" (16:4). Here the existence of a single, righteous, all-knowing, and sovereign God is simply taken for granted. In the second reference, this God is identified as the God of the Jews and the God who has directed the Persian kingdom: the Jews "are children of the living God, most high, most mighty [υἱοὺς τοῦ ὑψίστου μεγίστου ζῶντος θεοῦ]"; but this is the same God who has also "directed the kingdom both for us and for our ancestors in the most excellent order" (16:16). Both aspects of God reappear in the other two references: God is both the universal ruler (τοῦ τὰ πάντα ἐπικρατοῦντος θεοῦ [16:18]; ὁ πάντα δυναστεύων θεός [16:21]) and the defender of "his chosen people" (τοῦ ἐκλεκτοῦ γένους [16:21]) who has meted out swift and deserved punishment on Haman (16:18).

34. In Hebrew Esther Haman was an Agagite (Esth 3:1, 10). Elsewhere in Greek Esther he is described as a Bougean (Βουγαῖος [12:6; 3:1]), a term whose significance is unknown. For discussion, see C. Moore (1977, 178).

The capstone of Artaxerxes's transformation, then, is his acknowledgment of and submission to the God of Israel, who is also the universal sovereign. But as he does so, he remains fully a Gentile. He continues to be proud of his Persian blood (16:10). He acknowledges the righteousness of the Jewish laws (16:15) but seems to believe that all that is required of him as a God-fearing monarch is that he protect their right to observe them (16:19); there is no suggestion that he should adopt them for himself or for his kingdom as a whole. He recognizes that he is subject to the same God who has chosen the Jews but seems to believe that he can honor and relate to this God directly, without having to depend on Jewish mediation of some kind; there is no suggestion, for example, that to honor God it would be necessary for him to make an offering at the Jerusalem temple. This profile of Gentile piety comes close to the kind of ethical monotheism that is exemplified, for example, by King Ptolemy in the *Letter of Aristeas*. If piety had been one of the royal virtues on display in the first edict, prior to the king's recognition of the truth about the Jewish people, this passage might be classified as an example of ethical monotheism. But since the king's piety appears only in conjunction with his new attitude toward the Jews, it is more appropriate to treat it as an example of Jewish sympathization.

The addition of these two edicts, then, puts quite a different spin on the story. If the earlier supplements (i.e., Additions A, C, D, and F) have rendered the story more particularistic, setting Jew and Gentile over against each other, Additions B and E impose a more universalistic reading, inviting readers to identify Jews and Persians as distinct "nations" who nevertheless can live together under the sovereignty and protection of the same God. Of course, by the nature of the case, the fit between these final additions and the earlier version of the story is awkward. But this only underlines the striking significance of this final interpretive layer.

Tobit

Tobit is an obviously contrived but nevertheless highly entertaining tale of piety and misfortune, danger and deliverance, and romance and restoration. Since the story is set in the Diaspora, the relationship of Jews and Gentiles is an integral feature of the narrative. Further, since the experience of this particular Jewish family in exile is meant to reflect the experience of Israel as a whole, the place of Gentiles in the story is of more than passing significance.

As Nowell (1987) has observed, the place of Gentiles in the world of Tobit is mixed. On the one hand, the strong emphasis on Torah piety produces a sharp tone of separation and exclusivity. Unlike his compatriots, whose Torah-laxity was the reason for the exile, Tobit refrained "from eating the food of the Gentiles" (1:11). Marriage with a Gentile woman is strongly prohibited (4:12–13); indeed, the need to "marry a woman from among the descendants of your ancestors" (4:12) is one of the tracks on which the plot moves forward. It is Tobit's resolve in burying his kinsfolk according to the prescriptions of the

Torah that provokes the anger of Nineveh's king Sennacherib and contributes to Tobit's downfall (1:16–20). Nineveh itself, framing the story as the place of exile (1:3) that nevertheless was destined for destruction as the prophets had foretold (14:4), serves as a microcosm of the Gentile world set over against Israel as a whole.

But at the same time there is a certain generosity toward the Gentiles and a willingness to accord them a place within an Israel-centered world. As with Daniel, Tobit is rewarded for faithfulness to the Torah by receiving a position of prominence within Shalmaneser's court (1:12–14). While acknowledging that "none of the nations has understanding," Tobit nevertheless believes that "the Lord himself will give them good counsel" (4:19).[35] More specifically, Tobit contains three passages that qualify for more extended discussion here. One is a reference to "the proselytes who had attached themselves to Israel" (1:8). The other two—Tobit's prayer of thanksgiving as the story reaches its climax (ch. 13) and his deathbed speech to his family (ch. 14)—deal with the eschatological destiny of the Gentiles.

Before looking at these passage directly, we need to address an issue concerning the status of chapters 13 and 14. The emphasis in both chapters falls not on the particular circumstances of Tobit and his family but on the present misfortunes and future redemption of Israel as a whole. This has led some scholars to argue that these chapters were later additions. Zimmermann (1958, 24–27), for example, places both of them in the period after the destruction of the temple in 70 C.E., arguing that only in such circumstances would we find an interest in the rebuilding of Jerusalem and the temple (cf. 13:10; 14:5). The tendency in more recent scholarship, however, has been to view Tobit as a unity.[36] The expectation that Jerusalem and the temple would be rebuilt in the end times was undeniably present in the Second Temple period (e.g., *1 Enoch* 90:28–29); such an expectation by no means necessitates a post-70 C.E. dating. Further, Jewish tales and romances (e.g., Esther, Daniel, Judith), while enjoyable in themselves, are generally concerned in some way with the larger situation of the people as a whole. This is particularly true of Tobit. The opening of the work carefully places Tobit's personal story in the context of Israel's larger story, emphasizing the importance of Torah observance and temple worship (1:3–13), the rewards of faithfulness (1:12–13) and the consequences of unfaithfulness (specifically exile [1:2–5, 10]). Further, in the prayer that Tobit

35. This is based on a reconstruction of 4:19. ℵ has a lacuna between 4:7 and 19, and lacks any counterpart to "none of the nations has understanding" (BA). In place of "the Lord himself will give them good counsel" (ℵ), BA reads "the Lord himself will give every good thing." In either case, the Gentiles are the recipients of divine beneficence that compensates for their natural failings.

36. For a full discussion, see C. Moore (1996, 21–22); see also Spencer (1999).

offers at the point when his fortunes have reached their lowest ebb (3:1–6), he explicitly links his own troubles with those of Israel as a whole, who have been given over "to plunder, exile, and death, to become the talk, the byword, and an object of reproach among all the nations among whom you have dispersed us" (v. 4; see vv. 3–5). Thus it is perfectly fitting that the story should end as it does, with the restoration of Tobit's fortunes linked paradigmatically with the redemption of Israel as a whole. There is no pressing reason, then, to see either chapter as a later entity.[37]

Text: Greek: LXX (Rahlfs, 1979); Aramaic and Hebrew: 4Q196–200 (Fitzmyer 1995)
Translation: NRSV (based on Codex Sinaiticus[38])
Date: Circa 225–175 B.C.E.
Provenance: Probably the eastern Diaspora
Original Language: Aramaic or Hebrew[39]
Bibliography: Deselaers (1982); Di Lella (1979); Fitzmyer (2003); Kraus (1996, 77–79); Levine (1992); C. Moore (1996); Nowell (1987); Soll (1989); Spencer (1999); Zimmerman (1958).

§13 Tobit 1:8

A third tenth I would give to the orphans and widows and to the converts who had attached themselves to Israel.

Category: CONVERSION

This passage appears near the beginning of the narrative, where the author is establishing the faultless Torah- and temple-piety of the main character Tobit.

37. This is not to rule out the possibility that either 13:1–17 or 14:4–7 represent preexistent sources or traditions reworked and incorporated by the author. In fact, given Tobit's evident reworking of various folktales (Soll 1989; C. Moore 1996, 11–14), a similar reworking of Biblical tradition is perhaps to be expected. The point here, however, is that there is no reason to see these passages as later additions.

38. The text of Tobit is found in several forms: a shorter form, represented by Vaticanus (B), Alexandrinus (A) and the Latin Vulgate; and a longer form, represented by Sinaiticus (א) and old Latin. The evidence from Qumran—fragments in Aramaic (4Q196–199) and Hebrew (4Q200)—generally agrees with the longer form, indicating that it is to be preferred. The Qumran evidence, while important for issues of text and original language, does not have a significant bearing on the passages under discussion here. For a full discussion of the textual tradition, see Fitzmyer (2003, 3–15).

39. While Deselaers (1982) has recently revived older arguments for a Greek original, the evidence from Qumran (four fragments in Aramaic and one in Hebrew) has produced a widespread consensus that Tobit was written originally in a Semitic language (Hebrew or Aramaic).

Tobit is of the tribe of Naphtali in the northern kingdom and with his kinsfolk has been carried away into exile in Nineveh. At this point in the narration, however, Tobit is looking back at his pattern of life prior to the fall of the northern kingdom. What is striking here is Tobit's commitment to the Jerusalem temple; alone of all his kinsfolk, he would travel regularly to Jerusalem to celebrate the festivals, "as it is prescribed for all Israel by an everlasting decree" (1:6). It is in this context that he speaks of giving a third tithe to the orphans, widows, and "proselytes" (προσηλύτοις).

How is the term προσηλύτοις to be interpreted? The pertinent text in the Torah is Deut 14:28–29, which prescribes a third tithe to be given every third year to the גר, the orphan, and the widow.[40] As will be discussed in more detail later,[41] in its original usage גר designated not a religious convert to Judaism but a resident alien, a non-Jew living in the land and thus included in certain ways in the common life of the Jewish nation. Given the narrow ritual and biblical focus of Tob 1:8, then, it might be argued that προσηλύτοις should be interpreted in the same way; that is, that the passage is simply reflecting the Biblical language of resident aliens rather than the later reality of proselytes or full religious converts.

Two considerations make this unlikely, however. One is the Diaspora context of Tobit. Sociologically, the concept of a resident alien belongs to the situation of a nation at home in its own land. Admittedly, this is the narrative context of Tob 1:8; it is in Jerusalem that the προσήλυτοι in question are to be found. But in the actual setting of the author and his intended readers—the late third- or early second-century B.C.E. Diaspora—the term (in Aramaic and Hebrew, as well as Greek) would naturally have denoted a full convert. While it is not impossible that a Diaspora community might use the term in its older sense, it is not the most natural reading. The second, and more decisive, consideration is the descriptive phrase, "who had attached [προσκειμένοις] themselves to Israel." While not present in Deuteronomy, such language is commonly used in the Second Temple period of full proselytes.[42] It is likely, then, that Tob 1:8 refers to full converts to Judaism rather than simply to resident aliens.

§14 Tobit 13:11–14

> [11]*A bright light will shine to all the ends of the earth; many nations will come to you from far away, the inhabitants of the remotest parts of the earth to your holy name,*

40. For a discussion of the complexities of the Biblical laws of tithing, their interpretation in the Second Temple period, and the variations in the Greek versions of Tobit, see C. Moore (1996, 111–15).

41. See ch. 11.

42. E.g., Esth 9:27; Jdt 14:10; *Jos. Asen.* 16:14; 4QpNah frags. 3–4, 2.9; Philo *Spec.* 1.51; Josephus *Ant.* 13.319; see Kuhn (1968, 735). The point is also made by Fitzmyer (2003, 111), though without citing any references outside Tobit.

bearing gifts in their hands for the King of heaven. Generation after generation will give joyful praise in you, the name of the chosen city will endure forever. [12]*Cursed are all who speak a harsh word against you; cursed are all who conquer you and pull down your walls, all who overthrow your towers and set your homes on fire. But blessed forever will be all who revere you.* [13]*Go, then, and rejoice over the children of the righteous, for they will be gathered together and will praise the Lord of the ages.* [14]*Happy are those who love you, and happy are those who rejoice in your prosperity. Happy also are all people who grieve with you because of your afflictions; for they will rejoice with you and witness all your glory forever.*

Category: ESCHATOLOGICAL PARTICIPATION

Tobit's prayer in chapter 13 is a typical piece of restoration eschatology, containing strong echoes of Isaiah and related passages.[43] Here we find the gathering of the scattered exiles (vv. 5, 13), the restoration and glorification of Jerusalem and the temple (vv. 10, 11, 16–17), the light shining to the ends of the earth (v. 11), and, especially, the pilgrimage of "many nations" (ἔθνη πολλά) bearing gifts to God in Jerusalem (v. 11).[44]

As is often the case in passages of this kind, the situation and status of these Gentile pilgrims is not precisely indicated. Still, there are several indications that the Gentiles are expected to be actual participants in salvation and not simply observers, present only to acknowledge the special status of Israel and Jerusalem. Since Gentiles are also in view in v. 12—those "who conquer you and pull down your walls"—the whole of vv. 11 and 12 must be concerned with Gentiles. This means in particular that the generations who "will give joyful praise in you" are Gentiles. The fact, then, that joyful praise is to be offered in Jerusalem by generations of Gentile worshippers suggests ongoing participation in the worship of God. A similar observation can be made concerning v. 12b. Since the "cursed" are clearly Gentiles, so also are the "blessed" who "revere"[45] Jerusalem. Such a state of blessedness suggests that Gentiles are expected to receive some of the benefits of the age of salvation, not simply to observe them.[46]

A clearer statement of Gentile participation, however, is found in the second text of interest in Tobit.

43. E.g., note the echoes of Isa 49:6 and 60:1 in v. 11.

44. On the textual variations in v. 11, see Fitzmyer (2003, 313).

45. οἱ φοβούμενοι ("fear, reverence," Sinaiticus); οἱ ἀγαπῶντες ("love," Alexandrinus, Vaticanus). While 4Q196 contains portions of Tob 13:6–12, this portion of v. 12 is missing.

46. Cf. C. Moore's comment on v. 11: "Although Tobit may have confined most of his time and charity to his fellow Israelites, here Tobit's (or better, the author's) compassion and broad-mindedness are clearly evident" (1996, 280–81).

§15 Tobit 14:5–7

> [5]*After this they all will return from their exile and will rebuild Jerusalem in splendor; and in it the temple of God will be rebuilt, just as the prophets of Israel have said concerning it.* [6]*Then the nations in the whole world will all be converted and worship God in truth. They will all abandon their idols, which deceitfully have led them into their error;* [7]*and in righteousness they will praise the eternal God. All the Israelites who are saved in those days and are truly mindful of God will be gathered together; they will go to Jerusalem and live in safety forever in the land of Abraham, and it will be given over to them. Those who sincerely love God will rejoice, but those who commit sin and injustice will vanish from all the earth.*

Category: ESCHATOLOGICAL PARTICIPATION

In his deathbed farewell, before giving some final instructions and admonitions to his descendants, Tobit looks ahead and "predicts" Israel's subsequent history—from the fall of Nineveh, to the destruction of the temple, to the initial return from exile, and on to the final restoration. This example of restoration eschatology, typical in many respects, is nevertheless striking for the prominence given to the Gentiles. As much attention is paid to the turning of the Gentiles to God as to the restoration of Jerusalem and the temple, if not more. More specifically, there is no question about the Gentiles' full participation in the end-time state of bliss. "All the nations in the whole world" (πάντα τὰ ἔθνη τὰ ἐν ὅλῃ τῇ γῇ) will abandon[47] their idols (v. 6) and give true reverence (φοβ–ηθήσονται) to God (v. 6), praising God in righteousness (v. 7). Further, while v. 7 returns to the situation of Israelites ("All the Israelites who are saved in those days . . . "), the verse ends on a universal note ("all the earth"), suggesting that the company of those "who sincerely love God" and thus "rejoice" (v. 7) either includes Gentiles or perhaps even is exclusively Gentile.[48]

Where the text is not clear, however, is in the matter of the status of these Gentiles with respect to Israel and the law of Moses. The NRSV describes them as being "converted" (v. 6), thereby suggesting that the Gentiles are expected to be fully incorporated into the covenant people Israel—eschatological proselytes, as it were. While this position is held by some interpreters,[49] the word

47. ἀφήσουσιν. The shorter form (B and A) has κατορύξουσιν (bury); 4Q198 reads ירמון (cast away). The variation does not affect the sense of the verse.

48. It is possible that v. 7b refers exclusively to Gentiles; v. 7 can be understood as referring first to Jews ("All the Israelites who are saved in those days . . .") and then to Gentiles ("Those who sincerely love God"). Support for such a reading might be provided by the other text tradition (B and A); here "those who love the Lord God" are said to "show mercy to our brethren," which seems to imply an exclusively Gentile group.

49. McKnight speaks of "conversion to Judaism" (1991, 37; also p. 47). Likewise, C. Moore uses the term "converted," but without further comment (1996, 291). E. P. Sanders, more vaguely, describes these Gentiles as "added to Israel" (1985, 214).

(ἐπιστρέψει) simply means "to turn," and by no means implies full conversion (Kraus 1996, 79).

Some light can be shed on the issue by looking at the passage in the context of Tobit as a whole. As we have observed, there is no doubt whatsoever about Tobit's adherence to the Torah and about the sharp line of demarcation between Jew and Gentile that such Torah piety produces. One might expect, therefore, that Tobit would demand similar Torah piety of any Gentiles who wanted to "fear God in truth" (cf. 14:6). But this does not seem to be the case. To be sure, the terms used with reference to the Gentiles in 14:5–7 tend to be also predicated of pious Jews earlier in the book: "fear God" (v. 6; cf. 4:21); "in truth" (v. 6; cf. 1:3; 4:6); "in righteousness" (v. 7; cf. 1:3; 4:6; 12:8); "praise God" (v. 7 [εὐλογεῖν]; cf. 3:11; 4:19; 8:5, 15; 11:14–17; 12:6, 17, 18, 22; 13:6, 10, 15, 17). Thus these Gentile participants in end-time salvation are expected to share some basic elements of piety with the covenant people. But there is no indication whatsoever that these Gentiles are themselves to become full members of the covenant people. Abandonment of idolatry and worship of the God of Israel seem to be the only requirements. The striking absence in this passage of any reference to "law," "covenant," "circumcision," or "commandments" suggests strongly that these Gentiles are expected to share in the joys of the coming age as Gentiles, and not as end-time proselytes to Judaism (see Levine 1992, 108).

§16 Sirach 10:19–22

> *Whose offspring can be in honor? Human offspring. Which offspring are in honor? Those who fear God. Whose offspring can be in disgrace? Human offspring. Which offspring are in disgrace? Those who transgress the commandment. . . .* [22]*Be it sojourner, wayfarer, alien or pauper, his glory is the fear of the Lord.*

Text: Greek: Ziegler (1965); Hebrew: Beentjes (1997)
Translation: Skehan and Di Lella (1987)
Date: Early second century B.C.E.
Provenance: Judea
Original Language: Hebrew
Bibliography: Di Lella (1966); Kraus (1996, 47–50); Skehan and Di Lella (1987)
Category: CONVERSION

This rendering of Sir 10:22 is based on Hebrew readings found in the Cairo Genizah (גר זר נכרי ורש).[50] The Greek manuscripts contain no reference to sojourners or foreigners; instead, they speak of "the rich and the eminent and

50. Two of the six genizah manuscripts (A, B) contain 10:22 (A adds ו to זר). The verse is not found in the manuscripts from Qumran and Masada. See Beentjes (1997).

the poor" (πλούσιος καὶ ἔνδοξος καὶ πτωχός). The Qumran discoveries, however, have tended to confirm the general reliability of the Cairo genizah manuscripts (Di Lella 1966). This general consideration, together with the fact that other ancient versions make reference to foreigners in this verse,[51] makes it highly probable that the Hebrew version of 10:22 is original.

If this is the original reading, however, the verse is somewhat of an anomaly in Sirach, whose author displays little positive interest in the Gentiles. Sirach's goal is to convince his readers that true Wisdom is to be found only in the temple (24:10), the Torah (19:20; 24:23), and the people associated with both. While Wisdom might hold sway "over every people and nation" (24:6), she has chosen to dwell solely in Israel (24:1–12). Those who obey Wisdom "will judge the nations" (4:15), and Sirach calls on God to punish the nations so that they will know "that there is no God but you, O Lord" (36:1–22; here v. 5). While Wisdom (and therefore the Torah) is of universal significance, Sirach is primarily concerned to maintain the wall that separates Israel from the nations; for those outside the wall, Wisdom's universal role is experienced in a negative way. True, Sirach does make mention of God's promise to Abraham "that the nations would be blessed through his offspring" (44:21). But the statement simply paraphrases scripture (Gen 12:3), and the promise is quickly passed over.

The passage under discussion here, however, opens up a breach in the wall, albeit a narrow one. A line continues to be drawn between those "who fear God" and those "who transgress the commandment" (10:19). The parallelism implies that fearing God and keeping the commandments are closely linked, and vice versa. But the groups on either side of the line are described in curiously universal terms: in either case they are "human offspring" (σπέρμα ἀνθρώπου). The righteous here are described generically as the "seed of a human being" rather than, say, the seed of Abraham. Further, 10:22 seems to imply that non-Jews—specifically, the sojourner (גר), the foreigner (נכרי)—are able to "fear the Lord," presumably by keeping the commandments.

It needs to be noted, however, that the use of these terms does not go beyond their scriptural meanings. Specifically, there is no notion of proselytism at work here; גר does not have the sense of "proselyte." If it did, a נכרי who "feared the Lord" would by definition have become a גר, which would make the term redundant. גר and נכרי here retain their scriptural meanings of "resident alien" and "foreigner" respectively. The passage thus reflects the Biblical world in which resident aliens and foreigners were congenitally incapable of becoming Israelites, even if it was also possible for them to "fear the Lord" and "keep the commandments." To the extent that this represented a way of including the non-Jew within the sphere of righteousness and divine benevolence, Sirach can

51. Specifically the Sahidic and Syriac; see Ziegler (1965, 172), who, on these grounds, emends the Greek text so that it reads προσήλυτος καὶ ξένος καὶ πτωχός.

be described as sharing in such a pattern of inclusion. But Sirach represents no advance over the Biblical pattern.

2 Maccabees

The main section of 2 Maccabees (3:1–15:36) is an account of the Maccabean revolt that begins with the conflict between the high priest, Onias III, and Simon, the captain of the temple, during the reign of Seleucus IV (187–175 B.C.E.), and ends with Judas's victory over the Seleucid general Nicanor (161). This historical narrative is bracketed by a preface (2:19–32) and an epilogue (15:37–39), which describe the history as an abridgment "into a single book" of a five-volume work by a certain Jason of Cyrene (2:23). The abridger remains unnamed but speaks to his readers in the first person—plural in the preface and singular in the epilogue. The work is written in an elevated Greek style, indicating that, despite his evident concern to preserve Jewish particularity, the abridger was thoroughly conversant with traditions of Hellenistic rhetoric.[52] The work as it has come to us, however, begins not with the abridger's preface but with two letters from Jerusalem Jews addressed to the Jewish community in Egypt. Both letters exhort Egyptian Jews to join with the Jerusalemites in observing a festival on the twenty-fifth day of the month Chislev to celebrate the purification of the temple. Neither letter displays any awareness either of the other or of the historical narrative to follow, which suggests that the two letters and the abridged history were originally independent. Thus we need not concern ourselves here with issues arising from the letters themselves.[53]

Concerning the provenance of the abridgment, an important indicator is the treatment of the Maccabees in the work. While Judas is the central figure in the account and is treated positively, in contrast to 1 Maccabees the rest of the Hasmonean family is relegated to the shadows. Mattathias is not mentioned at all; although the abridger describes the account as "the story of Judas and his brothers" (2:19), the brothers are minor characters; Simon in particular is presented in less than glowing terms.[54] This feature of the account is probably to be linked with several others: the highly positive presentation of Onias III (e.g., 3:1); the presentation of Judas as the leader of the Hasidim (14:6; cf. 1 Macc 7:13–14); the emphasis on resurrection and miraculous intervention; and the

52. Hengel (1974, 1:95); Doran (1981, 24–46); van Henten (1997, 20–21).

53. On the letters, see Bickerman (1933); Hengel (1974, 100); Goldstein (1983, 157–59); Schürer (1986, 3:533); J. J. Collins (2000, 79–80).

54. In 10:18–23, Simon appears particularly inept. Judas left him to carry out a siege of two fortified towers, but the defenders were able to bribe some of Simon's men and thus to escape. It was Judas, not Simon, who punished the Jewish miscreants and who then "immediately captured the two towers" (10:22). See also 14:17, where again the emphasis falls on Simon's inability to succeed.

fact that the narrative concludes while Judas is still alive and thus prior to the developments under Jonathan, Simon, and their successors. 2 Maccabees should probably be seen as stemming from a group whose sociopolitical and theological outlook differed considerably from that of the Hasmoneans.[55] It was produced at a point in the story when the coalition hammered together by Judas was still intact, but when different parties in the coalition were competing to put their own theological spin on their common history. A date early in the reign of John Hyrcanus, or even in the time of Simon, is probably to be preferred.[56]

The major themes of 2 Maccabees are readily apparent at the opening (3:1–3) and close (15:28–36) of the narrative. The narrative begins with an idyllic situation: because of the piety and hatred of wickedness exhibited by the high priest Onias, the "holy city" lived in peace and its people lived in full conformity to the law, with the result that the temple was glorified and held in honor even by foreign kings. At the end of the narrative, as the last in a series of assaults on the temple comes to naught with the defeat of the foreign general Nicanor, all Jerusalem gives praise to God "who has kept his own place [τὸν ἑαυτοῦ τόπον] undefiled" (15:34).[57] The lesson of the narrative as a whole is that if Israel is faithful to the law, God will protect the temple and preserve the city in peace. The corollary, however, is that if the people fall away in sin, then God's protection will be withdrawn and punishment will follow.

Several suggestions have been made as to the structure of the narrative, but since the narrator is careful to note changes in the Seleucid regime, it seems simplest to divide the book into four blocks according to the successive reigns:

55. For the idea that 2 Maccabees is at best lukewarm in its attitude toward the Hasmonaeans, see Doran (1981, 112); van Henten (1997, 54); J. J. Collins (2000, 82–83). Some have suggested that the work was fundamentally opposed to the Hasmonaean regime: "Our writer opposes the doctrines of the Hasmonaeans quite as much as their dynastic pretensions" (Goldstein (1983, 18); also Nickelsburg (2005, 109–10). But this probably goes too far. For one thing, there is no indication in the epilogue, which brings the story up to the time of the abridgment ("and from that time the city has been in the possession of the Hebrews" [15:37]), that the abridger was opposed in any substantial way to the contemporary state of affairs. Further, at the conclusion of the abridgment itself, we find the temple in a pure and undefiled state (15:34–36), with no hint that its purity might be threatened by subsequent high priests. In other words, neither the abridger nor the abridgment display any sense of alienation from the temple establishment.

56. The epilogue reflects a situation where Jerusalem is fully under Jewish control (15:37), which seems to set the *terminus a quo* at the start of Simon's reign in 142 B.C.E. ("when the yoke of the Gentiles was removed from Israel" [1 Macc 13:41–42]); given the positive view of the Romans throughout 2 Maccabees, the *terminus ad quem* is the arrival of Roman rule with Pompey in 63 B.C.E.

57. ὁ τόπος appears frequently in 2 Macc. (some fifteen occurrences) as a term for the temple, both by itself and with modifiers (ὁ ἅγιος τόπος; ὁ ἑαυτοῦ τόπος).

Seleucus IV (3:3–4:6); Antiochus Epiphanes (4:7–10:9); Antiochus Eupator (10:10–13:26); Demetrius (14:1–15:36).[58] What binds the four blocks together, however, is that each of them contains one or more accounts of an assault on the temple.

The first block is in a way paradigmatic for the rest. Here we are presented with the story of Heliodorus, who was sent by the king (Seleucus) to confiscate funds from the temple for his own purposes. When the high priest Onias heard of this, he informed Heliodorus that the money had been deposited in good faith by people who "trusted in the holiness of the place and in the sanctity and inviolability of the temple" (3:12). When Heliodorus proved himself impervious to this appeal, brushing it aside with the comment that he had his orders, the "whole city" (3:14), led by the high priest, made earnest supplication to "the Almighty Lord that he would keep what had been entrusted safe and secure" (3:14–22; here v. 22). Their prayers were heard; when the royal envoy arrived at the temple, he was suddenly confronted with a manifestation of divine power—a frightful horse that "rushed furiously at Heliodorus and struck at him with its front hoofs" (3:25) and two angelic figures who pummeled him so severely that he would have died had not Onias prayed for his recovery. We will look more closely at Heliodorus's response a little later. For present purposes, what is important is the two-fold theme of the story: God's readiness to protect the Jerusalem temple from assault and Israel's (cf. "the whole city" [3:14]) commitment to the sanctity of the temple and dependence on God's protection. The relationship between these two themes—specifically, the extent to which the first is dependent on the second—remains unspecified in block 1, though it plays an essential part in what follows.

Block 2 (4:7–10:9) differs from the first block in that the assault on the temple is successful, at least initially. In two theological asides (5:17–20; 6:12–17), however, the narrator makes it clear that Antiochus's "success" was not inconsistent with the themes portrayed in the Heliodorus story. Antiochus was able to loot the temple (5:15–16) only because "the Lord was angered for a little while because of the sins of those who lived in the city" (5:17).[59] But God's anger had correction and discipline as its aim (6:12); indeed, in contrast

58. This corresponds to the fourfold structure of van Henten (1997, 25). Doran's threefold structure (3:1–40; 4:1–10:9; 10:10–15:36) differs only slightly; he combines the last two sections into one and takes 4:1 rather than 4:7 as the start of a new section (Doran 1981, 75). Nickelsburg (2005, 107) opts for a structure based more on plot sequence: blessing (3:1–40), sin (4:1–5:10), punishment (5:11–6:17), turning point (6:18–8:4), and judgment and salvation (8:5–15:36).

59. Sinful Israelites can be found in the Heliodorus story as well, at least in the person of "the impious Simon" (3:11). Presumably the difference here is one of degree; apart from Simon, "the whole city" was united in its distress over the intentions of Heliodorus (3:14) and, presumably, the impiety of Simon.

to the situation of "the other nations [τῶν ἄλλων ἐθνῶν]," where God waits to punish them "until they have reached the full measure of their sins," Israel is punished immediately, so that they might be disciplined, not destroyed (6:12–16). Once the punishment had had its desired effect, God would be "reconciled" (5:20), and the temple would once again fall under divine protection. As the narrative continues, it is apparent that what brought about this reconciliation was the faithfulness displayed by the martyrs, Eleazar, and the mother with her seven sons, all of whom willingly embraced death rather than betray the covenant (6:18–7:42). From this point on, the plot of block 2 conforms to that of block 1. Although Antiochus declared in his arrogance that he would "make Jerusalem a cemetery of Jews" (9:4), the "all-seeing Lord, the God of Israel," stopped him (literally) dead in his tracks (9:5).

This pattern is reproduced in the final two blocks of the narrative. During the reign of Antiochus Eupator (10:10–13:26), Lysias on two occasions launched attacks on Judea, intending "to make the city a home for Greeks, and to levy tribute on the temple . . . and to put up the high priesthood for sale every year" (11:2–3; cf. 13:1–2, 9–11). In each case, Judas led "all the people" to pray to God for deliverance "with lamentations and tears" (11:6; cf. 13:10–12). Likewise in each case, God responded—the first time by sending "a horseman . . . clothed in white and brandishing weapons of gold" to lead the charge (11:8), the second time by helping the army to fight bravely in battle (13:13–14). During the reign of Demetrius (14:1–15:36), the threat to the temple came in the form of Nicanor, the Gentile governor of Judea, who threatened to "level this shrine of God to the ground and tear down the altar, and build here a splendid temple to Dionysus" (14:33). This time the priests led the prayers to the "constant Defender of our nation" (14:34–36); Razis, a pious elder of Jerusalem, reprised the role of Eleazar and the seven brothers as he accepted death for the sake of the covenant (14:37–46); and God, as should be expected by now, came to the aid of faithful Israel, first by sending Onias and Jeremiah in a vision to reassure Judas (15:11–16) and then by sending "a good angel to spread terror and trembling before" the Judean army (15:23–27).

Thus the overarching theme of 2 Maccabees is that God will intervene, even in miraculous ways, to protect the sanctity of the temple and the security of its people as long as the people are faithful to the covenant and willing to act in dependence on God's provision. This theme gets worked out in a number of smaller narrative blocks that, as we have seen, have a somewhat similar structure. There is one additional element in these narrative blocks, however, that is of particular interest for our purposes. In each instance where God acts to defend the temple and to vindicate the Israelite faithful, there is a scene in which God's power is acknowledged in some way by the Gentile king or general who had led the assault. The most striking of these are the instances involving Heliodorus (3:33–39), Antiochus Epiphanes (9:11–17), and, to a lesser extent, Antiochus Eupator (13:23), where the Gentiles in question go beyond mere acknowledgment of God's power and actually engage in acts of veneration. We will look at these passages in more detail in a moment. In other instances the acknowledgment does not seem to be accompanied by any religious change of heart: after being defeated by Judas, Nicanor fled the scene of the battle incognito, and "proclaimed"—perhaps in words or, more likely, implicitly, by the mere fact of his ignominious flight—"that the Jews had a Defender, and that therefore the Jews were invulnerable, because they followed the laws ordained by him" (8:36); likewise Lysias, after his defeat and "disgraceful flight" (11:12), came to the realization "that the Hebrews were invincible because the mighty God fought on their side" (11:13); after the final battle, when Nicanor met his death, Judas displayed his body in Jerusalem as "a clear and conspicuous"—but this time certainly mute!—"sign to everyone of the help of the Lord" (15:35). Since these instances do not seem to involve any change in the religious disposition of the figures in question, we will not include them in the list of texts below. In addition to the texts involving veneration, however, there is a second category to be included—passages in which reference is made to more idyllic times in the past when Gentile kings had honored the temple by providing gifts and offerings (3:1–3, 12; 5:16).

Text: LXX (Rahlfs, 1979)
Translation: NRSV
Date: Second half of the second century B.C.E.
Provenance: Judea
Original Language: Greek
Bibliography: Balch (1998); Bickerman (1933); Bunge (1971); J. J. Collins (2000, 78–83); Doran (1981); Goldstein (1983); Gruen (2002, 174–81); Hengel (1974, 95–99); van Henten (1997); Nickelsburg (2005, 106–10); Schürer (1986, 3:531–36); D. Schwartz (1998).

§17 2 Maccabees 3:1–3

While the holy city was inhabited in unbroken peace and the laws were strictly observed because of the piety of the high priest Onias and his hatred of wickedness, [2]it came about that the kings themselves honored the place and glorified the temple with the finest presents, [3]even to the extent that King Seleucus of Asia defrayed from his own revenues all the expenses connected with the service of the sacrifices.

Category: SYMPATHIZATION

These verses constitute the opening of the historical narrative itself. They thus serve to present an idealized past against which the woes of the period to follow are to be measured. In this idealization, the piety and righteousness of the high priest served to produce an era of peace and law-observance within the "holy city." This, in turn, induced foreign kings to honor the temple with gifts and contributions toward its expenses. In view of the statement a little later that the temple was honored "throughout the whole world" (3:12), it is probable that the author intended the "kings" in question not to be limited to those of the Seleucid kingdom.

These verses, of course, represent an exaggerated and overly pious interpretation of what, for Hellenistic kings, was a normal part of the *Realpolitik* of the Mediterranean world. Seleucus was just continuing the practice of his father Antiochus III, who, when he finally took control of Judea, rewarded the Jews handsomely for support they had provided him during the war with the Ptolemies (Josephus *Ant.* 12.136–46). His benefactions included contributions toward the refurbishment of the temple, so that it might be "more splendid" (*Ant.* 12.141), and lavish provisions of money and material for the ongoing operation of the sacrificial cult in Jerusalem. Thus while the royal benefactions are not to be doubted, it is quite a stretch to see them as a response to Jewish Torah-piety and even more of a stretch to attribute them to the influence of Onias III, who had not yet succeeded his father Simon II when Judea came under Seleucid rule.

This opening statement, then, reflects the theological interests of the author-abridger. It provides his narrative with a kind of baseline or norm: when Israel lives as it should—in faithfulness to the law and in loyalty to a properly constituted temple establishment—then the honor and glory of the temple will be acknowledged by Gentile kings. The author does not seem to have any interest in the religious disposition *per se* of Seleucus or any of the others. Instead, it is a means of reassuring his readers of the intrinsic value of Torah-piety and of the ultimate certainty of divine protection and vindication.

§18 2 Maccabees 3:12

> *And he* [Onias] *said that it was utterly impossible that wrong should be done to those people who had trusted in the holiness of the place and in the sanctity and inviolability of the temple that is honored throughout the whole world.*

Category: SYMPATHIZATION

This statement forms part of Onias's response to Heliodorus when the latter arrived in Jerusalem to appropriate the temple deposits for the royal coffers. The statement echoes the introductory comments of the narrator that we have just examined, except that they have been generalized (the temple has been "honored" [τετιμημένου], but there is no reference to gifts) and universalized (the temple has been honored "throughout the whole world" [κατὰ τὸν σύμπαντα κόσμον]). The author thus draws a contrast between the ideal standard set out in the introductory statement and Heliodorus's sacrilegious intentions.

§19 2 Maccabees 3:33–39

While the high priest was making an atonement, the same young men appeared again to Heliodorus dressed in the same clothing, and they stood and said, "Be very grateful to the high priest Onias, since for his sake the Lord has granted you your life. [34]*And see that you, who have been flogged by heaven, report to all people the majestic power of God." Having said this, they vanished.* [35]*Then Heliodorus offered sacrifice to the Lord and made very great vows to the Savior of his life, and having bidden Onias farewell, he marched off with his forces to the king.* [36]*He bore testimony to all concerning the deeds of the supreme God, which he had seen with his own eyes.* [37]*When the king asked Heliodorus what sort of person would be suitable to send on another mission to Jerusalem, he replied,* [38] *"If you have any enemy or plotter against your government, send him there, for you will get him back thoroughly flogged, if he survives at all; for there is certainly some power of God about the place.* [39]*For he who has his dwelling in heaven watches over that place himself and brings it aid, and he strikes and destroys those who come to do it injury."*

Category: SYMPATHIZATION

Heliodorus's incursion into the temple is the first in the series of threats to the temple's sanctity that constitute the narrative spine of 2 Maccabees. As has been observed earlier, the story of Heliodorus establishes the theme that will govern the narrative to follow: to the extent that Israel is faithful to the covenant and devoted to the sanctity of the temple, God will protect both people and temple from foreign assault. In addition, however, the conclusion of the Heliodorus story underlines a characteristic feature of the way in which this theme is developed in the work. It is important, apparently, not only that the Gentile threat be turned back, but also that the Gentile antagonist bear witness to the supremacy of Israel's God. If the normative situation is one in which the glory of the temple is acknowledged "throughout the whole world" (3:12; cf. 3:1–3), then it is not enough that the threat be thwarted; the vindication of Israel and the temple must also effect a reversal in the attitude of the Gentile figure who led the assault.

Thus Heliodorus could not be allowed to die. After he was restored to life through the intervention of the high priest, the two "young men" who had pummeled him almost to death commanded him to "report to all people the majestic power of God" (3:34). This he proceeded to do (3:36), even informing the king himself that "there is certainly some power of God about the place" (3:38) and advising him that if he had any enemy or opponent who needed to be brought down a peg or two, the king should send him on a similar mission to Jerusalem, for God will "strike and destroy those who come to do it injury" (3:39). But Heliodorus's reversal of attitude was even more extensive than this. Before leaving the temple to bear witness to all people "concerning the deeds of the supreme God" (3:36), he first acknowledged the supremacy of God directly, by "offer[ing] sacrifice to the Lord and mak[ing] very great vows [εὐχὰς μεγίστας] to the one who had preserved [περιποιήσαντι] his life" (3:35). In this veneration of Israel's God, he went above and beyond the response that the young men demanded of him.

This reversal in Heliodorus's attitude is narrated not for its own sake, of course, but for the larger narrative purpose that it effects. His veneration of God underscores the theme of vindication and thus serves to encourage the Jewish readers of the narrative to honor the temple and to trust in God's readiness to protect it. There is no indication that the narrator presents Heliodorus as a model to be emulated by Gentiles in general. Still, from the author's perspective, such veneration on the part of a Gentile is considered to be quite appropriate. Indeed, as part of the normative state of affairs (cf. 3:1–3), it is to be expected.

§20 2 Maccabees 5:16

> *He [Antiochus] took the holy vessels with his polluted hands, and swept away with profane hands the votive offerings that other kings had made to enhance the glory and honor of the place.*

Category: SYMPATHIZATION

That the readers of 2 Maccabees were expected to see the story of Heliodorus as providing a frame of reference for the remainder of the narrative becomes apparent in the account of Antiochus's entry into the temple (5:15–21). Here the narrator makes explicit reference to the earlier account, noting that Antiochus was able to profane the temple only "because of the sins of those who lived in the city" (5:17) and that otherwise he "would have been flogged" and repulsed "just as Heliodorus had been" (5:18). But even though God was using Antiochus as a means of punishing Israel, his disregard for the sanctity of the temple was no more justifiable than Heliodorus's had been. Again the author contrasts the attitude of the Gentile antagonist with the reverence that had been demonstrated toward the temple by kings in the past. It was part of the normal state of things (cf. 3:1–3, 12) that kings would make "votive offerings [ἀνατεθέντα] . . . to enhance the glory and honor of the place [τοῦ τόπου]" (5:16). By carrying these off "with profane hands," Antiochus was simply demonstrating his impious arrogance (cf. 5:21) and sealing his own fate "when the great Lord became reconciled" to Israel (5:20).

§21 2 Maccabees 9:11–18

> *Then it was that, broken in spirit, he* [Antiochus] *began to lose much of his arrogance and to come to his senses under the scourge of God, for he was tortured with pain every moment.* [12]*And when he could not endure his own stench, he uttered these words, "It is right to be subject to God; mortals should not think that they are equal to God.* [13]*Then the abominable fellow made a vow to the Lord, who would no longer have*

mercy on him, stating [14]that the holy city, which he was hurrying to level to the ground and to make a cemetery, he was now declaring to be free; [15]and the Jews, whom he had not considered worth burying but had planned to throw out with their children for the wild animals and for the birds to eat, he would make, all of them, equal to citizens of Athens; [16]and the holy sanctuary, which he had formerly plundered, he would adorn with the finest offerings; and all the holy vessels he would give back, many times over; and the expenses incurred for the sacrifices he would provide from his own revenues; [17]and in addition to all this he also would become a Jew and would visit every inhabited place to proclaim the power of God. [18]But when his sufferings did not in any way abate, for the judgment of God had justly come upon him, he gave up all hope for himself. . .

Category: SYMPATHIZATION, CONVERSION

Although Antiochus was initially more successful than Heliodorus, in the end of the story as the author relates it, God intervened in as dramatic a fashion, first through the victories of Judas over Nicanor (ch. 8) and then directly, by afflicting Antiochus with an agonizing and incurable illness (9:5–12). As in the case of Heliodorus, this produced a dramatic reversal in Antiochus's attitude, resulting in a willingness not only to venerate God and to honor the temple, but even to "become a Jew" (9:17). Of course, in keeping with the differences between the two stories—on which more in a moment—the reversal of attitude had a strikingly different outcome in the case of Antiochus: Antiochus was now beyond the mercy of God (9:13), and so his change of heart was to no avail. Nevertheless, the reversal of attitude has the same narrative function: to bear witness to the theme that God will defend the temple from violation if Israel is faithful to the covenant.

As we have noted, despite the parallels, the story of Antiochus is more complex than that of Heliodorus. Because of Israel's sin, God allowed Antiochus to assault the temple, thus using him as a means of punishment. But Antiochus misinterpreted this, "thinking in his arrogance that he could sail on the land and walk on the sea, because his mind was elated" (5:21) with his victories in Judea. In the end it was his arrogance that was his undoing. The last of the seven brothers to suffer martyrdom identified "arrogance [τῆς ὑπερηφανίας]" (7:36)[60]—the unwillingness to "confess that he alone is God" (7:37)—as the king's fundamental error; and it was precisely the suffering of the martyrs that was able "to bring to an end the wrath of the Almighty" (7:38) that had fallen for a time on Israel. With the end of God's wrath came the end of Antiochus's success, and hence of his arrogance. Humbled by God, he came "to his senses," acknowledged his subjection to God (9:11–12), and made the grand vows of 9:13–17 that have been quoted earlier.

60. In addition to 5:21 and 7:36, the word group appears frequently in ch. 9 with reference to Antiochus (9:4, 7, 8, 11, 12).

In his vows, Antiochus goes a great deal beyond the level of veneration that had been exhibited by his father, Seleucus IV, and other kings before him (3:1–3). Not only would he underwrite the expenses of the sacrifices and adorn the sanctuary, but he would repay what he had plundered "many times over" (9:16), he would declare Jerusalem to be free (9:14), he would make the Jews "equal to citizens of Athens" (9:15),[61] he would "proclaim the power of God" in every inhabited place (9:17), and he himself would even "become a Jew" (literally, be a Jew: Ἰουδαῖον ἔσεσθαι; 9:17).

What are we to make of this final promise? As we have seen, such language appears in one other Jewish text—in Bel and the Dragon, where the king's subjects complain that he has become a Jew (there γίνομαι instead of εἰμί). In this other case, the text provides very little indication as to what would be involved in "becoming a Jew." Second Maccabees 9:17 is a little more forthcoming; for a Gentile to become a Jew involves something more (πρὸς δὲ τούτοις) than simply providing benefactions for the Jews, honoring the temple, and venerating God. What precisely is involved, the author does not say. Presumably he takes it for granted that his readers will know.

Even though Antiochus's proposed change of religious behavior involves conversion and not simply veneration, his response plays the same narrative role as that of Heliodorus. In both cases, the change of religious disposition on the part of the antagonist serves as a dramatic counterpoint to the change of circumstances on the part of Israel. By being brought to their theological senses, both Heliodorus and Antiochus function as means to underscore God's vindication of Israel and thus to add weight to the author's rhetorical purposes with respect to his readers. This intended rhetorical effect is not diminished in the least by the fact that Antiochus's change of heart comes too late. Either way, the point is made that God will in the end vindicate a faithful Israel. Again, this means that the author is not interested in a change of heart for its own sake. An Antiochus damned serves his rhetorical purposes as effectively as a Heliodorus transformed. Again there is no apparent interest in encouraging other Gentiles to emulate Antiochus's change of heart. Still, the rhetorical device demonstrates that the author-abridger can nevertheless contemplate—and consider to be quite appropriate—the possibility that a Gentile would venerate God and even be prepared to become a Jew (Cohen 1999, 129).

§22 2 Maccabees 13:23

> [The king] *called in the Jews, yielded and swore to observe all their rights, settled with them and offered sacrifice, honored the sanctuary and showed generosity to the holy place.*

Category: SYMPATHIZATION

61. On what these last two items might mean, see Goldstein (1983, 355–56).

This passage comes at the conclusion of yet another attempt to assault the temple, this time by Antiochus Eupator, the "son of that ungodly man" (2 Macc 10:10), Antiochus IV. The narrative conforms to the pattern that has by now been well established. The king had massive forces at his disposal (13:2); like his father before him he displayed "barbarous arrogance," threatening to do even worse things to the Jews than his father had done (13:9); Judas led the people in calling on God to defend the people from this threat to "the law and their country and the holy temple" (13:10); Judas and his forces won a mighty victory, "because the Lord's help protected him" (13:17). The author does not deal in any detail with the effect of this reversal of fortune on the king. Still, it is clear that the normal state of affairs—as the author understands things—has been re-established: the foreign king has come to recognize the power and sovereignty of Israel's God, which he demonstrates by allowing the Jews to live in peace, by making gifts (ἐφιλανθρώπησεν) to the temple, and by offering sacrifices to God. While the purpose of the account is to reaffirm Jewish values for Jewish readers, it is also clear that the author also thinks it to be quite appropriate for Gentiles to venerate the God of Israel.

JUDITH

§23 Judith 14:10

> *When Achior saw all that the God of Israel had done, he believed firmly in God. So he was circumcised and joined the house of Israel, remaining so to this day.*

Text: Greek: LXX (Rahlfs, 1979)
Translation: NRSV
Date: Late second or early first century B.C.E.
Provenance: Judea
Original Language: Hebrew
Bibliography: Cazelles (1951); Craven (1983); Enslin and Zeitlin (1972); Haag (1963); Levine (1995); C. Moore (1985); Roitman (1992); Steinmann (1953); White (1992); Wills (1995, 132–57)
Category: CONVERSION

The story of Judith is sufficiently well known that there is no need to summarize it here. In order to assess the significance of Jdt 14:10, however, we do need to examine the part played in the story by Achior the Ammonite. Achior appears twice in the narrative, first in chapters 5 and 6, where he is described as "the leader of all the Ammonites" (5:5), and then in 14:5–10. He is also referred to by Judith in her first encounter with Holofernes in 11:9–10. While he is clearly a secondary character, his role is essential to the story and to its overall impact on the reader.[62]

In Achior's first appearance he is part of a group of leaders from Moab, Ammon, and the coastlands, whom Holofernes has summoned to ascertain why it is that the Israelites are the only ones who have not submitted to him and, through him, to the lordship of Nebuchadnezzar (5:1–4). Achior takes the lead in responding, declaring to Holofernes that he will tell him "the truth about this people" (v. 5). How he has come by his knowledge of Israel, we are not told. Nevertheless, from the standpoint of the author, who evidently uses Achior as a spokesman for his own perspective, Achior's response is indeed the "truth." The response is a recitation of Israel's history from the time of Abraham down to the return from exile (vv. 6–19), followed by a piece of concluding advice for Holofernes (vv. 20–21).

Achior's interpretation of Israel's experience conforms to the familiar pattern of Deuteronomistic history: Israel fares well or badly in accordance with their faithfulness "to the way [their God] had prescribed for them" (5:18). His advice to Holofernes is that he attempt to ascertain whether Israel has sinned against their God. If so, victory is assured; but if not, "then let my lord [ὁ κύριός μου] pass them by; for their Lord [ὁ κύριος αὐτῶν] and God will defend them and we shall become the laughingstock of the whole world" (5:21). The implications of Achior's statement were not lost on Holofernes (Haag 1963, 32). Although Achior has been deferential to the foreign general throughout, addressing him as "my master" (v. 20) and "my lord" (vv. 5, 20, 21), the implicit assumption on which his discourse was based was that Israel's fate was in the hands of another god higher than Nebuchadnezzar, against whom Holofernes's power would be futile. Holofernes understandably reacts with anger ("What god is there except Nebuchadnezzar?" [6:2]), but his anger does not dull his sense of irony. He gives command that Holofernes be handed over to the Israelites so that he will share their fate and thus will perish with them at the precise moment when it becomes evident to all that it is Nebuchadnezzar who is "lord of the whole earth" (6:4). Of course, the victim of the irony eventually turns out to be Holofernes himself.

Since Judith's stratagem is to inform Holofernes that Israel, driven to desperate measures by the siege, is about to sin, Achior's response is essential to the forward movement of the plot; he provides Holofernes with the information necessary for Judith's offer to appear plausible.[63] The point is underlined by Judith herself when she assures Holofernes that what Achior has said "is true" (11:10). Of course, given Holofernes's belief in Nebuchadnezzar's divinity,

62. For studies of Achior's role in the book, see Cazelles (1951); C. Moore (1985, 59, 158, 161–62); Roitman (1992); Steinmann (1953, 55–62).

63. Cazelles (1951, 126–27); C. Moore (1985, 158).

Judith's offer should have been just as offensive to him as was Achior's discourse, but he apparently is too dazzled by her beauty to notice.

Achior makes his second appearance in the story at its highest point of dramatic intensity, just after Judith has displayed Holofernes's head to the dumbfounded residents of Bethulia. Here the irony unwittingly set in motion by Holofernes reaches its completion, as Achior—to whom Holofernes had said "you shall not see my face again from this day until I take revenge on [Israel]" (6:5)—sees his now-lifeless face and faints dead away (14:6). Again, however, Achior's role is not simply an ironic one. Since he is the only one in Bethulia who can confirm that this is indeed the head of Holofernes (14:5), his role is essential to the plot here, too (Roitman 1992, 44, n. 38).[64]

Thus, despite his secondary status, the character of Achior has an important part to play in the narrative as a whole. His speech to Holofernes and his later presence in Bethulia are both essential to the mechanism of the plot. Further, his speech provides the theological framework within which the story takes place and finds its meaning; Achior undoubtedly serves as the mouthpiece for the author himself. In addition, as a key component in the dramatic irony around which the narrative is constructed, his testimony to "all that the God of Israel had done" (14:10), which is given expression in his conversion, contributes powerfully to the overall impact of the narrative on its readers.

But what of his conversion? What is the significance of the fact that "he circumcised the flesh of his foreskin [περιετέμετο τὴν σάρκα τῆς ἀκροβυστίας], and was added [προσετέθη] to the house of Israel" (14:10)? At the most basic narrative level, the conversion is subservient to the main themes of the story—the demonstration that Israel's God, not Nebuchadnezzar, is the only God (cf. 6:2) and "lord of the whole earth" (6:4), and the vindication of those who remained faithful to this God. Achior's transformation—from one who aligned himself (albeit in a qualified way) with Holofernes (note the first person plural in 5:20: "then *we* can go up and defeat them"[65]) to a passive participant in Israel's fate, to an active convert to Israel and its God—serves as a means of highlighting and drawing attention to the victory of God and the vindication of a Torah-centered way of life.

But at another level of the narrative, the conversion of Achior is to be understood as more than simply a signpost to something else. The conversion

64. Since the summoning of Achior intrudes into Judith's instructions for battle (14:1–4), some have followed the Vulgate in placing the account of Achior's conversion between 13:20 and 14:1 (see Enslin and Zeitlin 1972, 158; C. Moore 1985, 235). But while it is awkward, the awkwardness attests to the importance of Achior's witness. (The text attested by the Vulgate is probably to be seen as an attempt to smooth over the awkwardness.)

65. Roitman has suggested that Achior undergoes a transformation in the course of his response to Holofernes (Roitman 1992, 33–34). Against this, however, is the fact that this use of the first person plural comes at the end of the speech.

is significant in its own right.[66] As many commentators have observed, the main characters in the story are presented not simply as individual characters but as typological figures. Judith's very name ("Jewess," the feminine form of Judah) points in this direction, as does the victory song in chapter 16, in which Judith takes on the voice of Israel itself (C. Moore 1985, 248). Judith personifies the ideal Israelite, exemplifying the kind of faithfulness and courage that should characterize Israel as a whole. Likewise, by constructing Nebuchadnezzar in such absurdly anachronistic terms,[67] the author signals to his readers that this "Nebuchadnezzar" is not the Babylonian king from the distant past, but instead is an amalgamation of all godless Gentile potentates from Nebuchadnezzar down to Antiochus IV.

But there is another type of Gentile in the narrative world of Judith besides Nebuchadnezzar and his feckless henchman Holofernes. While the latter typify those Gentiles who set themselves up against the God of Israel and—at least in Holofernes's case—are destroyed, Achior[68] embodies those Gentiles who recognize the God of Israel as the one true God and who thus come to attach themselves to Israel and to share Israel's salvation. Interestingly, Holofernes promises Judith that he would do the same—"If you do as you have said, your God shall be my God" (11:23)—but of course, by the time Judith had done what she really had set out to do, it was too late. Achior, on the other hand, stands as a kind of Gentile counterpart to Judith.[69] He boldly declares the truth of Israel's theology to a hostile Holofernes; she determinedly rallies a dispirited band of Israelites with the same theology. He is transferred from the camp of Holofernes

66. Cf. White (1992, 10): "Achior's conversion is one more symbol of the triumph of Yahweh in the book of Judith"; Roitman (1992, 39): "His conversion is meant to prove the main thesis of the book: the superiority of the Jews and their beliefs over the world of the pagans." While these statements are not inaccurate, they are not a full account of the matter.

67. For example, the story is set after the return from exile (5:19), and thus long after the death of the real Nebuchadnezzar. The fictional Nebuchadnezzar is not the king of the Babylonians in Babylon, but of the Assyrians in Nineveh. For a full discussion, see C. Moore (1985, 38–56).

68. While various attempts have been made to discern some symbolic significance in the name, none have been convincing. As it stands, the name in Hebrew would signify "my brother is light." Moore stretches a point when he says that the name is appropriate in that Achior "did finally become a Jewish 'brother,' i.e., a Jewish convert" (C. Moore 1985, 158). If this had been the author's intention, a name could have been chosen that would have made the point more clearly. In this connection, Steinmann, noting that LXX Num 34:27 uses Αχιωρ to render אחיהוד (resulting from a confusion of ד and ר), suggests that the name was originally אחי יהוד, "brother of the Jews" (Steinmann 1953, 56). But this would have required more than a simple confusion of letters. Cazelles (1951) has proposed that Achior is a transformed version of the popular ancient character Ahikar, but the differences seem to be too great.

69. On the structural parallelism of Achior and Judith, see Roitman (1992).

to the town of Bethulia, while she moves in the opposite direction. Each is welcomed by their new hosts with a feast.[70] Each in their own new place report to their new hosts the plans and activities of the other (though in Judith's case with a certain ironic deceptiveness). At the point when the truth of their theological interpretation of Israel's history has been demonstrated for all to see, Achior leaves his Gentile world behind, believes firmly in God, and is added to the house of Israel. Fittingly, this happens as he meets Judith for the first time in the story.

Since the narrative of Judith is played out on a larger symbolic stage, the conversion of Achior is more than simply "a colorful addition" (Enslin and Zeitlin 1972, 158). Instead, it expresses the conviction that there is a class of Gentiles who, like Achior, will be so impressed by the nature of God's dealings with Israel[71] that they will abandon the world of false gods represented by Nebuchadnezzar and become full converts to Israel. It is no coincidence that Achior's recitation of Israel's history begins by describing the founding members of the people (Abraham is not mentioned by name) as those who "abandoned the ways of their ancestors, and worshiped the God of heaven, the God they had come to know" (5:8). In other words, by becoming a proselyte,[72] Achior was simply following a pattern established by the first Israelites themselves.[73]

But while the world projected by the book of Judith is one in which Gentile converts have an established place, there is no indication that such converts are to be actively sought or encouraged. Israel's role is a passive one; moved by what they have seen of God's care for Israel, Gentiles turn to God and seek to join God's people. The dynamic is similar to that which underlies the eschatological pilgrimage tradition. Indeed, the story of Judith could easily be read as a kind of eschatological parable. While this certainly was not its original intention, one

70. For Achior, see 6:21. The same word πότος is used in 6:21 and 13:1.

71. The NRSV rendering of v. 7—"In every nation those who hear your name will be alarmed"(also C. Moore 1985, 235)—suggests that Achior expects other Gentiles to respond only with fear. But the translation is probably incorrect. The parallelism of the two prepositional phrases "in every tent of Judah" and "in every nation" suggests that they belong together: "Blessed are you in every tent of Judah and in every nation." The subsequent relative clause is awkward in either case (οἵτινες ἀκούσαντες: "who, hearing . . ."), but the awkwardness should not be used as a warrant to destroy the simple parallelism of the first clause. In other words, Achior is expressing the hope that other non-Jews will be as impressed with what God has done through Judith as he is.

72. The term itself is not used of Achior. Rather, his change in status is indicated by the mention of circumcision and the statement that he was "added to" (προσετέθη) the house of Israel. (The NRSV rendering "joined" perhaps makes Achior too much the agent of his own incorporation.) The same verb is used in LXX Esth 9:27.

73. See Roitman (1992, 39), who observes that the phrase ἐπίστευσεν τῷ θεῷ, used with respect to Achior in 14:10, is also used of Abraham in LXX Gen 16:6—its only appearance in the Septuagint.

can say, at least, that it represents the kind of idealized Deuteronomic history on which many eschatological scenarios are constructed.[74]

Perhaps this is the perspective from which to view one puzzling detail in the story of Achior: he is identified not simply as a Gentile but particularly as an Ammonite (5:5).[75] The problem arises from the tension between Jdt 14:10 and Deut 23:3, which explicitly excludes Ammonites (along with Moabites) from entering "the assembly of the Lord," "even to the tenth generation." It is hard to imagine that in choosing to make Achior an Ammonite, the author was unaware of this verse. At the same time, there is such an emphasis in Judith on conformity to the Torah that it is equally difficult to read Judith as a deliberate and explicit rejection of Deuteronomy. Perhaps it is to be understood as the same type of idealized hope for the future as is found in Isa 56:3, where—in a statement equally in tension with Deuteronomy 23 (v. 1)—the prophet envisages the day of salvation as one in which the eunuch (along with the foreigner) will have a place in the Lord's house.

Wisdom of Solomon

§24 Wisdom of Solomon 1:1–2

Love righteousness, you rulers of the earth, think of the Lord in goodness and seek him with sincerity of heart; [2]because he is found by those who do not put him to the test, and manifests himself to those who do not distrust him.

§25 Wisdom of Solomon 6:9–11

To you then, O monarchs, my words are directed, so that you may learn wisdom and not transgress. [10]For they will be made holy who observe holy things in holiness, and those who have been taught them will find a defense. [11]Therefore set your desire on my words; long for them, and you will be instructed.

Text: LXX (Rahlfs, 1979)
Translation: NRSV (adapted)
Date: 100 B.C.E.–30 C.E.
Provenance: Egypt
Original Language: Greek

74. Allegorical interpretations of Judith go back at least to Luther; see Metzger (1957, 51). For a discussion, see Craven (1983, 108–10).

75. For discussion, see Cazelles (1951, 127); Craven (1983, 103, n. 68); Enslin and Zeitlin (1972, 160); Haag (1963, 53–54); C. Moore (1985, 235–36); Roitman (1992, 39); Steinmann (1953, 62). For Qumran interpretation of Deut 23:1–3, see the discussion of 4QFlorilegium.

Bibliography: Barclay (1996, 181–91); J. J. Collins (1997, 178–221; 2000, 195–202); Kolarcik (1991); Nickelsburg (2005, 205–12); Reese (1970); Winston (1979).
Category: ETHICAL MONOTHEISM

The Wisdom of Solomon opens with an address to "you rulers of the earth," who are summoned to seek the Lord "with sincerity of heart" (1:1); it ends with an address to "the Lord," who has "exalted and glorified your people" (19:22). This contrast between beginning and end—a shift of focus from universal humanity, as represented by its rulers, to a particular people, chosen and cared for by God—illustrates what Collins has described as a "fundamental tension between universalism and particularism" in the work (J. J. Collins 2000, 201). One's reading of the work as a whole will depend on how one assesses the tension.

The Wisdom of Solomon comprises three distinct sections carefully constructed to form an integrated unity. The first section (1:1–6:11), framed by direct addresses to the rulers of the earth (1:1–13; 6:1–11), parts of which are cited above, deals primarily with the grand reversal of fortune that will be experienced by the righteous and the ungodly on the day of judgment. Like the apocalyptic literature that it resembles in some respects (Nickelsburg 2005, 207), the Wisdom of Solomon takes delight in exposing the folly of the wicked who have confused appearance for reality. Convinced by what they observe—both their own state of well-being and the ignominious lot of the righteous—that "might is right" (2:11), they are destined to be chagrined on the day of reckoning when they realize that these "persons whom we once held in derision" are "numbered among the sons of God" (5:4–5). The second section of the book (6:12–9:18) is a discourse in praise of Wisdom, delivered in the first person singular by a speaker whom a biblically literate reader will recognize as Solomon. This section is linked to the first both by its address to the "monarchs over the peoples," who are informed that the way to maintain their rule is to "honor wisdom" (6:21), and by the implicit presentation of Solomon as one whom the "kings of the earth" should emulate. The third section (chs. 10–19) contains a reflection on various aspects of Pentateuchal history. Again, the transition is smooth; Solomon's generalized conclusion that "people . . . were saved by wisdom" (9:18) leads into the more particular exposition of how wisdom was active in guiding and protecting Adam (10:1–2), Noah (10:4), Abraham (10:5), Lot (10:6–8), Jacob (10:9–12), Joseph (10:13–14), and the people of Israel as a whole (10:15–11:20). As the section proceeds, however, the figure of wisdom recedes into the background;[76] increasingly the focus shifts to Israel and the Egyptians, who are portrayed as models of the righteous and the ungodly

76. While Wisdom is mentioned explicitly ten times in ch. 10—σοφία four times and αὕτη six—there are only two other references in the rest of the book (14:2, 5). A similar figure reappears in 18:15, however, this time described as God's "all-powerful word [λόγος]."

respectively. In this section there is an emphasis on the justice of God's dealings with the wicked (11:21–12:27) and on the folly of idolatry (13:1–15:19).

The Wisdom of Solomon, then, opens by sounding a universalistic note: it invites the kings of the earth[77] to "love righteousness," to "think about the Lord in goodness," and to "seek [the Lord] with sincerity of heart." The initial impression is that the author is making a universal appeal for righteousness—to the world's rulers and, presumably, through them to their subjects—and is optimistic that his appeal will be heeded. This impression is confirmed by the corresponding appeal with which the first section of the work is brought to a conclusion, which is just as optimistic that the monarchs might "learn wisdom and not transgress" (6:9; also 6:21–25).

Many other aspects of the work as a whole might be adduced in support of the conclusion that it is optimistically universalistic in its orientation and intentions. From the richness of the vocabulary and the sophistication of the rhetorical style it is clear that the author has had a thorough Greek education. Further, the author's Hellenization is not simply a veneer; he has assimilated significant aspects of Hellenistic philosophy (e.g., the preexistence and immortality of the soul) and has incorporated them into a Hellenized reworking of Judaism similar to that of Philo in many respects.[78]

With respect to specific themes, God's activity is placed into a universal framework. God is the creator who continues to care for the whole creation (1:13–14; 6:7; 9:1). God's spirit, which "holds all things together," has also filled the οἰκουμένη—the world of human habitation and culture (1:7); Wisdom, likewise, is universal in its scope (8:1). God has created humankind—generically described (ἄνθρωπον)—to rule the world (9:2–3). Wisdom is characterized as φιλάνθρωπος, loving the whole human race (1:6; 7:23); the righteous are to be likewise (12:19). Further, while it is recognized that the human race is differentiated into the righteous and the ungodly, God is the "savior of all" (16:7) who does not desire the death of any creature (1:13–14; 11:25–26) but is eager for human repentance: God is "merciful to all, for you [i.e., God] can do all things, and you overlook people's [ἀνθρώπων] sins, so that they may repent" (11:23; also 12:2, 10). Wisdom, the key to righteousness, can be found by any who are willing to seek her (6:12).

Further, with respect to the righteous and the ungodly, there is no indication, at least in the first two parts of the book, that they are differentiated on

77. Literally, judges (οἱ κρίνοντες); elsewhere we find βασιλεύς (e.g., 6:1, 24) and τύραννος (e.g., 6:9, 21).

78. On the Hellenistic character of the Wisdom of Solomon, see Reese (1970); Winston (1979, 14–18, 25–64). The question of the relationship with Philo is partly dependent on dating but is complex in any case. It is clear, however, that they both are deeply embedded in the intellectual world of Middle Platonism.

ethnic grounds. True, the differentiation between the two has something to do with the "law" (νόμος): wicked kings are reproached for not having kept the law (6:4) and for their "sins against the law" (2:12);[79] the love of Wisdom is equated with keeping her laws, which, in turn, leads to immortality (6:18); wickedness is described as lawlessness (ἀνομία; 5:7, 23). But while this law is accepted by Israel (18:9), there is no mention whatsoever of those particularistic aspects of the law that differentiate Jew from Gentile (J. J. Collins 1997, 220; 2000, 199). Righteousness is presented as a form of ethical monotheism open to all, whose positive character is apparent from the kind of behavior that is condemned: idolatry (13:1–15:19) and a variety of sins seen to have arisen from idolatry (adultery, sexual immorality, "a raging riot of blood and murder, theft and deceit, corruption, faithlessness, tumult, perjury" [14:25] and so on [14:22–29]). While ethnic factors are prominent in the third part of the book, one could argue that Israel and Egypt have a paradigmatic function here—that is, that they simply serve as biblical examples of righteousness and impiety, rather than as an indication that the author identified the righteous with Israel in any fundamental way (J. J. Collins 1997, 214; 2000, 199–202). Israel's only significance as an ethnic entity, in this reading, is its role in making righteousness available to all; it is through Israel ("your sons") that "the imperishable light of the law was to be given to the world" (18:4).

On the basis of these considerations, the Wisdom of Solomon might be understood as the product of a thoroughly Hellenized form of Judaism, whose aim was to reinterpret the biblical tradition as a universally valid ethical monotheism that the Gentile world was invited to adopt for its own.[80] But it is unlikely that such a reading—one in which the Wisdom of Solomon is seen as an instrument of universal enlightenment—can be consistently maintained. Two features of the book are important here. First, beginning this time with the end of the book, it is just not the case that Israel and Egypt are treated in chapters 10–19 simply as paradigms for the righteous and the wicked, with

79. It has been suggested that 2:12 reflects tensions within the Jewish community, where one group rebukes another for sins against the law and against their "training" (Barclay 1996, 185–86; J. J. Collins 1997, 194). While this is possible, it would then be an isolated piece of evidence. Elsewhere in the book there is no evidence of criticism directed at other Jews. The treatment of the brass serpent (16:5–14; 18:20–25) offers an instructive case in point. Here there is no differentiation between sinners and the righteous within Israel, as one might have expected if this were an issue for the author. Israel's solidarity is maintained, as the incident is treated as God's discipline of Israel as a whole. It seems preferable to treat 2:12 as another instance where Gentiles are held accountable to the law (along with 6:4).

80. J. J. Collins's work (1997, 178–221; 2000, 195–202) represents the most recent and persuasive articulation of this reading.

no ethnic particularism in view.[81] Or, more correctly, while Egypt might function paradigmatically, ethnic particularism cannot be eliminated from the depiction of Israel. With respect to Egypt, as is demonstrated by the lengthy diatribe against the folly of idolatry (13:1–15:19), it does seem that Egypt simply serves as a particularly pertinent stand-in for the Gentile world as a whole. But in the case of Israel, as the following considerations demonstrate, the distinction between Israel as an ethnic entity and the other ἔθνη of the world is an essential element of chapters 10–19.

On the one hand, Israel is clearly presented as a particular ἔθνος (17:2) or λαός (10:15). They are the particular people ruled over by Solomon (9:7, 12), who descended from the patriarchs (12:6; 18:6, 22), who accepted the law at a certain point in their history (18:9), who are identified by the fact that they were the recipients of specific divine "oaths and covenants,"[82] whose king built the temple (9:8). Israel appears in all its ethnic particularity. But on the other hand, it is precisely this specific ethnic group that is identified in chapters 10–19 as "the righteous" (10:20; 11:14; 16:17, 23; 18:7, 20), as the people of God (16:2, 3, 20; 19:5, 22), as the children of God 16:21; 18:4), even as the son of God (18:13). It is the particular "people" (λαός) and "race" (σπέρμα) that was delivered from Egypt that is described as holy and blameless (10:15). This is a very particularistic view of the identity of the righteous. Nothing in this section of the book invites us to see the clearly indicated ethnic particularities as inessential to the identity of the righteous. While the author is open to the possibility that Gentiles might also be righteous, the second half of the book leaves little doubt that the community of the righteous is identified primarily with Israel as a particular ethnic group. Indeed, the effect of chapters 10–19 is to require the reader to reassess initial impressions and to redefine, in much more specific terms, the identity of "the righteous" who were encountered in the first part of the book. Even the righteous individual of chapter 2, identified as God's "son," can, in view of the similar description of Israel in 18:13, be seen as a personification of Israel as a whole, rather than as just a typical righteous individual.

The second feature of the book to be observed here is its pervasive pessimism about idolaters; if the possibility is held out that idolaters might repent and seek the light of the law, it is largely hypothetical. As Barclay has observed, the categories of the righteous and the ungodly are "sharply polarized" (Barclay 1996, 185); nowhere do we see any indication of someone actually heeding the

81. Of course, the Wisdom of Solomon is characterized by the absence of specific names for any of the individuals or nations treated in the work. But the effect is not to universalize the material; instead, it is assumed that the readers have the kind of considerable biblical knowledge that would be restricted to a much smaller circle of readers. As Barclay (1996, 190) has observed: "The anonymity of the characters is not designed to establish a broad typology capable of including the righteous of all nations."

82. διαθήκη in 18:22; συνθήκη in 12:21.

author's appeal to "learn wisdom and not transgress" (6:9). While the work might be described as universalistic in a formal way, it is much more difficult to describe it as universalistic in substance.

More specifically, when one examines the universalistic material in its context, it is readily apparent that its primary function is to make the point that divine punishment is both inevitable and just. To begin with, although the first part of the work (1:1–6:11) is framed by a positive-sounding appeal to the rulers of the earth, they are nevertheless identified categorically as those who "did not rule rightly, or keep the law, or walk according to the purpose of God." Consequently, God "will come upon you terribly and swiftly, because severe judgment falls on those in high places" (6:4–5). Judgment seems to have been already determined. Further, the main concern in this whole first section of the work is the end-time vindication of the righteous, who have suffered persecution at the hands of the powerful. The lines are sharply drawn, and there is little sense that there are any ungodly at all who are capable of learning wisdom and thus of being made holy (6:9–10).

Similar observations are to be made about the universal scope of God's activity and the universal role of Wisdom. While it may be true that "the spirit of the Lord has filled the world" (1:7), the author's reason for mentioning this ("therefore" [v. 8]) is to make the point not that the Lord is therefore universally accessible but that "those who utter unrighteous things will not escape notice." Likewise, although it is possible "from the greatness and beauty of created things" to arrive at "a corresponding perception of their creator" (13:5), the author provides us with no example of any who have done so. Rather, this possibility is put forward to leave idolaters without excuse (13:8), "for if they had the power to know so much that they could investigate the world, how did they fail to find sooner the Lord of these things?" (13:9).

The same conclusion is to be drawn from the statements about divine forbearance. Although God "did not make death" and "does not delight in the death of the living" (1:13), the ungodly have nevertheless chosen death for themselves (1:16–2:5). God may "overlook people's sins, so that they may repent" (11:23) and "correct little by little those who trespass . . . so that they may be freed from wickedness" and turn to God (12:2). But, with the notable exception of the Israelites (16:5–13; 18:20–25), this divine leniency does not produce the desired outcome. The ungodly remain ungodly to the end (12:11); failing to take advantage of the "opportunity to repent" (12:10), the wicked "experience the deserved judgment of God" (12:26). The purpose of God's forbearance is that no one can accuse God of treating the wicked unfairly (12:12–27). Only in the case of Israel does God's merciful treatment of sinners lead to repentance (12:18–22). The author emphasizes this point by turning on two occasions (16:5–13; 18:20–25) to the incident of the brass serpent (Num 21:4–9). Probably we are to see in this repetition a certain nervousness about a biblical text that could easily suggest that Israel too "set their hopes on dead things" (13:10).[83] But the explicit point that is made, especially in 16:5–13,[84] is that Israel responds positively to God's chastising (16:6, 11). Thus God deals with Israel "as a father does in warning" but with the ungodly "as a stern king does in condemnation" (11:10). The consequences—and perhaps even the intentions—of divine forbearance, then, are ethnically differentiated. In Israel's case it leads to repentance and restoration; in that of the idolaters, it results in justly deserved condemnation.

Thus while the Wisdom of Solomon might exhibit a "tension between universalism and particularism" (J. J. Collins 2000, 201), it seems that the particularistic forces at work in the piece are considerably stronger. To be sure, the author desires Gentiles to abandon their sinfulness and to turn to God. Further, there is certainly no indication that Gentiles are obligated to accept the law of Moses in all its particularity—in other words, to become proselytes to Judaism. Turning to God in this instance means embracing a way of life that can be described as ethical monotheism. But at the same time there is very little evidence that the author expected many to do so; such an outcome appears to be more a hypothetical possibility than a reality. The purpose of the work seems to be more one of reinforcing the identity of Hellenistic Jews as God's "people" (19:22) than of inviting Gentiles to "seek [the Lord] with sincerity of heart" (1:1).

3 Maccabees

Of interest to us in 3 Maccabees are passages at the beginning and end of the narrative in which the Gentile antagonist, the Egyptian king Ptolemy Philopator, acknowledges the God of Israel. The two most pertinent passages are these:

§26 3 Maccabees 1:9

> *After he had arrived in Jerusalem, he offered sacrifice to the supreme God and made thank offerings and did what was fitting for the holy place.*

§27 3 Maccabees 6:33

> *Likewise also the king, after convening a great banquet to celebrate these events, gave thanks to heaven unceasingly and lavishly for the unexpected rescue that he had experienced.*

83. Note 16:7: salvation was accomplished "not by the thing that was beheld, but by you, the Savior of all."

84. In 18:20–25 the emphasis is on Moses's role in acting as Israel's "champion." J. J. Collins (1997, 220; 2000, 202) sees universalistic significance in the fact that the "whole world" is depicted on Moses's robe (18:24). But there is very little hope expressed in this whole section of the work for the "world" outside Israel. The very next line underlines the particularism: "The glories of the fathers were engraved on the four rows of stones."

Text: LXX (Rahlfs, 1979)
Translation: NRSV
Date: Probably early in the era of Roman Egypt (30 B.C.E.–37 C.E.)
Provenance: Alexandria
Original language: Greek
Bibliography: H. Anderson (1985a); Barclay (1996, 192–203); J. J. Collins (2000, 122–31); Gruen (1998, 222–45); Hadas (1953); Kasher (1985, 211–32); Schürer (1986, 3:537–42); Tcherikover (1961)
Category: SYMPATHIZATION

Although 3 Maccabees does not deal with the Maccabees at all, it displays significant affinities with 2 Maccabees, on which it probably depends.[85] The most prominent of these has to do with the relationship between Gentile kings and the Jerusalem temple: both contain scenes in which desecrating incursions into the temple are prevented by divine intervention; both also contain scenes in which foreign kings honor God by making appropriate sacrifices at the temple. To be sure, there are some not unsubstantial differences as well, which will be important for our investigation. In either case, however, it will be convenient to keep 2 Maccabees in mind as we look at the pertinent material in 3 Maccabees.

The antagonist in 3 Maccabees is Ptolemy IV Philopator (c. 221–205 B.C.E.), who, although predating Antiochus IV in real life, nevertheless plays a role here that combines aspects of both Antiochus IV and Heliodorus in 2 Maccabees. The narrative begins, abruptly,[86] with an account of Philopator's victory over Antiochus III at Raphia (near Gaza), a battle that took place in 217 B.C.E. To consolidate his victory, the king decided to visit cities in the area and to bestow royal largesse on their sanctuaries. It was thus that he came to Jerusalem, where he "offered sacrifice to the supreme God and made thank offerings and did what was fitting for the holy place [τῷ τόπῳ]" (1:9). His admiration for the beauty of the temple, however, produced in him a desire to enter the holy of holies, a desire that only intensified after he was told that this

85. For the affinities, see Hadas (1953, 11–12). But as Hadas demonstrates, 3 Maccabees displays similarities with other literature as well, especially LXX Esther and the *Letter of Aristeas*.

86. The opening sentence ("When Philopator learned from those who returned . . .") assumes a knowledge of prior events that are nowhere described. A similar assumption is present in the reference to the king's "previously mentioned drinking companions" (2:25), who, however, have not been mentioned at all in the narrative to this point. Hadas (1953, 5) speculates that an opening chapter has been lost, which, in addition to providing the antecedents for these references, might also have provided some grounds for the link with the Maccabees in the traditional title. Such speculation, however, presumes a level of narrative skill on the part of the author that is not necessarily borne out by the rest of the book.

was restricted to all but the high priest. As in the case of Heliodorus in 2 Maccabees, the whole city responded to this threat against the sanctity of the temple with lamentation, protest, and prayer. In his prayer (2:1–20) the high priest Simon acknowledged Israel's sins (2:13, 19), reminded God of the divine promises that "you would listen to our petition when we come to this place and pray" (2:10), and called on God to punish "this audacious and profane man" (2:14) just as God had done with "the audacious Pharaoh who had enslaved your holy people Israel" (2:6). God heard this "lawful [ἐνθέσμου] supplication" (2:21) and proceeded to administer to the king the same sort of violent lesson on monotheistic omnipotence as was experienced by Heliodorus (2:21–22; cf. 2 Macc 3:24–28), except that this time the "scourging" was administered by God directly.

Like Heliodorus, Philopator recovered from the life-threatening punishment; unlike Heliodorus, however, he did not repent and recognize the power of Israel's God. Instead, the incident in the Jerusalem temple simply set the stage for the main part of the narrative, a threat to the Jewish community in Egypt. On his return to Egypt (2:25), the king decided to teach the Jews a lesson of his own (2:25–29). He enacted legislation that reduced Jews to the status of slaves and compelled them to offer (pagan) sacrifice, to be branded with a symbol of Dionysus, and to pay a poll tax (λαογραφίαν). At the same time, in what he thought was a magnanimous gesture (3:21), he offered "equal citizenship [ἰσοπολίτας] with the Alexandrians" to those who were willing to be initiated into "the mysteries" (2:30). When the majority of Alexandrian Jews refused to compromise their religious devotion in any way, the king gave orders that all Jews, both those in Alexandria and those in the countryside, "should promptly be gathered into one place and put to death by the most cruel means" (3:1).

What follows is by turns horrifying and ludicrous.[87] Spurred on by the king, the majority of "the Gentiles" (4:1) in Egypt turned on the Jewish residents,[88] participating in the mass round-up and celebrating their imminent destruction. The Jews themselves were interned in a large hippodrome, where Egyptian officials systematically began to register them in preparation for death (4:11–15). As a "cruel means" of death, the king ordered that his herd of elephants—some five hundred in total—should be turned loose in the hippodrome, after having been drugged and intoxicated, so as to trample the Jews to death. At this point in the story, however, the horrifying has begun to give way to the ludicrous. Although they had worked at a frenzied pace for forty days, the Egyptian officials had not been able to complete the task of registration, even exhausting their supply of pens and papyrus in the process (4:19–20). On

87. Gruen (1998, 222–45) does an admirable job of describing the comic elements in the narrative, but underplays the terror.

88. The only exceptions were "the Greeks" in Alexandria (3:8–10); this will be discussed later in this chapter.

the appointed day of the execution, the king overslept, God having sent a deep sleep upon him (not to mention the fact that he had been feasting more or less continuously from the time of his return to Egypt), with the result that the event had to be postponed until the next day (5:1–22). The next day, however, the king awoke with no recollection whatsoever of his plans against the Jews, for God had responded to their entreaties by "implant[ing] in the king's mind a forgetfulness of the things he had previously devised" (5:28). When told of what was about to happen, the king was angry with his officials, praising the Jews, "who give me no ground for complaint and have exhibited to an extraordinary degree a full and firm loyalty to my ancestors" (5:31). After returning to his feasting, however, the king reverted to his original state of mind, and gave orders for the third time that the elephants be prepared for their deadly assignment (5:36–47). For the third time the Jews called to God in prayer, this time led by a pious elderly priest by the name of Eleazar (5:48–6:15). Again God responded, this time by sending "two glorious angels of fearful aspect" (6:18), who threw the enemy into such "confusion and terror" (6:19) that the elephants began to trample their handlers and the rest of the king's soldiers.

At this point, the king had a final change of heart. Unlike Heliodorus and Antiochus IV, however, who in 2 Maccabees repented of their former folly even as they acknowledged Israel's God, Philopator acted as if the whole thing had been a thoroughgoing act of treason cooked up by his advisors (6:23–28).[89] When he saw the display of divine power, he turned on his advisers, reproaching them for their "outrageous treatment" of the Jews—"those who from the beginning differed from all nations in their goodwill toward us" (6:26), whose God had from the beginning "granted an unimpeded and notable stability to our government" (6:28). These themes are repeated in a letter sent by the king to all his officials (7:2–9). Again he denounced the "malicious intent" (7:3) of his advisors, cleared the Jews of any charges against them (7:7), recognized "the friendly and firm goodwill" that the Jews had always shown toward the royal house (7:7), and acknowledged that the God of the Jews was "the Ruler over every power, the Most High God" (7:9), the "God of heaven" who "surely defends the Jews" (7:6).

It is not clear how the intended reader of 3 Maccabees is supposed to interpret this change of heart. Of course, we have already seen a similar shift in the king's mental state in chapter 5, where the king woke up on the day of slaughter with no recollection whatsoever of his plans to annihilate the Jews, blaming it all on his advisors. In this case, however, the narrator clearly indicates that the king's new state of mind is simply a temporary "forgetfulness" of his true intentions, a mental "derangement" (5:30) brought about by the intervention of divine providence (5:27–30). This altered state of consciousness was short-lived;

89. In his letter, however, he does say that he has "come to realize" the folly of opposing those whom God defends (7:6).

very quickly the king reverted to his original murderous frame of mind. At the end of the story, however, although the king's mental transformation is similar in substance, there is no indication that his newfound admiration of the Jews and acknowledgement of their God is to be seen as a transitory "derangement" of his true mental state. The narrator provides no reason to believe that the king is simply shifting the blame to his advisors to save his own skin or reputation; one gets the impression that his new attitude is to be seen as sincere and to be taken at face value.

Third Maccabees, then, contains two distinct plot lines that are clumsily twisted together. On the one hand, Philopator is an Antiochus IV (as in 2 Maccabees)—an evil and arrogant tyrant, bent on the desecration of the temple and the destruction of Israel, but forced in the end to acknowledge God's power and his own folly. On the other, he is an Artxerxes (as in LXX Esther)—fundamentally well-disposed to the Jews for their piety and loyalty, but duped for a time by his advisors, who manipulate him into supporting their evil schemes. Our assessment of how the author views Philopator's acknowledgment of "the Most High God" will depend on how we sort out these conflicting plot lines.

There can be little doubt that 3 Maccabees was written in Alexandria and that it reflects the anxieties of the Jewish community there concerning its social and legal status under Gentile rule. The outer limits for its production are the battle of Raphia (217 B.C.E.) and the destruction of the temple by the Romans (70 C.E.). Attempts have been made to fix the date more precisely, either by identifying the poll tax (λαογραφία) of 2:28 with the new policies introduced by the Romans in 25–24 B.C.E. when Egypt was organized as a province[90] or by seeing in the figure of Philopator a clear reflection of Gaius Caligula (so J. J. Collins 2000, 125–29). But while these attempts to date the work precisely tend to cancel each other out,[91] a date sometime in the early Roman period is likely. It is possible that some kernels of the narrative go back to actual events in the time of Philopator,[92] but on the whole 3 Maccabees is best seen as a narrative reworking of stock themes and traditions gathered from a number of sources.[93] The sophistication and elegance of the Greek style[94] indicates clearly that Greek was the language of composition.

90. See Tcherikover (1961); Hadas (1953, 3).

91. The use of λαογραφία (which literally means "census") is not decisive, since the Ptolemies took regular censuses (Hadas 1953, 19). On the other hand, the absence of any reference to the installation of a royal image in the temple or to actual pogroms in the streets of Alexandria seems to require a date prior to Caligula. Further, the figure of Philometor in 3 Maccabees can be accounted for fully as a literary combination of Heliodorus and Pompey.

92. See Hadas (1953, 16–21); Barclay (1996, 194).

93. E.g., the story of the crazed elephants is similar to a story in Josephus (*Ag. Ap.* 2.51–55), though the latter is set in the reign of Ptolemy Physcon (Euergetes II), who came to power in 146 B.C.E.

94. Hadas (1953, 22–23); H. Anderson (1985a, 510).

What, then, are we to make of the veneration shown by Philopator to Israel's God and temple? This will depend on the relative weight that we give to the conflicting tendencies within the work. On the one hand, there is a sharp polarity between Jews and Gentiles in 3 Maccabees. "Gentiles" usually are presented as set over against either "the Jews" (4:1–2; 5:6, 13; 6:9) or against Israel's God (especially in Eleazar's prayer: 6:5, 13, 15). Further, Gentiles are described in categorically negative terms. They are arrogant (5:13), abominable, and lawless (6:9). When they heard of the king's decree against the Jews, "the Gentiles" responded with great jubilation and celebration, thus demonstrating the "inveterate enmity that had long ago been in their minds" (4:1). The narrator also expresses unrelenting animosity toward those Jews who betrayed their heritage by giving in to the king's decree and who thus "had wilfully transgressed against the holy God and the law of God" (7:11). But on the other hand, there are indications of a more positive relationship that might exist between Jews and Gentiles. For one thing, Gentile animosity was not uniform and total. Not only was there a widespread recognition of their "good deeds" (3:5), but one group of non-Jews—"the Greeks"—recognized the injustice of the situation, attempted "to console them," and offered private assurances of support (3:8–10). Further, Jewish loyalty to the king is emphasized, appearing near the beginning of the narrative in a comment by the narrator ("The Jews, however, continued to maintain goodwill and unswerving loyalty toward the dynasty" [3:3]) and at the end, in the king's own endorsement of the contribution that the Jews had made toward the security and stability of the nation (6:24–28; 7:7; also 5:31).[95] Finally, as we have seen, the conclusion of the narrative seems to absolve the king of blame, presenting the anti-Jewish measures as the work of ill-spirited and wrong-headed advisors.

Gruen's attempt to dismiss the anti-Jewish hostility by seeing it simply as burlesque comedy,[96] while true to some extent, nevertheless underestimates the real tension and anxiety present in the narrative. But Barclay seems to go too much in the other direction when he dismisses the positive portrayal of the Greeks as an aberration in a plot line constructed around "the binary contrast of 'Jews' and 'Gentiles,' whose relationship is chiefly defined by hostility" (Barclay 1996, 197). The author wants to have it both ways, and, while he is not able to incorporate both views of the relationship into a smooth narrative, we should probably allow both to stand.[97] On the one hand, the work reflects a real anxiety on the part of the Jews that suspicion about Jewish "differences in worship and foods" (3:7) will produce a situation where rulers and common

95. The king's statement in 6:26 that the Jews differed from all other nations "in their goodwill toward us" stands in contrasting parallel to his earlier statement that they were "the only people among all nations" who displayed "manifest ill-will toward" the king (3:19).

96. "Philopator emerges less as tyrant . . . than as buffoon" (Gruen 1998, 235).

97. See J. J. Collins (2000, 126–28).

people alike join in concerted hostility against them. But on the other, the work is not fundamentally hostile to the Gentile world. The "normal" situation is one where the Jews are able to combine faithfulness to their own traditional distinctives (3:3–7) with loyalty to the Gentile king, and where such faithfulness is respected and such loyalty appreciated. Royal veneration of Israel's God and temple is the normal way in which such respect and appreciation is expressed.

As in 2 Maccabees, then, the king's worship of Israel's God is not of interest for its own sake. While the author values the good opinion of "the Greeks" (3:8–10), for example, there is no suggestion that the Greeks should follow the example of their king and join in worshiping God as well. Instead, this aspect of the narrative serves to reassure Jewish readers of the intrinsic value of their own identity and to reinforce their commitment—albeit in different political circumstances than in 2 Maccabees—to remain loyal to the Jewish way of life. Still, again as in 2 Maccabees, the narrative nevertheless assumes that it is possible and appropriate for a non-Jew to "offer sacrifice to the supreme God" (1:9), the God of Israel.

4 Maccabees

§28 4 Maccabees 4:11–12

> *Then Apollonius fell down half dead in the temple area that was open to all, stretched out his hands toward heaven, and with tears begged the Hebrews to pray for him and propitiate the wrath of the heavenly army.* [12]*For he said that he had committed a sin deserving of death, and that if he were spared he would praise the blessedness of the holy place before all people.*

Text: LXX (Rahlfs, 1979)
Translation: NRSV
Date: Mid-first century C.E. to early second century C.E.
Provenance: Diaspora, perhaps Antioch
Original language: Greek
Bibliography: H. Anderson (1985b); Barclay (1996, 369–80); Breitenstein (1976); J. J. Collins (2000, 202–9); Hadas (1953); van Henten (1997); Klauck (1989); Schürer (1986, 3:588–93)
Category: SYMPATHIZATION

4 Maccabees presents itself as a philosophical treatise dedicated to the proposition that "devout reason is sovereign over the emotions" (1:1). The primary proof that the author adduces in support of this proposition is the example of the steadfast loyalty to the law demonstrated by the Maccabean martyrs (Eleazar, the mother, and her seven sons). While the author has a general familiarity with Greek philosophy and evidently has had some rhetorical training, his purpose is to encourage his fellow "offspring of the seed of Abraham" to "obey

this law" (18:1), that is, the law of Moses, rather than to effect any sort of rapprochement between this law and Greek philosophy.

While the work displays significant differences from 2 Maccabees (e.g., in the absence from 4 Maccabees of any notion of physical resurrection), it nevertheless depends on 2 Maccabees for its subject matter. In particular, the passage quoted above is a retelling of 2 Maccabees 3, except that the Seleucid official who attempted to seize the money from the temple is named Apollonius rather than Heliodorus; evidently the latter has been confused with Apollonius the governor of Coelesyria and Phoenicia, who appears in 2 Macc 3:5.

Although the story of Heliodorus/Apollonius is recounted in some detail in 4 Maccabees, its primary purpose is to provide the necessary background to the story of the martyrs. In particular, nothing in the story itself has any direct bearing on the theme of reason and the emotions. Thus the author shows very little interest in Apollonius's change of heart itself: he ignores completely Antiochus's deathbed change of heart, as found in 2 Maccabees 9. In other words, the author simply takes over from his source the detail of Apollonius's willingness to "praise the blessedness of the holy place [τοῦ ἱεροῦ τόπου] before all people [πᾶσιν ἀνθρώποις]," without making any attempt to incorporate it into his theme. Thus there is little to be gained here by any detailed examination of his work.

CHAPTER 3

PSEUDEPIGRAPHA

Introduction

"Pseudepigrapha" is not a particularly apt term, in that much of the literature typically assembled under this heading is not pseudepigraphal, and pseudepigraphal literature can be found elsewhere (e.g., Wisdom of Solomon). But in the absence of any suitable alternative, it is being used here to refer to Jewish literature from the period bracketed by the Bible and the Mishnah that does not belong to any other identifiable collection or grouping.

Texts and Commentary

1 ENOCH

The "book" that we know as *1 Enoch* is a composite work, comprising at least five major sections plus several postscripts,[1] which were written at various points from the late-third century B.C.E. to perhaps the mid-first century C.E.

1. These five sections are generally recognized: the Book of the Watchers (1–36); the Similitudes (37–71); the Astronomical Book (72–82); the Dream Visions (83–90); the Epistle (91–105), including the Apocalypse of Weeks (93:1–10 + 91:11–17). Chapter 108 represents a discrete unit, appended at some subsequent date. Charles also understood ch. 105 to be a later addition, but it is now generally seen as an integral part of the Epistle. There continues to be debate about chs. 106–07; the issue will be discussed further later.

The resultant collection, while falling into the general category of apocalyptic literature, nevertheless contains a striking diversity of subject matter. What holds this diverse collection together, of course, is its eponymous central figure, Enoch, whose cryptic story is recounted in Gen 5:18–24. But there are thematic links as well, one of which has to do with the Gentiles. There are at least eight separate texts, representing four of the major sections (Book of the Watchers [10:21–11:2]; Similitudes [48:4–5; 50:2–3]; Dream Visions [90:30–38]; Epistle [91:14; 105:1–2]), in which Gentiles are included within the sphere of eschatological blessing.[2] As Nickelsburg has observed (2001, 7, 54), this universalistic theme is striking, given the remnant mentality that pervades *1 Enoch* as a whole. *1 Enoch* tends toward an exclusive view of election, in which the community of the righteous has been narrowed—from Israel as a whole to a smaller group comprising those who subscribed to its own particular understanding of God's purposes. But alongside, we find a recurring expectation that the end-time vindication of the faithful will be followed by a wide-scale turning to God on the part of the Gentile nations. The texts will be discussed in their probable chronological order.

Text: Ethiopic (Ge'ez): Knibb (1978); Greek: Black (1970); Aramaic: Milik (1976)
Translation: Nickelsburg (2001) (except for the Similitudes)
Date: A composite work, dating from the late-third century B.C.E. to perhaps as late as the mid-first century C.E. (see further later)
Provenance: Palestine
Original Language: Aramaic (the complete work is extant only in Ethiopic, itself a translation from a Greek translation)
Bibliography: Black (1985); Charles (1913b, 2:163–281; 1917; J. J. Collins (1998, 43–84; 177–93); Isaac (1983); Nickelsburg (2001); VanderKam (1984)

§29 1 Enoch *10:21–11:2*

And all the sons of men will become righteous; and all the peoples will worship (me); and all will bless me and prostrate themselves. [22]*And all the earth will be cleansed from all defilement and from all uncleanness; and I shall not again send upon them any wrath or scourge for all the generations of eternity.* [11:1]*Then I shall open the storehouses of blessing that are in heaven; and make them descend upon the earth, upon the works and the labor of the sons of men.* [2]*And then truth and peace will be united together for all the days of eternity and for all the generations of men.*

2. *1 En.* 107:1 also speaks of the appearance in the future of "generations of righteousness." There is no explicit indication in this passage that Gentiles are included in this coming age, however, which means that the passage should be excluded from consideration.

Date: Mid-third century B.C.E.
Category: ESCHATOLOGICAL PARTICIPATION

1 Enoch 6–11 represents a distinct unit within the larger Book of the Watchers (chs. 1–36). While it is differentiated from the rest of these chapters by the absence of any reference to Enoch, its description of the activity and fate of the rebellious angels (Watchers) is foundational for the remainder. As several commentators have suggested, it is likely that there was an intended parallel between the activity of these angels and circumstances in the author's own day,[3] though it is difficult to identify these circumstances with any degree of confidence. Absence of any hints of persecution or of internal conflict suggests a date prior to the Maccabean era.

These chapters represent an expansion of Genesis 6, in which several strands of the Genesis account—the enigmatic account of the "sons of God" who had intercourse with the daughters of men (Gen 6:1–4), and the subsequent judgment of the flood—are woven into a detailed scenario describing the origin of evil, the final judgment, and the ultimate establishment of God's reign. The entry of evil into human affairs is depicted as the work of a band of renegade angels, who took wives from the "beautiful and comely daughters" who were born in the days "when the children of men had multiplied" (6:1–2), teaching them a variety of magical and martial arts, and producing with them a race of rapacious giants. When the resultant evil state of affairs comes to God's attention, the Most High responds by sending the flood (as in Genesis) and by giving commands that Azazel and the rest of the wicked angels be bound until the final day of judgment. While there is a passing reference to the future generations of Noah's offspring (10:3), attention shifts quickly to the final judgment of the Watchers and their offspring (10:9–15), and the ultimate establishment of God's rule of righteousness, prosperity, and peace (10:16–22). The whole course of human existence, then, is here both determined and overshadowed by these primordial and eschatological events.

One of the things that gets skipped over in this rush from the flood to the final state of affairs is the whole history of Israel. Indeed, covenantal particularism is strikingly muted in the Book of the Watchers as a whole, a fact that is only partly accounted for by the pre-Abraham setting of the Enoch story. While there is certainly a distinction made between the righteous and the sinners (e.g., 1:7–9; 10:17; 22:13), together with some reference to the "commandment of the Lord" (21:6) and rich allusion to Israel's scripture,[4] there is no explicit indication that the righteous are to be identified by their adherence to the commandments of the Lord set out in the Torah.

3. See Nickelsburg (2005, 49–50; 2001, 169–71); J. J. Collins (1998, 50–51).
4. Especially Ezekiel; see Nickelsburg (2005, 50) and Black (1985, ad loc).

This has a bearing on our passage of interest (10:21–11:2), which describes the turning of "all nations" to God in the last days. In keeping with the muted covenantal character of the Book of the Watchers, this description of end-time bliss lacks many of the usual features of the eschatological pilgrimage tradition. Absent are such themes as the restoration of Jerusalem and the temple, the gathering of the exiles, the pilgrimage of the Gentiles to Zion, and so on. Still, there is a clear distinction between the "righteous" who will escape the final woes (10:17) and the "sons of men" and "all the peoples" who subsequently "become righteous" and turn to worship God (10:21). Given the biblical framework of the text, its original readers would be inclined to see at least an implicit connection between these "righteous ones" and the community of Israel. Thus the passage belongs to the broader category of texts in which Gentiles are expected to turn to the God of Israel in the last days and to share in the blessings of the end time. Nevertheless, the emphasis in these verses falls on the universality of the final state of blessing. While Kraus probably goes too far in saying that the particular identity of Israel is dissolved in this passage,[5] there is no apparent interest in the status of these newly righteous nations with respect to Israel or its usual boundary markers.

§30 1 Enoch *91:14*

> *After this there will arise a ninth week, in which righteous law will be revealed to all the sons of the whole earth; and all the deeds of wickedness will vanish from the whole earth and descend to the eternal pit, and all humankind will look to the path of eternal righteousness.*

Date: Second century B.C.E., prior to the Maccabean revolt (167)
Additional bibliography: Dexinger (1977)
Category: ESCHATOLOGICAL PARTICIPATION

The vision of universal righteousness described in *1 Enoch* 91:14 appears toward the end of the Apocalypse of Weeks, a discrete unit within the Epistle of Enoch (chs. 91–105). Evidence from Qumran has confirmed Charles's earlier supposition that the Ethiopic text shows evidence of "severe dislocation" and that the conclusion to the apocalypse that begins in 93:1–10 is to be found in 91:11–17.[6] In the reconstructed apocalypse, the whole of human history from creation to

5. Kraus sees 10:21 as evidence for the same type of expectation as he finds in 90:30–38; see Kraus (1996, 55–56). But it is unlikely that this latter passage speaks of an end-time dissolution of the boundary between Israel and the Gentiles (see §32).

6. Actually Charles identified the Apocalypse as consisting of 93:1–14 and 91:12–17. But in the Aramaic fragments, 93:10 is followed immediately by 91:11, thus confirming that a dislocation had taken place but correcting slightly Charles' reconstruction of the original. See Charles, 1913b, 2.170, 263–64; Black (1985, 21–23, 287–88); Nickelsburg (2001, 414–15).

consummation is divided into ten periods ("weeks") of unequal length. Enoch was granted this knowledge of human history on his heavenly journey when he was allowed to read the "heavenly tablets" (93:2). Commentators are generally agreed that the Apocalypse had a separate existence prior to its being incorporated into the Epistle.[7] The absence of any explicit allusion to the Maccabean crisis suggests a date in the first third of the second century B.C.E.

The first seven "weeks" are demarcated by important events occurring at the end of each: Enoch's birth (week 1); Noah and the flood (week 2); the election of Abraham and his posterity ("a plant of eternal righteousness" [week 3]); the giving of the law (week 4); the building of the temple (week 5); the destruction of the temple and the exile (week 6); and the selection of "the chosen . . . from the eternal plant of righteousness" (93:10), evidently the group from whose standpoint the apocalypse was written (week 7). In contrast to the preceding weeks, the eighth is characterized as a week "of righteousness" (91:12); it begins with judgment ("a sword will be given to all the righteous, to execute a righteous judgement on all the wicked" [91:12]) and ends with the rebuilding of the temple ("the temple of the kingdom of the Great One will be built in the greatness of its glory for all the generations of eternity" [91:13]). In the ninth week righteous judgment becomes universal (91:14), suggesting that the wicked who were judged in the preceding week were the apostates within Israel (cf. the "perverse generation" of 93:9). There appears, then, to be a progressive, stage-by-stage character to the final judgment—first Israel (week 8), then the whole of humankind (week 9) and finally the angelic Watchers (week 10).[8]

Our passage of interest appears in the ninth week, where judgment is extended to the whole earth. This week is brought to an end by a state of affairs in which "all humankind will look to the path of eternal righteousness" (91:14). If Black's translation of the preceding lines were correct ("all workers of iniquity . . . will be cast into the eternal pit"), it would be surprising that there would be any people at all left to seek the true path. But the translation is based on a reconstructed text (וכול עב]די רשׁעיא]), and commentators have tended to favor the Ethiopic reading, where it is the "works" and not "the workers" of iniquity that will be cast into the pit.[9] Indeed, this reading is in keeping with the universal emphasis in the verse as a whole; the statement that "all the deeds of wickedness will vanish from the whole earth" is just another way of saying that "all the sons of the whole earth" or "all humankind" will seek the path of righteousness.[10]

7. E.g., J. J. Collins (1998, 62–63); Black (1985, 287–89); Nickelsburg (2001, 440). Milik (1976, 49–55, 255–56) and VanderKam (1984, 142–46) have argued for a unified composition, but they are definitely in the minority.

8. See Black (1985, 293–94); Nickelsburg (2001, 438).

9. See Knibb (1978, 219); Isaac (1983, 73; Nickelsburg (2001, 437). Cf. Black (1985, 294).

10. Nickelsburg (2001, 449) notes the repetition of כולה (all) in this verse.

But what will this path look like? What relationship will there be between these newly righteous Gentiles and the righteous people of Israel? Before this question is addressed directly, it is important to note that the people of Israel are more explicitly to the fore in the Apocalypse of Weeks than they were in the Book of the Watchers discussed above. Abraham is "chosen" to be the origin of "the plant of righteousness for ever and ever" (93:5); from this "eternal plant of righteousness" the elect of the end times are also "chosen" in the seventh week (93:10); the Mosaic "covenant" is mentioned explicitly in the fourth week (93:6); the Jerusalem sanctuary and its sanctity is a recurring theme (the tabernacle [93:6]; the Solomonic temple [93:7]; the destruction of the temple as the climax of a period of apostasy [93:8]; and the appearance of the eschatological temple at the end of the eighth week [91:13]). When in the ninth week the Gentiles turn *en masse* to the path of righteousness, it is the culmination and consequence of a process that takes place squarely within Israel.

But do the Gentiles end up squarely within Israel? Does the text envisage them as proselytes? If Nickelsburg's rendering is correct, the text of 91:14 seems to move in this direction when it speaks of the "righteous law" being revealed to the Gentiles. The same phrase (דין קשׁוט) appears in 91:5, 12. דין is normally rendered "judgment," and this is clearly the sense in 91:12. But Nickelsburg has adduced evidence that in Aramaic usage the word can be used of the law of Moses, and this is how he interprets both 93:5 (Abraham as the plant of "righteous judgment") and 91:14 (Nickelsburg 2001, 446, 449). If the "path of righteousness" is determined by the law of Moses, it would be plausible to argue that the Gentiles who look to this path in the end time do so by embracing the Torah and are thus in effect grafted into Abraham's "plant of righteousness."[11] But even if we grant this rendering of דין, it would not be wise to draw any firm conclusions about the status of the Gentiles in 91:14. In 93:4 there is also a reference to the "law" that was enacted at the time of Noah; one could just as plausibly argue that these end-time Gentiles are righteous according to the commandments given to the whole of humankind through Noah.[12] In addition, even earlier, the time of Enoch is characterized as an era of righteousness (93:3), which means that righteousness is not tied exclusively to the law of Moses.

The passage, then, is not concerned to determine the status of these Gentiles with any precision. On the one hand, the era of universal righteousness is made possible by the establishment of righteousness in Israel; this is a

11. See Nickelsburg (1985, 76–77).

12. See the discussion in Black (1985, 289–90). The description of this as a law "made for sinners" might tell against the idea that the Noachian decrees are in view here, since these are generally seen as describing those who, in contrast to the rest of the Gentile world, are righteous. Black points to *Jub.* 6:2 and 7:20, where Noah reaffirms commandments that had been forgotten, as an equally possible interpretation of the verse.

very particularistic form of universalism. On the other hand, the Gentiles seem to participate in this era of righteousness as Gentiles; there is no indication that they are incorporated into Israel and lose their identity as Gentiles.

§31 1 Enoch *105:1–2*

> *In those days, says the Lord, they will summon and testify against the sons of earth in their wisdom. Instruct them, for you are their leaders and . . . rewards over all the earth. For I and my son will join ourselves with them forever in the paths of truth in their life. And you will have peace. Rejoice, O children of truth. Amen.*

Date: Second century B.C.E., prior to the Maccabean revolt (167)
Category: ESCHATOLOGICAL PARTICIPATION

The place of *1 Enoch* 105 in the larger construction of the book as a whole has been variously assessed in the history of scholarship. Charles was of the opinion that chapter 104 brought the Epistle of Enoch to a conclusion and that chapter 105—along with 106–7 and 108—were later independent additions (1913b, 2:170). In part, his opinion was based on the phrase "I and my son" (105:2), which he took to be a reference to God and the Messiah (1913b, 2:170), unparalleled elsewhere in the Epistle. Evidence from Qumran, however, has rendered such an approach less tenable; 4QEn^{c} contains parts of chapters 104–7, indicating that chapter 105 belonged to the same Aramaic text that contained chapters 91–104.[13] "I and my son" is probably understood as a reference to Enoch and Methuselah.[14] VanderKam has taken this evidence one step further, arguing that the Epistle contained not only chapter 105 but chapters 106–7 as well. Observing that both chapters 106–7 and chapter 91 contain apocalypses in which Methuselah is addressed by Enoch, he argues that these chapters form an *inclusio*, with the result that there is a discernible literary unity to the whole of 91–107 (VanderKam 1984, 174–75). But such a conclusion is open to question. As Nickelsburg has demonstrated, chapter 91 can be separated from the Epistle, which properly begins with chapter 92; 92:1 and 105:1–2 function as an *inclusio*, framing the Epistle as a whole (Nickelsburg 2001, 22–24, 335–37). In addition, 4QEn^{c} contains a space between chapters 105 and 106, which suggests that the latter was seen as the start of an independent section (Nickelsburg 2001, 22). For present purposes, however, the important thing to note is that chapter 105 was most probably an integral part of the Epistle.

13. See Black (1985, 318–19); Nickelsburg (2001, 8, 22).

14. See Nickelsburg (2001, 535) and also Black (1985, 318–19). In this reading the phrase "says the Lord" is not seen as signaling a change in speaker that extends to the next sentence. Milik has argued that the sentence as a whole was a Christian interpolation (Milik 1976, 208); but his argument (based on the length of the lacuna in 4QEn^{c}, line 23) is unpersuasive (the lacuna is long, and his restoration is not the only possibility).

The Epistle of Enoch is characterized by a sustained contrast between the "righteous" and the "sinners." To a certain extent the contrast is worked out in general and typical terms, the line of demarcation being the readiness to "learn to do the commandments of the Most High, and to walk in the paths of his righteousness" (99:10). But several aspects of the text seem to signal a more specific reference. For one thing, the "righteous and pious and wise" are identified as those who possess "my [i.e., Enoch's] books" (104:12–13); that is, the "righteous" seem to be identified with a specific (Enochian) group within Israel. This is reinforced by the depiction of the sinners. This category includes not only the Gentiles (e.g., 99:6–9; 101:7), but apostates within Israel as well—those "who alter the true words and pervert the eternal covenant" (99:2; cf. 104:10–12). Further, there is a striking social character to Enoch's charge against the sinners. They amass gold and silver (97:8–9), build elaborate houses (94:6–7), and partake of sumptuous banquets (96:5), even as they persecute and oppress the righteous (95:7; 96:5, 8). The Epistle of Enoch, then, seems to have emanated from a particular segment of Judaism, characterized by a strong group identity and what might be termed a "remnant mentality," forged in the context of a conflict with the ruling elite.

The question of the date of the Epistle is related to that of its relationship with the Apocalypse of Weeks, which it contains. Charles (1913b, 2:171–72) felt that the Epistle reflected the conflict between the Pharisees and Sadducees in the Hasmonean era, while the Apocalyse, which seems to contain no allusion to the Hellenizing crisis at all, must have been a pre-Maccabean unit that was taken over and inserted into the Epistle.[15] The tendency more recently, however, has been to see the Apocalypse as more closely associated with the Epistle. On the one hand, the contrast between the sinners and the righteous is just as marked in the Apocalypse as in the rest of the Epistle; here we find a similar remnant mentality (93:10) and a similar expectation that the righteous will eventually execute judgment on the wicked (91:12; cf. 98:12). On the other hand, the details reflected in the Epistle are vague; they could just as easily apply to the period of the Hellenizing crisis as to the later Hasmonean period. While VanderKam has probably gone too far in arguing for a unified composition (VanderKam 1984, 142–46), it is probable that the Epistle postdates the Apocalypse of Weeks only slightly, and that they both emerged from a similar milieu.[16]

As has already been observed, the Epistle of Enoch is characterized by a strong remnant consciousness. The circle of the righteous is identified with those who possess and believe in the books of Enoch (104:12–13); all others are "sinners," whose final prospects seem bleak:

15. Charles (1913b, 2.171–72); a similar approach has been taken by Tcherikover (1959, 258–62) and, more recently, by Black (1985, 277–78).

16. Nickelsburg's reconstruction is convincing; see Nickelsburg (2001, 335–37; 425–29).

> And now know that you have been prepared for a day of destruction; and do not hope to be saved, O sinners; you will depart and die. [Know[17]] that you have been prepared for a day of great judgment and tribulation and very great shame for your spirits (98:10).

But, as is the case elsewhere in *1 Enoch*, this narrowed view of election stands alongside a more generous expectation concerning the ultimate destiny of the Gentiles. If chapter 105 is indeed part of the Epistle of Enoch, the Epistle concludes with the promise that "in those days" those who have received the books of Enoch (104:13) will "summon" and "instruct" the "sons of earth" in the ways of righteousness. The text is not without its difficulties. In addition to the reference to "I and my son," discussed earlier, the phrase translated "rewards over all the earth" (105:1) is problematic.[18] Nevertheless, the overall thrust of the passage is clear; as Nickelsburg has observed, the passage anticipates that the Gentiles will be converted to righteousness by means of "the testimony of the righteous based on the books of Enoch."[19]

What, though, about the status of these Gentile believers? Is it expected that they will conform to the same standard of righteousness as adhered to by the community to which the text is addressed? That is, are they to become full observers of the "eternal covenant" (99:2), end-time proselytes? The Epistle as a whole places a great deal of stress on the "paths of righteousness," which, in contrast to the Apocalypse of Weeks, are explicitly equated with "the commandments of the Most High" (99:10; also 91:4, 18, 19; 94:1, 3, 4). Thus, it would be in keeping with the tenor of the Epistle that these "sons of earth" who will be instructed "in the paths of truth" would be expected thereby to become full observers of the Torah. Nevertheless, the passage itself provides no explicit support for this expectation, which suggests that the question should be left open.

§32 1 Enoch *90:30, 33, 37–38*

> [30]*And I saw all the sheep that remained. And all the animals upon the earth and all the birds of heaven were falling down and worshiping those sheep and making petition to them and obeying them in every thing.. . .* [33]*And all that had been destroyed and dispersed [and*[20]*] all the wild beasts and all the birds of heaven were gathered in that house. And the Lord of the sheep rejoiced greatly because they were all good and had*

17. Nickelsburg uses angle brackets to indicate a textual emendation.

18. For discussion of the possibilities, see Black (1985, 318) and Milik (1976, 208).

19. Nickelsburg (2001, 535). It is not clear, then, why in his translation Nickelsburg renders it "they will summon and testify against the sons of earth"; cf. Black ("testify to," 1985, 99); Milik ("testify with regard to them" [1976, 207]); Isaac ("reveal it to them," 1983, 86).

20. This is a revision of Nickelsburg's translation. The Ethiopic reading is "and," but Nickelsburg has conjectured that it should be replaced with "by." For discussion, with refutation, see the following sections.

> *returned to that house.. . .* [37]*And I saw how a white bull was born, and its horns were large. And all the wild beasts and all the birds of heaven were afraid of it and made petition to it continually.* [38]*And I saw until all their species were changed, and they all became white cattle. And the first one became <leader> among them (and that <leader> was a large animal), and there were large black horns on its head. And the Lord of the sheep rejoiced over it and over all the cattle.*

Date: *Circa* 165 B.C.E.
Additional bibliography: Hengel (1974, 1:177–78); Kraus (1996, 53–57); Schnabel (2004, 97–98); Tiller (1993)
Category: ESCHATOLOGICAL PARTICIPATION

This remarkable passage forms part of the climax of the Animal Apocalypse (chs. 85–90), one of two dream visions that make up the fourth section of *1 Enoch* (chs. 83–90). The apocalypse, which recounts the whole of human history from the creation of Adam until the final consummation, derives its name from the fact that the human characters in the story are symbolized by beasts of various kinds—the preflood patriarchs by domesticated cattle (bulls, cows, oxen), Israel by sheep, and the Gentile nations by a variety of birds and beasts. In keeping with their role in the story, the latter are generally undomesticated, levitically unclean, and predatory or scavenging.[21] In addition to these human characters, two groups of angelic figures play important roles in the apocalypse. One group, obviously derived from Gen 6:1–4, is depicted by a number of "stars," who, having descended from heaven, had intercourse with female cattle and generated other beasts (elephants, camels, and asses) who began to devour the cattle (86:1–6). The other group of angelic figures, depicted as seventy shepherds, are those to whom God (the Lord of the sheep) entrusted the discipline and punishment of Israel in the period of the exile and beyond (89:59–64).

The events leading up to the end begin with the emergence of some sheep who "began to open their eyes and to see" (90:6), a description whose significance derives from the fact that, since the return from exile, "the eyes of the sheep were blind, and they did not see" (89:74). At the center of this group is a ram with a great horn, who is able to withstand the attacks of the "eagles and vultures and ravens and kites" (90:9–13). Scholarly opinion is unanimous in identifying this ram as Judas Maccabees.[22] Since at this point the narrative clearly shifts from the historical to the eschatological—the ram's cry for help precipitates the coming of the "Lord of the sheep" and the final defeat of the beasts (90:13–19)—the apocalypse can be dated to a point

21. See Tiller (1993, 28–36).

22. E.g., Black (1985, 20); Charles, 1913b, 2.170–71; J. J. Collins (1998, 69); Milik (1976, 43–44); Nickelsburg (2001, 396–401); Tiller (1993, 61–79); VanderKam (1984, 163).

sometime after the outbreak of the Maccabean revolt (167 B.C.E.) but before Judas's death (161 B.C.E.).[23]

The material of interest to us is contained within the eschatological scenario that unfolds from this point. The passage is typical of Jewish Zion eschatology in many respects, as it describes the defeat and destruction of the Gentile oppressors (90:18–19); the judgment of the wicked angels (both the "stars" and the "shepherds" [vv. 20–26]); the construction of a new Jerusalem (the "house" [vv. 28–29])[24]; the subjugation of the Gentiles (presumably those who were not involved in the oppression of Israel, since these have already been destroyed [v. 30]); the gathering of the exiles (the "dispersed" [v. 33]); and the resurrection of the righteous (the "destroyed" [v. 33]).[25]

To this point the references to Gentiles have been negative; the wicked have been destroyed (vv. 18–19), while the others have been subjugated to those sheep who had initiated the battle (v. 30). The situation is different, however, in v. 33, at least as the verse reads in the original manuscripts: "And all that had been destroyed and dispersed and all the wild beasts and all the birds of heaven were gathered in that house." If this reading is correct, the Gentiles join with redeemed Israel in the "house" (Jerusalem), to share in the blessings of the eschatological era.

Nickelsburg has argued, however, that the text should be emended; in his translation he replaces "and" with "by," so that the verse reads: "And all that had been destroyed and dispersed *by* all the wild beasts and all the birds of heaven . . . " This has the effect of eliminating any positive reference to the Gentiles; rather than being present with redeemed Israel in the new Jerusalem, they are mentioned simply as those who had been responsible for the dispersion and destruction of the Israelites in the old era. His reason for this emendation is the statement later on in v. 33 that they all "had returned to that house"; since it could not be said of Gentiles that they "returned" to Jerusalem, he argues, the first part of the verse cannot include them. The argument has a certain plausibility, and if there were no other reference to Gentiles in the passage, it might be convincing. But as we will see in more detail in a moment, the Gentiles come into view again in vv. 37–38, and in a startlingly positive manner. Thus it seems more prudent to let the text stand, and to see v. 33b as the start of a short section (vv. 33b–36) where the focus is on Israel. In other words, v. 33a introduces two groups that are present in the new Jerusalem—"all that had

23. Nickelsburg argues that the Animal Apocalypse was originally written earlier (either late-third century B.C.E. or after the death of Onias III in 169 B.C.E.) but was updated to the Maccabean period through additions to 90:6–19. The argument—plausible but probably incapable of proof—is based on the presence in 90:6–19 of two parallel (but now intertwined) structures.

24. The temple itself seems to be depicted as a tower within the house (e.g., 89:50)

25. On resurrection, see Tiller (1993, 380–81).

been destroyed and dispersed" (redeemed Israel) and "all the wild beasts and all the birds of heaven" (gathered Gentiles). If this reading is correct, while the Gentiles themselves do not come fully into focus until v. 37, they are nevertheless present in the "house." With the Jews who are also there they form a single assembly; indeed, the fact that they are mentioned along with the exiles (the "dispersed") and the resurrected righteous (the "destroyed") seems to suggest that their presence is necessary to make the assembly complete. Thus, while the focus shifts in the first instance to Israel, there is no reason to exclude the Gentiles from the sphere of divine joy. The passage clearly expects that Gentiles will be full participants in the blessings of the eschatological era.

In v. 37, attention shifts from Israel (the sheep who "had returned to that house," v. 33b) to the Gentiles ("all the wild beasts and all the birds of heaven"). This section begins with the birth of a white bull (v. 37). Since "all the wild beasts and all the birds of heaven were afraid of it and made petition to it continually" (v. 37), the white bull has usually been considered as a Messiah figure.[26] In the grammar of the apocalypse, however, this figure is closely aligned with the patriarchs of the pre-Israel period (Adam, the line of Seth, Noah, the line of Shem, Abraham, Isaac), who were also represented by white bulls (85:3, 7–10; 89:1, 9, 10). The appearance of the white bull sets the stage for a general transformation, for at this point "all their species were transformed, and they all became white bulls" (v. 38). Given the significance of white bulls in the apocalypse, then, this transformation has to do with the restoration of an original, patriarchal state of affairs.

But how inclusive is this transformation?[27] Tiller and Nickelsburg assume that "all their species" denotes the whole human menagerie, sheep included. In other words, the transformation is universal; the text anticipates "the transformation of the whole human race, Israelites and Gentiles, into primordial righteousness and perfection."[28] If this reading is correct, the Animal Apocalypse would have as its startling conclusion the eradication of the distinction between Jew and Gentile, an end-time scenario that would make it unique in the literature of the period (Kraus 1996, 53–57).

Even if this reading is correct, however, Tiller goes too far when he says, "The existence of the separate nations, one of which is Israel, is apparently seen

26. This goes back to Charles; 1913b, 2.260.

27. The interpretation of this transformation is made even more difficult by the confused description of the further transformation of the "messianic" white bull, in which it is said to become "a word" (v. 38b). The text is clearly corrupt; for discussion of the possible emendments, see Nickelsburg (2001, 403); Black (1985, 280); Tiller (1993, 385–86). But the nature of the original reading does not seem to bear directly on the issue under discussion here.

28. Nickelsburg (2001, 407); also Tiller (1993, 19–20, 385); Kraus (1996, 53–57); Rowland (1982, 163); Schnabel (2004, 97–98).

as one of the negative effects of human history that the ideal future will undo."[29] For the scenario is nevertheless one that is still centered very much on Israel. The transformation takes place, after all, in Jerusalem, to which all the nations have gathered. Further, despite the transformation, the God who rejoices over "all the cattle" is still described as the "Lord of the sheep." In addition, Abraham himself is depicted as a white bull. Consequently when the Gentiles are transformed into white bulls themselves, they become part of the family not simply of Adam, but more specifically of Abraham, a point that Tiller does not take sufficiently into account.[30] Even in this inclusive reading of the passage, then, the existence of Israel needs to be seen as a means to such an end-time transformation, rather than as one of the negative elements that this transformation will undo.

But it is not at all certain that this reading of the passage is correct. As has already been observed, God continues to be described as the "Lord of the sheep," a description that would seem out of place if the sheep had been transformed along with the others into an undifferentiated herd of cattle. Further, the most natural reading of v. 38 is that the group indicated by means of the personal pronouns ("all *their* species"; "*they* all became") is the same group introduced in v. 37, that is, "all the wild beasts and all the birds of heaven." There is no real reason to believe that "all" includes anything more than the various non-Jewish nations referred to in v. 37. In support of this one can adduce 89:10, where similar language ("every kind of species") is used to talk about the Gentile nations as distinct from Israel.[31] It seems more likely, then, that vv. 37–38 deals with Gentiles exclusively, just as vv. 33b–36 deals with Israel exclusively. In other words, what is undone in this end-time transformation is the initial degeneration of the family of Noah (89:9) into a state of wild rapacity.

If this reading is correct, then the Gentiles who are included in the end-time restoration continue to exist as Gentiles. Although they are restored to the state of righteousness that was characteristic of the patriarchs—Adam, Seth, Noah, and even Abraham—they are not absorbed into the family of Israel.[32]

29. Tiller (1993, 20). In the remainder of the paragraph from which this quotation is drawn, however, Tiller acknowledges the ambiguity of the symbolism and the difficulties in interpretation. Still, he tends to tilt the balance a little too far in the direction of undifferentiated universalism.

30. There is no mention of Abraham in his discussions of the "ideal, third age"; Abraham is eclipsed by Adam (see Tiller 1993, 19–20, 385). There is a similar tendency in Kraus (1996, 53–57).

31. The vocabulary, however, is not identical. In 90:38 the word translated "species" is *ʾazmādihomu* (their kindred, family group), while in 89:10 it is *ʾaḥzāb* (group of people, population). Still, the language is sufficiently similar to have some probative value. (I appreciate the assistance of Mesfin Atlaye with the Ge'ez text.)

32. Rowland (2002, 216) provides no justification for his statement that these Gentiles were expected to "submit to the Law of Moses and become proselytes, thus accepting circumcision."

They gather to the "house" of God in Jerusalem where they live peaceably with the "sheep" and presumably worship the God who is the "Lord of the sheep." But beyond this there is no indication that they adopt any practices or identifying marks that would serve to incorporate them into Israel.[33] They are full participants in this scene of end-time salvation; the Lord of the sheep rejoices over their presence; but they are there as Gentiles.

§33 1 Enoch *48:4–5*

> *He will become a staff for the righteous ones in order that they may lean on him and not fall. He is the light of the gentiles and he will become the hope of those who are sick in their hearts. [5]All those who dwell upon the earth shall fall and worship before him; they shall glorify, bless and sing the name of the Lord of the Spirits.*

§34 1 Enoch *50:2–5*

> *He heaped evil upon the sinners; but the righteous ones shall be victorious in the name of the Lord of the Spirits. He will cause the others to see this so that they may repent and forsake the deeds of their hands. [3]There shall not be honor unto them in the name of the Lord of the Spirits. But through his name they shall be saved, and the Lord of the Spirits shall have mercy upon them, for his mercy is considerable. [4]He is righteous in his judgment and in glory that is before him. Oppression cannot survive his judgment; and the unrepentant in his presence shall perish. [5]The Lord of the Spirits has said that from henceforth he will not have mercy upon them.*

Text: Ethiopic: Knibb (1978)
Translation: *OTP* (Isaac 1983)
Date: Mid-first century C.E. (?)

33. The issue is complicated somewhat by the fact that in the apocalypse as a whole, there is a distinct lack of emphasis on the usual marks of differentiation between Jew from Gentile. There is no mention of circumcision, not even—in striking contrast to the biblical account—in the story of Abraham himself (89:10–12). Even more striking is the absence of the law; we are told about Moses' ascent of Sinai (89:29) but not that the purpose of the climb was to receive the Torah. To be sure, in a footnote, Isaac suggests the possibility that the Torah is in view in v. 29 ("the Lord of the sheep sent it to them"), but this is unlikely, for the only possible antecedent for "it" is "that sheep" (i.e., Moses); see Isaac (1983, 66). (On the absence of the law, see Tiller 1993, 291–92). Instead, the emphasis in this section concerns the incident of the golden calf (89:32–35) and the building of the tabernacle (89:36). Consistent with this is the fact that the recurring blindness of the sheep has to do with false and impure worship at the "house" and "tower" (89:32, 51, 54, 73–74; cf. 90:6–7, 35), rather than with disobedience to the law in general. Likewise, there is no criticism of the Gentiles for their disobedience of God's commands; their fault is chiefly their oppression of Israel. But while the usual boundary markers are not to the fore, the author's choice of symbolism indicates that for him the boundary between Jew and Gentile is clear and distinct.

Provenance: Palestine
Original Language: Probably Aramaic
Bibliography: Black (1985); Charles (1917; 1913b, 2:163–281); J. J. Collins (1998, 43–84; 177–93); Isaac (1983); Nickelsburg (2001); VanderKam (1995)
Category: ESCHATOLOGICAL PARTICIPATION

These two passages are found in the Similitudes of Enoch, a section of *1 Enoch* (chs. 37–71) that is extant only in Ethiopic. Given its length, the absence of the Similitudes from the Qumran manuscripts cannot be fortuitous; the Qumran version of *1 Enoch* clearly did not contain the Similitudes. While the author of the Similitudes wrote in conscious awareness of other Enochic literature—it is described as the "second vision which . . . Enoch . . . saw" (37:1)[34]—the work is sufficiently well-defined and distinctive that it needs to be considered as a self-contained entity. Milik's hypothesis that the Similitudes was a Christian work dating from the latter part of the third century C.E. (Milik 1976, 89–96) has attracted considerable attention but not much of a following. The Similitudes should be read as a Jewish apocalypse, dating probably from the first century C.E.[35] and originating within a Jewish group related to, but distinct from, other Enochic groups.

The work receives its name from the three parables (or similitudes) that were revealed to Enoch in a heavenly vision and that he in turn reveals to those who dwell on the earth (37:1–5). The three similitudes are clearly demarcated (38–44; 45–57; 58–69) and constitute the major portion of the work. They are framed by an introduction (ch. 37) and conclusion (chs. 70–71). While distinct topics are indicated for each of the similitudes—"when the congregation of the righteous shall appear, sinners shall be judged for their sins" (38:1); "concerning those who deny the name of the Lord of Spirits and the congregation of the holy ones" (45:1); "concerning the righteous and the elect" (58:1)—there is an overall thematic unity to the Similitudes and little real difference among its three major sections. Our passages of interest are found in the second similitude.

34. Milik (1976, 89) identified the "first vision" as the whole Enoch collection reflected in the extant Greek and Aramaic manuscripts, i.e., the whole of *1 Enoch* minus the Similitudes. But this identification is driven more by his theory of a late origin for the Similitudes than by anything in the text itself. The phrase could refer just as easily to 1:2.

35. For a discussion of the date, see Suter (1979, 11–33). If "the city of my righteous ones" (56:7), which will withstand an attack by the Parthians and the Medes, is identified as Jerusalem—a plausible identification, given the prophetic allusions in the passage—a date prior to 70 C.E. seems likely; there is no hint whatsoever of the destruction of Jerusalem. Indeed, the absence from Ethiopic Enoch as a whole of any reflection of the war with Rome seems to suggest a pre-70 provenance for the version of *1 Enoch* on which the Ethiopic translation depends. If the collection were assembled later, one would expect some attention to be paid to these later climactic events.

Like much other apocalyptic literature, the Similitudes is concerned to describe a coming reversal of fortune, an end-time setting-to-rights in which the righteous, presently suffering oppression and tribulation, will be vindicated and blessed, and in which the sinners, presently enjoying wealth and ease despite their wickedness, will be brought low, forced to recognize the exaltation of the righteous and handed over for punishment. The purpose of such literature is to reassure its readership (who, of course, are assumed to be numbered among the righteous) that they will indeed be vindicated and thus to encourage them to hold firm.

But hold firm to what? In contrast to most other Jewish apocalyptic literature (though not unlike *1 Enoch* 1–36), many of the usual, Israel-centered components of righteousness are missing or sharply attenuated in this work. Neither the Torah nor the temple, usually central to Jewish understandings of righteousness, play any explicit role in the Similitudes. None of the typical Jewish boundary markers—Abrahamic descent, circumcision, Sabbath observance, food laws—serve to characterize the community of the righteous. Rather, the righteous are defined by their loyalty to and worship of the "Most High" or (more often) the "Lord of Spirits" and by their relationship to an exalted figure variously named "the Righteous One" (once[36]), "the Anointed One" (twice), "the Chosen One" (fifteen times) and—famously—"the Son of Man" (sixteen times).

Although there is a pattern to the distribution of these four titles within the various sections of the Similitudes, it is clear that a single figure is in view; the same role is assigned to each and the titles are treated as equivalents.[37] The Son of Man (to use the most prominent term) is a quasi-human personage ("son of a woman" [62:5]) who has been chosen by the Lord of Spirits from the beginning of creation (48:3, 6) to play a decisive, end-time role; he is the one who will vindicate the elect, judge and punish the wicked, and rule in righteousness. While he will remain hidden from the world at large until the end (48:6; 62:7), he has been revealed already to the righteous ones (62:7), who alone know his name (69:27).[38] Indeed, there is a tight connection—as is

36. The singular adjective appears in *1 En.* 47:1, 4, but here the sense is probably collective; see VanderKam (1992, 170).

37. On the pattern of distribution, see Hooker (1967, 34–37). On the equivalence of the terms: in *1 En.* 52 the same figure is called "the Anointed One" (v. 4) and "the Elect One" (v. 6); ch. 62 alternates between "the Elect One" (v.1) and "the Son of Man" (vv. 5, 7, 9, 14); in 53:6 we read of "the Righteous and Chosen One."

38. In 71:14 Enoch himself is identified as the Son of Man. The identification is awkward in that up to this point Enoch on his heavenly journeys has observed and described the Son of Man, i.e., the two have been distinct characters. Scholars have tended to see chs. 70–71 as a later addition (e.g., J. J. Collins 1998, 187–91), but the case can be made that chs. 70–71 were original, functioning as the intended—albeit surprising—climax to the apocalypse (so VanderKam 1995, 177–85).

implied by the terminology itself—between the righteous or chosen ones and the Righteous or Chosen One. The vision of the Righteous/Chosen One, already enthroned in glory though hidden from the sinners, is enough to assure the righteous/chosen ones that their vindication is sure.

Despite the attenuation of Jewish identifying markers, the close connection between the Son of Man and the community of righteous ones serves to identify the latter with biblical Israel. As VanderKam and others have demonstrated—and as the four terms themselves indicate—Enoch's description of the Son of Man is deeply rooted in Israel's scriptures. Especially prominent in this regard are Daniel 7, with its vision of "one like a son of man" (7:13; cf. *1 En.* 46), and the servant songs of Deutero-Isaiah (e.g., Isa 42:6; 49:6; cf. *1 En.* 48:4); but other texts are drawn in as well (VanderKam 1995, 188–91). To any reader familiar with Israel's scriptures, the Israel-centered identity of the Son of Man—and thus by extension of the community whose destiny is bound up with his—would be taken for granted. Of course, the central role played by Enoch himself already serves to locate the community within a world defined by Israel's scriptures. Such a conclusion finds further support in 56:5–7. This passage describes an incursion by "the Parthians and Medes" from "the east" into "the land of my chosen ones," an incursion which falters when it reaches "the city of my righteous ones." Clearly the "land" is Judea and the "city" is Jerusalem, which identifies the "righteous ones" as the people of this land and city. In other words, the righteous ones are clearly a community of Israelites. The attenuation of the usual Jewish identity markers is probably to be understood as an indication (1) that the community identified itself with reference more to Enoch than to Israel as a whole and (2) that this distinctive subgroup therefore represented a kind of Judaism for which "covenantal nomism" is not an appropriate description.

What then of the "sinners"? Through much of the Similitudes, "righteous" and "sinners" seem to be the only two options for human existence, which seems to suggest that the latter group was made up of all who were not part of the Enochian community. The first similitude begins: "When the congregation of the righteous shall appear, sinners shall be judged for their sins, they shall be driven from the face of the earth" (38:1), and this simple, two-fold classification frequently reappears through the work as a whole. This would seem to leave little room for the kind of third entity reflected in the texts under discussion here—the "nations," apparently distinct from "the righteous," who will be enlightened by the Son of Man (48:4), or "the others," apparently distinct from both "the sinners" and "the righteous," who will repent and find mercy before the Lord of Spirits (50:2).

On closer examination, however, it is apparent that "sinners" is a more focused and restricted entity in the Similitudes of Enoch. Even in chapter 38, the terms of reference slide quickly and easily from "the sinners" (vv. 1–3) to "the mighty and exalted" (v. 4) and "the mighty kings" (v. 5). This easy correlation is characteristic of the Similitudes as a whole. Not only are "the kings of the earth and the mighty landowners" (48:8) repeatedly singled out for denunciation,[39] but as a group they seem to be virtually equivalent to that of "the sinners." There is no indication that the powerful are sinners *par excellence* or even *par exemple*, that is, part of a larger group. For example, in chapter 53 the same group introduced as "the sinners" in v. 2 is described in v. 5 as "the kings and the potentates of this earth." It seems to be a case where two sets of terms are equivalent and interchangeable, rather than one being a subcategory of the other. While no doubt it was a large group, containing all whom the Enochian community found troublesome, there is no reason to believe that all outside the community were considered *ipso facto* to be sinners destined for destruction.

Charles was of the opinion that the "kings and the potentates" were the later Hasmonean kings and the Sadducees (Charles 1917, 67, 72–73). But no Jewish leaders would be described as those whose "devotion is to the gods which they have fashioned with their own hands" (46:7); it is clear that these "sinners" are Gentile. Their sinfulness, however, is not linked explicitly with their Gentile character. Rather, it consists primarily of their failure to recognize the Lord of Spirits (38:2; 41:2; 45:1; 46:6; 48:8), who is the true source of their power (46:5).[40] While one text castigates them for their denial of "the Lord of Spirits and his Messiah" (48:10),[41] this stands in tension with the statement that the Son of Man is hidden in the present age and has been revealed only to the chosen (62:7). The predominant picture in the Similitudes is that the Son of Man becomes apparent to the powerful only in the judgment, when they are forced to witness his enthronement (55:4; 62:1). At this point they recognize their sinfulness, worship the Son of Man (62:9) and the Lord of Spirits (63:1–4), and ask for mercy (62:9). But it will be too late.

Apparently, however, it will not be too late for everyone. As has been observed, there are two passages in the Similitudes that seem to hold out hope that others besides the "chosen and righteous ones" will have a share in the final state of righteousness. The first of these is 48:4–5. Drawing on the description of the servant in Isa 42:6 and 49:6, the author of the Similitudes describes the Son of Man in the latter part of v. 4 as "the light of the gentiles" (48:4). This seems to be a different group than the one in view in the first half of the verse. The first half of the verse has to do with "the righteous ones," for whom the Son

39. 46:4–6; 48:8–10; 53:5; 54:2; 55:4; 62:1–63:12; 67:8–13.

40. Two other aspects of their sinfulness are latent in the text but not emphasized: their oppression of the righteous, who apparently have suffered ("the blood of the righteous" [47. 1, 2, 4], taking "righteous" as a collective [so VanderKam 1992, 170–71]); and their association with the fallen angels who have led humankind astray (chs. 54, 69).

41. In 46:4–5 it is said that the Son of Man will cast down the powerful because "they do not extol and glorify him." In view of v. 6, however ("for they do not extol the name of the Lord of Spirits"), "him" probably refers to the Lord of Spirits rather than to the Son of Man.

of Man will provide support. But since there is nothing in the Similitudes to suggest that the community of the righteous would see themselves as among "the gentiles," the second half of the verse represents a shift. Here the significance of the Son of Man "in those days" (cf. v. 8) will be extended to a larger, more universal group. He will be "the light of the gentiles" and "the hope of those who are sick in their hearts" (cf. Isa 61:1: "to bind up the brokenhearted"). Black has attempted to minimize the significance of this, asserting that the "theme is not further developed" and going on to say: "[w]hile faithful to his Isaianic tradition, one has the impression that the author is not anxious to stress this universal role of his Elect Son of Man as *lux gentium*" (Black 1992, 159 and n. 44). But this is not persuasive. Not only does such a universalistic theme reappear in chapter 50, but even in chapter 48 it is "further developed." For v. 5 is a deliberate elaboration of v. 4b: "All those who dwell upon the earth"—note the universal scope—"shall fall and worship before him; they shall glorify, bless and sing the name of the Lord of the Spirits." Further, given the author's free use of scripture, which provides no reason to believe that he felt constrained to include material simply out of faithfulness to tradition, the choice to describe the Son of Man in such terms is of itself significant. The author clearly expects that the end-time revelation of the Son of Man will come as good news to a portion of humankind who, while not part of the "mighty of the earth," are nevertheless Gentiles, and who, while not part of the elect, will nevertheless worship the Son of Man and benefit from his light.

In the second passage (50:1–3), the central role is played not by the Son of Man but by the community of the righteous. "In those days" the chosen ones will be transformed: "the light of days shall rest upon them; and glory and honour shall be given back to the holy ones" (v. 1). This transformation, together with the ensuing downfall of the sinners and triumph of the righteous (v. 5), will cause "the others" to "repent and forsake the deeds of their hands" (v. 2). Actually, the active role here is played by the Lord of Spirits, who shows them the reversal of fortune precisely so that they might repent. Black translates "the others" as "the Gentiles" (Black 1985, 51). While the translation is not literal, it nevertheless captures the sense. The description of the "others" as those whose works need to be abandoned, and who "have no honour before the Lord of Spirits" but are solely dependent on his mercy, is a clear indication of their status as Gentiles. Once again, then, the author holds out hope that a group of Gentiles, distinct from both the elect (v. 1) and the sinners (v. 2a), will share in the final era of salvation. This passage conforms more closely to the pattern of the eschatological pilgrimage tradition; while no pilgrimage is in view, it is the vindication of (the elect within) Israel that prompts the Gentiles to repent and seek the Lord of Spirits.

The lack of interest in Jewish identity markers in the Similitudes of Enoch as a whole makes it difficult to say whether these repentant Gentiles are considered as full converts to Israel or as Gentiles still. Nevertheless, there is no indication that they are incorporated into "the holy and the chosen" (v. 1). They remain a distinct and separate entity. While "glory and honour will return to the holy," the others remain without "honour before the Lord of Spirits"; while the righteous have been "chosen," the others have received divine mercy because of their repentance. To the extent that the question can be asked at all, then, these end-time believers continue to be Gentile.

§35 1 Enoch *108:11*

> *And now I will summon the spirits of the pious (who are) from the generation of light; and I will transform those who <have descended into> darkness, who in their bodies were not recompensed with the honor appropriate to their faithfulness.*

Translation: Nickelsburg (2001)
Date: First century C.E.
Category: ESCHATOLOGICAL PARTICIPATION

While *1 Enoch* 108 is clearly an addition, it has evidently been composed to serve as a concluding exhortation to the collection as a whole, or at least to a collection that contained major portions of the book as we know it.[42] Addressed to Methuselah and "those who would come after him and keep the law in the last days" (108:1), the chapter holds out the promise of the final vindication of the righteous, in order to encourage its readers to hold firm to the end.

In its extant form, v. 11 reads: "I will transform those who were born in darkness, who in their bodies were not recompensed with the honor appropriate to their faithfulness." Charles understood this as a statement that some Gentiles (those who were born in darkness) had remained faithful and would be redeemed at the end. He has been followed in this reading by Sanders.[43] Here, however, unlike 90:33,[44] Nickelsburg's emendation seems to be justified. In the remainder of the chapter, there are only two categories in view—the righteous (those who keep the law [v. 1], the humble [v. 7], those who love [v. 8] and bless [vv. 9, 10] God, etc.) and the unrighteous (evildoers [v. 2], sinners and blasphemers and those who do evil [v. 6], etc.). "Those who were born in darkness" clearly belong to the latter group (v. 14). Their destiny is to be "cast into darkness," apparently en masse. There is nothing whatsoever in the passage as a whole to suggest that there existed a subsection of this group that would escape this fate and be transformed in the end. An emendation such as Nickelsburg has suggested, so that v. 11 refers to the righteous who

42. On the basis of explicit parallels, Nickelsburg identifies the version for which ch. 108 serves as a conclusion as containing at least chs. 1–71, 81:1–82:4 and 85–105.

43. Charles (1913b, 2.281); E. P. Sanders (1977, 359).

44. See §32.

have suffered in "darkness" despite their faithfulness, seems to be required. If so, the text does not provide any evidence for end-time redemption of Gentiles.

ARTAPANUS, THEODOTUS, ARISTOBULUS

Artapanus, Theodotus, and Aristobulus are among several Hellenistic Jewish writers whose work is known to us only through tantalizing fragments that have been preserved as excerpts in later Christian writings. Generally speaking, these writings reflect a positive view of Hellenistic culture,[45] as they attempt either to recast Jewish tradition in Hellenistic literary forms (e.g., Philo the Epic Poet, Theodotus, Ezekiel the Tragedian), to align the law or the Jewish way of life with the best of Hellenism (e.g., Aristobulus) or to present Moses and the patriarchs as cultural innovators and teachers of the nations (e.g., Eupolemus, Artapanus). Eusebius is our primary source for these authors (often at second-hand, especially through citations from the Greek historian Alexander Polyhistor), though in the case of Aristobulus there are citations by Clement of Alexandria as well.

§36 Artapanus (frag. 3; P.E. *9.27.4)*

> *As a grown man he* [Moses] *bestowed many useful benefits on mankind, for he invented boats and devices for stone construction and the Egyptian arms and the implements for drawing water and for warfare, and for philosophy. Further, he divided the state into 36 nomes and appointed for each the god to be worshiped, and for the priests the sacred letters, and that they should be cats and dogs and ibises. He also allotted a choice area to the priests.*

Text: Holladay (1983, 204–25)
Translation: *OTP* (J. J. Collins 1985b)
Date: Late-third to the end of the second century B.C.E.
Provenance: Egypt
Original Language: Greek
Bibliography: Barclay (1996, 127–32); J. J. Collins (1985b; 2000, 37–46); Freudenthal (1874); Gruen (1998, 155–60); Holladay (1983, 189–243); Schürer (1986, 3:521–25); Sterling (1992, 167–86).
Category: ETHICAL MONOTHEISM

The text forms part of a work attributed to Artapanus, probably entitled "On the Jews," which was summarized by Alexander Polyhistor and preserved in fragmentary form by Eusebius (*P.E.* 9.18, 23, 27). Eusebius has preserved three excerpts, dealing with Abraham, Joseph, and Moses, the latter of which is by far

45. As we will see, however, Theodotus uses a Hellenistic poetic genre to express a conventional—even rigid—form of covenantal Judaism.

the longest. In each, these Jewish heroes are presented as teachers of the Egyptians, having introduced them to various beneficial aspects of civilized life—astrology (Abraham), civil administration and measurement (Joseph), "boats and devices for stone construction and the Egyptian arms and the implements for drawing water and for warfare" (frag. 3; *P.E.* 9.27.4) and much more besides (Moses). In Moses's case, his beneficial influence extended far beyond Egypt in that the Greeks knew him as Mousaeus, the teacher of Orpheus. In his treatment of Moses, Artapanus selects certain aspects of the biblical account (Moses's upbringing in the king's household, his flight from Egypt, the plagues, the exodus, the passage through the Red Sea and the death of the Egyptians), gives them his own particular spin (e.g., when Moses strikes the Nile with his rod, instead of turning to blood, the river floods, which is the origin of the annual inundation of the Nile [*P.E.* 9.27.28; cf. Exod 7:14–24]), and weaves them into a highly entertaining narrative that departs from the biblical account both in detail and in ethos.

For our purposes what is most significant is the role that Artapanus assigns to Moses in the establishment of Egyptian religion. Before Moses arrived on the scene, Egypt was a land of social instability and disorganization. There were many kings in the land, and the masses were in the habit of deposing and appointing kings at will (*P.E.* 9.27.3, 5). One of these kings was Chenephres, whose wife Merris had the good sense to adopt "the child of one of the Jews" (*P.E.* 9.27.3), whom she named Moses. When he was grown, Moses directed all his energy and ingenuity to the organization and stabilization of his adoptive father's kingdom. His success earned him the love of the masses but the envious resentment of Cenephres. As the story unfolds, it is the conflict between Moses and Cenephres that results in the liberation of the Jews from Egypt.

Part of Moses's organizational activity involved religion. Although he is identified as a Jew at the outset and seems to be devoted to the God of the Jews throughout, he makes no attempt to use his position to introduce the Jewish God or to further Jewish religion. Instead, having organized the country into a number of "nomes," he "appointed for each of the nomes the god to be worshiped, and for the priests the sacred letters, and that they should be cats and dogs and ibises" (*P.E.* 9.27.4). In other words, Moses himself is the origin of Egyptian religion, complete with its polytheism, priesthood, and animal worship! To be sure, he does introduce circumcision (*P.E.* 9.27.10), but this is taken up into Egyptian religion rather than implying any connection with Judaism. Further, Moses was accorded divine status by the priests (ἰσοθέου; *P.E.* 9.27.6) and the rod that he used to call forth the various plagues became an object of veneration in the temples of Isis (*P.E.* 9.27.32). Here, as elsewhere (*P.E.* 9.27.16), the Isis cult is mentioned with no hint of criticism or derogation.

But this apparently positive view of Egyptian religion does not bring with it any blurring of Moses's Jewish identity. When he first appears he is mentioned as a "child of one of the Jews" (*P.E.* 9.27.3); when the Jews are next mentioned in the story, they are identified as Moses's "compatriots" (ὁμόφυλοι; *P.E.* 9.27.19) and from this point on he is their champion and defender; he prays to God on behalf of his people and "the master of the universe" commissions him to "rescue the Jews and lead them to their ancient homeland" (*P.E.* 9.27.21–22); the very name of this God, pronounced or written by Moses, is enough to produce fainting and even death (*P.E.* 9.27.24–26). While Artapanus's presentation of Moses leaves out what many Jews would have identified as the most significant feature of Moses's Jewish identity—namely, the giving of the law[46]—his Jewishness is nevertheless clear and unqualified.

What are we to make of this combination—a Moses who is both the leader and liberator of the Jews and the one who initiated and organized the religion of the Egyptians? Or, to put the question in a form that is closer to the concerns of this study: What does this combination suggest about the attitude of Artapanus toward the religion of the Egyptians and the religious status of those who embrace it?

On the one hand, it would be a mistake to try to eliminate or explain away the positive and uncritical way in which Egyptian religion is treated in the writing.[47] The references to religion are gratuitous; Artapanus's presentation of Moses as the one who brought culture and civilization to the Egyptians by no means depends on the religious component. The portrait would have remained full and intact without it. Further, since there is a negative element to the role of the Egyptians in the narrative—it is a version of the exodus story, after all—Egyptian religion could easily have been aligned with the negative side of the story if the author had been so inclined. For the author, polytheistic religion was a natural and non-controversial part of Egyptian life, and it posed no problem for him to think of Moses as having established and organized it.

But on the other hand, this does not imply any diminishing or relativizing of the God worshiped by the Jews. There is no suggestion that this God is to be seen as just one other god to be added to the Egyptian pantheon. Moses's God remains the "master of the universe" (*P.E.* 9.27.22), whose very name is powerful enough to overcome Egyptian king and priest alike. While Artapanus cannot be described as monotheistic, neither is he polytheistic. He is probably better described as henotheistic; that is, his view is that, while there are many lesser gods worshiped by the nations, the God of the Jews is supreme.[48] The attitude—if this is an accurate account of it—is not unlike the statement about

46. Since the concluding sentences of the fragment provide a summarizing statement about the forty years in the wilderness, the failure to mention Sinai must be seen as intentional and not simply as happenstance; that is to say, there is no reason to believe that Artapanus's narrative went on to narrate the giving of the law.

47. While Collins' observations are valid, his position tends to move a little too much in this direction (J. J. Collins 2000, 41–45).

48. Cf. Barclay (1996, 132): "even as a Jew he is both a monotheist and a polytheist."

the gods of the nations in Deut 32:8:[49] that non-Jewish religion is part of the divine order of things, under the ultimate sovereignty of the God of Israel. Of course, this is not to say that the two are equivalent. Artapanus seems not to share any of Deuteronomy's horror at the thought of Jewish participation in idol worship. If there is a similarity, Artapanus needs to be seen as an irenic extension, in quite a different cultural context, of the biblical idea.[50]

But what of the Gentile participants in the system of worship set up by Moses? The corollary of the view described in the previous paragraph would seem to be that nothing more was expected of non-Jews than that they live peaceably within this divinely ordered state of affairs, and that by doing so they would have done all that God required of them. Unfortunately, what Artapanus has to say about Egyptian religion does not allow us to press things this far. Nevertheless, what he does say represents probably the most positive assessment of non-Jewish religion to be found in the literature under discussion here.

§37 Theodotus (Fragment 4; P.E. 9.22.4–6)

> *And Dinah, still a virgin, came into Shechem when there was a festival, since she wished to see the city. But when Sychem the son of Hamor saw her, he loved her; and after seizing her as his own, he carried her off and ravished her. Then, coming back again with his father to Jacob, he asked for her in the partnership of marriage. Jacob said that he would not give her until all the inhabitants of Shechem were circumcised and became Jews. Hamor said that he would persuade them. Concerning the necessity of their being circumcised, Jacob says, "For this is not allowed to Hebrews to bring sons-in-law or daughters-in-law into their house from elsewhere but, rather, whoever, boasts that he is of the same race."*

Text: Holladay (1989, 106–27)
Translation: *OTP* (Fallon 1985)
Date: Between late-third and late-second centuries B.C.E.
Provenance: Uncertain
Original Language: Greek
Bibliography: J. J. Collins (1980; 2000, 57–60); Fallon (1985); Freudenthal (1874); Gruen (1998, 120–25); Holladay (1989, 51–204); Schürer (1986, 3:561–63); Standhartinger (1994)
Category: CONVERSION

Another of the writings treated by Polyhistor and cited by Eusebius is a work attributed to Theodotus entitled (or referred to as) *On the Jews*. Eusebius quotes no less than eight segments of Theodotus's work (*P.E.* 9.22.1–12), all of them

49. Following the readings in the LXX ("according to the number of the angels of God") and 4QDeut ("sons of God") rather than the MT ("sons of Israel").

50. See Goldenberg's study of Jewish attitudes toward other religions (1998), especially pp. 63–80 and the comments about Artapanus on p. 79.

dealing with the story of Dinah and the Shechemites in Genesis 34. Some of the Theodotus material seems to be quoted verbatim; some of it has been paraphrased by Polyhistor.

What can be glimpsed in these eight segments is a work that combines a Greek form—epic poetry of the Homeric style—with rigid adherence to traditional Jewish boundary markers. To be sure, an earlier school of opinion tended to doubt that the author was Jewish. The emphasis on Shechem, together with the description of Shechem as a "sacred town" (literally, "holy city"; frag. 1), was taken as an indication of a Samaritan viewpoint (Freudenthal 1874). But any praise of Shechem in the work is more than counterbalanced by the disparagement of its inhabitants. The present trend is to see this as the work of a Jewish writer.[51] Estimations of date have clustered around two points. On the basis of archaeological evidence suggesting that the walls of the city were in good repair up to 200 B.C.E. but then began to decay, the reference to "a smooth wall around the town" in frag. 1 has been used to argue for a date in the late-third to mid-second century B.C.E. Alternatively, the opposition to intermarriage and the emphasis on circumcision have been seen as evidence for a date in the time of John Hyrcanus.[52] The evidence is evenly balanced and any decision is difficult. For our purposes it is sufficient to see the work as written sometime in the period between the late-third and late-second centuries B.C.E. There is a similar uncertainty about the place of origin. Both Judea and the Diaspora have been suggested (Holladay 1989, 70–72), though in view of the Homeric form the burden of proof probably falls on the case for Judea.

As is usually the case with paraphrases of biblical narrative, what is of most interest is the way in which the paraphrase deviates from the biblical account. One such deviation in this case is the more positive portrait of Levi and Simeon. Genesis 34 appears to be critical of the two brothers of Dinah, who first persuaded the Shechemites that intermarriage was possible if they were willing to become circumcised, but then took advantage of their gullibility by slaughtering the Shechemites while they were still suffering the effects of the operation. Not only is this activity described as deceitful (34:13), but it is roundly condemned by Jacob (34:30).[53] In Theodotus's version, however, there is no suggestion of deceit. Not only is the offer of circumcision made by Jacob in good faith, but there is no indication that the Shechemites had actually carried out the act before they were attacked. Nor is there any indication that Jacob was displeased. Of course, we do not have access to the whole work, but the fact that the slaughter of the Shechemites is justified on the basis of an oracle from God (based on Gen 15:18–21) would seem to preclude any possibility of paternal disapproval.

51. For a thorough discussion of the issues, see Holladay (1989, 58–68).

52. Again, for a thorough discussion of the evidence, see Holladay (1989, 68–70).

53. Still, it is not without significance that Simeon and Levi get the last word (34:31).

But it is another addition in Theodotus's account that is of particular interest here—the use of the term "Judaize" with reference to circumcision. Jacob said that he would not give his daughter in marriage to Sychem "until all those living in Shechem were Judaized by becoming circumcised" (πρὶν ἄν πάντας . . . περιτεμνομένους Ἰουδαΐσαι). The reference to circumcision, of course, is found in Genesis; the term Ἰουδαΐζω, however, is not. Two questions need to be asked: What is meant by the term in its context? What is the attitude of the text toward such "Judaization" of Gentiles?

Since fragment 4 is Polyhistor's paraphrase rather than a direct quotation, there is uncertainty as to whether the term is due to Theodotus or Polyhistor.[54] In the quoted material Theodotus uses "Hebrews" rather than "Jews," which might suggest that the term is Polyhistor's. On the other hand, if *On the Jews* is the title of Theodotus's work and not simply a general description,[55] it is possible that the term is original. All we can say with certainty is that Theodotus provides us with an account in which Gentiles are offered the possibility of intermarriage with Jews on the condition of circumcision, and that either Theodotus or Polyhistor described this as an instance of Judaizing. It is on this basis that we will press our questions.

Theodotus clearly views circumcision as the definitive mark of membership in the "race" of the "Hebrews." This mark has been given to Abraham "and all his family" as a command given by God, a command that, for this very reason, "remains unshaken" (frag. 5). A corollary of this command is the injunction against intermarriage: it "is not allowed to Hebrews to bring sons-in-law or daughters-in-law into their house from elsewhere." Since Jacob makes this statement to Hamor the Shechemite in the process of explaining the condition of circumcision, the implication is that the injunction can be set aside if prospective Gentile sons-in-law are prepared to undergo circumcision. (Jacob has nothing to say about what would be expected of prospective Gentile daughters-in-law.) But what does the text tell us about the significance of this act? How does it make intermarriage possible?

Several observations can be made. First, the implication of Jacob's statement at the end of fragment 4 is that Gentiles who are circumcised thereby come to be considered as part of the "same race" (γενεῆς . . . ὁμοίης). The actual form of his statement, of course, is negative: Hebrews are allowed to marry only those of the same race and not those "from elsewhere." However, as already noted, since he makes this statement to Hamor to explain and justify the requirement that Sychem be circumcised, the implication seems to be that by virtue of circumcision he would thereby become part of the Hebrew race.

54. Given the way in which Eusebius cites his sources, there is no reason to suppose that the term is due to Eusebius, as Cohen has suggested (1999, 188).

55. The question is debated; see Holladay (1989, 54–58).

Further, this transition is not simply ethnic and cultural, but is one with religious and ethical dimensions as well. The practice of circumcision among the Hebrews is the result of a divine command, by means of which God has constituted the "family" (frag. 4) and "descendants" (frag. 6) of Abraham as a special community. The relationship between God and this community is an ongoing one: God has given promises to them that apparently begin to be fulfilled with the defeat of the Shechemites (i.e., promises that they would receive "ten nations" [ἔθνεα]; frag. 6). In other words, Theodotus presents us with a strongly covenantal view of the "Hebrews."[56] Correspondingly, Gentiles who become circumcised are becoming part of a covenant community, and thus are coming into a relationship with God and not just into a new ethnic group. Consistent with this is the statement in fragment 7 that the slaughter of the Shechemites was justified because they were "impious" (ἀσεβεῖς; frag. 7). The implication seems to be that what disqualified them from the possibility of becoming part of the "Hebrew race" was their impiety; piety was also a precondition of conversion. In addition, their impiety takes the specific form of immorality—dishonoring visitors, disregard of rights and laws, deadly works (frag. 7). Thus while the focus is on marriage, "Judaization" in Theodotus's view (whether the term is his or Polyhistor's) involves a more complete incorporation of Gentiles into the Hebrew race, understood as a religious community constituted by divine command.

But despite Hamor's apparent willingness, the Shechemites are slaughtered before they have the opportunity to be circumcised. When everything is taken into account, how positive is Theodotus toward those who are not part of the "Hebrew race"? One scholar who has ventured an opinion is John Collins, who sees Theodotus as narrowly particularistic: "Despite his use of the epic form, and a Greek style far superior to that of Philo the epic poet, Theodotus lacks the universalism which characterized most Hellenistic Jewish writers. His vision of Judaism is covenantal nomism of the narrowest variety" (J. J. Collins 2000, 59). Of course, if one is prepared to grant Collins's definition of universalism, the statement is accurate. One does not find in Theodotus the positive estimation of Greek philosophy that we encounter in Philo or the *Letter of Aristeas* or the attempt to place the patriarchs on a world stage as we do in Artapanus. But if we define universalism in such a way as to include proselytism, then we have to recognize that Theodotus is universalistic in his own way.

As we have observed, in contrast to the account in Genesis where the offer of circumcision is part of a deceptive ploy, in Theodotus the offer is made in good faith. Jacob is fully willing to give Dinah in marriage if the Shechemites "Judaize by becoming circumcised." Moreover, he implies that they would thereby become part of the "Hebrew race." The failure of this to happen comes about not because of any categorical exclusion of conversion but simply because

56. Cf. the quotation from Collins cited in the next paragraph.

the Shechemites did not meet the requirement of piety. Even if the offer did not come to anything in the narrative, there is no suggestion that the terms on which the offer was made were invalid. The offer to Gentiles that they can become part of the Hebrew race by "Judaizing" is nowhere rescinded. To be sure, the writing very definitely evinces a narrow covenantal view of the world. Further, there is very little in the fragments that have survived to suggest that Theodotus had any optimism about the possibility of Gentile conversion. The most that can be demonstrated is the negative argument that such a possibility is not precluded in the work. Nevertheless, Theodotus is at least open to the possibility that Gentiles could become part of the "Hebrew race" through circumcision. In this respect his work does contain an element of universalism.

§38 Aristobulus (frag. 4; P.E. *13.12.6–7)*

> *And Aratus also speaks about the same things thus: "Let us begin with God, whom men never leave unspoken; full of God are the streets, and all the marketplaces of humanity, and full the sea and the harbors; and we are all in need of God everywhere. We are all his children; and he gently to humanity gives good omens, and rouses people to work, reminding (them) of sustenance; and he tells when the soil is best for cattle and for pickaxes, and he tells when seasons are favorable both for planting trees and for sowing all seeds."[7] I believe that it has been clearly shown how the power of God is throughout all things. And we have given the true sense, as one must, by removing the (name) Zeus throughout the verses. For their intention refers to God, therefore it was so expressed by us. We have presented these things therefore in a way not unsuited to the things being discussed.*

Text: Holladay (1995, 128–87)
Translation: *OTP* (A. Y. Collins 1985)
Date: Mid-second century B.C.E.
Provenance: Alexandria
Original language: Greek
Bibliography: Barclay (1996, 150–58); A. Y. Collins (1985); J. J. Collins (2000, 186–90); Gruen (1998, 246–51); Hengel (1974, 163–69); Schürer (1986, 3:579–87); Walter (1964)
Category: ETHICAL MONOTHEISM, SYMPATHIZATION

The previous passage is one of five fragments from Aristobulus preserved by Eusebius.[57] The task of assigning a date to Aristobulus is complicated by the question of its relationship to the *Letter of Aristeas*, with which it displays a number of affinities—most notably the reference to the translation of the law

57. Frag. 1: *H.E.* 7.32.16–18; frag. 2: *P.E.* 8.9.38–8.10.17; frags. 3–5: *P.E.* 13.12.1–16. Portions of these fragments are also cited by Clement, though in a less precise form; for details, see Holladay (1995). On Polyhistor, see Rawson (1985, 61–63; 255–56).

under the supervision of Demetrius of Phalerum (frag. 3). Attempts to argue for direct dependence of one on the other, or vice versa, have tended to cancel each other out. Commentators are now more inclined to see both writings as dependent on a common tradition,[58] and to discuss the date of Aristobulus without linking it directly to the *Letter of Aristeas*. Aristobulus addresses his work to Ptolemy the king, whom he identifies as a descendant of Ptolemy Philadelphus (frag. 3; that is, Ptolemy II, 283–247 B.C.E.). The author of the letter found in 2 Macc 1:10–2:18 seems to have identified this king as Ptolemy VI Philometor (180–145 B.C.E.), for Judas (presumably Maccabaeus) is mentioned among the senders of a letter that is addressed "to Aristobulus, who is of the family of the anointed priests, teacher of King Ptolemy, and to the Jews in Egypt." While the historical value of this reference is debated, scholars generally agree with 2 Maccabees in dating Aristobulus to the time of Philometor.[59] The description of Aristobulus as a "teacher of Ptolemy," however, is probably to be seen as no more than an inference drawn from the fact that his apology was addressed to the king.

On the basis of the fragments, it is apparent that Aristobulus was concerned to present Judaism as a school of philosophy (ἡ καθ' ἡμᾶς αἵρεσις [frag. 4; *P.E.* 13.12.8]), one that is both similar and yet superior to those associated with the names of "Pythagoras, Socrates and Plato" (frag. 4; *P.E.* 13.12.4). One of his lines of approach is to provide rational explanations for aspects of the law that might have been viewed otherwise by Hellenistic observers. Thus he attempts to root the celebrations of Passover (frag. 1) and the Sabbath (frag. 5) in the very structure of the cosmos. In frag. 2, he deals with the apparently troublesome matter of biblical anthropomorphisms, arguing that such turns of phrase need to be understood metaphorically (μεταφέροντας; *P.E.* 8.10.8). God's "hand," for example, is really a reference to God's "power" (*P.E.* 8.10.7). He is thus critical of those who interpret solely with reference to the "letter" rather than on the basis of "understanding" (*P.E.* 8.10.5). One characteristic of his concept of "understanding" is that the specific injunctions of the Jewish law need to be interpreted "according to the laws of nature" (*P.E.* 8.10.2). These specific arguments allow him to make the broader case that, on the basis of generally accepted opinions about what makes for a legitimate school of philosophy, Judaism should receive high grades: "It is agreed by all the philosophers that it is necessary to hold holy opinions concerning God, a point our philosophical school makes particularly well" (frag. 4; *P.E.* 13.12.8). Likewise, "with reference to piety and justice and temperance and the rest of the things that are truly good"—which, he implies,

58. See Holladay (1995, 64–65).

59. For a thorough discussion, see Holladay (1995, 45–75), who concludes that there is probably a historical core to the passage. Holladay dates Aristobulus's apology to the early years of Philometor's reign (176–170 B.C.E.).

would also be seen by "all the philosophers" as "necessary" for real philosophy—Aristobulus claims that this is what the law is really all about (*P.E.* 13.12.8). In other words, all philosophical schools have ethical monotheism as their center and goal, and Judaism gets closer to this goal than most.[60]

But it is not simply that Judaism qualifies as a particularly good example of a philosophical school. Aristobulus argues in addition that the law of Moses was the source and origin of much that is commendable in Hellenistic philosophy. Philosophers and poets "took significant material from him" and "are admired" precisely because of the quality of the borrowed material (frag. 2; *P.E.* 8.10.4). Plato "imitated our legislation," having "investigated thoroughly each of the elements in it" (frag. 3; *P.E.* 13.12.1). "Pythagoras, Socrates, and Plato with great care follow him in all respects" (frag. 3; *P.E.* 13.12.4). To make the argument plausible, of course, Aristobulus has to maintain that parts of the law had been translated even before the time of Demetrius (frag. 3; *P.E.* 13.12.1). To make it convincing, he cites poems attributed to Orpheus and Aratus that, he claims, demonstrate an imitation of Moses (frag. 4).[61] The passage under discussion here is the citation of Aratus, an early Stoic poet (ca. 315–240/239 B.C.E.), whose poem *Phaenomena* is known from other sources.[62] The material cited by Aristobulus forms part of the opening section of the poem.

As we find it in the fragment from Aristobulus, the poem is a paean of praise to God. Its themes are simple: God is described as being everywhere present; human beings are said to be God's children (γένος); God provides humankind with gentle guidance and cares for their needs. What is striking about this poem is that in its original form all these attributes and activities were assigned to Zeus. Aristobulus informs us that he has taken the liberty of replacing Δίς and Ζεύς with God (θεός), claiming that the substitution is justified since this was the intention or the inherent meaning of the original.[63] Read in this way, he concludes, the poem demonstrates "that the power of God is throughout all things."

Aristobulus's revision should not be seen as an attempt to impose Jewish categories on a non-Jewish poem. For the "God" to whom Aristobulus refers is not the Jewish God specifically, but the God who is contemplated and known by Jews and "other" philosophical schools alike. The terminological substitution is

60. Also *P.E.* 13.12.11: "One of our ancestors, Solomon, said more clearly and better that wisdom existed before heaven and earth."

61. The reference to imitation comes in *P.E.* 13.12.4. The Orphic poem is cited only by Christian authors (in different versions); for a discussion of the attendant problems, see Holladay (1996, 128–33). In frag. 5, he also cites poems attributed to Hesiod, Homer and Linus.

62. For sources and secondary literature, see Holladay (1995, 221).

63. τὸ γὰρ τῆς διανοίας αὐτῶν ἐπὶ θεὸν ἀναπέμπεται; Holladay renders it literally as: "For the point of their meaning sends (our thoughts) upward towards God" (1995, 223, n. 113).

to be seen not as a criticism of Aratus (for an inferior conception of God or for using an inadequate name), but as a clarification. While the poem in its original form might give the impression that it was speaking just of a god known to the Greeks, the content of the poem indicates—so says Aristobulus—that Aratus was really talking about the one true divinity revered by all true philosophers, the Jews included. Thus Aristobulus's conception comes close to the statement in *Let. Aris.* 16, where Aristeas claims that the God whom the Greeks worship as Zeus is the same deity as is worshiped by the Jews; the names may differ, but the God to whom the names refer is the same. Aristobulus is not quite as explicit, but this seems to be the implication.

What does Aristobulus think, then, about the religious status of Aratus and those who share his perceptions of Zeus/God? While there is a sense in which Barclay is correct when he describes Aristobulus as "safeguard[ing] the uniqueness of his Jewish tradition" (1996, 156), Aristobulus does not thereby empty the philosophic tradition of its validity.[64] Plato and the others may have borrowed from Moses, but for that very reason their philosophical schools are also dedicated to "holy opinions about God" and to piety and justice and temperance and the rest of the things that are truly good" (frag. 4; *P.E.* 13.12.8). Unlike Philo or even the *Letter of Aristeas*, Aristobulus does not give explicit consideration to the religious status of non-Jewish philosophers. Still, at the implicit level, he seems to move in the same direction: Greek philosophy and Jewish law religion represent parallel routes to the same destination—a way of life characterized by virtue and monotheistic worship. The law may be prior, better, and even the source of what is good and true in the other philosophies. But those on the other route are legitimately on their way to the same destination.

The Letter of Aristeas

The *Letter of Aristeas* presents itself as a communication from a highly placed, Gentile official in the court of the Egyptian king Ptolemy II Philadelphus (283–247 B.C.E.)—whose name is eventually revealed to be Aristeas (19)—to his "blood-brother" (7) Philocrates, about "the meeting which we had with Eleazar, high priest of the Jews" (1). Actually, this meeting is just one element in a longer series of events that begins with the desire of the king's librarian to acquire a copy of the "lawbooks of the Jews" (10) and culminates with the translation of the law into Greek. While scholars in an earlier era were interested in the composition primarily for the light it might shed on the origins of the Septuagint, in more recent times scholarly attention has tended to focus more on its attempt to forge a kind of cultural convergence between Jews and Greeks.

64. Barclay (1996, 156); he is criticized on this point by J. J. Collins (2000, 190).

Despite its traditional ascription as the *Letter of Aristeas*, the author himself describes the work as a narrative (διήγησις).[65] After his introductory address to Philocrates (1–8), Aristeas begins his story, which is set in motion by the librarian Demetrius, who had been charged by the king to collect, "if possible, all the books in the world" (9), apparently in Greek translation. When he reports to the king that one of the desiderata is the Jewish law, the king enthusiastically undertakes to send a request to the Jewish high priest in Jerusalem, a request conveyed by Aristeas (and Andreas, another court official) and accompanied by a large number of costly gifts from the king (9–82). The delegation is warmly received by Eleazar the high priest, who for the task of translation chooses seventy-two highly qualified individuals (six from each tribe). Then, before sending them off, he responds to questions from the Alexandrians by presenting a discourse on the nature and characteristics of the law (83–171). On their arrival in Alexandria, the Jewish translators are given an elaborate and lavish welcome by the king (173–81), which includes a series of no less than seven banquets, at which he poses questions to each of them in turn. The questions have to do with virtue in general and prudent statecraft in particular; the responses display a degree of piety and wisdom that elicits praise and admiration from all who are present, especially the philosophers (172–300). After this lengthy build-up, the translation itself is described with surprising brevity (301–21). The translators are taken to the island of Pharos, where again they are given lavish provisions. They complete the work of translation in seventy-two days, the finished product being received with great approval by both the Jews of Alexandria and the king himself. A short concluding word to Philocrates rounds out the narrative (322).

There is a broad scholarly consensus that the *Letter of Aristeas* originated within the Jewish community in Alexandria. Despite the Gentile persona of its narrator, it is clearly the work of a Jewish author. With respect to the provenance of the work, while one should not rush to conclusions simply on the basis of the locale in which its narrative is set, an Alexandrian origin seems likely, especially in view of the conceptual affinities with other Jewish writings from Alexandria, particularly the work of Philo. There is less scholarly consensus on the date of the work, though most commentators place it sometime in the second century B.C.E.; for our purposes there is little to be gained by attempting to narrow this time-frame.[66] As is the case with most Diaspora literature, there is a debate as to whether the *Letter of Aristeas* was directed at a readership that

65. For other instances in Classical and Hellenistic Greek literature where the term is used to refer to historical narrative, see Fitzmyer (1981, 292).

66. Schürer (1986, 3:684) and Barclay (1996, 445) are content with this broader time frame. For the argument in favor of a date early in the second century (presented but not endorsed), see Schürer (1986, 3:680–82). Perhaps the narrowest time frame is that adopted by Goldstein (1991), who places it in the 130s. For a dating in the mid- to late-second century, see Bartlett (1985, 16–17); Boccaccini (1991, 165); J. J. Collins (2000, 98–101).

was primarily Gentile (see Schürer 1986, 3:679) or Jewish.[67] The evident concern to establish the legitimacy of the Greek translation lends support to the latter position; few Gentiles would need to be assured that the translation was an accurate rendition of the original (311). Even though this is not the major concern of the work, its more central concern—to depict Judaism as a way of life and thought that is respected and admired by discerning Gentiles—could also be read as directed at Jewish readers. Still, as Barclay has reminded us (1996, 148), we are not forced to choose between a Jewish or a Gentile readership. If the Jewish community for whom the *Letter of Aristeas* was intended had also attracted a company of Gentile admirers and sympathizers, then there is much in this work that would have been of interest to them as well.

Text: Thackeray (1914)
Translation: Author's own; *OTP* (Shutt 1985)[68]
Date: Second century B.C.E.
Provenance: Alexandria
Original language: Greek
Bibliography: Balch (1998); Barclay (1996, 138–50); Bartlett (1985, 11–34); Boccaccini (1991, 161–85); J. J. Collins (2000, 97–103, 191–95); Goldstein (1991); Gruen (1998, 206–22); Hadas (1951); Jellicoe (1974); Kraus (1996, 79–81); Pelletier (1962); Schürer (1986, 3:677–87); Tcherikover (1974 [1958]); Zuntz (1974)

§39 Letter of Aristeas *4–7*

It is worthwhile telling you this as well, [5]for I am convinced that because you are more favorably inclined toward the piety and disposition of those who live by the sacred Law, concerning whom we propose to write, you will gladly listen, since you have paid a special visit to us from your island, and wish to hear with us of matters pertaining to the edification of the soul. [6]I had previously sent the account of what I regarded as the most memorable matters. We received this account of the people of the Jews from the most renowned high priests in renowned Egypt. [7]You are studiously disposed toward what can help the mind and it is my duty to share this with all like-minded persons, and all the more so with you, for you have a kindred spirit, being not only a blood brother in character but also in the pursuit of beauty the same as we are.

Category: SYMPATHIZATION

67. Tcherikover (1974 [1958]); followed by Bartlett (1985, 12); Boccaccini (1991, 164–65).

68. Other citations from *Let. Aris.* will be taken from Shutt's translation. But for reasons that will become apparent as the discussion unfolds, it is preferable to provide my own translation of these key passages. Italicized material within square brackets is implied in the Greek text and has been supplied in the interest of clarity.

As the narrator of the work, Aristeas speaks with obvious admiration for the law, the temple, and the piety of the Jews. Further, he is willing to put his admiration into action: even before the translation project gets underway, he intercedes with the king on behalf of those Jews who had been sold into slavery by the king's father (12–37). He does not, however, engage in any reflection on the nature of his own piety. For such reflective comments we need to look at his presentation of his fraternal alter ego, Philocrates.

Philocrates is presented as a Gentile who has a special interest in Jewish religion. In Aristeas's description, he is "favorably inclined [ἔχοντα πρόσκλισιν] toward the piety and disposition of those who live by the sacred Law" (5). This interest has already led him to travel from his island[69] to Alexandria (5) and has been further stimulated by an account "of the people of the Jews" that Aristeas has already composed and sent to him (6). For these reasons, Aristeas knows that Philocrates will attach "great importance to hearing a personal account" of the events leading up to the translation of the law. Since in all these respects Aristeas obviously shares the same inclination and interest, both of them can be described as Jewish sympathizers.

At the same time, however, Philocrates is presented as one who aspires to the Greek philosophical ideal. Aristeas praises him for his love of learning (1, 171; φιλομαθῆ), his search for piety (εὐσέβειαν), "the highest of all ends" (2), his pursuit of "beauty" (τὸ καλόν; 7), his dedication to "culture" (παιδεία) rather than wealth (8), and his concern for the things that benefit the mind (322). Philocrates' admiration for Judaism thus stands side by side with his commitment to the highest ideals of Hellenism. Clearly the two characteristics are true of Aristeas as well.

But how are the two related? What relative value is assigned to each? How is it that these cultured Hellenists have come to admire Jewish piety and what importance does the author attach to this admiration? These questions lead us into the heart of the narrative and the values that undergird its world, aspects that can be seen clearly through the lens provided by three passages, *Let Aris.* 16, 140 and 176–78.

§40 Letter of Aristeas *16*

> *These people* [i.e., the Jews] *worship God, the overseer and creator of all things, whom all people, ourselves included, O king, also [worship], although naming him differently, Zeus and Dis.*

Category: ETHICAL MONOTHEISM

69. The island is unidentified; some have suggested Cyprus (e.g., Bartlett 1985, 19).

§41 Letter of Aristeas *140*

For this reason the leading priests of the Egyptians, having looked closely into many things and having participated in affairs, gave us the name "people of God," which is not attributed to the rest [of humankind], unless someone reverence the true God.

Category: ETHICAL MONOTHEISM

§42 Letter of Aristeas *176–78*

When the king saw the delegates, he proceeded to ask questions about the books, [177]*and when they had shown what had been covered and unrolled the parchments, he paused for a long time, did obeisance about seven times, and said, "I offer you my thanks, gentlemen, and to him who sent you even more, and most of all to the God whose oracles these are."* [178]*They all, visitors and the court present alike, said together and with one voice, "It is well, O King." At this the king was moved to tears, so deeply was he filled with joy.*

Category: SYMPATHIZATION

The first of these passages (*Ep. Aris.* 16), part of an address by Aristeas to the king, is widely acknowledged to represent one of the most generous Jewish statements about Gentile piety.[70] The second passage (*Ep. Aris.* 140), part of Eleazar's discourse to the Alexandrian visitors, has not received as much attention. But if the translation offered above is correct, as I believe it is, it also gives expression to the idea that there are Gentiles who, independent of any knowledge of or connection with Judaism, can be described as "people of God." But before looking at these passages directly, it will be helpful to look first at the ideal image of Jews and Judaism on display in the work.

While the most striking feature of the *Letter of Aristeas* is the generous universalism that comes to expression in these passages and elsewhere, it is also important to note that this generosity is not purchased at the expense of the law. While the Jewish translators may have cultivated a thorough familiarity with Greek literature (121), this only served to enhance their ability to interpret the law. Being conversant with Greek culture and being open to a certain kind of Gentile piety by no means implies any compromise of Jewish culture and Torah piety. Indeed, if there was compromise, it was on the part of the Gentiles. At the banquets, for example, the king commanded that everything be prepared "in accordance with the customs practiced by all his visitors from Judea" (184). Thus the food was in keeping (καθηκόντως) with Jewish observances, and was served to the king as well (181). Further, although it was the

70. *Ep. Aris.* 16 is not as "generous," however, as the claim of Artapanus that Moses established the polytheistic worship of the Egyptians. See §36.

custom for Egyptian priests to offer the initial prayers at state banquets, the steward dispensed with this custom and generously invited the oldest priest among the Jewish guests (also named Eleazar) to offer the prayer. The prayer itself, it should be noted, was generous in return: Eleazar prayed that "the almighty God" would pour out divine blessing on the king, his family and "those of the same mind" all the days of their lives (185). Still, the pattern of generosity remains asymmetrical; nowhere in the work are Jews presented as dispensing with their own customs so as not to offend non-Jewish sensibilities.

Further, such compromises in the Jewish direction are not to be attributed simply to Egyptian hospitality. Aristeas and the Egyptian delegation have already heard the high priest's uncompromising description of the law as a barrier interposed between Jew and Gentile. The regulations of the law, Eleazar said, function as "unbroken palisades and iron walls to prevent our mixing with any of the other peoples (ἐθνῶν) in any matter" (139). To prevent any inappropriate mixing, the lawgiver "hedged us in on all sides with strict observances connected with meat and drink and touch and hearing and sight" (142). One could well imagine, then, that if the meat and drink offered to the Jewish translators at the royal banquet contravened these strict observances in any way, the guests would have retreated behind these iron walls in short order. Readers are probably expected to understand the special arrangements at the banquet to be the result not simply of normal Egyptian hospitality but of a recognition on the Egyptians' part of the special barrier posed by Jewish law observance.

Nevertheless, from beginning to end the *Letter of Aristeas* has to do with a certain kind of "mixing" between Gentiles and Jews—or, better, a mixing between Gentiles of a certain kind and Jews. How, then, are we to understand this apparent gap in the iron walls? Here it is important to look at the larger context in which these statements concerning the fence-building character of the law are to be found (128–42). Eleazar's discourse on the law is prompted by questions from the Alexandrians about the rationale for some of the food laws. Why is it, they ask, that, although the created order is a unity, some things are considered clean and others not (129)? In his reply, Eleazar begins by making general observations about the consequences that can result from association with others: on the one hand, "through bad relationships men become perverted"; on the other, "if they mix with wise and prudent companions," they become wise and prudent themselves (130). The highest wisdom, says Eleazar,—the highest religious value—is the belief that "God is one" (132). Of all the nations, only the Jews have attained this wisdom; all others "believe that there are many gods" (134). Consequently, if Jews were allowed to mingle freely with such polytheists, it is inevitable that their beliefs would become corrupted. This, says Eleazar, is where the law comes in. God gave the law as a means of preserving the monotheistic belief of the Jews by keeping the Jews separate from those who do not share such beliefs. In Eleazar's (and the author's) view, then, the separation toward which the law is directed is a separation not from

Gentiles per se, but from polytheistic worship. Jewish separatism is not an end in itself; strict observances are imposed not simply to keep Jews apart and distinct from Gentiles, as if ethnic distinctiveness were the goal. The goal, rather, is the preservation of monotheism and the nurture of a kind of life appropriate for people who desire to live under the sovereignty of the one true God.

As Eleazar continues in his exposition of the law, however, it becomes apparent that the law serves this higher end not simply by keeping Jews separate from bad influences, but also because the particular commandments of the law work in a positive way to inculcate monotheism and virtue—at least if they are interpreted correctly. He denies that any of the ordinances have been constructed "without purpose or fancifully" (168). Rather, each law is consistent with "natural reasoning"; each law has a "profound reason for it" (143). For example, he says that since many of the birds designated as unclean are predatory, the purpose of the laws pertaining to them is to teach that people should not behave in a predatory way with other people, but that they should "practice righteousness" (147). Similarly, the cloven hoof of clean animals, with its differentiation of one part from the other, teaches that human beings need to differentiate good from evil, "with righteousness as our aim" in all human activity (151).[71] Thus, on the basis of a rudimentary form of allegorical exegesis, Eleazar argues that the whole of the law has as its "intent that through the whole of our lives we may also practice justice to all mankind in our acts, remembering the all-sovereign God" (168). That is to say, the goal of the law is the development of monotheistic virtue.

Further, this goal is one that Gentiles—some of them, at least—can recognize and approve on their own terms. This is present as a premise in Eleazar's discourse. He assumes that, while the laws may seem strange and foreign to his Alexandrian interlocutors on the surface, once their real purpose is explained to these Gentiles, they will readily recognize that the law is directed toward a goal that they themselves already share. It is also present in his statement that "the leading priests among the Egyptians," who are well qualified in these matters, have described the Jews as "people of God" (140); presumably these Gentiles would need to be "people of God" themselves in order to recognize the Jews as such. This is also implied in a statement made earlier to the king by Demetrius the librarian, to the effect that the law, because of its divine nature, "is very philosophical and genuine" (31).

A similar conclusion emerges from the question-and-answer sessions at the royal banquets. Each of the king's questions has to do with an aspect of the wisdom or virtue that is necessary for successful living, especially for successful

71. The High Priest even finds deep significance in what he takes to be an accepted fact of nature, namely, that female weasels conceive through their ears and deliver their young through their mouths (165)!

statecraft. Each answer is pithy and to the point, with a reference to God as either the source or the model for the virtue under discussion. The performance of these Jewish translator-philosophers is greeted with enthusiastic praise. At the end of the first set, the king addresses his own philosophers: "I think that these men excel in virtue and have a fuller understanding, because when asked questions of this sort unexpectedly they give appropriate answers, all making God the basis of their argument" (200). Rather than being offended by this invidious comparison, the spokesperson for the philosophers agrees wholeheartedly. Then after the third set, the audience applauds, "especially the philosophers, for these men far surpassed them in attitudes and eloquence, their starting point being God himself" (235). Again, the assumption in the narrative is that by virtue of their philosophy the philosophers already have a recognition and an understanding of a truth that, while perhaps expressed more eloquently by the Jews, is nevertheless accessible apart from any awareness of the law. The goal to which the law is directed is one that can be approached by other means. Jewish law and Greek philosophy, then, represent two routes to the same sort of truth.

Thus the striking statement in *Ep. Aris.* 16—that the God of the Jews is the same deity as the one whom Greeks worship as Zeus or Dis—is to be taken with all seriousness. Already at the outset of the work we find the idea that monotheism, while a Jewish distinctive, can be arrived at by other means. *Ep. Aris.* 16 is programmatic for the work as a whole. The same God who has given the law to the Jews is at work providentially in the wider Gentile world (15). Gentiles, even those with no knowledge of Judaism, can know something about this God even if they use different names for the deity.[72]

Further, it is clear that for the author the idea of a parallel route to virtuous monotheism is not simply a hypothetical possibility. The narrative presents us with real examples of Gentiles who have arrived at this destination without reference to Judaism or its law. The king himself is one example. At this early point in the narrative (i.e., 16), there is no indication that the king has any more than a rudimentary knowledge about the Jews. For example, it apparently comes as a surprise to him that there were considerable numbers of Jewish slaves in Egypt who had been sold into slavery unjustly. Aristeas's comment about the one God with various names is made as he is attempting to persuade the king that before asking the high priest for assistance with translation he should, as a sign of good faith, release these Jews from slavery. Since the statement comes before the king has had any real contact with Jews, its implication is that the king already can be counted among those who worship the same God as the Jews, even if he knows God by a different name. Consistent with this is the king's declaration that his "overall aim is that which promotes justice and piety in all things" (24), a declaration made in the course of his decree freeing the

72. See also Segal (1990, 90–91).

Jewish slaves. The monotheistic piety of the king is confirmed later on in the narrative, during the banqueting, when the Jewish translators make comments whose implication is that the king himself already displays the divine virtues that they are commending in their responses to his questions. For example, speaking of natural calamities, one of them said, "As for you, God-fearing [εὐσεβεῖ] as you are, none of these evils would befall you" (233); another, speaking of discernment, describes it as "an excellent gift from God—which indeed you possess, O king" (276); a third declares that God has already given the king "a crown of righteousness" (280).

Besides the king, the philosophers can probably be counted in the number of those who have found God via the route of philosophy. While there is no affirmation on the part of the author that they have actually achieved the kind of monotheistic virtue that they recognize in the Jewish visitors, the implication seems to be that they are already making good progress toward the same destination along their own independent path. Aristeas and Philocrates can probably be included as well, though, as we have already observed, when we first encounter them they are already admirers of the Jews and their laws. In other words, it is not clear that they arrived at their convictions about God and virtue independently of Judaism.

In addition to these specific examples, it is probably the case that *Ep. Aris.* 140 makes a more general statement about Gentiles who deserve the appellation "people of God." We have touched on this passage already, noting that Egyptian priests have described the Jews in these terms. But the narrator goes on to say of this appellation: ὃ τοῖς λοιποῖς οὐ πρόσεστιν, εἰ μὴ τις σέβεται τὸν κατά ἀλήθειαν θεόν. Shutt's rendering—"which is ascribed exclusively to those who worship the true God, and not to those who are concerned with meat and drink and clothes"—could be taken in an exclusive sense: the term applies exclusively to Jews.[73] But the clause more literally says of this appellation, "which is not attributed to the rest, unless someone reverence the true God." This seems to imply that there are some exceptions among the "rest," that is to say, non-Jews who nevertheless also worship the true God.[74] Since such exceptions can be found elsewhere in the work, this more literal rendering is probably to be preferred.

Thus for the author of the *Letter of Aristeas* not only does the law lead to the same goal as is sought by the adherents of Greek philosophy, but he is prepared to point to specific examples of non-Jews who have approached this goal along the parallel philosophical route. To be sure, the numbers are not large. Apart from the Jews, "all the rest of mankind" has gone astray by worshipping many gods (134–38). Thus it is not surprising that monotheistic Gentiles are

73. Barclay takes it in this sense (1996, 144).

74. See Boccaccini (1991, 177). See also J. J. Collins (2000, 193).

the exception (140). Still, such Gentiles exist; the parallel route to monotheistic virtue is not simply a hypothetical one.

But what precisely is expected of such Gentiles? One implication of the narrative is that they would be expected to give up their traditional polytheistic worship. The author is much more positive about Greek philosophy than he is about Greek or Egyptian religion (137–38). Aristeas and the king may address the "Most High God" as "Zeus or Dis," but this seems to be the limit of tolerance; nowhere in the work are these commendable Gentiles depicted as engaging in typical Gentile worship. Do they need to take the further step of becoming Jewish sympathizers? Since the king and the philosophers are presented as models of monotheistic virtue even before they encounter the Jews, the answer seems to be no. Nevertheless, when they do encounter Jews they are impressed; they seem to recognize that although the Jewish law and their own philosophy lead to the same goal, the Jewish law does so more effectively. For example, on receiving the Jewish delegation and viewing the as yet untranslated law, the king showed reverence (προσκυνήσας) and offered his thanks to the delegates, "to him who sent you even more, and most of all to the God whose oracles these are" (177). The implication seems to be that, in the author's view, once they come into contact with Jews, true ethical monotheists will recognize the superiority of the Jewish route, will respond with admiration (and even gifts!), and will be prepared to compromise in order to associate with such superior piety.

But this is not where the emphasis is to be placed. To the extent that the *Letter of Aristeas* recognizes the existence of Gentile "people of God" (cf. 140), this is a status that Gentiles may achieve via the route of Greek philosophy, without any reference to the Jewish law. Thus while the author wants to present himself as defending a traditional, Torah-centered way of life—the Torah as a set of "unbroken palisades and iron walls" separating Jews from others—his understanding of the character and goal of the life carried out behind those walls represents a significant reformulation. While in formal terms Eleazar's "palisades and walls" may resemble the kind of covenantal barrier between Jew and Gentile that, say, the author of 1 Maccabees was so zealous to defend, they were significantly different in substance.

Sibylline Oracles 3

Sibylline oracles were widespread in the Greco-Roman world. (The) Sibyl (originally a personal name, later a generic) was a female oracular figure who combined gloomy predictions of downfall and disaster with scornful denunciations of human folly and wickedness. Assuming the persona of a preternaturally aged woman, she was thereby able to present history in the form of prediction, which cast an aura of authority around her oracles as a whole. While the phenomenon was in the first instance oral, oracles were eventually written down and then circulated widely in a fluid and changeable form.

With its emphasis on present wickedness and future disaster, and its venerated status in the Greco-Roman world, the Sibylline tradition was tailor-made for Jewish writers who wanted to express Jewish views of the world in a Hellenistic genre. The first Jewish Sibyllines appeared in Egypt; other Jewish—and later, Christian—productions followed. They have been preserved in Christian collections, probably dating from the sixth century C.E. The earliest document is generally agreed to be *Sibylline Oracles* 3.[75]

In the form in which it has been handed down, *Sibylline Oracles* 3 is generally recognized as a composite work dating from different periods.[76] Lines 1–96, which in most manuscripts are described as "from the second book concerning God," are seen by almost all scholars as stemming from a separate work. Lines 350–488, containing assorted oracles against various nations, are also generally recognized to be a later addition, written in the first century B.C.E. The passages that will interest us here are all found in the material that remains, which, despite its disorderly arrangement, can be seen as a single work. John Collins (1983, 354) has argued convincingly that this work consists of a series of five discrete oracles (97–161; 162–195; 196–294; 545–656; 657–808), interspersed with other material and followed by a first-person conclusion (809–829), in which the Sibyl identifies herself as the daughter-in-law of Noah. Passages of interest here are found in three of the oracles—the second (162–195), fourth (545–656) and fifth (657–808).

These three oracles follow a similar pattern: a survey of human history and political empires with an emphasis on sinfulness; announcements of punishment and destruction; a promise of a coming kingdom of peace and true worship. Recurring references to the "seventh king" of Egypt, or a "seventh reign" (193, 318, 608), suggest a dating during the reign of Ptolemy VI Philometer (163–145 B.C.E.). Collins (2000, 88–96) has argued that the Sibyl viewed the seventh king as a messianic figure, somewhat akin to Cyrus in Deutero-Isaiah. But such an interpretation would require equating this king with the "king from the sun" (652–56), an identification that, while possible, is not demanded by the text. The most that can be said with confidence is that the Sibyl expects eschatological deliverance to take place during the reign of—not necessarily through the agency of—the seventh king.[77]

75. For general introductions, see J. J. Collins (1983, 317–26); Schürer (1986, 3:618–54); Barclay (1996, 216–19).

76. Nikiprowetzky (1970) has argued for a unified composition dating from the first century C.E., but he is virtually alone in this opinion. See the discussion in J. J. Collins (2000, 85–87); Schürer (1986, 3:632–38). But note Gruen's skepticism about attempts to identify a unified core that can be dated precisely (Gruen 1998, 268–80).

77. J. J. Collins further aligns *Sibylline Oracles* 3 with the house of Onias. Barclay (1996, 222–25), following Momigliano, sees *Sibylline Oracles* 3 instead as reflecting a pro-Maccabean orientation. This approach probably represents an over-specification in the other direction.

With respect to the Gentiles and their status vis-à-vis Israel's God, the most characteristic feature of these passages is the repeated expectation that Gentiles will turn to God in the eschatological future. In the last two of the oracles, however, we encounter injunctions directed at the Gentiles (particularly the "Greeks") in the present, encouraging them to abandon their misguided ways and accept the law of God even now. This intermingling of future expectation and present injunction is most pronounced in the final oracle, which therefore will receive most of our attention.

Text: Geffcken (1902)
Translation: *OTP* (J. J. Collins 1983)
Date: Mid-second century B.C.E.
Provenance: Egypt
Original Language: Greek
Bibliography: Barclay (1996, 216–26); J. J. Collins (1974; 1983; 2000, 83–97, 160–65); Donaldson (1990, 16–19); Gruen (1998, 268–90); Kraus (1996, 84–86); Nikiprowetzky (1970); Schürer (1986, 3:618–41)

§43 Sibylline Oracles *3:191–95*

Every kind of deceit will be found among them
until the seventh reign, when
a king of Egypt, who will be of the Greeks by race, will rule.
And then the people of the great God will again be strong
who will be guides in life for all mortals.

Category: ESCHATOLOGICAL PARTICIPATION

In this passage, which brings the second oracle to a conclusion, eschatological expectation is muted but is nevertheless clearly discernible when seen in the context of the work as a whole. Admittedly, the passage has sometimes been seen as a reference not to the eschatological future but solely to the present—specifically, to the Maccabean period when the Jews had become "strong" under the leadership of Judas and his brothers.[78] However, this time of strengthening is said to take place during the reign of a seventh king in Egypt (192–93), a time that elsewhere in the book coincides with the arrival of God's kingdom (318 and especially 608). Thus *Sib. Or.* 3:162–95 is probably to be seen as parallel in structure to two subsequent eschatological oracles (545–656, 657–808),[79] both of which survey a succession of human kingdoms, with an

78. See Lanchester (1913, 2:382); also Barclay (1996, 222–24), who adapts a position developed by Momigliano.

79. See J. J. Collins (1983, 354–55).

emphasis on sin and idolatry, and culminate in the arrival of a golden age ("[God] will raise up a kingdom for all ages" [767–68]). This suggests that the restoration of "the people of the great God" to a position of strength (καρτερόν) should be seen as a reference to Israel's eschatological vindication. Correspondingly, the statement that the people of Israel will also become "guides in life for all mortals" should be seen as an equally compressed but nevertheless clear reference to a time when the Gentiles would imitate the Jews in their piety and righteousness.

§44 Sibylline Oracles *3:545–50*

Greece, why do you rely on mortal leaders
who are not able to flee the end of death?
To what purpose do you give vain gifts to the dead
and sacrifice to idols? Who put error in your heart
that you should abandon the face of the great God and do these things?
Revere the name of the one who has begotten all, and do not forget it.

Category: ETHICAL MONOTHEISM

§45 Sibylline Oracles *3:556–72*

But when the wrath of the great God comes upon you,
then indeed you will recognize the face of the great God.
All the souls of men will groan mightily and
stretch out their hands straight to broad heaven
and begin to call on the great king as protector
and seek who will be a deliverer from great wrath.
But come and learn this and place it in your heart,
how many woes there will be as the years circle on.
Greece, also, by offering the holocausts of oxen
and loud-bellowing bulls, which she has sacrificed, at the Temple of the great God,
will escape the din of war and panic and pestilence
and will again escape the yoke of slavery.
But the race of impious men will survive up to this point:
whenever this fated day comes to pass.
You will certainly not sacrifice to God until everything happens.
What God alone has planned will not go unfulfilled.
A strong necessity will insist that everything be fulfilled.

Category: ESCHATOLOGICAL PARTICIPATION

§46 Sibylline Oracles *3:624–31*

But you, devious mortal, do not tarry in hesitation
but turn back, converted, and propitiate God.
Sacrifice to God hundreds of bulls and firstborn lambs

and goats at the recurring times.
But propitiate him, the immortal God, so that he may have pity
for he alone is God and there is no other.
Honor righteousness and oppress no one,
for so the Immortal bids wretched mortals.

Category: ETHICAL MONOTHEISM

The fourth oracle (545–656) contains an account of Gentile participation in end-time blessings (556–72) that is more explicit than the one just examined (191–95). The Sibyl anticipates a time when the Greeks "will recognize the face of the great God" (557) and will "escape the yoke of slavery" (567) by offering sacrifices "at the Temple of the great God (565)." But in so doing, the Gentiles will simply be behaving as they should have all along. For the eschatological section of the oracle is flanked by passages in which the Gentiles are admonished in the present to "revere the name of" God (550), and to "turn back," "sacrifice to God," "honor righteousness and oppress no one" (625, 626, 630). This combination of eschatological anticipation and present injunction is found in the final oracle as well, and we will postpone more detailed comment until we have cited this material.

§47 Sibylline Oracles *3:710–23*

And then all islands and cities will say,
"How much the Immortal loves those men!
for everything fights on their side and helps them,
heaven, divinely driven sun and moon"
(but the all-bearing earth will be shaken in those days).
They will bring forth from their mouths a delightful utterance in hymns,
"Come, let us all fall on the ground and entreat
the immortal king, the great eternal God.
Let us send to the Temple, since he alone is sovereign
and let us all ponder the Law of the Most High God,
who is most righteous of all throughout the earth.
But we had wandered from the path of the Immortal.
With mindless spirit we revered things made by hand,
idols and statues of dead men."

§48 Sibylline Oracles *3:732–33, 740*

But wretched Greece, desist from proud thoughts.
Entreat the great-hearted Immortal and take precautions.. . .
Serve the great God so that you may have a share in these things.

§49 Sibylline Oracles *3:762–75*

But urge on your minds in your breasts
and shun unlawful worship. Worship the Living One.
Avoid adultery and indiscriminate intercourse with males.

Rear your own offspring and do not kill it,
for the Immortal is angry at whoever commits these sins.
And then, indeed, he will raise up a kingdom for all
ages among men, he who once gave the holy Law
to the pious, to all of whom he promised to open the earth
and the world and the gates of the blessed and all joys
and immortal intellect and eternal cheer.
From every land they will bring incense and gifts
to the house of the great God. There will be no other
house among men, even for future generations to know,
except the one which God gave to faithful men to honor.

Category: ESCHATOLOGICAL PARTICIPATION

The final oracle (657–808) contains more extended descriptions of end-time realities, which correspond to a typical eschatological pilgrimage scenario. Again we encounter a pattern in which descriptions of end-time bliss (702–31, 741–61, 767–95) alternate with exhortations addressed to Gentiles (732–40, 762–66). The eschatological oracle begins with an assault by the "kings of the nations" (βασιλῆες ἐθνῶν; 663) on the temple in Jerusalem (657–68). This assault is forestalled by God and leads instead to cosmic disaster and the final judgment of the wicked (669–701). The Israelites in Judea, however, remain untouched by it all:

But the sons of the great God will all live
peacefully around the Temple, rejoicing in these things
which the Creator, just judge and sole ruler, will give.
For he alone will shield them, standing by them magnificently
as if he had a wall of blazing fire round about.
They will be free from war in towns and country.
No hand of evil war, but rather the Immortal himself
and the hand of the Holy One will be fighting for them. (702–9)

It is precisely this evidence of divine protection—not only of Israel, but also of the temple itself—that brings "all islands and cities" to their senses. They realize the futility of their idols and decide that they will "send [presumably sacrifices] to the Temple" and "ponder the Law of the Most High God." The pilgrimage of the Gentiles to the Jerusalem temple comes more clearly into view when the Sibyl picks up the theme of the Gentiles again in 772: "From every land they will bring incense and gifts to the house of the great God."[80] Travel conditions will be ameliorated by a transformation of the earth itself: "All the paths of the plain and rugged cliffs, lofty mountains, and wild waves of the sea will be easy to climb or sail in those days" (777–79). And not only

80. A historical prototype for this end-time procession of gifts might be found in 291, where the kings of the Persians are praised for helping with the rebuilding of the temple by bringing "gold and bronze and much-wrought iron."

travel conditions—the whole natural order will be marked by the kind of peace and harmony anticipated by Isaiah (780–95; cf. Isa 11:6–9).

It is clear that the Sibyl expects the Gentiles to live according to "the Law of the Most High God" (719) in this end-time age of bliss and to follow the "common law" that God will establish for all of humankind (757–59; cf. 767–71).[81] But what precisely is the content of this law? Before addressing this question directly, it needs to be noted that the exhortations contain no explicit references to the law at all. The closest we get is the reference to "unlawful worship" in 763. For the rest, the injunctions are phrased in very general terms. Gentiles are to abandon their worship of idols (548, 763); to worship the one true God (548–50, 733, 740, 763); to offer sacrifices to God (624–29), presumably at the Jerusalem temple (cf. 772–75: "no other house"), something that was always possible for Gentiles;[82] to honor righteousness (630); and to abstain from adultery, homosexuality, and infanticide (764–66). There is nothing in these injunctions to suggest that Gentiles are to observe those aspects of the law that differentiate Jew from Gentile.

On the basis of observations such as these, Nikiprowetzky (1970, 78, n. 1) has argued for a two-step process. In the present, he says, the Sibyl wanted the Gentiles to adhere only to the natural law, seen as those laws given to Noah for the whole of humankind. In the eschatological future, however, Gentiles are expected to embrace the whole law, in effect becoming proselytes. But while he is right in saying that the injunctions for the present are couched in terms of a natural law, his idea of a two-step process, with different expectations in effect for the future, is not supportable. Two considerations militate against it.

First, while law observance is not explicit in the exhortations themselves, elsewhere it is clear that Gentiles are expected to live according to the law. The pertinent texts appear in passages in which Gentiles are being denounced for their sins. Lines 595–600 contain a long list of Gentile nations, their misdeeds described as a transgression "of the holy law of immortal God." Gentile assaults against the temple will come to naught "because they knew neither the law nor the judgment of the great God" (685–87).[83] There can be little doubt, then, that law observance was expected of Gentiles in the present as well as the future.

The second observation, however, has to do with the nature of law observance itself. Certainly the law in view is the Jewish law, given through Moses

81. It is more likely that this common law is introduced primarily as the standard of the judgment described in the immediately subsequent lines (759–61) rather than as an aspect of the age of bliss described in the preceding lines (744–55); since the sentence goes on to talk about "wretched mortals" (759), the focus seems to be more on judgment than on blessing. But in either case it is clear that the law will be observed by all the coming era.

82. There is no mention in *Sibylline Oracles* 3 of those sacrifices that were distinctively Jewish in character.

83. Also 495–96: "Because of the unjust tongue and lawless (ἀνόμου), unholy life which all have carried out."

and instituted at Sinai (254–58). But even when speaking of the law as observed by Israelites, there is no mention of Jewish distinctives. Except for one vague reference to ablutions (591–93), we find no indication that the law contained regulations concerning circumcision, purity, dietary restrictions, and so on. What is in view, especially in two encomiums on the Jews (218–64; 573–600), are precisely those things that are enjoined on the Gentiles: rejection of idolatry; worship of the one, true God in the one, true place of worship in Jerusalem; and adherence to a universal moral code. How is it that the Jews fulfil "the word of the great God, the hymn of the law" (246)? By rejecting astrology and magic (221–33); not loving money (235); establishing just measurements (237); respecting boundary lines (240); caring for the poor (241–45). Why did they experience the evil of the exile? Because they "did not obey in [their] heart the holy law of the immortal God, but in error worshiped unseemly idols" (275–77). The Jews observe "the righteousness of the law of the Most High" (580) by worshiping God at the Jerusalem temple (575–79), rejecting idolatry (586–90), remaining faithful in marriage (595), and abstaining from pederasty (596).

Thus for the Sibyl the law of Moses functions as a universal law centered on three essential elements: monotheism, with its corollary, the rejection of idolatry; worship at the Jerusalem temple; and a set of basic moral injunctions. While the Sibyl does not share Philo's concern to demonstrate that these elements can be naturally perceived, her assumption that Gentiles should be aware of these requirements does give them the character of a natural law. But while the Sibyl does not seem to make any distinction between the "law" that is observed by the Jews and that which is incumbent on Gentiles, there is at the same time no indication that by observing the law Gentiles would thereby become part of the "race (γένος) of most righteous men" (219) who live around the temple of God. "Righteous" they may be (cf. 630), but Gentiles they remain.[84]

Testaments of the Twelve Patriarchs

The *Testaments of the Twelve Patriarchs* is modeled on Jacob's deathbed speech to his twelve sons (Gen 49), except that in this case the deathbed speech is given by the twelve patriarchs to their own sons. The individual testaments display a common pattern: a brief introduction, which identifies what follows as the words spoken by the respective patriarch to his sons; a biographical section, in which the patriarch surveys selected aspects of his life; a section of ethical exhortation addressed to the sons; and an eschatological section, which looks ahead

84. See also Segal (1990, 90). J. J. Collins's choice of "converted" (3.625) represents an overtranslation of παλίμπλαγκτος (driven back). Likewise, in describing these end-time pilgrims as "proselytes," Kraus (1996, 86) fails to take into account the distinctive view of the law in *Sib. Or.* 3.

to Israel's future of sin, exile, and restoration. Ethical exhortation is central not only to the structure of each testament but also to its purpose, as both biography and eschatology serve to underline the main ethical appeal of the whole. We will be interested primarily in the eschatological sections, nine of which contain positive references to Gentiles, though the biographical section of the *Testament of Joseph* also contains a passage of interest.

While the structure of the *Testaments* is relatively clear, any assessment of their contents is bedeviled by the vexed question of their provenance. The writing is extant primarily in Greek and Armenian (the latter a translation from the Greek)[85] and has been preserved and transmitted in Christian tradition. In this latter respect, it is not unlike many other Jewish pseudepigraphal writings. But over and above the Christian transmission of the work, the *Testaments* is distinguished by some explicitly Christian content. While most of the material would be at home in a Jewish environment, there is a set of statements—a dozen or so—that present apparently unambiguous Christian allusions.[86] The history of the tradition is further complicated by the existence of related Semitic documents: medieval Hebrew midrashim dealing with Naphtali and Judah; fragments of a Testament of Levi in Aramaic, found in the Cairo Genizah; and, from Qumran, further fragments of an Aramaic Testament of Levi and a Hebrew Testament of Naphtali.[87] There is no direct relationship between our Greek *Testaments* and any of these Semitic documents; the one is certainly not a translation of any of the others. Nevertheless, there is clearly an indirect relationship; as this material demonstrates, there was a Hebrew and Aramaic tradition concerning the twelve patriarchs that could have served as source material for the Greek *Testaments*.

Scholarly opinion concerning the origin of the *Testaments* has tended to cluster around two sharply differentiated alternatives: (1) that the *Testaments* is essentially a Jewish work with discrete Christian interpolations, a position identified most clearly with R. H. Charles; or (2) that the *Testaments* in its present form is a Christian work, albeit one that draws on Jewish tradition—a position developed in the numerous publications of M. de Jonge.[88] This is not the place to engage in any lengthy discussion of the issues involved. The position taken here is closer to Charles than to de Jonge: the work is probably to be seen as

85. There are also Slavonic, Serbian, and Latin versions. On the textual tradition as a whole, see de Jonge (1978, xi–xli).

86. For example: "For the Lord will raise up from Levi someone as high priest and from Judah someone as king, God and man" (*T. Sim.* 7:2); "He shall enter the first temple, and there the Lord will be abused and will be raised up on wood" (*T. Benj.* 9:3).

87. See Schürer (1987, 775–77). A Greek translation of the Genizah text has also been discovered (in the Monastery of Koutloumous on Mount Athos).

88. A third, much more minor, cluster sees the *Testaments* as Essene, either in its entirety (Dupont-Sommer 1959) or in the interpolations (Philonenko 1960).

essentially a Jewish product, dating from sometime in the Hasmonean period; it appears to have been composed in Greek (though no doubt depending on the kind of tradition represented in the Genizah and Qumran fragments);[89] while Syria is often suggested as its area of origin (e.g., Kee 1983b 778), the emphasis on Joseph in many of the testaments might suggest an Egyptian provenance; Christian redaction, in the form of discrete interpolation and a few more thoroughly reworked passages, can be identified with some measure of confidence and separated out from the Jewish work.[90]

Even if we approach the *Testaments* on these assumptions, however, questions remain about the place of Gentiles in the work, since it is apparent that the relationship between the Gentiles and Israel is one of the concerns of the Christian redactor. The clearest examples are in the *Testament of Benjamin*. *Testament of Benjamin* 9:3 describes how "the Lord" will be abused in the temple and will be "raised up on wood," and how "the temple curtain shall be torn." After this, "the spirit of God will move on to all the nations [τὰ ἔθνη] as a fire is poured out"[91]—an apparent allusion to the Pentecost account (Acts 2:3). A little further on, in *T. Benj.* 11:3, we read of someone, perhaps the apostle Paul, who "until the consummation of the ages . . . shall be in the congregations of the gentiles." A similar Christian thematization of Gentile salvation appears in *T. Levi* 10. Here, as a result of several Christian interpolations, the scattering of Israel among the nations (presumably after the war with Rome) comes to be seen as divine punishment for the mistreatment of "Christ, the Savior of the world" (10:2). Thus there is evidence that the Christian redactor has a special interest in the Gentiles, linking Gentile salvation with Israel's rejection of the Christ and God's subsequent punishment of Israel.[92]

This opens up the possibility that other references to Gentile salvation are Christian interpolations as well, especially in cases where there is evidence of Christian interference nearby and where such references could easily be excised from the text. A pertinent example is *T. Sim.* 7:2: "He will save all the gentiles and the tribe of Israel." The larger context (*T. Sim.* 7:1–3) contains two explicit Christian interpolations. Further, apart from this reference to Gentiles, the rest of the passage concerns itself with matters internal to Israel.[93] Thus one has to

89. Charles, however, argued for a Hebrew original.

90. For a similar position, see Schürer (1987, 770–75). Since the Armenian version has fewer Christian references than the Greek, Charles argued that it reflected an earlier stage of the textual tradition. More recent study, however (esp. Stone 1977; Hollander and de Jonge 1985, 412), has demonstrated that this was not the case.

91. Despite Kee's translation, πάντα does not appear. Further, the reference to the Gentiles is not present at all in the Armenian version.

92. For a study of this, see Jervell (1969).

93. *T. Sim.* 6:5 ("by himself he will save Adam") could well be a Christian interpolation, given that the preceding words in v. 5 ("as a man") are Christian.

view the phrase πάντα τὰ ἔθνη καί with suspicion; it should probably not be used as evidence for Jewish patterns of thought.

But not all references to Gentiles in the *Testaments of the Twelve Patriarchs* need to be removed from consideration. There are other cases where universalistic themes are integral to the passage as a whole and where references to Gentiles cannot be easily excised. For example, *T. Jud.* 24:4–6 hangs together as a unit, constructed largely around the theme of the "shoot" of Isa 11:1.[94] Since the text from Isaiah anticipates end-time blessings for the nations (see esp. vv. 9–10), and since the references to "all humanity" (πάσης σαρκός; v. 4) and "the nations" (τοῖς ἔθνεσι; v. 6) cannot be removed without damaging the rest of the text, it is probable that these references were part of the Jewish original.

Thus the texts in question need to be dealt with on a case-by-case basis. In addition to *T. Sim.* 7:2, there are six further passages where references to Gentiles fit awkwardly with their contexts and could easily have been interpolated: *T. Levi* 2:11; 4:4; *T. Jud.* 22:2; *T. Ash.* 7:3; *T. Benj.* 9:2.[95] These will not be included here. Four other instances are not as clear but nevertheless are sufficiently suspicious that they should also be set aside: *T. Levi* 8:14;[96] *T. Dan* 6:7;[97] *T. Benj.* 10:5–10;[98] *T. Benj.* 11:2–5.[99]

This leaves five passages where references to Gentiles and their future salvation seem to be integral to the text and thus can probably be taken as reflective of Jewish attitudes: *T. Levi* 18:2–9; *T. Jud.* 24:4–6; 25:5; *T. Zeb.* 9:8; *T. Naph.* 8:1–4.

94. While there are Christian references in *T. Jud.* 24:1–3, there are none in vv. 4–6. See J. J. Collins (1995, 92), who sees vv. 4–6 as the "Jewish core" of the larger passage.

95. "Through you and Judah the Lord will be seen by men, by himself saving every race of humankind" (*T. Levi* 2:11); "Blessing shall be given to you and to all your posterity until through his son's compassion the Lord shall visit all the nations, although your sons will lay hands on him in order to impale him" (*T. Levi* 4:4); "until the salvation of Israel comes, until the coming of the God of righteousness, so that Jacob may enjoy tranquility and peace, as well as all the nations" (*T. Jud.* 22:2); "He will save Israel and all the nations, God speaking like a man" (*T. Ash.* 7:3); "The twelve tribes shall be gathered there and all the nations, until such time as the Most High shall send forth his salvation through the ministration of the unique prophet. He shall enter the first temple, and there the Lord will be abused and will be raised up on wood." (*T. Benj.* 9:2).

96. This passage speaks of a king who will arise from Judah who "shall found a new priesthood in accordance with the gentile model and for all nations." Charles sees in this combination of priest and king a reference to the Hasmonaean line (Charles 1913c, 2.309). But it is difficult to imagine a priesthood "in accordance with the gentile model" (κατὰ τὸν τύπον τῶν ἐθνῶν) being presented by a Jewish writer as something worthy of praise. It is more likely that the whole sentence (and perhaps vv. 12–15 in its entirety) is to be seen as Christian (see J. J. Collins 1995, 90–91).

97. In Kee's rendering of *T. Dan* 6:7, the second half of the verse has the appearance of a Christian interpolation: "His name shall be everywhere throughout Israel; and the Savior

Text: de Jonge (1978); Charles (1908)
Translation: *OTP* (Kee 1983b)
Date: Disputed, but probably late second century B.C.E.
Provenance: Perhaps Syria; less likely, Egypt
Original Language: Greek
Bibliography: Becker (1970); J. J. Collins (1998, 133–43; 2000, 174–83); Hollander and de Jonge (1985); Hultgård (1977); Jervell (1969); de Jonge (1975a; 1975b; 1978); Kee (1978); Kraus (1996, 73–76); Kugler (2001); Philonenko (1960); Schnabel (2004, 98–101); Schürer (1987, 3:767–81); Slingerland (1977)

§50 Testament of Levi *18:2–9*

And then the Lord will raise up a new priest to whom all the words of the Lord will be revealed. He shall effect the judgment of truth over the earth for many days. [3]*And his star shall rise in heaven like a king; kindling the light of knowledge as day is illumined by the sun. And he shall be extolled by the whole inhabited world.* [4]*This one will shine forth like the sun in the earth; he shall take away all darkness from under heaven, and there shall be peace in all the earth.* [5]*The heavens shall greatly rejoice in his days and the earth shall be glad; the clouds will be filled with joy and the knowledge of the Lord will be poured out on the earth like the water of the seas. And the angels of the glory of the Lord's presence will be made glad by him.* [6]*The heavens will be opened, and from the temple of glory sanctification will come upon him, with a*

---

will be known among the nations." The Greek is less straightforward, however: τὸ δὲ ὄνομα αὐτοῦ ἔσται ἐν παντὶ τόπῳ Ἰσραὴλ καὶ ἐν τοῖς ἔθνεσι σωτήρ. Kee has taken the second half of the verse as an ellipsis; if the sentence is to be construed as elliptical, a more literal rendering of the ellipsis might be: "His name shall be in every place of Israel, and among the nations [his name shall be] Savior." Another construal, however, would be to take the two prepositional phrases as parallel: "His name shall be in every place of Israel and in the nations: savior" (see Hollander and de Jonge 1985, 290, 292). Here the term "savior" stands on its own and (although Hollander and de Jonge do not see it this way) could be considered in isolation as an interpolation. But in either case, the larger context in *T. Dan* is inwardly focused; the passage is concerned about the end-time fate of Israel, with little indication of an interest in the outer Gentile world (except for the curious statement in v. 9: "What you have heard from your father pass on to your children, so that the father of nations may accept you"). It seems safer to treat this as another example of Christian interpolation.

98. Kee's rendering of *T. Benj.* 10:5–10 contains several positive statements about Gentiles in the final judgment: "They gave us all these things as an inheritance, saying, 'Keep God's commandments until the Lord reveals his salvation to all the nations. . . . [T]he Lord first judges Israel for the wrong she has committed and then he shall do the same for all the nations. Then he shall judge Israel by the chosen gentiles as he tested Esau by the Midianites who loved their brothers." The translation is based on the Armenian version, however; all Greek manuscripts of this chapter are thoroughly riddled with Christian references. It seems prudent, therefore, to forego any attempt to discern a Jewish original, contra Schnabel

fatherly voice, as from Abraham to Isaac. [7]And the glory of the Most High shall burst forth upon him. And the spirit of understanding and sanctification shall rest upon him in the water. [8]For he shall give the majesty of the Lord to those who are his sons in truth forever. [9]And in his priesthood the nations shall be multiplied in knowledge on the earth, and they shall be illumined by the grace of the Lord, but Israel shall be diminished by her ignorance and darkened by her grief. In his priesthood sin shall cease and lawless men shall rest from their evil deeds, and righteous men shall find rest in him.

Category: ESCHATOLOGICAL PARTICIPATION

The eschatological section of the *Testament of Levi* is contained in chapters 14–18, where Levi conveys to his sons the knowledge that he has gleaned "from the writings of Enoch" (14:1) concerning the events of the end time (ἐπὶ τέλει). Chapters 14 and 15 contain a survey of Israel's sinfulness, with an emphasis on priestly infidelity, leading up to the destruction of the temple and the exile (chs. 14–15). In chapter 16, a chapter that has been heavily reworked by a Christian editor, Levi surveys the "seventy weeks" (v. 1) that will pass "until he will again have regard for you, and will take you back in compassion" (v. 5). Then, in a rather confused fashion, chapters 17 and 18 return to cover the same ground—from the appointment of Levi until the final consummation—using a system of jubilee-based priesthoods. Seven of these are recounted in chapter 17. Then in strikingly universalistic terms, chapter 18 describes the final redemption of the world in the days of an eschatological priest, whose "star shall rise in heaven like a king" (v. 2) and who "shall take away all darkness from under heaven" (v. 4). This expectation of a priestly messiah is part of a more widespread tendency in the *Testaments* to emphasize the role of Levi (*T. Reu.* 6:5–12; *T. Levi* 8:11–17; *T. Naph.* 5:3–5) and to look for end-time salvation from the house of Levi, a levitical messianism that usually stands alongside the more traditional expectation of a messiah from Judah (*T. Sim.* 7:1–3; *T. Dan* 5:10; *T. Naph.* 8:2–3; *T. Gad* 8:1; *T. Jos.* 19:11).[100]

There is some evidence of Christian reworking in chapter 18, especially in vv. 6–7, which contain clear allusions to Jesus's baptism.[101] The negative statement

(2004, 101), who includes this passage in his list of Jewish material. On the inferiority of the Armenian version, see n. 91.

99. This is a difficult text, with quite different wordings in each of the two families of Greek manuscripts identified by Charles and in the Armenian tradition. Following de Jonge's reconstruction of the text, the passage seems to refer to the apostle Paul—one who "will arise from my seed in later times [cf. Phil 3:5: "of the tribe of Benjamin"] . . . with a new knowledge enlightening all the Gentiles"; one who "until the consummation of the ages . . . will be in the gatherings of the Gentiles" (Hollander and de Jonge 1985, 441–44). If this interpretation is correct, the passage seems to have been thoroughly Christianized, and thus should be left out of account here.

100. On the levitical messianism, see J. J. Collins (1995, 74–101).

101. Some Greek manuscripts also contain the phrase "until his assumption" (ἕως ἀναλήψεως αὐτοῦ) at the end of v. 3.

about Israel in v. 9 ("diminished by her ignorance and darkened by her grief") also seems to be at odds with its context, which has to do with the universal era of peace, joy, and holiness inaugurated by this end-time priest-king. Indeed, except for the reference to Beliar and evil spirits in v. 12, this is the only negative note struck in the whole chapter. It is possible, then, that this negative statement can also be bracketed out as a Christian interpolation. Admittedly, the eschatological passage that would remain once this excision is effected is characterized by a certain generality and lack of Jewish particularity. Explicit references to Israel are surprisingly absent (the reference to Abraham, Isaac, and Jacob in v. 14 comes closest), and, despite the expectations generated by the description in earlier chapters of the temple's desecration (14:5, 8; 15:1; 16:1, 4) and reconstruction (17:10), there is no description in chapter 18 of any restored end-time temple over which this priest-king might officiate. Thus one has to be open to the possibility that chapter 18—its vision of universal salvation included—is the product of a more thoroughgoing Christian reworking.

Still, there are reasons to believe that the eschatological vision in chapter 18 is primarily Jewish rather than Christian. The idea of an eschatological priest is rooted in Jewish tradition, including the related Levi material from Qumran (see esp. J. J. Collins 1995, 74–101). Further, once vv. 6–7 and 9b are bracketed out, nothing in the remainder of chapter 18 would be out of place in a Jewish context. In addition, what remains is integrally connected to what precedes. This is true of the vision of a restored priesthood, which is suggested at the outset of the work ("You shall be his priest and . . . shall announce the one who is about to redeem Israel" [2:10]) and is required by the sin-exile-restoration theme as it is developed in *T. Levi* 14–17. It is true also of the universalism of chapter 18. Not only are earlier chapters of the work concerned with the wider Gentile world in its sinfulness,[102] but the Torah is also seen to be universal and intended for the enlightenment of all ("the light of the Law which was granted to you for the enlightenment of every man [παντὸς ἀνθρώπου]").[103] Thus, on the basis of chapters 1–17, one expects to find a description of eschatological consummation such as is found in chapter 18.

Levi's vision of the future, then, is one in which Gentiles are included. When Israel's priesthood is restored and purified in the figure of the "new priest" (v. 2), the benefits will spill out into the whole world. The "star" that "shall rise in heaven like a king" (v. 3) will "be extolled by the whole inhabited world [τῇ οἰκουμένῃ]" (v. 3), will "take away all darkness from under heaven,"

102. "I observed all human beings (πάντας ἀνθρώπους) making their way in life deceitfully. . . . I kept grieving over the race of the sons of men (2:3–4); "But the sons of men, being insensitive to these matters, keep sinning and provoking the anger of the Most High. Know, then, that the Lord will effect judgment on the sons of men." (3:10–4:1).

103. *T. Levi* 14:4; in *T. Levi* 13, the Torah is equated with Wisdom.

and will bring peace to "all the earth [πάσῃ τῇ γῇ]" (v. 4). The task of this priest is to kindle "the light of knowledge" (v. 3), and it is clear that both knowledge and enlightenment will be universal. "The knowledge of the Lord will be poured out on the earth (ἐπὶ τῆς γῆς) like the water of the seas," Levi announced in v. 5. During his priestly rule, "the nations [τὰ ἔθνη] shall be multiplied in knowledge on the earth, and they shall be illumined by the grace of the Lord" (v. 9). For the *Testament of Levi*, then, the time when God "will again have regard for you [Israel] and will take you back in compassion" (16:5) is a time that will benefit the Gentiles as well. They, too, will share the blessings of the end-time realm of light and knowledge.

But what of their relationship to Israel and the Torah? In the context of the work as a whole, it is probable that we are to see these end-time Gentiles as law observers of some kind. The theme is only touched on in chapter 18; the future era will be one in which "lawless men (οἱ ἄνομοι) shall rest from their evil deeds" (v. 9). But as we have seen, an earlier passage (*T. Levi* 14:4) explicitly identifies the law as having been given "for the enlightenment of every man." Thus it is reasonable to expect that if "the nations" are "illumined" in the end time (18:9), it is because the law has come to fulfil its enlightening purpose among them.

When we ask what this might mean, however, we encounter something that will be true of the *Testaments* as a whole. While *T. Levi* stresses the law as the way of life for the people of God ("Choose for yourselves light or darkness, the Law of the Lord or the works of Beliar" [19:1]), there is very little stress on those aspects of the law that differentiate Jew from Gentile.[104] Sin has to do with deceit (2:3), injustice (2:3), sexual immorality (9:9; 14:6), and plunder (14:5); sinners are those who are "idolaters, adulterers, money lovers, arrogant, lawless, voluptuaries, pederasts, and those who practice bestiality" (17:11). Except for laws concerning the proper functioning of the temple (chs. 8–9, 14),[105] the law is associated with such general virtues as piety (14:4; 16:2), righteousness (18:9), good deeds (13:6, 9), and, above all, wisdom (ch. 13). The only reference to circumcision—the story of Dinah and the men of Shechem (ch. 6)—is tangential to its covenantal role. While Levi is unique among the *Testaments* in its concern for "the law of the priesthood" (9:7), even here there is no evident concern that the temple serves as a place where the Gentiles might worship God. In short, while the *Testament of Levi* expects the Gentiles to walk in the light of the law in the end time, this seems to mean little more than that they abandon idolatry and live virtuous lives.

§51 Testament of Judah *24:4–6*

> *This is the Shoot of God Most High; this is the fountain of life for all humanity.* [5] *Then he will illumine the sceptre of my kingdom,* [6] *and from your root will arise the Shoot,*

104. This has been observed by Kee (1983b 779–80) and J. J. Collins (2000, 174–83).
105. On which see Slingerland (1986).

and through it will arise the rod of righteousness for the nations, to judge and to save all that call on the Lord.

§52 Testament of Judah *25:5*

And the deer of Jacob shall run with gladness; the eagles of [Israel][106] *shall fly with joy; the impious shall mourn and sinners shall weep, but all peoples shall glorify the Lord forever.*

Category: ESCHATOLOGICAL PARTICIPATION

These two passages form part of the eschatological section with which the *Testament of Judah* concludes. It follows a section (chs. 18–23, esp. 23) in which Judah recounts what he has learned from "the books of Enoch the Righteous" about "the evil things" his descendants will do "in the last days" (18:1). This sinfulness will precipitate divine punishment (23:3–4), which will last until Israel repents and "turns to the Lord in integrity of heart" (23:5). At this point, "the Lord . . . will free you from captivity under your enemies" (23:5), and "there shall arise for you a Star from Jacob in peace" (24:1).

As was observed above, while *T. Jud.* 24:1–3 contains clear Christian allusions, there are good reasons to see vv. 4–6 as the "Jewish core" (J. J. Collins 1995, 92) of the chapter. The passage develops the theme of the "branch" or the "shoot" of the house of David (Isa 11:1; also Jer 23:5; 33:15; cf. Zech 3:8; 6:12; CD I, 7). Since the text in Isaiah goes on to describe a situation where the earth is "full of the knowledge of the Lord" (v. 9) and where "the nations shall inquire" of the root of Jesse (v. 10), it is not surprising to see a universalistic theme in the *Testament of Judah* as well. The "Shoot" will be both "the fountain for the life of all humanity [πάσης σαρκός]" (24:4) and the one who wields "the rod of righteousness for the nations [τοῖς ἔθνεσι], to judge and to save all [πάντας] that call on the Lord" (24:6). Israel's restoration, then, has as one of its consequences the salvation of the Gentiles, at least as many of them as "call on the Lord."

Chapter 25 goes on to describe the resurrection of the patriarchs (vv. 1–2) and of the righteous dead (v. 4). Verse 5 brings the section to a conclusion by restating, in poetic fashion, the content of 23:5–24:6: the restoration of Israel ("the eagles of Israel shall fly with joy") will be accompanied by the blessing of the nations ("all peoples (πάντες οἱ λαοί)[107] shall glorify the Lord forever").

These passages do not provide us with any clear indication of what is required of these Gentiles who are to be "saved," other than that they "call on

106. Kee follows the reading "Jacob," found in only one MS (*g*); Ἰσραήλ is to be preferred (see de Jonge 1978, 78; Charles 1908, 104).

107. Charles translates this as a singular form ("all the people," 1913c, 2.324), which could be then read as a reference to Israel. But the Greek text—including his own edition—is plural.

the Lord" (24:6). While this certainly implies that they are to abandon their idolatry, there is no indication of their relationship to Israel's law. Even if it be assumed that they are expected to embrace the law, the "law" that Judah enjoins on his sons (26:1) seems to be a matter of avoiding such moral transgressions as idolatry, drunkenness, sexual promiscuity, and the love of money (11:2; 12:3; 13:2, 6; 16; 17; 19:1). Judah's autobiographical survey concentrates on his failings in these areas (except for idolatry, which is presented in more hypothetical terms); he declares these things (sexual promiscuity and the love of money in particular) to be the things that "distance you from the law of God" (18:3). For the most part, the law as Judah presents it is a universal moral code. While the implication might be that this law is binding on Gentiles as well, this is not clearly stated and, in any case, would not mean any Gentiles who accepted it would thereby become Jews. The one particularistic note in the *Testament of Judah* is the "evil" (11:1) of exogamy. What implication this might have for relations with Gentiles in the end times who have "called on the Lord" is not spelled out. But it is clear that the nations continue to exist as nations, rather than being incorporated into Israel.[108] There is no indication that they become full law observers, especially with respect to those aspects of the law that are peculiar to Israel.

§53 Testament of Zebulon *9:8*

> *And thereafter the Lord himself will arise upon you, the light of righteousness with healing and compassion in his wings. He will liberate every captive of the sons of men from Beliar, and every spirit of error will be trampled down. He will turn all nations to being zealous for him.*

Category: ESCHATOLOGICAL PARTICIPATION

The eschatological section of the *Testament of Zebulon* is relatively brief, occupying just a portion of chapter 9. Zebulon passes on to his sons what he has learned "in the writing of the fathers" (v. 5)—that Israel will allow themselves to be divided by following after two kings. This will lead to abomination and idolatry (v. 5), which in turn will lead to divine punishment in the form of exile (v. 6). But then Israel "will remember the Lord and repent" (v. 7), in response to which the Lord will redeem Israel, the redemption being described in v. 8 as cited above.

Before we look at the place of the Gentiles in this scenario, it needs to be noted that Christian influence is present in the remainder of the chapter (vv. 8b–9). Specifically, the phrase "God in a human form" (v. 8) is clearly a Christian

108. *T. Jud.* 25:3—"you shall be one people of the Lord, with one language"—seems to speak of Israel; Gentiles come into the picture only in v. 5 ("all peoples"), and here the plural stands in contrast with v. 3.

interpolation; likewise, the anti-Israel statement in v. 9—"you will provoke him to wrath by the wickedness of our works, and you will be rejected until the time of the end"—stands in jarring contrast to the scene of redemption in v. 8 and is thus to be seen as a Christian addition. This raises the possibility that the universalistic statement in v. 8—"He will turn all nations to being zealous for him"—is also a Christian interpolation, the first part of a pro-Gentile, anti-Israel pair.

Since similar pairings are found elsewhere in the Christian redaction of the *Testaments* as a whole, such a possibility cannot be ruled out. Nevertheless, this is not the only universalistic element in v. 8. Zebulon expects that the Lord will liberate from the power of Beliar "every captive of the sons of men [υἱῶν ἀνθρώπων]," a phrase that cannot be suspected of Christian influence. The context requires some description of the Lord's action once he has "arisen," and the description that does appear displays a nicely balanced parallelism that must have been original. If the first universalistic statement ("sons of men") is original, there is no reason to doubt the second.

Zebulon expects, then, that God's compassionate redemption of Israel will be accompanied by a liberation of "all nations" (πάντα τὰ ἔθνη) as well. These Gentiles will exhibit "zeal" for God, but we are given no further indication as to the nature of their zeal. Of course, it is to be taken for granted that zeal for God means abandonment of idolatry. But, as was the case with the *Testament of Judah*, even if we were to assume that the Gentiles are expected to embrace the law, Zebulon's view of the law tends in the direction of a universally applicable morality rather than of any Jewish distinctives. Zebulon's ethical injunctions have to do with the importance of showing compassion (chs. 5–8), a lesson that he learned from his brothers' contrary treatment of Joseph (ch. 4). When he instructs his children "to keep the Lord's commands" (5:1), what he means is that they should "show mercy to [their] neighbour, have compassion on all" (5:1). So even if the Gentiles are expected to become law-observers—and there is no explicit indication of this—the "law" in view would be a universal moral code rather than anything the observance of which would turn Gentiles into Jews. The Gentiles are present in the end-time scenario of 9:8 as Gentiles.

§54 Testament of Naphtali *8:1–4*

> *Behold, my children, I have shown you the last times, all things that will happen in Israel. [2]Command your children that they be in unity with Levi and Judah, for through Judah will salvation arise for Israel, and in him will Jacob be blessed. [3]Through his kingly power God will appear [dwelling among men on the earth], to save the race of Israel, and to assemble the righteous from among the nations. [4]If you achieve the good, my children, men and angels will bless you; and God will be glorified through you among the gentiles.*

Category: ESCHATOLOGICAL PARTICIPATION

The eschatological section in the *Testament of Naphtali* is less coherent and self-contained than in other testaments. The section begins with a typical reference to "the writing of holy Enoch" (4:1). What follows is also typical—a brief account of Israel's sin (v. 1), the punishment of the exile (v. 2), and Israel's repentance and restoration (v. 3). The return to the land, however, is presented in negative fashion; again they act impiously (v. 4), and again they are dispersed, until a second restoration is effected by "a man who effects righteousness" (v. 5). Verses 3–4 strike a jarring note and are probably to be seen as the result of Christian reworking. The eschatological theme is continued in a different form in chapters 5–7, as Naphtali recounts two dreams that he had and subsequently related to his father Jacob. Chapter 8, in which our passage of interest is found, contains a set of final exhortations that Naphtali addresses to his children.

Once again, we need to reckon with Christian interference. Verse 3 contains a clause with an incarnational ring to it—"dwelling among men on the earth"; it is clearly a Christian addition. The second half of v. 4 also seems to be Christian, with its unmistakable allusion to the account of Jesus's temptation (Mark 1:12–13). This part of the verse, however, is intrusive, as v. 5 clearly is meant to follow v. 4a. In v. 4a Naphtali declares that if Israel behaves well, the nations will glorify God; verse v. 5 amplifies this with an analogy: "Just as anyone who rears a child well is held in good esteem." Thus it is possible to see v. 4b (with its parallel in v. 6b) as a Christian interpolation.

The passage as it appears without these interpolations contains two references to the Gentiles. In v. 3, Naphtali asserts that, through the royal line of Judah, God will come "to save the race of Israel, and to assemble the righteous from among the nations (ἐκ τῶν ἐθνῶν)." It needs to be noted that the reference to the nations is not as tightly integrated into the syntax of the verse as Kee's rendering suggests; a more accurate translation would be, "Through his kingly power God will appear to save the race of Israel; and he will gather the righteous from among the nations." The statement about the nations is a separate principal clause, which might create a suspicion that this is a Christian interpolation. Still, the second reference to the Gentiles, which appears in the following verse, is certainly part of the Jewish original, and this provides some justification for retaining this statement as well. But who is being "gathered"—Gentiles, or Diaspora Jews? Either sort of eschatological pilgrimage would fit the context. Moreover, taken by itself, the final clause in v. 4 could be understood as a statement that God will "gather the righteous ones [of Israel] from [their dispersion among] the nations." But the preceding clause speaks of God saving, not those resident in Judea, but "the *race* [τὸ γένος] of Israel," that is, Israel as a whole. It seems more likely that v. 3b refers to an eschatological pilgrimage of Gentiles, who will be assembled by God to share in Israel's salvation.[109]

The second reference to Gentiles appears in the next verse—the statement previously referred to above in which Naphtali declares that if Israel achieves

109. See Gaston (1987, 24).

"the good, . . . God will be glorified through you among the nations [ἐν τοῖς ἔθνεσι]." While the statement is general, the eschatological context created by the preceding verse tends to put this statement into an end-time framework as well: the "good" performed by the "race of Israel" under its royal savior will prompt the nations to glorify God.

What of the status of these end-time pilgrims? The picture is similar to what has been observed already, though in the *Testament of Naphtali* the idea of a natural law is a little more pronounced. A reference to his physical prowess (2:1) leads Naphtali into a consideration of how God has apportioned and appointed the various parts of the human body (2:2–10); this, in turn, leads him to identify various forms of Gentile sinfulness—specifically, idolatry and homosexual behavior—as deviations "from the order of nature" (3:4) and thus as a departure from "the Law of God" (3:2). The implication seems to be that those Gentiles who in the end time come to "glorify" God will do so by turning to the law of God. But the nature of this law as Naphtali has described it provides no reason to believe that these Gentiles are to be incorporated into "the race of Israel."

§55 Testament of Joseph *4:4–6*

> *When she achieved nothing by means of it, she began to approach me for instruction, so that she might learn the Word of God.* [5]*And she kept saying to me, "If you want me to abandon the idols, have intercourse with me, and I shall persuade my husband to put away the idols, and we shall live in the [law] of your Lord."* [6]*But I kept telling her that the Lord did not want worshipers who came by means of uncleanness, nor would he be pleased with adulterers, but with those who were pure in heart and undefiled in speech.*

Category: SYMPATHIZATION, ETHICAL MONOTHEISM

Joseph occupies an important place in the *Testaments* in that many of them deal centrally with the role of the respective patriarchs in selling Joseph into slavery.[110] Somewhat surprisingly, then, the autobiographical focus in the *Testament of Joseph* is his self-control in face of the repeated attempts of Pentephris's wife to seduce him. While Joseph's refusal to dishonor his brothers by telling the truth about his circumstances is present as a secondary theme—again with an emphasis on Joseph's self-control (10:3–6; 15:3; 17:1)—the relationship with "the Egyptian woman of Memphis" (3:6) takes up a major portion of the work.

In this version of the story, the woman was besotted with Joseph from the outset; indeed, it was because of her illicit desire for him that she persuaded her husband to buy him in the first place (16:1). To have her way with Joseph, she

110. *Testaments of Simeon, Zebulon, Dan, Naphtali, Gad* and *Benjamin*. There is also a reference in *T. Reu.* (4:8–10), but here with reference to Joseph's sexual purity rather than to Reuben's role in his being sold into slavery.

employed various tactics: threats (3:1), promises of promotion (3:2), pretense (3:7–9), flattery (4:1–2), gifts (5:4), "food mixed with enchantments" (6:1), and even threats of suicide (7:3). One of her ploys was the promise to abandon idols and to live according to the law, as recounted in the passage quoted above.

If in 4:5 "law" is to be preferred on text-critical grounds,[111] then on the face of it the woman is promising that both she and her husband would become proselytes if Joseph would have sexual intercourse with her.[112] (One wonders what would have been in it for the husband!) But as with the other *Testaments*, the tendency in the *Testament of Joseph* is to see the law more as a set of universal moral virtues in accordance with "the order of nature" (*T. Naph.* 3:4) than a set of particularistic commandments that set Jews apart from Gentiles. As we have seen, Joseph's behavior is presented as a model of self-control—more of a Stoic virtue than a Jewish one. When he is exhorting his children to follow his example, law observance ("everyone who does the Law of the Lord" [11:1]) is presented as a matter of "self-control and purity with patience and prayer with fasting in humility of heart" (10:2). He refuses to eat the food she sends him not because of any dietary considerations but because he perceives that it has been mixed with "enchantments" (6:1). Likewise, the problem with the proposed sexual relationship itself is not that she is Gentile but that she is married (4:6; 5:1–3); adultery, not exogamy, is the problem. Her offer to follow the law seems to consist only in the abandonment of idols (4:6; 6:5), which for Joseph would qualify her as a worshiper (σεβομένους) of God (4:6). One observes a sharp contrast with respect to the things that separate Joseph from his would-be paramours in this work and in *Joseph and Aseneth*.

Thus while "the Egyptian woman from Memphis" offers to become a law observer, the proposed course of action would not have turned her into a proselyte. A pattern of life based on this law would have involved the abandonment of idolatry and—at least from the perspective of the author—the abandonment of attempts to seduce young men with promises of conversion! It would not have involved incorporation into the people of Israel.

Psalms of Solomon

§56 Psalms of Solomon *17:29–32, 34b–35*

He will judge peoples and nations in the wisdom of his righteousness. Pause. [30]*And he will have gentile nations serving him under his yoke, and he will glorify the Lord in (a*

111. Kee follows those MS (*c*, *h*, and *j*) that read ἐνώπιον κυρίου σου (in the presence of your Lord). The preferred text, however, is ἐν νόμῳ κυρίου σου; see de Jonge (1978, 148).

112. The statement attributed to her by Joseph in 6:5—"I do not go near the idols, but only to the Lord"—assumes that she led Joseph to believe that she had already abandoned idolatry.

place) prominent (above) the whole earth. And he will purge Jerusalem (and make it) holy as it was even from the beginning, [31]*(for) nations to come from the ends of the earth to see his glory, to bring as gifts her children who had been driven out, and to see the glory of the Lord with which God has glorified her.* [32]*And he will be a righteous king over them, taught by God. There will be no unrighteousness among them in his days, for all shall be holy, and their king shall be the Lord Messiah. . . . He shall be compassionate to all the nations (who) reverently (stand) before him.* [35]*He will strike the earth with the word of his mouth forever; he will bless the Lord's people with wisdom and happiness.*

Text: Greek: Rahlfs (1979)
Translation: *OTP* (Wright 1985)
Date: Mid-first century B.C.E.
Provenance: Judea
Original Language: Hebrew
Bibliography: J. J. Collins (1995, 49–56); Hann (1982; 1988); Holm-Nielsen (1977); Klausner (1955, 321); Kraus (1996, 50–52); Ryle and James (1891); E. P. Sanders (1977, 387–409); Schnabel (2004, 103); Schüpphaus (1977); Schürer (1986, 3:192–97); Trafton (1994); Viteau (1911); Winninge (1995); Wright (1985)
Category: ESCHATOLOGICAL PARTICIPATION

In contrast to much other pseudepigraphal literature, the *Psalms of Solomon* allow for relatively clear answers to the usual introductory questions (date, language, provenance, etc.). While the text is extant only in Greek and Syriac (the latter a translation from the Greek), there is clear evidence of a Hebrew original (Winninge 1995, 9–12). The psalms originated among "the assemblies of the devout" (17:16), a Jewish group whose piety is defined by its loyalty to the law and the temple cult on the one hand and, on the other, by its opposition to Jewish "sinners" who usurped the monarchy (17:6) and defiled the temple (1:8; 2:3–5; 8:8–13). Since these sinners were routed by a Gentile leader (8:14–22) who, after having defiled the temple himself (2:1–2), met his own death on the seashore in Egypt (2:26–27), one can readily identify the "sinners" as the Hasmonean dynasty and their supporters, and the Gentile conqueror as Pompey. Because of both their opposition to the Hasmoneans and their religious emphases—the law, the covenant (9:10; 10:4; 17:15), and resurrection (3:12; 13:11; 14:8–10; 15:10–13)—the *Psalms of Solomon* have traditionally been associated with the Pharisees (e.g., Gray 1913, 2:627–30). But these characteristics were by no means restricted to Pharisaic circles, nor do the *Psalms* exhibit any interest in oral tradition, either in general or in specific topics known from later sources (e.g., tithing). The interest in purity and cultic matters (1:8; 2:3; 8:11–13, 20–22; 17:45) has led others to suggest a link with Qumran (Dupont-Sommer 1959, 308, 347) or—since no trace of the *Psalms* has turned up at Qumran—to the wider Essene movement (e.g., Hann 1988). But opposition to the Hasmoneans has more to do with their usurpation of the monarchy (17:6) than of the high priesthood. Further, the unproblematical way in which the psalmist identifies with Israel as a whole (e.g., 7:8; 8:26, 34; 9:11; 10:5–8) does not suggest a narrowly sectarian viewpoint. Thus, while the *Psalms* should probably not be associated with the Pharisees in any strict or exclusive sense, the form of piety that they represent is characteristic of a "broad religious movement" (E. P. Sanders 1977, 388) in which the Pharisees would be included.

One of the most striking features of the *Psalms of Solomon* is the sharp contrast that is drawn between the righteous and the sinners, not only in individual verses but also in whole psalms (3, 13, 14). The company of sinners certainly includes the Gentiles, who are sinners (e.g., 2:1–2, 16; 17:22–25) almost by definition: they are "lawless" (παράνομα [17:24]), having been rejected by God (7:2). But the line between sinners and the righteous does not coincide exactly with that between Jew and Gentile. On the one hand, the *Psalms* save their fiercest denunciation of sinners for those found among the Jews themselves (4:8; 17:5–6), who in their desecration of throne and sanctuary—"their lawless actions"—have completely "surpassed the gentiles before them" (1:8; 8:13). On the other, in the previously cited passage, the author apparently is able to contemplate at least some space for Gentiles in the age of holiness and righteousness to be established by the "Lord Messiah."[113]

The first half of *Ps. Sol.* 17 surveys Israel's history: the election of David and his descendants (v. 4); Israel's sin (v. 5a), which made possible the emergence of the Hasmonean monarchy (vv. 5b–6); and divine punishment of this arrogant monarchy through the agency of "a man alien to our race" (v. 7), who not only routed the Israelite sinners (vv. 7–10) but also, in his own arrogance, defiled Jerusalem and persecuted the righteous (vv. 11–20). At this point the psalmist turns in petition to God, asking that God will "raise up for them their king, the son of David, to rule over your servant Israel" (v. 21). What follows is a lengthy description of the actions and character of the Messiah and of the righteous kingdom that he sets in place. The description draws heavily on Davidic scriptures, especially Psalm 2 and Isa 11:1–4 (see J. J. Collins 1995, 54).

As Winninge has observed (1995, 98), there is a real ambiguity in the statements concerning the relationship of the Gentiles to the Messiah and his program of end-time restoration. At the outset of the prayer their situation is described in completely negative terms. The coming king will "purge Jerusalem from gentiles" (v. 22), who "will flee from his presence" (v. 25); he will "destroy the unlawful nations with an iron rod" (v. 24). In view of statements elsewhere

113. χριστὸς κύριος. Many interpreters have taken this as a mistranslation of an original Hebrew construct form and thus have emended it to χριστὸς κυρίου (the Anointed/Messiah of the Lord), but there is no pressing reason why the text should not be accepted as it stands (see Hann 1985).

about the ultimate destruction of the wicked,[114] one might expect this destruction to be final and complete. A few verses later, however, we read that as righteous Israelites are gathered and restored in the land (vv. 26–28), "the alien and the foreigner [πάροικος καὶ ἀλλογενὴς] will no longer live near them" (v. 28). While foreigners might be expelled from the land of Israel, it appears that they are expected to continue living somewhere else. This is confirmed two verses later, where we read that the messianic king "will have gentile nations [λαοὺς ἐθνῶν] serving him under his yoke" (v. 30).

At this point in the prayer, then, Gentile prospects have brightened somewhat, the nature of their end-time circumstances having shifted from sheer destruction to survival and subservience. In v. 31 another shift is apparent in that, despite having been excluded from Jerusalem, Gentiles (ἔθνη) are described as coming "from the ends of the earth to see his [presumably, the king's] glory." Their journey is the result—or perhaps even the purpose[115]—of Jerusalem's restoration. The purpose of their journey, in turn, is that "they might bring as gifts her children who had been driven out." This does not necessarily involve anything more than subservience; one way in which the Gentile nations serve under the yoke of the messianic king (cf. v. 30) is to bring the scattered exiles back to the land.[116] Still, several features of the passage seem to move beyond mere subservience and to suggest that these Gentiles are on an end-time pilgrimage to Zion.[117] The description of the exiles as "gifts" (δῶρα) brought by the Gentiles to Jerusalem seems to echo the language of Isa 66:20 (cf. Isa 60:9). Further, the Gentiles come "from the ends of the earth" not simply to bring the exiles but also to see the "glory"—the glory of the messiah (τὴν δόξαν αὐτοῦ), but also "the glory of the Lord with which God has glorified her [αὐτήν]," presumably Jerusalem. Of course, this does not necessarily imply that they are worshiping the God of glory or even that they benefit from this demonstration of glory in any particular way. Still, the fact that this language contains further echoes of the eschatological pilgrimage tradition in Isaiah—coming to see God's glory (Isa 42:12; 66:18) and the ends of the earth (Isa 42:10–12; 45:22; 48:20; 49:6; 52:10)—might suggest that similar expectations are at work here.[118]

Such an interpretation would be confirmed if we could follow Viteau (1911, 361) in seeing v. 32 as referring to the Gentiles. His argument is that the pronouns in v. 32 should most naturally be taken as referring back to the

114. E.g., 14:9: "Therefore their inheritance is Hades, and darkness and destruction; and they will not be found on the day of mercy for the righteous."

115. The pilgrimage of the nations is expressed by means of an infinitive (ἔρχεσθαι).

116. In *Ps. Sol.* 11, the return of the exiles is accomplished by God directly.

117. Some authors see only subservience in *Ps. Sol.* 17; e.g., Davies (1948, 62); Holm-Nielsen (1977, 104); Kraus (1996, 50–52); Russell (1964, 300–01); Schnabel (2004, 103).

118. See Klausner (1955, 321); Viteau (1911, 357–61); cf. Volz (1934, 358).

collective that precedes, that is, the Gentiles who come "to see the glory of the Lord." If so, then, "there will be no unrighteousness among" the Gentiles in the days of the king, "for all shall be holy." While this reading is possible, however, it is probably not to be accepted. Elsewhere in the psalm, the phrase "their king" is used with reference to Israel (v. 21; cf. v. 46). It seems more likely that the statement "their king shall be the Lord Messiah" refers to Israel as well, especially since the antecedent of the pronouns could just as legitimately be "the children" of v. 31.[119]

There is an additional reference to the Gentiles, however, which may serve to confirm a more positive reading of the passage. Verse 34 declares that the messianic king "shall be compassionate to all the nations (who) reverently (stand) before him." Taken at face value, the verse seems to provide evidence that these end-time pilgrims will be the recipients of messianic mercy. There is a problem with the face-value reading, however; verse 35 goes on to say: "for[120] he will strike the earth with the word of his mouth forever." Some commentators find it impossible that the smiting of the earth could somehow be the cause of or occasion for the king's compassion and thus believe that ἐλεήσει is the result of some corruption (e.g., Gray 1913, 2:650; Holm-Nielsen 1977, 104). Admittedly, elsewhere in the psalm the "word of his mouth" has negative connotations for the Gentiles, as it is the means of their destruction (v. 24). Also, as Wright's translation indicates, the Greek is awkward as it stands: literally, "and he shall have compassion on all the nations before him in fear" (καὶ ἐλεήσει πάντα τὰ ἔθνη ἐνώπιον αὐτοῦ ἐν φόβῳ). Still, the manuscript evidence unanimously supports ἐλεήσει. Further, elsewhere in the *Psalms of Solomon* fear (of the Lord) is a characteristic of the devout.[121] In addition, the language echoes Isa 11:4, where a statement concerning judgment (v. 4b) is likewise sandwiched between promises of blessings (vv. 4a, 5) and where the larger context also contains hope for the nations (vv. 9–10). While the connection between vv. 34 and 35 remains puzzling,[122] there seems to be no pressing reason to discount the reference to mercy in v. 34, especially in view of the evident allusions to eschatological pilgrimage material in v. 31.

Thus *Ps. Sol.* 17 can be counted among those texts that anticipate end-time blessings for the Gentiles. Prompted by the glorification of Jerusalem, the Gentiles gather "from the ends of the earth" to escort the returning exiles, to witness God's glory, and to experience divine mercy. They are present in Jerusalem just as visitors; the land is reserved for Israel (v. 28). There is no suggestion that

119. See Holm-Nielsen (1977, 104).

120. Wright ignores γάρ, but there are no grounds for doing so.

121. *Ps. Sol.* 2:33; 4:12; 4:21, 23; 5:18; 6:5; 8:5; 12:4; 13:12; 15:13; 17:40; 18:7–9.

122. Winninge (1995, 95) suggests a change in subject, v. 34b referring to God and v. 35 to the king: "Thus the nations, brought to reverence for God by the judgement of the Messiah, will receive mercy from the Lord himself."

they become incorporated into Israel. To the extent that they benefit from the end-time rule of the messianic king, they do so as Gentiles.

Joseph and Aseneth

Since *Joseph and Aseneth* recounts the story of a conversion—indeed, it is the longest and most elaborate conversion story to be found in the Jewish literature of the period[123]—the whole story is pertinent. It would be impractical, however, to reproduce the whole story here.[124] Two passages, representing key moments in Aseneth's conversion, will lead us into the writing as a whole. The first is a portion of her prayer of repentance (12:3–5); the second is the announcement of her acceptance before God, conveyed to her by her heavenly visitor (15:2–7).

§57 Joseph and Aseneth *12:3–5*

> *With you I take refuge, Lord, and to you I will shout, Lord, to you I will pour out my supplication, to you I will confess my sins, and to you I will reveal my lawless deeds.* [4]*Spare me, Lord, because I have sinned much before you, I have committed lawlessness and irreverence, and have said wicked and unspeakable (things) before you.* [5]*My mouth is defiled from the sacrifices of the idols and from the tables of the gods of the Egyptians.*

§58 Joseph and Aseneth *15:2–7*

> *And the man said to her, "Courage, Aseneth, chaste virgin. Behold, I have heard all the words of your confession and your prayer.* [3]*Behold, I have also seen the humiliation and the affliction of the seven days of your want (of food). Behold, from your tears and these ashes, plenty of mud has formed before your face.* [4]*Courage, Aseneth, chaste virgin. For behold, your name was written in the book of the living in heaven; in the beginning of the book, as the very first of all, your name was written by my finger, and it will not be erased forever.* [5]*Behold, from today, you will be renewed and formed anew and made alive again, and you will eat blessed bread of life, and drink a blessed cup of immortality, and anoint yourself with blessed ointment of incorruptibility.* [6]*Courage, Aseneth, chaste virgin. Behold, I have given you today to Joseph for a bride, and he himself will be your bridegroom for ever and ever.* [7]*And your name shall no longer be called Aseneth, but your name shall be City of Refuge, because in you many nations will take refuge with the Lord God, the Most High, and under your wings many peoples trusting in the Lord God will be sheltered, and behind your walls will be guarded those who attach themselves to the Most High God in the name of repentance.*

123. The only other extended story is Josephus's account of Izates' conversion (*Ant.* 20.17–53).

124. The Greek MSS fall into four families (*a*, *b*, *c*, and *d*). Family *d* is much shorter than the other three. Philonenko's text is based on the shorter version (Philonenko 1968), Burchard's (1996) on the longer (an eclectic text based primarily on *b*). While there is more text-critical work to be done, most contemporary scholars have found Burchard's position to be more persuasive. His text and translation will be used in what follows.

Text: Burchard (1996, 161–209); Philonenko (1968)
Translation: *OTP* (Burchard 1985)
Date: Between 100 B.C.E. and 115 C.E.
Provenance: Egypt
Original Language: Greek
Bibliography: Barclay (1996, 204–16); Bohak (1996); Burchard (1965; 1985; 1996); Chesnutt (1995); J. J. Collins (2000, 103–10, 230–39); Goldenberg (1998, 75–78); Gruen (1998, 89–99); Humphrey (1995; 2000); Kee (1983a); Kraemer (1998); Kraus (1996, 82–84); Pervo (1991); Philonenko (1968); Schürer (1986, 3:54652); Segal (1990, 91–92); Wills (1995, 170–84)
Category: CONVERSION, ETHICAL MONOTHEISM, SYMPATHIZATION

The point of departure for this tale of piety and romance is the statement in the biblical story of Joseph that Pharaoh "gave him Asenath [LXX: Ἀσεννεθ] daughter of Potiphera [LXX: Πετεφρη], priest of On [LXX: Heliopolis], as his wife" (Gen 41:45; cf. 41:50–52; 46:20). While the biblical narrator relates this detail without comment, later readers evidently were troubled by the idea that a patriarch of Israel would be linked in marriage to the daughter of an Egyptian priest. But *Joseph and Aseneth* is more than simply the smoothing out of a troubling biblical wrinkle. By spinning an elaborate story that turns on the social consequences both of avoiding idolatry (on Joseph's part) and of turning to "the God of the Hebrews" (on Aseneth's part [11:10]), the author has made it clear that the story addresses social concerns in the world of its readers.

The story begins "in the first year of the seven years of plenty" (1:1), when Joseph had already been elevated by Pharaoh and put in charge of the Egyptian grain supply. The abruptness of this beginning indicates that the readers of the story were expected to have a thorough familiarity with the biblical account. After a brief introduction of Joseph and of Pentephres, priest of Heliopolis and "chief of all the satraps and the noblemen of Pharaoh" (1:3), the attention of the narrator turns to Aseneth, the daughter of Pentephres, where it remains for most of the story to follow. Renowned for her beauty, Aseneth is sought after by all the young noblemen of the land, even the son of Pharaoh himself. None of them has even so much as seen her, however, since she lives in seclusion behind the protective walls of a tower built by her father to protect her virginity. Shielded from male gaze, Aseneth has grown disdainful of all men, her would-be suitors included. Instead, her devotion is reserved for the gods of the Egyptians, whose images and names adorn her walls and her jewelry.

Into this situation of brittle equilibrium comes Joseph, whose project of gathering surplus grain brings him to Heliopolis and the house of Pentephres. Pentephres is overjoyed "that my Lord Joseph thought me worthy to come to us" (3:3), and immediately makes plans to offer Aseneth to him as his bride. She, predictably, rejects the proposed marriage, countering her father's encomium on Joseph's virtues (4:7) with her own jaundiced account of his rise to power (4:9–10). When she catches sight of him from her tower window, however, she has a dramatic change of heart. Instead of the opportunistic poseur she had described to her father ("the shepherd's son from the land of Canaan" [6:2]), what she saw from her window was "the sun from heaven" (6:2), even a "son of God" (6:3), a luminous figure of such beauty that she is now willing for her father to give her to Joseph not so much as a wife but "as a maidservant and slave" (6:8). Now, however, it is her turn to be rejected. When Joseph had arrived at the house he had been seated at a separate table, since it "was an abomination to him" to eat with idolaters (7:1). When Aseneth is presented to Joseph for a sisterly kiss, he continues to insist on social separation, rebuffing her with the words:

> It is not fitting for a man who worships God [ἀνδρὶ θεοσεβεῖ], who will bless with his mouth the living God and eat blessed bread of life and drink a blessed cup of immortality and anoint himself with blessed ointment of incorruptibility to kiss a strange [lit. "foreign"; ἀλλοτρίαν] woman who will bless with her mouth dead and dumb idols and eat from their table bread of strangulation and drink from their libation a cup of insidiousness and anoint herself with ointment of destruction." (8:5)

Seeing her distress, however, Joseph blesses her (apparently it is "fitting" for him to put his hand on her head!), asking that God would "renew her by your spirit . . . and let her eat your bread of life, and drink your cup of blessing, and number her among your people" (8:9).

With this blessing ringing in her ears, Aseneth retreats to her room in distress and confusion. She puts on garments of mourning, destroys her idols, covers herself in ashes, and spends seven days lamenting her idolatry and foolishness (10:1–17). On the eighth day—the day when Joseph had promised to return—she finally gathers sufficient courage to open her idol-defiled mouth and to cry to Joseph's God for deliverance (11–13). Her prayer is answered in the form of a man from heaven, whose appearance was "in every respect similar to Joseph" (14:9), except for his heavenly radiance. He announces to her (in the words previously cited) that her prayer has been heard and that her name has been written in the heavenly book of life. She invites him to stay for some bread and wine (15:14–15), whereupon he miraculously produces a honeycomb, produced by the "bees of paradise" as food for "all the angels of God . . . and all the chosen of God and all the sons of the Most High" (16:14). When she has eaten a portion of the honeycomb, he declares to her that she has now "eaten bread of life and drunk a cup of immortality, and been anointed with ointment of incorruptibility" (16:16).

Nothing now stands in the way of marriage. Joseph returns, the long-delayed kiss finally takes place (three times, for good measure [19:11]), and the marriage is performed by Pharaoh himself (21:2–8). They live happily ever after, but not before having to foil a plot hatched by Pharaoh's son—aided, surprisingly, by several of Joseph's brothers—to kill Joseph and to take Aseneth for himself (23–29).

Joseph and Aseneth is thus a strange mixture; mundane and generic Jewish concerns (idolatry, intermarriage) appear side by side with exotic and mystical details of plot and characterization (the exalted status of Joseph,[125] the mysterious honeycomb, "the ineffable mysteries of the Most High" that are revealed to Aseneth, and so on). Several of these details have a Christian ring to them, especially the description of Joseph as "son of God" and the emphasis on the "bread of life and cup of immortality." Indeed, Batiffol, the scholar who first brought the work to wider attention, saw it as a fifth-century Christian symbolic account of Christ (Joseph) and the church (Aseneth) (Batiffol 1889–1890). Such an interpretation, however, requires a level of allegorizing that is not supported by the text itself. Most contemporary scholars see *Joseph and Aseneth* as a Jewish work, originating probably in Egypt sometime between 100 B.C.E. (because of its allusions to the LXX, especially the prophetic material) and 115 C.E. (the start of the Jewish uprising in Egypt).[126]

For our purposes, the important question has to do with the nature of Aseneth's conversion. Here two tendencies can be identified in scholarly discussion. One approach centers on the climactic scene between Aseneth and her heavenly visitor, understanding it as reflecting an actual ritual of initiation. Since the elements of the putative ritual—bread, wine, oil—find no real counterpart in other accounts of proselyte initiation, interpreters tend to identify *Joseph and Aseneth* with some more particular segment within Judaism—for example, Therapeutae (Delcor 1962), Essenes (Beckwith 1984), Merkabah mysticism (Kee 1983a) or an otherwise unknown Jewish mystery cult (Philonenko 1968).

Such an approach, however, is open to question. For one thing, the story as a whole is replete with elaborate descriptions of material and accoutrements (e.g., the furnishings of Aseneth's room [2:1–12]) that lend the tale a sense of the exotic without seeming to carry any symbolic weight.[127] Further, Joseph speaks of the bread, the wine, and the oil as elements that are consumed and used by everyone who "worships God," himself included (8:5); in other words, they probably are to be seen as part of the ordinary life of piety, rather than as constitutive elements of an initiatory ritual.[128] Moreover, in her encounter with

125. Joseph is described as the "powerful one of God" (3:4; 4:7); a "son of God" (6:3, 5; 13:13); God's "firstborn son" (18:11; 21:4; 23:10); "the sun from heaven" (6:2), who has a "great light . . . inside him" (6:6). He has a heavenly counterpart, in that, except for his heavenly radiance, the angelic visitor is "a man in every respect similar to Joseph" (14:9).

126. For the history of scholarship, see Chesnutt (1995, 20–93) and Humphrey (2000, 17–79). Kraemer (1998) has reopened the issue of provenance, arguing for a non-Jewish and perhaps Christian origin and a date in at least the third century C.E.

127. Also her clothing and adornments (3:6); the fruit of the field (4:2).

128. See Chesnutt (1995, 130); J. J. Collins (2000, 233).

the man from heaven, Aseneth does not partake of bread or wine at all, nor is she anointed with oil. Instead, in the act of eating the honeycomb itself she is said to have eaten the bread, drunk the wine, and been anointed with the oil (16:16). This suggests that the purpose of the scene is to equate ordinary Jewish food with the food of immortality consumed by heavenly beings (16:14; J. J. Collins 2000, 235), rather than to describe a ritual about which nothing else is known and which must therefore be reconstructed from the text itself.

This leads to the other approach, in which the interpretive center of the work is found in the more everyday, pan-Jewish concerns about idolatry and intermarriage, and the exotic elements are seen as literary embroidery on a pattern that is concerned primarily with the preservation of Jewish identity in a Gentile world, social differentiation between Jew and Gentile, and the possibility of conversion.[129] While the mystical and apocalyptic elements are not to be overlooked,[130] it seems better to take the work as an idiosyncratic reflection on a type of experience that was characteristic of the Jewish Diaspora more generally, than as the product of a more narrowly circumscribed Jewish subgroup.

Looking at Aseneth's conversion from this perspective, one is struck by two, somewhat divergent, features of the narrative. On the one hand, the author is concerned to emphasize the ineradicable social barrier separating Jews from Gentiles. While there is some unevenness and inconsistency in the way in which this barrier functions in the narrative itself, there can be little doubt that Aseneth's conversion involves a separation from one social milieu, constituted by the worship of Egyptian gods, and a full incorporation into the "people" (8:9) who worship the "God of the Hebrews" (11:10). In other words, although the term itself does not appear, Aseneth is depicted as a proselyte, one who not only gives exclusive devotion to the God of Joseph but is also fully incorporated into the Jewish people.

Owing to the nature of the story, the barrier between Jew and Gentile has to do primarily with sexual relationships and marriage: it would be an "abomination" for one who worships God even to kiss, let alone marry, one who is devoted to "dead and dumb idols" (8:5–6). But the barrier itself is more generally constituted. It was equally an "abomination" for Joseph to eat with Egyptians (7:1);[131] when he came into the house of Pentephres he ate by himself (at a table that was considerately provided by his host, who seems to have accepted this stricture without demur). To be sure, such eating arrangements are not carried out consistently through the rest of the story. There is no indication that Joseph insisted on

129. This is essentially the approach of Burchard in his various writings on *Joseph and Aseneth*; it also characterizes Chesnutt's significant work on Aseneth's conversion (Chesnutt 1995).

130. A point emphasized rightly by Humphrey (2000, 40–44).

131. Readers familiar with the Genesis account would have recognized an inversion of Gen 43:32, where Joseph and his Egyptian companions would not eat with his brothers newly arrived from Canaan, "for that is an abomination to the Egyptians."

similar arrangements at the wedding banquet, even though it was given by Pharaoh (at Joseph's insistence!) and was attended by "all the chiefs of the land of Egypt and all the kings of the nations" (21:8). Perhaps the deference shown by both Pentephres and Pharaoh to the God of Jacob has put them in a different category as far as table fellowship is concerned (on which more later). More likely it is simply due to the constraints of the narrative; not only does the biblical account specify that it was Pharaoh who gave Asenath to Joseph as his wife (Gen 41:45), but also by this point in the story, with Aseneth safely on the other side of the barrier separating Jew from Gentile, there is no need to belabor the point. In any case, the narrative leaves no doubt about the fact that since Joseph's God "hates all those who worship idols," those who worship this God need to remain separate in significant ways from "those who worship strange gods" (11:7).

Another indication of the social barrier between these two groups of worshippers is found in the alienation from her own family and people that Aseneth experiences—or, at least, reports—as a result of her renunciation of idolatry. In her prayer of repentance she cries out:

> Rescue me, Lord, the desolate and solitary, because my father and my mother disowned me and said, "Aseneth is not our daughter," because I have destroyed and ground (to pieces) their gods, and have come to hate them. And I am now an orphan and desolate, and I have no other hope save in you, Lord, and I have no other refuge except your mercy, Lord, because you are a father of the orphans, and a protector of the persecuted and a helper of the afflicted. (12:12–13; also 11:4–5)

Again, however, we encounter a ragged seam in the narrative. This theme of Aseneth's rejection and social ostracism is found only in her prayer and not in the narrative itself.[132] Indeed, her family does not seem even to be aware of her week-long ordeal and its outcome. Just after she retires to her room, they head off to their estate (10:1), from which they return only after all is resolved (20:6). Far from disowning her, they are amazed at her transformation and overjoyed at the prospect of marriage (20:6–8). Nowhere do they even allude to the fact that she has abandoned the gods of the Egyptians, let alone hate her "because she has destroyed our gods" (11:5).

What are we to make of this? Burchard has suggested that Aseneth's parents are to be seen as converts as well. He points to the fact that they "gave glory to God" and joined with Aseneth (and presumably Joseph) in a meal of celebration (20:7–8).[133] But while this is not impossible, the argument is not persuasive. Since Pentephres has been introduced as "priest of Heliopolis" (1:3)—the problematic detail which, after all, occasioned the story in the first place—it is hardly to be expected that he would be presented as a convert without some explicit indication that he abandoned his priestly role in Egyptian idolatry. The positive

132. See Chesnutt (1995, 115).

133. Burchard (1985, 234); also Pervo (1991, 154).

depiction of Aseneth's parents seems to be the result of narrative necessity: their approval is necessary for the story to move forward. The disjunction between their role in the narrative and her depiction of them in her soliloquies is probably just an indication of the author's clumsiness as a storyteller. It seems clear that the prayers and soliloquies provide us with a surer indication of the author's viewpoint than do the details of the narrative itself.

But not only is Aseneth alienated from her own people—"an orphan and desolate and abandoned and hated" (11:3); in her conversion she is fully incorporated into the people of Israel. To be sure, some commentators have been struck by the individualistic nature of her experience:[134] the climax of her conversion comes while she is alone; there is no larger Jewish community in the story to which she is linked by her marriage to Joseph. These features of the story notwithstanding, the author has provided clear indication that precisely by means of her marriage to Joseph, Aseneth has been joined to the Jewish people. It is significant that at the beginning of the story, each characterizes the other as a "foreigner" (4:9: ἀνδρὶ ἀλλοφύλῳ; 8:5: γυναῖκα ἀλλοτρίαν). Then in his prayer for her, Joseph not only petitions God for her own personal renewal and rebirth but also asks that God might "number her among your people [τῷ λαῷ σου] that you have chosen before all (things) came into being, and let her enter your rest which you have prepared for your chosen ones" (8:9). Thus her renewal is not to be accomplished without incorporation into God's people. Further, this "people" is elsewhere clearly identified as the people of the "Hebrews." For one thing, the God to whom she turns for refuge is not only "the Lord God of Heaven," the "Mighty One of the powerful Joseph," but "the God of the Hebrews" (11:10). For another, Aseneth herself is not at all "similar to the virgins of the Egyptians, but she was in every respect similar to the daughters of the Hebrews, and she was as tall as Sarah and handsome as Rebecca and beautiful as Rachel" (1:5); in other words, her renunciation of idolatry just completes an assimilation to the Hebrew people that was already foreshadowed in her own physical appearance. This full assimilation is confirmed when she meets Jacob and is allowed to address him as her father (22:3–9).

In addition, it needs to be recognized that any individualism in the story is sharply qualified by the representative role played by Aseneth and, by extension, Joseph. Aseneth is not simply an isolated convert. Rather, she is a prototype and representative of a whole company of proselytes. In the passage cited above—a text replete with biblical language (proselytism, the cities of refuge in Mosaic legislation, the eschatological pilgrimage tradition)[135]—the heavenly emissary declares to her:

134. Burchard (1985, 193); cf. Barclay (1996, 212).

135. Proselytism: προσκείμαι; "under your wings." Cities of refuge: Num 35:10–15; Josh 20:1–9. Eschatological pilgrimage: esp. LXX Zech 2:15 (καὶ καταφεύξονται ἔθνη πολλὰ ἐπὶ τὸν κύριον ἐν τῇ ἡμέρᾳ ἐκείνῃ καὶ ἔσονται αὐτῷ εἰς λαόν); see also Philonenko (1968, 55).

> And your name shall no longer be called Aseneth, but your name shall be City of Refuge, because in you many nations [ἔθνη πολλά] will take refuge with the Lord God, the Most High, and under your wings many peoples [λαοὶ πολλοί] trusting in the Lord God will be sheltered, and behind your walls will be guarded those who attach themselves [οἱ προσκείμενοι] to the Most High God in the name of Repentance. (15:7)

The importance of this representative role is underscored by the fact that it is referred to on two subsequent occasions—once by the man from heaven (16:16) and again by Aseneth herself when she meets Joseph and gives him a brief summary of her experience (19:5). At a symbolic level, then, the marriage of Joseph and Aseneth represents not simply the union of two individuals but also the incorporation of a whole company of ἔθνη into the people of Israel.

What is striking about Aseneth's conversion, however, is not a supposed individualism but the degree to which it depends on repentance and forgiveness. Aseneth's incorporation into the people of Israel is not a matter simply of her desire to become a proselyte and Israel's (or even just Joseph's) acceptance of her as such. The fundamental assumption underlying Joseph's prayer for her (8:9), her own troubled soliloquies (11:3–14, 16–18), and her own prayer itself (12–13) is that God has the decisive role to play. Aseneth is painfully aware of her "sin" (11:7–11, 18; 12:3–5) and of God's consequent anger (11:8, 16–18), though she is also aware that God is reputed to be merciful (11:10). Her petition to God centers on her confession of sinfulness (12:3–5) and her appeal for mercy and forgiveness (12:14; 13:1, 13). As is indicated by the words of her heavenly visitor, the decisive moment of her conversion comes when her prayer of confession is heard in heaven (15:3). Just as this visitor seems to be the heavenly counterpart of Joseph, so Aseneth has her own counterpart, an "exceedingly beautiful and good daughter of the Most High," known as Repentance (Μετανοία [15:7]). While the importance of social incorporation is not to be downplayed, *Joseph and Aseneth* is distinctive in the heightened role assigned to repentance and divine forgiveness.

Still, the end result of the process is that the barrier between Jew and Gentile is traversed and Aseneth is fully incorporated into God's people. But when we look more particularly at the way in which this barrier is traversed and this incorporation is effected, we encounter a second—and contrasting—aspect of Aseneth's conversion. The barrier separating Aseneth from Joseph—and thus Gentile from Jew—has to do almost entirely with the matter of idolatry. Even in the matter of food, there is no indication that Joseph's separatism is motivated by a concern for levitical food laws or tithing regulations. The difference between the "bread and wine" of the Hebrews and that of the Egyptians is that the latter comes from the table of "dead and dumb idols" (8:5), not that the former is selected and produced in conformity with the law of Moses. To be sure, the concern with "strangulation" (8:5) means that cultic elements are not completely absent. But this is quite overshadowed by the emphasis on idolatry.

Further, except for a few references to the "lawless" character of Aseneth's former way of life (ἀνομίας, 12:3; ἠνόμησα, 12:4), there is no indication that the Jewish way of life is shaped by the Torah, either in general or in any of its particulars.[136] While the author is evidently concerned with behavior that is "fitting for one who worships God" (8:5; 21:1; 23:9, 12; 29:3), such behavior is limited to the rejection of idolatry, separation from idolaters, sexual purity, and considerate treatment of enemies (cf. J. J. Collins 2000, 234). Likewise, there is nothing to suggest that proper worship of the one true God is somehow associated with the one true temple in Jerusalem. While Aseneth is clearly a convert, the Judaism to which she converts has the profile more of an ethical monotheism than of a religious group centered on Torah and temple.

It is in this context that we should view the oft-noted absence from *Joseph and Aseneth* of any reference to circumcision, immersion, and temple sacrifice—the constitutive elements of the rabbinic conversion ritual. Chesnutt is correct in arguing (against Kee and others) that this ritual was by no means universal, so that its absence does not imply a sectarian origin for the work (Chesnutt 1995, 153–84). Nevertheless, he does not take sufficiently into account the more general and more fundamental eclipse of Torah piety in this conversion story. While the boundary between Jew and Gentile is clearly marked, the typical Torah-based boundary markers are strikingly effaced.[137] *Joseph and Aseneth* thus has much in common with that body of Hellenistic Jewish literature that seeks to downplay the ethnos-specific aspects of the law of Moses and to reinterpret it as a kind of "natural law"—a universal *politeia* of ethical monotheism. What sets *Joseph and Aseneth* apart, however, from other such material is the emphasis on social integration. Unlike, say, Philo's "righteous men" (*Spec. Laws* 2.42–48), Aseneth is clearly a proselyte in the sense that she is incorporated into God's own "people" (8:9).[138]

This raises a question, however, about the status of other Egyptians who appear in the story, a question that has been touched on already. There are several additional characters in the story who, unlike Aseneth, are not incorporated into Israel but who nevertheless speak of Joseph's God in terms of respect and

136. While there is a reference to God's "commandments" (τὰς ἐντολάς σου; 12:3), these are injunctions observed by elements of the created order, not by human beings.

137. Of course, the circumstances of the story—the fact that the convert is a woman and the pre-Sinai setting—means that some of these boundary markers are less pertinent. But as Burchard has observed (1985, 190), if Torah and circumcision were important for the author, they could easily have been incorporated. On this aspect of *Joseph and Aseneth* more generally, see Goldenberg (1998, 75–78).

138. In my preliminary treatment of Jewish patterns of universalism, I included *Joseph and Aseneth* in this other category (Donaldson 1997, 62–63). Subsequently, however, I have come to recognize that social integration should be given greater weight in the interpretation of the work.

a degree of acknowledgement. Pentephres, Aseneth's father, refers to Joseph as "the Powerful One of God" (3:4; 4:7); further: "the spirit of God is upon him, and the grace of the Lord (is) with him" (4:7). When he hears that Joseph is on his way, he exclaims: "Blessed (be) the Lord, the God of Joseph, because my lord Joseph thought me worthy to come to us" (3:3). Likewise, one of the household servants describes Joseph as "the Powerful One of God" (18:1) and speaks without qualification of "the Lord God of heaven" who has chosen Aseneth as Joseph's bride (18:11). When the story reaches its resolution and the forthcoming marriage is announced, Pentephres is joined by his whole family in "giv[ing] glory to God" (20:7). Even Pharaoh himself, who presides over the wedding and provides the banquet, asks that "the Lord God the Most High bless you and multiply you and magnify you and glorify you forever" (21:6).[139] Indeed, while Egyptian idolaters generally are described in harshly negative terms (7:1; 8:5–7; 12:9), every individual Egyptian who appears to this point in the story[140] speaks of God with respect; conversely, but with similar effect, no Egyptian (Aseneth before her conversion excepted) engages in idolatrous practice of any kind.

Since there is no indication that any of these characters become proselytes in the sense of full incorporation into the people of Israel, it is appropriate to ask whether they are to be viewed as sympathizers (or ethical monotheists). Certainly the language put on the lips of these characters would be consistent with such an interpretation; anyone who is able to bless "the Lord, the God of Joseph" (3:3) or to say that "the spirit of God" is upon Joseph (4:7) can be described as a "sympathizer" in some sense of the term.[141] But as we have already observed with respect to Pentephres, there is no indication at all that he has abandoned his role as "priest of Heliopolis" (1:3). Given the categorical status of idolatry in the work, one would expect that if this was the author's intention, it would have been signaled in some explicit way. After all, it took Aseneth six chapters, seven days, and much anguish of soul to abandon her idolatrous past. Why should we assume that Pentephres and Pharaoh reached much the same point without causing a ripple on the surface of the narrative? Part of the answer is probably that a distinction is being made between marriage and lesser degrees of association with Israel: since Aseneth is in some sense incorporated into Israel through marriage, a higher standard of conformity to Jewish ways is required of her than of those who acknowledge the God of Israel as outsiders.

139. On Pharaoh, see Gruen (1998, 95).

140. There is a second part of the story in which Pharaoh's son attempts to kill Joseph and to take Aseneth as his own wife.

141. Several scholars suggest that Pentephres and Pharaoh should be seen as "sympathizers" (J. J. Collins 2000, 232; Philonenko 1968, 51). A weakness in Chesnutt's otherwise exemplary treatment is the absence of any attention to the issue of "God-fearers" or "righteous Gentiles."

But in addition, we probably have to reckon once again with a certain lack of skill on the part of the author. The positive disposition of these characters is necessary for the development of the story. The fact that their characterization is not consistent with the values projected by the central section of the story should probably be seen simply as the result of narrational clumsiness. While such an intermediate status—that is, a sympathizer (or ethical monotheist) who nevertheless is not incorporated into Israel—would not be inconsistent with the author's world of values, it probably is not present in the story.

Finally, before leaving *Joseph and Aseneth*, one can ask about its rhetorical intention. To whom was it addressed and to what end? Chesnutt is probably right in rejecting the suggestion that this is a "missionary novel" addressed to Gentiles in the hopes of attracting proselytes.[142] For one thing, the narrative assumes too much biblical knowledge on the part of the reader. For another, Aseneth's ethnic uniqueness—she "had nothing similar to the virgins of the Egyptians, but she was in every respect similar to the daughters of the Hebrews" (1:5)—would hardly commend the work to a wide outside readership (Boccaccini 1991, 255). Nor can the story be read as an attempt to encourage Jews to engage in mission. There is no missionary initiative in the narrative; as Burchard has observed (1985, 192), all Joseph does for Aseneth is pray for her. Before that, the initiative was her father's, at least to the extent that he suggested marriage; after that, the initiative is all hers. But Chesnutt probably goes too far in his argument that the work is directed exclusively towards Jews (encouraging them to welcome proselytes as equal members of the community).[143] The work would speak just as effectively to proselytes and to sympathizers. It is likely that all three groups were in view—native Jews, sympathizers, and proselytes—and that the narrative was written, at least in part, to emphasize for all three groups both the importance of social segregation from idolatry and the equal status to be accorded all those who, like Aseneth, turn to the God of the Hebrews for refuge.[144]

Pseudo-Phocylides

§59 Pseudo-Phocylides 1–2

> [1]*Phocylides, the wisest of men, sets forth*
> [2]*these counsels of God by his holy judgments, gifts of blessing.*

Text: Young (1961)
Translation: *OTP* (van der Horst 1985)

142. The term is Philonenko's (1968, 53); for further bibliography and full discussion, see Chesnutt (1995, 256–65).

143. Chesnutt (1995, 262); a similar position is taken by Barclay (1996, 215–16).

144. See Burchard (1985, 194–95); J. J. Collins (2000, 238).

Date: Uncertain, but probably 100 B.C.E.–100 C.E.
Provenance: Probably Alexandria
Original Language: Greek
Bibliography: Barclay (1996, 336–46); Bockmuehl (2000, 156–57); J. J. Collins (2000:168–74); van der Horst (1978; 1985); Schürer (1986, 3:687–92).
Category: ETHICAL MONOTHEISM

Pseudo-Phocylides is a puzzling piece of literature. Comprising a series of ethical instructions in poetic form, it presents itself as the "counsels of God" set forth by "Phocylides, the wisest of men" (1–2). The puzzle presented by this work is reflected already in this introductory combination of "God" and "Phocylides." On the one hand, the "counsels" of this "God" display an unmistakable Jewish character.[145] For one thing, there are clear echoes both of Septuagint language and of Mosaic legislation.[146] Further, the reference to monotheism (εἷς θεός; 54), the injunctions against homosexuality (190–92, 213–14), and the discussion of resurrection (103–4) are also characteristically Jewish. But on the other hand, to the extent that the work is Jewish in its character and origins, the author takes pains to disguise the fact, attributing it to a Gentile (Phocylides was a sixth century B.C.E. poet from Miletus, well-known for his ethical maxims) and avoiding all references to anything that would be explicitly and identifiably Jewish. Further, the poem lacks the polemic against idolatry that is usually present in Hellenistic Jewish literature. Indeed, in its casual use of language that could readily be understood by non-Jewish readers as polytheistic,[147] it seems to lean in the opposite direction. While the monotheistic commitments of the author are nevertheless not in doubt (Barclay 1996, 340–43), the author apparently felt it unimportant to guard against the possibility that his readers would read this language in a polytheistic way.

Further, who these intended readers are and why the author is addressing them is also puzzling.[148] Some have seen the work as addressed to Gentiles, and

145. Barclay (1996, 338–40); J. J. Collins (1997, 158–77); van der Horst (1978).

146. Line 53 provides an example of the former: "Do not pride yourself on wisdom nor on strength nor on riches" (cf. LXX Jer 9:22); also the analogy of the industriousness of the ants in 164–70 (cf. Prov 6:6–8). For the latter, see, e.g., the injunction against taking the mother bird along with her young (84–85; cf. Deut 22:6–7) and the command to hold the stranger in equal honor with the citizen (39), discussed at the end of this section. For more examples, see the marginal notes in van der Horst (1985, 574–82).

147. Especially the references to "the heavenly ones" (71) and "the blessed ones" (75, 162); also the statement that in their resurrection people become "gods" (104).

148. An Alexandrian provenance is often suggested, though the evidence is scanty. It is usually dated in the period 100 B.C.E.–100 C.E. See the discussions in Barclay (1996, 344–46); J. J. Collins (1997, 175–77); van der Horst (1985, 565–66; 1988).

thus as a means of inculcating greater respect for Judaism or even of encouraging Gentiles to adopt some aspects of Jewish practice and belief (i.e., to become "sympathizers"). But it is difficult to see how an author could ever hope to achieve such purposes by means of a text that studiously avoids any reference to Judaism whatsoever. On the other hand, since Jewish readers might well be expected to recognize the biblical underpinnings of the work, it is more plausible to think of it as addressed to such readers as a means of reassuring them that Hellenistic tradition at its best is in line with Jewish ideals. But even here, the absence of any explicit indication that this is how the work is to be read probably puts too much of an interpretive burden on its putative readers. It is hard to imagine any Jewish reader carrying out the interpretive steps necessary to detect the echoes of Moses in the sayings of Phocylides and thus to conclude that Jewish law and Hellenistic moral teaching are compatible. The tendency in recent scholarly discussion has been to emphasize the gnomological form of Pseudo-Phocylides—that is, its character as a collection of short ethical maxims—and thus to see it as having been produced for the purpose of educational instruction.[149]

Still, taken on its own terms, the work presents itself as addressed to a universal audience. As is evident from the lines quoted above, the author takes his place among humankind in general: "we humans live [ἄνθρωποι ζῶμεν]" (114). Further, the "counsels of God" (2) that the author commends to this universal readership can be described as a kind of ethical monotheism. The existence of God is assumed from the outset (2). Also assumed is the oneness of this God (54), together with God's roles as creator (106, 125), provider (29), and judge (11). Further, the whole work is presented as a discourse on "the mysteries of righteousness" (229). While the author does not draw a sharp line between the righteous and the wicked, nevertheless readers are encouraged to separate themselves from the ways of the wicked (132–34), and the impression is given that those readers who follow the "mysteries of righteousness," as they have been described in the work, will be pleasing to God. By choosing to put these "mysteries" in the mouth of Phocylides, the author avoids rather than addresses the question of how this universal ethic relates to the law of Moses and the people of Israel, both of which are central to the scriptures that are assumed throughout the work. Still, even if the author sidesteps some of the concomitant difficulties, he nevertheless takes the position that there is a monotheistic morality that is incumbent upon all.

One other statement in Pseudo-Phocylides requires a brief comment, since it uses a term (strangers [ἔπηλυς]) that appears elsewhere (especially in Philo) with reference to proselytes. The saying is found towards the end of a section in which readers are exhorted to care for the poor and those otherwise in need (22–41). It reads: "Strangers [ἐπήλυδες] should be held in equal honour [ὁμότιμοι] among citizens [πολιήταις]." In view of the strong biblical echoes

149. See esp. J. J. Collins (1997, 158–77).

in this whole section,[150] it is likely that the saying is dependent on such biblical injunctions concerning resident aliens as are found, for example, in Lev 19:34: "The alien who resides with you shall be to you as the citizen among you." This conclusion finds support in evidence from Philo, whose language when commenting on biblical legislation concerning resident aliens is very similar to that in Ps.-Phoc. 39.[151]

But while Philo understands this biblical tradition as having to do with converts, Pseudo-Phocylides transforms it into a generalized maxim, universal in its applicability. He goes on to say: "For we all experience the poverty of much wandering" (40); in other words, the reason that we should be concerned for the stranger in our midst is that each of us might find ourselves in a situation where we are the strangers. While there is probably an echo of the biblical text in this line as well ("for you were aliens in the land of Egypt"), here all traces of ethnic particularity have been effaced.[152] Thus, even if the text is rooted in the same biblical soil that nourished the idea of proselytism, it has become something quite different through Pseudo-Phocylides' cultivation. Here it is a general truth, valid for all (πάντες) without differentiation and, in particular, having nothing to do with the incorporation of Gentile "strangers" into the specific community of Israel. Thus, whatever the purpose of Pseudo-Phocylides, this line has no evidential value for the issue of Jewish proselytism.

On Jonah

The whole of *On Jonah* is relevant to our purposes here. The theme of the work, however, is clearly conveyed by God's final words to Jonah (216–19), part of the longer divine speech with which the work concludes (183–219). At this point in the speech, God's dealings with the Ninevites are being compared with the activity of a gardener, who will not destroy a plant as long as there is the possibility that it might become fruitful but will take various measures to attempt to restore the plant to fruitfulness.

150. On *Ps.-Phoc.* 22 ("Give to the poor man at once, and do not tell him to come tomorrow"), cf. Prov. 3:28: "Do not say to your neighbour, 'Go, and come again, tomorrow I will give it,' when you have it with you." See further van der Horst (1978, 126–30).

151. He too uses ἔπηλυς to refer to resident aliens and speaks of the "equal rank" (ἰσοτιμία, ἰσοτέλεια) and "equal privilege" (ἰσονομία) that they should enjoy (*Spec. Laws* 1.52–53).

152. J. J. Collins (1997, 159) suggests that the line might reflect the conflict between Jews and Alexandrians over civic rights in the first century. While this is plausible, it appears here in a much more generalized form.

§60 On Jonah *216–19*

For one cuts down a plant that does not produce fruit; but if it is fruitful, one leaves it standing. The Ninevites were once without the fruits of piety. They did not know the fruit of divine righteousness and the honour that was due to the Creator they rendered to the created world. [217]*But now they no longer render thanks to nature for its fruits nor do they worship the elements; but they confess the one who provides the fruits and render to him the honour that is due for his gifts. Instead of venerating this world, they are engaged in venerating its Architect.* [218]*How then could I hold to the sentence of death that had been pronounced in the case of those who have changed their lives? If I have sent an unpitying word against the deplorable conduct of human beings, I will now pronounce a benevolent word for a pious life.* [219]*For as their conduct in the past deserved a severe message, their repentance deserves the proclamation of God's love for human beings.*

Text: Armenian: Lewy (1936)
Translation: My own, based on the German translation of Siegert (1980) and the French of Siegert and de Roulet (1999)
Date: Early first century C.E.
Provenance: Probably Alexandria
Original Language: Greek
Bibliography: Kraus (1996, 90–92); Siegert (1980, 1992, 1994); Siegert and de Roulet (1999)
Category: ETHICAL MONOTHEISM

On Jonah is one of several anonymous writings that have been preserved in Armenian as part of a collection of Philo's works.[153] In substance, it consists of an interpretive retelling of the narrative found in the canonical book of Jonah. The Armenian collection contains two other similar works, one a treatment of Samson (*On Samson*) and the other an additional, but fragmentary, treatment of Jonah. This collection first came to scholarly attention in the early nineteenth century through the efforts of J. B. Aucher, who prepared an edited version and Latin translation. It was recognized from the outset that these were not authentic works of Philo, and as a result they received little scholarly attention.[154] Through the more recent efforts of Siegert and others, however, they are beginning to be studied in their own right.

In view of the fact that the narrator in *On Jonah* speaks in the first person singular (e.g., 2, 4), addressing his audience directly[155] and with apparent homiletical

153. The collection includes *Questions on Genesis* and *Questions on Exodus*, which are extant only in Armenian.

154. Lewy's preparation of a critical text in 1936 was an exception, but his long-promised English translation never appeared. The writings were not included in Charlesworth's *Old Testament Pseudepigrapha*.

155. "[M]es amis"/"ihr frommen Zuhörer" (60); Siegert suggests that the original was ὦ ἄνδρες (Siegert 1980, 18).

intent, Siegert has argued that it should be identified as a synagogue sermon. Dependence on LXX Jonah requires a *terminus a quo* of sometime near the beginning of the second century B.C.E.; the absence of any evidence of conflict with Gentiles and foreign empires suggests the destruction of the temple as a *terminus ad quem*. Although the work might have emerged in any sizable Diaspora community, Siegert suggests that Alexandria is the place where one is most likely to find the combination of rhetorical sophistication and universal outlook that is reflected in *On Jonah*. If so, it is difficult to imagine the work emerging after the civic disturbances in 37 C.E. Siegert thus suggests a date roughly contemporaneous with Philo (Siegert 1992, 39–52). Such conclusions about the provenance of the work may have to be revised as the material is studied further, but they seem to be reliable at this stage in the discussion.

Although *On Jonah* is of interest primarily in areas where its content differs from that of canonical Jonah, in its form it follows the narrative structure of Jonah quite closely. Except for an opening proem (1–9) and the preacher's reflection on Jonah's plight after he had thrown himself into the sea (60–63), the sequence of the narrative conforms to that of canonical Jonah: God's initial address to Jonah (10–19; cf. Jon 1:1–2); Jonah's flight, the storm, and his leap into the sea (20–59; cf. Jon 1:3–15); Jonah in the belly of the beast (64–68; cf. Jon 1:17); Jonah's prayer (69–98; cf. Jon 2:1–9); Jonah's deliverance and journey to Nineveh (99–102; cf. Jon 2:10–3:3); Jonah's preaching (103–7; cf. Jon 3:4); the response of the Ninevites, convicted by Jonah's preaching (108–10; cf. Jon 3:5a); a public assembly of Ninevites (111–40, replacing the king's proclamation in Jon 3:6–9); three days of penitence (141–50; cf. Jon 3:5b); Nineveh's celebration of deliverance (151–52) and prayer to God (153–56; cf. Jon 3:10); God's final dealings with Jonah (157–219; cf. Jon 4:1–11). There are only two additional variations from the canonical sequence. First, in 111–40, where canonical Jonah has a proclamation by the king, in *On Jonah* it is the whole city that responds, gathering in a great civic assembly (of "men and women, elders and aediles, slaves and masters, all those with rank and nobility"; no king is mentioned) to reflect on their misdoings and to call on God for mercy. Second, in 151–56, where Jonah just has a brief statement saying that God "changed his mind" (Jon 3:10), *On Jonah* describes the great celebration that ensued when the three days had elapsed without judgment (151–52)[156] and the Ninevites' subsequent prayer of thanksgiving (153–56).

In its homiletical reworking of the Jonah story, *On Jonah* develops a strikingly positive view of the Gentiles and their status with respect to God.[157] To a certain extent, of course, such a view is determined by the biblical subject matter itself: by extending God's covenantal character—"gracious and merciful,

156. While according to the MT there were to be forty days until judgment (Jon 3:4), *On Jonah* follows the LXX, which has "three days."

157. See Kraus (1996,90–92); Siegert (1994).

slow to anger and abounding in steadfast love, and ready to relent from punishing" (Jon 4:2)—so that it applies also to non-Jews—"Nineveh, that great city, in which there are more than a hundred and twenty thousand persons who do not know their right hand from their left" (Jon 4:11)[158]—canonical Jonah achieves one of the high-water marks of biblical universalism. Still, *On Jonah* picks up this theme and develops it into one of the most generous expressions of ethical monotheism to be found in Jewish Diaspora literature.

To begin with, it is a little misleading to speak of the view of the *Gentiles* in *On Jonah*, since the term does not appear. To be sure, the Jewish orientation of the work is not in doubt; it is a sermon on Jonah, after all. But the story of Jonah itself and the few additional references to Israel's larger story are placed into a universal framework. At the outset, while the proem mentions the writings of the prophets and the functioning of the law, both are oriented towards humankind as a whole. With respect to the prophets, the author says that many of those who read them are interested in them for the things they contain that are "useful to human beings" (1); in other words, the typical reader of the prophets is a "human being" rather than a member of any particular subgroup to which the prophets might have belonged. Similarly, while there is also a reference to the law,[159] it is compared to a well-made boat that its pilot steers "on the right path for the salvation of each one" (4); that is, the law is universal in its scope and intention. A little later in the work (94), there are references to the divine deliverance of various biblical figures—Noah, the patriarchs, "the Hebrews" in the Red Sea and (presumably) Daniel in the lion's den.[160] But these are adduced not to set the Hebrews apart as a privileged group but to convince a generic "man" that God has the power to save even those who have been separated from the body in death. Further, in the preacher's perspective Nineveh's role as Israel's cruel conqueror (surely the backdrop to canonical Jonah) has completely fallen away. Instead he presents Nineveh as the "origin of every city"—that is, as a kind of urban prototype.[161]

Closely connected to this universal anthropology is the preacher's universal theology. The primary characteristic of God in *On Jonah* is God's "love for humanity" (presumably φιλανθρωπία). As can be seen from the passage previously quoted, God's φιλανθρωπία is the note on which the sermon ends: because of their repentance, the Ninevites deserve to hear a message concerning "God's love for human beings" (219). This note is sounded at the outset of the

158. Not to mention the "many animals"!

159. Siegert suggests that the original was νομοθεσία (legislation).

160. The text speaks of "how the righteous play with wild beasts." Siegert (1980, 25) links this with Daniel 6.

161. Siegert (1992, 102) refers us to LXX Gen 10:12, where Nineveh is described as the "great city." But between a "great city" and the "origin of every city" there is certainly some interpretive added value.

work as well: when God first decides to take steps towards the salvation of the Ninevites, "the friend of human beings" (ὁ φιλάνθρωπος) chooses Jonah as a divine collaborator (8). And in the intervening narrative God's philanthropy is repeatedly stressed. Indeed, Jonah's refusal to acknowledge God's φιλανθρωπία is one of his two failings (the other is his foolish belief that one can hide from the all-present one) and thus one of two lessons that he needs to learn through his dealings with the Ninevites (61–63, 69, 73, 87). Likewise, God's "love for humanity" is one of the things that the Ninevites come to realize through Jonah's preaching (136), and this even before they experience God's mercy and forgiveness. This does not mean that God condones sin and unrighteousness (on which more in a moment), but as long as people are repentant, God can be described as merciful (162) and benevolent (87); God is "severe towards sinners, but soft towards those who pray" (138; cf. 71).

Indeed, divine severity in *On Jonah* is fully in the service of divine "softness." While the story begins with God's perception of Nineveh's "evil way of life" (5), God's intentions from the beginning are for the salvation and preservation of the city. Just as a physician might use painful means in order to effect a cure, so God used the threat of destruction as the means by which Nineveh might be "saved" (7) and "delivered" (8). Even though Jonah is commissioned to announce judgment on Nineveh—"announce to this city the ruin and cruel death that is about to strike them" (19)—this is simply a means to an end: "In the intention of saving and preserving Nineveh, God sent a prophet though whom he threatened the destruction of the city" (6). Jonah, of course, is not unaware of God's ultimate intentions. Precisely because of his gift of prophecy, he can see what God is up to and thus runs away (20). Consequently, before God could use Jonah for the healing of Nineveh, the divine physician had first to heal the prophet (9). God's softness towards human disobedience is universal, encompassing Jonah as well as the Ninevites.

Still, divine severity has its part to play in the story. In the preacher's view, God's threat of judgment on Nineveh is justified because of the equally universal way in which sin is defined. Nineveh's sin is described in detail at three points in the narrative. The story begins with God's commissioning of Jonah, in which we are presented with a thorough description of their sinful culpability. Their sinfulness takes two forms. First, although the Ninevites have been abundantly blessed—good crops, fruitful land, pleasant climate (10)—they have refused to recognize God and to give God thanks for the blessings received: "Not that I demand repayment for such great goodness, only words of thanks. But they have become unthankful to such an extent that they not only neglect to thank; they do not know any longer who their Benefactor is" (12). While they have been given eyes precisely so that they might recognize the architect of the world, they refuse to see (14). Second, this sin along the vertical axis has its counterpart along the horizontal—their culpable misdeeds towards each other (15–17). The young are consumed with pleasures of the flesh; men use their power for robbery and women their beauty for seduction; even the aged, deprived of strength and charm, use their minds to plot deceit. Each stage of life exhibits its own kind of sin and unrighteousness.

These themes are expanded in Jonah's preaching (105–7) and in the subsequent deliberations of the Ninevites (111–40). While Jonah begins by denouncing them for their refusal to recognize God and to render thanks for their blessings, he spends more time on their ethical failings: corruption of justice, oppression of the poor, sexual immorality, the seeking of pleasures that are "contrary to the law" (probably παράνομους), transvestitism, embezzlement, and so on. The Ninevites, by contrast, are more remorseful about their failure to recognize God. Although they have received from God the ultimate gift—that they "are human beings" (120)—they have sunk to the level of beasts in that they "enjoy the fruits of the earth without remembering the One who has produced them" (120). Making explicit what to this point has been implicit, the Ninevites fully admit their culpability, acknowledging that the character of God is readily apparent from the natural order. "We cannot object that He is invisible and that it is impossible to see with perishable eyes the Imperishable One" (125), they confess, for God's presence and might can be discerned in the created order itself: "If we cannot see the architect, we can nevertheless recognize him from what he has skilfully made" (126). Human beings have been given the faculty of reason precisely so that they might recognize God (135), but the Ninevites acknowledge that they have failed to see the obvious: "We have not recognized the Creator of the world, for all our observation of the world; we have not recognized the Steersman, for all our scrutinizing of the contents of the boat" (135).

At the heart of *On Jonah*, then, is a concept of natural law based on a natural theology. Human beings dwell in a building whose Architect is discernible in the order and grandeur of its architecture. The inhabitants of this building have been given reason precisely so that they might recognize God and live in such a way as to please God (118)—both by giving thanks to God for blessings received and by treating each other with righteousness and benevolence. Although the author makes reference to the "Hebrews," cites scripture explicitly (e.g., 47, 176), and refers to the law (4, 105, 176), he does not seem to make any fundamental differentiation within humankind. Whatever might be present in scripture or in the law is, in principle, apparent to all through the rational observation of the created order. Conversely, whatever might be naturally discerned about God and moral behavior is incumbent on the whole of humankind without distinction or differentiation. Although the author does not use the term "Gentile," still the implication of the work is that they can be full and equal recipients of divine *philanthropia* to the extent that they live in accordance with this universally accessible ethical monotheism. In contrast to what we have seen in the *Letter of Aristeas* (and will see in a more thoroughgoing way in Philo), however, the author of *On Jonah* does not seem to be concerned with identifying the Law as given through Moses as a more accessible and reliable way to this universal end. To a considerable extent, Jewish particularities are suppressed in this work.

They are suppressed, perhaps, but not effaced. For in the context of the story itself, the Ninevites come to their ethical and monotheistic senses not by dint of their own rational contemplation of the universe but as a result of the preaching carried out in their midst by a divinely chosen and commissioned prophet. Jonah's own experience is a very important part of the narrative as a whole. The author seems particularly concerned with drawing out the parallelism between God's dealings with Jonah and those with the Ninevites. Just as the Ninevites had two types of sin from which they needed salvation, so Jonah had two "maladies" (9) for which he needed healing. Jonah's maladies were not the same as those of the Ninevites, though they were not unrelated. In place of the failure to recognize God at all, Jonah's failure was the belief that he could flee from God's presence and knowledge. In place of malicious behavior towards humankind, Jonah's problem was an unwillingness to recognize God's universal love for humankind. Thus before Jonah could heal others, he had to be healed himself by learning "not to assume that God was ignorant and not to oppose God's love for humankind [φιλανθρωπία]" (63). As a consequence, having experienced God's *philanthropia* himself in his deliverance from the sea, he could not begrudge the Ninevites the same treatment (62), even though it took him a while to get to this point (cf. 182).

Jonah plays this role of the "healed physician" (cf. 9), however, not as a human being in general but as a Jewish prophet in particular. To be sure, the portrayal is subtle; as we have seen, the author goes out of his way to speak in universal terms, referring to "the Hebrews" only in passing and avoiding any characterization of the Ninevites as "Gentiles." Still, since the author can confidently assume that his readers will know what he is talking about when he refers to "scripture" (47) or to what is written "in the law" (176), we can confidently assume that other features of Jonah's portrayal will not be lost on the intended readers, either. Jonah is not an otherwise unknown prophet of a generically universal deity; since the prophet is one whose story is contained in "scripture" (47) and since the deity is one who speaks in "the law" (176), both are to be understood with reference to the story contained in this larger collection of Israel's scripture. Further, in the only explicit reference to particular aspects of Israel's history, the author is careful to establish the links with Jonah. In 91–94 we find a list of people who had been delivered from danger or death by divine power. The list contains Noah, the patriarchs, the Hebrews at the Red Sea, Daniel in the den of lions,[162] and, as the last and most convincing example of God's power to deliver the righteous, Jonah himself (95–96). Any reader

162. Presumably this is what is meant by the vague reference to "the righteous men who played with savage beasts" (94); so Siegert and de Roulet (1999, 69).

who is familiar with "scripture" or "the law" will recognize the larger story within which the story of Jonah is to be read and understood.

The point should not be overstressed. Nothing in *On Jonah* would justify any attempt to smuggle any form of covenantal particularity in by the back door. The universal form of ethical monotheism that is on display in the work needs to remain intact. Still, the fact that this message of ethical monotheism comes to Nineveh precisely through the agency of Jonah, a "prophet" whose story is recounted in the "scriptures" of the "Hebrews," also needs to be given due weight. If Nineveh is the prototype of "every city" (5), Jonah is at least the representative of something larger than himself. For the preacher, what Jonah comes to learn about the universality both of God and of God's love for humankind is consonant with the message of "scripture" itself. Further, Jonah is eager that his story be included "in the holy scriptures" so that all those who read it will learn of God's benevolence towards sinners (86–87). His scripturally enshrined story serves as "as a witness" (95) for God's power to save and thus also as a kind of guarantee for the ultimate deliverance of all who turn to God: just as he experienced a kind of "new birth" from the belly of the sea monster, so God will be able to "preserve intact" those who have died (96).[163] Thus Jonah's story is presented here as directed towards a universal readership. But while the message is universal, the Jewish particularity hinted at and apparently assumed by the author has its own part to play in bringing it to the attention of the various "cities" for which Nineveh is "origin" and prototype (5). By means of his sermon (if sermon it is), the author of *On Jonah* hopes to do his part—it would appear—to make this message known.

Testament of Abraham

§61 Testament of Abraham *10:12–14 (A) / 12:12–13 (B)*

> *And immediately a voice came down from heaven to the Commander-in-chief, speaking thus, "O Michael, Commander-in-chief, command the chariot to stop and turn Abraham away, lest he should see the entire inhabited world.* [13]*For if he were to see all those who pass their lives in sin, he would destroy everything that exists. For behold, Abraham has not sinned and he has no mercy on sinners.* [14]*But I made the world, and I do not want to destroy any one of them; but I delay the death of the sinner until he should convert and live."* (Recension A)

> *Then the Lord God spoke to Michael, saying, "Turn Abraham away to his house, and do not let him go round all the creation which I made, because his heart is not moved for sinners,* [13]*but my heart is moved for sinners, so that they may convert and live and repent of their sins and be saved."* (Recension B)

163. Siegert interprets this as a reference to a kind of resurrection (Siegert and de Roulet 1999, 161).

Text: Schmidt (1986); Stone (1972)
Translation: *OTP* (E. P. Sanders 1983)
Date: Probably first century C.E., but uncertain
Provenance: Probably Egypt
Original Language: Probably Greek
Bibliography: J. J. Collins (1998, 251–55); Delcor (1973); James (1892); Ludlow (2002); Munoa (1998); Nickelsburg (1976); E. P. Sanders (1983); Schürer (1987 3:761–67)
Category: ETHICAL MONOTHEISM

The *Testament of Abraham*, extant in Greek and in a number of other languages dependent on the Greek version, has come down to us in two recensions. Recension A, the longer of the two, is generally held to be more reliable with respect to the content and order of the original, even though it contains later vocabulary and evidence of Christian reworking; Recension B, however, has probably preserved more original wording in a number of places.[164] While some have argued for a Semitic original (e.g., Schmidt 1976), the work most probably originated in Greek. Date and provenance are uncertain, but the suggestion of an origin in Egypt sometime in the first century C.E. is probably not far from the mark.[165]

The *Testament of Abraham* consists of a curious, and perhaps intentionally humorous, account of the circumstances leading up to Abraham's death. Abraham is presented as the epitome of righteousness, described as such not only by the narrator (1:1; 2:1) but also by the archangel Michael (4:6), God (1:5), and even by personified Death himself (17:7).[166] The narrative gets underway when God summons Michael and commissions him to tell Abraham that his death is near so that he can "arrange for the disposition of his possessions" in a timely manner (1:4). Readers thus are led to expect that the narrative to follow will be testamentary in form. In the course of his instructions to Michael, God calls Abraham "my beloved friend" (1:6) and describes him as "righteous in all goodness, (having been) hospitable and loving until the end of his life" (1:5). Abraham's reaction to this news, however, after Michael has finally found a way to communicate his message, is not what we might expect from such a venerable and noble friend of God. Abraham simply refuses to go

164. This was the conclusion of James (1892), who produced the first critical edition of the Greek texts. While there have been dissenting voices—e.g., Schmidt (1976), who argues for the priority of Recension B—James' approach has been generally accepted. Most recently Ludlow (2002) has argued for the priority of Recension A on the basis of a narrative critical analysis of *T. Ab.*

165. For recent and thorough discussions of introductory issues, see Munoa (1998, 13–27) and Ludlow (2002, 1–7, 152–80). See also E. P. Sanders (1983, 871–81).

166. Except where otherwise indicated, passages cited or referred to are from Recension A.

(7:12), with the result that Michael has to return to God empty-handed (8:1–3). In accordance with God's instructions Michael returns, informing Abraham that if he refuses to come this time, the next divine emissary will be Death himself (8:12–9:2). As if to buy time, Abraham asks that first, while he is still "in this body," he be allowed "to see all the inhabited world [πᾶσαν τὴν οἰκουμένην] and all the created things" that God had established (9:6). But even after God has granted this request, Abraham still refuses to go (15:8–10), which results in Michael's second empty-handed return to the heavenly courts (15:11–15). At this point God, who remains curiously patient throughout the whole affair, carries through on the earlier threat to hand the commission over to Death (16:1–6). Death is successful in the end, even though Abraham initially refuses (16:16) and Death has to resort to a subterfuge (20:8–10). Death's success is not complete, however; Abraham dies without ever making a will and arranging for the disposition of his goods! The story ends with the glorious reception of Abraham's soul in heaven, and God's command that the angels "take . . . my friend Abraham into Paradise, . . . where there is no toil, no grief, no moaning, but peace and exultation and endless life" (20:14). One is left wondering why Abraham had been so reluctant to go!

What is of most interest for our purposes is what transpires on Abraham's cosmic journey (chs. 10–14). In accordance with Abraham's request, Michael takes Abraham in "a chariot of cherubim" to view "the entire inhabited world" (10:1). They see "everything which was happening in the world, both good and evil" (10:3). Abraham, however, seems to be more upset by the evil than he is impressed by the good. One after another, as he sees human beings engaged in evil acts (murder, sexual immorality, robbery), he requests that they immediately be punished and put to death. God grants his request on three occasions, but with this God's patience is exhausted. God commands that Michael bring the tour to a halt, "lest he should see the entire inhabited world"; for if Abraham were allowed to see "all those who pass their lives in sin, he would destroy everything that exists" (10:13–14). Abraham's righteousness is now revealed to be a kind of fault; because he has not sinned (!), "he has no mercy on sinners" (10:13)—unlike God, who presumably has not sinned either but who nevertheless does "not want to destroy any one of them" (10:14). At this point Abraham is conveyed to "the first gate of heaven" (11:1) so that he might see divine judgment in action and thus learn something about divine mercy.

Certainly there is a hardness in God's mercy: human destiny is determined by the relative balance of sins and righteous deeds (12:12–18; 13:9–10), and the ones who are saved are vastly outnumbered by the ones who are destroyed (11:11–12). In some respects, then, the picture is as bleak as it is in *4 Ezra* (cf. J. J. Collins 1998, 254). Yet the picture is softened in several ways. As has already been mentioned, God desires that sinners "turn [ἐπιστρέψαι]" from their sin and "live" (10:14). Presumably sins that are repented of are not counted in the final tally. Further, those who die in an untimely manner, whose opportunity to repent has therefore been foreshortened, are not further punished (14:15). Also, the prayers of the righteous can help to tip the balance when sins and righteous deeds are equal (14:4–8). God's mercy is particularly in view in the conclusion of this part of the narrative. After having been granted this glimpse of the final judgment, Abraham comes to see his zeal for immediate punishment as a sin, and so he appeals to God on behalf of those he had destroyed (14:10–13). God hears his prayer, forgives his sin, and grants salvation to those who had perished: "those whom you think that I destroyed, I have called back and have led them into life by my great goodness" (14:14). The emphasis in the *Testament of Abraham*, then, is placed on divine goodness and mercy—on God's eager desire that sinners repent and turn from their sinfulness and God's willingness to forgive and save those who do.

What is most striking about this portrait of divine mercy is the contrast between the Jewish framework of the writing and its universalistic content. On the one hand, the world in which the story takes place is distinctively Jewish. Unlike other Diaspora literature, there is no attempt here to bring Abraham into a relationship with the wider Gentile world. While Josephus (*Ant.* 1.161–68) and Artapanus[167] might use Abraham's sojourn in Egypt as an opportunity to depict him as a cosmopolitan who brought culture and learning to the Egyptians, the *Testament of Abraham* makes no mention of this aspect of the biblical account whatsoever. Except for those whom Abraham sees on his (foreshortened) tour of the inhabited world, the story is populated solely by biblical figures: Abraham, Sarah, Isaac, Adam, and Eve (8:8), Abel (13:2), Jacob (20:14), the "forefathers" (8:9), the prophets (8:9), the twelve tribes of Israel (13:6), and Michael the angelic "commander-in-chief." In addition, the author clearly expects that readers will be familiar with the biblical narratives from which these figures are drawn. Further, the writing is as devoid of polemic against Gentile religion (idolatry, polytheism) as it is of attempts to appropriate the positive aspects of Gentile philosophy.

But on the other hand, distinctively Jewish considerations play no part whatsoever in Abraham's tour of the inhabited world and the lessons he has to learn about divine mercy and judgment. The human world in the end is divided into two categories—the sinners, who are driven through the wide gate into destruction; and the righteous, who pass through the narrow gate into life (chs. 11–14). There is no indication whatsoever that this dual categorization might correspond in any way to a differentiation of humankind into the two camps of Jew and Gentile. Indeed, apart from the reference to the twelve tribes of Israel (13:6; lacking from Recension B) and passing references to his "seed" (3:6; 8:7), there is very little to suggest that Abraham was the progenitor of a distinctive nation. Nor is there any mention of the observances that differentiate Jew from Gentile (circumcision, food laws, endogamy, etc.). While one

167. See §36.

might stretch a point to excuse the absence of any reference to the Torah on the grounds that Abraham lived earlier than Moses, this is of no avail with respect to circumcision (cf. Gen 17). The closest one gets to the idea of the covenant are vague references to promises (of blessings and land) made to Abraham and his seed (1:5; 3:6; 4:11; 8:5). In keeping with this, the line separating sinners and righteous is drawn on the basis of universal ethical norms rather than particular covenantal ones. What identifies the sinners is that they engage in robbery, sexual immorality, destruction of property, and murder (ch. 10); on the other side of the scale, what identifies the righteous is that they live up to the standard set by Abraham, who is "merciful, hospitable, righteous, truthful, God-fearing [θεοσεβῆ], refraining from every evil deed" (4:6).[168] There is no role for the covenant whatsoever—either as a factor in the salvation of the righteous or as a criterion in the determination of the wicked.

What was the purpose of this curious story? The absence of any attempt to engage with the Gentile world suggests strongly that the author was aiming at a Jewish audience (so Schürer 1987, 3:762). Further, the overall thrust of the narrative seems to be directed at anxiety about death; readers are reassured both that a happy fate awaits the righteous (20:14) and that God is merciful towards repentant sinners. John Collins's suggestion that the intended function of the work was "primarily consolation" (J. J. Collins 1998, 254) is probably close to the mark. The comedic features that have been so perceptively described by Ludlow also contribute to the process of "diffusing fear in such fearful situations" (Ludlow 2002, 44).

If the *Testament of Abraham* was intended for internal consumption, its non-ethnic and non-covenantal presentation of righteousness and salvation becomes even more impressive. The world reflected or projected by the narrative is one which is both implicitly Jewish and strikingly universalistic. The Jewish author and his readers matter-of-factly assume that Jews and non-Jews alike will enter paradise on the basis of generically human standards of righteousness and universally impartial divine mercy. While the author provides no indication of how this outlook is to be coordinated with the particularistic and ethnos-specific elements of the biblical narrative that is also assumed in a matter-of-fact way, his ethical monotheism is clear and beyond dispute.[169]

168. This description is missing from some mss. (see Schmidt 1986, 106), but is nevertheless an accurate summary of the way Abraham's righteousness is defined throughout the work (see, e.g., 1:1–2, 5; 17:7).

169. Contra Schürer (1987, 3:762), where it is argued that the intended audience (Jewish) and purpose (consolation in the face of death) account for the universalistic features of the work, without any need to posit "a universalistic form of Judaism." On the universalism of *T. Ab.*, see Boccaccini (1991, 258–59); J. J. Collins (1998, 254–55); E. P. Sanders (1983, 876–78).

SIBYLLINE ORACLES 4

Sibylline Oracles 4 is quite evidently a composite work. The core is a survey of human history arranged according to ten generations (49–101). The tenth generation also coincides with the fourth empire, that of the Macedonians (86).[170] But since the oracle goes on to describe the Roman empire (102–151), which perforce falls outside the ten-generation scheme, this section at least must have been added later. Further, 1–48 and 152–192 introduce a religious element not present in the historical core. Thus it is likely that an original anti-Macedonian oracle, dating from a period not long after Alexander, was supplemented and adapted for a more religious purpose by someone in the later first century C.E.[171]

The religious sections in their entirety are relevant for our purposes here, but the most important evidence is contained in two shorter passages.

§62 Sibylline Oracles *4:24–39*

Happy will be those of mankind on earth
who will love the great God, blessing him
before drinking and eating, putting their trust in piety.
They will reject all temples when they see them;
altars too, useless foundations of dumb stones
(and stone statues and handmade images)
defiled with blood of animate creatures, and sacrifices
of four-footed animals. They will look to the great glory of the one God
and commit no wicked murder, nor deal in
dishonest gain, which are most horrible things.
Neither have they disgraceful desire for another's spouse
or for hateful and repulsive abuse of a male.
Other men will never imitate their way
or piety or customs, because they desire shamelessness.
On the contrary, they deride them with mockery and laughter.
Infantile in their foolishness, they will falsely attribute to those
what wicked and evil deeds they themselves commit.

§63 Sibylline Oracles *4:162–70*

Ah, wretched mortals, change these things, and do not
lead the great God to all sorts of anger, but abandon
daggers and groanings, murders and outrages,
and wash your whole bodies in perennial rivers.

170. The Assyrians occupy six generations (49–53), the Medes two (54–64), and the Persians one (65–87).

171. There are references to the destruction of Jerusalem (115–17, 125–27), the legend of Nero's flight to Parthia (119–24), and the eruption of Vesuvius (130–34).

Stretch out your hands to heaven and ask forgiveness
for your previous deeds and make propitiation
for bitter impiety with words of praise; God will grant repentance
and will not destroy. He will stop his wrath again if you all
practice honorable piety in your hearts.

Text: Geffcken (1902)
Translation: *OTP* (J. J. Collins1983)
Date: *Circa* 80 C.E.
Provenance: Uncertain[172]
Original Language: Greek
Bibliography: J. J. Collins (1983; 2000, 166–67); Schürer (1986, 3:641–43)
Category: ETHICAL MONOTHEISM

In its final form, *Sibylline Oracles* 4 consists of a survey of five world empires (49–151) framed by an introduction (1–48) and conclusion (152–192) that set human history in a particular religious context. The Sibyl divides humankind into two groups—the pious (εὐσεβέες) and the impious (ἀσεβεῖς); in the framing material, she is concerned with describing their nature and ultimate fate. The passages previously cited form part of the framing material. The introduction consists of a denunciation of idolatry (6–23), a eulogy on the pious (24–39, cited above), and a description of the final judgment (40–48). The conclusion brings the historical survey to an end by describing the widespread impiety of the last days (152–161); then, before a description of the final judgment of the impious and vindication of the pious (171–192), the Sibyl exhorts her readers to turn from impiety and to seek forgiveness (162–70, the second passage cited above).

It is clear that *Sibylline Oracles* 4 is a Jewish work. A constellation of features—the rejection of idolatry; the corresponding emphasis on monotheism; the special interest in the destruction of Jerusalem and the temple (115–129); the statement that the eruption of Vesuvius was divine punishment for Rome's destruction of Jerusalem (130–36); and the absence of any explicitly Christian content—all indicate a Jewish provenance. Two features of the work, however, have elicited surprise from commentators. One is the categorical rejection of temple worship, phrased in such a way as to suggest also a rejection of the Jerusalem temple:

For he does not have a house, a stone set up as a temple,
dumb and toothless, a bane which brings many woes to men,

172. On the basis of the attitude to the temple and to ritual washing, Syria or the Jordan valley have been suggested (see J. J. Collins 1983, 382). These features of the work will be discussed below. Perhaps the address of the work to "people of boastful Asia and Europe" (1) should be given more consideration in discussions of provenance.

> but one which it is not possible to see from earth nor to measure
> with mortal eyes, since it was not fashioned by mortal hand. (8–11)

The other is the injunction that the impious give expression to their repentance by washing their "whole bodies in perennial rivers" (165). On the basis of these two features, some have argued that the work reflects the outlook of the Essenes or of "Jewish baptist circles."[173]

Any assessment of these two features of the work needs to be carried out in connection with a third observation, one which is of central concern here—namely, its non-covenantal definition of piety. It is clear that the Sibyl identifies the "pious" closely with Israel: the people of Jerusalem are called "the blameless tribe of the pious" (136). But piety is elsewhere defined in terms that make no reference to Israel's distinctive identity markers. Piety involves a rejection of idolatry; worship of the one "great God" (25); blessing God before meals (26); abstention from murder, dishonesty, adultery, and male homosexual behavior (30–34). Further, there is no attempt to link this pattern of piety to the law; the term does not appear. Still, it is a pattern of piety that characterizes present-day Israel; as "the blameless tribe of the pious," Israel seems to be thought of as more or less identical with "the pious." And it is a pattern of piety that is incumbent on Gentiles as well; the oracle, including its appeal for conversion (162–170), is addressed to the "people of boastful Asia and Europe," that is, to a significant segment of the Gentile world. In other words, Gentiles are urged to convert to a pattern of piety that, on the one hand, is identified closely with Israel, but that, on the other, is to be described as an ethical monotheism rather than as a covenantal nomism.

Thus *Sibylline Oracles* 4 displays characteristics similar to those found in *Sibylline Oracles* 3. At the same time, however, there are differences. There is no attempt to align this universal pattern of piety, incumbent on Jew and Gentile alike, with the law of Moses. Nor is there any attempt to glorify the Jerusalem temple or to identify it as the center of monotheistic worship. And, as has been observed, Gentiles are required to "wash [their] whole bodies in perennial rivers." Which brings us back to the question of the Jewish milieu reflected in the work.

Concerning the attitude to the temple, it presses the evidence too hard to say that the Sibyl rejects temple worship in a categorical way. After all, she describes the Jerusalem temple as "the great Temple of God" (116); because they destroyed it, the Romans are subject to "the wrath of the heavenly God" (135). If she speaks of God as inhabiting a heavenly house, "not fashioned by mortal hand" (8–11), such an emphasis is understandable in the period after the war with Rome and is not without parallel in other Jewish literature of the

173. See J. J. Collins (1983, 383). See also Schürer (1986, 3:642) for references to the suggestion of an Essene origin.

period.[174] The emphasis on ritual washing is more surprising (but cf. *Sib. Or.* 3:591–93). Since Gentiles are not being encouraged to become proselytes in any ordinary sense of the word, comparisons with proselyte baptism[175] are not particularly germane. The reference remains enigmatic, but the suggestion of a link with "Jewish baptist groups" should probably be seen as an attempt to account for the enigmatic on the basis of the obscure.

One other difference from *Sibylline Oracles* 3 is the absence of any expectation of a turning to God on the part of the Gentiles in the eschatological future. In order to have a share in the future age, when the pious are resurrected and behold "the delightful and pleasant light of the sun" (191), Gentiles need to join the company of the pious in the present. Otherwise, they will be numbered among those who "sinned by impiety" (184), whose fate is destruction (40–44, 171–175, 184–185).

Sibylline Oracles 5

After an introductory survey of Roman history (1–51), *Sibylline Oracles* 5 consists of a series of oracles that seem to be grouped into five structured collections (52–110, 111–178, 179–285, 286–434, 435–531), each of which concludes with a depiction of end-time destruction and redemption. The first four of these have additional features in common: the expectation of Nero's "return" from the east (93–110, 137–154, 214–227, 361–385), and the expectation of a savior/king sent by God (108–109, 155–161, 256–259, 414–425). The introductory survey traces the succession of Roman emperors down to Hadrian, who is seen in surprisingly positive terms (46–50). The positive attitude towards Hadrian suggests a date for this section prior to the Bar Cochba war; if so, then line 51, referring to Marcus Aurelius, seems to have been tagged on later. In contrast, the oracles that follow are marked by their bitterness towards both Rome and Egypt. They make explicit reference to the destruction of Jerusalem (150, 397–413), which tends to be depicted as the prelude to the events of the end. There is no explicit reference, however, to the Jewish uprising in the time of Trajan (115–117 C.E.). These oracles are probably to be dated, then, in the latter part of the first century, reflecting the sort of animosity towards both Rome and Egypt that led to the uprising in the early part of the second century.

Such animosity notwithstanding, *Sibylline Oracles* 5 shares with *Sibylline Oracles* 3 the expectation that the future glorification of Jerusalem will be the occasion for (some) Gentiles to abandon their wicked ways and to honor the God of Israel. Two such passages appear (247–280, 420–431), in the eschatological conclusions of the third and fourth sections. In addition, the final section

174. E.g., *2 Bar.* 4:1–7; see §71 below.

175. E.g., Schürer (1986, 3:642).

contains a curious account of a temple to the one true God, erected by Gentiles in Egypt (489–503). The first two passages can be treated together; we will begin with them.

§64 Sibylline Oracles *5:247–80*

But whenever the Persian land desists from war, pestilence, and groaning,
then on that day it will come to pass that the divine and heavenly race of the blessed Jews,
who live around the city of God in the middle of the earth,
are raised up even to the dark clouds,
having built a great wall round about, as far as Joppa.
. . .

260 *Blessed one, no longer weary your spirit in your breast,*
divinely born, wealthy, sole-desired flower, good light, holy shoot, beloved plant,
delightful Judea, fair city, inspired with hymns.
No longer will the unclean foot of Greeks revel around your land
but they will have a mind in their breasts that conforms to your laws.
But glorious children will honor you exceedingly,
and they will attend table with devout music,
all sorts of sacrifices and with prayers honoring God.
. . .

276 *All will remain unsown and unplowed until mortal men*
pay attention to the immortal eternal God, ruler of all,
and no longer honor mortal things, neither dogs nor cultures,
which Egypt taught men to revere with vain mouths and foolish lips.

§65 Sibylline Oracles *5:420–31*

And the city which God desired, this he made more brilliant than stars and sun and moon,
and he provided ornament and made a holy temple, exceedingly beautiful in its fair shrine,
and he fashioned a great and immense tower over many stadia
touching even the clouds and visible to all,
so that all faithful and all righteous people could see the glory of eternal God, a form desired.
East and West sang out the glory of God.
For terrible things no longer happen to wretched mortals,
no adulteries or illicit love of boys, no murder, or din of battle,
but competition is fair among all.

Text: Geffcken (1902)
Translation: *OTP* (J. J. Collins1983)
Date: Late first century C.E.

Provenance: Egypt
Original Language: Greek
Bibliography: Barclay (1996, 226–28); J. J. Collins (1974; 1983; 2000, 143–50, 166–67); Schürer (1986, 3:643–45)
Category: ESCHATOLOGICAL PARTICIPATION

The first passage appears in a section that strikes a universalistic note at the outset, as it looks back to a kind of golden age, when the words of the prophets brought enlightenment and nourishment to "all mortals" (238–41). In the passage under discussion here, the future is seen as a renewal of this golden age. "On that day" (248) the "divine and heavenly race of the blessed Jews" will be exalted (249–51), the walls of Jerusalem will extend as far as Joppa (252), and Judea will bask in the light of divine favor (260–63). The establishment of this state of affairs is linked with the appearance of an "exceptional man from the sky" (256). The text as it stands is Christian, especially line 257. But it is probable that the present text is a Christian reworking of a messianic reference that was present in the Jewish original.[176]

For our purposes, the significant aspect of the passage is that this beatific state of affairs is expected to extend to Gentiles as well. "Greeks" will no longer desecrate the land; rather "they will have a mind in their breasts that conforms to your laws" (265). Given the extremely negative attitude in *Sibylline Oracles* 5 towards both the Romans (e.g., 162–178, 386–396) and the Egyptians (e.g., 179–199), there is probably some significance in the fact that Greeks are singled out here. Nevertheless, as the passage continues, the language becomes less specific and more general: those who turn to honor God are "glorious children" (266), "righteous men" (269), "mortal men" (276). Thus the Sibyl's expectations do not seem to be limited to Greeks per se.

The Sibyl expects, then, that some Gentiles will turn to the laws of the Jews. The word here is not νόμος but ὁμόσθεσμον, an adjective formed from ὁμός (one and the same, common) and θεσμός (that which is laid down; thus, a law or an ordinance). The sense is that these Gentiles will have an inner inclination that conforms to a common set of divine ordinances incumbent on all humanity. We get a hint of what this means a little further on in the oracle, when the Sibyl declares that the time of woe will last until "mortal men" abandon their idolatry and honor "the immortal eternal God, ruler of all" (277). The most important of these "common ordinances," then, are injunctions for monotheistic worship and against idolatry.

176. Line 257 is clearly Christian: "who stretched out his hand on the fruitful wood." Some have seen the whole of 256–59 as a Christian interpolation, but in view of the presence of such a savior figure elsewhere in the work, it is preferable to see this section as a Christian reworking of an original messianic oracle rather than an interpolation in its entirety. See the discussion in J. J. Collins (1974, 87–92).

The second passage also describes the end-time glorification of Jerusalem ("more brilliant than stars and sun and moon") and of the temple ("exceedingly beautiful") with its sanctuary ("a great and immense tower"). Here the role of a messianic figure ("a blessed man . . . from the expanses of heaven with a scepter in his hands which God gave him") is more explicit. The inclusion of Gentiles, however, is less so, at least at first glance. While the renewed temple is "visible to all" (425), these are further specified as "all faithful and all righteous people" (426), which could be taken as a reference to Israelites alone. However, the next line strikes a more clearly universal note, as it describes how "east and west sang out the glory of God" (428). The universal character of this end-time set of events is especially apparent in the reason given (γάρ) for the singing. What prompted this outburst of praise was the disappearance from the world as a whole (cf. "wretched mortals") of precisely the type of immorality that, in the Sibyl's view, characterized Gentile behavior and rendered them liable to divine punishment (sexual immorality, pederasty, etc.). Whether those who were doing the singing were Jews or—as is more likely, given the universal flavor of "east and west"—the Gentiles themselves, the expectation is that Gentiles will abandon their wickedness and exhibit the type of behavior that will cause God to be glorified.

As these passages indicate, this behavior centers on the abandonment of idolatry (278–80), the worship of the one true God (277) and the observance of basic moral standards (429–31). This is consistent with the model of piety that is found in the work as a whole. As in the other Sibylline Oracles, we find no emphasis on those aspects of the law that differentiate Jew from Gentile. Rather, the style of life that the Gentiles are expected to adopt in the end times is precisely that for which the Jews are praised in the present: rejection of idolatry (403–405), worship of God alone (406–7) at God's temple in Jerusalem (150, 397–402). While there is less interest here than in *Sibylline Oracles* 3 to link this pattern of life with the law of Moses, this work shares with the other Sibyllines the vision of a common form of piety—what we might call a temple-centered ethical monotheism. While the Gentiles come to share this piety in the end, there is nothing to suggest that they thereby become Jews.

§66 Sibylline Oracles *5:484–503*

Isis, thrice-wretched goddess, you will remain by the streams of the Nile alone,
a speechless maenad on the sands of the Acheron.
No longer will memory of you remain throughout the whole earth.
And you, Sarapis, reposing on many unwrought stones,
will lie, a very great casualty in thrice-wretched Egypt.
But as many as brought the desire of Egypt to you will all bewail you bitterly,
turning their attention to the imperishable God.
Those who sang out your praises as a god will know that you are nothing.
Then a man clad in linen, one of the priests, will say,

"Come, let us erect a sanctuary of the true God.
Come, let us change the terrible custom we have received from our ancestors
on account of which they performed processions and rites
to gods of stone and earthenware, and were devoid of sense.
Let us turn our souls, singing out the praises of the imperishable God
himself, the begetter who is eternal, the ruler of all, the true one, the king,
the begetter who nourishes souls, the great eternal God."
Then there will be a great holy temple in Egypt,
and a people fashioned by God will bring sacrifices to it.
To them the imperishable God will grant to reside there.

Text: Geffcken (1902)
Translation: *OTP* (J. J. Collins1983)
Bibliography: J. J. Collins (1974, 74–76, 93–94)
Category: ESCHATOLOGICAL PARTICIPATION

This anticipation of a temple in Egypt, erected by a Gentile priest in honor of the God of Israel is indeed a "remarkable prediction" (J. J. Collins 1974, 76). The passage is found in the final section of the work (435–531), a collection of oracles that contain some of the same elements as the previous sections (oracles against the nations, end-time destruction) but that contain no vision of the eschatological redemption of Israel. In its place is a passage dealing with the future of Egypt (484–511), which begins with the portion cited above. The conclusion of the passage is just as remarkable, in that the Sibyl also expects this temple to be destroyed by the Ethiopians (504–507), which in turn will lead to their own judgment by God (508–511).

Even though the anticipated state of affairs is only temporary, the scenario is startling. The Sibyl anticipates a time when the cult of Isis and Sarapis will be no more, as Egyptians turn "their attention to the imperishable God" (490). A priest, evidently an Egyptian because of his reference to "our ancestors" (494), calls on his countryfolk to abandon their ancestral idol worship and to "erect a sanctuary of the true God" (493). The Sibyl evidently fully endorses the idea. The temple is "great" and "holy" (501); the people who offer sacrifice there are "fashioned by God" (502); it is God who has granted them the right to abide there (503).

Of course, the scenario has not been conjured up out of thin air. In all probability it depends heavily on Isaiah 19, with its anticipation that "on that day" there will be "an altar to the Lord in the center of the land of Egypt" (v. 19). And it probably has drawn some of its inspiration from the "altar to the Lord" that had existed until recently in Leontopolis. In addition, the temporary character of this state of affairs needs to be taken fully into account. This Egyptian temple will not endure indefinitely into the eschatological period, but will be destroyed. Further, while the destruction will be carried out by the Ethiopians, the Egyptians themselves seem also to be culpable: the destruction will happen "because they [the Egyptians] did not guard what God entrusted to them" (511). Thus the passage does not expect a permanent turning to God on the part of these Gentiles; their end-time change of heart will be short-lived. Nevertheless, despite its anomalous character, the passage needs to be included in any documentation of the expectation that in the end times Gentiles will turn in significant numbers to worship the God of Israel. Here there is no question whatsoever about the status of these Gentiles; with their own separate sanctuary to "the true God" (493), they remain distinct from the people of Israel.

2 Enoch

§67 2 Enoch *48:6–9*

> *Thus I am making it known to you, my children; |and| you must hand over the books to your children, and throughout all your generations, <and to (your) relatives>, 7 and |among| all nations who are discerning so that they may fear God, and so that they may accept them. And they will be more enjoyable than any delightful food on earth. And they will read them and adhere to them. 8 But those who are undiscerning and who do not understand <|the Lord|> neither fear God nor accept them, but renounce them, and regard themselves as burdened by them—|a terrible judgment is awaiting them|. 9 Happy is |the person| who puts their yoke on and carries it around; for he will plow on the day of the great judgment.*

Text: Slavonic: Vaillant (1976)
Translation: *OTP* (Andersen1983)[177]
Date: Perhaps first century C.E., but very uncertain
Provenance: Uncertain; perhaps Palestine or Egypt
Original Language: Perhaps a Semitic original (Slavonic based on a Greek version)
Bibliography: Andersen (1983); J. J. Collins (1998, 243–47); Nickelsburg (2005, 221–25); Schürer (1987, 3:746–50)
Category: ETHICAL MONOTHEISM

2 Enoch (or the *Slavonic Apocalypse of Enoch* or the *Book of the Secrets of Enoch*) presents the interpreter with so many unresolved questions as to the circumstances of its origin that one needs to exercise considerable caution in any appeal to its evidence. Still, there seems to be enough of a preliminary consensus on its character (Jewish) and date (first or early second century C.E.) that it should be included here.

177. The manuscript tradition contains both a longer and a shorter version. Andersen presents translations of each, the longer based on manuscript J and the shorter based on A. Each has been supplemented with readings from other manuscripts. In the translation cited above, based on J, supplemental readings from R are indicated as {. . .} and from P as | . . . |.

2 Enoch recounts Enoch's ascent to the throne room of the Lord, where the secrets of creation are revealed to him and where he is commissioned to return to his sons for a brief period to instruct them concerning what he has seen and heard. The work thus has a narrative spine that supports a series of visions and exhortations. Enoch's journeys and relocations serve to divide the work into five discernible sections. It begins on earth, with a brief introduction to the whole story (1a); an account of Enoch's dream, in which two angelic figures ("two huge men"; 1:4) inform him of his imminent departure (1:3–10); and some final instructions to his sons (2:1–10), ending with a promise that he would return. Then Enoch is led by the two angelic figures on an ascent through the seven heavens[178] (3:1–22:10). Along the way he sees the fallen angels in their imprisonment (second heaven; chap 7); the final abodes of the righteous (paradise) and the wicked, both in the third heaven (8–10); the courses of the sun and moon (fourth heaven; 11–17); the rebellious angels (fifth heaven; 18); and the righteous angels (sixth heaven; 19). Enoch's arrival in the seventh heaven culminates in his direct encounter with "the Lord" and his transformation into angelic form ("like one of his glorious ones" [22:10]).

This leads into the third section (22:11–35:3), in which God reveals to Enoch the structure of creation, secrets that had been explained "not even to my angels" (24:3). The account is structured according to the six-day pattern of Genesis, but contains fantastical elements without parallel in the biblical tradition. After the description of the creation itself, there is an account of Adam and Eve (30:8–32:2) and of the coming flood (34–35). Before the revelatory session begins, Enoch is instructed to write everything in books; fortunately, he is given "a pen for speed-writing" (22:11)! The pen must have been effective, for he produces no less than 366 books.[179] The books are produced for the benefit of Enoch's children, so that "they will acknowledge me as the Creator of everything" and "understand that there is no other God except myself" (33:8). His sons are to preserve the books so that they can be revealed to the generation living in the time before the final judgment (35:1–3; cf. 33:11–12). The scene ends with God's commissioning of Enoch to return to earth for thirty days to prepare his sons for their task.

The next section, then, takes place back on earth (37–66). It consists of a tedious series of exhortations, addressed first to the sons (39–56), then to Methosalam, his brothers and a company of elders (57–63), and finally to a larger gathering—two thousand strong—from "all his people, near and far" (64:1; 64–66). With Enoch's return to heaven (67), attention turns to the period leading up to the flood (68–73), a section (perhaps an originally

178. The longer MSS make confusing mention of a tenth heaven. See the discussion in Andersen (1983, 134–35).

179. There are only 360 in the shorter manuscripts (a difference that has no bearing on the nature of the pen!).

independent tradition) that includes an account of the miraculous—and bizarre—birth of Melkisedek.

As can be seen from the preceding description, the revelation entrusted to Enoch and contained in his (small library of) books is of great significance, especially for the last generation before the final judgment—that is, the time of *2 Enoch*'s intended readers. While the author acknowledges the existence of other books (scripture?), Enoch's books—the content of which is presumably conveyed in *2 Enoch* itself—are paramount:

> There have been many books since the beginning of creation, and there will be until the end of the age; but not one of them will make things as plain to you as <the books in> my handwriting. If you hold on firmly to them, you will not sin against the Lord. (47:2)

More explicitly, a few verses later, the message contained in Enoch's books is identified as that which will determine the ultimate fate of humankind. Those who "read them and adhere to them" (48:7) will find happiness "on the day of the great judgment" (48:9); those who "neither fear God nor accept them [i.e., the books], but renounce them, and regard themselves as burdened by them" will experience "a terrible judgment" (48:8).

It is in this context that we find the explicit reference to "the nations" as cited above. Enoch instructs his sons to "hand over the books" not only to their relatives and descendants but also to "all nations who are discerning" (48:7). If the text can be relied on, then Enoch's books are presented as determinative not merely for a limited group of his descendants but for the whole of humankind. The matter is uncertain, however, in that the shorter recension makes no mention of the nations at this point.[180] But while a final decision will have to wait for a more thorough examination of the textual tradition, it is worth asking about the place of the Gentiles in *2 Enoch* and their relationship to Enoch's revelation.

Two observations are to be made. The first is the universalistic character of *2 Enoch* as a whole. The story of Enoch is placed within the context of the human story grounded and initiated in Adam, with no attempt to align either Enoch or Adam with the subsequent story of Israel. In the description of Adam's creation (30:8–14), the universal significance of Adam is apparent in the way the language shifts back and forth between "Adam" and "man": "I created man . . . and called his name Adam" (vv. 10, 14). Adam, in other words, represents generic humanity. Later, the whole creation is said to have taken place "for the sake of man" (65:3). Further, while God is quite prepared to inform Enoch about events that would not take place until after his death (e.g., the flood), there is not even a hint of anything beyond Genesis 11. Abraham,

180. "And deliver these books to your children, and the children to the children, and to [all] your relatives, and all your generations, who have the wisdom and who will fear the Lord, and they will accept them."

Moses, the Torah, the temple, the people of Israel itself—all are strikingly absent. This is not to deny the essential Jewishness of the work, a point to which we will return. But on the whole *2 Enoch* seems to be interested in humankind in a universal and undifferentiated way.

Or, more precisely, the only differentiation that counts is the one between the righteous and the wicked. Adam is given free will not only that God might know whether Adam loves him but also "so that it might become plain who among his race loves me" (30:15). Adam is the progenitor of a single "race," and while a differentiation is to be made among his descendants, it has nothing to do with God's election of a special covenant people, and not even with the giving of a particular law. Rather, it is a differentiation arising from individual choice based on human free will. The differentiation is not ethnic or covenantal, but ethical.[181]

Which brings us to the second observation, having to do with the basis on which the righteous and wicked are differentiated. *2 Enoch* envisages a single set of requirements incumbent on the whole of humankind, consisting of the abandonment of idolatry and worship of "the Lord" on the one hand, and the observance of some basic moral commandments on the other. These requirements are first fully articulated in Enoch's ascent through the third heaven as he observes the final abodes of the righteous and the wicked (8–10). The righteous are those who suffer hardship patiently, who "avert their eyes from injustice," who care for the needy (the hungry, the naked, the fallen, the orphans) and who "worship him only" (9:1). The wicked are those who have engaged in homosexuality, in witchcraft and sorcery, in the oppression of the poor, and in idolatry (10:4–6). Similar catalogs of righteous and wicked deeds appear throughout the work—in God's revelation to Enoch concerning the reason for the flood (34:1–3), and in Enoch's instructions to his sons (42:6–14; 49–51), to Methusalam and company (63), and to the larger assembly (66:1–8). While these catalogs are similar in most respects to lists found in other analogous material, *2 Enoch* is unique in its emphasis on social ethics—generosity (2:2; 51:1–2), care for the needy and oppressed (42:8–9; 50:6; 51:1–2; 63:1), willingness to suffer injustice rather than taking vengeance (9:1; 50:4), respect for human beings as created in God's image,[182] and so on.

At the same time, however, in addition to this dominant strand of universalistic ethical monotheism, there are also reflections of particular Jewish concerns in *2 Enoch*. The focus on a biblical figure, together with the thoroughgoing reliance on biblical material in the work as a whole, marks this as a Jewish work.

181. Also 42:14: "For the works of the Lord are right, but the works of mankind—some are good, but others are evil; and by their works those who speak lying blasphemies are recognized."

182. "He who treats with contempt the face of any person treats the face of the Lord with contempt" (44:2).

In addition, there is a strong emphasis on sacrifice and offerings.[183] To a certain extent this could be seen as generic and non-specific. In 68:5–7, for example, Methusalam erects an altar on the spot where Enoch had departed to heaven, clearly somewhere other than Jerusalem; also, the author is more concerned with the ethical rather than the geographical context for sacrifice: sacrifice needs to be carried out with a pure heart and the right intentions.[184] Nevertheless, there are fairly clear allusions to Jewish particularities: the offering of first fruits (2:2); the distinction between clean and unclean animals and birds, both for sacrifice and for food (59:1–5); and, strikingly, a reference to the temple: "In the morning of the day and in the middle of the day and in the evening of the day it is good to go to the Lord's temple |on account of| <|the glory of|> |your| <|creator|>" (51:4). Further, while there is no explicit reference to the law of Moses, the ethical requirements that receive so much emphasis in the work are described as God's commandments (2:2; 34:1). Thus a case can be made that, despite its universal outlook, *2 Enoch* is nevertheless to be located within a world defined by Jewish particulars.

Still, to the extent that the work reflects the particulars of Jewish existence, the author has chosen to ignore the social and ethnic differentiations that such particulars produce and to present God's "commandments" in the form of a universal ethical monotheism equally binding on all of Adam's descendants without distinction.

4 Ezra

Like *Jubilees* or Pseudo-Philo, *4 Ezra* is unrelentingly pessimistic about the ultimate fate of the Gentiles. Like the Qumran literature, it restricts salvation to a small remnant within Israel, thus lumping the majority of Jews in with the Gentiles. Unlike these other writings, however, the author of *4 Ezra* is distressed by the smallness of the company of the redeemed. The literary result of this distress—a sustained struggle with issues of theodicy, including the justice of God's dealings with the Gentiles—is without parallel in the literature here under review.

Written towards the end of the first century C.E., probably during the reign of Domitian (81–96), *4 Ezra* is patently a response to the crisis of faith precipitated by the war with Rome and its outcome, the destruction of the temple, and the shattering of Jewish national existence. In one respect, this crisis of faith was the common experience of Judaism as a whole. But for the author of *4 Ezra*, it has assumed a form unique within the literature of the period. The point of departure for the book is a deep pessimism about the ability of human beings—even within Israel—to keep the law. The law was given in glory

183. 2:2; 42:6; 45:1–3; 46; 59:2–5; 61:4–5; 62:1; 66:2–4.

184. 45:3; 46; 61:4–5; 62:1; 66:3–4.

(3:17–19); but because of the "grain of evil seed [that] was sown in Adam's heart from the beginning" (3:30), human beings are afflicted with an "evil heart" (e.g., 3:20; 7:48), making it impossible for all but a very few to keep the law and so attain salvation. The consequence of this is that "many have been created, but few will be saved" (8:3; also 7:45–48, 59–61, 116–31; 9:14–16; etc.). Such pessimism is unusual in Jewish literature, where it is generally assumed that the law can readily be kept by those who desire to do so and that the covenantal provisions for repentance, atonement, and forgiveness are sufficient to deal with Israel's sin.[185]

If such pessimism is the point of departure of the book, the journey is the process by which Ezra comes to terms with it. The book is tightly constructed, comprising seven visions or episodes. The first three (3:1–5:20; 5:21–6:34; 6:35–9:25) consist of Ezra's anguished yet bold case against God for allowing such a situation to exist, together with the patient yet unyielding defense of God's ways by the angel Uriel. In the first two episodes, where Ezra assumes the role of a spokesperson for the Jewish people, the nations come in only as a foil for Israel. Like the prophets of old, Ezra laments that "those who opposed [God's] promises" (5:29) have not only prospered (3:2) but have also prevailed over Israel (3:28–36; 4:22–25; 5:28–30). In the third episode, however, the vision broadens; Israel's dilemma is placed in the larger context of the created order, and Ezra begins to speak on behalf of Adamic humanity as a whole. The assessment of the human situation remains unchanged: the "evil heart [which] has grown up in us" will work to bring death to "not just a few of us but almost all who have been created" (7:48). But Ezra identifies with doomed humanity as a whole and thus is led to question God's wisdom in creating the world at all (e.g., 7:62–69). In such a situation it is not enough for Uriel simply to reassure Ezra that the nations will be judged in due course; now their judgment needs to be justified. At this stage of the book, then, theodicy takes on universalistic dimensions, which adds significant additional dimensions to the treatment of the Gentiles in *4 Ezra*.

By the fourth vision (9:26–10:59), however, it has become apparent that a transformation has taken place in Ezra, as he now begins to defend the views he had previously challenged. After glimpses of the ultimate vindication of the remnant of Israel in visions five and six (11:1–12:39; 13:1–58), he emerges in the final episode (14:1–48) as a kind of new Moses, commissioned by God to console the people and to instruct them in the law.

Since the only change to take place in the course of the book is Ezra's acceptance of the position he once questioned, there is no softening of the pessimism regarding the Gentiles: from beginning to end they form part of the "many" destined for destruction. There are two slight exceptions to this gloomy

185. This point has been made, perhaps in an exaggerated fashion, by E. P. Sanders (1977, 409–18). For a recent re-examination of the matter, see Longenecker (1991).

outlook, however. One is the possibility that the author has made use of pre-existing traditions containing material that in its earlier context was much more optimistic about the eventual fate of the Gentiles. Two such passages in particular (i.e., 6:25–28; 13:12–13a) will be discussed below. The other is the following grudging admission that here or there may be individual Gentiles who have kept God's commandments.

Text: Latin: Klijn (1983a)
Translation: *OTP* (Metzger1983)
Date: Late first century C.E.
Provenance: The land of Israel
Original Language: Hebrew
Bibliography: J. J. Collins (1998, 195–212); Longenecker (1991; 1995); Metzger (1983); Myers (1974); E. P. Sanders (1977, 409–18); Schreiner (1981); Schürer (1986, 3:294–306); Stone (1990); A. Thompson (1977).

§68 4 Ezra *3:31b–36*

> *Are the deeds of Babylon better than those of Zion?* [32] *Or has another nation known you besides Israel? Or what tribes have so believed your covenants as these tribes of Jacob?* [33] *Yet their reward has not appeared and their labour has borne no fruit. For I have traveled widely among the nations and have seen that they abound in wealth, though they are unmindful of your commandments.* [34] *Now therefore weigh in a balance our iniquities and those of the inhabitants of the world; and so it will be found which way the turn of the scale will incline.* [35] *When have the inhabitants of the earth not sinned in your sight? Or what nation has kept your commandments so well?* [36] *You may indeed find individual men who have kept your commandments, but nations you will not find.*

Category: CONVERSION

The assertion that "the nations [*gentes*] . . . are unmindful of your commandments" echoes a theme that recurs in *4 Ezra*, especially in the third vision. Apparently the author felt some concern to justify the bleak outlook for the Gentiles that dominates the work. The answer given in several passages (especially 7:20–24, 72–74; 8:55–61; 9:9–12) is that the Gentiles were culpable because, although they knew God's requirements, they scorned them and refused to follow them. Each of these passages assumes that Gentiles were fully aware of God's requirements, that they nevertheless willfully ignored them, and that, as a result, their ultimate condemnation is justified.

But two questions present themselves. First, how is it that the Gentiles should have been aware of God's law in the first place? The passages provide very little indication of how this might have come about. While Uriel declares that humankind as a whole has "received the commandments" and "obtained the law" (7:72), he tells us nothing about the mode in which the commandments were received or the law obtained. Where similar language is used of Adam ("when Adam transgressed my statutes" [7:11]), the usage is more understandable in that Jewish tradition often understood the divine injunction given to Adam in the garden "as the Mosaic Law *in nuce*" (Stone 1990, 195). But in *4 Ezra* such a tradition seems to be extended to the Gentiles as a whole without further ado. Perhaps there is some affinity between this aspect of *4 Ezra* and the rabbinical idea that the law had been offered to the nations but they rejected it.[186] In any case, what seems to have been more important to the author was the "fact" that the Gentiles knew the law and thus could be held accountable for their sin, rather than any theory as to how they acquired this knowledge in the first place.

The second question has to do with the extent to which the Gentiles were expected to conform to the law. Are they condemned because they failed to embrace it fully, that is, to become proselytes? Or did they fall short of some lesser set of requirements that were incumbent on them as Gentiles? The answer to this question is not readily apparent. On the one hand, these passages make little reference to those ethnos-specific aspects of the law by which Jews were differentiated from Gentiles. The "law," and the Gentiles' transgression of it, are described in very general terms: "what they should do to live, and what they should observe to avoid punishment" (7:21); "they . . . forsook his ways" (8:56). The only transgressions mentioned explicitly are the denial of God's existence (7:23; 8:58) and the oppression of God's "righteous ones" (8:57). On the other hand, however, we need to note that while Ezra's language may not be ethnos-specific, it certainly is covenant-specific:[187] what the Gentiles refused to follow is described as God's "law" (7:24), the "commandments" (7:72), God's "covenants" (7:24), even God's "covenant" in the singular (7:46). Thus it is difficult to decide whether *4 Ezra* condemns the Gentiles because they failed to become proselytes or because they failed to honor God as Gentiles. Probably the question should not be pressed. For the author of this work the Gentiles fell so far short of either mark that the distinction was one not worth worrying about.

But in order for this argument of Gentile culpability to work, it is logically necessary that the Gentiles possess a real possibility of turning to God and embracing the divine law. Such a possibility is hinted at in a couple of verses: "those who dwell on earth shall be tormented, because though they had understanding they committed iniquity, and though they received the commandments they did not keep them, and though they obtained the Law they dealt unfaithfully with what they received" (7:72); "as many as scorned my Law while they still had freedom, and did not understand but despised it while an opportunity

186. E.g., *Sipre Deut* 343 (to Deut 33:2); Mek. Baḥodesh 1 (to Exod 19:2).
187. On this whole point, see Stone (1990, 194–95).

of repentance was still open to them, these must in torment acknowledge it after death" (9:11–12). But since the "opportunity of repentance" has now passed, the possibility in these passages is only hypothetical.

Things are a little different, however, in 4 Ezra 3:31b–36, the passage cited above. Of particular interest is v. 36, where the reference to "individual men who have kept your commandments"[188] seems to recognize the existence of actual Gentiles who have observed the law. But the reference is obscure; it is not possible to discern whether the author is thinking of contemporary proselytes, or of noteworthy Gentiles in scripture,[189] or of something else. Thus while the passage seems to be less hypothetical than the others, it does little to relieve the pessimism of *4 Ezra* as a whole. The Gentiles were aware of God's requirements; they had every opportunity to repent and turn to God; but, except for the slight possibility left open by the statement in 3:36, they did not do so. Thus their condemnation and destruction is justified.

§69 4 Ezra *6:25–28*

> [25]*It shall be that whoever remains after all that I have foretold to you shall be saved and shall see my salvation and the end of my world.* [26]*And they shall see the men who were taken up, who from their birth have not tasted death; and the heart of the earth's inhabitants shall be changed and converted to a different spirit.* [27]*For evil shall be blotted out, and deceit shall be quenched;* [28]*faithfulness shall flourish, and corruption shall be overcome, and the truth, which has been so long without fruit, shall be revealed.*

Category: ESCHATOLOGICAL PARTICIPATION

This description of eschatological redemption—the first to appear in *4 Ezra*—concludes a larger section (6:18–28) which opens with a collection of signs indicating the approach of the end. Like 5:1–13, another collection of signs to which the present passage makes reference (6:11–12), the style is strikingly different from the larger visions in which they are located. Elsewhere the style is dialogical, Ezra and Uriel engaging in a back-and-forth dialog on theodicy. In these two passages, however, we encounter straightforward apocalyptic oracle, of a style that is common in apocalyptic literature. These considerations have led many scholars to conclude that the author is here drawing on already existing material, even if it has been fully incorporated into its present context.[190]

In the context of *4 Ezra*, of course, the group that survives the tumult of the end and remains to experience divine salvation is made up of the few

188. The text is difficult: "by names" (Latin); "by name" (Georgian); "with names" (Syriac); "few" (Armenian). Two possibilities present themselves: "few enough to be enumerated by name," and "famous." The issue does not have a real bearing on the present point. For a discussion of the options, see Stone (1990, 60, 77).

189. For the suggestion of Job, see the comment by Box (1913, 2:564).

190. See Stone (1990, 107, 167); Longenecker (1995, 45).

law-observant righteous within Israel.[191] But abstracted from its context, the reference to the "earth's inhabitants" whose heart "shall be changed and converted to a different spirit"[192] takes on a decidedly universalistic ring. The term "inhabitants of the earth" appears earlier in v. 18, where it is clearly universal in its reference. Here it either refers to the earth's inhabitants as a whole, Jews and Gentiles together, or, given the distinction in v. 19 between the doers of iniquity on the one hand and humiliated Zion on the other, it is possible that "the inhabitants of the earth" is to be equated with the former and seen as a reference to the non-Jewish inhabitants. If this reading were valid, then in vv. 25–28 there would be a distinction between the group that "remains after all that I have foretold to you" (v. 25)—that is, the remnant of Israel, who are finally vindicated—and "the earth's inhabitants" whose heart is "changed and converted to a different spirit" (v. 26)—that is, the Gentiles, who are subsequently included in end-time salvation. But even if it were to be conceded that this distinction is forced, so that "whoever remains" (v. 25) and "the earth's inhabitants" (v. 26) both refer to the same group, the clearly universalistic sense of the latter term (already established in v. 18) suggests that, in the underlying source, at least, Gentiles are to be included in eschatological redemption.[193]

§70 4 Ezra *13:12–13a*

> [12]*After this I saw the same man come down from the mountain and call to him another multitude which was peaceable.* [13]*Then many people came to him, some of whom were joyful and some sorrowful; some of them were bound, and some were bringing others as offerings.*

Category: ESCHATOLOGICAL PARTICIPATION

4 Ezra 13 contains a vision (vv. 1–13), Ezra's request for interpretation (vv. 14–20), and the interpretation itself (vv. 21–58). In the vision, Ezra sees "something like the figure of a man come out of the heart of the sea" (v. 3), an image with clear reflections of Dan 7:13–14. Then "an innumerable multitude of men" gather to make war against this "man," but they are annihilated on a "great mountain" that the man "carved out for himself" (cf. Dan 2:34–35). It is at this point that the "man" calls to himself the "peaceable" multitude described in the text under discussion here.

The presence of significant disjunction between the vision itself (vv. 1–13a) and the interpretation of the vision (vv. 21–56) is a strong indication that the

191. For other references to those who survive the difficult time of trial to come, see 7:27; 9:7–8, 21–22; 12:34.

192. "Earth's" is missing from the Latin, but it should probably be taken as original; see Stone (1990, 163).

193. See Feldman (1993, 554, n. 9).

former represents an already-existing tradition. On the one hand, significant elements of the vision itself are either ignored in the interpretation (e.g., the wind that stirred up the sea; the flying on the clouds of heaven [both in v. 3]) or are touched on briefly and awkwardly (e.g., the carved mountain [vv. 6–7; cf. v. 36]). Conversely, the interpretation is at points only loosely connected to the vision, especially the section dealing with the lost tribes of Israel (vv. 39–47). This lack of fit between the vision (vv. 1–13a) and its interpretation (vv. 13b–56) is a clear indication that the vision itself has been drawn from already existing material.[194]

For our purposes, the point of interest concerns the two groups which gather in turn around the "man" at the conclusion of the vision: first a peaceable multitude (v. 12); then "many people" (v. 13a), a group further subdivided into the joyful and the sorrowful, and the bound and those bringing others as gifts. While there is a diversity of scholarly opinion concerning some of the details here, there is general agreement on one element, which provides us with a fixed reference point. The statement that "some were bringing others as offerings" is clearly based on Isa 66:20, a pilgrimage text in which Gentiles hear of God's glory and thus bring the scattered exiles "as an offering to the Lord,. . . just as the Israelites bring a grain offering in a clean vessel to the house of the Lord." This seems to suggest that despite the negative attitude towards the Gentiles in *4 Ezra* as a whole, the author has incorporated a much more positive piece of tradition.

Admittedly, it might be possible to construe this traditional piece in a consistently negative way. Klausner (1955, 360–61) identifies the "bound" with the returning exiles, which would make it possible to read the latter part of v. 13a as an instance of parallelism, the "bound" (i.e., Israelites) being identified with the "joyful" and those bringing the exiles (i.e., Gentiles) as the "sorrowful"; Stone seems to read the text in this way.[195] If "sorrowful" were taken in a strictly negative way, any element of hope might be excluded from the passage, the Gentiles appearing only as the means by which the exiled Jews were returned to Zion, with no hope of sharing in salvation (and thus sorrowful indeed).

But such a pessimistic reading is unlikely.[196] The fact that the Gentiles bring the exiles as "offerings" puts a more positive complexion on their role, echoing the positive features of Isa 66:18–21. Further, there is no support in the

194. For a full discussion, see Stone (1990, 396–400).

195. At least, he identifies the joyful as the Israelites and the sorrowful as the Gentiles (Stone 1990, 387).

196. Indeed, both Stone and (apparently) Klausner take the text as an example of the eschatological pilgrimage tradition. For Klausner, the second group in v. 13a consists entirely of Gentiles; as in *2 Bar* 72:2–6, the joyful are those who did not oppress Israel, while the sorrowful are those who did (Klausner 1955, 360). Stone (1990, 387) is a little harder to interpret. While he equates the sorrowful with the Gentiles, he seems to agree with "the general

tradition for an identification of the "bound" with the returning exiles; where it appears in eschatological texts, this feature refers only to Gentiles (Isa 45:14; *2 Bar* 40:1). The latter part of v. 13a is more plausibly to be taken as a chiasm: A: joyful; B: sorrowful; B*: bound (= those Gentiles destined for destruction);[197] A*: some (= redeemed Gentiles) bringing others as offerings (= Diaspora Jews). Thus the text is probably to be taken as an example of the eschatological pilgrimage tradition. Some Gentiles come in joy to the mountain of the Lord bringing Israelite exiles with them as part of their worship. The distinction between the two groups is maintained; the Gentiles retain their identity as Gentiles.

2 Baruch

2 Baruch contains three passages of interest. Two of these are found in the Cloud and Waters Apocalypse (chs. 53–74), which, as we will see, is undoubtedly to be understood as a preexisting source that the author of *2 Baruch* has taken up and refitted for his own use. One reason for this conclusion is that the attitude towards Gentiles in the Cloud and Waters Apocalypse differs from the viewpoint that is dominant in *2 Baruch*. The dominant viewpoint comes into view in the passage with which we begin.

Text: Syriac: Dedering (1973)
Translation: *OTP* (Klijn 1983b)
Date: Late first or early second century C.E.
Provenance: The land of Israel
Original Language: Probably Hebrew
Bibliography: Bogaert (1969); J. J. Collins (1998, 212–25); Klijn (1983b); Murphy (1985); Sayler (1984); Schürer (1987, 3:750–56)

§71 2 Baruch *41:1–42:5*

[41:1]*And I answered and said: For whom and for how many will these things be? Or who will be worthy to live in that time?* [2]*I shall now say before you everything that I think, and I shall ask you about the things of which I meditate.* [3]*For behold, I see many of*

opinion of the commentators" that "this verse describes the ingathering of the converted Gentiles who bring with them the dispersed of Israel" (assuming that the statement "the language typical of that idea is not to be found" refers to the idea of the "survivors" and not to that of the "ingathering of the converted Gentiles").

197. In Isa 45:14, the idea of "bonds" appears in a more positive setting, Gentiles making pilgrimage to Zion "in chains" as a sign of submission. But here the distinction between those who are bound and those who are making pilgrimage with the returning exiles seems to suggest a more negative interpretation of the bonds (as in *2 Bar.* 40:1).

your people who separated themselves from your statutes and who have cast away from them the yoke of your Law. [4]Further, I have seen others who left behind their vanity and who have fled under your wings. [5]What will, therefore, happen with those? Or how will that last time receive them? [6]Their time will surely not be weighed exactly, and they will certainly not be judged as the scale indicates?

[42:1]And he answered and said to me: [2]Also these things I shall show you. As for what you said: "To whom and to how many will these things be?" The good that was mentioned before will be to those who have believed, and the opposite of these things will be to those who have despised. [3]And as for that which you have said with regard to those who have drawn near and to those who have withdrawn, this is the explanation. [4]As for those who have first subjected themselves and have withdrawn later and who mingled themselves with the seed of the mingled nations, their first time will be considered as mountains. [5]And those who first did not know life and who later knew it exactly and who mingled with the seed of the people who have separated themselves, their first time will be considered as mountains.

Category: CONVERSION

Like *4 Ezra*, to which it is linked in some form of literary interdependence, *2 Baruch* uses the setting of the first destruction of the temple at the hands of the Babylonians to address questions raised for faithful Jews by the second destruction at the hands of the Romans. And as in the case of *4 Ezra*, these questions have to do with God's apparent unfaithfulness to Israel and the prospect that the covenantal promises will come to naught. But Baruch displays much less agony over these questions than Ezra and is much more confident that the covenantal story is unfolding as it should.[198] Such differences are apparent with respect to the Gentiles as well. On the one hand, Baruch displays none of the concern of Ezra over the bleak fate of the bulk of humankind. But this is because, on the other, Baruch is much more confident that the law can be obeyed, not only by Jews but also by Gentile proselytes as well.

Still, the destruction of Jerusalem and the temple is a calamity, and it raises real questions. What will become of Israel and its role as witness to God's glorious deeds "if you destroy your city and deliver up your country to those who hate us" (3:5–6)? Will everything "which you said to Moses" about Israel come to nothing (3:9)? How can it be true that the world was made for the righteous (15:7) if it is the sinners who live happily until the day of their deaths (14:2)? What justice can be found in a situation where Babylon is happy but Zion is destroyed (11:2)?

198. For example, since Baruch is informed of the destruction before it happens (1:1–5), and further, is allowed to see that the destruction is carried out by God's angels before the enemies enter but only after the sacred vessels have been removed (5:1–7:1), the events do not have the same unsettling potential that they do in *4 Ezra*. See J. J. Collins (1998, 216–17); also Bogaert (1969, 1:402–05).

In God's response to Baruch, any concern over the fate of Jerusalem is disposed of quickly. Baruch is not to lament the destruction of the city and the temple, because the real Jerusalem, of which Adam and Moses had only the merest of glimpses, is hidden away in God's presence, ready to be revealed in the coming age (4:1–7). Indeed, the destruction of Zion is almost to be welcomed, in that it makes it possible for the coming age to appear more quickly (20:1–2). The real issue is faithfulness to the law. The law, which is eternal (59:2) and the source of life (38:2), has been given to Israel alone of all the nations (48:20–24; 77:3). It is because of Israel's transgression of the law that it has suffered these calamities (1:2; 13:9; 77:8–10; 78:5; 79:2). These sufferings are intended to have a chastening effect (4:1; 13:9–10) so that Israel will return to the path of righteousness and not suffer the same fate as the nations (78:6). For the present prosperity of the nations is illusory (82:3–9); their time of punishment will come in due course (13:6–12; 40:1) and the wicked will receive their due reward (30:4–5; 51:4; 54:14–19). A similar fate awaits those within Israel who have abandoned the law (41:3), but those who live according to the law can be assured that they will enter into the joys of the coming age (32:1; 44:3–8; 48:20–24; 51:3; 77:3–10).

The law also governs the framework within which *2 Baruch* conceives of the nations. While Israel alone has received the law (48:20–24; 77:3), the law nevertheless is universal in its scope:

> For each of the inhabitants of the earth knew when he acted unrighteously, and they did not know my Law because of their pride. . . . And concerning all of those, their end will put them to shame, and your Law which they transgressed will repay them on your day. (48:40, 47)

Thus the Gentiles should have kept the law, are culpable for having spurned it (also 15:5–6; 51:4), and will ultimately be condemned by it (also 82:6). Consistent with the universal scope of the law is the fact that it predates Sinai: on the positive side of things, the patriarchs lived in accordance with the law in its unwritten form (57:2); on the negative side—and more importantly for our purposes—Adam's sin itself was a transgression of the commandment (4:3). Indeed, the situation of Adam (Eve is included at one point [48:42]) is prototypical for that of humankind as a whole. Because Adam and Eve have sinned, "this whole multitude [i.e., of their descendants] is going to corruption" (48:42–43). But this is no proto-Augustinian conception of original sin. Each of Adam's descendants has, by failing to love God's law (54:14), "prepared for himself the coming torment" (54:15) and thus will bear individually the responsibility for their transgression of God's law (48:47). "Adam is, therefore, not the cause, except only for himself, but each of us has become our own Adam" (54:19).

To this point, *2 Baruch* resembles *4 Ezra*, where in a similar manner the universality of the law is used to justify the ultimate condemnation of the

Gentiles. But whereas in *4 Ezra* the possibility of Gentile adherence to the law is little more than a hypothetical corollary of Ezra's grim theodicy, in *2 Baruch* this possibility is a very real one.[199] Baruch's more optimistic outlook is apparent in the passage cited in the previous paragraph, where we find a much more balanced treatment of the wicked and the righteous. Alongside those of Adam's posterity, each of whom "has prepared for himself the coming torment," is another company of "believers" (cf. 54:16), each of whom "has chosen for himself the coming glory" (54:15). Of course, there is nothing in this passage to indicate that Gentiles might be included among these believers; those who "love your Law" (54:14) might simply be the faithful within Israel. Still, the passage displays a surprisingly universal tone, and the groups are described in terms that are decidedly not ethnos-specific.[200] Moreover, the reader of *2 Baruch* has already been given an explicit indication that proselytes form a significant group in the demography of the apocalypse—that is, in 41:1–42:5, the passage to which we now turn our direct attention.

This passage appears in the dialog that follows the apocalypse of the forest, the vine, the fountain, and the cedar (chs. 36–38). Baruch has just been given an interpretation of the vision having to do with the appearance of God's Anointed One and the arrival of the messianic era (chs. 39–40). After inquiring "For whom and for how many shall these things be?" Baruch inquires about two groups of people in particular—apostates (those "who separated themselves from your statutes and who have cast away from them the yoke of your Law") and proselytes. While the latter term does not appear explicitly, the group is described in terms usually used of proselytes: they have "drawn near" (42:3), a term that is etymologically linked to προσήλυτος; they have "mingled with the seed of the people who have separated themselves" (42:5); the "vanity" that they have left behind (41:4) is no doubt that of idolatry;[201] like Ruth (Ruth 2:12), they have taken shelter under God's wings (41:4). Further, the contrast with the first group suggests that they have submitted to God's statutes and taken on the yoke of the law (cf. 41:3).[202]

199. Bogaert attempts to correlate the contrasting views of *4 Ezra* and *2 Baruch* with those of Rabbis Eliezer and Joshua (respectively) in *t. Sanh.* 13.2 (1969, 1:412–13). But this is a confusion of categories. *T. Sanh.* 13.2 has to do with the possibility of righteous Gentiles, and has nothing to do with proselytism. Given its dominant position that only proselytes will have a share in the age to come, *2 Baruch* is closer to R. Eliezer than to R. Joshua.

200. A similar generalized characterization of the righteous and the wicked is found throughout ch. 51.

201. As it is frequently in the OT; see Deut 32:21; 1 Kgs 16:13, 26; 2 Kgs 17:15; Jer 2:5; 8:19; Jonah 2:8.

202. The two groups are treated in antithetical parallelism in 42:4–5 as well. In view of the fact that the total number of Adam's descendants, wicked and righteous, has been decreed beforehand (*2 Bar* 23), this parallel treatment of apostates and proselytes might suggest that the proselytes come in to take the place in the appointed number of the righteous formerly

Concerned about the ultimate fate of these two groups, Baruch receives divine assurance that it is only their final disposition that will count in the end. While chapter 42 is confused and the text probably corrupt, the overall thrust of the passage is that the first state of the apostates ("those who have first subjected themselves"; v. 4) and of the proselytes ("those who first did not know life"; v. 5) will have no significance in the final reckoning.[203] In answer to Baruch's question, then, Gentile proselytes (but not Jewish apostates) will be included among those who "will be worthy to live in that time" (41:1).

2 Baruch represents a strain of thought, then, that is optimistic about the possibility of Gentiles becoming proselytes and treats proselytes as an important group in the overall scheme of salvation. In addition to the explicit reference in chapters 41–42, it is possible that proselytes are in view in the prayer that God might "save all those who come to you" in 48:19.[204] Further, it is at least possible that the attraction of proselytes is one of the ways in which the scattered people of Israel will "do good to the nations" (1:4).[205]

§72 2 Baruch *68:5–6*

> *And at that time, after a short time, Zion will be rebuilt again, and the offerings will be restored, and the priests will again return to their ministry. And the nations will again come to honor it.* [6]*But not as fully as before.*

Category: SYMPATHIZATION

The Cloud and Waters Apocalypse (chs. 53–74) is a lengthy apocalyptic vision in which Baruch sees the whole of human history, from the creation to the final consummation, depicted by means of an alternating series of dark and bright waters. This Apocalypse stands in tension with the rest of *2 Baruch* at several points. One disjunction between the two concerns the absence from the Apocalypse of any reference to the destruction of the temple by the Romans, an

---

occupied by those who have left. Such an idea would be consistent with Baruch's outlook, but it nowhere becomes explicit.

203. Taken as it stands, the final phrase in 42:4, 5 is obscure in the Syriac ("considered as mountains" [*ramata*]). Commentators have tended to take this as a rendering of the Greek ὑψηλοφρονεῖν, either "to be highly thought of" or "to be seen from on high." Bogaert, however, suggests a plausible emendation from *ramata* to *remta* (dust): their past will be considered as dust, i.e., as of no further significance; see Bogaert (1969, 2:76). (On this point I am grateful for the assistance of James P. Wagner, a friend and student of Syriac.)

204. Suggested on etymological grounds by Bogaert (1969, 2:89).

205. Bogaert says that the Syriac could also be rendered, "pour qu'il leur porte un message," which would make this possibility more explicit (1969, 2:10); Sayler's suggestion—that the "good" is the opportunity (through the exile) for the Gentiles to pile up even more transgressions—is unlikely (Sayler 1984, 46–47).

event that obviously loomed large in the author's own view of history. Another disjunction has to do with its attitude towards the Gentiles. As we have seen, outside the Cloud and Waters Apocalypse *2 Baruch* places great stress on the law as the sole and universal means of pleasing God, an approach which has a strict form of proselytism as its corollary: only by becoming proselytes to Judaism in this age will Gentiles have any hope of sharing in the blessings of the age to come. In the Apocalypse, however, Gentiles receive divine blessing in one way or another but without any indication that they have become proselytes. Indeed, in one passage (*2 Bar.* 72:1–6, to be discussed below) the criterion for participation in the messianic age is simply the fact of not having oppressed Israel in this age.

In all probability, this disjunction is to be accounted for on source-critical terms. That is, it is likely that the Cloud and Waters Apocalypse represents a pre-70 C.E. source taken over by the author and adapted for use in its present context. It is true that scholarship has developed a much higher tolerance for inconsistencies in apocalyptic literature than was the case in the past; the older tendency to exaggerate differences and then to postulate multiple sources to account for them has largely been abandoned.[206] Nevertheless, it is still generally recognized that the Cloud and Waters Apocalypse represents traditional material stemming from the pre-70 C.E. period.[207]

The passage under discussion here appears in the twelfth period, whose "bright waters" symbolize the return from exile and the rebuilding of Zion. This is followed by a black period, darker than all those that preceded (69:1), and then by the final bright period of messianic bliss (72:1). According to the usual pattern found in such apocalyptic periodizations, the author no doubt understood his own time to be that period of greatest blackness, which would soon give way to the brightness of the end. In its context, then, 68:5–6 refers to Gentile worship at the temple in the post-exilic period.

There are several things of interest in this passage. First, as mentioned above, there is no indication that these Gentiles have become proselytes; they are present as Gentiles, there simply to honor the temple of Israel. Second, in the view of the Apocalypse, this is something that had happened to a greater extent "before," that is, in the pre-exilic period. Bogaert (1969, 2:122) suggests that the text might have in mind the age of Solomon, in which "all the kings of the earth sought the presence of Solomon, to hear his wisdom" (2 Chr 9:23). But the temple is mentioned only in passing in this section of 2 Chronicles (cf. 9:4). A more likely background is to be found in 1 Kgs 8:41–43, Solomon's prayer of dedication for the temple, where he petitions God to hear the prayer

206. R. H. Charles, e.g., postulated no less than six sources (Charles 1913d, 2:474–76). For criticisms of such an approach, see Sayler (1984, 4–6), Murphy (1985, 2–3) and J. J. Collins (1998, 214–16).

207. See Murphy (1985, 66); Klijn (1970, 65–76; 1983, 617–18).

of "a foreigner, who is not of your people Israel, [but who] comes from a distant land because of your name." The third element of interest has to do with the phrase "not as fully as before." The idea that the second temple fell short of the first is a common theme in Biblical and post-Biblical texts (Ezra 3:12–13; Hag 2:3; Zech 4:10; Tob 14:5). But in contrast to these other texts, where the inadequacy has to do with lack of grandeur of the temple itself, in *2 Bar.* 68:6 it has to do with the degree to which Gentiles come to honor it.

In his treatment of the passage, Murphy has argued that in the original Cloud and Waters Apocalypse this account of a Gentile pilgrimage to the temple formed part of the eschatological climax, but that the author of *2 Baruch* retrojected the pilgrimage into the past as part of a thoroughgoing program of undercutting any expectation of a restored this-worldly temple and of shifting attention instead to a heavenly future (Murphy 1985, 112–13). But this argument is overly subtle and unconvincing. For one thing, as is evident from the material presented in this chapter, the idea of a Gentile pilgrimage is by no means restricted to eschatological contexts. Jews took great pride in the degree to which Gentiles honored the temple in the present, which means that there is no reason whatsoever to suspect that vv. 5–6 were originally eschatological in orientation. Further, the qualitative contrast between this age and the age to come is not as sharp in *2 Baruch* as Murphy would have it.[208] Note, for example, the earthly dimensions of the consummation in chapters 73–74. Why would the author have chosen as the climactic segment of his work an apocalypse (i.e., the Cloud and Waters Apocalypse) whose conclusion stands in such considerable tension with his own supposedly heavenly hopes? Further, given the earthly nature of the consummation in chapters 73–74, it is difficult to see that this putative rearrangement (i.e., shifting the idea of Gentile temple pilgrimage from the eschatological future into the historical past) would do what Murphy claims it does, viz., to redirect hopes for salvation from the earthly sphere to heaven. The absence of the temple from chapters 73–74 does nothing to eliminate the very earthly context of the consummation.

But even in the unlikely event that Murphy were right, the text as we have it refers to the present age and thus is to be added to the catalog of those texts that describe Gentiles as worshipping at the present earthly temple.

§73 2 Baruch *72:2–6*

> [2]*After the signs have come of which I have spoken to you before, when the nations are moved and the time of my Anointed One comes, he will call all nations, and some of them he will spare, and others he will kill.* [3]*These things will befall the nations which*

208. "The radical difference between the two worlds as seen by our author leads him to see heaven as the place of the final abode of the righteous. Heaven is permanent. The earth is corruptible." The two "are ontologically different." (Murphy 1985, 67).

will be spared by him. [4]Every nation which has not known Israel and which has not trodden down the seed of Jacob will live. [5]And this is because some from all the nations have been subjected to your people. [6]All those, now, who have ruled over you or have known you, will be delivered up to the sword.

Category: ESCHATOLOGICAL PARTICIPATION

This passage, also found in the Cloud and Waters Apocalypse, clearly offers some form of participation in the age to come to those Gentiles who have not oppressed Israel in this age. The nature and terms of this participation, however, are not as clear. If one were to focus narrowly on v. 5, it would be possible to see this purely as subservience to Israel; "some from all the nations" will be spared solely in order to be "subjected to your people" (so Volz 1934, 356). While this is possible, several features of the larger context seem to point to a more positive future for these Gentile non-combatants.[209] First, the description of the messianic age in chapters 73–74 is strikingly universalistic in its tone: various sources of distress "will pass away from *among men*" (v. 2); "joy will encompass *the earth*" (v. 2); "*nobody* will again die untimely" (v. 3); various sources of evil that have afflicted the "life *of men*" will be uprooted (v. 5); and enmity between beasts and "*men*" will come to an end (v. 6). Second, the notion of Gentile subservience, introduced unexpectedly in 72:5,[210] is just as quickly dropped. There is no hint in chapter 73 that the "men" who experience this age of bliss are subdivided into dominant Israelites and subservient Gentiles. One even wonders whether 72:5 might have been added by the author in taking over and adapting the passage for his own purposes.

In any case, in the Cloud and Waters Apocalypse it is expected that while those nations that have afflicted Israel will be destroyed, the others will be spared and will share with Israel the joys of the messianic age. This idea of a precondition for eschatological blessing is unusual. In that the fate of non-Jews in the future is somehow dependent on their disposition in the present, this passage has some affinities to the other patterns of universalism that are being documented here. But this precondition—to have neither known nor oppressed Israel[211]—falls far short of ethical monotheism or conversion or righteous sympathy. This,

209. The positive view is taken by most interpreters; see, e.g., McKnight (1991, 38); E. P. Sanders (1976, 18); Feldman (1993, 333).

210. Why should the reward for not making Israel subservient be subservience to Israel?

211. The text as it stands reads: "every nation which has not known Israel and which has not trodden down the seed of Jacob." The element of knowledge is curious. Those who did not know the people of Israel could not have trodden them down, so that the second element is redundant. But surely there were many nations who knew Israel but were not oppressive; those who came to honor the temple (68:5) would fall into this category. Bogaert (1969, 2:127–28) makes the plausible suggestion that the translator mistook a form of ἐφίσταμαι (to stand upon, be set over) for ἐπίσταμαι (to know).

then, must be seen as just a preliminary qualification; the passage also assumes some sort of decisive transformation yet to take place in the eschatological future. Further, there is nothing to suggest that this transformation would involve conversion. In chapter 72 these Gentiles continue to exist as Gentiles and not as newly arrived members of Israel.

CHAPTER 4

QUMRAN

Introduction

Despite their overall pessimism concerning the spiritual status and ultimate destiny of all those outside its membership, the Qumran scrolls are not completely devoid of more positive references to Gentiles. For one thing, in three texts—*11QPsalms*[a] (11Q5), *4QPrayer of Nabonidus* (4Q242) and *4QWords of the Luminaries* (4QDibHam / 4Q504)—Gentiles appear in the guise of sympathizers, that is, as non-Jews who stand in a positive relationship with the God of Israel. While the absence of any sectarian tendencies in these texts suggests that they originated outside the community, the fact that they were included in the community's library at all is not without significance. Further, the literature contains five instances of the word גר (sojourner, proselyte), together with two other passages dealing with the incorporation of non-Jews (slaves, captured women) into the community. These passages provide substantial evidence that the Qumran community was prepared to accept (at least the idea of) Gentile proselytes.

Apart from these few texts, however, the overwhelming sense of the Qumran material is negative, as far as the present spiritual status and ultimate destiny of the Gentiles is concerned. Humankind is divided into two divinely determined camps—the children of righteousness and the children of injustice, under the sway of the angel of truth and the angel of darkness, respectively (1QS III, 15–26)—and the line between the two coincides more or less with the boundary of the community itself. In the present, all outside the community are "the men of the lot of Belial" (1QS II, 4–5), "sons of deceit," who are under the "total dominion" of the "Angel of Darkness" (1QS III, 19–20) and who thus are accursed for their "wicked, blameworthy deeds" (1QS II, 5). As for the future, the dominant expectation is for the complete destruction and annihilation of the wicked. The *War Scroll* looks forward with great enthusiasm to the end-time "war of extermination against the sons of darkness" (1QM I, 10); the sons of light will head into the final battle carrying trumpets emblazoned with the motto "God has struck all the sons of darkness; he shall not cause his wrath to return until they are exterminated" (1QM III, 9). The expectation of the end-time extermination of the wicked is most prominent in the *War Scroll*,[1] but it comes to expression in other texts as well.[2]

Of course, for the Qumran community "the wicked" is not quite the same category as "the Gentiles." Since they believed that the company of sinners headed for destruction also included a majority of Jews, they drew the fundamental dividing line not between Jew and Gentile but between their own community and the rest of the human world. The sectarian nature of the Qumran community has the effect, then, of relativizing the line separating Jew from Gentile to a certain extent.

Nevertheless, the line by no means disappears, and whatever relativization there may have been does not result in any discernible benefit for Gentiles. On the one hand, as Schiffman has observed (Schiffman 1997, 170), the Jew-Gentile distinction is not called into question in any fundamental way. Even in their state of blindness and deception, those outside the community are not deprived of the name "Israel."[3] While it is true that to join the community is equivalent to "joining with the house of Judah" (CD IV, 10–11)—which might be taken to imply that Jewish outsiders are no better than Gentile sinners—the two nevertheless continue to be differentiated. Specifically, a Jew who presents himself as a candidate for membership in the community is described as being "from Israel" (1QS VI, 13), while any Gentile who might do likewise (as we will see) would be called a proselyte. On the other hand, in their denunciation of the wicked in general, the Qumran covenanters do not fail to single out the Gentiles in particular. When they march out for the final battle, the "sons of light" will carry banners declaring "God's destruction of every futile people [גוי]" (1QM IV, 12); a victory hymn acclaims Israel's God, who "has gathered the assembly of peoples [קהל גויים] for destruction with no remnant" (1QM XIV, 5; cf. also XV, 12). While the Gentiles are absorbed into a larger company of the wicked, they do not thereby lose their identity, and the prospects of the Gentiles as Gentiles are unrelentingly grim.

1. See also I, 5–7, 16; IV, 12; XIV, 5; XV, 12–14.

2. E.g., 1QS IV, 11–14; 1QH XIV, 29–20; 4QpPs^{a} (4Q171) II, 5–8.

3. CD XVI, 2–3 speaks of "the blindness of Israel"; CD VI, 1–2 refers to those who "prophesied deceit in order to divert Israel from following God."

Annihilation is not the only prospect, however. While this is the dominant theme, there are a few texts that anticipate instead the end-time subjugation of the nations and their subservience to Israel. 1QSb (1Q28b) V, 27–29 addresses this benediction to the messianic "prince of the congregation":

> May you gore like a bu[ll . . . and may you trample the nation]s like mud of the streets. For God has raised you to a sceptre for the rulers be[fore you . . . all the na]tions will serve you, and he will make you strong by his holy Name, so that you will be like a li[on . . .] your prey, with no-one to give it back.

The *War Scroll* contains two versions of a victory hymn that sounds a similar note:

> "Rejoice, Zion, passionately! Shine with jubilation, Jerusalem! Exult, all the cities of Judah! Open your gate[s] continuously so that the wealth of the nations [גואים] can be brought to you! Their kings shall wait on you, all your oppressors lie prone before you, the dust [of your feet they shall lick.][4]

Deines has argued on the basis of these texts that the Qumran community anticipated an end-time pilgrimage of the nations to Zion, that is, they expected Gentiles ultimately to be included in the blessings of the age to come.[5] But such an argument lacks textual support. While these texts stand somewhat in tension with the expectation elsewhere in the scrolls that the Gentiles would be simply annihilated along with the rest of the wicked, one should not make much of the tension; the theme of subjugation is simply determined by the language of scripture itself.[6] Whether subjugation or annihilation, the prospects for the Gentiles are bleak indeed.

Nevertheless, there are some glimmers of light in the Qumran material, to which we now turn.

4. 1QM XII, 13–15. Virtually the same hymn is found in 1QM XIX, 5–7 (also 4QM^{b} [4Q492] 5–7). See also 1QSb (1Q28b) III, 18–21, 27–28.

5. Deines (1994). His argument is that the Qumran community held to a two-stage eschatological scenario. In the first stage, the time in which the community found itself, it was necessary to separate from the Gentiles in the interests of creating a restored and purified remnant of Israel. But the fulfillment of this first-stage goal would make possible a second stage in which salvation would become universal. By means of this two-stage scenario, Deines argues, the Qumran authors were able to combine two conflicting strands in Israel's scriptures—one anticipating universal salvation (e.g., Isaiah), the other advocating particularistic exclusion (e.g., Ezra and Nehemiah). The idea is winsome but without any real basis in the texts he puts forward in support.

6. The hymns in the *War Scroll*, for example, are clearly based on Isa 60:10–14.

Texts and Commentary

§74 Psalms Scroll[a] *(11QPs[a], 11Q5) XXIV, 8–9*

> [8]*Instruct me, YHWH, in your law, and teach me your precepts* [9]*so that many may hear your deeds and nations may honour your glory.*

Text and translation: García Martínez and Tigchelaar (1998, 1172–79)
Date: Third century B.C.E.
Provenance: Judea
Original Language: Hebrew
Bibliography: Flint (1997), García Martínez, Tigchelaar and van der Woude (1998, 29–36); James A. Sanders (1965; 1967); G. Wilson (1985)
Category: SYMPATHIZATION

In addition to canonical psalms, the *Psalms Scroll* contains seven other psalms not found in the Hebrew Psalter. Four of these were already known through other sources in translated form;[7] three represented previously unknown compositions. The compilers of the document evidently considered all of them to be "psalms of David," which indicates that the precise limits of the Psalter had not yet been established.

The text of interest here is a portion of the psalm known in the Syriac version as Ps 155. In the *Psalms Scroll*, however, it follows immediately after Ps 144. The absence of any sectarian features, together with the fact that the psalm was preserved in other circles, indicates that it was not a Qumran composition but rather part of a larger collection of psalms belonging to a still-fluid Psalter tradition. It thus pre-dates the formation of the Qumran community, though a more precise date is difficult to determine (James A. Sanders 1967, 103).

Couched in thoroughly biblical language, the psalm is a call for deliverance and preservation. While much of the psalm is centered on the psalmist's own concerns and circumstances, line 9 puts these in a much larger context: if God grants his request, many will hear of God's deeds and "peoples" will honor God's glory. The word here is not גוים, the most common biblical term for the Gentile nations, but עמים. But while עם can be used of Israel, especially in the singular, its plural form is often used of the Gentile nations, especially in the Psalms. Psalm 96 is an instructive case in point: "Declare his glory [כבודו] among the nations [גוים], his marvellous works among all the peoples [עמים]." Not only is עמים (peoples) in parallel with גוים (Gentile nations),[8] but we find

7. Three of them were contained in the Syriac Psalter (151, 154, 155), the other in Sir 51:13–19.

here a similar concern that the nations recognize God's works and glory[9] (כבוד appears in line 9 of the Qumran psalm as well). There can be little doubt, then, that 11QPs[a] XXIV, 8–9 is giving voice to a similar thought.[10] While there is no indication of the form in which the "honour" is expected to take, the psalmist nevertheless believes that if the Gentiles hear of God's deeds they will thus honor God's glory. Moreover, it is clear that the psalmist sees himself as playing a role in bringing this about.

§75 Prayer of Nabonidus *(4QPrNab ar, 4Q242)*

> *Words of the pr[ay]er which Nabonidus, king of [the] la[nd of Baby]lon, the [great] king, prayed [when he was afflicted]* [2]*by a malignant inflammation, by decree of the G[od Most Hi]gh, in Teiman. [I, Nabonidus,] was afflicted [by a malignant inflammation]* [3]*for seven years, and was banished far [from men, until I prayed to the God Most High]* [4]*and an exorcist forgave my sin. He was a Je[w] fr[om the exiles, who said to me:]* [5]*"Make a proclamation in writing, so that glory, exal[tation and hono]ur be given to the name of [the] G[od Most High." And I wrote as follows: "When]* [6]*I was afflicted by a ma[lignant] inflammation [. . .] in Teiman, [by decree of the God Most High,]* [7]*[I] prayed for seven years [to all] the gods of silver and gold, [of bronze and iron,]* [8]*of wood, of stone and of clay, because [I thoug]ht that t[hey were] gods [.]* (García Martínez and Tigchelaar 1997, 476)

> *The words of the p[ra]yer which Nabonidus, king of [baby]lon, [the great]king, prayed [when he was smitten]* [2]*with a bad disease by the decree of G[o]d in Teima. [I, Nabonidus, with a bad disease]* [3]*was smitten for seven years and sin[ce] G[od] set [his face on me he healed me]* [4]*and as for my sin, he remitted it. A diviner (he was a Jew fr[om among the exiles) came to me and said:]* [5]*'Pro[cla]im and write to give honour and exal[tatio]n to the name of G[od Most High', and I wrote as follows:]* [6]*'I was smitten by a b[ad] disease in Teima [by the decree of the Most High God.]* [7]*For seven years [I] was praying [to] the gods of silver and gold, [bronze, iron,]* [8]*wood, stone, clay, since [I thoug]ht that th[ey were] gods.* (J. J. Collins in Brooke et al. 1996, 89)

Text and translation: García Martínez and Tigchelaar (1997, 486–88); J. J. Collins (in Brooke et al. 1996, 83–93)
Date: Third century B.C.E.
Provenance: Judea
Original Language: Aramaic

8. Also Ps 96:10; 33:10. See also Ps. 47:1, 3; 57:9; 108:3.
9. Also Ps 97:6; 105:1.
10. James Sanders seems to be of the opinion that the line refers to Israel: "He [the psalmist] in turn would teach the congregation of God's glory" (1967, 109). But this seems unlikely.

Bibliography: Cross (1984); García Martínez (1992); Kraus (1996, 68–69); Milik (1956); Puech (1996); van der Woude (1978);
Category: SYMPATHIZATION

The *Prayer of Nabonidus* was first published by J. T. Milik in 1956, on the basis of four fragments from Cave 4. Since then there has been considerable scholarly disagreement as to how the fragments are to be arranged and how the lacunae are to be filled.[11] Nevertheless, enough of the text is discernible to gain a sense of the character of the text and to see its significance for our purposes.

Nabonidus was the last king of Babylonia before the victory of Cyrus the Persian. Babylonian evidence indicates that Nabonidus was absent from Babylon for at least ten years (553–43 B.C.E.), part of which was spent in the Arabian city Teiman; his son Belshazzar ruled in his place. The tradition reflected in the prayer, then, seems to have developed on the basis of these historical circumstances. The tradition is similar in many respects to the account of Nebuchadnezzar's madness and healing in Daniel 4. Indeed, even before the Qumran discovery, there was scholarly speculation that Daniel 4 was based on a tradition having to do with Nabonidus. Publication of the *Prayer of Nabonidus* has been taken as a confirmation of this; that is, the *Prayer of Nabonidus* probably reflects an earlier form of the tradition that also lies behind Daniel 4. This, together with the absence of any sectarian tendencies, leads scholars to date the prayer to the third century B.C.E. (García Martínez 1992, 136).[12]

The first line states that what is to follow is a prayer. The extant text falls into two parts: a first-person narration of the events leading up to the writing of a royal proclamation concerning the king's illness and healing (XI, 1–4); and the proclamation itself, which begins with its own narration of events and presumably would have concluded with the prayer mentioned in the first line. In both parts of the text, Nabonidus informs the reader that while he was in Teiman he was afflicted with a serious ailment for seven years. In the first part and, according to most reconstructions, the second part as well, the king attributes his ailment to "the decree of God." The second part indicates that during the seven years of his illness, he prayed to various gods. No doubt the text would have gone on to indicate that these prayers were ineffectual.

Details of the king's healing are extant only in the first part of the text, but there are uncertainties concerning several aspects of it. In García Martínez's reconstruction, there is no explicit mention of healing. The king took the initiative by

11. Three of the fragments, represented by the translation above, evidently link up with each other; the fourth, more fragmentary in nature, stands apart in scholarly reconstructions. Cross (1984) has proposed a placement of the fragments that require shorter lacunae than in Milik's reconstruction. While Cross's version has not been widely accepted (see Puech 1996, 210), it has been endorsed by J. J. Collins in DJD XXII (83–93).

12. The MS itself is dated on paleographic grounds to 75–50 B.C.E. (Cross 1984: 260).

praying to "the God Most High," whereupon a Jewish adviser (whom he calls an "exorcist") forgave his sin and instructed him to make a written proclamation. As John Collins renders it, there is no mention of a prayer on the part of the king. The initiative is taken by God, who gratuitously healed the king and then forgave his sin. The role of the Jewish adviser (whom Collins calls a "diviner") is to enlighten the king as to the source of his healing and to instruct him to give praise to God.

While this text will inevitably remain uncertain in many respects, some aspects of Collins's reconstruction are more convincing. As Puech has observed, to make the Jewish adviser the one who offers forgiveness both introduces a theological notion without parallel in Jewish tradition (i.e., a human being forgiving sin) and is syntactically unnecessary (Puech 1996, 216–17). Collins's reconstruction also has the advantage of an explicit mention of healing, without which the text as a whole makes little sense. While there is no explicit indication of the adviser's role in this reconstruction, Collins's suggestion is at least plausible.

For our purposes, however, what is important is the apologetic nature of the text—something that is readily apparent, despite the uncertainties. As Collins has indicated, by virtue of its polemic against idolatry and its evident desire to "affirm that the God of Israel is also sovereign over the Gentiles," the text has a "propagandist quality" (J. J. Collins in Brooke et al. 1996, 87). As with other apologetic literature, the primary audience for this affirmation was probably (some segment of) the Jewish community itself. But even if the text was directed towards a Jewish readership in the first instance, it nevertheless reflected and sought to reinforce a set of attitudes that were directed towards the wider Gentile world. Several things are to be observed. First, Nabonidus is presented as a commendable figure solely on the basis of his renunciation of false gods and his recognition of the true God, the God of the Jews. The text makes no mention of the Torah, of circumcision, or of any other of the Jewish identity markers. In other words, Nabonidus is not presented as a proselyte, nor is there any indication that he should become one. He seems to have done all that is required of him by rejecting idolatry and acknowledging the one true God. Second, the activity of the Jewish adviser[13] is also presented in positive terms. While he appears on the scene abruptly, he is evidently operating in concert with God's own activity in the situation. The text thus conveys the message that it is appropriate for a Jewish person to assist a Gentile to come to the kind of recognition of God displayed by Nabonidus.

13. The term rendered "exorcist" by García Martínez and "diviner" by J. J. Collins is גזר. The term appears in a list of Babylonian wise men, magicians, and other court functionaries in Dan 2:27; 4:4; 5:7, 11. A cognate substantive (גזרה) has the sense of "decree" in Dan 4:14, 21. While "adviser" is perhaps too bland a term, we have insufficient evidence to render it with any greater precision.

§76 Words of the Luminaries[a] *(4QDibHam 4Q504) 1–2 IV, 2–13*

. . . a place of rest [3]in Jerusa[lem the city which] you [cho]se from the whole earth [4]for [your Name] to be there for ever. For you loved [5]Israel more than all the peoples. And you chose the tribe of [6]Judah, and established your covenant with David so that he would be [7]like a shepherd, a prince over your people, and would sit in front of you on the throne of Israel [8]for ever. And all the countries have seen your glory, [9]for you have made yourself holy in the midst of your people Israel. And to your [10]great Name they will carry their offerings: silver, gold, precious stones, [11]with all the treasures of their country, to honour your people and [12]Zion, your holy city and your wonderful house. And there was no opponent [13]or evil attack, but peace and blessing.

Text and translation: García Martínez and Tigchelaar (1997, 1008–20)
Date: Mid-second century B.C.E.
Provenance: Judea
Original Language: Hebrew
Bibliography: Baillet (1982, 137–75; 1961); Davila (2000, 239–66); Falk (1998, 60–94); Kraus (1996, 67–68); Schiffman (1997); Schnabel (2004, 107–8)
Category: SYMPATHIZATION

Words of the Luminaries is a liturgical work containing prayers for each day of the week, culminating in special prayers for the Sabbath. Each prayer seems to begin with a call to remembrance of some mighty act of God in the past, followed by an appeal that God show mercy to Israel in its present distress. The biblical allusions appear in more or less chronological order, beginning with a reference to Adam in the first prayer (Davila 2000, 241). The passage under discussion here refers to the establishment of the Davidic dynasty and the construction of the temple in Jerusalem. The prayer looks back on this era as a golden age of "peace and blessing" (L, 13)—in particular, one in which "all the countries" (literally, nations [כול הגוים]) recognized God's glory and journeyed to Zion to bring offerings to the temple. While the description is similar in many respects to the eschatological pilgrimage tradition, in which the Gentiles come to honor the restored temple in the future, it is clear that the pilgrimage in view here is one that had already taken place in the ideal past. There is no suggestion that these Gentiles had become converts to Israel in any sense of the term. While the goal of their pilgrimage was clearly to revere the temple and the God of Israel, it is just as clear that they did so as Gentiles.

On paleographical grounds, the fragment can be dated to the middle of the second century B.C.E. With respect to content, the prayer differs from the typical Qumran attitude towards Gentiles, not only in the general aspect of its positive tone, but also in the particular matter of the acceptability of Gentile offerings: evidence from 4QMMT (3–7 I, 6, 10) indicates that one of the distinctive viewpoints of the sect was its rejection of Gentile offerings at the temple (Schiffman 1997, 164–65). Thus arguments on the basis both of paleography and of content converge in support of the position that 4Q505 is a pre-sectarian work adopted by the Qumran community for its own use.

The remaining texts deal with proselytism, either explicitly or by implication. Before we look at the individual texts, several questions need to be raised about the set of texts as a whole.

First, there is the question of the precise meaning of גר in these texts. As Wise has observed, it is not immediately clear whether the term should be translated as "proselyte" or whether it should have the older biblical sense of "sojourner" (Wise 1991, 116).[14] The uncertainty is reflected in the choices made by the English translators. García Martínez and Tigchelaar render it three times by "proselyte" and twice (CD VI, 21; 11QT[a] XL, 6) by "foreigner"; Vermes translates it in every instance as "stranger," except for CD XIV, 4, where we find "proselyte."

What makes "sojourner" a real possibility is the tendency in the Qumran literature to engage in an imaginative recreation of the world as the authors would have liked it to be, based on their understanding of the covenant and interpretation of scripture. For example, the *War Scroll* envisages a situation where twelve levites will be on duty in the temple, "one per tribe" (1QM II, 2–3), even though the idea of "twelve tribes" no longer corresponded to any actual social reality. Similarly, their community rules call for a division into "thousands, hundreds, fifties and tens" (1QS II, 21–22; 1QSa I, 14–15; cf. Exod 18:21, 25; Deut 1:15), even though their numbers would scarcely have necessitated any four-digit enumeration.[15] This opens up the possibility, at least, that the texts cited above could be read in similarly antiquarian terms, that is, as part of an attempt to recreate the world of the biblical past—sojourners included—according to their own ideals rather than as an indication of any readiness (real or hypothetical) to incorporate Gentiles into their own actual world as full converts to the covenant.

Another possibility for the meaning of גר has been put forward by Davies, who suggests instead that the Qumran sectarians used the term in an extended sense, to refer to someone who was "in the process of initiation into [the sect], who does not yet have a full place in 'Israel' or 'Aram'" (Davies 1994, 75). The assumption here is that all outside the sect are viewed as non-Israelites; in order to be part of the true community of Israel, all need to enter it as "proselytes." Used in this sense, the term theoretically might include Gentiles; but since most recruits to the sect were Jews, the force of Davies's suggestion is that the term primarily refers to Israelites.

14. On the development of the term, see ch. 11 below.

15. On this point, see Vermes (1981, 88).

In conjunction with questions of meaning, we can also ask about social reality. Whatever is decided about the meaning of גר (sojourner, proselyte, initiate), it is also necessary to ask whether the term is just a theoretical construct or whether it refers to real people associated with the community in some way. The situation is simplest in the case of Davies's suggestion, which carries with it a corresponding social reality. The other alternatives, however, where non-Jews are in view, are trickier.

Decisions on these issues, of course, need to be made on the basis of the texts themselves. One issue, however, can be dispensed with at the outset. Davies's suggestion that גר refers to Israelites who were in the process of incorporation into the community is quite unlikely. To be sure, the suggestion has a certain plausibility. Because of the sectarian nature of the Qumran community, there is a certain relativizing of the line separating Jew from Gentile. Since, in their view, the majority of Jews also belong to the company of sinners destined for destruction, the crucial line of demarcation falls not between Jew and Gentile but between their own community and the rest of humankind. To join the community is equivalent to "joining with the house of Judah" (CD IV, 10–11), which might be taken to imply that Jewish outsiders are no better than Gentile sinners. More specifically, it might be taken to imply that all outsiders needed to enter the community as "proselytes."[16]

But there is no evidence in the text that גר was being used in this way. For one thing, neither in the older sense of "resident alien" nor in the later sense of "proselyte" is there an element of liminality in the term גר. There is nothing in the term that would lend itself to the category of a novice or an initiate-in-process. If גר were being used in the kind of extended way that Davies suggests, it would more probably be used of full community members rather than of novices undergoing initiation. After all, the גר is one who has already completed the process of initiation. In addition, as Schiffman has observed, the Qumran community did not push its sectarian logic to the extreme conclusion that Jewish outsiders were to be seen as Gentiles. In his words, "the distinction between Jews and non-Jews is never blurred in the Dead Sea Scrolls, and the sect's Jewish opponents are never accused of non-Jewish status" (Schiffman 1997:170). For example, in 1QS VI, 13 a potential convert is said to be "from Israel" even before having "enter[ed] into the covenant." Thus, whatever we might conclude about its more precise meaning, גר in the Qumran literature refers to people who, in ethnic origin at least, were Gentiles, not Jews.

§77 Damascus Document *VI, 14–21*

> [14]*They should take care to act in accordance with the exact interpretation of the law for the age of wickedness: to keep apart* [15]*from the sons of the pit; to abstain from*

16. Christiansen (1995, 137) understands the term as referring to "*converts* to the community from within Judaism."

wicked wealth which defiles, either by promise or by vow, [16]*and from the wealth of the temple and from stealing from the poor of his people, making widows their spoils* [17]*and murdering orphans;. . .* [20] *. . . for each to love his brother* [21]*like himself; to strengthen the hand of the poor, the needy and the foreigner.*

Text and translation: García Martinez and Tigchelaar (1997, 551–627)
Date: Mid-second to mid-first century B.C.E.
Provenance: Judea
Original Language: Hebrew
Bibliography: Christiansen (1995, 135–38); Davies (1983; 1994); Deines (1994); Hempel (1998; 2000); Schiffman (1997).
Category: CONVERSION

This passage appears in a section of the *Damascus Document* in which historical allusions to the emergence of the sect are interwoven with exhortations for proper behavior among the members of the sect ("all those who have been brought into the covenant" [VI, 11]). Among the latter is this exhortation "to strengthen the hand of the poor, the needy and the foreigner" (גר). The association of גר with "widows" (אלמנות), "orphans" (יתומים), "poor" (עני), and "needy" (אביון) is strongly reminiscent of Pentateuchal language (e.g., Lev 19:10; 23:22; Deut 14:29; 16:11, 14; 24:17–21), even though there are no specific citations. This, together with the absence of any indication of conversion in the passage, means that גר here could simply be rendered "sojourner" or "resident alien." Still, there is nothing in the passage that would necessarily exclude "proselyte."

§78 Damascus Document *XIV, 3–6*

[3]*Rule of the assembly of all the camps. All of them shall be enlisted by their names: the priests first,* [4]*the levites second, the children of Israel third and the proselyte fourth; and they shall be inscribed by their [na]mes,* [5]*each one after his brother; the priests first, the levites second, the children of Israel* [6]*third and the proselyte fourth. And thus shall they sit and thus shall they be questioned about everything.*

Category: CONVERSION

The situation is clearer, however, in CD XIV, 4, 6, where the גר is integrated into the covenant community. This text is found in a section of the *Damascus Document* (XIV, 3–18^{a}) that deals with a collective meeting of "all the camps" (XIV, 3); it follows on from a section dealing with meetings of individual "camps" (XII, 22^{b}–XIV, 2). As is typical of the Qumran community, this gathering is tightly structured according to rank; priests are at the head, followed by levites, ordinary Israelites, and then the גר.[17] A גר who sits alongside priests,

17. 4QD^{b} (4Q267) contains a slightly different version of CD XIII, 22–14.9. גר is lacking from the parallel to CD XIV, 4 (9 VI, 8) but is present in the parallel to CD XIV, 6 (line 10).

levites, and children of Israel to be "questioned about everything"—that is, who is included within the life and activities of the community—conforms more closely to the usual idea of the proselyte.[18]

§79 Damascus Document *XII, 8–11*

> [8]*No one should sell clean animals* [9]*or birds to the gentiles lest they sacrifice them.* [10]*And he should not sell them anything from his granary or his press, at any price. Neither should he sell his servant and his maidservant* [11]*to them, for they entered the covenant of Abraham with him.*

> **Category:** CONVERSION

A similar element of incorporation into the covenant community is found in CD XII, 11, albeit without the use of גר. The text is part of a larger passage dealing with a variety of concrete situations—commerce with Gentiles, food and purity regulations, the treatment of an apostate, and so on. Included in a list of things not to be sold to a Gentile are male and female slaves, "for they entered the covenant of Abraham with him (באו עמו בברית אברהם)." While the slaves in question are not explicitly identified as Gentiles, both the language of "entering the covenant" and the Biblical injunctions against the owning of Hebrew slaves (Lev 25:35–46) suggest that Gentile slaves are in view.[19] As with the rabbinic category of the "Canaanite slave" (*m. Giṭ* 4.6), the concern seems to be that such a slave sold to a Gentile master would no longer be able to live according to the Torah (Schiffman 1997, 156–57). In other words, despite the absence of the term, the slaves in question appear to have joined their masters as full members of the covenant and thus can be described as proselytes.[20]

§80 Nahum Pesher *(4QpNah 4Q169) 3–4 II, 7–9*

> [7][Nah 3:4]*On account of the many fornications of the prostitute, full of elegance and mistress of enchantment, who misled nations with her fornications and clans with her [enchant]ment.* [8]*[Its] interpretation [con]cerns those who misdirect Ephraim, who with their fraudulent teaching and lying tongue and perfidious lip misdirect many;* [9]*kings, princes, priests and people together with the proselyte attached to them. Cities and clans will perish through their advice, nobles and le[aders]* [10]*will fall [due to the fero]city of their tongues.*

18. See Hempel (1998, 135). Deines (1994, 83, n. 69) argues, unconvincingly, that the text is deliberately using the term in the archaic sense of "Fremdling" ("sojourner").

19. Davies has suggested that the slaves were Jewish (members of the covenant of Abraham) but not members of the covenant of Damascus (Davies 1994, 76). But it is hard to understand how it could be said of Jewish slaves that they "entered" the covenant of Abraham "with" their master.

20. See Hempel (2000, 80); Schiffman (1997, 156–57); Davies (1994, 76).

Text and translation: García Martínez and Tigchelaar (1997, 334–41)
Date: First century B.C.E.
Provenance: Judea
Original Language: Hebrew
Bibliography: Allegro (1969, 37–42); Dupont-Sommer (1963); Horgan (1979); Schiffman (1997)
Category: CONVERSION

In *Nahum Pesher*, גר appears as one constituent element in a description of "Ephraim" as a whole: "kings, princes, priests and people together with the גר attached to them." While the phrase is stylized, it is found in a highly "realistic" context: the commentary on Nahum bristles with references to the actual history of Judea and the experiences of the sectarian community within it. Although the identity of "those who misdirect Ephraim" is not as clearly discernible as that of some of the other persons referred to in the text, real situations are nevertheless in view, which makes it more difficult to read the passage in an archaizing way. Further, language of joining or attachment ("the גר attached [נלום] to them") is often used to describe full converts in other texts; note in particular Esth 9:27, which uses the same verb (the niphal form of לוה) to speak of "themselves and their descendants and all who joined them (כל הנלוים עליהם)."[21] Thus "proselyte" is the more natural rendering here.

§81 Temple Scroll[a] *(11QT[a] 11Q19) XL, 5–6*

> [5]*You shall make a thi[r]d courtyard [. . .]* [6]*[. . .] for their daughters and for foreigners who were bo[rn . . .]*

Text and translation: García Martínez and Tigchelaar (1997, 1228–1307)
Date: Second century B.C.E.
Provenance: Judea
Original Language: Hebrew
Bibliography: Baumgarten (1982); Christiansen (1995, 135–38); Kraus (1996, 64–65); Maier (1985); Schiffman (1997); Wise (1990; 1991); Yadin (1983)
Category: CONVERSION

The *Temple Scroll* can be described as a kind of Torah for the ideal temple. Drawing on and reworking sections of the Pentateuch dealing with the cultic

21. LXX Esth 9:27 renders נלוטם with προστίθημι, found in a similar context in Jdt 14:10; cf. Tob 1:8.

observance, it sets out an authoritative[22] description of a temple that in its layout and functioning does not correspond exactly to any of Israel's actual temples or to the eschatological temple envisaged by Ezekiel. 11QT[a] XL, 5–6 appears in a section of the document that deals with the courts of the temple. In contrast to Herod's temple with its four courts, the *Temple Scroll* envisages only three. The third, described in the text under discussion here, corresponds in function to the court of women in Herod's temple, though it is considerably larger in size. In effect, it displaces the court of Gentiles, which has no counterpart in the *Temple Scroll.* The third court of the *Temple Scroll* differs from the Herodian court of women in one additional way, which is of primary concern here. This court is designated not only for women but also for גרים; women and גרים alike are allowed to enter this court but cannot proceed to the second court, which is restricted to ritually pure Israelite males.

There can be little doubt that the גרים in the text are proselytes or converts.[23] The fact that they are placed into the same category as Israelite women points in this direction. This seems to be confirmed by XLIV, 5–8, which describes a platform that is to encircle the outer courtyard, whose gates contain steps "upon which the children of Israel [בני ישׂראל] will ascend to enter my temple" (XLIV, 7–8). In other words, the assumption seems to be that access to the temple complex is restricted to Israelites, of whom the גרים are presumably a special class. In addition, the concern for purity in Jerusalem as a whole (XLV, 7–18)[24] could be taken to imply that Gentiles would not have been allowed even into the city itself. Finally, Wise has observed that, in its use of material from Deuteronomy, the *Temple Scroll* has systematically omitted all passages where גר clearly refers to resident aliens living in the land. He argues that the author of the *Temple Scroll* was aware of the two possible senses of the word. On the one hand, Gentile sojourners

> were to have no part in the eschaton. On the other hand, the redactor had no intention of excluding "proselytes" from the land of the eschaton, where they

22. An indication of the authority that the *Temple Scroll* claims for itself is provided by a slight revision of passages taken from Deuteronomy. Legislation in Deuteronomy is presented in the voice of Moses, who refers to God in the third person (e.g., "Justice, and only justice, you shall pursue, so that you may live and occupy the land that the Lord your God is giving you" [Deut 16:20]). By contrast, the *Temple Scroll* is written in the first person singular; its legislation is presented as the direct utterance of God ("Justice, justice shall you pursue, so that you can live and enter and take possession of the land which I give you as an inheritance for all days" [11QT[a] LI, 15–16]).

23. Yadin rendered it as resident aliens (Yadin 1983, 2.170), but subsequent interpreters have understood the passage to be referring to proselytes; so Baumgarten (1982), Maier (1985, 37); Schiffman (1997, 162); Wise (1990, 169–72).

24. Those excluded from the city: the blind, lepers, and those defiled by a corpse or by sexual intercourse.

> could even enter the temple. True, their legal status was only that of a woman in terms of entry into the temple, but in other respects they were doubtless not distinguished from other Jews. (Wise 1990, 171)

Wise's assumption that the *Temple Scroll* refers to an eschatological state of events is questionable; we will pick this up in the next paragraph. This aside, his argument is convincing and lends support to the conclusion that גרים in 11QT[a] XL, 6 should be rendered "proselytes."

As was just observed, Wise interprets the passage in an eschatological sense. In fact, he sees 11QT[a] XL, 6 as an example of eschatological pilgrimage expectation—the expectation "that finally, after all the wars, nations would come to the light and kings to the Holy One of Israel (Isa. 60:3)" (Wise 1990, 172). But this is quite unlikely.[25] In XXIX, 8–10 a clear distinction is made between the temple described in the *Temple Scroll* as a whole, and a future, everlasting temple:

> I shall sanctify my [te]mple with my glory, for I shall make my glory reside over it until the day of creation, when I shall create my temple, establishing it for myself for all days, according to the covenant which I made with Jacob at Bethel.

The proselytes in view in XL, 6, then, are not end-time pilgrims but this-age converts to Israel.

In that they are classified with women as far as access to the temple is concerned, these converts occupy a status lower than that of a natural-born Israelite. But there is some evidence that this status was not considered to be perpetual. The evidence has to do with the phrase "the fourth generation" (דור רבי[ע]), appearing in a fragmentary section of col. 39 (line 5). Since the passage goes on to enumerate those who are not allowed to enter the second court—a list that includes women (XXXIX, 7)—Yadin may well be right in his suggestion that "fourth generation" referred to proselytes; that is, that fourth-generation male descendants of proselytes were allowed to enter the middle court[26] and thus were considered to be of the same purity status as natural-born Israelites.

§82 Temple Scroll[a] *(11QT[a], 11Q19) LXIII, 10–15*

> [10] *When you go out to war against your enemies and I place them in your hands, and you make prisoners,* [11] *and you see among the prisoners a woman of beautiful appearance, and you desire her and you take her as a wife for yourself,* [12] *you shall bring her into your house, and shave her head and cut her nails, and you shall remove* [13] *the prisoner's clothes from her. And she will live in your house, and she will weep for her father and her mother a full month.* [14] *Afterwards you shall enter her, and marry her, and she will become your wife. But she is not to touch your purities for* [15] *seven years, nor may she eat the peace offering until seven years pass; afterwards she may eat.*

Category: CONVERSION

25. On this point see Maier (1985, 86); Schürer (1986, 3:414); Yadin (1983, 1:412).
26. Yadin (1983, 2:170); also Maier (1985, 102); Schiffman (1997, 162).

This is the second passage to be discussed in this section in which גר does not appear. As in CD XII, 11 (discussed above), the text deals with a foreigner who is incorporated into the covenant community. This case deals not with a slave but with a foreign woman captured in war and taken as wife by an Israelite. The text is an expanded version of the regulations set out in Deut 21:10–14, though the regulations in lines 14–15, concerning the seven-year purity period, have no counterpart in Deuteronomy and reflect the purity concerns evident in the document as a whole. Since the woman is allowed to partake of the pure food of the community when the seven-year period has been completed, it appears that at this point she becomes a full (female) member of the community. For this reason, despite the absence of גר, the woman can be seen as a kind of "proselyte."

§83 4QFlorilegium *(4QFlor 4Q174) I, 1–7*

> [1]*"[Not] [will] an enemy [strike him any] more, [nor will] the son of iniquity [afflict] him [aga]in as in the past. From the day on which* [2]*[I appointed judges] over my people, Israel." This (refers to) the house which [he will establish] for [him] in the last days, as it is written in the book of* [3]*[Moses, "The temple of] YHWH your hands will est[a]blish. YHWH shall reign for ever and ever." This (refers to) the house into which shall not enter* [4]*[. . . for] ever either an Ammonite, or a Moabite, or a bastard, or a foreigner, or a proselyte, never, because his holy ones are there.* [5]*Y[HW]H [shall reign for] ever." He will appear over it for ever; foreigners shall not again lay it waste as they laid waste, in the past,* [6]*the tem[ple of I]srael on account of their sins. And he commanded to build for himself a temple of man, to offer him in it,* [7]*before him, the works of thanksgiving.*

Text and translation: García Martínez and Tigchelaar (1997, 352–54)
Date: Mid-first century C.E.[27]
Provenance: Judea
Original Language: Hebrew
Bibliography: Allegro (1969, 53–57); Baumgarten (1972; 1982); Blidstein (1974); Brooke (1985); Deines (1994); Dimant (1986); Gärtner (1965); Kraus (1996, 66–67); Schiffman (1997); Wise (1991); Yadin (1959)
Category: CONVERSION

4QFlorilegium is a midrash on several biblical texts; the extant portion deals with 2 Sam 7:10–14 (I, 1–13), Ps 1:1 (I, 14–17) and Ps. 2:1 (I, 18–19). The

27. Paleographic evidence suggests that the manuscript itself dates from the first century C.E. or the latter part of the first century B.C.E. Taking matters of content into consideration as well, Brooke argues for a date "in the second or third quarter" of the first century C.E.; see Brooke (1985, 83–84, 217).

biblical texts are interpreted eschatologically. Second Samuel 7:10, which deals with the "house" (= temple) that David wants to build for God, is understood with reference to the temple that God will establish "in the last days" (I, 2–3). Likewise, the "house" (= dynasty) that God promises to build for David is understood as a reference to the messianic "branch of David, who will arise with the Interpreter of the law . . . in the last days" (I, 11–12). Somewhat surprisingly, given the royal theme of Psalm 2, the Psalms passages are understood with reference not to a Davidic messiah but to "the elect ones of Israel in the last days" (I, 9), also described as the "sons of Zadok and the men of their council" (I, 7). This communal interpretation is perhaps connected to the enigmatic and oft-discussed phrase "a temple of man" (מקדש אדם) in lines 6–7, which has been understood as a reference to the community itself. It is not immediately clear why this combination of texts was selected for interpretation. The thematic connection between 2 Sam 7:10–14 and Psalm 2 suggests the possibility that they had already been linked in some liturgical setting,[28] a possibility that receives further support from the fact that the midrash ignores the thematic linkage.

The passage of interest here appears near the beginning of the extant text, in the section where 2 Sam 7:10 is linked with Exod 15:17–18, both being interpreted as referring to the eschatological temple. The passage contains a list of those who will be excluded from this "house"; entrance will be refused to "an Ammonite, or a Moabite, or a bastard, or a foreigner [בן נכר], or a proselyte [גר],[29] never, because his holy ones are there" (I, 4). The list is apparently based on a combination of Deut 23:2–3 (which excludes "from the assembly of the Lord" Ammonites, Moabites, and those born of an illicit union, "even to the tenth generation") and Ezek 44:9 (which bars any "foreigner" [בן נכר] from the sanctuary). As Baumgarten (1972, 87) has observed, the appearance of גר in this list of excluded categories is surprising, both because of the absence of the term in Deut 22:2–3 and Ezek 44:9, and because elsewhere in Qumran material the גר tends to be incorporated into the community. The contrast with the *Temple Scroll* is particularly striking. As we have seen, in 11QT^a XL, 6 the גר is included among those permitted to enter the temple. Admittedly, גרים are classed with women and are not allowed to penetrate any further than the third court. Still, with respect to the line dividing Israel from the Gentiles, in 11QT^a XL, 6 the גרים are clearly on the Israel side of the line. In 4QFlor, by contrast, not only are the גרים excluded from the temple but they are also explicitly lumped in with Gentiles in the process.

28. Brooke describes it as "a midrash on festival texts for the latter days" (Brooke 1985, 164).

29. The word is obscured by a crease in the manuscript; וגר, יגר, and ועד have all been suggested. For a thorough discussion, and a convincing argument in favor of וגר, see Brooke (1985, 84, 101–03).

Perhaps, then, we are to interpret this text as an instance in which גר should be understood in its older, biblical sense of sojourner, that is, not as a convert to the Jewish religion but as a foreigner who has taken up residence in the Jewish land and who thus represents a distinct category of Gentile.[30] Two considerations, however, render this unlikely. One is that, as we have observed, elsewhere in the Qumran material the גר seems to be included within Israel, that is, to be a proselyte. While a homogenizing approach to Qumran material is to be avoided, the meaning of the term elsewhere needs to be given some interpretive weight. The other consideration is that the term does not appear in Deut 22:2–3 and Ezek 44:9; the authors of 4QFlor have deliberately added it to the biblical list. This seems to indicate that they were not simply replicating biblical categories in an antiquarian sort of way but were using the term with the sense it had acquired subsequently. In other words, it seems preferable to conclude that a full proselyte is in view here.

But what are we to make of the fact that the proselyte is excluded from the temple, along with the "Ammonite, Moabite and foreigner"? The question takes on added significance when we draw 4QFlor I, 6 into the discussion, with its reference to the "temple of man" (מקדש אדם). If this indeed is a reference to the Qumran community itself, as many believe, then exclusion from the eschatological temple might also imply an analogous exclusion from the community.[31]

Discussion of 4QFlor I, has been carried out in conjunction with 1QS VIII, 4–10 and IX, 4–5. These passages in the *Community Rule* describe the community itself as a "holy house" (בית קודש; VIII, 5; IX, 6) and use sacrificial language to refer to its life of prayer and study. The implication seems to be that the community saw itself somehow as equivalent to, or as a replacement for, the temple in Jerusalem. This suggests an interpretive framework for the more enigmatic statements in 4QFlor I, 6. The "temple of man" can be understood as a "human temple," that is, a temple of human beings or, in other words, the community itself. In this temple what are offered to God are "the works of thanksgiving"(מעשי תודה)—or, perhaps, "the works of the Torah" (מעשי תורה);[32] in either case, their communal activities are equivalent to sacrifice. But equivalent in what way? Prior to the publication of the *Temple Scroll*, there was a tendency

30. Deines (1994, 80–81) reads the text in this way. He also argues, unconvincingly, that the exclusion of Gentiles from the temple was only an interim measure; in the second stage of eschatological fulfilment, Gentiles would make pilgrimage to the temple there to worship the God of Israel.

31. See McKnight (1991, 38).

32. The manuscript is unclear, making it difficult to differentiate between a ד and a ר. Brooke (1985, 87, 108) opts for "works of thanksgiving." The publication of 4QMMT, with its phrase מעשי התורה (4QMMT[e] [4Q398] 14–17 II, 3), has provided some support to the reading "works of the Torah" (so Baumgarten 1972, 95; Dimant 1986, 177). But "works of thanksgiving" is still preferred by many (see García Martínez 1996, 24; Kampen 1996, 138, n. 40).

to think that the community saw itself as the eschatological temple without remainder, so that their spiritualization of sacrifice was categorical and final (e.g., Gärtner 1965, 31–32). But with the publication of the *Temple Scroll* and the subsequent recognition of the importance of cultic and legal matters in Qumran thought, scholarly interpretation has been more cautious in this regard. The sacrificial and cultic dimensions of communal life tend to be seen as an interim arrangement, a temporary compensation for the fact that worship in the Jerusalem temple had been hopelessly polluted.[33]

Nevertheless, if the community itself functions as a kind of interim replacement until the temple might be restored in the coming age, it would follow that those who were to be excluded from the eschatological temple would also be excluded from its interim communal replacement. In what sense, then, was the גר of 4QFlor I, 4 a proselyte? Should the term be translated as "resident alien" after all?

Two things can be said by way of response. First, the issue here is one of purity, not membership in Israel. Note that the list of those to be excluded from the eschatological temple also includes one born of an illicit sexual union (ממזר, "bastard"), even though such a person would be in some sense an Israelite. In other words, the presence of the גר in this list does not imply that the גר is being treated as a non-Israelite.

To expand on this point, 4QFlor I, 6 seems to be similar in intent to several other Qumran texts where classes of people are excluded on the basis of what appears to be purity considerations; that is, the exclusion is from a sphere of sanctity (especially the temple) and not from membership in Israel per se. The closest parallel seems to be 4QMMT 8 III, 9–10. While the text is not fully decipherable, it appears to speak of "the Ammonite and the Moabite and the bastard and the one with crushed testicles and one with severed penis" in a context clearly concerned with the preservation of temple purity. Also to be mentioned is 1QSa II, 3–10, which lists several groups of people to be excluded from the community meal in the messianic days:

> No man, defiled by any of the impurities of a man, shall enter the assembly of these; and no-one who is defiled by these should be established in his office amongst the congregation: everyone who is defiled in his flesh, paralysed in his feet or in his hands, lame, blind, deaf, dumb or defiled in his flesh with a blemish

33. E.g., Vermes (1999, 162–63). Dimant goes too far, however, when she argues that the community saw itself not as a substitute for the temple itself but as a re[-]creation of "the 'congregation of priests' officiating in the holy enclosure of the Tabernacle or the Temple-city" (Dimant 1986, 188). For a parallel was drawn not only between the community itself and the community of priests in the temple but also between activities—of prayer, worship and study on the one hand and sacrifice on the other. The Qumran counter-community was significant not simply for its mere existence but also for what it did.

> visible to the eyes, or the tottering old man who cannot keep upright in the midst of the assembly; these shall not en[ter] to take their place [a]mong the congregation of the men of renown, for the angels of holiness are among their [congre]gation. And if [one of] these has something to say to the holy council, they shall question [him] in private, but the man shall [n]ot enter in the midst of [the congregation,] because [h]e is defiled.

Here the exclusion of these various classes of people functions to preserve the purity of the community. There is nothing to suggest that such persons were ipso facto excluded from the covenant and considered as non-Israelites. Indeed, the fact that provision is made for the possibility of such persons addressing the assembly indirectly suggests that they were still considered part of the wider community. Likewise, as we have seen, 11QT[a] XL, 6 refers to a third courtyard of the temple, beyond which women and proselytes were not allowed to proceed. While women and proselytes were restricted from entering the more sacred areas of the temple, this does not meant that they were thereby excluded from the covenant itself. Again the exclusion is relative, conforming to Qumran notions of rank[34] and purity, and not absolute or having to do with membership in Israel itself.

It is probable, then, that 4QFlor I, 1–7 is concerned primarily with purity. Because of the purity of the eschatological temple and of the covenantal community that substitutes for it in the present, certain classes of people are excluded. Baumgarten (1972) has made the observation that in rabbinic tradition, the same set of Biblical texts (i.e., Deut 23:2–3; Ezek 44:9) has been interpreted with reference to permissible and forbidden marriage unions.[35] The phrase "assembly of the Lord" (Deut 23:2–3) is ambiguous; the rabbis interpreted it with reference to marriage, the Qumran community with reference to the temple.

But by extension, the Qumran community interpreted these passages with respect to the community itself. This leads to the second observation concerning the presence of "proselyte" in the list of 4QFlor I, 4. If גר is indeed to be translated as "proselyte," the text contains a fundamental tension. How can a full convert to the community of Israel be excluded from the community of Israel? Admittedly, the text does not say this explicitly, but as soon as the

34. On the concern for rank in the Qumran material, see, e.g., 1QS VI, 8–11; CD 14:3–6.

35. See, e.g., *m. Qidd.* 4.1, which lists ten classes of Israelites, grouped according to who can marry whom. Proselytes stand fifth in the list, able to marry all Israelites except for priests. Cohen (1999, 249–50) observes that both interpretations of Deut 23:2–3 are present within the biblical material itself: 1 Kgs 11:1–2 echoes Deut 23:3–4 (along with Deut 7:3–4) while criticizing Solomon for his marriages to foreign women; in contrast, Lam 1:10 evokes Deut 23:2–3 in connection with the entry of Gentiles into the temple.

"house" from which the גר is excluded (I, 4) it is reinterpreted as the community itself ("the human temple," I, 6), this is the clear implication. One could readily imagine a Gentile convert to this self-proclaimed "assembly of the Lord" feeling that the community was speaking out of both sides of its mouth.

But perhaps this is the point. Real converts would draw attention to the inconsistency by their very presence; hypothetical converts would not. Rather than understanding גר in 4QFlor I, 4 as an archaizing re-creation of the older biblical category of the resident alien, it is more likely to be seen as part of the construction of an idealized Israel, one which included the category of proselytes but as an idealized, hypothetical construct, rather than as a group of flesh-and-blood Gentile converts to Israel. If such converts had been materially present in the Qumran community, there would have been a natural check against the development of a tradition in which a category of community members was categorically excluded from the community. In support of this conclusion one could cite 1QS VI, 13–14, which seems to assume that new community members will be drawn from Israel itself rather than from among the Gentiles: "And anyone from Israel who freely volunteers to enroll in the council of the Community, the man appointed at the head of the Many shall test him with regard to his insight and his deeds."

In other words—and this conclusion pertains to the full set of Qumran texts discussed in this section—there were proselytes within the Qumran worldview but not within the Qumran community.[36] גר should be translated as proselyte rather than as resident alien, but the proselytes who appear in the texts are probably to be understood as hypothetical figures rather than as real community members. It is unlikely that the community actually incorporated Gentile converts.

36. This conclusion agrees with that of Schiffman on the former and disagrees with him on the latter; see Schiffman (1997, 170).

Chapter 5

Philo

Introduction

On the basis of most status indicators—family, wealth, education, ability, and influence—Philo belonged to the highest stratum of the Jewish community in Alexandria. His family was extremely wealthy: his brother Alexander had the resources to loan Herod Agrippa two hundred thousand drachmae without blinking[1] and to donate gold plating for nine massive gates in the Jerusalem temple (Josephus *J.W.* 5.205). Alexander was also well-connected, serving as overseer[2] for Antonia, the mother of Claudius (Josephus *Ant.* 19.276), and occupying the office of *alabarch*, apparently a significant position in Egypt's tax administration (Schürer 1986, 3:136). Philo himself had received a thorough Greek education in the gymnasium and school system, which was evidently coupled with an equally thorough grounding in the Scriptures and traditions of Judaism.[3] For one with such a love of learning, his social status proved to be a

1. Aware of Agrippa's profligacy, however, he actually entrusted the money to Agrippa's wife Cypros (Josephus *Ant.* 18.159–60).

2. ἐπιτροπεύσαντα; Jos. *Ant.* 19.276. Barclay (1996, 68, n. 44) suggests that he managed her Egyptian estates.

3. On the Greek side, note the assumption that parents provide for the education of their children's body through the gymnasium and soul through the school curriculum (*Spec. Laws* 2.230; also Barclay 1996, 160; Morris 1987, 819, n. 27). On the Jewish side, Philo identifies himself as one who was "reared under laws which incite to every virtue, trained from our earliest years under divinely gifted men" (*Spec. Laws* 1.314).

mixed blessing. On the one hand, his financial security meant that he was able to devote himself to his primary joy—the study of philosophy and the development of his writing projects (*Spec. Laws* 3.1). On the other, his prominence meant that he was unable to avoid entanglement in "civil turmoils" (*Spec. Laws* 3.5). The most notable of these was his role as the head of the Jewish delegation that was sent to the emperor in Rome to appeal the actions of the governor Flaccus (*Flaccus, Embassy*). His account of this undertaking (which took place in 39–40 C.E.) provides us incidentally with our only solid piece of information concerning his biographical chronology. Writing shortly afterwards, he describes himself as one of "the aged" (οἱ γέροντες) who have "grown grey" (*Embassy* 1). Since he elsewhere describes the threshhold of old age as fifty-seven years,[4] his date of birth can be identified as somewhere in the vicinity of 20 B.C.E. .

Philo's extant works run to twelve volumes in the Loeb edition, comprising some thirty-five separate tractates. Most of his work is exegetical in nature, though this body of work falls into three distinct subcategories.[5] The *Allegory*, occupying the first five volumes in the Loeb edition, is aimed at a readership thoroughly familiar with both Scripture and philosophy. In form, these treatises consist of a running commentary on various Pentateuchal texts, mainly from Genesis; in content, their primary theme is the struggle of the soul to free itself from earthly passions, to acquire virtue, and to arrive at the vision of God. Given the decidedly non-philosophical content of Genesis, with its rambling patriarchal narratives, it is not surprising that to accomplish his purposes Philo has to subject the text to a sustained allegorical interpretation.[6] In the *Exposition*, however (vols. 6–8 in the Loeb edition), Philo deals much more prosaically with the text, providing the less sophisticated reader with a systematic introduction to Moses and his legislation. A third set of writings, *Questions and Answers on Genesis and Exodus* (not fully extant), comes at the text from yet another angle, responding to a series of questions on the biblical text with a combination of literal and "symbolical" responses. In addition to his exegetical works, Philo produced a miscellany of other treatises, including his political works, *Against Flaccus* and *On the Embassy to Gaius*, with their valuable insight into Alexandrian politics, and *That Every Good Person is Free* and *On the Contemplative Life*, with their descriptions of the Essenes and the Therapeutae, respectively.

In all his writings Philo reveals himself as a devoted servant of two masters, Plato and Moses; the constant thrust of his intellectual and exegetical agenda

4. Dividing the stages of life into multiples of seven; *Creation* 105.

5. On the arrangement of Philo's works, see Morris (1987, 825–32, 840–44).

6. He finds justification in the reference to the "tree of life" (Gen 2:9): "This description is, I think, intended symbolically (συμβολικῶς) rather than literally; for never yet have trees of life or of understanding appeared on earth, not is it likely that they will appear hereafter" (*Creation* 154). On his allegorical interpretation generally, see Morris (1987, 876–78).

was to demonstrate that these two masters ultimately spoke with the same voice. In Goodenough's memorable way of putting it (Goodenough 1962, 10),

> Out of the two strands [Jewish tradition and Greek philosophy] he had woven himself a single cloth, warp and woof. He read Plato in terms of Moses, and Moses in terms of Plato, to the point that he was convinced that each had said essentially the same things.

To be sure, other philosophical influences are readily apparent;[7] Philo wants to make common cause with what he sees to be the highest elements in Greek philosophy, no matter what their origin. Still, it is clear that for him Plato holds pride of place on the one side, just as Moses does on the other.

But how could Philo expect educated Alexandrians, whether Jewish or Gentile,[8] to read the Pentateuch and be convinced that Moses "had attained the very summit of philosophy" (*Creation* 8)? Such an agenda might seem to be so quixotic and his two masters so disparate that allegorical interpretation would have to be his only possible option. But a striking feature of his exegetical work, especially the *Exposition*, is that his philosophical enterprise is grounded on a fairly literal reading of the text. Philo packages the material of the Pentateuch so that it accords with common perceptions of the goal and achievement of philosophy, thus constructing a philosophical-expositional edifice that he—and presumably many of his readers—would have found to be plausible and compelling.

Philo's isomorphic presentation of Plato (or philosophy) and Moses (or Jewish ideals) is anchored at three points. One is the attainment of virtue. On one side of it, the description of virtue and how to attain it is clearly a dominant preoccupation of the philosophical tradition. On the other, the laws of Moses, which attempted to guide and regulate all of life, could readily be presented as a handbook of virtue. In his treatment of the law (*Spec. Laws*; *Virtues*), Philo first argues that all the "special laws" can be organized under the general heading of the Decalogue (*Spec. Laws* 1.1–4.131); then he goes on to argue in the remainder that all of the laws so classified can be subsumed under "the virtues of universal value": "For each of the ten pronouncements separately and all in common incite and exhort us to wisdom and justice and godliness and the rest of the company of virtues" (*Spec. Laws* 4.134).

A second point of connection is that of a civic constitution or πολιτεία, something that all thoughtful people deemed essential for "a well-ordered city" (*Creation* 143). Using the Stoic notion of the whole world as a "city" with natural law being its constitution,[9] Philo presents Moses's laws as a πολιτεία fully

7. Barclay (1996, 163–65); Birnbaum (1996, 21–22); Morris (1987, 871–72).

8. On the question of Philo's intended audience, see the comments later on in this introductory section.

9. On the Stoic concept, see Borgen (1997, 147–48).

in keeping with the natural law. Indeed, Moses started where he did—with an account of the world's creation—precisely so as to indicate that "the Father and Maker of the world was in the truest sense also its Lawgiver" (*Moses* 2.48). Thus Philo can present the laws of Moses as the blueprint for a social order that is the best expression of the universal πολιτεία that philosophers had long sought to identify and describe.[10]

The third point of connection that Philo establishes between philosophy and Mosaic Scripture is the vision of the Uncreated One, the one true God.[11] The connection, as he sets it out, is a tight one: "For what the disciples of the most excellent philosophy gain from its teaching, the Jews gain from their laws, that is to know the highest, the most ancient Cause of all things and reject the delusion of created gods" (*Virtues* 65). What philosophers arrive at by dint of strenuous thought (cf. *Abr.* 57), Jews receive naturally through their Mosaic inheritance.

By presenting the law of Moses as both a handbook of virtue and a civic constitution coherent with the laws of the cosmos, by aligning the divine character of the law (in both its origin and goal) with philosophical strivings towards monotheism, and by doing all of this with conviction, sophistication, and elegance, Philo portrays a Moses who would at least have been seen as congenial to those whose primary master was Plato or to those who—like Philo himself—wanted to serve both. But this raises a question that has been hinted at once or twice already. For whose benefit was Philo carrying out this portrayal? Were his intended readers primarily people like himself—bi-cultural Jews who were searching for an intellectual framework that would accommodate and combine both poles of their cultural allegiance? Or was he addressing a wider readership, one that would include Gentiles who were, or who might be persuaded to become, interested in Judaism?

This question, of course, is not unique to Philo, but it has been often raised with respect to Jewish apologetic literature more generally.[12] While it is best to leave the question open until we have looked at Philo's writings more directly, a few preliminary comments are in order. The question takes a different shape depending on whether it is being raised with respect to the *Allegory* or to the *Exposition*. The *Allegory* assumes such a familiarity with Judaism and the Mosaic Scriptures that if Gentiles are included among the intended readership, they must be understood as proselytes, or at least as having had a long and intimate association with the Jewish community. It is with respect to the *Exposition*,

10. On Philo's use of πολιτεία, see Birnbaum (1996, 51–52).

11. On Plato's conceptions about God, see Morris (1987, 880–81), with the literature cited there.

12. First raised in a pointed form by Tcherikover (1956). For discussions of Philo's audience in particular, see the surveys in Birnbaum (1996, 17–21) and Morris (1987, 3:817–18, 840, 878–79).

then, with its more accessible discussion of the material, that the question must first be addressed.[13] Here one finds a considerable spectrum of opinion, ranging from Goodenough's belief that these writings were addressed primarily to Gentiles[14] to the contention of Will and Orrieux that Philo's works provide no real evidence that he had ever even seen a proselyte, and thus that he wrote solely for the benefit of his co-religionists.[15] But both extremes distort the evidence of the texts. While there is no clear evidence that Philo addresses himself to Gentiles directly, the Jewish community to which he addresses himself is clearly one with a significant penumbra of interested Gentiles. Borgen's suggestion that Philo is addressing himself to the kind of community reflected in *Moses* 2.41–42 (albeit with some probable exaggeration), where "multitudes of others" join with Jews in an annual celebration of the translation of the Scriptures into Greek, is probably not far from the mark (Borgen 1997, 143).[16]

But whatever we decide about the intended beneficiaries of Philo's attempt to bring Moses and Plato into coherence, the attempt is inherently problematic, and the difficulties become especially apparent as he attempts to work both ends towards the middle. That is, he attempts to chart a course both from a starting point in Moses moving outwards towards Plato, and from Plato back towards Moses, but the two courses are not well aligned, and his navigational deficiencies become apparent precisely at those points at which they should join up with each other.

A particular case in point is Philo's universalism—the ways in which Gentiles are drawn into his program. As Birnbaum (1996) has demonstrated in detail, each of Philo's starting points leads to a form of universalism,[17] but when one attempts to coordinate or align them, one is confronted with significant tensions and inconsistencies. On the one hand, Philo's claim that the law of Moses represents the best route to virtue and the best civic constitution leads naturally to an emphasis on proselytism. For Philo the law is not simply an

13. Nevertheless, one should not exaggerate the differences between the two works and their intended audiences. Since Philo is quite prepared to refer readers of his *Exposition* back to a section in the *Allegory* (*Spec. Laws* 2.40), we need to think of overlapping audiences rather than as two distinct and separate circles of intended readers. In her attempts to resolve tensions within Philo's writings, Birnbaum perhaps tends to resort too quickly to the notion of different intended audiences (Birnbaum 1996, 118, 220–30).

14. E.g., Goodenough (1933); see also the comment by Morris (1987, 3:840–41, n. 111).

15. Will and Orrieux (1992, 97); Niehoff (2001, 13).

16. Dickson (2003, 37–39) also draws attention to *Spec. Laws* 1.320–23, where Philo contrasts the secrecy of the mystery religions with those, presumably like himself, who are prepared to speak openly in the marketplace.

17. Birnbaum actually concludes that Philo cannot be described as a universalist, because he believes that for individuals to be included within that group of people who stand in a positive relationship with God they "would first have to relinquish their wrong beliefs and adopt the monotheistic premise" (Birnbaum 1996, 226). But with such a definition, no

abstract intellectual structure, existing on its own apart from the people whose constitution it was. The law is the special possession of a particular nation (ἔθνος) or people (λαός), that of the "Jews" or the "Hebrews." While the law is a reflection of the universal law of nature and thus is open to all, those who accept it fully as their own necessarily become incorporated into this ethnic entity. Philo speaks with great pride of the Jews' willingness to welcome proselytes as "our dearest friends and closest kinsmen" (*Virtues* 179).

On the other hand, Philo presents the quest to "see" God in a manner that would seem to apply to all who are devoted to the philosophical life, irrespective of ethnic identity. Especially in the *Allegory*, Philo takes texts dealing with Israel in particular and interprets them in universal terms. For example, in *Migration* 56–59, the "great nation" of Israel (Deut. 4:6–7) is taken to refer to "all the lovers of wisdom and knowledge," a group made up of "world-citizens" (κοσμοπολίτης). Similarly, in *Dreams* 2.250–51, he locates Jerusalem, the city where God dwells, not "among the regions of the earth" but "in a soul . . . whose sight is keen, which has set before it as its aim to live in contemplation and peace." Further, when pressed to give examples of people past and present "who took God for their sole guide and lived according to a law of nature's right reason" (*Good Person* 62), the list that he puts forward contains groups that clearly were not Jewish.[18] At the same time, elsewhere in his works the primary examples of those who have seen God are such Jewish figures as Abraham and Moses, and he never gives his readers explicit reason to believe that they can become part of this company of God-seeing ones without embracing the particular revelation in which Abraham and Moses are central figures.

Thus, depending which of Philo's two poles functions as the primary point of reference, one ends up with two quite different portraits of Gentile inclusion. How is one to correlate the figure of the proselyte, for whom Moses makes provision on the literal surface of his "most excellent" law (*Moses* 2.12), with that of the "one who sees God," to whom Moses's writings are addressed at the level of "the hidden and inward meaning" (*Abraham* 147)? Are they the same in Philo's conception? If so, are his "proselytes" really just ethical monotheists, living a life committed to virtue and the vision of the one God, and thus becoming part of "Israel" in the etymological sense but not adopting those practices

---

Jew in our period could be described as "universalist." Since her only other category is particularism, defined as the belief that one has to be a Jew in order to related positively to God, her categories are too few and too polarized to be helpful. What is needed are categories that recognize that Jews could be "universalistic"—in the sense of believing that non-Jews might, in one way or another, stand in a positive relationship with the God of Israel—while still being "particularistic"—in the sense of believing that Israel has been chosen by God for a very particular relationship.

18. *Good Person* 72–74; see §101 below.

that would turn them into Jews? Or does he assume that those who seek to "see God" become part not only of "Israel" in an abstract sense but also of "the Jews" in a very real sense? Is the tension only apparent, as Birnbaum (1996) has argued, a reflex of the fact that different sections of his opus are addressed to different audiences? Or is the tension inherent to his work, reflecting the fact that he had not really sorted these issues out for himself? Are these tensions the inevitable result of his attempt to serve two masters? Is it the case that when he begins with Plato as his primary frame of reference, he can say that Judaism and philosophy are parallel tracks to the same goal (*Virtues* 65), but when he begins with Moses, he believes that the Jews have been given through their election what reason by itself is not able to attain (*Embassy* 3–6; also *Moses* 2.6)?

These are complex questions, and any attempt at an answer will need to emerge from a close reading of the pertinent passages.

Texts and Commentary

Text and translation: LCL (Colson, Whitaker and Marcus 1929–62), occasionally modified for clarity
Date: First half of the first century C.E.
Provenance: Alexandria
Original language: Greek
Bibliography: Barclay (1996, 158–80); Birnbaum (1996); Bockmuehl (2000, 107–9); Borgen (1984; 1997); Goodenough (1962); Kraus (1996, 86–90); Leonhardt (2001); McKnight (1991); Mendelson (1988); Morris (1987, 3:809–89); Niehoff (2001); Sandmel (1979); Will and Orrieux (1992, 81–99); Wolfson (1948)

§84 Dreams *1.160–61*

And Isaac is a dweller on his native soil, while Abraham is an emigrant and an incomer in the land. [161]*For, abandoning the foreign alien tongue of Chaldaea, the tongue of sky-prating astrology, he betook him to the language that befits a living creature endowed with reason, even the worship of the First Cause of all things.*

Category: CONVERSION

Apparently a sequel to a treatise that is no longer extant, *On Dreams* contains allegorical interpretations of those biblical dream accounts in which the human mind is actively engaged (1.1). The passage cited here is found in the context of a discussion of Jacob's vision of the ladder reaching to heaven. Citing Gen 28:13—"I am the Lord God of Abraham thy father and the God of Isaac: fear not"—Philo draws our attention to the different language for God with respect to the two patriarchs—"Lord God" in the case of Abraham, but "God" in the case of Isaac. For Philo, all such textual details are full of significance. In this case, they highlight differences between Abraham and Isaac, one of which is expressed in the passage cited here.

In contrast to Isaac, who lived in the land as indigenous and native-born (αὐτόχθονι καὶ αὐθιγενεῖ), Abraham was an "emigrant and a stranger" (μετανάστῃ καὶ ἐπηλύτῳ). The descriptions are true of Abraham and Isaac in a literal sense, but in 161 Philo goes on to add a level of meaning in which Abraham appears as a "convert." As we will see, ἐπήλυτος ("incomer") is one of several derivations from ἐπέρχομαι (also ἐπηλύτης and ἔπηλυς) that Philo often uses in place of the less familiar biblical term προσήλυτος (which nevertheless also appears). What Abraham "abandoned"[19] was not simply the land and the language of the Chaldeans but also their idolatrous worship; what he "came to" was not only a new land but also a new worship—"the worship of the First Cause of all things." In other words, Abraham appears here not simply as a sojourner but also as a proselyte. If Isaac is the prototypical native-born Israelite, Abraham is the prototypical proselyte, a depiction that will be presented more emphatically in *Virtues* 212–19.[20] The essence of Abraham's conversion, however, is his abandonment of idolatry and his worship of the one true God.

§85 Dreams *2.273*

> *These are the Levites and the proselytes, the orphans and widows; the first suppliants, the second those who have left their homes and taken refuge with God, the others those who are as orphans and widows to creation, and have adopted God as the lawful husband and father of the servant-soul.*

Category: CONVERSION

In the second book of the treatise *On Dreams*, Philo considers those dreams that require human interpretation. The passage cited here appears in the context of his discussion of Pharaoh's dream and its interpretation by Joseph. The passage itself is a comment on LXX Deut 26:13, which prescribes a tithe in the third year to be given to the Levite, the "proselyte" (τῷ προσηλύτῳ), the orphan, and the widow. There is no need to retrace the long and circuitous route by which Philo moves from Pharaoh's dream to the third-year tithe of Deut 26:13.

19. The term (ἀπολείπω) appears in other proselyte passages (*Spec. Laws* 1.52; *Virtues* 102, 181).

20. In *Moses* 1.7, Abraham is described as "the first settler [ἐπηλύτης], who became the founder of the whole Jewish nation." Given use of similar language in *Dreams* 1.161 and *Virtues* 212–19 to describe Abraham as the first proselyte, it is possible that ἐπηλύτης should be given such a sense in *Moses* 1.7 as well. But since there is no explicit indication of this in the passage, it has been left out of account here.

The only pertinent point is his description of proselytes as wanderers and refuge-seekers (μετανάσται καὶ πρόσφυγες). While the language appears elsewhere with reference to proselytes,[21] thus justifying the inclusion of the passage in our discussion, the statement adds very little to the investigation.

§86 Moses *1.147*

> *They were accompanied by a promiscuous, nondescript and menial crowd, a bastard host, so to speak, associated with the true-born. These were the children of Egyptian women by Hebrew fathers into whose families they had been adopted, also those who, reverencing the divine favour shewn to the people, had become incomers, and such as were converted and brought to a wiser mind by the magnitude and the number of the successive punishments.*

Additional bibliography: McKnight (1989).
Category: CONVERSION

With the treatise *On the Life of Moses*, we are moving into the *Exposition* portion of Philo's work. Although the Loeb edition groups this treatise with biographies of Abraham and Joseph, it is not certain that it really belongs here. These others, along with lost biographies of Isaac and Jacob, clearly were intended to function as an introduction to the exposition of the law proper, which begins with *On the Decalogue*.[22] But the biography of Moses stands more on its own and is not tightly integrated into the sequence of treatises constituting the *Exposition*. Nevertheless, it is clear from cross-references to it in other sections of the *Exposition* (*Rewards* 53; *Virtues* 52) that it belongs to this work in some way.

In a manner consistent with the more straightforward approach taken in the *Exposition*, here he deals with the life of Moses in a non-allegorical manner; book 1 is essentially chronological, while book 2 is thematic. The passage cited here is his comment on LXX Exod 12:37–38, where it is said that when the Israelites departed from Egypt, a great mixed group (ἐπίμικτος πολύς) went up with them.

There is a puzzling tension in Philo's description of this accompanying multitude. As the passage begins, this multitude is described in pejorative terms (e.g., συγκλύδων: washed together by the waves; thus, a mixed rabble),

21. μετανάστης appears also in *Dreams* 1.160; *Spec. Laws* 2.118; 4.178; *Virtues* 105, 218. πρόσφυγες appears also in *Spec. Laws* 2.118.

22. At the beginning of his treatise on Abraham, Philo indicates that before dealing with the particular laws he wants to present the patriarchs who, with their "good and blameless lives" exemplified the "originals," of which the written laws were copies (*Abraham* 3–4). It is clear from *Abraham* 60 that he intended to deal with Isaac and Jacob as well; he presents the treatise on Joseph as kind of an extension of the original triad (*Joseph* 1). On the question of the place of *Moses* in the structure of the *Exposition* as a whole, see Morris (1987, 854–55).

especially in the contrast drawn between the bastard or counterfeit (νόθον) group of hangers-on and the company of genuine (γνησίου) Israelites. As the passage proceeds, the multitude seems to be divided into three subgroups. The contrast between counterfeit and genuine seems to provide an appropriate description of the first of these subgroups—the children of Egyptian mothers and Jewish fathers. But there does not seem to be any hint of criticism in his description of the other two subgroups—those who were impressed in a positive way by the signs of divine favor and as a consequence became "incomers" (ἐπηλύται), and those who were impressed in a negative way by the plagues and as a consequence "were converted [or changed, μετεβάλοντο] and brought to a wiser mind [σωφρονισθέντες]." Since these terms (μεταβάλλω, σωφρονίζω) are frequently used elsewhere with reference to proselytes or incomers,[23] these two subgroups should both be seen as consisting of proselytes.

McKnight (1989) has suggested that the passage should be seen as a precursor of later rabbinic traditions that treat certain types of proselytes with disapproval—namely, the dream (or advantage) proselyte (one who seeks conversion simply to share in Israel's blessings) and the lion (or fear) proselyte (one who seeks conversion to escape some form of negative consequence). But there is no hint in Philo's description of these two groups that he disapproves of their motives. Indeed, later in the same treatise he takes it as quite natural that Gentiles would find Judaism more attractive when the Jews were flourishing (*Moses* 2.43–44) and clearly sees this as a desirable state of affairs. Analogously, in the treatise *On Rewards and Punishments* he presents as worthy of praise the proselyte who, impressed by the promise of reward and the threat of punishment, comes over to the "camp of God" (152).

What, then, are we to make of this tension? On the face of it, the pejorative description at the beginning of the passage seems to apply to all three subgroups. But as will become clear throughout this chapter, if proselytes are viewed in a negative light here, the passage is an anomaly in the Philonic corpus; Philo generally refers to them with great enthusiasm and looks on them with approval. Indeed, in the very next paragraph Philo describes Israel as "a nation destined . . . to offer prayers for ever on behalf of the human race that it may be delivered from evil and participate in what is good" (*Moses* 1.149). No ambivalence about proselytes here! At the same time, Philo's antipathy towards ethnic Egyptians (in contrast to Greeks) is well documented.[24] Later in this same treatise he charges the Egyptians of being "almost alone among the nations" in the

23. Especially μεταβάλλω: *Spec. Laws* 1.51; *Virtues* 177, 217; *Rewards* 152. Other verbs compounded with μετα- are used with reference to proselytes: μεταλλάσσω and μεταδίδωμι (both in *Virtues* 108); μεθορμίζω (*Spec. Laws* 1.51; cf. *Rewards* 152). σωφρονίζω also appears in *Rewards* 152.

24. See Birnbaum (1996, 226); Mendelson (1988, 118).

nature of their idolatrous worship of the created order (*Moses* 2.193–96), a passage especially pertinent because it deals (in caustic terms) with Jewish-Egyptian intermarriage. Thus, while pejorative overtones cannot be eliminated entirely, it can reasonably be concluded that Philo's invective is aimed specifically at the first subgroup, that is, "illegitimate" children of Jewish-Egyptian marriages; we probably should not see it as carrying over in any considerable degree to his description of the other two subgroups, that is, to proselytes.

§87 Moses *2.17–24*

> *Yet, though it may be rightly thought a great matter in itself that the laws should have been guarded securely through all time, we have not reached the true marvel. There is something surely still more wonderful—even this: not only Jews but almost every other people, particularly those which take more account of virtue, have so far grown in holiness as to value and honour our laws. In this they have received a special distinction which belongs to no other code.* [18] *Here is the proof. Throughout the world of Greeks and barbarians, there is practically no state which honours the institutions of any other. Indeed, they can scarcely be said to retain their own perpetually, as they adapt them to meet the vicissitudes of times and circumstances.* [19] *. . . We may fairly say that mankind from east to west, every country and nation and state, shew aversion to foreign institutions, and think that they will enhance the respect for their own by shewing disrespect for those of other countries.* [20] *It is not so with ours. They attract and win the attention of all, of barbarians, of Greeks, of dwellers on the mainland and islands, of nations of the east and the west, of Europe and Asia, of the whole inhabited world from end to end.* [21] *For, who has not shewn his high respect for that sacred seventh day, by giving rest and relaxation from labour to himself and his neighbours, freemen and slaves alike, and beyond these to his beasts?. . .* [23] *Again, who does not every year shew awe and reverence for the fast, as it is called, which is kept more strictly and solemnly than the "holy month" of the Greeks?*

Category: SYMPATHIZATION

On the Life of Moses is laid out in two distinct parts. The first deals with Moses's life in a more or less chronological way; the second treats aspects of Moses's person under the headings of lawgiver, high priest, and prophet (*Moses* 2.2). The passage under discussion here appears near the beginning of the treatment of Moses as lawgiver, as part of Philo's argument for the thesis that Moses "was the best of all lawgivers [νομοθετῶν]" (2.12). Before defending this thesis on the basis of the laws themselves (beginning at 2.45), he provides two preliminary arguments. The first of these has to do with the unchangeable character of the Mosaic legislation; unlike the laws of other nations, which have been altered in various ways, those of Moses "remain secure from the day when they were first enacted to now" (2.14), because "all have clearly paid honour to their venerable and godlike character" (2.15).

The second preliminary argument concerns the "honour" that has been shown to the laws of Moses by "almost every other people" (2.17), people from "the whole inhabited world from end to end" (2.20). After drawing a contrast with the rest of the world, where nations generally disdain the laws and customs of other nations (2.18–19), Philo illustrates the attractiveness of the Jewish law by citing several observances that have been adopted by Gentiles—specifically the Sabbath (2.21–22) and the "fast" (i.e., Day of Atonement; 2.23–24). These are followed by a third illustration, having to do with the translation of the Scriptures into Greek (2.25–43), which will be taken up below.

Philo's claims are as exaggerated (cf. Goodman 1994, 74–75) as they are vague. The claim to universality is qualified only slightly, in that it is "particularly those which take more account of virtue" (2.17) who admire the Jewish laws. While both examples are introduced with a universal rhetorical flourish ("Who has not shown his high respect for that sacred seventh day?" 2.21), in neither case does he provide any specific information. Indeed, in the case of the "fast," he seems to be more intent on demonstrating the superiority of this Jewish observance to Gentile festivals than on demonstrating that there actually were Gentiles who observed the Jewish festival. It is worth noting that he continues his argument by reproducing the fanciful tradition that the Septuagint translation was carried out at the impetus of an admiring Ptolemy Philadelphus (2.25–40; cf. *Letter of Aristeas*). This strengthens the impression that the evidential value of the material in 2.17–24 for the question of Gentile attraction to Judaism has to do more with general Jewish opinion than with the phenomenon itself. Still, there is enough evidence elsewhere, especially of Sabbath observance, to indicate that such a climate of opinion was not self-generated. The passage provides at least some second-level evidence for the phenomenon (Cohen 1999, 149; Feldman 1993, 348–49).

But what of Philo's own opinion? While his main purpose here is to glorify the law, his statements provide some indication of how he viewed such Gentiles. On the one hand, they clearly remain Gentiles; there is no suggestion that their admiration reached the point that they became proselytes or "incomers." On the other hand, Philo sees their admiration of the law as an indication both of their virtue and of the extent to which they have progressed towards holiness (2.17). In other words, he extends to them some sort of religious approval. Still, any approval is qualified by the statement with which this whole section of the treatise is brought to a conclusion. In this passage (2.44), which will come up for more discussion below, Philo anticipates a day when Gentile adoption of Jewish law will be total rather than partial: "*each* nation" will abandon its own ways and "turn to honouring our laws *alone*." Philo is happy when Gentiles sympathize with Judaism, but he reserves his full approval for full acceptance.

§88 Moses *2.25–43*

> *That the sanctity of our legislation has been a source of wonder not only to the Jews but also to all other nations, is clear both from the facts already mentioned and those which I proceed to state.* [26] *In ancient times the laws were written in the Chaldean tongue, and remained in that form for many years, without any change of language, so long as they*

had not yet revealed their beauty to the rest of mankind. [27]*But, in course of time, the daily, unbroken regularity of practice exercised by those who observed them brought them to the knowledge of others, and their fame began to spread on every side. For things excellent, even if they are beclouded for a short time through envy, shine out again under the benign operation of nature when their time comes. Then it was that some people, thinking it a shame that the laws should be found in one half only of the human race, the barbarians, and denied altogether to the Greeks, took steps to have them translated. . . .* [31]*[Ptolemy] having conceived an ardent affection for our laws, determined to have the Chaldean translated into Greek . . .* [36] *. . . [T]aking the sacred books, [the Jewish translators] stretched them out towards heaven with the hands that held them, asking of God that they might not fail in their purpose. And He assented to their prayers, to the end that the greater part, or even the whole, of the human race might be profited and led to a better life by continuing to observe such wise and truly admirable ordinances.. . .* [41]*Therefore, even to the present day, there is held every year a feast and general assembly in the island of Pharos, whither not only Jews but multitudes of others cross the water, both to do honour to the place in which the light of that version first shone out, and also to thank God for the good gift so old yet ever young.* [42]*But, after the prayers and thanksgivings, some fixing tents on the seaside and others reclining on the sandy beach in the open air feast with their relations and friends, counting that shore for the time a more magnificent lodging than the fine mansions in the royal precincts.* [43]*Thus the laws are shewn to be desirable and precious in the eyes of all, ordinary citizens and rulers alike, and that too though our nation has not prospered for many a year.*

Category: SYMPATHIZATION

This passage continues the argument begun in 2.17–24, where Philo adduces Gentile admiration for the law of Moses as evidence for the greatness of the legislator. After dealing with Gentile observance of Jewish festivals (Sabbath, Day of Atonement), he turns his attention to the Septuagint, treating both the process of translation itself (2.25–40) and a contemporary Alexandrian celebration (2.41–42).

Philo's account of the translation process generally follows the story as it is presented in the *Letter of Aristeas*. He seems to take the story at face value and thus assumes that the impetus for the translation came not from Jews but from some (unnamed) Gentiles, who admired the law and thought it "a shame" (2.27) that it was not readily accessible to the Greeks. Given the fanciful character of this account, we cannot say that it provides us with any direct evidence of Gentile sympathy; its evidential value has to do more with its reflection of Jewish attitudes and beliefs.

Several things are of particular interest here. One is Philo's readiness to believe that Gentiles found the Jewish Scriptures to be sufficiently appealing that they would undertake to have them translated. Such a sympathetic attitude is displayed in its highest form by the king, Ptolemy Philadelphus. Not only did he possess "all the qualities which make a good ruler" (2.29), but he had them in such measure that he stood at the head of the whole body of the world's kings

(2.30). The crowning virtue of this noble king is that he had conceived "an ardent affection [ζῆλον καὶ πόθον] for our laws" (2.31). Philo makes no attempt to turn the king into a convert; it is as a Gentile that he admires the Jewish law and thus is used by God to carry out a larger purpose.[25]

This leads directly to a second point. Using the common Greek conceit that the human population can be divided into two groups—the Greeks and the barbarians—Philo presents the translation as a virtual counterpart of the initial revelation to Moses. Through Moses the laws were given to one-half of the "human race" (τοῦ γένους ἀνθρώπων), the implication being that Israel somehow represented all of the "barbarian" nations (27). By designating the language of Scripture as Chaldean rather than Hebrew, Philo was no doubt attempting to give a more universal (or at least demi-universal) complexion to a text emanating from the single nation of Israel.[26] The translation of Moses's Scriptures into Greek, then, was an "event in revelatory history" (Borgen 1997, 142), one that brought the initial revelation to completion by making it available to the rest of the human race. The island of Pharos, where the translation is said to have taken place (2.35, 37, 41–42), thus becomes a kind of second Sinai.

The momentous and universal significance of this event comes into view again a few sentences later where Philo recounts the prayer of the translators "that they might not fail in their purpose" (2.36). This reference to a divine purpose for the translation is Philo's own addition; the narrative in the *Letter of Aristeas*, which he is following, simply mentions daily prayers without giving any indication of their content (305–6). As Philo continues, he specifies the nature of this purpose: "that the greater part, or even the whole, of the human race" might come to accept the law. Further, he goes on to say that the prayers of the translators are granted (ἐπινεύει; 36) by God, though how it is that "the greater part, or even the whole, of the human race might be profited and led to a better life" (36) will become apparent only later in the passage.

Israel's role in this grand universal purpose is not limited to prayer on behalf of the nations. It was the "daily, unbroken regularity" (2.27) of Israel's law observance that attracted the attention of the other half of the world in the first place, leading to the initiatives that resulted in the translation itself. And, of course, it was through the agency of Israel—first in the person of the high priest who recognized God's purposes at work in the king's request (2.31–32) and then through the translators themselves—that these initiatives were brought to a successful conclusion. To be sure, there is no suggestion here that Jews should engage in any sort of active "mission" to attract and win proselytes; Goodman and others are correct on this point.[27] Still, Philo does see Israel as

25. The high priest believes "that God's guiding care must have led the king to busy himself in such an undertaking" (2.32).

26. On Philo's use of "Chaldean" see Birnbaum (1996, 48–49, 109).

27. Goodman (1994, 68, 74–75); Will and Orrieux (1992, 90–91).

caught up in a grand divine purpose in which the glories of the law "shine out" (ἀναλάμπει; 2.27) in the wider world, both through Israel's own visible devotion to the law and through its readiness to make it available, through translation, to "the whole human race" (2.36). No doubt Philo would have seen his own interpretive enterprise as contributing in no small way to this grand purpose.

To this point the passage provides evidence primarily for Philo's own convictions. The second part of the passage, however, provides us with a glimpse into the social realities of Philo's own day. After describing the process of translation (in dependence on the *Letter of Aristeas*), he goes on to describe a contemporary festival to commemorate the translation, held annually on the island of Pharos, where the translation had actually taken place (2.41–42). The event as Philo depicts it is quite appealing—feasting with friends and family on the beach, either in tents[28] or in the open air. And apparently its appeal extended to Gentiles as well, for he says that the celebrants included "not only Jews but multitudes of others." Here any tendencies Philo might have towards idealization and exaggeration are held in check. While he could make extravagant claims (and apparently believe them) about a single event in the distant past, claims that were not readily open to falsification, he could hardly assert that there was such an annual local festival without there being some substance to the claim. The Jewish community in Alexandria must have attracted a perennial body of Gentile sympathizers, on whom Philo looked with favor and to whom he pointed with pride (2.43). As Borgen (1997, 143) has suggested, this social phenomenon needs to be kept in mind in any assessment of the intended audience for Philo's work.

§89 Moses *2.43–44*

> *Thus the laws are shewn to be desirable and precious in the eyes of all, ordinary citizens and rulers alike, and that too though our nation has not prospered for many a year. It is but natural that when people are not flourishing their belongings to some degree are under a cloud. But, if a fresh start should be made to brighter prospects, how great a change for the better might we expect to see! I believe that each nation would abandon its peculiar ways, and, throwing overboard their ancestral customs, turn to honouring our laws alone. For, when the brightness of their shining is accompanied by national prosperity, it will darken the light of the others as the risen sun darkens the stars.*

Additional Bibliography: Scott (1995).
Category: ESCHATOLOGICAL PARTICIPATION

This passage is a continuation of the one just discussed. Philo has been discussing the translation of Israel's scriptures into Greek and has just described

28. The reference to tents leads Leonhardt (2001, 47–48) to speculate that the festival was linked to the Feast of Booths (Sukkoth) and thus was a local variation of a known festival rather than an innovation. But the fact that the tents were optional suggests that they can be accounted for on the basis of function rather than symbolism.

the annual celebration of the event on the island of Pharos (where the translation was said to have taken place). Then, in a kind of *a minori ad maius* form of argumentation, he goes on to say that if the law has proved to be so appealing even in the present inauspicious state of the Jewish nation, should Jewish fortunes begin to shine more brightly, then all other nations would abandon their own ways and "turn to honouring our laws alone."

Except for the general orientation towards the future, this passage contains no readily apparent indication that this transformation of Jewish fortunes and Gentile commitments, which Philo puts forward as a future possibility, is linked in any way to Jewish eschatological expectation. Indeed, given Philo's philosophical and exegetical agenda, one might think that eschatology would have had no place in his thinking at all, except perhaps in an allegorized Platonic form. His treatise *On Rewards and Punishments*, however, contains a full-scale eschatological scenario (162–72), one that conforms in most respects (with, of course, some typically Philonic twists) to more traditional Jewish eschatology. While this eschatological scenario does not contain any explicit reference to the inclusion of Gentiles in the coming state of affairs, there is enough similarity between the two passages to suggest that a similar eschatological framework is present in *Moses* 2.43–44.

As we will see in more detail below, *On Rewards and Punishments* functions as a kind of conclusion to the *Exposition*. The latter part of the treatise (79–172) is based on passages in Leviticus (chs. 26, 28) and Deuteronomy (chs. 28–30) in which Moses sets out the blessings or curses that Israel would experience in consequence of its obedience or disobedience respectively. Philo deals with rewards and blessings in 79–126 and with punishments and curses in 127–61; 162–72 functions as a conclusion to the whole.

One of the striking features of this treatise is the presence of what can only be described as an "eschatological vision."[29] Expressions of such a vision are not restricted to the passage mentioned above (162–72) but have already become apparent at several previous points (also 87–97, 115–17). Some scholars have attempted to downplay this material, arguing that it simply reflects the biblical texts with which Philo is dealing (e.g., Kraus 1996, 86–87). But such an argument fails to convince. While the blessing and curse passages contain material that might be suggestive of eschatological themes for those so inclined (e.g., the return from exile anticipated in Deut 30:1–5), Philo's passages go so far beyond the biblical text as to demonstrate that he was definitely open to suggestion. In other words, the eschatological vision needs to be taken seriously.[30] Still, it is only in the final passage (162–72) that Israel as a national and ethnic entity is clearly in view.

29. Barclay (1996, 176): "a rare but significant eschatological vision."

30. See Barclay (1996, 176); Borgen (1997, 260–81); J. J. Collins (2000, 134–38); Scott (1995); Wolfson (1948, 2:407–26).

The first of these sections (87–97) seems to have been precipitated by the promise in Lev 26:6 that if Israel keeps the commandments, God "will remove dangerous animals from the land." Apparently linking this to the end-time vision of peace in Isa 11:6–9, Philo anticipates an era "when savage creatures become tame and gentle" (88). This state of affairs will be brought about when a certain number of people are so attuned to virtue that for them "the wild beasts within the soul shall be tamed" (88). This peaceable state of affairs within human souls will not only bring to an end the age-old war between beasts and humans but will also lead to an era of peace in the human world as well (91). Those who live in "the land of the godly" (93) will be delivered from their human enemies, either because the latter cannot stand before a virtuous people who "have in justice an irresistible ally" (93) or because the virtuous will be aided by "a man . . . [who] leading his host to war . . . will subdue great and populous nations" (95). This "man," whose activity Philo finds described in an "oracle"—clearly LXX Num 24:7[31]—is a messianic figure[32] who, apparently, will come to the aid of the godly only if the presence of virtue is not sufficient in itself to "allay the onsets of evils" (93).

While traditional Jewish eschatology is recognizable here, it has also been transformed in distinctively Philonic ways. For one thing, virtue is given a dominant role, even to the point that a messianic figure will be necessary only as a last resort, if virtue alone is not sufficient to carry the day (Borgen 1997, 275). Further, while the "godly" live in a "land" (93) and are beset by enemy "nations" (95), they are not clearly identified as Jews in the land of Judea. Still, the emphasis on the land and on the keeping of God's commandments (98) mean that such an identification is by no means closed off.

The second passage with an eschatological tinge is 115–17, where, in evident dependence on Deut 30:3–5, Philo speaks of the possibility that "God with a single call may easily gather together from the ends of the earth to any place that He wills the exiles dwelling in the utmost parts of the earth" (117). Here, however, his interest is primarily allegorical; the gathering of the exiles is used simply as an image of how the mind, straying in sinful exile, might be called back to the path of virtue. Thus the passage is of interest here only in that it anticipates the conclusion of the treatise (162–72), in which a literal return of Jewish exiles to their own land is envisaged.

As mentioned above, 162–72 serves as a conclusion to the whole treatise. The section begins with a summary of the "curses and penalties" that the disobedient will "deservedly suffer" (162). It is important to note that the disobedient

31. "There will come forth a man from his seed and he shall rule over many nations." Cf. MT: "Water shall flow from his buckets, and his seed shall have abundant water." Philo also cites and discusses the text in *Moses* 1.289–91.

32. So, e.g., Borgen (1997, 269–76); J. J. Collins (2000, 135); Wolfson (1948, 2:414–15).

are described in very ethnos-specific terms: they are those who "have forgotten the teaching of their race and of their fathers [τῆς συγγενοῦς καὶ πατρίου διδασκαλίας], in which they were trained [ἐπαιδεύθησαν] from their earliest years" (162). References to race, to patrimony, and to training indicate that Philo clearly has Jews in view here. The fact that in an earlier passage (152) the disobedient were explicitly contrasted with proselytes (see §100 below) only serves to underscore the fact.

After this retrospective look at the punishments that he has just described, however, Philo goes on to describe what will happen if the disobedient "accept these chastisements as a warning rather than as intending their perdition" (163). He holds out the possibility that the disobedient might repent, confess their sin, and look to God for forgiveness. The rest of the treatise is given over to a description of what will happen as a result. As the passage unfolds, it is clear that Philo is thinking in national and ultimate terms rather than simply of individual repentant sinners. Indeed, what follows is a traditional piece of Zion eschatology, albeit decked out in Philonic dress.[33]

The passage begins with a reference to the exile: "even though they dwell in the uttermost parts of the earth, in slavery to those who led them away captive" (164). That Philo intends this situation of captivity in foreign lands to be taken quite literally, rather than as an allegorical description of the soul, is clear from the explicit geographical terms in which the exile is described in the next paragraph: "those who but now were scattered in Greece and the outside world [ἐν Ἑλλάδι καὶ βαρβάρῳ] over islands and continents" (165). These exiles will be liberated, not by direct divine intervention, but as a consequence of their "conversion [μεταβολῆς] . . . to virtue"; when their masters see the change, they, awestruck, "will set them free, ashamed to rule over men better than themselves" (164). Thus liberated, the exiles will stream "in their pilgrimage" (lit. "guided as strangers"; ξεναγούμενοι) "to the one appointed place." While the "place" is not specified, the language of exile implies that they are returning home, that is, to the land of Judea;[34] subsequent reference to the land once inhabited by "their fathers and ancestors" (168) confirms it. When they arrive home, "everything will suddenly be reversed" (169): the land will be transformed into a place of fruitfulness and plenty (168), their enemies will be forced to confront the fact that those whom they had mistreated were in reality "men of high lineage" and "noble birth" (171), and the curses that Israel had formerly experienced because of its sin will now fall on its enemies (169).

33. As is generally recognized; see Borgen (1997, 276–80); Scott (1995).

34. The phrase "the appointed place" (τὸν ἀποδειχθέντα χῶρον) does not appear elsewhere in Philo. The verb ἀνασῴζομαι—rendered by Colson in the LCL as "pass from exile to their home"—appears elsewhere in Greek literature with reference to the homecoming of exiles (LSJ). On Jerusalem as the "metropolis" of the Jews, see Scott (1995, 558–59).

While the passage is clearly patterned after traditional eschatological expectations, one common component of Zion eschatology—the end-time turning to God of the Gentiles—is not present in this passage.[35] This lack seems to be supplied, however, by *Moses* 2.43–44. Here Philo looks ahead to a time of "national prosperity" (εὐτυχίᾳ τοῦ ἔθνους; 44), a time of dazzling brightness when the circumstances of Israel's national existence will be at their peak (ἐν ἀκμαῖς; 44). Clearly, what is in view here is a situation similar to that described in more detail in *Rewards* 162–72.[36] In this case, however, Philo focuses on the positive consequences that Israel's restoration brings about for the Gentiles. Here the result is not curse but blessing. The nations will all abandon their own ways and "turn to honouring our laws alone." Gentile adoption of Jewish law, already happening in partial and preliminary ways in the present, will in this ideal future become wholehearted and complete. Thus, for Philo, these end-time converts have the character of proselytes—or, as he prefers to call them, "incomers" (ἐπηλύται)—rather than simply ethical monotheists.

§90 On the Special Laws *1.51–52*

All of like sort to him, all who spurn idle fables and embrace truth in its purity, whether they have been such from the first or through conversion to the better side have reached that higher state, obtain his approval, the former because they were not false to the nobility of their birth, the latter because their judgement led them to make the passage to piety. These last he calls "proselytes," or newly-joined, because they have joined the new and godly commonwealth. [52] Thus, while giving equal rank to all incomers with all the privileges which he gives to the native-born, he exhorts the old nobility to honour them not only with the marks of respect but with special friendship and with more than ordinary goodwill. And surely there is good reason for this; they have left, he says, their country, their kinsfolk and their friends for the sake of virtue and religion. Let them not be denied another citizenship or other ties of family and friendship, and let them find places of shelter standing ready for refugees to the camp of piety. For the most effectual love-charm, the chain which binds dissolubly the goodwill which makes us one is to honour the one God.

Category: CONVERSION

This passage, part of a larger treatment of proselytes and apostates (1.51–58),[37] appears at a crucial juncture not only in the treatise itself but also in the *Exposition* as a whole. Thus we need to begin by setting the passage in its larger context.

35. Of course, Gentiles are implicitly present, in the form of the proselytes who have already come "over to the camp of God" (152).

36. For the connection between these two passages, see Borgen (1997, 278–80); J. J. Collins (2000, 135); Scott (1995, 573). A similar national restoration is hinted at in *QE* 2.76.

37. The theme of proselytes is continued in 1.53, where Philo comments on LXX Exod 22:28 (unlike the MT, the LXX has the plural, "gods").

The structure for Philo's treatise *On the Special Laws* is provided by his assumption that all of the Mosaic legislation can be arranged under the general headings provided by the Decalogue (*Decalogue* 154; *Spec. Laws* 1.1). The treatise thus exists as a sequel to *On the Decalogue*, to which it refers in its opening sentence. To be sure, no sooner does he introduce this structure than he sets it aside, presenting an introductory preamble on circumcision (1.2–11). But with this out of the way he turns back to his announced procedure, beginning with the first commandment and the related set of special laws "the subject of which is the sole sovereignty of God" (1.12). Before describing any of these special laws in any particularity, however, he slides almost imperceptibly into the second commandment concerning idolatry (1.21–31). When he finally turns to the special laws directly (1.59), he first discusses legislation prohibiting divination (1.59–65) and then deals at length (1.66–298) with laws regulating the temple and other aspects of Israel's worship. In other words, combining the first two commandments, he uses them more or less as a single heading under which he deals with the way in which the one true God is to be worshipped.

Our passage, then, forms part of a bridge section (1.32–58) in between the commandments themselves and the special laws associated with them. This section begins with a general discussion of two philosophical questions introduced in 32—"whether the Deity exists" (32–35) and "what the Deity is in essence" (35–50). In the latter part of his discussion of this second question, Philo presents Moses as a model of one who desires, and is granted, the vision of God. Actually, the vision is not that of God directly, for this is not "within man's power to take" (43); rather, the vision is of the impress of God's nature that can be perceived in the "forms" or "ideas" embedded in the created order itself. This vision is "a spectacle apprehended not by the eye of the body but by the unsleeping eyes of the mind" (49).

At this point in the treatise, Philo turns to a discussion of those who follow Moses in this "constant and profound longing for wisdom" (50). This company is made up of two distinct groups—those who have been part of "the new and godly commonwealth [πολιτείᾳ]" from birth and those who have joined it as proselytes (51–53). Both are contrasted to the apostates (54–57), who have abandoned "the ranks of piety and religion" (54) and are worthy of death. And both are presented as exemplifying the kind of piety to which the special laws point. For at just that point in his discourse where Philo moves on to a discussion of "everything else" that "the most holy Moses" has to say, he does so with a backward reference to Moses's "disciples [γνωρίμοις]": "The like principle is clearly maintained in the case of everything else by the most holy Moses, who loves and teaches the truth which he desires to engrave and stamp on all his disciples" (59). In other words, this passage is located at a crucial spot, right at the outset of Philo's treatment of the special laws. Proselytes, along with faithful Jews, are presented as models of the kind of piety and worship that is the goal of all of the special laws pertaining to the first two commandments of the Decalogue.

But as we will see a little later, this is not all. Just prior to the conclusion of the treatise *On Rewards and Punishments*, which itself brings the *Exposition* to a conclusion, the contrast between proselytes and apostates appears again (152). In this treatise, Philo concludes his lengthy *Exposition* of the law by focusing attention on what is at stake—blessings for those who follow the path of virtue laid out in the law and curses for those who do not—and by pointing to proselytes and apostates as evidence that these outcomes are dependent not on circumstances of birth but on human response. The two passages—*Spec. Laws* 1.51–59 and *Rewards* 152—thus function as a kind of *inclusio* for the *Exposition* as a whole.

Turning to the passage itself, one is struck by two—somewhat conflicting—features. On the one hand, the transformation experienced by the proselyte[38] is described in very general and abstract terms. Proselytes are counted among those "who spurn idle fables and embrace truth in its purity"; they have made a "passage to piety"; they have joined a "new and godly commonwealth" (1.51); they have made a decision "for the sake of virtue and religion"; they have found "places of shelter" (καταφυγαί) as "refugees [τοῖς αὐτομολοῦσι] to the camp of piety" (1.52);[39] they have joined with those who "honour the one God" (1.52). While in doing so they have become "of like sort to" Moses (1.51), this language by itself does not imply anything more than a commitment to monotheism and virtue. In particular, there is no explicit reference to any of the "special laws" that differentiate Jew from Gentile.

But on the other hand, the proselyte experience as Philo describes it involves a very real social dislocation and relocation, such as one would not readily associate with a simple commitment to ethical monotheism. Impiety and idle fables are not the only things that these proselytes have left behind; they have also had to abandon their "country and friends and kinsfolk" (πατρίδα καὶ φίλους καὶ συγγενεῖς; 1.52). In return, what they have entered is not simply an abstract class of those who are seeking a vision of God; instead, they have been incorporated into a distinct social entity. In exchange for what they have left behind, they have become part of new "civic bodies and households and friendships" (πόλεων καὶ οἰκείων καὶ φίλων; 1.52). In their new set of circumstances they are, at least theoretically, equal in status to the native-born: they have been given "equal rank" (ἰσοτιμίαν) and the same privileges (1.52).[40] Of course, the very terms in which Philo describes the reception and equality of status offered to proselytes suggest that reality did not always conform to the ideal; if the native-born need to be

38. The smooth transition from προσηλύτους (1.51) to ἐπηλύταις (1.52) demonstrates their semantic equivalency for Philo.

39. Both καταφυγή (*Spec. Laws* 1.309; *QE* 2.2) and αὐτομολέω (*Virtues* 181; 221; *Rewards* 152) are used elsewhere with reference to proselytes.

40. The theme of equality continues in 1.53: proselytes have been granted ἰσονομίαν καὶ ἰσοτέλειαν.

"exhorted" (παραινεῖ) to welcome the incomers (1.52), such welcome was evidently not always freely offered. But this only underlines the essentially social character of the change in status under discussion here. What Philo presents us with is not simply a case of Gentiles who have pursued the philosophical route with such diligence that, while remaining embedded in Greek culture, they have achieved a commitment to virtue and a conception of the one God that is analogous to that of the Jews. Instead, the outcome of their new commitments is that they have been alienated from their native social environment and have been incorporated into a new one.

Despite the abstract and idealized language, then, it appears that Philo is talking about real proselytes, converts who have been fully incorporated into the Jewish community. But what are we to make of his failure to mention circumcision or any of the other Torah-based markers that normally differentiated Jew from Gentile? While any conclusions at this point need to remain tentative, there is no reason to believe that Philo would have seen these things as inessential or as not to be required of proselytes. The passage, after all, is found in the context of a treatise extolling the virtues of the "special" and very specific laws of the Torah. Further, as we have seen, at the outset of this treatise Philo even postpones his declared procedure in order to begin with an exposition of the significance and meaning of circumcision itself. In this excursus on circumcision, he first lists four traditional arguments for the beneficial nature of circumcision (1.3–7) and then supplements these with two allegorical arguments concerning the symbolic (cf. σύμβολον; 1.8) significance of circumcision (1.8–11), each of which would be as applicable to the proselyte as to the native-born. One would expect, then, that those who have been granted ἰσονομίαν (1.53) with other members of the "new and godly commonwealth" (1.51) would be expected to follow the same νόμους, including that of circumcision. At the same time, however, this is not where Philo chooses to place the emphasis. The thing that binds these newcomers most closely to the native-born is not their shared marks of membership but their shared honor of the one God (1.52).

§91 On the Special Laws *1.308–9*

> *Yet vast as are his excellences and powers, he takes pity and compassion on those most helplessly in need, and does not disdain to give judgement to strangers or orphans or widows. He holds their low estate worthy of His providential care, while of kings and despots and great potentates He takes no account.* [309]*He provides for the incomers because forsaking the ancestral customs in which they were bred, customs packed with false inventions and vanity, they have crossed over to piety in whole-hearted love of simplicity and truth, and rendering to Him that truly exists the supplication and service which are His right, partake in due course of His protecting care in the measure that fits their case, and gain in the help that He gives the fruit of making God their refuge.*

Category: CONVERSION

At this point in his discussion of the "special laws," Philo turns from "direct commands and prohibitions" to injunctions that are in the form of "homilies giving admonitions and exhortations" (1.299). The passage cited here appears in the context of an extended treatment of Deut 10:12–22, a biblical text that deals with the orphan, the widow, and the stranger (ὁ προσήλυτος [LXX Deut 12:18]). The topic comes up naturally, then, because of its presence in the biblical text under discussion.

The passage does not add a great deal to our investigation, though it is consistent with what we have observed to this point. Once again we see the equivalence of Philo's terminology; he reproduces the LXX's προσηλύτοις ("strangers"; 1.308) but in commenting on the text replaces it with his own preferred but evidently synonymous term, ἐπηλύτων ("incomers"; 1.309). While the biblical passage contains the injunction that Israel is also to "love the stranger" (Deut 10:19), Philo passes this by without comment,[41] since his expositional point in 1.307–10 has to do with the character of God (both beneficent and punitive) rather than the corresponding obligations of the people. Once again the language that Philo uses to describe the proselyte's change in circumstances is a combination of social reality and ideological abstraction. On the one hand, proselytes have left[42] "the ancestral customs in which they were bred" (τὰ πάτρια οἷς ἐνετράφησαν); the terms denote socialization, education, and patrimony. But on the other, what they come over to is piety, the love of simplicity and truth, and the worship of the One who truly exists.

Still, there is no reason to believe that Philo would exempt these incomers from the more specific aspects of the "service which [is] His by right."[43] Particularly instructive are two passages, closely adjacent to the text under discussion, in which he sets forth the character of the Jewish people. A few sentences earlier we find a remarkable passage that contains Philo's version of Israel's election: "Yet out of the whole human race He chose as of special merit and judged worthy of pre-eminence over all, those who are in a true sense men, and called them to the service [θεραπείαν] of Himself" (1.303). This "service" is described in abstract and philosophical terms: the elect are those who have "feasted to the full on virtue's draught" (1.304). Yet in a passage just subsequent to the text under discussion, a passage also descriptive of the Jews as a distinct people, he presents these virtues as the outcome of an upbringing and education in the "special laws" of Moses: "we who, born as citizens of a godly community [πολιτείᾳ], reared under laws which incite to every virtue, trained from our earliest years under divinely gifted men . . . " (1.314). In other words, while Philo

41. He does, however, deal with this aspect of the text elsewhere; see *Virtue* 102–03; *QE* 2.2.

42. καταλιπόντες. The verb is used of proselytes in *Virtues* 219 as well.

43. The Greek is construed a little differently: proselytes become "supplicants and worshippers of the One who truly exists" (ἱκέται τε καὶ θεραπευταὶ τοῦ ὄντως ὄντος).

lays stress on virtue as the outcome of the Jewish way of life, this emphasis should not be allowed to eclipse his conviction that it is precisely by means of adherence to the laws of Moses in all their particularity that this outcome is produced.

Philo thus presents us with two patterns of education and socialization—one in "false inventions and vanity" (1.309), which proselytes have experienced and now have to leave behind in their transition to "piety," and another in the "laws which incite to every virtue." One is led to expect that proselytes will need not only to abandon the one but also to engage in the other. The path to piety for proselytes will require a re-education in the same laws that have provided the primary education for Jews.

§92 On the Special Laws *2.42–48*

When the law records that every day is a festival, it accommodates itself to the blameless life of righteous men who follow nature and her ordinances.. . . [44]*All who practise wisdom, either in Grecian or barbarian lands, and live a blameless and irreproachable life, choosing neither to inflict nor retaliate injustice . . .* [45] *. . . are the closest observers of nature and all that it contains;. . . While their bodies are firmly planted on the land they provide their souls with wings, so that they may traverse the upper air and gain full contemplation of the powers which dwell there, as behoves true "cosmopolitans" who have recognized the world to be a city having for its citizens the associates of wisdom, registered as such by virtue to whom is entrusted the headship of the universal commonwealth.* [46]*Such men filled with high worthiness, inured to disregard ills of the body or of external things, schooled to hold things indifferent as indeed indifferent, armed against the pleasures and lusts, ever eager to take their stand superior to their passions in general, trained to use every effort to overthrow the formidable menace which those passions have built up against them, never swerving under the blows of fortune because they have calculated beforehand the forces of its assaults, since the heaviest adversities are lightened by anticipation, when the mind ceases to find anything strange in the event and apprehends it but dully as it might some stale and familiar story—such men, we say, in the delight of their virtues, naturally make their whole life a feast.* [47]*These are indeed but a small number left in their cities like an ember of wisdom to smoulder, that virtue may not be altogether extinguished and lost to our race.* [48]*But if only everywhere men had thought and felt as these few, and become what nature intended them to be, all of them blameless and guiltless and lovers of sound sense, rejoicing in moral excellence just because it is what it is and counting it the only true good and all the other goods but slaves and vassals, subject to their authority, the cities would have been brimful of happiness, utterly free from all that causes grief and fears, and packed with what produces joy and states of well-being, so that each season as it comes would give full opportunity for cheerful living and the whole cycle of the year would be a feast.*

Category: ETHICAL MONOTHEISM

As we have already observed, in *On the Special Laws* Philo arranges the various items of the Mosaic legislation under the ten headings provided by the Decalogue. Under the heading of the Sabbath, Philo deals with a variety of things, including ten feasts or festivals (*Spec. Laws* 2.41–14). The second of these is the Sabbath itself; but before dealing with this feast, Philo treats something that he calls "the feast of every day" (2.41). He recognizes that objections could be raised against the idea of treating every day as a festal—and thus special—day ("the mention of which may perhaps cause some surprise"; 2.41), but the idea derives from the biblical text with which he is dealing. Philo derives his list of ten feasts in large measure from the legislation in Numbers 28 and 29. Numbers 28 begins with instructions for the daily burnt offering, which provides him with the idea of a feast that is to be celebrated every day (thus, "the law records that every day is a festival"; 2.42). In his exposition of this feast, however, the daily temple sacrifice does not come into view at all. Instead, he uses this text as an opportunity to develop the theme that for the truly virtuous, the whole of life is a feast (2.42, 46, 48).

This passage is remarkable in several respects. First, the group that Philo has in mind clearly includes Gentiles. The group comprises "all who practise wisdom, either in Grecian or barbarian lands" (2.44); while the numbers are few, each city in the civilized world has its own representatives (2.47). It would probably not be accurate to describe this group as Gentile *in toto*, since presumably Philo would include himself and other like-minded Jews in its number. Still, the group is characteristically human, not Jewish; the group represents "our race" (τοῦ γένους ἡμῶν; 2.47), that is, the human race.[44]

Closely related to this is a second observation: there is no suggestion whatsoever that the law of Moses has played any necessary part in the cultivation of the wisdom and virtue that characterizes this group. Not only is this implied by the presence of Gentiles among the group of the virtuous, but it is also clearly indicated by the language Philo uses to describe the group. They are those "who follow nature and her ordinances" (2.42); they "are the closest observers of nature and all that it contains" (2.45); they are "true cosmopolitans" (τοὺς τῷ ὄντι κοσμοπολίτας), citizens of a "world city" in which citizenship is granted solely on the basis of wisdom and virtue (2.45); they are those who have "become what nature intended them to be" (2.48). To the extent that wisdom and virtue are further described, it is in terms of an ability to "disregard ills of the body or of external things" (2.46) so that the soul might engage itself in contemplation of higher things (2.45). As we have seen, Philo elsewhere presents the written law as a means to the same ends—it gives explicit expression to the law of nature, it teaches its adherents to disregard the body and cultivate the soul, and so on. However, in this passage there is no reference to the written law; these ends can evidently be achieved in other ways.

Third, this alternative route to virtue is not merely a hypothetical possibility. The set of "the righteous who follow nature and her ordinances" (2.42) is

44. On Philo's use of γένος to refer to humankind (or some subset thereof) in a generic way, see Birnbaum (1996, 52–54, 56–58).

not a null set; the passage clearly assumes that such people exist. While the numbers may be few (2.47), there are nevertheless a few—in each city (2.47) throughout the land of the Greeks and barbarians (2.44). They are not present in sufficient numbers to avert the effects of "all that causes griefs and fears" (2.48), which otherwise would be the case. But they nevertheless exist as a "smouldering ember," whose presence ensures that "virtue may not be altogether extinguished and lost to our race" (2.47).

The passage provides solid evidence, then, that what seems to be implied by Philo's project as a whole was a real possibility. What "the Jews gain from their laws"—namely, a life of virtue and wisdom—could really be attained by "the disciples of the most excellent philosophy" who were prepared to follow "its teaching" (*Virtues* 65). Examples can be found in every city "in Grecian or barbarian lands."

§93 On the Special Laws *2.118–19*

> *His reason is that he wishes to give the newcomers also a basis on which they may feel themselves firmly established in the country. For since they have no apportionment of land as they were not counted when the holdings were distributed, the law assigned to them their houses in fee simple in its anxiety that those who had come as suppliants and refugees to the laws should not be cast adrift.*[119] . . . *And of these, as I have said, they assigned a share to the newcomers, to prevent them finding themselves cut off from holding property both in the country and in the cities.*

Category: CONVERSION

In this portion of the treatise, Philo continues to deal with those "special laws" that he has classified under the heading of the fourth commandment, pertaining to the Sabbath (2.39–222). His treatment of the Sabbath itself (2.56–139) includes a discussion of the jubilee legislation of Lev 25:8–55 (2.110–23), in the context of which we find the passage quoted above.

In this passage, Philo is commenting on a portion of the jubilee legislation (Lev 25:29–31) having to do with the sale and redemption of houses. The biblical text makes a distinction between houses located in walled cities and those found in unwalled villages. The latter are held to be the equivalent of buildings in the open country and thus are subject to the regular jubilee legislation; that is, if they have been sold by their original owner, they can be redeemed at any time up to the jubilee year, at which point they are returned to the original owner. City houses, however, can be redeemed only up to a year from the time of sale; after that point the sale becomes final.

In the biblical account, no reason is given for this exemption. Philo, however, provides a reason: it was to give "newcomers" (ἐπηλύταις) an opportunity to acquire property in the land. Since their ancestors were not present when the land was apportioned, they have no rights to the land; any land that they might acquire would revert to its ancestral family in the jubilee year. But the exception made for city property, Philo declares, was precisely to compensate for this lack of ancestry; incomers could acquire houses and land in the city to which they would have clear title after a redemption period of just a year.

The interpretation is striking for its gratuitous character. There is no suggestion whatsoever in the text that the exception was made for the benefit of sojourners; as has been noted, the text provides no rationale for the law whatsoever. Nor is there evidence to suggest that Philo is drawing on an already-existing interpretation of the text.[45] He seems to have gone out of his way to introduce a concern for proselytes into his reading of the text. This underlines both the importance that he attached to the phenomenon and his desire to believe that the law was ready at every turn to receive them and to make them feel welcome. Of course, his interpretation also reflects the fact that, declarations of equality notwithstanding (e.g., *Spec. Laws* 1.52–53), proselytes were subject to an ineradicable difference in status; they would never be "equal" with reference to an ability to trace their ancestry back to those who first settled in the land. But his interpretation also reflects an assumption that proselytism involved full integration into the social reality of the Israelite people; the world envisaged by the lawgiver was one in which proselytes lived cheek-by-jowl with native-born Jews in the cities of Israel.

§94 On the Special Laws *4.176–78*

> *Lowliness and weakness are attributes of the widow, the orphan and the incomer. It is to these that the supreme king who is invested with the government of all should administer justice, because according to Moses God also the ruler of the Universe has not spurned them from His jurisdiction.* [177]*For when the Revealer has hymned the excellences of the Self-existent in this manner, "God the great and powerful, who has no respect to persons, will receive no gifts and executes judgement"* [Deut 10:17–18], *he proceeds to say for whom the judgement is executed—not for satraps and despots and men invested with power by land and sea, but for the "incomer, for orphan and widow."* [178]*For the incomer, because he has turned his kinsfolk, who in the ordinary course of things would be his sole confederates, into mortal enemies, by coming as a pilgrim to truth and the honouring of One who alone is worthy of honour, and by leaving the mythical fables and multiplicity of sovereigns, so highly honoured by the parents and grand-parents and ancestors and blood relations of this immigrant to a better home.*

Category: CONVERSION

At *Spec. Laws* 4.131, Philo completes his declared agenda of arranging and discussing the laws of Moses under the headings of the ten commandments. At this point he shifts to a more panoramic view, looking at the Mosaic legislation as a whole and arguing that, despite its variety, it is held together and undergirded

45. Belkin (1940) makes no reference to this text in his study of parallels between Philo and the oral law.

by a common concern for the cardinal virtues. All of the laws "incite and exhort us to wisdom and justice and godliness and the rest of the company of virtues" (4.134). Concerning the first three members of this company—piety, wisdom, and temperance—Philo believes that he has said enough already. The remainder of this treatise (4.32–238) is given over to a consideration of justice. In the subsequent treatise, *On the Virtues*, which begins by referring back to his discussion of justice (1), he goes on to consider several others.[46] In Philo's program of systematization, then, the whole array of Mosaic legislation can be arranged under the ten commandments of the Decalogue, which in turn exemplify and inculcate a set of the most important virtues.

The passage cited above is found in a context where Philo is discussing the role of the ruler in dispensing justice, which includes the important matter of choosing capable assistants so that the ruler is not so burdened with petty matters that he has no time or energy for the "greater questions" (170–72). The greater questions, says Philo, are not, as one might suppose, those in which both parties are equally rich and powerful but rather those in which there is an imbalance, where "the commoner or the poor or the obscure" are engaged in a lawsuit with the powerful and "where their one hope of escaping a fatal disaster lies in the judge" (4.172). To illustrate this point, Philo cites the example of the Supreme Ruler, who, as Moses says (Deut 10:17–18), is not only completely impartial but also executes justice "for the incomer [ἐπηλύτῳ], for the orphan and the widow" (4.177).

What Philo goes on to say about the incomer is similar to what we have seen already. Again we see the synonymity in his usage of προσήλυτος and the ἐπηλυ- set of terms. Indeed, in contrast to several other passages we have looked at, in which he first cites an LXX text that uses the former and then goes on to discuss it as if it read the latter (e.g., *Spec. Laws* 1.51–53, 308–9), here he uses ἔπηλυς at the outset, freely substituting it for the LXX's προσήλυτος. In addition, in his description of the proselyte experience we again encounter the puzzling combination of real social translocation on the one hand and a more general transition from idolatry to monotheism on the other. On the one hand, the proselyte is presented as one who has exchanged the world of "mythical fables and multiplicity of sovereigns" for the "truth and the honouring of One who alone is worthy of honour." On the other, this exchange at the level of truth and piety has resulted in real and radical social dislocation; the proselyte is now alienated from "kinfolk"—from "parents and grand-parents and ancestors and blood relations"—who have now become "mortal enemies," but in exchange have found a "better home"—literally, a better "home away from home" or "home in exile" (ἀποικίαν). It is interesting to note that Philo can use the language of pilgrimage or migration

46. On the uncertainty concerning the content of *On the Virtues*, see n. 48 below.

for both aspects of the proselyte experience:[47] the proselyte is both a "pilgrim [μετανάστας] to truth" and one who has found a home within a new social group.

What do we make of this combination? Again, then, it is clear that Philo is talking about real proselytes, in the sense of persons who have dissociated themselves—or who have had to dissociate themselves—from their native social group and have been resocialized into the community that worships the one God revealed by Moses. Are we to imagine that by failing to mention circumcision, food laws, and the other particular laws that differentiate Jews from Gentiles Philo believed that the abandonment of polytheism and the acceptance of monotheism was sufficient? The emphasis with which he describes law observance as the distinguishing characteristic of the Jewish people makes this difficult to imagine. In the next paragraph he describes "the Jewish nation" as one that "lives under exceptional laws which are necessarily grave and severe, because they inculcate the highest standard of virtue" (4.179). It is hard to see how a Gentile could find a home in exile among this community without living under the same "exceptional laws." Still, Philo chooses to place the emphasis on the acceptance of monotheism and the desire for truth and virtue rather than on such particularities.

§95 Virtues *102–4*

> *Having laid down laws for members of the same nation, he holds that the incomers too should be accorded every favour and consideration as their due, because abandoning their kinsfolk by blood, their country, their customs and the temples and images of their gods, and the tributes and honours paid to them, they have taken their journey to a better home, from idle fables to the clear vision of truth and the worship of the one and truly existing God.* 103 *He commands all members of the nation to love the incomers, not only as friends and kinsfolk but as themselves both in body and soul: in bodily matters, by acting as far as may be for their common interest; in mental by having the same griefs and joys, so that they may seem to be the separate parts of a single living being which is compacted and unified by their fellowship in it.* 104 *I will not go on to speak of the food and drink and raiment and all the rights concerning daily life and necessary needs, which the law assigns to incomers as due from the native born, for all these follow the statutes, which speak of the friendliness shown by him who loves the incomer even as himself.*

Category: CONVERSION

The treatise *On the Virtues* is a continuation of the discussion of the virtues with which Philo concludes *On the Special Laws*. As mentioned in the previous section, his theme here is that all of the laws should be understood as exemplifying

47. On this point see Birnbaum (1996, 202–03); on the use of ἀποικία, in Philo and elsewhere, see Gruen (2002, 241–42).

and inculcating a number of cardinal virtues. In this section of the treatise he is discussing the sixth of these[48]—humanity or humankindness (φιλανθρωπία), "the virtue closest akin to piety" (51). This passage concerning the treatment of proselytes is one of several that Philo puts forward as evidence of the φιλανθρωπία evident in the law of Moses. The text he has in mind seems to be Lev 19:34 ("The alien [προσήλυτος] who resides with you shall be to you as the citizen among you; you shall love the alien as yourself, for you were aliens in the land of Egypt"), though in the next section, where he takes up the closely related topic of the resident alien (μέτοικος), he shifts to Deut 23:7–8.

Several aspects of the passage are similar to things we have seen in other proselyte passages: Philo's assumption that the LXX προσήλυτος is a reference to converts and is thus synonymous to ἐπήλυτος and related terms ("incomers"); monotheism as the primary constituent element of a proselyte's transformation ("from idle fables to the clear vision of truth and the worship of the one and truly existing God"); at the same time, an emphasis on proselytes' dissociation from their native social environment (they have abandoned "their kinsfolk by blood, their country, their customs and the temples and images of their gods"); migration imagery ("they have taken the journey to a better home"); and full incorporation into a new social environment. In keeping with Philo's theme here, this last point receives particular emphasis. Not only does the law make all sorts of provisions for the daily needs of these newcomers (104), and not only are they to be given the status of "kinfolk" (συγγενεῖς), more than this, the native-born (αὐτοχθόνων; 104) are to love proselytes as they love themselves. Philo draws the idea from the Torah (Lev 19:34), but he amplifies it in a striking way: incomers and native-born together form a single living entity (ἓν ζῷον; 103), in which they each have a share (κοινωνίας). While it is legitimate to doubt whether the reality was ever as idyllic as Philo presents it, his gloss on Lev 19:34 reflects the degree of significance that he attaches to the phenomenon.

§96 Virtues *108*

> *And if any of them should wish to pass over into the Jewish community, they must not be spurned with an unconditional refusal as children of enemies, but be so far favoured that the third generation is invited to the congregation and made partakers in the divine revelations, to which also the native born, whose lineage is beyond reproach, are rightfully admitted.*

Category: CONVERSION

48. In the manuscript tradition, *On the Virtues* deals with four virtues: courage, human kindness, repentance and noble birth. Since Eusebius seems to speak of this treatise as dealing with three virtues (*H.E.* 2.18.2), various proposals have been made concerning the rearrangement of the material in it. See the discussion in Morris (1987, 850–53). Proposals that would have the effect of removing the latter two sections (on repentance and noble birth) from the treatise are not persuasive. Here we will consider the treatise as a single entity.

This statement forms the conclusion of the passage (105–8) that follows on from the passage just discussed. Here Philo continues his argument that the virtue of humankindness (φιλανθρωπία) is apparent throughout the law of Moses. Having pointed to the reception of proselytes as one example (102–4), he turns in this passage to the treatment of resident aliens or "settlers" (μέτοικοι) as another. The text that he cites in this connection is LXX Deut 23:7: "You shall not abhor an Egyptian because you were a sojourner [πάροικος] in Egypt." This text is closely related to Lev 19:34, which was the centerpiece of his discussion of proselytes in the preceding passage; indeed, the Hebrew version uses גר in both texts. But since the LXX uses μέτοικοι to render גר in Deut 23:7 (in contrast to Lev 19:34, where we find προσήλυτοι), Philo cites the text as evidence for Israel's benevolent treatment of resident aliens.

At the end of this passage, Philo moves on to Deut 23:8, which states that "children of the third generation" of Egyptian and Edomite settlers "may be admitted to the assembly of the Lord." While he does not describe such persons as proselytes, it is clear from the language that he uses of them that he considers them as such. They have "passed over" (μεταλλάξασθαι) into the Jewish "community" (πολιτείαν); they are called into the "assembly" (ἐκκλησίαν); they are given a share (μεταδιδόναι; used of proselytes in *Spec. Laws* 2.119) along with the native-born in the "divine revelations." As full participants in the Jewish *politeia*, they are clearly assumed to be proselytes,[49] even if Philo does not use the specific term. What is not so clear is what Philo thought of the three-generation waiting period for Egyptians. Since the idea does not appear in any of his other discussions of proselytes, perhaps he thought of it as an injunction applicable only in Judea.

§97 Virtues *175–82*

> *Our most holy Moses, who so dearly loved virtue and goodness and especially his fellow-men, exhorts everyone everywhere to pursue piety and justice, and offers to the repentant in honour of their victory the high rewards of membership in the best of commonwealths and of the felicities both great and small which that membership confers.. . .* [179] *So therefore all these who did not at the first acknowledge their duty to reverence the Founder and Father of all, yet afterwards embraced the creed of one instead of a multitude of sovereigns, must be held to be our dearest friends and closest kinsmen. They have shown the godliness of heart which above all leads up to friendship and affinity, and we must rejoice with them, as if, though blind at the first they had recovered their sight and had come from the deepest darkness to behold the most radiant light.. . .* [181] *For it is excellent and profitable to desert without a backward glance to the ranks of virtue and abandon vice that malignant mistress; and where honour is rendered to the God who is, the whole company of the other virtues must follow in its train as surely as in the sunshine the shadow follows the body. The proselytes become at once*

49. *Pace* Birnbaum (1996, 204), who treats them as "interested non-Jews."

temperate, continent, modest, gentle, kind, humane, serious, just, high-minded, truth-lovers, superior to the desire for money and pleasure, just as conversely the rebels from the holy laws are seen to be incontinent, shameless, unjust, frivolous, petty-minded, quarrelsome, friends of falsehood and perjury, who have sold their freedom for dainties and strong liquor and cates and the enjoyment of another's beauty, thus ministering to the delights of the belly and the organs below it—delights which end in the gravest injuries both to body and soul.

Category: CONVERSION

This passage is part of Philo's discussion of repentance (μετάνοια; 175–86), the seventh in a series of virtues that he sees as inherent in the law of Moses.[50] While he makes no explicit reference to proselytes until his discussion is half-complete, it is clear from the manner in which the term is introduced that proselytes are his central concern. His discussion has to do not with repentance in general but with that exhibited by proselytes in particular.

This is hinted at already in the first sentence (175), where the reward of repentance is said to be "membership in the best of commonwealths" (πολιτείας κοινωνίαν τῆς ἀρίστης). To be sure, when he goes on to suggest that, apart from God, only a divine man such as Moses stands in no need of repentance (177), he seems to be implying that rank-and-file Israelites would also need to repent. But as he goes on from here to indicate more precisely what repentance entails, it is apparent that Israelites are not in view. For what needs to be repented of is not sin in general but polytheism in particular. The repentant are those who "rise in rebellion against the mythical fables impressed on their yet tender souls from their earliest years by parents and nurses and tutors and the multitude of other familiars" (178). In other words, they are those who have been socialized as polytheists from birth; it is only Gentiles who can be described as those "who did not at the first acknowledge their duty to reverence the Founder and Father of all" (179). If Jews come into the picture here, they should be seen as the healthy body "free from disease," rather than the body afflicted by disease that is therefore in need of "recovery" and "rectification" (176). Thus it is not surprising that in 182 Philo speaks of "proselytes" (ἐπηλύται) in a matter-of-fact way, thereby implying that this is what he has had in mind all along.

What is involved, then, in becoming a proselyte? In this passage there appears to be less emphasis on the social aspects of conversion. Philo defines repentance as involving two things—first the abandonment of polytheism, and then the life of virtue that follows in its wake. The "first and most essential form of repentance" has to do with "revering created things before the Creator and Maker" (180). But this necessarily accompanied by the abandonment of vice

50. On the total number of these virtues, and the related issue of the composition of *On the Virtues* and the placement of the discussion of repentance and noble birth, see n. 48 above.

and the embrace of virtue: "Where honour is rendered to the God who is, the whole company of the other virtues must follow in its train" (181). It is actually in the context of this second phase of repentance that Philo first mentions proselytes explicitly.

The emphasis in this passage, then, is on monotheism and virtue—the proselyte as ethical monotheist. Nevertheless, there are some indications that Philo still sees the proselyte as one who is incorporated into the Torah-defined social realities of the Jewish people. The reference at the outset of this section to "membership in the best of commonwealths [πολιτείας]" (175) is one such indication. Another is at least implicit in the negative statement that these repentant ones have risen "in rebellion" against their native world as constructed by "parents and nurses and tutors and the multitude of other familiars" (178). The note of social dislocation is not sounded as strongly here as in some other passages, but it is nevertheless present. Another bit of negative evidence is the contrast drawn between the proselytes and the apostates (182); since the latter are depicted as "rebels from the holy laws," the proselytes (who for their part have been rebels against their own cultural heritage) are by implication those who have become virtuous precisely because they have adopted those "holy laws" (τῶν ἱερῶν νόμων) which are the primary route to virtue. But perhaps the strongest indication of the social—and thus Torah-shaped—character of proselytism is the central role played by these two figures of the proselyte and the apostate in the remaining section of the treatise, in which Philo deals with nobility of birth.

§98 Virtues *212–19*

The most ancient member of the Jewish nation was a Chaldean by birth, the son of an astrologer, one of those who study the lore of that science, and think that the stars and the whole heaven and universe are gods, the authors, they say, of the events which befall each man for good or for ill, and hold that there is no originating cause outside the things we perceive by our senses.. . . [214]*Perception of these truths and divine inspiration induced him to leave his native country, his race and paternal home, knowing that if he stayed the delusions of the polytheistic creed would stay within him and render it impossible for him to discover the One, who alone is eternal and the Father of all things, conceptual and sensible, whereas if he removed, the delusion would also remove from his mind and its false creed be replaced by the truth.. . .* [216]*And, therefore, he is the first person spoken of as believing in God, since he first grasped a firm and unswerving conception of the truth that there is one Cause above all, and that it provides for the world and all that there is therein. And having gained faith, the most sure and certain of the virtues, he gained with it all the other virtues,. . .* [219]*He is the standard of nobility for all proselytes, who, abandoning the ignobility of strange laws and monstrous customs which assigned divine honours to stocks and stones and soulless things in general, have come to settle in a better land, in a commonwealth full of true life and vitality, with truth as its director and president.*

Category: CONVERSION

The final section of *On the Virtues* (187–227), in which Philo deals with nobility of birth, is tightly connected to the preceding discussion of repentance (175–86). In this discussion he emphasizes the high value that Moses places on repentance—specifically, repentance exhibited by the proselyte who turns to the one true God and to a life of virtue—and contrasts this with its negative counterpart, as exhibited by the apostate (182). The lesson to be drawn from this, Philo declares at the beginning of the final section of the treatise, is that ancestry is no sure indicator of nobility or ignobility and that "those who hymn nobility of birth [εὐγένειαν] as the greatest of good gifts" are open to censure (187). He develops this theme first by dealing with various negative examples from biblical tradition—Cain, one of the sons of Noah,[51] Adam himself, Abraham's other sons, and Esau. Then at 212 he turns to positive examples, beginning with Abraham in the passage cited above.

For our purposes what is most significant about this passage is Philo's presentation of Abraham as the first and model proselyte; he is the "standard of nobility for all proselytes" (ἅπασιν ἐπηλύταις εὐγενείας ἐστι κανών; 219). Once again, the emphasis is placed on the linked characteristics of monotheism and virtue; if Abraham is the standard, proselytes are those who abandon the worship of many gods, gain a vision of the one God and thus enter into a life of virtue. Reared by those who "think that the stars and the whole heaven and universe are gods" (212), Abraham was aware that as long as he lived among such people his vision would be clouded by "the delusions of the polytheistic creed" (214) and he would never be able to see "the One, the Primal, the Uncreated and Maker of all" (213), "the One, who alone is eternal and the Father of all things" (214). His journey thus was not simply a geographical migration but also a journey in search of the one God. Having received visions of God—though "not of His essence, for that is impossible, but of His existence and providence" (215)—Abraham can be described as the first one who believed in God, the first to have "grasped a firm and unswerving conception of the truth that there is one Cause above all, and that it provides for the world and all that there is therein" (216). And having grasped this, "the most sure and certain of the virtues, he gained with it all the other virtues" (216), so that he was held in awe by all those with whom he came in contact in his new land (216–18). Proselytes who conform to Abraham's "standard," then, also are marked by the same nobility (219), one based not on birth but on a similar commitment to monotheism and virtue.

In keeping with this emphasis on ethical monotheism as the hallmark of the proselyte is the absence of any of the more specific Jewish boundary markers. To a certain extent this is not surprising, in that Abraham predates Moses and the giving of the law. But one of the highlights of the Abraham narrative

51. Ham, though Philo does not name him. The reference is to Gen 9:20–27.

in Genesis is the introduction of circumcision (Gen 17). Even though Philo describes him as "the most ancient member of the Jewish nation" (212), he passes over in silence the defining requirement for membership (cf. Gen 17:9–14, esp. v. 14), choosing instead to highlight Abraham's belief in the one God and his resultant life of virtue.

Did Philo therefore believe that circumcision was not required of proselytes? We will leave a direct treatment of this question for our discussion of *QE* 2.2 below. For the present, however, it is important to observe that the passage also contains an emphasis on socialization and dissociation. Abraham's initial polytheism was the direct result of his early socialization; it was because he "was a Chaldaean by birth, the son of an astrologer" (212) that he first formed the false conceptions that he later had to abandon and unlearn. As long as he stayed in this social context, it would be impossible for him to discover the one God (214). And thus he had "to leave his native country, his race and paternal home" (214); his migration was not simply a journey of the mind but also a real social translocation. Likewise, proselytes need to abandon "the ignobility of strange laws and monstrous customs" and "to settle in a better land," a "commonwealth" (πολιτείαν) of truth (219). While the "land" may be figurative and metaphorical, there is no mistaking the social dimensions of the transformation that Philo has in view. And given the fact that the new commonwealth is one based on the law of Moses, it is at least implicit that proselytes will not only abandon the "strange laws" (ἀλλοκότων νόμων; 219) of their native commonwealth but will take on the divine laws of their new one.

Still, the hallmark of the proselyte is ethical monotheism; the proselyte is one who, with Abraham, has exchanged the worship of the many for the worship of the One and has received along with this primary virtue all of the others in its train.

§99 Virtues *220–22*

> *To this nobility not only did men beloved of God aspire, but women also, who unlearnt the errors of their breeding, the ignorance which led them to honour the works of men's hands, and became schooled in the knowledge of the monarchical principle by which the world is governed.* 221 *Tamar was a woman from Palestinian Syria, bred in a house and city which acknowledged a multitude of gods and was full of images and wooden busts and idols in general. But when passing, as it were, from profound darkness she was able to glimpse a little ray of truth, she deserted to the camp of piety at the risk of her life, caring little for its preservation, if it were not to be a good life. This good life she held to mean nothing else than to be the servant and suppliant of the one great Cause.* 222 *Although she was married to two brothers in turn, both of them wicked, to the elder as her husband in the usual way, to the younger under the law of the duties of the next of kin, as the elder had left no issue, she nevertheless kept her life stainless and was able to win the good report which belongs to the good and to become the original source to which the nobility of all who followed her can be traced.*

Category: CONVERSION

This passage is a continuation of the one just discussed. Here Philo presents Tamar as a kind of female counterpart to Abraham. While he does not refer to her explicitly as a proselyte, his language indicates that he clearly considers her as such.[52] He presents her as a "foreigner" (ἀλλόφυλος; 222), one who was on the same quest for nobility as was Abraham (220). His purpose in introducing her was to demonstrate that women as well could "unlearn the errors of their breeding" (220)—specifically, the error of idolatry—and could come over "to the camp of piety" (πρὸς εὐσέβειαν; 221), there to become "schooled" in monarchical worship (220). But her significance for Philo is more than the evidence she provides (in his reading of the account) for female proselytes. After recounting her story, he concludes by presenting her not simply as one among many but as the prototype for all to follow: she is the "original source of nobility" (εὐγενείας ἀφορμή) for all who followed her.

Such an elevated status is surprising. There is little in the Genesis account that could be taken as suggesting that Tamar was even a proselyte, let alone a prototypical one. The passage (Genesis 38) contains no explicit indication that she had been a polytheist or an idolater. To be sure, her mother-in-law—the wife of Judah and the mother of Er, Onan, and Shelah—was a Canaanite, and Philo may have inferred from this that she was Canaanite as well. But the Biblical account displays no interest whatsoever in her religious background or practices. There her motivation is simply the material security and status that come from having a husband. For Philo, in contrast, she was motivated by the "little ray of truth" that she had been able to glimpse in the midst of her polytheistic darkness. One wonders why Philo would have chosen Tamar for this prototypical role rather than, say, Sarah.[53] Nevertheless, his depiction of her in this passage is in keeping with her profile elsewhere in his writings, where she consistently appears as a figure or a symbol of virtue.[54]

This construction of Tamar as a prototypical proselyte, despite the absence of any explicit grounding in the biblical text itself, is a striking indication of the importance of the category for Philo. Again, the primary features of this category are monotheism and virtue: Tamar desired above all else to become "the servant and suppliant of the one great Cause" (221) and as a result was able to keep herself "stainless" and to be classed with the "good" (222). At the same time, however, the social dimensions of her transformation are also present: she had been a "foreigner" (222), a "woman from Palestinian Syria" (221); she had

52. Birnbaum (1996, 201, 214, 216). See also Niehoff (2001, 29–31).

53. Especially since he goes on to describe Jacob's concubines—who, of course, predated Tamar—in terms suggesting that they too were proselytes (223–25). Since his description does not mention religious transformation (the emphasis is on their equality with Jacob's wives and the surprising lack of discord in the household), the passage has not been included for discussion here.

54. See *Alleg. Interp.* 3.74; *Unchangeable* 136–37; *Prelim. Studies* 124; *Flight* 149–56.

to unlearn the errors of her upbringing (ἀμαθίαν τὴν σύντροφον; 220); she deserted (ηὐτομόλησεν; 221) her native house and city and became part of a new family through marriage.

§100 Rewards *152*

> *The proselyte exalted aloft by his happy lot will be gazed at from all sides, marvelled at and held blessed by all for two things of highest excellence, that he came over to the camp of God and that he has won a prize best suited to his merits, a place in heaven firmly fixed, greater than words dare describe, while the nobly born who has falsified the sterling of his high lineage will be dragged right down and carried into Tartarus itself and profound darkness. Thus may all men seeing these examples be brought to a wiser mind and learn that God welcomes the virtue which springs from ignoble birth, that He takes no account of the roots but accepts the full-grown stem, because it has been changed from a weed into fruitfulness.*

Category: CONVERSION

This passage does not add in any substantial way to the profile of the proselyte that has been emerging from the passages discussed thus far. It has more significance than some of these other passages, however, because of the context in which it is found and what it therefore has to tell us about the importance of proselytes for Philo's larger agenda.

In the treatise *On Rewards and Punishments*, Philo begins with a retrospective survey of the material covered in the *Exposition* as a whole (1–2) and then states that, since this material has "been discussed as fully as was needful in the preceding treatises" (3), he can now go on to discuss "the rewards and punishments which the good and the bad have respectively to expect" (3). The treatise, then, is intimately tied in with the *Exposition*, for which it serves as its intended conclusion.[55] The first part of the treatise discusses individual cases of reward and punishment in the biblical narrative. For the most part, the discussion of rewards is carried out with respect to the two triads encountered elsewhere in the *Exposition*—Enos, Enoch, and Noah; Abraham, Isaac, and Jacob (13–56; cf. *Abraham* 7–59). The discussion of punishment begins with the cases of Cain and Korah, but there appears to be a lacuna in the text beginning at 78. After the lacuna, the text resumes with a discussion of the blessings (79–126) and curses (127–61) described by Moses in Leviticus 26 and Deuteronomy 28–30. A relatively brief—but, as we will see, highly significant—conclusion (162–72) brings the treatise to an end.

As we might expect on the basis of the material discussed to this point, as Philo develops his discourse, the categories "good" and "bad" display a striking

55. Morris (1987, 853) designates it as "a kind of epilogue," but this fails to do justice to the tight connection that is apparent.

combination of generic and ethnic characteristics. On the one hand, he defines "goodness" according to his usual twin criteria of monotheism and virtue. At birth, "before the reason in us is fully grown," human beings "lie in the borderline between vice and virtue" (62). The "good" are both "true athletes of virtue" (5) and those who have set their hope on God as their creator and preserver (13). They are those who have chosen the "immaterial and conceptual" over the merely "visible," "casting aside all the irrational part of the soul and employing only the part which is called mind and reasoning" (26). Enoch is a model of those who have left "covetousness and injustice" and have "come over to soberness and justice and the other virtues" (15). Abraham, "the leader in adopting the godly creed [τῆς θεοφιλοῦς δόξης]," achieved this status by means of "virtue gained through instruction, and he received for his reward belief in God" (27). Jacob, as his other name Israel suggests, is one who achieved a vision of the one true God (according to Philo's etymology, "Israel" means the one who sees God [ὁρῶν θεόν; 44]),[56] which sets him apart from those who merely infer the existence of the Creator from the creation (36–46). And so on.

But on the other hand, Philo's ideal of ethical monotheism is inextricably bound up with the *politeia* of Moses and thus is embedded in the people of Israel. This is apparent in the passage dealing with proselytes (152), to which we will turn in a moment. But it is also apparent at the outset of the treatise, where the "good" are described not only as "citizens of [Moses's] polity" (τοὺς κατ᾽ αὐτὸν πολιτευομένους; 4) but more specifically as those who have become "athletes of virtue" by holding firm to "the laws which had trained them" (τοὺς ἀλείπτας νόμους; 5). Given the retrospective note on which the treatise begins (3), this reference to the law and its formative role serves to anchor the discussion of the "good" and the "bad" in the Mosaic law, Philo's theme in the *Exposition* as a whole. The implication is that the good—those who can be described as worshipping the one true God and living a life of virtue—are to be found in the first instance and most naturally among the nation whose *politeia* is the law of Moses.

The ethnic matrix of Philo's ethical monotheism is strikingly present in the concluding section (162–72) as well. This section begins with a retrospective look at the treatise as a whole (162), in which he makes it clear that in his discussion of the "bad" he has had in view not the wicked in general but Jewish apostates in particular. The "curses and penalties" pertain to those "who have forgotten the teaching of their race and of their fathers" and who have abandoned the worship of the supreme God for "the polytheistic creeds which finally lead to atheism." The language of race (συγγενοῦς), patrimony (πατρίου), and upbringing (ἐπαιδεύθησαν) serves to underscore the ethnic particularity of the discussion. Further, as we have already observed (§89 above),

56. For a discussion of Philo's etymology, see Birnbaum (1996, 67–77).

this initial comment about Jewish apostates leads into a surprising eschatological vision; Philo brings both the treatise and therefore the *Exposition* as a whole to a stunning conclusion with a vision of what will happen when Israel turns to God in a wholehearted way (ὅλῃ ψυχῇ) and is converted "in a body to virtue" (163–64). In our discussion of the passage we have noted the ethnic particularity of the vision. What Philo has in view here is not some abstract, symbolic entity but the real Jewish nation. While he reshapes Jewishness in conformity with his ideals of monotheism and virtue, he certainly does not abandon it.

This is the context in which we need to read the passage in 152, where Philo introduces the figure of the proselyte. At first glance, this paean of praise to the proselyte (ὁ ἔπηλυς) seems to be out of place in a passage whose purpose is to enumerate the curses that will befall those who are disobedient to the law. On closer inspection, however, it becomes apparent that he has taken advantage of an opportunity provided by the biblical text with which he has been dealing. Deut 28:43 sets up a contrast between sinful Israel and the resident alien (MT גר); as a result of Israel's punishment, there is a reversal of status: "Aliens residing among you shall ascend above you higher and higher, while you shall descend lower and lower." The LXX translates גר as προσήλυτος, which Philo, in keeping with his consistent tendency, takes as a reference to the proselyte, for which he substitutes his preferred term ἔπηλυς. Read in this way, the text provides him with an opportunity to draw out a contrast between the proselytes, who have "come over to the camp of God" (αὐτομολῆσαι πρὸς θεόν), and the apostates, who have been unfaithful to their noble birth.

Philo does not say much about proselytes here, but it is clear that, as in passages discussed already, he is referring specifically to non-Jews who have left the world of their birth and have become part of the ethnic group whose *politeia* is provided by the law of Moses. That this is the case can be seen from the way in which each group is defined in terms of birth. Those who end up in "profound darkness" are there because they have abandoned their noble lineage (εὐπατρίδης) and noble birth (εὐγενείας). Those who come "over to the camp of God" have overcome the deficiencies of their "ignoble birth" (δυσγενείας) so that, while their root was originally weed-like, their full-grown stem has become fruitful.

But while the passage does not add anything to the profile of the proselyte in Philo's perception, it is highly significant for our understanding of the place of the proselyte in his work. The significance of this passage arises first from its function in *On Rewards and Punishments* itself and then—in view of the role of this treatise as a conclusion to the *Exposition*—its implication for our reading of the *Exposition* as a whole.

The first thing to note is the definition of the "good" and the "bad" that becomes apparent by the end of the treatise. As we have observed, Philo describes his theme at the outset as having to do with "the rewards and punishments which the good and the bad have respectively to expect" (3). Some aspects of his discourse might lead the reader to believe that these are generic categories, that "the human race" (τῷ γένει τῶν ἀνθρώπων; 9; cf. "we men"; 62) as a whole can be divided into these two groups without any reference to the categories of Jew and Gentile whatsoever. But at the end of the treatise, when he is summing up his argument, a quite different definition appears. As we have observed already, the "curses and penalties" are said to fall not on a particular portion of generic humanity but on "those who have forgotten the teaching of their race and of their fathers, in which they were trained from their earliest years" (162). In other words, for Philo "the bad" are not wicked people in general but apostates from the Jewish people in particular. Presumably he would classify most Gentiles as "bad" as well, but that is not his focus here.

The immediate implication of this is that for Philo the "good" are not to be seen simply as a generic company of ethical monotheists (ethical monotheists though they be). Instead, the primary implication is that they are "non-apostates," native-born Jews who have remained faithful to their ancestral heritage and teaching. Of course, he wants to include proselytes in this company as well, a point to which we will return in a moment. But the first consequence of his identification of the "bad" with apostates is that the "good" are to be seen as faithful Jews.

And yet, when he first brings the figure of the apostate into view (152), he goes out of his way to balance this figure with its positive counterpart, that of the proselyte. Although he does this by taking advantage of an opportunity presented to him by the biblical passage with which he is dealing (Deut 28:43), the fact that he disregards the negative thrust of the original and gives it his own positive spin indicates the independent value that the proselyte has in his pattern of thought. Together, the figures of the apostate and the proselyte serve to define the group that Philo describes more generally at the outset of the treatise as "the citizens of his [Moses's] polity" (τοὺς κατ᾽ αὐτὸν πολιτευομένους; 4). This company of "citizens" is closely associated with the *ethnos* of Israel. But to this ethnic group one needs to add the proselytes who come in from outside; and from this group one needs to subtract the apostates who have forfeited their native heritage. Still, apostates and proselytes are exceptions to what is essentially an ethnic norm. If the "bad" are those who abandon their Mosaic heritage, the "good," by implication, are the faithful members of the people of Israel, together with those proselytes who have become incorporated into this people. At the same time, however, the importance that Philo assigns to the categories of the apostate and the proselyte signifies that what is essential for membership in this people is not Jewish birth per se but a willingness to remain committed to—or to adopt—the laws that are the natural possession of the Jewish commonwealth. Philo transforms the traditional idea of the Jewish commonwealth by recasting it as a route to ethical monotheism. But at the same time he gives no indication whatsoever that one could arrive at this destination without remaining or becoming part of the *ethnos* whose *politeia* is the law of Moses.

The passage under discussion, then, has an important part to play in the treatise *On Rewards and Punishments* as a whole. It comes at an important juncture, just as Philo is about to bring his discourse to a conclusion. The purpose of the treatise is to articulate both the blessings that will come to those who remain in or join this nation and the curses that will fall on those who abandon it. And, as the conclusion makes clear, these blessings and curses are experienced not simply in the mundane present but ultimately in the eschatological future. By introducing the figures of the apostate and the proselyte where he does, he both clarifies the true character of the "good" and the "bad" who have stood at the center of the treatise from the outset and prepares the ground for the nation-centered conclusion to follow. The passage is thus essential to the whole argument.

But in view of the fact that *On Rewards and Punishments* functions as a conclusion to the *Exposition* as a whole, the passage takes on added significance. As we have already observed, Philo begins his exposition of the "special laws" in a similar fashion, by drawing a contrast between proselytes and apostates.[57] The "new and godly commonwealth" brought into being by Moses consists of those who have become part of it at birth and those who have come into it as proselytes (*Spec. Laws* 1.51). Over against them stand the apostates (1.54–57), those "members of the nation" who have betrayed "the honour due to the One" and have abandoned "the ranks of piety and religion" (1.54). The *Exposition* begins and ends, then, with passages dealing with proselytes and apostates; *Rewards* 152 represents the closing member of an *inclusio* that frames the *Exposition* as a whole.

Philo's purpose in the *Exposition* is to articulate, explain, and extol this "new and godly commonwealth." While this commonwealth is more or less equivalent to the nation of the Jews, the fact that membership in it is determined in the end not by birth but by individual commitment serves to highlight the importance for Philo of proselytes (and apostates). Thus the references to proselytes in the *Exposition* are to be seen not as casual comments made in passing but as essential to the work as a whole. While it would be going too far to describe the *Exposition* as a missionary tractate, it would also be wrong to exclude potential proselytes from the intended readership. If one of the purposes of the work is (evidently) to prevent native-born Jews from abandoning "the ranks of piety and religion," then the categorical and rhetorical symmetry with which Philo treats apostates and proselytes suggests that another is to encourage Gentile sympathizers (such as are reflected in *Moses* 2.41–43) to join the ranks as full members.

§101 Good Person *62, 72–74*

> *These people often ask "who have there been in the past, and who are there living now of the kind that you imagine?" An excellent answer is that in the past there have been*

57. See *Spec. Laws* 1.50–57, and above, §90.

> *those who surpassed their contemporaries in virtue, who took God for their sole guide and lived according to a law of nature's right reason, not only free themselves, but communicating to their own neighbours the spirit of freedom: also in our own time there are still men formed as it were in the likeness of the original picture supplied by the high excellence of sages.. . .* [72]*Consequently land and sea are full of the rich, the distinguished and the men of pleasure, but of the wise and just and virtuous, the number is small. But this small body though scanty is not absolutely non-existent.* [73]*For this we have the testimony, both of Greece and the world outside Greece. In Greece there flourished the sages known also by the appropriate name of the Seven, and we might expect that both before them and after them, others had their day, though the memory of the more ancient has vanished in the lapse of many years, and is dimmed in the case of those whose lives are still recent through the widespread neglect of their contemporaries.* [74]*In the outside world where are those who spread the message by words and deeds, we find large associations of men of the highest excellence. Among the Persians there is the order of the Magi, who silently make research into the facts of nature to gain knowledge of the truth and through visions clearer than speech, give and receive the revelation of divine excellency. In India, too, there is the order of the Gymnosophists, who study ethical as well as physical philosophy and make the whole of their lives an exhibition of virtue.*

Category: ETHICAL MONOTHEISM

Philo's most thoroughgoing assertion that there are Gentile "ethical monotheists" who conform to the ideal towards which he encourages his readers to strive is found in his treatise *That Every Good Person Is Free*. The extant portion is the second part of a longer treatise, the first part of which argued the converse thesis "that every bad man is a slave" (*Good Person* 1). The passage of interest for present purposes is not limited to what is quoted here, but continues on down at least to paragraph 130.

Philo begins to argue his thesis by differentiating between a slavery of the body, in which a person is subject to a human master, and a slavery of the soul, in which a person is subject to the mastery of "vices and passions" (17). His thesis is that those are truly free who are not slaves in the second sense—people who "have never fallen under the yoke of desire, or fear, or pleasure or grief" (18). As he goes on to describe such people, it is apparent that they are "good" in an ultimate sense; that is, they conform to Philo's ideal of virtuous monotheism. The "good person" is one "who has God alone for his leader" (20); such a one belongs to God and thus has chosen "eternal order and happiness" and is unmoved by "the tossing surge of circumstance" (24); Moses speaks of such a person as one "who was possessed by love of the divine and worshipped the Self-existent only" (43); or, in the passage cited above, they are "those who surpassed their contemporaries in virtue, who took God for their sole guide and lived according to a law of nature's right reason" (62). Clearly, the "good person" on display in this treatise is one who fully exhibits the characteristics of virtue and monotheistic devotion that represent Philo's religious ideal.

In the first portion of the treatise (16–61), Philo argues his case using "the methods of logical deduction" (62). A striking feature of this portion of the treatise is the presence of frequent appeal to Hellenistic authors, whom Philo puts forward as unquestioned authorities. He cites Plato ("the sacred authority of Plato"; 13), Sophocles (whose words "are as true as any Delphic oracle"; 20), and Zeno ("who lived under the direction of virtue to an unsurpassed degree"; 53), along with Antisthenes (28) and Homer (31). To be sure, he also cites "the law-giver of the Jews" (29; also 43, 68), even going so far as to suggest that Zeno derived his insights from Moses (57; cf. 160). Still, for the most part Moses appears simply as one authority among many.

In the next portion of the treatise, Philo accommodates himself to those "who have no understanding of the methods of logical deduction" (62) by providing specific examples of the kind of good person that he has been discussing. He promises to provide examples not only from the past but also from "our own time." After some preliminary comments, in which he laments the fact that most people have not taken the trouble to search out such good persons (63–71), he finally turns to specifics. He begins by asserting that even though the number "of the wise and just and virtuous" is small, such a group nevertheless exists (72). Then he lists specific examples: the seven sages of Greece (73); the Persian Magi, who "gain knowledge of the truth" both through the investigation of nature and through visions and revelations (74); and the Gymnosophists of India, who "make the whole of their lives an exhibition of virtue" (74).

At this point Philo turns to a Jewish group, the Essenes, though he introduces them somewhat offhandedly as a group from "Palestinian Syria" (75). While this example is notable for its length (74–91), the Jewish identity of the group is underplayed. In particular, there is no suggestion that the Essenes were categorically distinct because of the law of Moses, nor that they as Jews had any special insight into the nature of virtue or the oneness of God. After his treatment of the Essenes, Philo turns from examples having to do with groups to those pertaining to "the lives of good individual men" (92). There is no need here to list these and to discuss them one by one. In fact, the focus seems to fall away from the ideal of ethical monotheism, as the examples cited tend increasingly to demonstrate only the ability of human beings to endure physical suffering rather than to abandon their commitments—a tendency that reaches its extreme form in the argument that "the freedom of the wise" can even be seen in "irrational animals," such as cocks that are prepared to fight to the death (131–35).

Nevertheless the main point is clear. The passage stands as clear evidence that for Philo it was really possible for Gentiles to attain his religious ideal—virtue, freedom from bodily passion, the cultivation of the soul, devotion to the one true God—as Gentiles and apart from the law of Moses. Even if Moses points in the same direction, even if Moses represents "an oracle higher than Zeno" (160) and the other philosophers, there nevertheless are actual examples of people who have reached this destination apart from Moses, by following the philosophers or by cultivating their own sense of the "law of nature's right reason" (62).

§102 Embassy *157*

> *Indeed so religiously did he* [Augustus] *respect our interests that supported by wellnigh his whole household he adorned our temple through the costliness of his dedications, and ordered that for all time continuous sacrifices of whole burnt offerings should be carried out every day at his own expense as a tribute to the most high God.*

Category: SYMPATHIZATION

On the Embassy to Gaius is Philo's account of Emperor Gaius, his various mistreatments of the Jews, and the experience of the Alexandrian delegation to Rome, led by Philo himself. There is no need here for a detailed discussion of the treatise itself or of the circumstances it relates.[58] The delegation formed part of a response to a series of difficulties experienced by the Jewish community in Alexandria. The Jewish desire for the rights of full citizenship met with resentment from the other residents of the city, which boiled over during a visit of the newly ascendant Herod Agrippa in 38 C.E. A violent riot ensued, in which much Jewish property was destroyed and many Jews were killed. Synagogues that were not destroyed were desecrated, as statues or busts of Gaius were forcibly erected. The governor Flaccus, in an ineffectual attempt to deal with the crisis, stripped the Jews of whatever citizenship rights they had, declaring them to be "foreigners and aliens" (*Flaccus* 54). After Flaccus had been recalled by Gaius, two Alexandrian delegations made their way to Rome to seek redress from the emperor—Philo's Jewish delegation and a Greek delegation led by Apion. While they were waiting for a hearing, the Jewish situation took a desperate turn, with news of Gaius's intention to erect an image of himself in the Jerusalem temple. Since the treatise ends with a statement of Philo's intention to describe the "palinode" (τὴν παλινῳδίαν; usually "recantation")—presumably an account of the outcome, with Gaius's death and Claudius's succession—it was written sometime after the crisis had subsided.

One of Philo's lines of argument in the treatise is to adduce various Roman figures who, by their respectful and sympathetic treatment of Jews and Judaism, stand in sharp contrast to Gaius. The first example is Augustus, whom Philo puts forward as an example of a king who was worthy of the greatest honor but who steadfastly rejected any attempts on the part of his subjects to worship him as a god (143–58). Augustus's policies towards the Jews are brought in as evidence of this attitude; Philo argues that Augustus's benevolent treatment of a

58. There are many discussions of the latter; see, e.g., Barclay (1996, 48–71); Delia (1991); Kasher (1985); Modrzejewski (1995); Sly (1996); Smallwood (1981, 220–55).

people "who he knew full well regarded all such things with horror" (154) demonstrates his own antipathy towards emperor worship. While the argument is specious, Augustus's benevolence towards the Jewish community is well known. In addition to the honors shown to the temple, Philo mentions tolerance of the Jewish prayer houses in Rome, permission to transmit temple tax money to Jerusalem (155–57), and a provision concerning the distribution of benefactions to residents of Rome, according to which Jews were allowed to receive these on the following day when distribution happened on a Sabbath (158).

Philo's statement that Augustus demonstrated reverence towards Jewish tradition (ὡσίωτο περὶ τὰ ἡμέτερα; 157) derives maximum apologetic value from what was Augustus's normal policy towards Roman provinces.[59] Josephus also mentions daily sacrifices carried out on behalf of the emperor (*Ag. Ap.* 2.77; *J.W.* 2.197, 409), but he claims that they were paid for by the Jews themselves (*Ag. Ap.* 2.77). Perhaps, as Smallwood has suggested (1981, 148, n. 20), the sacrifices were paid for out of provincial taxes, so that both accounts have some claim on the truth.[60] Concerning gifts to the temple, Augustus's visit to Herod's domain in 20 B.C.E.[61] would have provided a likely occasion.

In contrast to the treatment of Augustus's gifts to the temple in the letter of Agrippa I, Philo here does not attempt to account for the emperor's "reverence" in terms of his love of "philosophy" (310, 318). Here it is sufficient for his argument that he can present Augustus's actions towards the temple as standing in sharp contrast to those proposed by Gaius.

§103 Embassy *210–11*

For all men guard their own customs, but this is especially true of the Jewish nation. Holding that the laws are oracles vouchsafed by God and having been trained in this doctrine from their earliest years, they carry the likenesses of the commandments enshrined in their souls. [211] *Then as they contemplate their forms thus clearly represented they always think of them with awe. And those of other races who pay homage to them they welcome no less than their own countrymen, while those who either break them down or mock a them they hate as their bitterest foes.*

Category: CONVERSION

59. On these various concessions and policies, see Smallwood (1981, 136–43).

60. In a subsequent reference to the daily sacrifices for the emperor (*J.W.* 2.409), Josephus describes them in terms that are closer to Philo. The context is an account of the cessation of these daily sacrifices in 66 C.E., which Josephus sees as a virtual declaration of war. In Josephus' account, this was the outcome of a more general policy initiated by Eleazar, the captain of the temple, that they "accept no gift or sacrifice from a foreigner." This gives the impression that the sacrifices were being made by the emperor rather than on his behalf (though the genitive construction—μηδενὸς ἀλλοτρίου δῶρον ἢ θυσίαν ("no foreigner's gift or sacrifice")—is perhaps a little less definite than the LCL translation.

61. Both Dio Cassius (54.7.6) and Josephus (*Ant.* 15.354–63) say that Augustus visited Herod in Syria. The statement that Herod "escort[ed] Caesar to the sea" (*Ant.* 15.363)

This passage appears at the point in the narrative where Philo is describing the reaction of Petronius, the Roman legate in Syria, to the letter from Gaius commanding him to erect an image of the emperor in the Jerusalem temple. The legate, whom Philo will go on to describe not only as thoroughly familiar with Judaism but even as a sympathizer (see the next entry), is distressed because "he knew that the Jews would willingly endure to die not once but a thousand times" (209) before they would see their temple desecrated in this way. The passage cited above is part of an explanatory aside in which Philo elaborates on the "zeal" (σπουδή; 212) of the Jews for their law. To make the point that any hatred on their part towards those who would threaten their "customs" (210) is due to their devotion to the law and not to any innate animosity towards outsiders, he points to the fact that the Jews are eager to "welcome [ἀποδέχονται][62] no less than their own countrymen [τῶν ἰδίων πολιτῶν]" those "of other races [τοὺς ἀλλοφύλους]" who are prepared to "pay homage [τιμητικῶς ἔχοντας]" to the Jewish laws.

The first question to be asked is whether Philo thinks of such foreigners as proselytes. The term itself does not appear, and Birnbaum, for one, is of the opinion that the passage refers instead to "interested non-Jews" (Birnbaum 1996, 204). Certainly Philo can use the language of "homage" or "honour" with reference to Gentiles who admire and adopt aspects of the law without becoming full converts. *Moses* 2.17–44 is the most pertinent case in point. As we have seen (§87), in that passage Philo puts forward a variety of evidence to demonstrate that everywhere people of virtue "have so far grown in holiness as to value and honour our laws" (πρὸς τὴν ἀποδοχὴν αὐτῶν καὶ τιμήν; 2.17). Both by the examples he puts forward and by the fact that he anticipates a time in the future when, in contrast, other nations will "turn to honouring our laws *alone*" (ἐπὶ τὴν τούτων μόνων τιμήν; 2.44), it is clear that these are not full proselytes.

Still, as the text just cited demonstrates, proselytes can also be described as honoring the Jewish law.[63] Further, the language of full incorporation into the Jewish *politeia* is elsewhere used only of proselytes. As we have seen, proselytes enjoy "equal rank," having received "all the privileges which he [Moses] gives to the native-born" (*Spec. Laws* 1.52); native-born Jews are to love them "not only as friends and kinsfolk but as themselves" (*Virtues* 102); they are "our dearest friends and closest kinsmen" (*Virtues* 179). Since Philo does not use such language with reference to casual admirers of Judaism, it is probable that when he

should probably be taken as a reference to Caesarea Maritima; it is difficult to imagine that Herod would not have taken this opportunity to showcase this lavish architectural homage to his patron.

62. Used of proselytes also in *Rewards* 152.

63. Proselytes are also described as honoring God (*Spec. Laws* 4.178; *Virtues* 181; *QE* 2.2) or as having formerly honored false gods (*Spec. Laws* 2.164–65; *Virtues* 179, 219, 220).

speaks of Gentiles whom the Jews "welcome no less than their own countrymen," he has proselytes in view. While the language by which he describes their attitude towards the law—τιμητικῶς ἔχοντας (holding in honor)—could by itself indicate something less than full acceptance, we should not use this passage as evidence that Philo would recognize as a proselyte a Gentile whose acceptance of the law was any less in extent or degree than that of the native-born "citizens."

§104 Embassy *245*

> *Indeed it appears that he* [Petronius] *himself had some rudiments of Jewish philosophy and religion acquired either in early lessons in the past through his zeal for culture or after his appointment as governor in the countries where the Jews are very numerous in every city, Asia and Syria, or else because his soul was so disposed, being drawn to things worthy of serious effort by a nature which listened to no voice nor dictation nor teaching but its own. But we find that to good men God whispers good decisions by which they will give and receive benefits, and this was true in his case.*

Category: SYMPATHIZATION, ETHICAL MONOTHEISM

Both Josephus and Philo depict Petronius as a figure of piety. In Josephus's case (*Ant.* 18.261–88; cf. *J.W.* 2.185–203), piety makes its appearance in the later stages of the crisis. After Petronius decided to intervene with Gaius on behalf of the Jews—having been persuaded that Jewish resistance to the emperor's order would result in disaster—he witnesses an event (a sudden and unexpected rainfall) that convinces him of God's providential care for the Jews.[64] In Philo's account, however, Petronius's willingness to listen to the appeal of the Jews was the result of an appreciation of "Jewish philosophy and religion" that was there at the outset.

It is clear from both accounts that Petronius was motivated by *Realpolitik* rather than by any personal sympathy for Jewish religion. But while it is doubtful that Philo has any real information about Petronius's religious proclivities—the vagueness of his language is telling—it is interesting to see how he interprets the information he does have. Taking Petronius's temporizing actions as evidence of an internal disposition, he concludes that Petronius must have adopted some "glimmers" (ἐναύσματα) of "Jewish philosophy and piety [εὐσεβείας]." How did this come about? Philo offers several possibilities, not necessarily mutually exclusive: his early education, in which he exhibited a zeal for "culture" (παιδεία); his later contacts with Jews in his capacity as provincial governor; and a soul naturally predisposed to seek out worthy things. But however it came about, Philo is convinced that by his actions in the crisis Petronius

64. "He said, moreover, that the Divinity who was in charge of them had shown His power to be unimpaired and was quite unambiguous in displaying this power" (*Ant.* 18.287).

has shown himself to be among the company of the "good" with whom God communicates in a special way. In other words, Petronius emerges as a particular representative of the ideal Gentile world with which Philo wants to align his own reconstructed Jewish world. The fact that this portrait has been constructed on so flimsy a basis should both caution us against too hasty an acceptance of other Philonic accounts of actual Jewish sympathizers and impress on us the importance for Philo of the template on which this portrait rests.

§105 Embassy *291, 294–97, 309–10, 317–20*

> [291] *Your grandfather Agrippa visited and paid honour to the temple, and so did Augustus by the letters in which he ordered the first fruits to be sent from every quarter and by instituting the perpetual sacrifice . . . .*
>
> [294] *For instance, your maternal grandfather M. Agrippa, being in Judea when Herod my grandfather was king of the country, saw fit to come up from the coast to the capital situated in the centre of the land.* [295] *But when he surveyed the temple and the rich array of the priests and the worship paid by the native population he was filled with wonder thinking that he had seen something to be profoundly reverenced, something greater than words could describe. His discourse to those of his friends who were there with him consisted of nothing else but praise of the sanctuary and all that pertained to it.. . .* [297] *After decking the temple with all the dedicatory gifts which the law made permissible . . .*
>
> [309] *But what of your greatgrandfather the best of the emperors that ever were to this day, he who first received the title of Augustus for his virtue and good fortune, who disseminated peace everywhere over sea and land to the ends of the world?* [310] *Did he not, hearing by report the story of the temple and that it had no work of men's hands, a visible effigy of an invisible being, marvel and pay it honour? For he had not taken a mere sip of philosophy but had feasted on it liberally and continued so to feast almost every day, partly by the memories of the lessons which his mind had conned from its earlier instruction in philosophy, partly by intercourse with the learned who from time to time were in his company. For in the gatherings at his table most of the time was assigned to listening to men of culture so that not only the body but also the soul might be nourished by the food proper to each . . . .*
>
> [317] *Another example no less cogent than this shows very clearly the will of Augustus. He gave orders for a continuation of whole burnt offerings every day to the Most High God to be charged to his own purse. These are carried out to this day. Two lambs and a bull are the victims with which he added lustre to the altar, knowing well that there is no image there openly or secretly set up.* [318] *Indeed this great ruler, this philosopher second to none, reasoned in his mind that within the precincts of the earth there must needs be a special place assigned as sacred to the invisible God which would contain no visible image, a place to give us participation in good hopes and enjoyment of perfect blessings.* [319] *Under such an instructor in piety your great-grandmother Julia Augusta adorned the temple with golden vials and libation bowls and a multitude of other sumptuous offerings.*

Category: SYMPATHIZATION, ETHICAL MONOTHEISM

The passages quoted above are presented by Philo as excerpts from a letter of Agrippa I, written to Gaius shortly after he had arrived in Rome and received news of the emperor's intentions. Josephus makes no mention of a letter; in his account, Agrippa's intervention is face to face and oral (*Ant.* 18. 289–97). But because of his proximity to the events, Philo is probably to be preferred here—at least on the general point that Agrippa first approached Gaius with a written appeal. The Alexandrian delegation was in Rome at the same time, which means that Philo, who knew Agrippa (*Embassy* 179), was in all probability in contact with him there. Thus there is no pressing reason to doubt that Philo has preserved at least the gist of Agrippa's appeal to Gaius, even if it has been recast in Philo's own language.[65] At the same time, however, Philo's own language is clearly evident—the letter "owes a good deal to Philo's own pen" (Smallwood 1981, 179, n. 120)—which means that we can take it as reflective of his own viewpoint.

The letter repeats points that were made earlier by Philo directly about Augustus's concessions towards the Jews (291, 311–16) and his gifts to the temple (291, 317). But it goes beyond the earlier passage in two respects. First, it describes similar honors paid to the temple by other members of Augustus's household—Marcus Agrippa (294–97), Augustus's powerful assistant and (after 21 B.C.E.) son-in-law, and Julia Augusta (319–20), Augustus's wife.[66] Marcus Agrippa's visit to Jerusalem took place in 15 B.C.E., after Augustus had commissioned him to take charge of imperial matters in the east;[67] Livia Julia's benefactions are mentioned by Josephus (*J.W.* 5.562). Secondly, (Herod) Agrippa's letter goes beyond Philo's earlier statements by interpreting Augustus's actions in particular as evidence of his piety, virtue and commitment to monotheism.

This idealized portrait of Augustus comes into view at the beginning (309–10) and the end (318) of the section in Agrippa's letter that deals with "the best of the emperors that ever were to this day" (309). The section begins with a declaration that the title Augustus was well deserved, in view of his "virtue and good fortune." Then the letter goes on to account for the emperor's gifts to the temple (310) on the dual basis of his admiration for aniconic worship (he marveled that it had no "visible effigy of an invisible being") and his love of philosophy (deriving both from his initial education and from his almost daily association with the learned). Both points are picked up again at the end of the section (318). After describing the daily sacrifice that the

65. One or two scholars have raised questions about the historicity of the letter; e.g., Zeitlin (1965–1966). But see Grabbe (1992, 401–05); Schürer (1973, 1:394–96); Smallwood (1981, 178–79).

66. Augustus' daughter Julia was with Marcus Agrippa when he visited Jerusalem; but Julia Augusta was the emperor's wife (Livia), not his daughter.

67. For Josephus' account of this visit, see *Ant.* 16.12–57; see also Richardson (1996, 262–64).

emperor had commissioned—knowing full well "that there is no image there openly or secretly set up"—the letter writer takes us inside Augustus's mind. He "reasoned" that "the invisible God" deserved such a place of worship, a place for "participation in good hopes and enjoyment of perfect blessings." In Colson's translation these hopes and blessings are for "us"—presumably "us Jews." But there is no pronoun in the Greek version; Augustus seems to be included in the "participation" and "enjoyment." The main point of the passage, then, is that Augustus's philosophical bent has led him to recognize not only the existence of the one "invisible God" but also that this God is uniquely to be encountered in the temple at Jerusalem. Further, this recognition is one that he does not want to keep to himself. He in turn becomes an "instructor in piety" to his wife Julia (318), leading her to honor the temple in similar ways.

Again, of course, the portrait is completely fanciful. Augustus's gifts to the temple were matters of imperial policy, not indications of the emperor's personal piety. What makes the portrait especially interesting, however, is the fact that for Philo's rhetorical purposes an appeal to policy would have been sufficient; to make the point that Gaius's actions were unprecedented and improper, it would have been enough to point to the contrasting actions of Augustus. As is the case of Petronius, Philo is keen not only to relate actions favoring the Jews but also to interpret them as expressions of an underlying form of piety that can be described as ethical monotheism.

§106 Questions on Genesis *3.62*

> *Why does Abraham circumcise those of foreign birth? The wise man is helpful and at the same time philanthropic. He saves and calls to himself not only his kinsmen and those of like opinions but also those of foreign birth and of different opinions, giving them of his own goods with patience and ascetic continence, for these are the firm foundations to which all virtue hastens and finds rest.*

Category: CONVERSION

Questions and Answers on Genesis (*QG*) is part of a larger work that is no longer fully extant and whose original scope remains unclear. Formally, the work comprises a series of units in which Philo poses brief questions arising from a Pentateuchal text, to which he provides relatively brief responses. The responses regularly address the "deeper" (e.g., *QG* 3.50) or allegorical meaning of the text, though frequently after having first commented on the "literal meaning" (*QG* 3.50). The work thus has a catechetical character, which probably reflects its original function. What remains of the work are portions of the books dealing with Genesis and Exodus; it is not clear whether the work originally dealt with the Pentateuch as a whole. The most extensive extant portions are in Armenian, but these are supplemented by fragments in Latin and Greek.

Happily, for present purposes, there are Greek fragments for the texts under discussion here and in the next entry.[68]

This section of *Questions and Answers on Genesis* deals with questions arising from Genesis 17, a text that recounts the institution of circumcision. Circumcision of Gentiles comes up at two points in the chapter—in v. 12, where Abraham is commanded to circumcise Gentile slaves, and in v. 27, where he carries out the command. Philo's discussion concerning the first of these passages (*QG* 3.50) stays within limited parameters, restricting itself to the case of purchased slaves.[69] In *QG* 3.62, however, the discussion is carried out in terms that are both more general and seem to include the experience of proselytes, at least by implication. In Philo's response, the idea of purchased slaves has fallen away; he seems to be dealing more generally with "those of foreign birth" (τοὺς ἀλλογενεῖς) who have come to share with Abraham's natural kinsfolk the life of virtue that the patriarch desires to share. While these foreigners whom Abraham "saves and calls to himself" are not explicitly designated as proselytes, this seems to be the implication. If so, the passage provides evidence that, for Philo, proselytes are expected to become circumcised.

The final passage to be considered here, however, is one that many commentators have taken as providing evidence to the contrary.

§107 Questions on Exodus *2.2*

> *Why does (Scripture) in admonishing," Thou shalt not oppress a sojourner," add, "For ye were sojourners in the land of the Egyptians"? (Scripture) first makes it clearly apparent and demonstrable that in reality the sojourner is one who circumcises not his uncircumcision but his desires and sensual pleasures and the other passions of the soul. For in Egypt the Hebrew nation was not circumcised but being mistreated with all (kinds of) mistreatment by the inhabitants in their hatred of strangers, it lived with them in self-restraint and endurance, not by necessity but rather of its own free choice, because it took refuge in God the Saviour, Who sent His beneficent power and delivered from their difficult and hopeless situation those who made supplication (to Him). Therefore (Scripture) adds, "Ye yourselves know the soul of the sojourner." But what is the mind of the sojourner if not alienation from belief in many gods and familiarity with honouring the one God and Father of all? In second place, some call strangers "newcomers." But strangers are also those who by themselves have run to the truth, not in the same way as those who made their sojourn in Egypt. For these are newcomers* [ἐπήλυδες] *to the land, while those are (newcomers) to laws and customs. But the common name of "newcomers" is ascribed to both.*

68. On the textual tradition and other technical issues, see Morris (1987, 826–30). The Greek fragments are included in the Loeb edition; for a more critical edition, see Petit (1978).

69. At least as far as the "literal" meaning is concerned. The passage does go on to discuss a "deeper" meaning, but there is no definite indication that proselytes are in view.

Additional Bibliography: McEleney (1973–1974); Nolland (1981)
Category: CONVERSION

Like *QG* 3.62, *QE* 2.2 discusses proselytism by making explicit reference to circumcision. Unlike *QG* 3.62, however, *QE* 2.2 does so in such a way as to suggest that the one is not necessarily a requirement for the other. The defining characteristic of the sojourner (προσήλυτος), Philo declares, is not the circumcision of the foreskin (ἀκροβυστίαν) but the "circumcision" of "desires and sensual pleasures and the other passions of the soul." Further, since scripture describes the Hebrew nation as προσήλυτοι in the land of Egypt (LXX Exod 22:20), even though they were (in Philo's understanding) still uncircumcised, Philo presents us with one instance, at least, of "proselytes" who were still in an uncircumcised state.

The passage has prompted extensive discussion and debate, resulting in several clearly discernible schools of opinion. One group of scholars understands the passage as providing evidence for two levels of proselytism in Philo's conception. Alongside the idea of the full proselyte, readily apparent in those passages that emphasize full incorporation into the Jewish people, *QE* 2.2. provides evidence (it is argued) that Philo could also describe as a proselyte one who abandoned idolatry and worshiped the God of Israel. In contrast to most of the other passages discussed in this chapter, then, the "proselyte" of *QE* 2.2 is in reality a "semi-proselyte" (Wolfson 1948, 2:369), a "sympathizer" (Feldman 1993, 348), a "monotheistic proselyte" (Cohen 1999, 151) or the equivalent of the rabbis' *ger toshab* (Belkin 1940, 44–48). McEleney (1973–1974), in contrast, argues that Philo provides us with no reason whatsoever to believe that he was prepared to use προσήλυτος and related terms to denote two quite distinct levels of attachment to Judaism and the God of Israel. Convinced, however, that *QE* 2.2 provides evidence for "uncircumcised proselytes," McEleney argues that this passage should serve as a key to the interpretation of the other passages; in other words, for Philo generally, circumcision was not an essential requirement for becoming a proselyte in the full sense of the term.[70] A third body of opinion holds that the passage, when seen in its rhetorical context, provides no reason to believe that Philo would dispense with the usual practice of requiring the circumcision of would-be male proselytes (e.g., Nolland 1981), even if the passage also demonstrates the subordinate place that it occupies in Philo's thinking (J. J. Collins 1985a, 173–74). Aspects of this approach will come up as the discussion unfolds.

The first step in assessing the passage is determining the question that is being addressed. As Nolland has observed, quite rightly, Philo's question is not

70. Or, at least, this is how Nolland (1981, 173–74) reads him; McEleney himself is somewhat more cryptic. Nevertheless, Nolland's reading seems simply to draw out the clear implications of McEleney's argument.

"Is it necessary for a Gentile to be circumcised in order to be considered a proselyte?" Of course, this does not necessarily rule out the possibility that an answer to this question might be inferred from his response. Still, we need to begin by discerning what is under discussion.

Philo's question arises precisely because he assumes the later, religious sense of προσήλυτος. Marcus's choice of "sojourner" in the Loeb translation serves to obscure the question that the text poses for Philo. It becomes clearer if we render it as follows: "You shall not oppress a proselyte; for you were proselytes in the land of Egypt."[71] Philo's question, then, appears to be, "In what way was the experience of the Israelites in Egypt similar to that of a proselyte?"

The shape of Philo's reply is constrained by two assumptions that he brings to the text. Both are introduced without any apparent need to justify them; in other words, he takes them for granted as self-evident to his readers. One of these is the assumption that proselytes are normally defined by circumcision. There is no mention of circumcision in the biblical text; as Nolland (1981, 175) has observed, the casual way in which circumcision comes up in Philo's response indicates that he takes it for granted that proselytes are normally expected to be circumcised. If Philo is indeed arguing for the possibility of "uncircumcised proselytes," he is setting himself over against what he recognizes to be the generally accepted expectation. The second assumption at work in the passage is the curious belief that during their time in Egypt, Israelites were not circumcised. For present purposes it is not necessary to inquire into the basis of this belief.[72] What is significant here is that this is what introduces the idea of uncircumcision into the discussion. How is Israel's experience in Egypt similar to that of the proselytes? The similarity, says Philo, cannot involve circumcision, since the Israelites were not circumcised in Egypt. Instead, the similarity has to do with the fact that both abandoned "belief in many gods," both "took refuge in God" ("the one God and father of all"), and both chose to strip away the "desires and sensual pleasures and the other passions of the soul." Philo affirms that it is just such a commitment to ethical monotheism—and not physical circumcision—that characterizes a proselyte and that is held in common by proselytes and the Israelites in Egypt.

But does this mean that Philo is ready to dispense with circumcision as a requirement for proselytism? If "a proselyte is not the one who circumcises the

71. This wording is not found precisely in the LXX. It seems to be a conflation of LXX Exod 22:20 ("You shall not do wrong to a προσήλυτον nor shall you oppress him; for you were προσήλυτοι in the land of Egypt") and LXX Exod 23:9 ("And you shall not oppress a προσήλυτον; for you know the heart of a προσηλύτου, for you yourselves were προσήλυτοι in the land of Egypt"); cf. Lev 19:33–34; Deut 10:19; 24:17–18.

72. Curiously, the question has not been explored by commentators. Perhaps the origin of this belief is LXX Josh 5:2–5, which describes an event in which Joshua is commanded by the Lord to "circumcise the sons of Israel." According to the MT, this was necessary because,

foreskin but the one who (circumcises) pleasures and desires and the other passions of the soul" (my translation), would Philo count as a proselyte one who did only the latter and not the former? It must be conceded that, taken in isolation, the statement would be consistent with the conception of an "uncircumcised proselyte."[73] Nevertheless, it is quite unlikely that Philo is here advocating—or even assuming—a form of "proselytism" that would run so significantly counter to the accepted norm. Several considerations are pertinent.

First, one notes the absence of any contentiousness in Philo's reply. He seems to assume that his reply will be readily accepted by anyone interested, as he is, in the "deeper" sense of the scriptural text. This is understandable if the intention of his response was to assert that ethical monotheism is what is at the heart of the making of a proselyte. It would be much less understandable if he also wanted to assert that this is all that would be required of a proselyte—more specifically, that such an "ethical monotheist" should be accepted as a full proselyte without the requirement of circumcision. If this had been Philo's intention, one would have expected some recognition of the extent to which this contravened the normal Jewish practice that he himself took for granted.

Second, a few sentences farther on in *QE* 2.2, Philo describes the proselyte (here he shifts to his preferred ἐπήλυδας) as one who is an "incomer" to the "laws and customs" (νομίμων καὶ ἐθῶν) of the "Hebrew nation." There is not even a hint of the idea that such incomers were nevertheless exempt from one of the most characteristic of the Jewish "laws and customs." Even if the Jews were uncircumcised in Egypt, Philo assumes that this state of affairs came to an end with the Exodus; in other words, circumcision was part of the "laws and customs" by which Jewish life was defined. This description of what is expected of proselytes, then, is quite conventional. If in this passage as a whole Philo were truly advocating the unconventional idea of uncircumcised proselytes, one would not have expected such a conventional description at this point. He provides no indication that circumcision is to be excepted from the "laws and customs" that were incumbent on proselytes.

---

although those who had left Egypt had been circumcised, those born during the wilderness wanderings were not. The MT also describes this as a "second" act of circumcision (v. 2). The LXX account, however, is different in several respects. Those who were circumcised are described in these terms: "as many as were born in the way and as many as were uncircumcised of those that came out of Egypt" (v. 4)—which implies that at least some Israelites in the land of Egypt were uncircumcised. In addition, there is no mention of a second circumcision. Thus Philo could easily have inferred from the LXX that the Israelites had not been circumcised in Egypt.

73. There is no basis in the text itself for Kuhn's use of "merely": "the (true) proselyte is one 'who is circumcised not *merely* in the foreskin but in lusts and desires and other passions of the soul'" (1968, 732).

Third, as we have seen, on two occasions in *Questions and Answers on Genesis* Philo speaks quite matter-of-factly about the circumcision of Gentiles (*QG* 3.50; 3.62). As I have indicated, at least in the second of these passages Philo seems to be dealing with the experience of proselytes. If my reading of *QG* 3.62 is correct, the passage provides evidence that Philo took for granted the fact that proselytes were circumcised. In any case, he evidently felt no need to make the point that even if "Abraham circumcise[d] those of foreign birth," circumcision was not essential for those who wanted to receive the virtuous "goods" that Abraham had to offer.

Finally, wherever Philo speaks of circumcision elsewhere in his work, while he usually interprets it as symbolizing some deeper level of meaning, he nowhere allows this deeper level to be divorced from the literal practice. To take a passage close to hand, we can cite the discussion of Genesis 17 in *QG* 3.39–62, much of which deals with the institution of circumcision (specifically, 3.46–51, 61–62). In each instance, Philo provides some allegorical interpretation of circumcision. Yet at the same time, he consistently assumes that the command to circumcise is obeyed at the literal level. This is true as well of the passage at the start of *On the Special Laws* (1.2–11), where Philo defends the practice of circumcision against its detractors.[74] While he provides allegorical reasons for the significance of circumcision (1.8–11), he does so only after putting forward traditional arguments that defend the literal practice. The most famous instance of Philo's defense of the literal sense of the law, of course, is in *Migration* 89–93. Here Philo is rejecting the approach of a group of people who can be described as extreme allegorizers, Jews who take the position that since the laws really are to be understood as "symbols of matters belonging to the intellect" (σύμβολα νοητῶν πραγμάτων), the literal observance of the laws can be treated "with easy-going neglect" (*Migration* 89). Such a divorce of the literal and the symbolic Philo rejects outright. Among the examples he takes up is that of circumcision:

> It is true that receiving circumcision does indeed portray the excision of pleasure and all passions [ἡδονῆς καὶ παθῶν πάντων], and the putting away of the impious conceit under which the mind supposed that it was capable of begetting by its own power: but let us not on this account repeal the law laid down for circumcising. (*Migration* 92)

He goes on to compare the two aspects of the law with the two components of the human person, the body and the soul: "It follows that, exactly as we have to take thought for the body, because it is the abode of the soul, so we must pay heed to the letter of the laws" (*Migration* 93).

In all of these passages, Philo is talking about circumcision as it applies to Jews, not to proselytes. Nevertheless, since when he is talking about proselytes,

74. On this passage, see §90 above. A version of this defense is reproduced in *QG* 3.48.

he presents the deeper meaning of the law in precisely the same terms—note, for example, the reference to "pleasures" and "passions" in both *QE* 2.2 and *Migration* 92—we are justified in extending the point to the case of Gentiles as well. Just as Philo expects Jews to retain the "body" of the law even as they strive to ascertain its "soul," so he would expect proselytes to adhere to the literal form of the "laws and customs" that they have adopted—circumcision included—even if the more fundamental meaning of circumcision has to do with the excision of "desires and sensual pleasures and the other passions of the soul."[75] In other words, *QE* 2.2 provides no evidence that Philo would countenance the possibility of uncircumcised proselytes. Even if the deeper meaning of proselytism is to be found in ethical monotheism, this meaning is to be approached only within the sphere of a literal observance of the law.

Concluding Observations

The material that we have surveyed both provides us with evidence for several distinct patterns of universalism and at the same time presents us with a number of questions about how Philo himself held them together in his mind.

First, we have encountered two types of Gentile sympathizers in Philo's world (whether real or ideal): those who adopt aspects of Jewish law and practice to a greater or lesser extent and those who show honor to Jews and their God by various kinds of benefaction, at least some of whom seem to act on the basis of an already-existing ethical monotheism. While such sympathizers are of interest for their own sake, in Philo's writings they tend to appear as attenuated versions of more significant types: those who adopt Jewish ways fully and thus become proselytes or "incomers" and those who through philosophy attain a life of virtue and a vision of the one true creator God.

The second category that we have observed, then, has to do with converts. Philo uses προσήλυτος with reference to converts on six occasions,[76] usually

75. Thus J. J. Collins goes too far when he says (with reference to *Migration* 89–94): "we may assume that Philo would 'blame' a convert who did not fulfil the literal commandments, including circumcision, but the ritual is not an entrance requirement and its omission does not necessarily exclude the proselyte from the Jewish community, at least in theory" (J. J. Collins 1985, 174). For Philo, however, the role of the law as it pertains to proselytes is precisely the same as in the case of native-born Jews. Even though the law is only a means to an end, Philo would "blame" the proselyte who ignored these "means" in as categorical a way as he does the native-born Jew. In other words, he would not be prepared, even in hypothetical terms, to countenance the idea of a member of the *politeia* who did not fulfill the law in a literal sense—neither in the case of native-born Jews nor in that of proselytes.

76. *Dreams* 2.273; *Spec. Laws* 1.51, 308; *QE* 2.2 (three times). In addition the term appears twice in *Cherubim* (108, 119), both times in a quotation of Lev 25:23, where the term is used with reference to Israel: "The land shall not be sold in perpetuity, for the land is mine; with me you are but aliens and tenants."

under the influence of the scriptural text. He prefers, however, to use a different set of closely related terms that would have been more familiar for Greek readers: ἐπηλύτης (10x), ἐπήλυτος (9x) and ἔπηλυς (6x).[77] In some of these passages, the terms are used literally of resident aliens (including Israelites themselves). In as many as twelve passages, however, the terms are used in the extended sense of Gentiles who have "come to" the Jewish way of life.[78] In addition, Gentile "incomers" are referred to in four other passages but without the use of any technical terminology.[79] These passages taken together contain additional terminology that belong to a larger vocabulary set by means of which Philo describes the proselyte experience.[80]

In all of these passages, it is assumed that proselytes are fully incorporated into the social entity of the Jewish people. While circumcision is explicitly mentioned in only two passages, there is no reason to believe that Gentile incomers would be exempt from such a defining mark of the Jewish social entity. All members of the godly *politeia* are expected to live according to the norms of the *polis*, provided by the law of Moses.

At the same time, however, it is clear from our discussion of these passages that for all members of the *politeia*—native-born Jews and proselytes alike—the law of Moses is not an end in itself but instead is one—or more accurately, the best—route to a higher end. This higher end, which we have described as ethical monotheism, involves a life of virtue, of liberation from the encumberments of the body and its passions, of worship of the one true God, and, ultimately, of attaining a clear vision of the Existent One. While literal observance of the law is not to be abandoned, it is equally the case that mere adherence to the law with no awareness that it points to something beyond itself would be, for Philo, a failure to respond to the real purpose of the law. As Mendelson (1988, 2) has observed, the community of the truly virtuous represents a subset of the Jewish *politeia* as a whole. Virtue does not come automatically with law observance; rather, it is acquired by those who use the law as a

77. ἐπηλύτης: *Mos.* 1.7, 147; *Spec. Laws* 1.52, 53; 2.118, 119; *Virtues* 102, 103, 182, 219); ἐπήλυτος: *Cherubim* 120, 121 (2x); *Dreams* 1.160; *Spec. Laws* 1.309; 4.176, 177; *Virtues* 104 (2x); ἔπηλυς: *Cherubim* 121; *Rewards* 152; *Flaccus* 54; *QE* 2.2 (2x).

78. *Dreams* 1.160–61 (ἐπήλυτος); 2.273 (προσήλυτος); *Spec. Laws* 1.51–53 (ἐπηλύτης, προσήλυτος); 1.308–09 (ἐπήλυτος, προσήλυτος); 2.118–19 (ἐπηλύτης); 4.176–78 (ἐπήλυτος); *Virtues* 102–04 (ἐπηλύτης, ἐπήλυτος); 175–82 (ἐπηλύτης); 212–19 (ἐπηλύτης); *Rewards* 152 (ἔπηλυς); *QE* 2.2 (ἔπηλυς, προσήλυτος).

79. *Virtues* 108, 220–22; *Embassy* 210–11; QG 3.62. For a similar list of references to proselytes, including both those where the terms appear and those where the reference is contextually apparent, see Birnbaum (1996, 195–204). She excludes *Dreams* 2.273 from her first list, though as we have seen there are good reasons to include it; she also includes *Spec. Laws* 2.256 in the second list, though here the reference is too vague to warrant inclusion.

80. Including: ἀποδέχομαι; ἀπολείπω; αὐτομολέω; καταλείπω; καταφυγή; μεθορμίζω; μεταβάλλω; μεταδίδωμι; μεταλλάσσω; μετανάστης; πρόσφυξ; σωφρονίζω.

means to this higher end. It is incumbent on Jews and proselytes alike to use the law in its literal sense as a means towards this more sublime end. There is a sense, then, that the proselyte—who freely chooses the law and its *politeia* as a means of achieving the higher life of the soul—provides the model for membership in this *politeia*, rather than serving as a special case (so Kraus 1996, 89).

In addition to the idea that the law was just a means to a higher end, Philo also seems to argue that this higher end could be pursued, and even attained, without reference to the written law at all. Two aspects are of particular importance. First, he equates the higher end to which the law is directed with the goal of the philosophical quest, so that Moses and Plato represent two routes to the same destination: "For what the disciples of the most excellent philosophy gain from its teaching, the Jews gain from their laws, that is to know the highest, the most ancient Cause of all things and reject the delusion of created gods" (*Virtues* 65). Likewise in *Spec. Laws* 2.165, speaking of the "invisible and inscrutable" nature of God, Philo not only declares that "every student of astronomical science and other philosophy" strives "to discern it and do it service," but also seems to suggest that their quest is to some extent successful: this God, "the supreme father of gods and men and the Maker of the whole universe," is one whom "all Greeks and barbarians unanimously acknowledge." If philosophy and the Mosaic law represent two routes to the same destination, it would seem to follow that one could reach this destination by means of philosophy alone, without following the route provided by the law, that is, without becoming a proselyte. Indeed, as we have seen, on two occasions[81] Philo adduces actual instances of people who have done just that; the possibility of an alternative route is not simply hypothetical for him.

Second, in addition to presenting the law and philosophy as parallel paths, Philo treats the written law in a universalizing way, especially in the *Allegory*, which in its own way also suggests the possibility of a second route to the religious ideal. What is in view here is his tendency to see the real meaning of the text itself as having to do with human existence in general. For example, in *Migration* 57–59, Philo is discussing a text (Deut 4:6–7) that speaks of Israel as a "wise and understanding people [λαός]," a "great nation [ἔθνος] . . . which has God drawing nigh to it" (56). Who are the people to whom God draws nigh and "who are worthy to receive His benefits," Philo asks (57)? In his reply to his own question, the nation of the Jews disappears entirely from view: "Is it not clear that all the lovers of wisdom and knowledge are so?" (57). In Philo's reading the people of God are redefined as all who love wisdom and knowledge. It is a people made up not of Jews (and proselytes) but of "wise world-citizens" (ὁ κοσμοπολίτης σοφός; 59). Likewise Birnbaum has shown how Philo interprets "Israel" etymologically as "the one who sees God" (of course, using the eyes of the soul, unclouded by the distorting effect of the senses and the passions of the

81. *Spec. Laws* 2.42–48; *Good Person* 62, 72–74.

body); "Israel" thus comes to refer to all who strive for a vision of God. Only rarely is "Israel" linked with the particular people of the Jews (*Embassy* 4); characteristically, the term is used generically of all who "see God," without any indication that one has to be—or become—Jewish in order to be worthy of the name (Birnbaum 1996, 30–127). Thus in Philo's reading of the Pentateuch as a handbook of philosophy and a guide to the life of virtue, its particular character as the story of a specific ethnic group falls away. As Barclay puts it: "This move from history to philosophy represents a shift from the particular to the universal; to dehistoricize is to deJudaize" (Barclay 1996, 170).

Thus Philo presents us with two quite distinct patterns of universalism—one by means of proselytism and the law of Moses, the other by means of philosophy and reason. What are we to make of this combination?

At the outset we should note that the combination is by no means an impossible one. While it is common—and no doubt accurate—to speak of tensions between the two,[82] they are not necessarily incompatible. One could be both eager to welcome proselytes and prepared to affirm the possibility that Gentiles might also attain the same goal through philosophy. Even so, Philo does not give us any clear indication as to how he perceives the relationship between the two. Birnbaum is correct when, referring to these two patterns of universalism, she concludes:

> We therefore cannot determine precisely the relationship between those who see God—"Israel"—and those who worship Him in the Jewish way—the Jews. Although the two entities may overlap or be one and the same, the exact connection between them remains unclear (Birnbaum 1996, 212).

Further, when we turn from general considerations to Philo's particular development of the two patterns of universalism, we observe definite signs of tension. In contrast to *Virtues* 65, with its declaration that the law and philosophy are two parallel routes to the same end, other passages clearly suggest that the destination can be attained only through the law. In *Embassy* 4–6, Philo declares that while "reason cannot attain to ascend to God," the vision of God has been achieved within the Jewish nation.[83] In another passage he states that God has provided "prophecy" so that human beings might grasp "what the mind fails to reach" (*Moses* 2.6). Thus with one part of his mind Philo believed that the law and philosophy are two routes to the same destination, while with another he held that the destination could be attained only through the law.

82. E.g., Birnbaum (1996, 118); Barclay (1996, 177).

83. More precisely, Philo speaks here of the "race (γένος) of "Israel" (*Embassy* 4), a formulation that usually has a general, rather than ethnic, sense (the race of those who see God). Nevertheless, given the fact that *Embassy* deals in a very specific way with the Jews of Alexandria, it is clear that in this passage at least Israel is linked with the Jewish people (so Birnbaum 1996, 105–07, 189–92).

Thus the tension between these two patterns of universalism must be allowed to stand. Nothing is to be gained by attempting to eliminate one in favor of the other.[84] Still, it is possible to ask about the relative importance of the two for Philo. One way to formulate the question would be to ask what Philo would be likely to say to a Gentile who approached him for advice about God and virtue. To make the example concrete, we might consider one of those Gentiles who gathered with Jews on the island of Pharos to celebrate the translation of the law into Greek (*Moses* 2.41–42). Would Philo advise such a person to pursue philosophy or to learn from the school of Moses?

The answer would probably depend on how far the person had advanced along the route provided by the philosophers. If the person were Philo's equal in the ways of monotheism and virtue, Philo would probably be prepared to recognize the person as a fellow traveler on the road to virtue, though he would probably also appeal for a recognition in return that the law leads to the same goal. For the most part, however, I tend to think that Philo would encourage a Gentile inquirer to follow the path laid out by Moses and to become a proselyte. Several considerations are pertinent here.

First, while it is true that Philo can point to actual examples of Gentiles who conform to his religious ideal, he nowhere explicitly entertains the possibility that a Gentile might, by assiduous devotion to philosophy, make the transition from a life dominated by the passions to one of virtue. He recognizes those who have arrived at this goal but shows little interest in the possibility that someone might seek to abandon the world of the senses by setting off on the philosophic road to virtue. In contrast, as we have seen, he speaks with great enthusiasm of those who have made a parallel transition by becoming proselytes. In addition to his enthusiasm, he also expresses the hope that proselytism will become universal. In *Moses* 2.36, he says that the divine purpose at work in the translation of the Scriptures into Greek as that "the greater part, or even the whole, of the human race might be profited and led to a better life by continuing to observe such wise and truly admirable ordinances." A little later in the same treatise, he looks forward to a time in the future when "each nation" adopts, not the ways of reason and philosophy, but "our laws alone" (*Moses* 2.44). In other words, the only transition that he contemplates in real terms is that of proselytism.

Second, while Philo can describe his religious ideal in terms that are generic, universal and non–ethnos-specific—especially in the *Allegory*—it would be wrong to see this ideal as existing in complete independence of the law. Certainly in the *Allegory* ethnic particularities fall away as Philo universalizes the law and treats it as a general guide to ethical monotheism. Yet at the same time the *Allegory* also assumes a high level of familiarity with the law on the part of its

84. E. P. Sanders (1976, 27) goes much too far when he claims: "Philo in fact not only insists that all Jews except apostates are on the royal road, but he seems to think that no Gentiles are."

readers; he seems to be addressing himself to people who are already devoted to the law of Moses and who he believes are also capable of coming to see that the law is a route to this higher ideal.[85] While Philo might be prepared to see the law and philosophy as parallel routes to the same destination, his primary concern in the *Allegory* seems to be to encourage those already on the route provided by Moses to recognize the higher destination to which the law points.

Further, it is not without significance that the term Philo chooses for this generic group of ethical monotheists is "Israel." Birnbaum (1996) has demonstrated that there is a clear pattern in Philo's use of the terms "Israel" and "the Jews," corresponding to his two models of the religious ideal. He uses "Jews" to refer to the specific nation (ἔθνος) that is characterized by its adherence to the law of Moses; this term is more common in the *Exposition*. "Israel," on the other hand, appearing more frequently in the *Allegory*, is used of the "race" (γένος) of those who "see God." But Birnbaum also tends to minimize the ethnic significance of the latter term, suggesting that Philo would include within "Israel" anyone who was able to "see God," even "non-Jews like the Persian Magi and other unnamed sages from Greek and foreign lands" (Birnbaum (1996, 224). This, however, overstates the evidence and undervalues the significance of Philo's choice of term. There is no occurrence of "Israel" where Gentiles are explicitly included;[86] indeed, on the one occasion where an ethnic entity is in view (*Embassy* 6; admittedly, not in the *Allegory*), "Israel" clearly refers to the Jewish people. Given that the *Allegory* seems to be addressed to a readership fully conversant with the law, it is significant that Philo's preferred term for this "race" of ethical monotheists and proselytes is "Israel." If a distinction is to be made between "Israel" and "the Jews," the former is probably the more elite group that not only adheres to the law of Moses but also strives to reach the higher destination to which it points.[87] The purpose of the *Allegory* is to encourage members of the Jewish *ethnos* (both native-born Jews and proselytes) to attain the goal held aloft etymologically by the designation "Israel"—to arrive at a vision of God.

I suggest, then, that if a Gentile approached Philo and sought his counsel on how to attain a vision of God, Philo would encourage such a person to become a proselyte. Consistent with this conclusion is the fact that Abraham is presented both as the first one to have seen God (*Virtues* 215–16) and as the prototypical proselyte (*Virtues* 219). Like Abraham, the first proselyte, Gentiles

85. On the presumed audience of the *Allegory*, see Birnbaum (1996, 18); Morris (1987, 840).

86. Birnbaum recognizes that Philo does not refer explicitly to these non-Jews as "Israel"; still, she says that "his description of them would lead one to think that they meet the requirement for belonging [to Israel], namely, that they have the spiritual ability to apprehend the existing God" (Birnbaum 1996, 224).

87. Cf. Mendelson's argument that the truly virtuous represent a smaller group within the nation as a whole (Mendelson 1988, 2).

who have an "ardour to seek for the one" (*Virtues* 215) should probably follow Abraham's example in becoming a proselyte. While Philo recognizes that there are non-Jews who have also arrived at a vision of God apart from any connection with Judaism, there is no evidence that he would recommend this as an alternative route to a destination that could be reached more directly and surely through Jewish practice and belief.

Such an interaction between Philo and an interested Gentile is hypothetical, but it does lead to the question of whether Philo was aware of or would have advocated an active proselytizing mission to the Gentile world. Certainly Philo saw Israel as having been entrusted with a positive role with respect to the other nations. This comes to clear expression in his discussion of the translation of scriptures into Greek, where he sees the translation as part of a divine purpose by means of which "the whole of the human race might be . . . led to a better life" (*Moses* 2.36). In keeping with this there is a set of passages in which the Jewish nation is seen as offering prayers and sacrifice on behalf of the whole human race (*Moses* 1.149; *Spec. Laws* 1.97, 168, 190; *Embassy* 306) or as functioning as a kind of national priesthood to the world as a whole (*Spec. Laws* 2.163) or as the "first fruits" from "the whole human race" (*Spec. Laws* 4.180) or as a "chosen race" that functions as a kind of sample for the whole (*QE* 2.42). But in all of this, Israel's role is one that is carried out through its sheer existence as a distinct nation rather than through any active program of mission or proselytization. If there is Jewish initiative involved, it is more reactive than proactive.[88] The translation of the scriptures into Greek, for example, is the result of Gentile initiative; Israel's initial part in the process was simply the attractive character of its law-observant life.[89] Still, even if we cannot speak of active mission, Philo definitely sees Israel as having a positive role to play in making the glories of the law accessible to the wider world.

This comes into view as well in the final category, having to do with the eschatological future. As we have seen, on one occasion Philo seems to contemplate a time in the future when "each nation would abandon its peculiar ways, and, throwing overboard their ancestral customs, turn to honoring our laws alone" (*Moses* 2.44). Lines of connection with the treatise *On Rewards and Punishments* suggests that Philo is reworking eschatological traditions here. If so, it is precisely the "conversion to virtue" (*Rewards* 164) of Israel as a whole that precipitates this end-time transformation of the nations.

88. See the references to Goodman and Will and Orrieux above. Nevertheless, Will and Orrieux go too far in the direction of subordinating Philo's statements about proselytes to those about the priestly role of Israel (which they understand as a purely passive role); see Will and Orrieux (1992, 90–93).

89. "But, in course of time, the daily, unbroken regularity of practice exercised by those who observed them [the laws] brought them to the knowledge of others, and their fame began to spread on every side" (*Moses* 2.27).

CHAPTER 6

JOSEPHUS

Introduction

In contrast to Philo, whose literary career was the logical culmination of his origins and early life, Josephus's role as an author was more the result of contingent circumstances. Most prominent among them, of course, were Josephus's experiences in the war with Rome and its aftermath: his role as a military commander in Galilee, his defection to the Romans after the conquest of Jotapata, his shift in status from prisoner of war to imperial client with the acclamation of Vespasian as emperor, his role as advisor to Titus and mediator with the Judeans during the siege of Jerusalem, and his transfer to Rome, where he lived out the rest of his days under the patronage of the Flavian emperors.

But Josephus's subsequent career was also shaped by an event that happened just prior to the outbreak of war. As he recounts it in *Life* 13–16, at the age of twenty-six (i.e., in 63 C.E.) he journeyed to Rome to seek the release of some Judean priests whom Felix, the Roman procurator of Judea (c. 52–60 C.E.), had sent for trial before Nero and who had been languishing in prison for some time. Through the influence of a certain Jewish actor, Aliturus, who moved in the highest circles, Josephus was able to make contact with Poppaea Sabina, Nero's onetime mistress and now (since 62 C.E.) wife. Poppaea, who seems to have had a certain sympathy for Jews and Judaism,[1] not only used her influence to see that his request was granted but also sent him on his way with other benefactions.

1. See *Ant.* 20.195, a passage to be discussed below.

With this experience of Roman power and goodwill fresh in his mind, Josephus arrived back in Judea to find, however, that the country was gripped by quite a different mood towards the Roman reality, anti-Roman revolutionary fervor having by this time reached the boiling point. As he continues his narrative, Josephus claims that he attempted to cool the fervor and to convince his compatriots that any uprising against Rome was reckless folly (*Life* 17–19). Reckless folly or not, when the uprising passed the point of no return, Josephus nevertheless emerged as one of the Jewish commanders. The question of how Josephus the opponent of war became Josephus the military commander has generated considerable debate, especially because he himself gives two conflicting accounts of the sequence and character of the events.[2] But however we understand his place in the social and political dynamics in the early phases of the war, it seems reasonable to conclude that his recent experience in Rome, which would have given his voice a certain added force and authenticity, served to propel him to the fore in a way that probably would not have been the case had he simply remained in Jerusalem in the years leading up to the war as just another young priest in the temple establishment.

In addition to its possible role in the sequence of events that culminated in Josephus's career as a writer, this early experience probably also affected his writings in another, more direct way. In his first sojourn in Rome, he experienced firsthand the benefit that could accrue for the Jewish people as a whole from the success of local Jews in cultivating the friendship and patronage of highly placed Romans who, in turn, were sympathetic to Jews and Judaism. The question of Josephus's purposes in writing is contentious and needs to be taken up in more detail as we proceed. But there are reasons to believe that the fostering of such attitudes among influential Romans was at least one of his purposes in writing. In all likelihood, then, the agenda that he set for himself when he arrived in Rome for the second time was probably influenced in significant ways by his first experience of the city.

So while Philo viewed involvement in public life as an unwelcome distraction from the literary pursuits and ambitions for which his upbringing had prepared him (*Spec. Laws* 3.1–5), Josephus's writings would not have come into existence at all if he had not been caught up in public affairs in this way. Still, it was not just any young Jerusalemite who would have found himself on such

2. In *Life* Josephus claims that he was commissioned by "the leading men in Jerusalem" to travel to Galilee to encourage the revolutionary faction to lay down their arms (28–29); in *War*, he describes himself as one of the generals appointed by a coalition of moderates and rebels "to conduct the war" (2.562–68). For full discussion of the two accounts, see Cohen (1979), Bilde (1988), and Mason (2003). While the tensions between the two are not easily resolved, they nevertheless reflect the tensions that the whole Jewish aristocracy must have experienced as they attempted to negotiate between the *Realpolitik* of the Roman empire and their loyalty to the Jewish state.

a mission to Rome. Josephus's own upbringing as a member of the priestly aristocracy was certainly a necessary precondition for his later career. According to his account in *Life* (2–7), he came from a prominent Jerusalem family, his father being "among the most notable men in Jerusalem" (*Life* 7), a priest who, with his ancestors, enjoyed the special status that came with membership in the first of the twenty-four priestly courses. His additional claim to a Hasmonean pedigree is weakened somewhat by conflicting details in the genealogy he presents in support of the claim, but the claim itself is probably to be accepted.[3] Generally speaking, although Josephus's purpose in this work is to defend his reputation against certain opponents who were harshly critical of his conduct in the war, there is no indication that there was any question about his family's character and status, which would have been a matter of public record in any case. We should be less inclined to take at face value his claim to have been a *Wunderkind* in his mastery of Jewish learning and the account of his extensive "personal experience of the several sects into which our nation is divided" (*Life* 8–9). Still, there can be little doubt that he had received a thorough Jewish education and was thus well equipped to take his place within the priestly "aristocracy" that he believed to be the divinely ordained form of Jewish polity.[4] Further, he probably would not have been able to undertake his mission to Rome and to bring it to a successful conclusion if he had not received at least the rudiments of a Greek education (Rajak 1983, 11–45).

In 71 C.E., Josephus arrived in Rome for the second time. This time he was not a supplicant but part of the retinue of a victorious Roman general and a client of the new emperor. Vespasian honored him with Roman citizenship, a pension, and living quarters in the house that he had vacated when he became emperor (*Life* 423). While these benefactions did not confer on Josephus the kind of elevated status that has sometimes been claimed for him,[5] they nevertheless represented the makings of a comfortable existence that he was able to enjoy for the next thirty years or so.

3. In *Life* 2 he says that he is descended from the Hasmonaeans on his mother's side, but as he goes on to provide the supporting "pedigree" (τὴν διαδοχήν), he establishes the link instead through an ancestor on his father's side who married a daughter of Jonathan the high priest (*Life* 4). Josephus's evident uncertainty about his genealogy probably does not invalidate the basic claim (see Mason 2003, 38–39), though the Hasmonaean connection would have been diluted in any case.

4. In a summary of the Mosaic law (*Ant.* 4.196–301), which he characterizes as the Jewish "constitution" (πολιτεία; *Ant.* 4.196), he describes Jewish government as an aristocracy (ἀριστοκρατία; *Ant.* 4.223), which he defines further as rule by God rather than by a king. In *Ag. Ap.* 2.165–67 he coins the term "theocracy" to describe this polity. What he means in either case, however, is rule by a hereditary priesthood rather than by a monarchy (*Ant.* 11.111; 14.91; 20.251).

5. See Mason (2000, xviii), who points out that, unlike some other imperial clients, Josephus was not given equestrian status.

But instead of using this as an opportunity for indolence, Josephus redefined himself as a historian[6] and plunged into his new role with considerable industry. Sometime before the death of Vespasian in 79 C.E., he completed both an Aramaic version of the *Jewish War* and then a full revision in Greek,[7] which he carried out with the aid of Greek assistants.[8] In the introductory section of the *Jewish War*, Josephus declared that there was no need for an account of the "ancient history of the Jews," since this had already been provided by others and since the work of historians who wrote of events in their own lifetime was much more worthy of praise (*J.W.* 1.13–18). Apparently he had a quick change of heart, however, for it could not have been long after the completion of the *Jewish War* that he began work on his magnum opus, the *Jewish Antiquities*.[9] This work, which included a biographical account (*Life*) as an appendix or final chapter, appeared in "the thirteenth year of the reign of Domitian Caesar" (*Ant.* 20.267), that is, 93–94 C.E.[10] Sometime after this, Josephus published his final extant work, known to us as *Against Apion*, though this was not its original title.

These four works contain some fifty references that will be of interest to us here. Our interest in these texts will operate at two levels. First, in accordance with Josephus's intentions to write history, we will be interested in these texts for the evidence they provide concerning the historical realities to which they

6. He describes both the *Jewish War* and *Antiquities* (at least by implication) as works of "history" (ἱστορία; *J.W.* 1.2, 7; *Ant.* 1.1).

7. In *Ag. Ap.* 1.50 Josephus states that he presented the Greek version to Vespasian and Titus. Some have argued for later dates for the final, seven-volume version—during the reign of Titus for books 1 to 6 and after Domitian's succession for book 7 (e.g., Cohen 1979, 84–90). But although the nature of the book trade in antiquity lent itself to the production of successive editions, it is probable that books 1 to 6 were finished in more or less their present form during the reign of Vespasian and that book 7, even if it were later, was part of Josephus's original conception of the work (Mason 2003, 66).

8. On the original Aramaic version, see *J.W.* 1.3. At the start of *Antiquities* he speaks of his hesitation at undertaking such a large project in "a foreign and unfamiliar tongue" (*Ant.* 1.7); at the end he refers to his lifelong difficulty with proper Greek pronunciation (*Ant.* 20.263). On his Greek assistants, see *Ag. Ap.* 1.50.

9. In *Ant.* 1.6 he claims that this had been his intention from the outset, but that, considering the excessive length of the proposed project, he decided instead first to deal with the war in a self-contained work.

10. Some authors (esp. Cohen [1979], following Laqueur [1920]) have argued that *Life* first appeared as part of a second edition, published sometime after the turn of the century. This theory is based on a combination of the assumption in *Life* (359–60) that Agrippa II has already died and of the statement in Photius's *Bibliotheca* (ninth century C.E.) that Agrippa died "in the third year of Trajan," a statement contained in Photius's summary of the history written by Justus of Tiberias. The evidence from Photius, however, is too tenuous to bear the weight of the theory (Bilde 1988, 104–06; Schürer 1973, 1:481–83).

refer, even if their evidential value needs first to be assessed with respect to the biases and tendencies of Josephus's work as a historian. But these biases and tendencies are themselves significant at a second level, in that the texts under consideration also inform us about Josephus's own attitudes toward Gentiles and their religious status.

Until relatively recently, scholarly attention has been focused more on the first level than the second. In other words, the tendency has been to treat Josephus's writings as a repository of historical information rather than as literary works with their own rhetorical and ideological purposes.[11] Fortunately, this has begun to change in recent years.[12] Of particular interest here is that, while the scholarly discussion of Josephus as an author is still in its early stages, one of the nodes of the discussion thus far has to do with his attitudes and intentions concerning the attraction of Gentiles to Judaism. Conclusions about these issues will need to emerge from a study of the pertinent passages themselves, but to provide a framework for this study it will be helpful to sketch the positions of two authors who represent distinctive alternatives at opposing ends of the scholarly spectrum. One of these is Shaye Cohen; the other, Steve Mason.

Cohen's 1987 article "Respect for Judaism by Gentiles according to Josephus" was one of the first studies devoted to the topic. While he posits a variation in Josephus's attitude towards Gentile sympathizers and converts from one work to another, his general tendency is nevertheless to minimize the significance of the pertinent references and to downplay any evidence that might seem to suggest that Josephus was interested in encouraging the phenomena.

He divides the evidence into two categories, "tolerant monarchs and dignitaries" and "adherents and converts." With respect to the first, he sees a uniformly positive presentation throughout the corpus. Josephus consistently points with pride to foreign monarchs and Gentile rulers of Judea who "guarantee Jewish rights and privileges, sacrifice to God, worship in his temple, recognize that God protects and punishes his people, and believe that God appoints and removes the kings of both the Jews and the Gentiles" (Cohen 1987a, 413). None of this, however, is to be seen as evidence of Gentile attraction to Judaism. Rather, it was, for Josephus, simply the mark of a good ruler. Josephus shared with his Greek and Roman contemporaries the belief that respect for the gods and temples of other peoples was something to be expected of a virtuous monarch or dignitary. By pointing to examples of respect for Jews and Judaism on the part of rulers whom the Gentile world would recognize as

11. See, e.g., Mason (1998, 11), who points, lamentingly, to the example of the new Schürer, which devotes twenty pages to Josephus as a historical source (Schürer 1973, 1.43–63) but just two paragraphs to Josephus in the section dealing with "Jewish literature composed in Greek" (Schürer 1986, 3. 545–46), compared to eighty pages for Philo.

12. For *Antiquities*, see the account in Mason (2000, xiii–xvi).

virtuous, Josephus was simply seeking to demonstrate that Judaism was therefore worthy of honor and respect by all.

Cohen deals with the second category—adherents and converts—in separate sections, corresponding to Josephus's three major works. While such an approach is not inappropriate, it also conveniently reflects Cohen's belief that Josephus's career was marked by dramatic shifts in his stance vis-à-vis Rome and Judaism. The version of events presented in the *Jewish War*, in which "a period of moderation and legitimacy [was] sandwiched between periods of terror and anarchy" (Cohen 1979, 100), Cohen sees as Josephus's own invention, created to mask the extent to which Josephus himself was complicit in rebellion. After going over to the Roman side, Josephus became an apologist for the Romans, writing the *Jewish War* as propaganda for the new Flavian imperial family. By the time he published the *Jewish Antiquities*, however, his original patrons had been succeeded by the less sympathetic Domitian, and Josephus had made the transition "from a Roman apologist to a Jewish nationalist" (Cohen 1979, 240). In *Jewish Antiquities*, he addressed a Roman readership, seeking to commend Judaism as worthy of Roman favor and to commend the Pharisees as the natural leaders of the Jews. By the time he wrote *Against Apion*, the character of Roman anti-Judaism had become more pronounced (reflected a little later in the writings of Tacitus and Juvenal), and Josephus responded by becoming even more forthright in his Jewish nationalism.[13]

It is with respect to this reconstruction of Josephus's shifting circumstances and agendas that Cohen interprets his references to Gentile adherents and converts. In the *Jewish War*, Josephus keeps references to such Gentiles to a minimum, making no attempt to differentiate adherence from conversion and implying that the presence of such Gentiles was one of the factors resulting in "the troubles which befell the Jews in the cities of Syria in 66 and 67 C.E." (Cohen 1987a, 417). In *Jewish Antiquities*, Josephus does differentiate between adherence and conversion. However, in order to allay Roman fears about conversion to Judaism, Josephus's writing conveys what Cohen describes as "coolness towards the former and disapproval of the latter" (Cohen 1987a, 417). The only exception is the conversion of the royal house of Adiabene, whose more positive tone Cohen attributes to a combination of Josephus's dependence on more enthusiastic source material and the fact that, since Adiabene lay outside the Roman empire, Roman fears about conversion did not have to be taken so much into account. With respect to *Against Apion*, Cohen cannot get around the fact that here Josephus positively exults in the extent to which Gentiles have adopted Jewish ways. To some extent Cohen attributes this more aggressive tone to the fact that Josephus was responding to a new, more overtly anti-Jewish

13. Cohen's approach stands in an interpretive tradition that includes Laqueur (1920), Thackeray (1929), and S. Schwartz (1990).

mood in Rome. Even so, he attributes most of the material in question to Josephus's putative sources, which—he suggests—Josephus was following much more closely than had been his usual practice.[14]

Mason's reading of Josephus stands in sharp contrast to that of Cohen at almost every point. Where Cohen's Josephus zigzags from anti-Roman rebellion to pro-Roman propaganda and back to Jewish nationalism, Mason presents us with a Josephus who is more consistent in his life and continuous in his purpose. While we may never be able to reconstruct an accurate account of Josephus's role in the war, Mason maintains that the tensions in his biographical accounts should be seen more as reflective of the real tensions that he would have experienced—between his national loyalty as a Jewish aristocrat and his sober respect for the Roman reality—than as the result of deliberate attempts to conceal his past (Mason 2003, 44). During his years in Rome he was neither as close to Vespasian and Titus nor as alienated from Domitian as Cohen and others have maintained (Mason and Feldman 2000, xviii). The Jewish king Agrippa II seems to have played a larger role in the production and promotion of *Jewish War* than did either Vespasian or Titus (*Life* 359–67; Mason 1998, 78–79). In keeping with this, far from writing simply out of "flattery for the Romans" (c.f. *J.W.* 1.2) or out of an attempt to whitewash his own involvement, Josephus wrote his *Jewish War* in order to convince his primarily Roman readership (*J.W.* 1.3, 16) of the dignity and respectability of the Jewish people. In contrast to other accounts of the war, Josephus maintained that the cause of the war was not the national character of the Jews but the activity of a small revolutionary party who, overreacting to the corrupt and capricious rule of certain Roman governors, produced civic strife of a kind not unknown in Rome itself (*J.W.* 1.4). The destruction of Jerusalem was due not simply to Roman might but also to the will of Israel's God, who used Roman might to punish Israel for the heinous misdeeds of the rebels (e.g., *J.W.* 4.323). Even so, Israel's defenders displayed great fortitude and skill, while the natural ruling class conducted themselves with honor (Mason 1998, 72–74; 2003, 64–99).

While this represents quite a different reading of the *Jewish War* than that of Cohen, it does not affect our study all that directly, since, on either reading, Josephus's various references to Gentile adherence and conversion tend to take the form of incidental narrative details that do not have much direct bearing on his overall purpose. The situation is different, however, with *Jewish Antiquities* and *Against Apion*. In each case, Mason argues that Josephus is addressing himself primarily to a readership comprising converts, adherents, sympathizers and other interested outsiders, and that his purpose is precisely to encourage and support such Gentile attachment to Judaism.

14. Cohen identified this source as stemming from Alexandria in the first half of the first century C.E. (Cohen 1987, 425).

With respect to *Jewish Antiquities*, Mason stresses the significance of the Adiabene story (*Ant.* 20.17–96), seeking to deconstruct the interpretive firewall within which Cohen has attempted to contain it (Mason 1998, 90–95). Not only does the story display clear evidence of Josephus's own style and themes, he argues, but it also has an important part to play in the structure of the work as a whole. After describing how king Izates went ahead with his desire to become circumcised, despite the fears of his family and his Jewish adviser Ananias that this would result in undesirable consequences among his people, Josephus sums up the moral of the story as follows:

> It was God who was to prevent their fears from being realized. For although Izates himself and his children were often threatened with destruction, God preserved them, opening a path to safety from desperate straits. God thus demonstrated that those who fix their eyes on him and trust in him alone do not lose the reward of their piety. (*Ant.* 20.48).

The passage is strongly reminiscent of a passage at the beginning of *Jewish Antiquities*, in which Josephus describes the "main lesson to be learned" from his work as a whole:

> [T]he main lesson [τὸ σύνολον] to be learned from this history by any who care to peruse it is that men who conform to the will of God, and do not venture to transgress laws that have been excellently laid down, prosper in all things beyond belief, and for their reward are offered by God felicity; whereas, in proportion as they depart from the strict observance of these laws, things otherwise practicable become impracticable, and whatever imaginary good thing they strive to do ends in irretrievable disasters. (*Ant.* 1.14)

At the very least, it is difficult to avoid the conclusion that Josephus has presented Izates as a particular case of one who "conformed to the will of God" and who thus "prospered" as the recipient of divine "felicity" (εὐδαιμονία). Indeed, the counsel of his other adviser Eleazar, who had a reputation for "the strict [ἀκριβοῦς] observance of these laws,"[15] was, in effect, that Izates not "transgress" a law (i.e., that of circumcision) that had "been excellently laid down."[16]

This resonance between the Izates story and the introductory statement of the "main lesson" of the work gains in intensity, Mason argues, when one looks at other aspects of the Proem to *Jewish Antiquities*. After a some brief comments on the writing of history in general and on his previous account of the war,

15. "Eleazar . . . had a reputation for being extremely strict [ἀκριβὴς] when it came to the ancestral laws" (*Ant.* 20.43).

16. When Eleazar found Izates "reading the law of Moses, he said: 'In your ignorance, O king, you are guilty of the greatest offence against the law and thereby against God. For you ought not merely to read the law but also, and even more, to do what is commanded in it'" (*Ant.* 20.44).

Josephus describes his present work as an account of "our entire ancient history [ἀρχαιολογίαν] and political constitution [πολιτεύματος]," an account that he is addressing to "the whole Greek-speaking world" (*Ant.* 1.5). He says that he was urged to carry out the task by a group of people, the most prominent of whom was his patron Epaphroditus (*Ant.* 1.8–9). He goes on to compare his situation to an earlier attempt to make Israel's ancient history and constitution available to the Greek-speaking world—namely, the translation of the law as described in the *Letter of Aristeas*. In part, this provides him with a precedent for his own task, as he presents himself as reprising the role of Eleazar, the high priest, to Epaphroditus's Ptolemy, the Egyptian king who wanted "to have our Law and the political constitution [πολιτείας] based thereon translated into Greek" (*Ant.* 1.10). In part, however, he sees himself as completing the process of translation, since what Ptolemy received "was only the portion containing the Law" (*Ant.* 1.12).

Still, the law is important. Josephus wants to present it as the best of all possible constitutions, because it is based on Moses's philosophical insights into the character of God and the nature of the created order (*Ant.* 1.18–25). He invites his readers "to fix their thoughts on God and to test whether our lawgiver has had a worthy conception of his nature" (*Ant.* 1.15). The Proem, then, provides the frame within which Josephus wants to set all that is to follow. In the *Jewish Antiquities*, says Mason, Josephus "offers Judaism as an alternative political constitution and as an alternative philosophical system" (Mason 1998, 80). It is thus no accident that he begins the final volume of the work with a lengthy account of a king who is prepared to accept the offer. This story "at the end of the *Antiquities* narrative serve[s] to fulfill the expectations created at the beginning" (Mason 1998, 94). Readers are invited to emulate King Izates and to confirm for themselves that "those who fix their eyes on [God] and trust in him alone do not lose the reward of their piety" (*Ant.* 20.48).

But who are these readers? Gentiles, certainly. But only a particularly motivated Gentile would be prepared to plow through twenty long volumes of history in order to reach this point. Mason argues that the primary intended readers of *Jewish Antiquities* were Gentiles who already had a strong interest in Judaism but were in need of a more thorough exposition—Gentiles such as we know existed in considerable numbers in Rome at the time. Drawing a parallel with the "protreptic discourse" (λόγος προτρεπτικός), whose purpose was to attract newcomers to philosophy, Mason argues that *Jewish Antiquities* was written as "a primer in Judean law and culture for interested outsiders" (Mason 1998, 97).

This reading of *Jewish Antiquities* is confirmed, Mason claims, by a consideration of *Against Apion*, especially in its relationship to *Jewish Antiquities*. Against Cohen's attempts to drive a wedge between the two, Mason points out that Josephus himself ties them together in the tightest of ways: in the introduction to *Against Apion*, he says that in this new work he "will try again to do what his magnum opus had failed to do" (Mason 1996, 196). In this new work, of course, not only does Josephus present Judaism once again as both a philosophical way of life and an ideal constitution, but he also points with unguarded pride to the extent to which "the masses have long since shown a keen desire to adopt our religious observances" (τῆς ἡμετέρας εὐσεβείας; *Ag. Ap.* 2.282). Mason argues that Josephus's desire to encourage conversion is clearly apparent here; *Against Apion* is therefore also to be seen as a protreptic discourse, whose purpose was "to encourage potential converts to Judaism" (Mason 1996, 222). Further, if Josephus's purposes in *Against Apion* are properly to be seen as a continuation of those at work in *Jewish Antiquities*, then a desire for conversion was at work in his magnum opus as well. He concludes: "Whether Judaism was a missionary religion or not, Josephus tried to be a Judean 'missionary' in Rome."[17]

While the approaches of Cohen and of Mason serve to mark the limits within which Josephus's attitudes and intentions are to be assessed, any assessment needs to wait until we have examined the texts themselves.

Texts and Commentary

Text and translation: LCL (Thackeray, Marcus, and Feldman 1926–65)
Date: Late first century C.E.
Provenance: Rome
Original language: Greek
Bibliography: Barclay (1996, 346–68; 1998); Bilde (1988); Cohen (1979; 1987); Droge (1996); Feldman (1984; 1998); Feldman and Levison (1996); Feldman and Mason (2000); Kasher (1996); Mason (1991, 1996, 1998, 2003); Matthews (2001); Rajak (1983); Schreckenberg (1968; 1979); S. Schwartz (1990); Spilsbury (1998a); Sterling (1992); Wander (1998, 143–54)

§108 Jewish Wars *2.201*

"Either, God aiding me, I shall prevail with Caesar and have the satisfaction of saving myself as well as you, or, if his indignation is roused, I am ready on behalf of the lives of so many to surrender my own."

Category: SYMPATHIZATION

The speaker here is Petronius, the Syrian legate who found himself charged with the task of carrying out Gaius's orders to erect a statue of the emperor in

17. Mason (1996, 223); here he cites approvingly Bilde's earlier suggestion that *Against Apion* had a missionary purpose (Bilde 1988, 120).

the Jerusalem temple. Philo's discussion of the incident, with its emphasis on Petronius's piety, has already been discussed (*Embassy* 245; above §104). Petronius's piety also features strongly in Josephus's account of the incident in *Antiquities*, to be discussed below (§148). In *Jewish War* the theme is muted, appearing only in this passage, where Petronius refers in passing to God's assistance (τοῦ θεοῦ συνεργοῦντος). Since he is addressing Jews, the assumption is that the "God" referred to is somehow held in common by both Petronius and his Jewish hearers. In other words, he is casting his fate into the hands of the Jewish God.

§109 Jewish Wars *2.214*

> *On receiving this message, Claudius . . . went off with them without delay to sacrifice thank-offerings to God on his accession to the empire.*

Category: ETHICAL MONOTHEISM

As is apparent from the passage itself, the context of this statement is the assassination of Gaius and the emergence of Claudius as his successor. The details of the account—including the important part played by Agrippa, the source of the "message" referred to—are not important here. What is significant is the casual way in which Josephus describes Claudius's sacrifice as being offered "to God." This is clearly a pagan sacrifice: it is offered in Rome, presumably in a pagan temple; despite the crucial role played by a Jewish prince, Josephus gives us no indication that Claudius was sacrificing thank-offerings to Agrippa's God. Nevertheless, by speaking of "[the] God" without qualification (τῷ θεῷ), Josephus seems to imply that by engaging in his own religious observance this particular non-Jew was nevertheless worshipping the same "God" revered by the Jews.

§110 Jewish Wars *2.340–41*

> *Having traversed the city and satisfied himself as to the amenable temper of the inhabitants, Neapolitanus went up to the Temple. Here he called the multitude together, highly commended them for their loyalty to the Romans and earnestly exhorted them to keep the peace; then, after paying his devotions to the sanctuary of God from the permitted area, he returned to Cestius.*

Category: SYMPATHIZATION

The first instance in *Jewish War* in which a Gentile venerates the God of the Jews at the Jerusalem temple takes place, somewhat incongruously, as events have begun to spiral irremediably towards war. After the procurator Florus had lost control of Jerusalem, precipitating a massacre and his subsequent withdrawal to Caesarea, Cestius, the governor of Syria, sent the tribune Neapolitanus to investigate the situation in Jerusalem and to return with a report. As Josephus describes the scene, it unfolds as a model of how relations should take place between the Jewish populace and their Roman rulers; Neapolitanus thus serves as a pointed contrast to Florus. With Agrippa II playing an intermediary role, the residents of Jerusalem invite Neapolitanus to tour the city with only a single attendant so that they might have the opportunity to demonstrate by their peaceable reception of him that they "were duly subordinate to all the Roman officials, Florus alone excepted" (*J. W.* 2.340). After this tour had made its intended point, the tribune went to the temple, where he commended the people for their loyalty and then reciprocated by demonstrating reverence (προσκυνήσας) towards the sanctuary of God, taking care to remain within the area allotted to Gentiles for the purpose (ὅθεν ἐξῆν).

Josephus's description is matter-of-fact: the precise form of the reverence exhibited by the tribune remains unspecified, and there is little in the way of editorial comment on his action or attitude. Nevertheless, this does not justify Cohen's conclusion—that no great significance should be attached to the demonstration of reverence since Neapolitanus was simply behaving as a virtuous ruler should (Cohen 1987a, 412–15). While such behavior may have been common practice in the Greco-Roman world, it was just as common for Jews to set themselves apart from generally accepted Greco-Roman religious practices. Thus the matter-of-fact way in which Josephus accepts and commends the tribune's display of reverence at the temple is not without significance, a point that is reinforced by the following passage.

§111 Jewish Wars *2.409–17*

> *Another incident occurred at the same time in the Temple. Eleazar, son of Ananias the high-priest, a very daring youth, then holding the position of captain, persuaded those who officiated in the Temple services to accept no gift or sacrifice from a foreigner. This action laid the foundation of the war with the Romans; for the sacrifices offered on behalf of that nation and the emperor were in consequence rejected. The chief priests and the notables earnestly besought them not to abandon the customary offering for their rulers, but the priests remained obdurate. . . .* [411] *Thereupon the principal citizens assembled with the chief priests and the most notable Pharisees,. . . called the people together . . .* [412] *[and] then proceeded to expose the absurdity of the alleged pretext. Their forefathers, they said, had adorned the sanctuary mainly at the expense of aliens and had always accepted the gifts of foreign nations; not only had they never taken the sacrilegious step of forbidding anyone to offer sacrifice, but they had set up around the Temple the dedicatory offerings which were still to be seen and had remained there for so long a time. . . .* [417] *In the course of these remonstrances they produced priestly experts on the traditions, who declared that all their ancestors had accepted the sacrifices of aliens.*

Category: SYMPATHIZATION

In a previous passage (*J. W.* 2.197), Josephus has mentioned the daily sacrifices offered on behalf of the emperor and the Roman people, but in that instance he described it as if it were completely a Jewish initiative. Indeed, elsewhere he states that the Jews paid for the sacrifices out of their own funds (*Ag. Ap.* 2.77). But the clear implication of the scene described here—Eleazar's new policy of refusing to accept any "gift [δῶρον] or sacrifice [θυσίαν] from a foreigner [ἀλλοτρίου]," which resulted in the cessation of the daily sacrifices for Rome—is that the offerings were underwritten by Rome itself, something confirmed by Philo (*Embassy* 157, 317). Perhaps the money came out of taxes due to Rome, in which case it could be interpreted either way.[18]

There can be little doubt that Josephus is in full sympathy with the position taken by those objecting to Eleazar's innovation; the people allied against the "revolutionary party"—"principal citizens," "chief priests," "notable Pharisees," and "priestly experts"—are precisely his sort of people. Nor can there be much doubt that Josephus is right in his claim that this group had tradition on their side. The Torah assumes that Gentiles may bring animals for sacrifice (Lev 22:25), and—as is amply demonstrated by texts discussed in this work—it was commonly assumed that Gentiles offered gifts and voluntary sacrifices.[19]

But the passage provides evidence for two other attitudes towards Gentile sacrifice that can be differentiated from the traditional view to a greater or lesser extent. On one side stands the opinion of Eleazar. It is important to note that Eleazar's decision was categorical, not circumstantial. What was rejected was not simply the sacrifices made on behalf of the Romans, something that might have been readily understood as a particular response to an egregious situation. Instead, the decision was "to accept no gift or sacrifice from a foreigner"—presumably any foreigner. Even if Rome was the ultimate target, the cessation of the sacrifice for Rome was presented simply as the corollary of a more categorical decision concerning Gentile sacrifices per se. The fact that Eleazar chose this route to achieve his ultimate goal—together with the fact that he was able to garner enough support to carry the day—seems to indicate the presence within Judaism of another opinion concerning the legitimacy of Gentile sacrifice, according to which such offerings were categorically to be rejected.[20] How this position was justified scripturally is not immediately apparent; perhaps Lev 22:25 was subordinated to the more restrictive view found in Ezek 44:7–9.[21]

18. See Smallwood (1981, 148, n. 20).

19. Obligatory sacrifices, of course, were restricted to Jews.

20. 4QMMT (3–7 I, 6, 10) apparently takes a similarly negative attitude toward Gentile sacrifice.

21. In an article on Gentile sacrifices, Schwartz assumes that an uneasy conscience about such sacrifices was widespread among the priests (D. Schwartz 1992). He argues that the temple priests engaged in a kind of mental subterfuge in order to legitimize the practice for themselves. Since Gentiles were barred from actually participating in the sacrifice itself, the priests could think of the sacrificial animals simply as gifts, which they as priests were free to dispose of as they saw fit. While the Gentiles might have thought that they were offering sacrifice, to the priests the sacrifices were being made by the priests themselves. But Schwartz does not provide any real explanation as to the source of this uneasy conscience.

As he relates the opposition to Eleazar's innovation, however, Josephus gives voice to another opinion concerning Gentile sacrifices, one that stands in a sense on the far side of the traditional view. Although he attributes it to the "principal citizens," the "chief priests," and the "most notable Pharisees," it is more probable that it reflects his own particular viewpoint. The argument, as he relates it (*J. W.* 2.414), is that if Eleazar's decision were allowed to stand, the Jews would be "the only people to allow no alien the right of sacrifice or worship" and thus would be "open to the charge of impiety" (ἀσέβειαν). What is interesting here is that acceptance of Gentile worship is justified not on scriptural grounds nor by appeal to the character of Jewish religion itself, but on the basis of a universal standard of piety. The argument assumes that all nations recognize and adhere to a particular standard of piety, one which is incumbent on Judaism as well and by which Jewish practice can be assessed and judged. The argument, in other words, seems to reflect a way of thinking in which Jewish law and tradition is seen as a particular manifestation of a more universally accessible natural law.

It is also important to note that, throughout the passage, sacrifice offered by the Roman emperor is treated simply as an aspect of the more general topic of sacrifice by Gentiles. Neither Eleazar, nor the temple establishment, nor Josephus himself see the sacrifice offered on behalf of the emperor as belonging to a special category, distinct from worship offered by the common Gentile populace. In other words, Cohen's attempt to erect a barrier between the two, so that veneration offered by foreign potentates has nothing to do with Gentile attraction to Judaism,[22] is not consistent with this passage.

§112 Jewish Wars *2.454*

> *Thus, brutally butchered, perished all save Metilius; he alone saved his life by entreaties and promises to turn Jew, and even to be circumcised.*

Category: SYMPATHIZATION, CONVERSION

Metilius was the commander of a Roman garrison that took refuge in the royal towers after the Jerusalem rebels captured the Antonia fortress at the outset of the revolt. Seeing that their situation was hopeless, Metilius negotiated a surrender with Eleazar, one in which they would "surrender their arms and all their belongings" in exchange for their lives (*J. W.* 2. 449–50). Once divested of their weapons, however, they were treacherously set upon by the rebels, who put them all to death—all except Metilius, who in effect saved his skin by being willing to part with a small portion of it. To translate Josephus more precisely, he promised "to Judaize as far as circumcision" (μέχρι περιτομῆς ἰουδαΐσειν).

22. See the discussion in the introduction to this chapter.

Metilius's offer presupposes that Judaization refers to a range of activity that might not extend "as far as circumcision," even though circumcision would mark the extreme end of the range. The passage tells us little about what would be involved in forms of Judaization that fell short of conversion, but the term itself—Ἰουδαΐζειν—will repay some consideration.[23] As we have seen (§11), Cohen has shown that verbs of this pattern, where the ending -ιζειν is added to an ethnic indicator, were used to indicate three ways in which foreigners might accommodate themselves to or show sympathy with the ways of a particular ethnic group: by giving political support, by adopting their customs, and by speaking their language (Cohen 1999, 175–93).

Cohen's analysis is helpful, as is his suggestion that it was the spread of Hellenism—a cultural-political entity which non-Greeks could choose to adopt and into which they could be incorporated as full participants—that provided the model and stimulus for the developing patterns of conversion to Judaism.[24] But, as is apparent in his study of the Metilius incident, he tends to treat the political and the cultural aspects of Judaization (including conversion) as distinct entities—at least to the extent that he is prepared to see individual cases of Judaization as involving one and not the other.[25] We will need to deal with the individual cases as they come up, but one wonders at the outset whether Judaism itself can be so neatly divided into political-civic aspects on the one hand and cultural-religious aspects on the other.

With respect to Metilius, Cohen presents the two aspects as alternatives: "Metilius is promising either to side with the Jews (a political meaning) or to adopt Jewish customs and manners (a cultural meaning)" (Cohen 1999, 183). While he concedes that the promise could be understood in the latter sense—circumcision being a central Jewish custom—he argues instead that the former sense is preferable: "Metilius promises to defect from the Romans and to join the Jews, and as a sign of his change of politics he declares that he is prepared to go as far as circumcision." In support of this reading, he cites a passage a little later in which Josephus describes some Jerusalem Jews who continued to side with the Romans rather than with the Jewish rebels as "those who were still Romanizing (τῶν ἔτι ῥωμαϊζόντων; *J.W.* 2.562).

But while this parallel provides an instructive illustration of the political dimension of the lexical pattern, it should not be allowed to determine the meaning of Ἰουδαΐζειν in the earlier passage. The Jewish and Roman nations were quite different as political-cultural entities, and a determination of what it might have meant to "Judaize" or to "Romanize" will depend not only on the

23. Josephus also uses the term in *J.W.* 2.463 (see the next entry) but omits it in his account of the Esther story (*Ant.* 11.285; see §132 below).

24. Cohen 1999, 109–39; see also ch. 1 above.

25. Cohen's position is dependent to a certain extent on that of Smith (1996).

constituent circumstances in individual cases but also on the distinctive characters of the Jewish and Roman entities. Neither Josephus nor his Gentile readers would have seen a promise to be circumcised simply as a military defection or a shift in political allegiance. Because of the cultural and religious significance of circumcision within Judaism, Metilius's proposed course of action necessarily carried with it cultural and religions implications. Presumably he was motivated by a desire for self-preservation rather than an admiration for Jewish culture or a desire to worship the Jewish God. Nevertheless, what he was proposing to do to preserve his life was to identify fully with the Judeans, a social entity that was as much cultural and religious as it was political.

Of course, given the isolated character of the event, we have no way of confirming that it actually happened. It is by no means implausible. Josephus simply reports the incident without attaching any rhetorical significance to it, which suggests that the account did not originate with him. Further, an event that was part of the decisive early slide toward war could well have been widely reported and remembered. In any case, at least as Josephus presents the scene and as his readers would have understood it, what Metilius was proposing in exchange for his life was to become a convert. But given the terms of his proposal—conversion as an extreme form of Judaization—the assumption underlying his proposal is that one could Judaize—that is, identify with the Jewish community as a political, cultural and religious entity—in ways that stopped short of full conversion. Thackeray's translation, with its implication that one could "turn Jew" (i.e., become a full convert) without circumcision, is misleading.

§113 Jewish Wars *2.462–63*

> *For, though believing that they had rid themselves of the Jews, still each city had its Judaizers, who aroused suspicion; and while they shrunk from killing offhand this equivocal element in their midst, they feared these neutrals as much as pronounced aliens.*

Category: SYMPATHIZATION

At the same time as the Jewish rebels were taking control of Jerusalem, Josephus reports that there was a massacre of the Jewish population at Caesarea (*J.W.* 2.457). This precipitated fierce conflict in city after city: "every city was divided into two camps, and the safety of one party lay in their anticipating the other" (*J.W.* 2. 462). There were bloody reprisals against Gentiles in various Hellenistic cities in Judea and further slaughter of Jews in Syrian towns and cities. It is in this latter context that Josephus mentions the situation of people who fell somehow in between the "two camps" (δύο στρατόπεδα). The passage contains the second of the two appearances of Ἰουδαΐζειν in Josephus.

The first question to be faced concerns the number of groups in view. The Greek original of the passage cited above comprises three principal clauses linked by καί, with different descriptive terms in each: τοὺς ἰουδαΐζοντας (the

Judaizers); τὸ παρ' ἑκάστοις ἀμφίβολον (the ambiguous element alongside each of them); and μεμιγμένον (mixed). Thackeray's translation, cited above, takes the three terms as referring to a single group, made up of Gentiles whose Jewish sympathies result in "equivocal" loyalties or a "neutral" stance in the conflict. Smith, however, has interpreted the three differently worded clauses as referring to three distinct groups—those who had unambiguously adopted Jewish practices; those who were suspected of Jewish sympathies; and those of mixed (i.e., Jewish and Gentile) ancestry (Smith 1996, 316–17, n. 161). Cohen, persuaded by Smith in part, has argued instead for two groups—Judaizing Gentiles on the one hand, and an ambiguous group of mixed ancestry on the other.[26]

But the suggestion of a plurality of groups is unconvincing in either form. First, Smith speaks of "*to memigmenon*," taking the participle as a substantive ("the mixed element") even though no article is present.[27] Without an article, however, the participle has to be taken as circumstantial, so that the clause is linked to what precedes: "and although it was a mixed element, each one feared [it][28] as if it were decidedly foreign." Thus Cohen is right in taking the latter two clauses as referring to the same group. But there is no compelling reason to take this group as distinct from the Judaizers. For one thing, while each of the three clauses makes some reference to the attitude of the Gentile inhabitants, there is no real distinction to be made among the three. Each of the clauses describes an action or attitude that stands in contrast to their actions against the Jews, whom they slaughtered outright: they were suspicious, they were not prepared to go as far as killing, and they feared. A single stance seems to be in view, which suggests a single object. Further, the description of the group in the second clause—"the ambiguous element in their midst"—is itself so vague in comparison with "the Judaizers" that it is difficult to see it as introducing a distinct group. Finally, nowhere does Josephus use μείγνυμι to refer to mixed ancestry. The term denotes mixtures of various kinds[29] and, while its use here is determined by its contrast to ἀλλόφυλον (foreign), mixed ancestry is by no means

26. Cohen (1999, 184–85). In an earlier article (Cohen 1987, 416), he took the three clauses as referring to a single group.

27. Cohen (1999, 184, n. 38) rightly criticizes Smith on this point, though it is to be noted that in his earlier article he added an article to μεμιγμένον, albeit in brackets (Cohen 1987, 416).

28. The participle thus is tied to the direct object of ἐφοβεῖτο, unstated but understood. Cohen's rendering, in which the unstated element is taken as the subject of the verb ("it was feared as if it were truly foreign, although it was mixed"), is unlikely. φοβέω in the middle and passive normally has the sense "to (be seized with) fear, to be afraid of," with an object in the accusative (see LSJ *ad loc.*).

29. E.g., hot and cold water (*J.W.* 7.189), good wishes and prayers (*Ant.* 15.52), arguments of different kinds (*Ag. Ap.* 2.7), as well as the mingling of bodies in sexual intercourse (*J.W.* 1.498; *Ant.* 3.274; 16.256) and of armies in battle (J.W. 5.487; 6.77). Cohen and Smith are right, however, in rejecting Thackeray's rendering "neutral."

the only way in which a group might fall between the "two camps" of foreigners and citizens.

Thus it is probable that Josephus has a single group in view here—or, since he is generalizing about the situation in cities throughout Syria, a set of groups that he treats as a single phenomenon. As in the previous passage, Josephus does not attach any rhetorical valence to the account, a fact that is significant in two respects. First, even though the phenomenon is connected with "the troubles which befell the Jews in the cities of Syria" (Cohen 1987a, 417), there is no indication that Josephus is therefore critical of the phenomenon itself. Cohen's attempt to read the passage in this way is not convincing. Second, the absence of any explicit rhetorical agenda in the passage means that we can read it as a straightforward account of the phenomenon as Josephus perceived it.

What can we say about these Judaizers? Clearly their Judaizing had not reached the point of full assimilation. Otherwise, they would have shared the fate of the Jews. Evidently they were perceived as distinct from the Jewish community, which is in keeping with Josephus's description of the group as existing "alongside" (παρ' ἑκάστοις) the Gentiles rather than as in the other "camp." But what was it that made the group "ambiguous"? In what way was it "mixed," as opposed to belonging to one "camp" or the other? Again Cohen sets out two possibilities—either siding with the Jews politically or adopting Jewish customs; again he treats them as distinct alternatives and opts for the political. Of course, Cohen is dealing here only with the "Judaizers," whom he sees as distinct from the "ambiguous," "mixed" group. But if we see only a single phenomenon in view here, then the fact that Josephus contrasts "mixed" with "foreign" seems to favor a more cultural reading. A foreign group that adopts a political stance vis-à-vis one's enemy (for or against) does not thereby become any more or less "foreign." If it is necessary to choose between the cultural and the political—a choice that would in any case be a matter simply of emphasis—it is more likely that cultural sympathy is in view here. The Judaizers had adopted some Jewish practices and thus became an "ambiguous" entity in a polarized environment, an entity characterized by a mixture of cultural identity markers and religious observances.[30]

§114 Jewish Wars *2.521 (and passim)*

. . . Simon, son of Giora . . .

Category: CONVERSION

This marks the first appearance of Simon, one of the leaders of the Jewish rebellion. Giora (Γιώρα) is probably a transliteration of גיורא, the Aramaic equivalent of גר (proselyte). This is clearer in two other references, where we find the

30. They "mixed Jewish customs with those of the pagans" (Feldman 1993, 350).

full Aramaic form "bar-Giora" (son of the proselyte). One is found as a textual variant in Tacitus (*Bargioram*; *Hist.* 5.12), though here the term is mistakenly attributed to John; the other appears in Dio Cassius (Βαργιορᾶς; *Hist.* 66.7.1). Josephus, however, chooses not to use "bar," replacing it with υἱός or the genitive. In no case does he comment on Simon's origins or identify him as the son of a proselyte.[31] Still, there can be little doubt that this was the origin of the appellation. If so, the case of Simon the rebel leader indicates both that the son of a proselyte could become deeply involved in Jewish affairs and that proselyte origins could continue to be a mark of identification into the second generation.

§115 Jewish Wars *2.559–61*

> *Meanwhile, the people of Damascus, learning of the disaster which had befallen the Romans, were fired with a determination to kill the Jews who resided among them. As they had for a long time past kept them shut up in the gymnasium—a precaution prompted by suspicion—they considered that the execution of their plan would present no difficulty whatever; their only fear was of their own wives who, with few exceptions, had all become converts to the Jewish religion, and so their efforts were mainly directed to keeping the secret from them.*

Category: SYMPATHIZATION

This incident takes place a little later in the narrative, after the rout of Cestius's army. It is another example of the ethnic conflict that Josephus has been describing as raging throughout the cities of Syria. In contrast to his generalized description of the situation in the cities of Syria, where he speaks of an undefined company of "Judaizers" (see the preceding entry), here he presents us with a very specific group—the women of Damascus, almost all of whom "had been drawn away [ὑπηγμένας] to the Jewish religious observances [τῇ Ἰουδαϊκῇ θρησκείᾳ]." Because of their Jewish sympathies, their husbands had to keep secret from them their plans to slaughter the Damascene Jews.

The scenario is undoubtedly exaggerated. Were there really only a few out of all the women of Damascus who had not adopted Jewish customs? Did these women have no success whatsoever in persuading their husbands to join with them? Were there no male sympathizers or converts in Damascus? Still, if its exaggerations are trimmed away, the passage is generally consistent with the picture that emerges from other passages in Josephus, where we find references both to the presence of Gentile sympathizers with Judaism in Syrian cities and to the special attractiveness of Judaism to Gentile women.[32]

31. The appellation appears also in *J.W.* 2.652; 4.503; 5.11; 6.114; 7.25, 154, 265.

32. Feldman (1993, 328) suggests that the animosity of the husbands against the Jews was fueled by their success in attracting converts. The fact that Roman writers could express animosity against the Jews for this reason (see ch. 7 below) means that the suggestion cannot be dismissed out of hand. Still, the widespread character of ethnic conflict throughout

Thackeray describes these women as having become converts, but this is perhaps too categorical a rendering. The verb is a form of ὑπάγω, whose most basic meaning is to lead or bring under. What these women had been led to "come under" was "the Jewish θρησκεία"—the set of religious rituals and observances that characterize "the Jews."[33] One could imagine a proselyte being described in these terms—one who had taken on the characteristic rituals and observances of the Jews—and so the clause as a whole could plausibly be understood as describing conversion. However, the line between sympathizer and convert is much blurrier in the case of women, for whom circumcision, the decisive mark of conversion, is not a possibility. Further, these women clearly have not been assimilated into the Jewish community. It is better, then, to think of them as sympathizers rather than as converts,[34] though presumably there would have been a considerable range of adherence to Judaism within their ranks.

As in the previous passage, although Josephus refers to these sympathizers in the context of a narrative that recounts difficulties experienced by the Jewish population at the hands of Gentile citizens, there is no indication that Josephus saw any sort of causal link between the two. Indeed, the widespread sympathy for Judaism among the women of Damascus actually served to hinder the maltreatment of the Jews.

§116 Jewish Wars *3.444*

> *There for twenty days he rested his troops, while he was being fêted himself and rendering thankofferings to God for the successes which he had obtained.*

Category: ETHICAL MONOTHEISM

The one offering thanks to God here is Vespasian, who has retired to Caesarea Philippi for a little rest and relaxation (and religion) after a successful first phase of the war in Judea. As with the incident involving Claudius discussed above (*J.W.* 2.214), it is clearly pagan sacrifice that is in view. Again Josephus speaks of it without qualification as sacrifice offered "to [the] God" (τῷ θεῷ). Somehow he can conceive of Gentiles offering appropriate worship to "God" by engaging in their own forms of religious observance.

Syria at this time means that proselytizing success would have been at most just one factor among many.

33. θρησκεία appears in *Jewish War*, usually in the singular (*J.W.* 7.45 is one exception), sometimes of Jewish religious observance generally (e.g., 2.198, 391; 7.45), sometimes of temple worship in general (e.g., 4.324; 5.198, 199; 6.100, 442) and sometimes of particular observances (e.g., Sabbath [1.146; 2.456]; Passover [2.10]; Pentecost [2.42]; temple sacrifice [1.148, 150; 4.275; 5.229; 6.427]). In the passage under discussion, the term refers to Jewish religious practice in general.

34. See Cohen (1987a, 417) and Feldman (1993, 328).

§117 Jewish Wars *4.181*

> *Is it not enough to bring tears to the eyes to see on the one hand in our Temple courts the very votive offerings of the Romans, on the other the spoils of our fellow countrymen who have plundered and slain the nobility of the metropolis, massacring men whom even the Romans, if victorious, would have spared?*

Category: SYMPATHIZATION

This reference to Roman respect for the temple appears in a speech (*J. W.* 4.163–92) delivered to the Jerusalem populace by Ananus the high priest, shortly after the Zealot insurgents had taken control of the temple and chosen their own high priest.[35] It can be inferred from Josephus's admiration of Ananus[36] that he fully endorsed the words that he placed in the high priest's mouth.

In the speech Ananus expresses a theme that will recur throughout the narrative. He draws a contrast between Roman respect for the temple and Jewish religion on the one hand, and the desecration wreaked by the Jewish rebels on the other (*J. W.* 4.180–84). He observes ironically that the Romans, who always took care not to overstep the boundary restricting Gentile access to the temple, appear as the upholders of the law, while the Jewish rebels who had encamped within the sanctuary turn out to be its enemies. It is in this context that he refers to votive offerings that had been donated by the Romans and set up in the temple, contrasting this visible sign of veneration for the Jewish God with the spoils of war (τὰ σκῦλα) that the Jewish rebels had stripped from the bodies of their murdered co-religionists and had set out on display.

§118 Jewish Wars *4.262*

> *That has now become their base and refuge, the magazine for their armament against us; and the spot which is revered by the world and honoured by aliens from the ends of the earth who have heard its fame, is trampled on by these monsters engendered in this very place.*

Category: SYMPATHIZATION

This passage is similar both in form and in theme to the preceding. Again it appears in the context of a speech, this time one given by Jesus, "the chief priest next in seniority to Ananus" (*J. W.* 4.238), to a company of Idumeans who have been summoned by the Zealot insurgents to help them in their struggle for control of Jerusalem. Idumea seems to have been caught up in the same kind of conflict between the ruling class and revolutionary groups (*J. W.* 2.653–54).

35. It is only at this point that Josephus begins to use "Zealot" as the name of a distinct group; see Donaldson (1990).

36. See Josephus's lament over Ananus's death in *J. W.* 4.318–23.

The group of Idumeans who come into view here apparently represent a revolutionary faction who are just as eager as the Zealots to fight for freedom from the Romans and who are thus the Zealots' natural allies (*J. W.* 4.231–34).[37] The chief priests have barred the city gates, but before resorting to armed defense they decide to attempt persuasion, specifically by means of a speech addressed by Jesus to the Idumeans gathered outside the walls of the city (*J. W.* 4.239–69).

Jesus appeals to the Idumeans not to provide support to the Zealots but to choose one of three alternative courses of action: to join with the moderates against the desecration of the revolutionary faction, to enter the city "in the form of kinsmen" (σχήματι συγγενῶν; *J. W.* 4.265) in order to play the role of neutral arbiter, or to withdraw and allow the other two groups to fight it out on their own (*J. W.* 4. 258–69). (The description of the Idumeans as kinsmen is interesting and will come up for more attention in the next entry.)

In the context of the speech, again a contrast is drawn between Gentile reverence towards the temple and Zealot desecration. This time the reference is not simply to the Romans but to the whole inhabited world (τῆς οἰκουμένης) and to foreigners (ἀλλοφύλοις) who have come from the ends of the earth (ἀπὸ περάτων γῆς). The fame of the temple has spread to such an extent that it is "revered" (προσκυνούμενος) by the world and "honoured" (τετιμημένος) by foreigners. In contrast to such universal veneration, the Zealots, says Jesus, have turned the sanctuary into storehouse for weapons and a refuge for villains.

§119 Jewish Wars *4.275*

> *At any rate, this city, which flung wide its gates to every foreigner for worship, is now barricaded by you against your own people.*

Category: SYMPATHIZATION, CONVERSION

This passage represents a variant on the theme that has come to expression in the two preceding passages. This time the speaker is Simon, the leader of the Idumeans, who is responding to the speech of Jesus; and this time the target of the pointed contrast between Gentile reverence and Jewish impiety is not the Zealots but the more moderate party led by Ananus and Jesus.

In *Antiquities*, Josephus describes how the Idumeans submitted to circumcision and the Jewish law after their territory was annexed by John Hyrcanus (*Ant.* 13.257–58; §139 below). In this section of the *Jewish War*, however, he simply takes it for granted that the Idumeans and the Judeans are co-religionists.

37. Josephus gives the impression that the Idumeans as a whole were eager for revolution, but his account earlier of attempts by the "local magistrates" to defend the countryside against the activity of Simon bar Giora (*J. W.* 2.652–54) seems to suggest a society just as divided as that of Jerusalem.

In his own narration of the Idumean incursion, he describes Jerusalem as their "mother city" (μητρόπολις; *J.W.* 4.234), a usage that is repeated three times in Jesus's speech to them (*J.W.* 4.239, 245, 258). Further, as noted above, one of the courses of action that Jesus proposes to the Idumeans is that they lay down their weapons and enter the city not as combatants but as kinfolk (σχήματι συγγενῶν), playing the role of neutral arbiters (*J.W.* 4.265). In his reply, Simon continues the theme, describing himself and the Idumeans as "fellow-countrymen" (ὁμοφύλων) and "nearest kinsfolk" (συγγενεστάτοις), referring to Jerusalem as the "mother city" and characterizing temple worship as their shared patrimony (τῶν πατρίων ἱερῶν; *J.W.* 4.276, 278, 279). Thus in the passage under discussion here, Simon's characterization of himself and the Idumeans as "your own people"—people of the same household or family (τοῖς οἰκείοις)—is part of a theme running through the whole narrative.

It is this assumption—that the Idumeans are kinsfolk and not foreigners—that gives shape to Simon's derisive reply. He mocks Jesus and his company for daring to prevent their own kinsfolk from entering the city, even as they conspire secretly to admit the Romans. Throwing Jesus's own rhetoric back at him (see *J.W.* 4.262), Simon also points to the tradition of Gentile participation in temple worship and uses it as a way of accusing Jesus and his group—instead of the Zealots—of betraying temple ideals. While the city has always "flung wide its gates to every foreigner [ἅπασι τοῖς ἀλλοφύλοις] for worship," Jesus's group keeps the gates firmly closed, even "against your own people."

This speech, like the ones by Jesus and Ananus before it, is Josephus's own composition. While these events were taking place, he was Vespasian's prisoner of war in Galilee. Although he no doubt had his sources of information on what transpired in Jerusalem, these speeches tell us more about Josephus's own perceptions than about the people on whose lips they appear.

Still, two aspects of Josephus's perceptions are of particular interest here. One is his presentation of the Idumeans. He treats them as members of the Jewish family, heir to the same traditions and oriented around the same mother city. Further, he assumes this to be the view of Judean priests and Idumeans alike. The second aspect has to do with Gentile worship at the temple. In this passage, as in the two preceding ones, Josephus takes it for granted that Gentiles admired the temple, that they came regularly and in considerable numbers to participate in its worship, and that such worshipers were warmly welcomed by the Jews. Further, the way in which this theme is used rhetorically in these three passages indicates that he takes considerable pride in the tradition; only if such Gentile participation in temple worship were highly valued would it be useful as a stick to beat Jewish groups whose actions were perceived or portrayed as a betrayal of temple ideals. And again, Josephus assumes that his views are widely shared by his compatriots.

§120 Jewish Wars *4.324*

> *So they who but lately had worn the sacred vestments, led those ceremonies of world-wide significance and been reverenced by visitors to the city from every quarter of the earth, were now seen cast out naked, to be devoured by dogs and beasts of prey.*

Category: SYMPATHIZATION

This statement appears a little further in the narrative, after the Idumeans gained access to the city and joined forces with the Zealots to overthrow the moderate party and to take control of the city. After Ananus and Jesus are killed, Josephus reflects at length on the significance of their death for the course of events that followed (*J. W.* 4.318–25).[38] The passage under discussion here, referring to the shameful way in which the bodies of Ananus and Jesus were discarded without burial, forms part of his reflection.

Again a contrast is drawn between the positive significance of the Jerusalem temple for the Gentile world and the negative behavior of Jewish combatants. On the negative side of the contrast, while it is the Idumeans who are primarily responsible for the death of the high priests, Josephus treats them not simply as allies of the Zealots but explicitly as part of the larger Jewish community; they are kinfolk (τὴν συγγένειαν) of the Judeans, and with them they share a "common temple" (τοῦ κοινοῦ ἱεροῦ; *J. W.* 4.311). On the positive side, the high priests, now treated with such ignominy, were until recently venerated (προσκυνούμενοι) by people who had come to the city "from the whole inhabited world" (ἐκ τῆς οἰκουμένης). The worldwide significance of the Jerusalem cult is also indicated—albeit ambiguously—in the description of Jerusalem worship (θρησκείας) as κοσμικῆς. Thackeray has suggested that a parallel might be found in two texts from *Antiquities*, where Josephus describes both the tabernacle and the vestments of the high priest as having universal or cosmic significance,[39] but this is improbable. These other cases have to do not with religious observance (θρησκεία) but with physical objects (the tabernacle; the vestments of the high priest; cultic vessels). Further, in these cases universal significance is expressed not by κοσμικός—found nowhere else in Josephus—but by a form of ὅλος. Even apart from these considerations, evidence from a work written considerably later should be treated with considerable caution, especially when the context provides us with a perfectly plausible reading: the ceremonies can be described as κοσμικῆς precisely because they were attended by people "from the whole inhabited world."

38. "I should not be wrong in saying that the capture of the city began with the death of Ananus. . . . In a word, had Ananus lived," the outcome would have been significantly different (J.W. 4.318, 321).

39. *Ant.* 3.123, 180. See Thackeray's footnote to the passage.

The main point, however, is that this passage reinforces the theme found in the previous three passages concerning the universal appeal of the Jerusalem temple.

§121 Jewish Wars *5.15–18*

For although these frenzied men had stopped short of no impiety, they nevertheless admitted those who wished to offer sacrifices, native Jews suspiciously and with precaution, strangers after a thorough search; yet these, though successful at the entrances in deprecating their cruelty, often became casual victims of the sedition. For the missiles from the engines flew over with such force that they reached the altar and the sanctuary, lighting upon priests and sacrificers; and many who had sped from the ends of the earth to gather round this far-famed spot, reverenced by all mankind, fell there themselves before their sacrifices, and sprinkled with libations of their own blood that altar universally venerated by Greeks and barbarians. The dead bodies of natives and aliens, of priests and laity, were mingled in a mass, and the blood of all manner of corpses formed pools in the courts of God.

Category: SYMPATHIZATION

The context of this passage is the internal conflict that emerged within Jerusalem after the revolutionary group had split into three factions (under Eleazar son of Simon, John of Gischala and Simon bar Giora) but before the arrival of Titus. The scene as Josephus describes it is somewhat hard to imagine—Jewish and Gentile worshippers being prepared to risk death in order to offer sacrifice in a temple that had become a battlefield. Any of these who had come from outside Jerusalem would have had to traverse, successively, terrain held by three rival combatants—the city, held by Simon; the outer temple court, under the control of John; and the sanctuary proper, held by Eleazar. While none of the groups, presumably, would have wanted to be seen as preventing temple worship from continuing,[40] the worshippers themselves, after the first deaths, would inevitably have been increasingly unwilling to put themselves at risk. This would have been especially true of Gentiles, who, unlike Jews, were not under the same obligations to worship at the temple. While there may well have been some deaths, Josephus's presentation of this as an

40. According to *J. W.* 6.94, the daily sacrifice was offered continually right up to the final weeks of the war. The textual variant in *J. W.* 5.15, which has the revolutionaries admitting "native Jews after a suspicious and cautious search, strangers with less apprehension" (τοὺς δὲ ξένους ἀδεέστερον; see Thackeray's note), seems more plausible than the text cited above. In these circumstances, the rebel groups would have been more suspicious of Jews than of Gentiles. The variant is adopted by Williamson and Smallwood (1981).

ongoing phenomenon, resulting in many casualties,[41] should probably be seen as an exaggeration, especially in the case of Gentiles.

Exaggerated or not, the passage continues the theme sounded in previous passages, in which the impiety of the Jewish rebels is emphasized by means of ironic contrast with the veneration demonstrated towards the temple by Gentile worshippers. The temple is "reverenced by all mankind" (πᾶσιν ἀνθρώποις ἅγιον), "venerated" (σεβάσμιον) by all Greeks and barbarians. "Strangers" (τοὺς ξένους) have come to worship "from the ends of the earth." When the worshippers fell victim to the battle, the bodies of "aliens" (ἀλλόφυλοι) were mixed with natives, those of priests with lay people.

Throughout the passage, Josephus assumes that his readers are well aware of the temple's reputation as a place venerated by Gentiles from near and far. In the editorial aside that follows (*J.W.* 5.19–20), one can see how he uses this theme as part of a larger program of vilification and theodicy: the "pollution" of the temple by the revolutionaries, which appears even more heinous when seen in contrast to the veneration of the temple by pious Gentiles, has made it necessary for God to use the Romans to "purge [it] with fire."

§122 Jewish Wars *5.519*

> *When Titus, going his rounds, beheld these valleys choked with dead and the thick matter oozing from under the clammy carcases, he groaned and, raising his hands to heaven, called God to witness that this was not his doing.*

Category: ETHICAL MONOTHEISM

This grim scene takes place when the siege of Jerusalem has almost reached its climax and the bodies of those who had died from hunger and civil strife have been simply tossed over the walls into the ravines. Describing Titus's dismay at the sight, Josephus depicts him as calling on God to witness that the responsibility for this horror lay with the rebels, not with the Romans and their general. As in the cases of Claudius and Vespasian above (§§109, 116), we encounter a non-Jew who elsewhere in Josephus's account exhibits no sympathies towards Jewish life and practice but whose pagan piety he describes as being offered to "[the] God."[42] Here the expression of piety is different, involving lament rather than sacrifice. But the point is the same: Gentiles can revere the true God by means of their own religious observance and practice.

41. Note the "many" of *J.W.* 5.17, the confused tangle of bodies in 5.18, and the implication of the imperfect ἐγίνοντο (5.15; which Thackeray renders as "often became") that this happened repeatedly.

42. Something similar may be at work in two of the famous decrees cited in *Antiquities* 14, in which the people of Halicarnassus (*Ant.* 14.257) and of Sardis (*Ant.* 14.260) describe Jewish religious observance as being directed "to God" (τῷ θεῷ). But since Josephus does not elaborate on this aspect of the decrees, the references probably do not tell us much about *Jewish* patterns of universalism. On the decrees in general, see Rajak (1985).

§123 Jewish Wars *5.562–64*

John, when the plunder from the people failed him, had recourse to sacrilege, melting down many of the temple-offerings and many of the vessels required for public worship, bowls and salvers and tables; nor did he abstain from the vessels for pure wine sent by Augustus and his consort. For the Roman sovereigns ever honoured and added embellishments to the temple, whereas this Jew now pulled down even the donations of foreigners, remarking to his companions that they should not scruple to employ divine things on the Divinity's behalf, and that those who fought for the Temple should be supported by it.

Category: SYMPATHIZATION

This passage appears during Josephus's account of the final siege of Jerusalem. One of the by-products of the siege, of course, was famine, and Josephus has recounted in great detail the desperate measures to which people would resort to attain food and the atrocities inflicted on the starving populace by the rebels and their leaders (*J. W.* 4.420–45, 512–18). John's plunder of the temple is set against this background; when there was nothing left to plunder from the people themselves, he turned to the temple, appropriating for his own use not only the vessels and votive offerings but also the sacred wine and oil (*J. W.* 5.565).

Josephus expresses horror at this sacrilege (ἱεροσυλίαν), going on to imply that the Romans served as God's instruments of punishment. "I believe that, had the Romans delayed to punish these reprobates," he declares, Jerusalem would have been swallowed up like Korah and his band of rebels (Num 16:32) or swept away in a flood like Noah's generation or incinerated like Sodom (*J. W.* 5.566). Once again he appeals to the theme of Gentile veneration to make his point stand out even more sharply.[43] Among the items appropriated by John were gifts given by Augustus and Livia. Josephus draws an explicit contrast between the impious arrogance of "this Jew," who plundered "the donations of foreigners" (τὰ τῶν ἀλλοφύλων), and the Roman emperors, who "ever honoured [ἐτίμησαν] and added embellishment to the temple." The sacrilege of the Jewish rebels is even more reprehensible when set alongside the piety of the Romans.

§124 Jewish Wars *7.45*

Continuing to receive similar treatment from later monarchs, the Jewish colony grew in numbers, and their richly designed and costly offerings formed a splendid ornament to the temple. Moreover, they were constantly attracting to their religious ceremonies multitudes of Greeks, and these they had in some measure incorporated with themselves.

Category: SYMPATHIZATION, CONVERSION

43. This passage deals only with veneration exhibited by foreign rulers, with no explicit reference to Gentile worship in general. Nevertheless, the rhetorical structure is the same as in previous passages dealing with Gentile worship, which works against Cohen's attempt to treat foreign potentates as a special category (Cohen 1987a, 417).

The larger context in which this passage is found deals with a difficult situation faced by the Jewish community in Antioch shortly after the fall of Jerusalem. A serious fire broke out in the center of the city, the Jews were blamed, and there was a threat of imminent violence against them. The primary instigator of the anti-Jewish fury was a certain Jewish apostate by the name of Antiochus. In order to provide the background for this situation, Josephus finds it necessary to relate an earlier incident of anti-Jewish violence, also instigated by Antiochus. The passage under discussion here is part of this flashback.

The earlier incident took place "just at the time when war had been declared and Vespasian had recently landed in Syria, and when hatred of the Jews was everywhere at its height" (*J. W.* 7.46). In other words, this incident was contemporaneous with those discussed already (*J. W.* 2.462–63, 559–61), part of the ethnic conflict that took place in city after city at the start of the war. Presumably Josephus chose to delay the narrative so that he could link it to this later incidence of conflict in Antioch.

As already mentioned, the link between the two was the Jewish apostate Antiochus. The son of the leading member of the Jewish community in Antioch, he publicly renounced his patrimony and sacrificed to Greek gods. Accusing the Jews of a plot to set fire to the city, he used the resultant uproar to incite both Greek and Roman officials to take repressive measures against the Jews. Or at least this is the way Josephus tells the story (*J. W.* 7.46–53). But the alacrity with which the general populace followed his lead indicates that, as in other Syrian cities, anti-Jewish sentiment was sufficiently widespread that there probably would have been ethnic conflict even apart from the agitation of a Jewish apostate.

In Josephus's account, Antiochus stands as a negative counterpart to the "multitudes [πολὺ πλῆθος] of Greeks" who had come to be associated with the Jewish community. He introduces this group as the final detail in a description of the way in which the Jewish community had grown and thrived since the dark days of the apostate's namesake, Antiochus IV Epiphanes (*J. W.* 7.44–45). Antiochus's successors restored Jewish property, granted them rights of citizenship, and provided an environment in which the Jewish community could expand, prosper, and even draw Greeks into its corporate and religious life.

There are several observations to be made about Josephus's description of this phenomenon. First, while Thackeray's translation speaks of Gentiles being attracted to Jewish worship,[44] the Greek (προσαγόμενοι) suggests a more active role: the Jews were "leading" the Greeks "to" the religious ceremonies. The main verb attributes just as active a role to the Jews: to some measure they "incorporated" the Greeks with themselves. Josephus seems to see the presence of Gentile adherents as the result not simply of passive attraction but of a more

44. See also Williamson and Smallwood (1981).

active initiative on the part of the Jewish community. While the term "mission" is probably to be avoided, Josephus's own language suggests a posture more of active initiative than of passive attraction.[45]

Second, there is considerable ambiguity in the way in which this large group of Greeks is described. The ambiguity is reflected in the fact that some interpreters have seen them as converts (e.g., Cohen 1987a, 417) while others (e.g., Feldman 1993, 350) see them as sympathizers. On the one hand, these Gentiles identified with Judaism both by adopting the "religious observances" (ταῖς θρησκείαις) of the Jews[46] and by being incorporated into their community—made part of them (μοῖραν αὐτων πεποίηντο). The identification is thus both religious and social. Josephus is speaking not simply of the adoption of customs and religious observances, but of social incorporation. Still, the description seems to fall short of full incorporation: the Greeks were incorporated "in a certain manner" (τρόπῳ τινί) into the community. This qualification might be taken to suggest that Josephus intends these Greeks to be seen as adherents or sympathizers, rather than as full converts. Still, it is perhaps significant that he speaks of "manner" rather than of extent. Even if we were dealing with full proselytes, a "multitude" of them would not simply blend into the Jewish community without a trace; instead, it would inevitably be incorporated "in a certain manner." Perhaps the significant thing here is that Josephus is speaking of the Gentile group as a whole rather than to individuals within it. One should expect that such a group as is described here would include various levels of adherence, so that at least some would have been led fully into Jewish life—that is, would have become full converts. It is not part of Josephus's narrative purpose here to make these finer distinctions within the larger group. Probably we should read the passage as presenting us with a large group of Gentiles associated with the Jewish community and containing within it a range of adhesion and incorporation.

Third, it is again to be noted that Josephus does not seem to attach any value judgment to the phenomenon. He does not use it to score other rhetorical points; even the contrast between the Gentile adherents and the Jewish apostate is implicit. In particular, he gives no indication that the presence of Gentile adherents led to negative consequences for the Jews. Indeed, unlike the similar accounts concerning other Syrian cities, in this case, Gentile sympathizers seem to play no role at all in the ethnic conflict.

45. Cf. McKnight (1991, 65).

46. For θρησκεία, see n. 33 above. Josephus uses the term to refer both to specific observances and to Jewish religious life in general. Since the term is often used of temple worship, in view of the reference to the temple in the preceding clause it is tempting to read the sentence as saying that the Gentiles were being "led" to the temple and its worship. But since the main clause speaks more generally of incorporation into Jewish life, probably ταῖς θρησκείαις is to be taken generally as well.

§125 Antiquities *3.214–17*

> [Moses] *left to God supreme authority whether to attend the sacred rites, when it so pleased Him, or to absent himself; and this he wished to be made manifest not to Hebrews only but also to any strangers who happened to be present. . . .* [216]*By means of the twelve stones, which the high-priest wore upon his breast stitched into the* essen, *God foreshadowed victory to those on the eve of battle. For so brilliant a light flashed out from them, ere the army was yet in motion, that it was evident to the whole host that God had come to their aid. Hence it is that those Greeks who revere our practices, because they can in no way gainsay them, call the* essen *logion ("oracle").*

Category: SYMPATHIZATION

The first passage of interest in *Antiquities* appears just as Josephus has completed his account of the events at Sinai, including a lengthy description of the tabernacle, the ark, and the vestments of the high priest (*Ant.* 3.102–87). He will follow this with a survey of Mosaic legislation (*Ant.* 3.224–86), but he bridges these two sections with a brief narrative recounting the appointment of Aaron, the dedication of the tabernacle, and the start of normal cultic activity (*Ant.* 3.188–223). In the middle of this intervening narrative he provides a brief encomium on Moses as a legislator, emphasizing both his humility and his dependence on the inspiration of God (*Ant.* 3.212–14). Perhaps it is this reference to divine inspiration that prompts Josephus to return to the topic of the high priest's vestments (*Ant.* 3.214–18), and in particular to the marvelous stones by which the divine presence and will were made manifest.

The description of the high priest's vestments in Exodus 28 refers to two sets of precious stones, both of which contain the names of the twelve tribes—two onyx stones on the shoulder of the high priest's ephod (Exod 28:6–14) and twelve stones on the breastplate (Exod 28:17–21). In Josephus's version, which seems to reflect post-biblical interpretive traditions (Feldman and Mason 2000, 288–89), both sets of stones were designed by Moses in such a way that they shone with a brilliant divine light in certain circumstances.[47] With respect to the first set, which he mistakenly equates with the Urim and Thummim (cf. Exod 28:30),[48] Josephus states that one of the two stones, presumably the Urim,[49] would begin to shine whenever God chose to be present at the cultic ceremonies. With respect to the second, all twelve of them would flash on the eve of a successful battle, indicating that God was present and would lead the army to victory.

47. However, he also states that because of Israel's disobedience, both phenomena ceased two centuries prior to his own day (*Ant.* 3.218).

48. The Urim and Thummim are placed within the "breastplate"; see Feldman and Mason (2000, 289).

49. In the LXX, Urim is glossed as "manifestation" (τὴν δήλωσιν); the rabbis saw אורים as linked with אור (light); see Feldman and Mason (2000, 289).

Gentiles are drawn into this odd interpretive description at two points.[50] First, it was God's intention that the Urim would shine, and thus make the divine presence manifest, for the benefit not only of the Hebrews but also of "any strangers [τῶν ξένων] who happened to be present" (*Ant* 3.214). The second reference to Gentiles has to do with the fact that the Septuagint renders the unusual word חשן (generally translated in English as "breastplate"; cf. Josephus's ἐσσῆν) as λόγιον. He seems to attribute this rendering not to the Jewish translators but to "those Greeks who revere our practices" (οἱ τὰ ἡμέτερα τιμῶντες ἔθη). In his view such Gentiles recognized the oracular nature of the event. In the first reference, Josephus provides us with no indication of the circumstances under which non-Jews might be present. Although he does not say so explicitly, it is plausible that these should also be seen as Gentiles who "revere" Jewish practices—in other words, who are present for this divine manifestation out of reverence and not simply as a result of happenstance.

§126 Antiquities *3.318–19*

> *Certainly there is not a Hebrew who does not, just as if he were still there and ready to punish him for any breach of discipline, obey the laws laid down by Moses, even though in violating them he could escape detection. Many other proofs of that superhuman power of his might be adduced; and only recently certain persons from beyond the Euphrates, after a journey of four months, undertaken from veneration of our temple and involving great perils and expense, having offered sacrifices, could not partake of the victims, because Moses had forbidden this to any of those not governed by our laws nor affiliated through the customs of their fathers to ourselves. Accordingly, some without sacrificing at all, others leaving their sacrifices half completed, many of them unable so much as to gain entrance to the temple, they went their way, preferring to conform to the injunctions of Moses rather than to act in accordance with their own will, and that from no fear of being reproved in this matter but solely through misgivings of conscience.*

Category: SYMPATHIZATION

Josephus ends Book III with another encomium on Moses the legislator and originator of an ideal constitution (*Ant.* 3.316–22). Here he is concerned to emphasize the authority with which he spoke, so much so that people both in the past and in the present yield to his word completely and without question. The words of praise are oddly placed, coming as they do between accounts that seem to describe precisely the opposite—Israel's lack of faith after the return of the spies, recounted just prior to this, and Korah's rebellion, recounted at the

50. The earlier description of the high priest's vestments, to which Josephus alludes at the outset of this section, is replete with universal signification. As with the tabernacle, the design of the vestments "is intended to recall and represent the universe" (τῶν ὅλων; *Ant.* 3.180; see the whole passage, 179–87). The implications of this universal symbolism for the rest of humankind, however, are left unstated in this passage.

start of Book IV. Still, this just serves to underline the deliberation with which Josephus reminds his readers of his main theme—"that our constitution was established by God himself, through the agency of Moses and of his merits," something recognized even by Israel's enemies (*Ant.* 3.322).

To prove his point, Josephus provides three examples of the continuing power of Moses's utterances. Two of them involve Jews; the other one, however, is this curious account involving some non-Jews "from beyond the Euphrates." What is odd about this passage is the contrast with passages elsewhere in Josephus—some that we have seen already, others yet to be considered—that speak without hesitation of Gentiles offering sacrifice to God in the temple.[51] Here, however, these pilgrims are turned back, "some without sacrificing at all, others leaving their sacrifices half completed, many of them unable so much as to gain entrance to the temple," precisely because they were "not governed by our laws nor affiliated through the customs of their fathers [τῶν πατρίων] to ourselves." In other words, sacrifice seems here to be restricted to native-born Jews and proselytes.

Perhaps the key is to be found in the statement that these visitors "could not partake of the victims." This suggests that a distinction is to be made between the provision of a sacrificial animal, which Gentiles were permitted to do, and the consumption of the sacrifice, which was restricted to Jewish worshippers.[52] If this distinction is valid and is applicable here, then these Gentile pilgrims (or at least a certain number of them) had somehow been able to begin the process of sacrifice before it was discovered that they were not Jewish.

Even so, significant questions remain. Did these Gentiles actually enter the inner courts of the temple? If so, would they not have been subject to the strict penalties of which Josephus himself was well aware?[53] If not, in what way could they have been treated as Jews and allowed to consume the sacrifice? Further, the point Josephus wants to draw from the incident is the persuasive power of Moses's words. But if the incident has to do with Gentiles who somehow had been allowed to sacrifice as if they were Jews, then the aborting of the process would have been due not to the inner power of Moses's words on their "conscience" (see *Ant.* 3.319) but to the coercive power of the temple guards.

51. *J.W.* 2.409; 5.15; *Ant.* 11.336; 16.14;18.122; *Ag. Ap.* 2.48.

52. D. Shwartz (1992) has suggested that the priests engaged in a kind of holy subterfuge, in which the Gentiles believed that they were offering sacrifice to the God of Israel, while the priests saw their animals simply as gifts to the temple which the priests then sacrificed on their own behalf. He notes that the relevant passage in Leviticus speaks of Israelites as "sacrificing" (e.g., Lev. 22:21), but describes Gentile sacrifice in more passive terms; priests are described as "accept[ing] such animals from a foreigner to offer as food to your God" (Lev 22:25). While this part of his argument is compelling, his suggestion that Josephus has exaggerated the extent to which Gentiles were involved in such sacrificial practice is not.

53. *J.W.* 5.194; 6.124–28; *Ant.* 15.417; *Ag. Ap.* 2.103.

The passage, then, remains puzzling. Certainly it provides us with further evidence of Josephus's own belief that the temple was venerated by Gentiles from far and wide. And the very oddness of the account seems to suggest that some real incident lies behind it. But the precise character of the incident remains hidden behind the opacity of the account.

§127 Antiquities *8.116–17*

> *And this help I ask of Thee not alone for the Hebrews who may fall into error, but also if any come even from the ends of the earth or from wherever it may be and turn to Thee, imploring to receive some kindness, do Thou hearken and give it them. For so would all men know that Thou Thyself didst desire that this house should be built for Thee in our land, and also that we are not inhumane by nature nor unfriendly to those who are not of our country, but wish that all men equally should receive aid from Thee and enjoy Thy blessings.*

Category: SYMPATHIZATION

This passage forms part of Solomon's prayer at the dedication of the temple (*Ant.* 8.107–17; cf. 1 Kgs 8:22–53; 2 Chr 6:1–42). Josephus has reworked the prayer considerably, rearranging the sequence of the biblical material somewhat and revising it in accordance with several of his characteristic tendencies, especially his avoidance of covenantal themes.[54] The passage cited here is Josephus's reworked version of 1 Kgs 8:41–43 (cf. 2 Chr 6:32–33).

In the biblical version, Solomon's petition on behalf of "a foreigner [τῷ ἀλλοτρίῳ], who is not of your people," follows a petition in which he asks God to hear the prayers of Israelites when they call out to God in various circumstances of distress. God's concern for the foreigner who comes and prays "towards this place" is treated as a kind of extension of God's covenantal concern for Israel. Then Solomon goes on to provide a rationale: "so that all peoples might know your name and might fear you, just as your people Israel [do], and might know that your name has been called upon this house that I have made." In other words, the positive response that Solomon asks God to display towards individual Gentile petitioners is to have a kind of quasi-missionizing effect; the desired result is that "all peoples" (πάντες οἱ λαοί) might recognize the temple as God's dwelling place and come to know and fear God in the same way that Israel does.

Josephus follows the biblical account to some extent. The petition concerning the foreign supplicant follows a petition (greatly abbreviated) concerning

54. While the biblical version of Solomon's prayer places emphasis on God's election of Israel and ongoing covenantal faithfulness (1 Kgs 8:15–16, 23–24), Josephus makes no mention of the covenant whatsoever. Spilsbury argues convincingly that Josephus presents the relationship between God and Israel more as that between a patron and a client (Spilsbury 1998b).

Israelites in distress. Further, the divine assistance that Solomon requests for the Gentiles ("any who come even from the ends of the earth") is also an extension of the assistance that God is asked to display to "the Hebrews." But Josephus deviates considerably from his biblical source in the rationale that he provides. To be sure, he reproduces the biblical theme that, as a result of God's beneficence, Gentiles will recognize the divine character of the temple. But in place of the quasi-missionizing character of the biblical prayer, Josephus's version is concerned with Gentile attitudes towards the Jews. Solomon asks God to grant the petitions of Gentiles, so that "all" (πάντες) might recognize that Jews are neither "inhumane" (ἀπάνθρωποι) by nature nor "unfriendly" to foreigners and that they wish divine beneficence equally for all. In contrast to the biblical account, where Solomon hopes that the Gentiles might have a change of heart towards God, in Josephus's account he hopes simply for a change in attitude towards the Jews.

If, as Mason has argued, Josephus composed the *Antiquities* with a missionizing intent, he has missed a prime opportunity to make his intentions clear. His reworking of Solomon's prayer represents one of the stronger aspects of Cohen's argument to the contrary. Still, the universalistic character of the passage should not be overlooked. Josephus believes that the temple is a place of prayer not only "for the Hebrews" but also for Gentiles, "even from the ends of the earth." Further, Jews are people who wish that God's assistance might be experienced equally by all (literally, might be common [κοινήν] to all). Even if Josephus's concern here is primarily with Gentile attitudes towards Judaism, one of the attitudes that he would like Gentiles to adopt is precisely the recognition that they are welcome to offer prayer and worship to the God of Israel.[55] It is just a short step from such a wish to an implied invitation.

§128 Antiquities *11.3–5*

> *For he stirred up the spirit of Cyrus and caused him to write throughout all Asia, "Thus says King Cyrus: Since the Most High God has appointed me king of the habitable world, I am persuaded that He is the god whom the Israelite nation worships, for He foretold my name through the prophets and that I should build His temple in Jerusalem in the land of Judaea." These things Cyrus knew from reading the book of prophecy which Isaiah had left behind two hundred and ten years earlier.*

Category: SYMPATHIZATION, ETHICAL MONOTHEISM

In this section of his narrative, Josephus is following the account in 1 Esdras of Israel's return from exile in the Persian period. His sources present a positive

55. A point that Cohen fails to stress: in his reading of the passage from Josephus, the reason why God should respond to the prayers of Gentiles is simply "so that they will know that the Jews are not hostile to them" (Cohen 1987a, 422).

portrait of the Persian kings (Cyrus, Darius, and Xerxes), but Josephus extends this by emphasizing their piety in general and their veneration of Israel's God in particular.

This passage contains Josephus's version of Cyrus's decree as it is found in 1 Esdras 2:3–7. In the biblical account, Cyrus declares that "the Lord of Israel, the Lord Most High, has made me king of the world and commanded me to build him a house at Jerusalem" (1 Esd 2:3). The account says nothing about how the command came to Cyrus, nor does it provide any explanation as to why Cyrus would attribute his enthronement to the God of Israel. Josephus fills both gaps by rooting Cyrus's action in Isaiah's "prophecy" (Isa 44:28–45:1) and quaintly imagining a scene in which the Persian king actually reads the biblical passage in which his own role in the rebuilding of Jerusalem is prophesied. As a result of the experience, Cyrus "wondered at the divine power and was seized by a strong desire and ambition" to play the role that had been foreordained for him (*Ant.* 11.6). The experience also persuaded him that "the Most High God," who had appointed him as "king of the habitable world," was precisely the same god as "the god whom the Israelite nation worships."

In Josephus's account, then, Cyrus was one who already recognized "the Most High God," but who subsequently came to recognize this god as the God of Israel, as he experienced the "power" at work in Isaiah's prophecy.

§129 Antiquities *11.87*

> *They would, however, allow them to worship there, they said, but the only thing which they might, if they wished, have in common with them, as might all other men, was to come to the sanctuary and revere God.*

Category: SYMPATHIZATION

This passage is part of Josephus's account of the initial conflict between the Judeans and the Samaritans, as he found it in 1 Esdras 5:65–73. In the biblical passage, the "peoples of the land," who claim to have been worshipping the Lord ever since they had been settled there by the Assyrians, approach Zerubbabel and Jeshua and offer to share in the building of the temple. Their offer is brusquely turned aside; according to Cyrus' decree, it was the returning exiles alone who were authorized to rebuild the temple, which means that those already in the land "have nothing to do with us in building the house for the Lord our God" (1 Esd 5:70). As a result they carried out a campaign of obstruction, "preventing the completion of the building as long as King Cyrus lived" (1 Esd 5:73)

Josephus varies the account in two ways. One is by identifying the opponents explicitly as Samaritans. The other is the addition of the concession quoted above. After Zorobabelos and Jesus refuse the Samaritans' offer, they soften the rejection with this statement that they could nevertheless worship (προσκυνεῖν) at the temple, presumably once it had been completed. This right "to come to the sanctuary and revere God" (σέβειν τὸν θεόν) was something that the Samaritans shared with "all men" (πᾶσιν ἀνθρώποις), though it was only on such terms that they had anything in common with the Jews as far as the temple was concerned. In keeping with his view of the Samaritans on display elsewhere (e.g. *Ant.* 9. 290–91; 10.184), Josephus categorizes them as non-Jews, having nothing in common with the Jews except for those things enjoyed by Gentiles generally.

Still, one of the things enjoyed by Gentiles is the right to worship at the temple. It is noteworthy that Josephus chooses to soften the harshness of the biblical text by reminding his readers of this right.

§130 Antiquities *11.103*

> *Furthermore he* [Cyrus] *prayed to God that, if anyone should attempt to prevent the building of the temple, he should strike him down and restrain him from his wicked deed.*

Category: SYMPATHIZATION

After Darius had succeeded Cyrus as king, the Samaritans sent a letter to the new king objecting to the temple reconstruction project. Darius searched through his archives and found the original decree issued by Cyrus.[56] Josephus's version of the decree also includes the substance of the decree that, in 1 Esdras, Darius is said to have issued to the governor of Syria and Phoenicia in response (1 Esd 6:27–34). The result is that the portion of the decree cited above is attributed to Cyrus rather than to Darius.

What is of interest here is the fact that, in Josephus's account, this portion of the decree is described as a prayer: "He prayed to God" (κατεύξατο τῷ θεῷ). In 1 Esdras, it is simply a wish: "may the Lord, whose name is there called upon," punish any who would interfere with the work. While the point is minor, the alteration nevertheless serves to bring Cyrus into a closer supplicatory relationship with the God of Israel.

§131 Antiquities *11.120–32*

> *When Darius died, his son Xerxes, who took over the royal power, inherited also his piety toward God and his way of honouring him. . . .* [132]*When they learned of the king's orders and of his piety toward God as well as his goodwill toward Ezra, they were all greatly pleased.*

Category: SYMPATHIZATION

56. In 1 Esdras the letter was written by the Persian governor Sisinnes and his associates; furthermore, it was they who suggested that the king look in the archives (1 Esd 6:7, 21). The scenario is odd in both accounts, since in both 1 Esdras (4:43–46) and *Antiquities* (11.31–32) Darius is said to have made a vow to God, either before (Josephus) or when (1 Esdras) he became king, that he would rebuild the temple.

In this section of his narrative, Josephus is recounting the commissioning of Ezra by the Persian king Xerxes, using 1 Esd 8:1–27 as his source. Already in 1 Esdras the king (here Artaxerxes) is portrayed as engaging in acts of benefaction and veneration. He sends votive offerings to the temple (1 Esd 8:13); he provides funds out of his own treasury (1 Esd 8:18) and that of the province (1 Esd 8:19–20) for the refurbishment and maintenance of the temple; and he urges that all be done in accordance with the law lest "wrath" might come on "the king and his sons" (1 Esd 8:21).

Josephus carries all of this over into his account, adding several touches that are pertinent here. He begins and ends the account with a reference to Xerxes' piety. The king is introduced as someone marked by "piety and honour towards God" (τὴν πρὸς τὸν θεὸν εὐσέβειάν τε καὶ τιμήν); when the Jews of Babylon heard the letter, they discerned his "piety toward God." The term is used not simply to describe some particular actions taken by the king but to designate his basic character. Further, this characteristic was inherited from his father Darius; piety ran in the family. But this was not the only virtue on display here. In Josephus's version, Xerxes himself describes his benevolent treatment of the Jews as an outworking of his love of humankind (φιλανθρωπίας; *Ant.* 11.123).

Because Josephus clothes Darius and Xerxes in these virtues, it is difficult to follow Cohen in his argument that veneration towards God displayed by foreign monarchs is something of a special case—the sign of a good monarch rather than the model of behavior that might be expected of foreigners in general. In the Proem to *Antiquities*, Josephus presents the law as a means by which those who follow it might be schooled "in piety and the exercise of the other virtues" (*Ant.* 1.6), holding it out to "the whole Greek-speaking world" as a model to be admired. The first lesson that Moses teaches in Genesis is that "we men" are to be obedient "to the dictates of piety" (*Ant.* 1.21). Piety, for Josephus, is a universal virtue, albeit expressed most clearly in the law of Moses. Further, while we will look at the story of Izates in due course, we have already had occasion to note how Josephus presents him as a model of virtue to be emulated by all.[57] The piety exhibited by Darius and Xerxes toward the God of Israel, then, is not simply the mark of a good monarch but a model of what is expected of people in general.

§132 Antiquities *11.285*

> *And, when the letter of the king was published, joy and the light of salvation came upon the Jews both in the city and in the provinces, so that many of the other nations also, from fear of the Jews, had themselves circumcised and thereby managed to avoid danger.*

Category: CONVERSION

57. See the introduction to this chapter, above.

As we have observed above in our discussion of LXX Esther 8:17 (§11), the Hebrew version of the Esther story says that when events had reached their climax and the king had issued an edict in support of the Jews, "many of the peoples of the country professed to be Jews [מתיהדים], because the fear of the Jews had fallen upon them" (8:17). In the Septuagint, מתיהדים is rendered Ἰουδαΐζειν (to Judaize), but with the interpretive addition "they were circumcised" (περιετέμοντο). Josephus speaks only of circumcision,[58] omitting any mention of Judaizing. Since he seems to be aware of the longer version of Esther,[59] he may be dependent on the Greek version for the reference to circumcision. The substitution of a result—"and thereby managed to avoid danger"—for a motivation—"because the fear of the Jews had fallen upon them"—is presumably his own.

There is little to be derived for our purposes from this brief paraphrase. Presumably, given references to circumcision elsewhere in his writing, Josephus's audience would have understood this act of self-preservation as at least having the form of proselytism. Still, his cryptic language betrays little of what he might have thought of it. The elimination of ἰουδαΐζειν might be interpreted as an attempt to differentiate this from forms of "Judaizing" that he thought to be more appropriate, but there is no certain indication of this in the text.[60]

§133 Antiquities *11.331–36*

For when Alexander while still far off saw the multitude in white garments, the priests at their head clothed in linen, and the high priest in a robe of hyacinth-blue and gold, wearing on his head the mitre with the golden plate on it on which was inscribed the name of God, he approached alone and prostrated himself before the Name and first greeted the high priest. Then all the Jews together greeted Alexander with one voice and surrounded him, but the kings of Syria and the others were struck with amazement at his action and supposed that the king's mind was deranged. And Parmenion alone went up to him and asked why indeed, when all men prostrated themselves before him, he had prostrate himself before the high priest of the Jews, whereupon he replied, "It was not before him that I prostrated myself but the God of whom he has the honour to be high priest,. . ." [336]After saying these things to Parmenion, he gave his hand to the high priest and, with the Jews running beside him, entered the city. Then he went up to the

58. περιτεμνόμενα τὴν αἰδῶ: they were "circumcised" or "had themselves circumcised" "with respect to their modest parts." For αἰδώς as a euphemism for genitalia, see, e.g., *Ant.* 1.44; 11.285.

59. On Josephus' Bible, see Spilsbury (1998a, 23–25). His Esther narrative contains material found only in the longer LXX version (see *Ant.* 11.216, 229).

60. Spilsbury (1998a, 215) says that "Josephus' phrasing betrays the fact that he did not consider these to be true conversions, but rather acts of expedience in a time of crisis"; he provides us with no indication, however, of what it is about Josephus's phrasing that might lead to this conclusion.

temple, where he sacrificed to God under the direction of the high priest, and showed due honour to the priests and to the high priest himself.

Category: SYMPATHIZATION

In the opinion of most historians, Josephus's account of Alexander's visit to Jerusalem has no historical basis.[61] Thus the account is of interest here solely for what it reflects of the assumptions and attitudes of Josephus (and the traditions on which he depends).[62]

As Josephus tells the story, when Alexander had taken Damascus and was laying siege to Tyre, he sent a letter to the high priest Jaddus demanding allegiance and material assistance (*Ant.* 11.317). Because of his commitment to Darius, however, the high priest refused. Thus, when Alexander, having captured Tyre and Gaza, set out for Jerusalem, Jaddus understandably "was in an agony of fear" (*Ant.* 11.326). Wisely, he led the people in offering prayers and sacrifice to God, and this display of corporate piety saved the city. In a dream, God directed the high priest to go out to meet Alexander, the people wearing white garments and he himself his high-priestly vestments. Meanwhile, God appeared to Alexander as well in a dream, in which the king saw an elaborately dressed figure who assured him that he would defeat Darius and become master of Asia (*Ant.* 11.334). When Alexander saw the great company of Jerusalemites coming out to meet him, he immediately recognized the high priest as the figure who had appeared to him in his dream. Whatever plans he might have had to punish Jerusalem for its previous "disobedience" (*Ant.* 11.326) evaporated, and instead he "prostrated [προσεκύνησε] himself before the Name" of God that was inscribed on the high priest's miter. Somehow Alexander knew already that it was Jaddus' God who was responsible for the dream and who thus was deserving of veneration. After this, he went up to Jerusalem, where he "sacrificed to God under the direction of the high priest" and made displays of honor to the priests. While in Jerusalem he had an experience similar to that of Cyrus earlier (§128 above), being shown the scriptural passage (in Daniel this time) in which his own career was prophesied. Rejoicing, he offered generous benefactions to the people of the city.

As can be seen from this description, Josephus's account of Alexander's visit to Jerusalem represents a narrative form found elsewhere (e.g., 2 Maccabees, 3

61. In non-Jewish sources, Alexander went directly to Egypt after the conquest of Gaza (cf. *Ant.* 11.320). Since there would be no reason whatsoever to omit a trip to Jerusalem, it is much more likely that this is a legendary embellishment. For a lucid discussion of the issues, see Grabbe (1992, 174, 181–83, 208).

62. Versions of the story appear in other Jewish sources (see Grabbe 1992, 182), which suggests that Josephus is relaying tradition here rather than creating something out of whole cloth.

Maccabees), whose theme is that God will act to defend the city and the temple from foreign threat as long as the high priest and people are righteous and pious and call out to God for deliverance. Veneration of God and temple such as is displayed by Alexander here is a common element in this narrative form; by engaging in acts of worship, the foreign monarch recognizes the legitimacy of Israel's claim to be God's people and submits to the supremacy of Israel's God. Thus Alexander's veneration is recounted here because of its role in a story of vindication and not for its own sake. Still, for the story to work, Josephus has to assume that his readers will see such veneration as appropriate and desirable. For this reason, the passage is significant for our purposes.

§134 Antiquities *12.22*

> *For both they and we worship the God who created the universe, whom we call by the appropriate term Zena, giving him that name from the fact that he breathes life into all creatures.*

Category: ETHICAL MONOTHEISM

In *Ant.* 12.11–18 Josephus provides his readers with a lengthy recitation of the narrative found in the *Letter of Aristeas*. While he follows his source for the most part, two aspects of his redaction are of interest here (see also the next entry). The first is his version of the startling statement in *Let. Aris.* 16 that both Jews and (certain pious) Gentiles worship the same God, even if they use different names for the divinity. Josephus provides a certain etymological justification: it is appropriate that Greeks call God Ζῆνα (the accusative form of Zeus), since the creator is the one who has implanted the ability to live (τὸ ζῆν, the infinitive of ζάω) in all creatures. This embellishment demonstrates that Josephus is fully prepared to endorse the idea and to retail it in his own way.

§135 Antiquities *12.58*

> *However, as for the magnificence and workmanship of the dedicatory offerings which the king sent to the temple of God, I have thought it not inappropriate to describe them, in order that the king's eagerness to honour God may be apparent to all.*

Category: SYMPATHIZATION

The second aspect of interest in Josephus's version of the story found in the *Letter of Aristeas* is this editorial statement in which he refers to the king's "eagerness to honour" (φιλοτιμία) God, the only instance where Josephus adds his own commentary on *Aristeas*'s description of Gentile religiosity. While the editorial statement does not add much to our understanding of Josephus's attitudes, the larger narrative of which it is a part is quite significant. As we have seen, in the introductory Proem to *Antiquities*, Josephus cites the narrative recounted in *Aristeas* as justification for his own literary project. When he was asked by his patron Epaphroditus to present a full account of the history and political constitution of the Jews, Josephus, wondering whether it would be proper for Jews to undertake such an enterprise and whether Greeks would be interested in it when it was completed, found a fitting precedent in the story of the Egyptian King Ptolemy and the Jewish the High Priest Eleazar. This section of book 12, then, is not only part of the history that Josephus is in the process of recounting but also a full description of the model that he has set out to emulate.

§136 Antiquities *13.69–71*

> *And one may get a notion of the king's piety and that of his sister and wife Cleopatra from the letter which they wrote in reply,. . .* [70] *"King Ptolemy and Queen Cleopatra to Onias, greeting. We have read your petition asking that it be permitted you to cleanse the ruined temple in Leontopolis in the nome of Heliopolis, called Bubastis-of-the-Fields. We wonder, therefore, whether it will be pleasing to God that a temple be built in a place so wild and full of sacred animals. But since you say that the prophet Isaiah foretold this long ago, we grant your request if this is to be in accordance with the Law, so that we may not seem to have sinned against God in any way."*

Category: SYMPATHIZATION

This is one of several passages in Josephus dealing with the origins of the temple at Leontopolis in Egypt. There is no need here to enter into the difficulties posed by these passages with their conflicting details.[63] In this passage, Ptolemy (VI Philometor) replies to a letter from Onias IV requesting permission to build the temple. In his reply, the king raises questions as to whether such a project would be "pleasing to God" (τῷ θεῷ κεχαρισμένον) and demonstrates a concern that he not appear "to have sinned against God in any way." He grants the request on the grounds that, according to Onias (who cites Isa 19:19), the project was indeed "in accordance with the Law." This reference to the law indicates that the God whom Ptolemy was concerned to please was the God of Israel. Josephus understands the letter to be a rebuke of Onias for a transgression against the law[64] and sees this rebuke as a sign of the king's "piety" (εὐσέβεια). The evidential value of the passage is slight, but it nevertheless indicates Josephus's readiness to assume that a king who had a reputation of treating Jews favorably[65] and whom he himself believes to be "a good and upright

63. *J.W.* 7.423–36; *Ant.* 12.237–38, 397; 13.62–73. For a description, see Grabbe (1992, 266–67).

64. While one would expect the "sin" to consist in the construction of a second temple, the only question raised in the king's letter has to do with the appropriateness of the site ("so wild and full of sacred animals").

65. See the next entry. In *Ag. Ap.* 2.48–49, Josephus goes so far as to claim that Philometor placed his entire army under the command of Jewish generals. For a summary of the evidence concerning Philometor and the Jews, see Barclay (1996, 35–38); see also Schürer (1986, 3:135–36).

person by nature" (*Ant.* 13.114) is also prepared to recognize and defer to the God of Israel.

§137 Antiquities *13.78*

> *But as Sabbaeus and Theodosius permitted Andronicus to make the first speech, he began with proofs from the Law and the succession of the high priests, showing how each had become head of the temple by receiving that office from his father, and that all the kings of Asia had honoured the temple with dedicatory-offerings and most splendid gifts, while none had shown any respect or regard for that on Gerizim, as though it were not in existence.*

Category: SYMPATHIZATION

This passage also has to do with the reign of Ptolemy VI Philometor. According to Josephus, a dispute broke out between Jews and Samaritans in Alexandria concerning the relative legitimacy of the two temples. The king is apparently interested in the dispute and accepts a request from both parties that he "sit in council with his Friends" and decide which claim is "in accordance with the laws of Moses" (*Ant.* 13.75). The king decides in favor of the Jews and, in accordance with the terms requested by the two parties at the beginning of the hearing, has the Samaritan advocates put to death.

While Philometor's friendliness toward the Jews is substantially attested elsewhere, the passage raises some questions. How, for example, could the king accept both the argument of Andronicus (the Jewish advocate) that the temple specified by the law of Moses was the one in Jerusalem and Onias's argument that his proposed temple at Leontopolis was "in accordance with the Law" (see the preceding entry)? The significance of the passage, however, has to do not with the attitude of the king but with a comment made by Andronicus in the course of his argument. To support his case, he points to the recognition accorded the Jewish temple by "all the kings of Asia," who "honoured the temple with dedicatory offerings and most splendid gifts" (ἀναθήμασιν καὶ λαμπροτάταις δωρεαῖς), while disregarding the Gerizim temple entirely. The passage does not add anything to the evidence that we have seen already in Josephus, but it does attest to the commonplace character of this belief and to its rhetorical versatility.

§138 Antiquities *13.242–44*

> *And Hyrcanus sent to Antiochus, requesting a truce of seven days on account of the festival, which Antiochus, deferring to his piety toward the Deity, granted and moreover sent a magnificent sacrifice, consisting of bulls with gilded horns and cups of gold and silver filled with all kinds of spices. And those who were at the gates received the sacrifice from the men who brought it, and took it to the sanctuary, while Antiochus feasted his army, being very different from Antiochus Epiphanes who, when he captured the city, sacrificed swine upon the altars and bespattered the temple with their grease, thus*

perverting the rites of the Jews and the piety of their fathers, by which acts the nation was driven to war and became his implacable enemy. This Antiochus, on the other hand, because of his exaggerated devoutness was by all men called Eusebes *(the Pious).*

Category: SYMPATHIZATION

This account appears early in the reign of John Hyrcanus. Shortly after Hyrcanus succeeded his father Simon, the Syrian king Antiochus VII (Sidetes) invaded Judea with the intent of completing some unfinished business left over from Simon's reign. Under siege in Jerusalem, Hyrcanus calls for a truce. Antiochus responds magnanimously, going so far as to donate a luxurious sacrifice to the temple. This leads to negotiations between Antiochus and Hyrcanus and to a peace settlement (*Ant.* 13.236–48).

While Josephus interprets this as a sign of Antiochus' piety (on which more in a moment), the king's actions are clearly driven by political considerations. When he first succeeded his brother Demetrius, Antiochus made generous concessions to Simon and the Jews in order to gain support in his struggle against Tryphon. Once he had gained in strength, however, he broke with Simon, demanding that the Jews pay tribute and surrender significant portions of conquered territory. His attempts to enforce these demands were initially rebuffed, as Simon's sons John Hyrcanus and Judas defeated a Syrian force sent for this purpose. Once Hyrcanus had assumed the throne, however, Antiochus renewed his demands, invaded, and laid siege to the city. At the very least, Antiochus' gift to the temple was purely a strategic move, a ploy to bring Hyrcanus to the bargaining table. There is a strong possibility, however, that it was also motivated by pressure from Rome; the senate decree that Josephus reports a little later (*Ant.* 13.260–66) probably dates to this period.[66]

What is of particular interest to us here, however, is how Josephus interprets this incident. Antiochus' willingness to grant Hyrcanus' request for a truce is dictated not by hard-headed military strategy but by the king's "piety toward the Deity" (τῇ πρὸς τὸ θεῖον εὐσεβείᾳ). In fact, says Josephus, so widely was his piety recognized that he was even given the nickname "the Pious"; the fact that the epithet is not attested by anyone besides Josephus serves to underline the tendentiousness of the account. And while Josephus's use of "the deity" rather than "God," together with the statement that the king's piety was recognized by "all," might suggest simply a generic form of Hellenistic piety, Josephus sees this piety as manifested in particular by the sacrifice that he donates to the Jewish temple. Likewise, Hyrcanus' request for terms is based not on a political-military assessment but on a recognition of Antiochus' "reverence for the deity" (τὴν περὶ τὸ θεῖον σπουδήν; *Ant.* 13.245). While the fact is probably not to be

66. See the discussion in Rajak (1981) and Schürer (1986, 3:204–05). For the history of the relations between Antiochus VII and Judea, see Schürer (1986, 3:197–207) and Grabbe (1992, 297–301).

doubted that the Syrian king made a gift to the temple as part of a complicated set of political negotiations, it is striking to see how Josephus interprets it as another example of temple veneration by foreign monarchs.

§139 Antiquities *13.257–58*

> *Hyrcanus also captured the Idumaean cities of Adora and Marisa, and after subduing all the Idumaeans, permitted them to remain in their country so long as they had themselves circumcised and were willing to observe the laws of the Jews. And so, out of attachment to the land of their fathers, they submitted to circumcision and to making their manner of life conform in all other respects to that of the Jews. And from that time on they have continued to be Jews.*

Category: CONVERSION

In his account of how the Idumeans came to be attached to Judea in the Hasmonean period, Josephus stresses the coercive character of the event: Hyrcanus subjugated them and imposed Jewish observances on them as a condition of surrender. A similar coercive element is found in a passing statement about the Idumeans in *Ant.* 15.254 (see §143 below). This emphasis on coercion is odd, partly because elsewhere Josephus says that he disapproves of forced conversions (*Life* 113) and partly because Josephus at the same time seems to see the Idumeans as wholehearted converts to a Jewish way of life.

Such a depiction of the Idumeans—as full and legitimate converts—is present in the text under discussion: "from that time on they have continued to be Jews" (εἶναι Ἰουδαίους). Josephus's language is strikingly categorical and unqualified. No matter how it came about, the enduring result was that the Idumeans could be described simply as "Jews," people who continue to circumcise themselves and to live "in all other respects" in accordance with "the laws of the Jews." In addition, as we have seen already, this view of the Idumeans is strikingly present in Josephus's account in *Jewish War* of the Idumean intervention into the struggle for Jerusalem (§§118, 119). Even if he understands the conversion to have been forced, Josephus sees the results—from his perspective a number of generations later—as fully legitimate. He does not see them as a nation of Metiliuses, submitting to circumcision merely to save (the rest of) their skin. He sees them rather as "Jews" (*Ant.* 13.258), as "nearest kinsfolk" (*J.W.* 4.278), and thus as converts.

Until recent times scholarly interpretation of this passage and of the events it relates has tended to focus on the coercive element and to understand this as an instance of "forced conversion."[67] Adding heft to this interpretation is the figure of King Herod, whose supposedly superficial attachment to Judaism is

67. E.g., Schürer (1973, 1:207): Hyrcanus "forced the Idumeaeans to submit to circumcision and to accept the Jewish law." Also G. Moore (1927–1930, 335–36).

often taken as typical of Idumeans generally and thus as evidence that this "forced conversion" produced only superficial attachment to Judaism. More recently, however, a convincing case has been made that circumcision and Jewish observance was not so much imposed as willingly accepted.[68] One argument in favor of this thesis is the fact that Idumean support for Judea and Jewish causes continued long after the disappearance of the Hasmonean regime, something that would be difficult to explain if the relationship was simply the result of subjugation and forced conversion.[69] Another is Strabo's description of the annexation of Idumea, which lacks any sense of coercion.[70] In this interpretation, the Idumeans willingly came under Hasmonean rule, adopting Jewish religion in the process.

This line of approach should probably not be taken to an extreme. The Hasmoneans were definitely expansionist, and a willingness on the part of some of their new subjects to adopt Judaism does not mean that they had no interest in imposing it. Still, in the case of the Idumeans at least (and probably of the Itureans; see the next entry), we probably should see them as being willing to adopt Jewish religion.

If this was the case, what do we make of Josephus's account, with its odd combination of coercion and conversion? His purpose was hardly to allay the Roman suspicion about the political ramifications of conversion (as is argued by Cohen [1987, 423]). If this had been his aim, he would not have portrayed the Idumeans so clearly and positively as converts. Nor can the coercive element simply be sloughed off onto his sources;[71] the fact that he repeats it later seems to indicate that it is part of his own interpretation of events. Instead, both elements must be allowed to stand. Despite what he says about forced conversion elsewhere (*Life* 113), Josephus believed both that there was an element of coercion in Hyrcanus' annexation of Idumea and, from his perspective a number of generations later, that the results were nonetheless fully

68. Kasher (1988, 46–78), followed by others (e.g., Grabbe [1992, 329–31]; Richardson [1996, 55–56]). Smith (1996) takes a somewhat similar view, though he makes a sharp distinction between "conversion" as membership in a political alliance and religious conversion. For a restatement of the older opinion, with a response to Kasher, see Feldman (1993, 324–26).

69. Of course, support for Judea was not total, as the case of Costobar illustrates (*Ant* 15.253–58). Although he was appointed by Herod as governor of Idumea, he "did not think that it was proper . . . for the Idumeans to adopt the customs of the Jews and be subject to them" (*Ant* 15.255). Presumably the attitude was more widely shared. See further below, §143.

70. Strabo *Geog.* 16.2.34, discussed below §176. The evidence from Strabo, however, is counterbalanced somewhat by the presence of an element of coercion in one other text, an otherwise unknown *History of King Herod*, attributed to a certain Ptolemy; see §175 below.

71. Grabbe (1992, 330) attributes it to Josephus' source, Nicolaus of Damascus.

legitimate. Even if conversion was imposed on them as a condition of surrender, the conversion "took," producing real converts as a result.

§140 Antiquities *13.318–19*

> *[H]e conferred many benefits on his country, for he made war on the Ituraeans and acquired a good part of their territory for Judaea and compelled the inhabitants, if they wished to remain in their country, to be circumcised and to live in accordance with the laws of the Jews. He had a kindly nature, and was wholly given to modesty, as Strabo also testifies on the authority of Timagenes, writing as follows. "This man was a kindly person and very serviceable to the Jews, for he acquired additional territory for them, and brought over to them a portion of the Ituraean nation, whom he joined to them by the bond of circumcision."*

Category: CONVERSION

The ruler in question here is Aristobulus I, the short-lived successor to John Hyrcanus, who emulated his father in this respect at least, that he annexed neighboring territory (this time part of Iturea) and imposed Judaism on them as a condition of surrender. The passage raises the same questions as arose in the case of Idumea, just discussed, and probably is to be interpreted in the same way.[72] It is striking that the statement attributed to Timagenes (via Strabo; see below, §176) also lacks any sense of coercion: Aristobulus "brought over to them"—literally, "made into kinsfolk" (ᾠκειώσατο)—some of the Itureans, "joining them together with the bond of circumcision." Thus it is at least possible that these Itureans were willing to take on a Jewish way of life as one of the conditions of becoming part of the growing Hasmonean kingdom.

Likewise, we probably should interpret Josephus's account in a manner similar to that carried out in the case of the Idumeans. On the one hand, he seems to interpret the annexation of this portion of Iturea in coercive terms: if they wanted to live in peace, they had "to be circumcised and to live in accordance with the laws of the Jews." But on the other, while he is not as expansive as he was in the case of the Idumeans, he gives us no reason to believe that the Itureans did not accept these terms in a wholehearted way. That is, he sees them as converts to a Jewish way of life.

§141 Antiquities *13.397*

> *Pella . . . Alexander's men demolished because the inhabitants would not agree to adopt the national customs of the Jews.*

Category: CONVERSION

72. See Grabbe (1992, 331), who notes that this portion of Iturea had long been linked with Galilee.

The previous two passages described how Idumeans and Itureans willingly adopted "the national customs of the Jews" (τὰ πάτρια τῶν Ἰουδαίων ἔθη) as a condition of their submission to Hasmonean rule. In this passage we see the other side of the coin. In the context of a list of Gentile territory that had been annexed by the Hasmoneans, Josephus mentions Pella, adding that Alexander Jannaeus had it destroyed because it would not accept a Jewish way of life. If we take the statement at face value and in combination with Josephus's previous statements about the Idumeans and Itureans, it could be taken to imply that all the other cities and territories in the list had become "kinsfolk" and converts in as thoroughgoing a way as the Idumeans. This seems highly unlikely. What seems more probable is that Pella was destroyed because of overt resistance to Hasmonean rule. Presumably the Hasmoneans imposed some restrictions on subjugated territory arising from Jewish sensitivities, so that Pella's resistance could be read as a refusal to adopt Jewish customs. But probably the Idumeans (and less certainly, the Itureans) were exceptions—not only conforming to whatever Torah-inspired restrictions the Hasmoneans imposed, but willingly embracing the whole Jewish way of life.

§142 Antiquities *14.110*

> *But no one need wonder that there was so much wealth in our temple, for all the Jews throughout the habitable world, and those who worshipped God, even those from Asia and Europe, had been contributing to it for a very long time.*

Category: SYMPATHIZATION

Josephus makes this comment on the wealth in the temple in the context of his description of Crassus's short-lived term as governor of Judea (54–53 B.C.E.). In order to finance his ill-fated campaign against the Parthians, Crassus plundered the temple, carrying off a sum of two thousand talents in gold. Lest any of his readers doubt the sum, Josephus explains that it is the accumulation of gifts sent to the temple over a period of time by "all the Jews throughout the habitable world and those who worshipped God [πάντων τῶν κατὰ τὴν οἰκουμένην Ἰουδαίων καὶ σεβομένων τὸν θεόν]."

Since this is the earliest appearance outside the Acts of the Apostles of the construction "worshipper of God" (σεβόμενος τὸν θεόν) in a context where it might plausibly refer to non-Jews, the passage has had a significant part to play in the controverted discussion of "God-fearers."[73] There has been some attempt to argue that the phrase does not refer here to Gentiles at all. Lake has argued that if Josephus had two groups in mind, Jews and Gentiles, he would have repeated the definite article before σεβομένων. As it stands, the phrase—he

73. See the section on Luke-Acts in ch. 8, below.

argues—refers also to the Jews.[74] But Lake's reading is even more problematic. Not only does it fail to account for the conjunction καί; more than this, even if the conjunction were absent, Lake's reading would require the definite article just as much as the alternative (i.e., "the Jews, the ones reverencing God"). Further, after having described the gifts of the Jews as coming from the whole inhabited world, there would be no need for the more restricted geographical phrase "even those from Asia and Europe." Marcus' translation, which assumes two distinct groups, is probably to be accepted.[75] Since the first group is specifically designated as Jewish, this second group of "God-reverencers" must be Gentile.

As far as activity is concerned, the passage adds little to the portrait that has been emerging from Josephus's work; he has already informed us repeatedly about Gentile veneration of God and Gentile gifts to the temple. In fact, this repeated information serves to reinforce the interpretation of the phrase as referring to Gentiles. But terminologically the passage does represent an advance. Josephus assumes that his readers will understand σεβομένων τὸν θεόν as a reference to Gentile worshippers. This does not mean that the term is a technical one; the reference to Gentiles is determined not simply by the term itself but also by its conjunction with the contrasting term "Jews." Still, the significance of the term is not to be minimized.

§143 Antiquities *15.254–55*

> *Now Hyrcanus had altered their way of life and made them adopt the customs and laws of the Jews. . . . For he* [Costobarus] *did not think that it was proper for him to carry out the orders of Herod, who was his ruler, or for the Idumeans to adopt the customs of the Jews and be subject to them.*

Category: CONVERSION

Here Josephus is describing Herod's troubled relationship with Costobar, whom he had appointed governor of Idumea and to whom he had given his sister Salome as wife. According to Josephus, Costobar belonged to one of the highest-ranking families in Idumea, his ancestors having been priests in the Idumean cult of the god Koze. Once in power, Costobar adopted a policy of Idumean nationalism, trying to win Cleopatra's support for an independent Idumea. Although he was able to maintain his position for a while because of his connections with the Herodian family, eventually he overplayed his hand and was put to death by Herod.

In his introduction to the story, Josephus reminds his readers of the way in which Hyrcanus had "changed their constitution into the customs of the Jews"

74. Lake (1933, 85); Feldman also held this view originally (Feldman 1993, 350).

75. In addition to the LCL translation, see Marcus (1952). See also Feldman (1993, 350); J. J. Collins (2000, 266).

(Marcus' "made them adopt" is overstated). There is no need to repeat what was said above about the conversion of the Idumeans (see §140). The thing to note from this passage is its indication that the conversion was not as unanimous and thoroughgoing as Josephus seems to imply in some of his comments. Presumably Costobar was not alone in his views. No doubt part of his temporary success was due to the support of others who supported the traditional Idumean cult and who also believed that it was not "proper . . . for the Idumeans to adopt [μεταλαβοῦσιν] the customs of the Jews and be subject to them."

§144 Antiquities *16.14*

> *He also brought him to the city of Jerusalem, where all the people met Agrippa in festival attire and welcomed him with acclamations. Then Agrippa sacrificed a hecatomb to God and feasted the populace, which was not less in number than any of those in the greatest (cities).*

Category: SYMPATHIZATION

In 15 B.C.E., Herod prevailed upon Marcus Agrippa, Augustus' powerful second in command, who was then in the province of Asia, to pay a visit to Judea. Herod gave him the grand tour of his realm, proudly showing him his architectural accomplishments and sparing no expense in his provision of hospitality. The tour ended in Jerusalem, where Agrippa responded in kind, paying for a lavish sacrifice at the newly rebuilt temple and a feast for the people of the city.

No particular piety towards Israel's God attached to Agrippa's donations. He was simply following the conventions associated with such official visits between powerful patrons and clients. Presumably there were similar lavish sacrifices in the temple to Roma and Augustus in Caesarea. Nor does Josephus attempt to exaggerate the significance of the temple visit; it is simply one detail in a longer narrative illustrating Herod's loyal support of Agrippa (*Ant.* 16.12–26). Neither, however, does he eliminate the element of veneration, describing the gift in a straightforward manner as an offering made "to God."

§145 Antiquities *16.225*

> *But when they asked Syllaeus to be initiated into the customs of the Jews before the wedding—otherwise, they said, marriage would be impossible—, he would not submit to this but took his departure, saying that if he did submit, he would be stoned to death by the Arabs.*

Category: CONVERSION

After the death of her husband Costobar (at the hand of her brother Herod), Salome was courted by Syllaeus, a leading figure in the court of Obadas, king of Arabia. This is one of several cases where marriage into the Herodian royal family was made conditional on a form of conversion to Judaism. Elsewhere the emphasis is on circumcision. Here, perhaps because, as an Arab, Syllaeus was already circumcised (cf. *Ant.* 1.214), the condition is the more general one of accepting "the customs of the Jews." In contrast to the other cases, Syllaeus refused, with the result that Herod was not able to get his troublesome sister out of the household.

One detail of the account is worthy of comment. The word that Marcus renders as "initiated" is ἐγγραφῆναι, literally, "written on or in." Josephus uses it frequently in this basic sense; for example, the words of Isaiah the prophet were "written in books" (*Ant.* 10.35). Sometimes what is written has the character of an official decree (e.g., *Ant.* 12.416; 19.291). The closest parallels to the use of the word in this passage, however, are found in two places where people's names are said to be written in a document. In both cases the document is a will, specifically, that of Herod. In both cases, the reference is to the naming of his successor—Antipater in one instance ("I nominated him in my will, in the public eye, heir to my throne"; *J.W.* 1.625), Archelaus in the other ("He . . . had been named king by their father in the codicil to his will"; *Ant* 17.226). The implication seems to be that Syllaeus be "inscribed" in the customs of the Jews—in other words, that there be some sort of official record of his conversion. One wonders whether there was some sort of official register (in the temple? in a synagogue?) in which the names of proselytes were entered.[76] In the absence of any other evidence, however, it is probably safer to conclude that the "inscription" took the form of a clause in a marriage contract. Still, the phrasing "to be inscribed in the customs of the Jews" would be an odd way to refer to something that was to be inscribed in a marriage contract. The detail remains curiously suggestive.

§146 Antiquities *18.81–82*

There was a certain Jew, a complete scoundrel, who had fled his own country because he was accused of transgressing certain laws and feared punishment on this account. Just at this time he was resident in Rome and played the part of an interpreter of the Mosaic law and its wisdom. He enlisted three confederates not a whit better in character than himself; and when Fulvia, a woman of high rank who had become a Jewish proselyte, began to meet with them regularly, they urged her to send purple and gold to the temple in Jerusalem. They, however, took the gifts and used them for their own personal expenses, for it was this that had been their intention in asking for gifts from the start.

Additional Bibliography: Abel (1968); Barclay (1996, 298–301); Dickson (2003, 26–31); Feldman (1993, 303); Gruen (2002, 30–34); Matthews (2001, 11–14); Smallwood (1981, 202–9); Williams (1989)

Category: CONVERSION

76. For a discussion of the possibility, with generally negative results, see Cohen (1999, 49–52).

The outcome of the act of fraud recounted in this passage was that Tiberius banished "the whole Jewish community" from Rome and conscripted four thousand of them for military duty. Similar accounts of a major disruption of the Jewish community in Rome during the rule of Tiberias are found in Roman sources. Two of these—one by Tacitus (*Ann.* 2.85.4) and the other by Suetonius (*Tib.* 36.1)—will be considered in the next chapter,[77] though we will keep all of the references in view in each case. All of them refer to the banishment of the Jewish community from Rome (Josephus, Suetonius, Dio Cassius) or Italy (Tacitus) in the time of Tiberius (19 C.E., according to Tacitus). All but Dio Cassius refer in addition to the conscription of a certain number (Tacitus also says four thousand) into the army, to serve in Sardinia (Josephus, Tacitus) or "provinces of less healthy climate" (Suetonius). Presumably those experiencing conscription were citizens or *Latini Juniani*, who could not be expelled without a trial (Smallwood 1981, 207). All but Dio Cassius link the expulsion of Jews with similar measures taken against Egyptian cults (according to Josephus, that of Isis in particular). And most significantly for our purposes, all of them refer, in one way or another, to the attraction of converts as a factor in the expulsion.

In addition to the similarities just mentioned, there are differences as well. In the case of Josephus, his account is the only one to refer to Fulvia and to make the (unlikely) claim that the banishment of the Jewish community took place simply "because of the wickedness of four men" (*Ant.* 18.84). Josephus presents Fulvia as "a woman of high rank" who had "come over to the Jewish laws" (νομίμοις προσεληλυθυῖαν τοῖς Ἰουδαϊκοῖς). Fulvia thus conforms to a pattern—an upper-class woman attracted to Jews, Judaism and a Jewish way of life—that is frequently encountered in this study. While Feldman's "proselyte" is an overtranslation, the phrasing seems nevertheless to suggest a full conversion. Presumably in the interest of deepening her understanding of the Jewish way of life, she engaged the services of a Jew who presented himself as a teacher "of the Mosaic law and its wisdom." Together with his three associates, he encouraged her to make significant gifts to the Jerusalem temple. This she was apparently quite prepared to do, but the four Jews, in reality con artists rather than wisdom teachers, pocketed the gifts for their own use. When the fraud came to light, Fulvia's husband, Saturninus, complained to his "friend" the emperor, who promptly expelled "the whole Jewish community" (πᾶν τὸ Ἰουδαϊκόν) from Rome.

It is difficult to believe, however, that such extreme measures would have been taken simply to deal with a small-scale swindle. Why would a whole community have been expelled simply because of a fraud perpetrated by a few scoundrels in its midst? While there is no reason to dismiss Josephus's account

77. The other account is that of Dio Cassius (*Hist.* 57.18.5), who wrote early in the third century.

out of hand, if the duping of Fulvia was connected to the expulsion of the Jews from Rome, it must have been just one in a larger set of factors. Since there are other texts that deal with the incident, we can leave the issue open until we have discussed them all. Anticipating that discussion, however, it is significant that according to both Tacitus and (especially) Suetonius the expulsion affected Gentile adherents as well, which lends support to Dio Cassius' statement that the expulsion took place precisely because the Roman Jews were "changing [μεθιστάντων] many of the natives" over to their customs. It is easy to understand how an incident such as Josephus has described—one involving a high-status woman, in contrast to the freedmen mentioned by Tacitus—in a context where there was already suspicion and resentment over the popular appeal of Judaism, could have helped to trigger an expulsion.[78]

What then of Josephus's account? Either he was misinformed about the real reason for the expulsion, which would be hard to imagine, given its magnitude; or, as is more likely, he has suppressed the real reason, rooting the event not in the popularity of Judaism but in the misdeeds of a few Jewish scoundrels. One can well understand why he would want to interpret the event in this way. His version avoids any suggestion that Gentile attraction to Judaism was inherently problematical or that the success of the Jewish community in attracting sympathizers and converts led Roman authorities at the highest level to see it as subversive and dangerous. At the same time, however, he gives no indication that he disapproves of conversion or believes that Fulvia was not to be emulated in her desire to learn about the Mosaic law or to send gifts to the temple.[79] The blame is borne in its entirety by the gang of four, set apart from the rest of the Jews and Gentile converts alike by their particular wickedness.

Before we leave the story, it is appropriate to observe two other details that, at least in Josephus's perception of things, were part of Fulvia's experience as a convert to Judaism. One is the role of the teacher. While this one in particular turned out to be unscrupulous, he probably would not have been able to attract such a student as Fulvia if the role that he claimed for himself—"an interpreter of the Mosaic law and its wisdom"—were not widely recognized. What Eleazar and Ananias were doing in Adiabene and Charax Spasini, others were doing in

78. See Barclay (1996, 298–99); Georgi (1986, 95); Smallwood (1981, 202–10). Gruen has asserted that the expulsion had nothing to do with proselytism but was rather part of Tiberius' attempt to allay any suspicion that he had something to do with the death of Germanicus, which was also connected in popular thought to the influence of magic and other foreign "superstitions" (Gruen 2002, 30–36). But even if this were a factor in Tiberius' repression of foreign cults, it does not rule out other factors and certainly does not account for the aspect of the texts that are under discussion here. Williams' attempt to eliminate proselytism as a factor is equally unconvincing (Williams 1989), as is Abel's argument in the other direction that only proselytes were affected (Abel 1968).

79. Contra Cohen (1987a, 422–23).

Rome. Second, it seems to be taken for granted that someone who had "come over to the Jewish laws" would send gifts—in Fulvia's case, costly gifts of "purple and gold"—to the temple. Again, the unscrupulousness of the advisers does not negate the more general point. The fraud could not have been perpetrated if there had not been a general recognition that sending gifts to the temple was an appropriate thing for a sympathizer or convert to do. There is no indication, however, that this was anything other than a voluntary offering. In particular, no connection should be made with the sacrifice that, in later rabbinic tradition, was part of the conversion process.[80]

§147 Antiquities *18.122*

> *Yielding to their entreaty, he abandoned his original plan and ordered his army to march through the Great Plain, while he himself, together with Herod the tetrarch and his friends, went up to Jerusalem to sacrifice to God during the traditional festival which the Jews were celebrating there. When he arrived there, he was greeted with special warmth by the Jewish multitude.*

Category: SYMPATHIZATION

This is another matter-of-fact account of a situation in which a Roman official offers sacrifice "to God" at the Jerusalem temple. In this case the official is Vitellius, governor of Syria, leading a military expedition against Aretas the Nabatean (37 C.E.), who had recently defeated Herod Antipas in a skirmish over a boundary dispute. Originally planning to travel through Judea, he deferred to Jewish sensitivities about the images on Roman military standards and decided to take an alternative route. Vitellius' visit to Jerusalem was no doubt part of an attempt to mollify those "Jews of the highest standing" (*Ant.* 18.121) who had objected to his plans to march through the land and to consolidate his position as defender of the Jews against Nabatean aggression. Still, Josephus has chosen to highlight the act of veneration, making it the purpose of his visit to Jerusalem.[81]

§148 Antiquities *18.286, 288, 309*

> *Petronius, on his part, was struck with great amazement when he saw unmistakable evidence that God's providence was over the Jews and that he had shown his presence so abundantly. . . . [288]He said, moreover, that the Divinity who was in charge of them had shown his power to be unimpaired and was quite unambiguous in displaying this power. . . . [309]He rejoiced at the coincidence that Gaius' disaster came when it did, and marvelled at the providence of God, who swiftly and punctually had paid him his reward for showing honour to the temple and coming to the rescue of the Jews.*

Category: SYMPATHIZATION

80. *Sipre Num.* §108 (on Num 15:14); *m. Ker.* 2.1.

81. The future participle (θύσων) has intentional force.

The story of Petronius has come up for consideration twice already, once with reference to Philo's account of it (*Embassy* 245; §104) and once, briefly, with reference to Josephus's account of it in the *Jewish War* (*J.W.* 2.201; §108). In his earlier account, Josephus alludes to Petronius' piety briefly. Here, however, it is a more dominant theme.

Petronius, successor to Vitellius as governor of Syria, was commissioned by Gaius to erect a statue of the emperor in the Jerusalem temple. In contrast to Philo's version of the story, where Petronius appears as sympathetic to Jewish religion from the outset, here his piety emerges only gradually, as his support for the Jewish cause grows. At the outset he took the position of the obedient civil servant: "I am Caesar's emissary and bound to carry out the decision he has already made, since to disregard it would bring on me irretrievable punishment" (*Ant.* 18.265). After witnessing the intransigent resistance of the Jewish multitudes and hearing the persuasive appeals of Jewish leaders, however, he decided to intervene on their behalf with the emperor. At this point, Josephus describes him as "a man who made virtue his goal" (*Ant.* 18.278) and who, as such, was prepared to risk death on behalf of a multitude of others.

In announcing his decision to a convened assembly of Jews in Tiberias, Petronius made several direct references to God. The Jews, he said, were "serving the sovereign of all, almighty God"; he went on to express this wish: "May God assist you, since his might is above any human ingenuity or strength" (*Ant.* 18.280, 281). The assumption in these statements is that the same God is acknowledged by both Petronius and his Jewish hearers. Shortly afterwards, Petronius experienced what Josephus presents as a direct manifestation of divine power. "God showed Petronius his presence and his control over all things" (*Ant.* 18.284)[82] in the form of a miraculous—or at least timely—downpour that fell without warning on a parched land just as he had completed his address to the Jewish assembly. He perceived this, says Josephus, as "unmistakable evidence that God's providence was over the Jews" (*Ant.* 18.286) and included an account of this in his letter to Gaius, thereby informing the emperor "that the Divinity who was in charge of them had shown his power to be unimpaired and was quite unambiguous in displaying this power" (*Ant.* 18.288). When events turned out happily for Petronius—the news of Gaius' death happened to arrive before the letter from Gaius commanding him to

82. Feldman renders this "God, on His part, showed Petronius that He was with him and would lend His aid in all matters." But since Petronius goes on to talk about God's providential presence with the Jews (*Ant.* 18.286), it is better to render παρουσίαν τὴν αὐτοῦ as referring to God's presence more generally. Also, while σύλληψις can refer to assistance (LSJ *ad loc.*), its basic sense is "inclusion, comprehension"; the phrase τὴν ἐπὶ τοῖς ὅλοις σύλληψιν is perhaps better understood as referring to the inclusion of all things within the divine purview and hence control.

commit suicide—he "marvelled at the providence of God" (*Ant.* 18.309), the God who rewards those who honor the temple and defend the Jews.

What Petronius' actual motivations were is difficult to say. One would not have had to be a Jewish sympathizer to recognize the folly of Gaius' command. At the same time, the fact that both Philo and Josephus refer to his respect for the Jews and their God should not be dismissed out of hand. Nevertheless, for our purposes what is more striking is Josephus's readiness to attribute Jewish sympathies to Petronius, even presuming to be privy to his mental thoughts and perceptions. In Josephus's perspective, Petronius clearly recognized the God of the Jews as the universal sovereign and saw himself to have been rewarded by God for the honor he had shown to the temple.

§149 Antiquities *20.34–48*

Now during the time when Izates resided at Charax Spasini, a certain Jewish merchant named Ananias visited the king's wives and taught them to worship God after the manner of the Jewish tradition. It was through their agency that he was brought to the notice of Izates, whom he similarly won over with the co-operation of the women. When Izates was summoned by his father to Adiabene, Ananias accompanied him in obedience to his urgent request. It so happened, moreover, that Helena had likewise been instructed by another Jew and had been brought over to their laws.. . . [38] *When Izates had learned that his mother was very much pleased with the Jewish religion, he was zealous to convert to it himself; and since he considered that he would not be genuinely a Jew unless he was circumcised, he was ready to act accordingly. When his mother learned of his intention, however, she tried to stop him by telling him that it was a dangerous move. For, she said, he was king; and if his subjects should discover that he was devoted to rites that were strange and foreign to themselves, it would produce much disaffection and they would not tolerate the rule of a Jew over them. Besides this advice she tried by every other means to hold him back. He, in turn, reported her arguments to Ananias. The latter expressed agreement with the king's mother and actually threatened that if he should be unable to persuade Izates, he would abandon him and leave the land. For he said that he was afraid that if the matter became universally known, he would be punished, in all likelihood, as personally responsible because he had instructed the king in unseemly practices. The king could, he said, worship God even without being circumcised if indeed he had fully decided to be a devoted adherent of Judaism, for it was this that counted more than circumcision. He told him, furthermore, that God Himself would pardon him, if constrained thus by necessity and by fear of his subjects, he failed to perform this rite. And so, for the time, the king was convinced by his arguments. Afterwards, however, since he had not completely given up his desire, another Jew, named Eleazar, who came from Galilee and who had a reputation for being extremely strict when it came to the ancestral laws, urged him to carry out the rite. For when he came to him to pay him his respects and found him reading the law of Moses, he said: "In your ignorance, O king, you are guilty of the greatest offence against the law and thereby against God. For you ought not merely to read the law but also, and even more, to do what is commanded in it. How long will you continue to be uncircumcised? If you have not yet read the law concerning this matter, read it now, so that you may know what an impiety it is that you commit." Upon hearing these words, the king postponed the deed no longer. Withdrawing into another room, he summoned his physician and had the prescribed act performed.*

Additional bibliography: Dickson (2003, 33–37); Gilbert (1991); McEleney (1973–1974); Nolland (1981); Schiffman (1987); D. Schwartz (1996); Segal (1990, 99–100).

Category: SYMPATHIZATION, CONVERSION

The story of the royal family of Adiabene occupies a significant portion of Book XX (*Ant.* 20.17–96), appearing as a kind of excursus within the account of Fadus' term as procurator. The centerpiece of the story is the conversion of Helena, the queen mother, and King Izates, her son. But the story is significant for the topic of sympathization as well, both because the conversion of Izates (and presumably the others as well) comes as the culmination of a lengthy process in which he gradually took on more and more of a Jewish way of life, and also because of the special attention given to the differing opinions of his two advisors concerning his status as he hesitated over taking the final step of circumcision.

The narrative is coterminous with the life of Izates, beginning with his conception (*Ant.* 20.18) and ending with his death and, shortly after, that of his mother (*Ant.* 20.92–96). Despite the scope of the narrative, however, it is the religious element that is paramount. Josephus introduces it as a narrative describing how Helena and Izates "changed their way of life over to the customs of the Jews" (εἰς τὰ Ἰουδαίων ἔθη τὸν βίον μετέβαλον; *Ant.* 20.17), and the theme of the narrative is "that those who fix their eyes on [God] and trust in Him alone" will prosper under the providence of God and will win the admiration of all (*Ant.* 20.48, 49, 75, 91).

Since the story is well known, a brief summary will suffice. Before his accession to the throne, when Izates was living as a guest of the king in the neighboring city of Charax Spasini, the king's wives[83] were "taught to worship God [τὸν θεὸν σέβειν] as was the hereditary custom for Jews" (*Ant.* 20.34). Through the influence of these women, Izates was introduced to Ananias, who "persuaded him likewise" (*Ant.* 20.35). When Izates returned to Adiabene to take the throne, he found that his mother, coincidentally, "had likewise been instructed by another Jew and had been brought over [μετακεκομίσθαι] to their laws" (*Ant.* 20.35). While the extent to which she "had been brought over" is not specified here, when Josephus refers to her piety a few lines later, he implies that she has become a full convert: seeing how pleased his mother was with Jewish customs, Izates was eager to "change" (μεταθέσθαι) to that way of life

83. D. Schwartz (1996, 265) is probably correct in seeing these women as wives of the king of Charax Spasini rather than of Izates. At this point in the story, Izates is not yet king.

"himself" (*Ant.* 20.38). The use of the intensifier αὐτός implies that what Izates was eager to do his mother had already done. Since he had already been taught to worship God, the "change" that Izates was now considering was that of full conversion; he wanted to become "genuinely a Jew" (βεβαίως Ἰουδαῖος) through circumcision. And since he "also" was eager to make this change, his mother must have become a full convert by this point.

While the story from this point on centers on Izates, Helena's piety comes up for attention at several points. Josephus recounts her journey to Jerusalem "to worship at the temple of God, which was famous throughout the world, and to make thank-offerings there" (*Ant.* 20.49). Worship at the temple is presented as something that Helena desires to do and something that is appropriate for her as a convert to do, rather than something that needs to be done to confirm her status as a convert. Josephus also mentions her significant benefactions to Jerusalem (*Ant.* 20.51–53); her residency in the holy city, along with his five sons (*Ant.* 20.71); and her burial there in an elaborate family tomb (*Ant.* 20.95).[84]

But what Helena had embraced gladly for herself she was less enthusiastic about for her son. She feared that his subjects would be displeased and "would not tolerate the rule of a Jew over them" (*Ant.* 20.39). She found a supporter in Ananias (who had accompanied the king back to Adiabene), who also opposed the move for similar reasons, fearing moreover that the people would be displeased with him as well. But in his argument for the religious status quo Ananias went on to say something that has occasioned much scholarly discussion and dispute. He said that the king "was able to worship the deity [τὸ θεῖον σέβειν] even apart from circumcision, if indeed he had decided to be zealously devoted to the traditions of the Jews [ζηλοῦν τὰ πάτρια τῶν Ἰουδαίων]; this is more decisive than circumcision" (*Ant.* 20.41). He added that God would "show lenience to him" if he refrained from circumcision out of fear for his kingdom.

The king's mind was made up, however, by another adviser, Eleazar, who was "extremely strict [ἀκριβής] when it came to the ancestral laws."[85] He denounced Izates for his reticence, declaring that by ignoring "the law concerning this matter" (*Ant.* 20.45) Izates was "guilty of the greatest offence against the law and against God" (*Ant.* 20.44). Accordingly, the king immediately "had the prescribed act performed" (*Ant.* 20.46).

This story is of particular interest here both for its detailed account of a conversion and for its explicit debate about the religious status of pious Gentiles: Is it possible for an uncircumcised Gentile to "worship God" (τὸν θεὸν σέβειν; *Ant.* 20.34) in a manner pleasing to the deity? Eleazar's position is

84. Still extant in Jerusalem, known popularly as the Tomb of the Kings.

85. Some have identified Eleazar as a Pharisee (e.g., Garland 1979, 130; Hengel and Schwemer 1997, 64). The identification is supported, though not required, by Josephus's use of ἀκριβής and related terms as descriptors of the Pharisees (e.g., J.W. 1.110; *Ant.* 17.41).

clear: the only possible form of piety (cf. *Ant.* 20.45: ἀσέβεια) for a Gentile, the only way to please God (cf. *Ant.* 20.44: ἀδικῶν), was through adherence to all the commands, including that of circumcision. Of course, none of the biblical "commands" concerning circumcision apply explicitly to Gentiles. In the primary passage, for example, the injunction has to do with membership in Abraham's "seed" (Gen 17:14).[86] Eleazar's position, then, was that the only legitimate religious option for Gentiles was incorporation into the Jewish people.

But what of Ananias? Some scholars have understood him to be saying that in these circumstances Izates would be fully a Jew even without being circumcised.[87] Such a reading rests primarily on the statement that, except for this one observance, Izates had decided "to be zealously devoted to the traditions of the Jews." While circumcision is normally required for one to be "genuinely a Jew," in this case—so it is argued—an exception could be made because of the attendant dangers. Parallels are drawn with later rabbinic rulings that dispense with circumcision in the case of hemophiliacs.[88] But this reading is hard to maintain.[89] After all, the whole interchange rests on the assumption that if Izates were to be circumcised his subjects would consider him a Jew and would react accordingly, but if he did not take this step they would continue to view him as a Gentile. Those who understand Ananias to be offering Izates the status of an "uncircumcised proselyte" thus are implying some theological/sociological sleight of hand: as far as the citizens of Adiabene were concerned, he would be considered as a Gentile, but from the perspective of the Jewish community, he would be a full convert. But would this mean that he would enjoy all the privileges of a proselyte—the right to enter the court of Israel in the temple? to eat the Passover? to marry a Jewish woman? If so, then it is hard to believe that his subjects would not view him as fully a Jew, foreskin or not. It seems necessary to conclude that what Helena and Ananias were suggesting for Izates is not that he become a Jew in every respect but circumcision, but that he continue to worship the God of the Jews as a Gentile. Being "zealously devoted to the traditions of the Jews" cannot be given its maximal interpretation in any case, since circumcision is certainly one of these traditions. Thus the "zeal" that Ananias

86. In rabbinic accounts of the story, the specific passage of scripture that Izates was reading was Gen 17; see *Gen. Rab.* 46.10–11 and Schiffman (1987, 294).

87. See Borgen (1996, 53); McEleney (1973–74, 323–24); Gilbert (1991). McKnight (1991, 80), J. J. Collins (1985a, 179), and Goldenberg (1998, 60) hold it open as a possibility.

88. Several Mishnaic texts refer to uncircumcised Israelites (*m. Ned.* 3.11; *m. Yeb.* 8.1). In the Talmud these are identified as brothers of those who had died as a result of circumcision (*b. Yeb.* 64b; *b. Ḥul.* 4a).

89. Those who understand Ananias to be proposing something other than proselytism include Feldman (1993, 333); Gaston (1987, 25); Goodman (1994, 87); Kraus (1996, 98–99); Nolland (1981); Schiffman (1987, 302–03); Schürer (1986, 3:169); D. Schwartz (1996, 269); Segal (1990, 99).

expects of him is probably to be understood as a level of observance that would be appropriate for a Gentile but that would fall considerably short of what was required for a Jew.

This conclusion, however, should not be understood as implying a simple either/or status—either a full proselyte or a single, well-defined alternative (e.g., "God-fearer"). As with other passages discussed already, the picture that emerges here is more one of a spectrum. In a manner not unlike that of Metilius, who was prepared "to Judaize as far as circumcision" (*J.W.* 2.454), Izates moved along a spectrum that began with initial attraction, moved to various degrees of reverence towards God, and ended in full conversion.

One other aspect of the narrative that needs to be noted is the appearance of named individuals who engage interested Gentiles in an enterprise of teaching, advising, and persuading. While one should avoid the problematic term "mission," one should not overlook the element of initiative displayed by both Ananias and Eleazar.

But what of Josephus's attitude toward the narrative? As we have seen, Cohen has argued that Josephus has simply reproduced a source here, so that the enthusiasm for proselytism reflected in the account is simply that of his source.[90] But as we have already noted, the recurring theme in the Izates account—that "those who fix their eyes on [God] and trust in Him alone do not lose the reward of their piety" (*Ant.* 20.48; see also 49, 75, 91)—is so resonant of what Josephus presents at the start of his narrative as the "main lesson" to be drawn from the whole work[91] that the Izates story must be seen as carrying Josephus's full endorsement.[92] To be sure, there are differences. The Adiabene narrative makes no reference to the law's character as a constitution (πολιτεία), a theme that was prominent in the introduction to the work. Izates may have been "pleased with the customs of the Jews" (*Ant.* 20.38) for himself, but the suggestion does not even arise that he might think of the Jewish law as a constitution for his own nation. Still, Josephus is proud to be able to point to this example of a prominent Gentile who risked a considerable amount to become a convert to Judaism and who nevertheless flourished as a result.

But this does not necessarily mean that Josephus's primary purpose in telling this story is to encourage his readers to do likewise. For one thing, while

90. Cohen (1987a); see the discussion in the introduction to this chapter. For a similar approach, see Feldman (1993, 329) and Schiffman (1987, 294). Schiffman goes so far as to see the references to other discussions of the Adiabene story (*Ant.* 20.48, 53, 96) not as Josephus' own promises of further accounts but as cross-references within the original source that Josephus has clumsily retained.

91. *Ant.* 1.14; see the discussion in the introduction to this chapter.

92. "The story hints at Josephus's opinion: all things being equal, being Jewish is better than being God-fearing" (Segal 1990, 100).

he is pleased with the outcome of Izates' decision (*Ant.* 20.48), he gives no indication of disapproval when Ananias suggests that it was perfectly acceptable for the king to continue to worship God as a Gentile. In other words, he does not endorse Eleazar's position that Gentiles can please God only through conversion (a fact that has already become apparent in *Antiquities*). Further, not even while Izates was still just a Gentile sympathizer does Josephus present him as a model for all to emulate; he makes no explicit invitation to his readers to follow Izates' example, either as a sympathizer or as a convert. The lesson he wants to take from the narrative is that God will preserve those who "trust in Him alone" (*Ant.* 20.48)—a lesson that applies to Jews no less than to Gentiles. Nevertheless, it does apply to Gentiles as well, and if we cannot go so far as to say that Josephus's purpose was to encourage Gentiles to apply this lesson to themselves, we are justified to say that he was pleased when Gentiles did trust in Israel's God alone, either as Gentile worshippers or as full converts.

§150 Antiquities *20.75*

> *Izates' brother Monobazus and his kinsmen, seeing that the king because of his pious worship of God had won the admiration of all men, became eager to abandon their ancestral religion and to adopt the practices of the Jews.*

Category: CONVERSION

This passage appears in the midst of the larger Adiabene narrative (*Ant.* 20.34–96). Seeing the positive results of the king's conversion—he "had won the admiration of all"—his brother and other members of his family were also eager (ζηλωτόν) to "abandon their ancestral religion and to adopt the practices [ἔθεσι χρῆσθαι] of the Jews." The story that unfolds from here, however, actually serves to undercut the thesis of this introductory sentence. When the "high nobles" of the land get wind of what the king's brothers have done (the story assumes that they carried through with their desire to convert), they fiercely resent this new incursion of Jewish piety and thus concoct a plot to overthrow the king with the aid of the Arabs. This plot, however, together with a subsequent one, is foiled "by the providence of God" (*Ant.* 20.91). The story thus serves to increase the list of converts from the royal family of Adiabene, even as it indicates that the "admiration" of Izates for his piety was not as widespread and unanimous as Josephus would like his readers to believe.

§151 Antiquities *20.139*

> *After receiving this gift from the emperor, Agrippa gave his sister Drusilla in marriage to Azizus king of Emesa, who had consented to be circumcised. Epiphanes, son of King Antiochus, had rejected the marriage since he was not willing to convert to the Jewish religion, although he had previously contracted with her father to do so.*

Category: CONVERSION

This is the second of a series of incidents having to do with the marriage of Gentiles into the Herodian family. Previously, Syllaeus the Arab wanted to marry Herod's sister Salome but backed away from the union when he learned that he would be required to convert (i.e., to accept "the customs of the Jews"; *Ant.* 16.225). This incident has to do with Herod's grandson Agrippa II, shortly after Felix appointed him to the tetrarchy formerly ruled by Philip (along with some other territory). He had arranged a marriage for his sister Drusilla to Epiphanes, son of Antiochus king of Commagene, but Epiphanes withdrew from the engagement, like Syllaeus before him, because he was not willing "to take on the customs of the Jews" (τὰ Ἰουδαίων ἔθη μεταλαβεῖν). Azizus, the king of Emesa, had no such scruples apparently, for he agreed to be circumcised as a condition of marriage to Drusilla. The marriage was short-lived; within a year or so she divorced him in order to marry none other than Felix himself. Presumably Azizus's conversion (though not his circumcision!) was equally a short-term affair. Josephus is critical of the marriage to Felix, describing it as "transgress[ing] the ancestral laws" (*Ant.* 20.143). Presumably the transgression was the fact that Felix, in contrast to Azizus, did not undergo circumcision.[93]

§152 Antiquities *20.145–46*

> *After the death of Herod, who had been her uncle and husband, Berenice lived for a long time as a widow. But when a report gained currency that she had a liaison with her brother, she induced Polemo, king of Cilicia, to be circumcised and to take her in marriage; for she thought that she would demonstrate in this way that the reports were false. Polemo was prevailed upon chiefly on account of her wealth. The marriage did not, however, last long, for Berenice, out of licentiousness, according to report, deserted Polemo. And he was relieved simultaneously of his marriage and of further adherence to the Jewish way of life.*

Category: CONVERSION

This is another instance of conversion for the sake of marriage, involving yet another member of the Herodian family—Berenice, sister of Agrippa II. Her brief marriage to Polemo, king of Cilicia, was but one chapter in a crowded sexual and matrimonial biography. Although at this point she was no more than twenty, she had already been married (and widowed) twice—to Marcus Julius Alexander, a wealthy nephew of Philo (and brother to Tiberius Julius Alexander), and then to her uncle Herod, king of Chalcis (*Ant.* 19.277). Later, spectacularly, she became the mistress of Titus, the conqueror of Judea and son of the emperor, though public sentiment in Rome forced him eventually to send her back to Judea. The one male constant in her life, however, was her brother Agrippa, with whom she was so closely associated that the relationship

93. See Mason (2001, 75).

was widely believed to be incestuous. It was to dispel such rumors, says Josephus, that she entered into a marriage with Polemo. As his readers would by now have come to expect, a condition of the marriage was that Polemo be circumcised. That circumcision was just the definitive part of a more general acceptance of "the customs of the Jews" (τοῖς ἔθεσι τῶν Ἰουδαίων) becomes clear in the conclusion of the story: when the marriage came to an end—reportedly because of her licentiousness, Josephus informs us—so also did Polemo's obligation to live according to Jewish custom.

Such a rapid abandonment of Judaism indicates that these conversions for the sake of marriage were only (shall we say) skin deep. Still, the three instances of marriage into the Herodian family are interesting in several ways. One is the power of popular expectation. While none of the women involved seem to have displayed any particular devotion to Jewish piety, the Herodian family evidently felt that their legitimacy would have been questioned if they allowed their sisters or daughters to enter into a pagan marriage. A second is the importance of circumcision. While one doubts how devoted to the "customs of the Jews" Polemo would have been when he was off in his own realm, in the eyes of Agrippa's Jewish subjects it was his willingness to be circumcised that qualified him as an convert to Jewish customs and that therefore rendered his marriage acceptable. But third, even if Polemo's observance of Jewish customs was much less rigorous than that of, say, Izates, Josephus's narrative takes it for granted that circumcision was not simply a one-time prerequisite for marriage but carried with it an ongoing obligation to live according to the "customs of the Jews."

§153 Antiquities *20.195*

> *In this he showed favour to his wife Poppaea, who was a worshipper of God and who pleaded on behalf of the Jews.*

Category: SYMPATHIZATION

We have already observed how, when Josephus journeyed to Rome for the first time, he was able to find support for his cause (the release of certain Jerusalem priests) from Nero's wife Poppaea. In his account of this event (*Life* 16), there was no hint of any specifically religious motivation to Poppaea's action, though her patronage of the Jewish actor Aliturus and her readiness to assist Josephus might suggest a degree of more general sympathy towards Jews. In *Ant.* 20.193–96, however, we read about another embassy of Jerusalemites whose petition was granted through Poppaea's intervention, and here a religious element is present, though its sense is disputed.

The issue had to do with a conflict that had erupted in Jerusalem between Agrippa II and the temple authorities during the procuratorial rule of Festus. Agrippa had built an addition to his palace that afforded him a commanding view not only of the city as a whole but also of the activity within the temple. Not happy that sacred activity had thus become visible to prying eyes, "the eminent men of Jerusalem" built a wall to block the view. But because the wall also blocked the view of the Roman soldiers who kept watch on festival crowds from the western portico, the dispute spilled over into Roman jurisdiction. Festus first ordered the wall to be demolished but then relented under pressure and allowed the Jerusalem authorities to send an embassy to Nero. The emperor ruled in their favor and allowed the wall to stand, thus "showing favour to his wife Poppaea—for she was θεοσεβής—who had pleaded on behalf of the Jews."

But what does it mean that she was θεοσεβής? The issue is disputed. Feldman, whose LCL translation is given above, takes θεοσεβής as indicating devotion towards the God of Israel in particular and thus argues that Poppaea was a Jewish sympathizer. He even draws into his argument Josephus's curious statement that she retained two of the delegation as "hostages"; in Feldman's view she retained them "not as hostages but as teachers" who would provide her with "further instruction about Jewish practices" (Feldman 1993, 351–52). On the other side, Smallwood, seeing no evidence of Jewish piety in Roman accounts of Poppaea's life (in which her immorality and involvement in pagan religion feature prominently), denies that she was a "Judaizer" or Jewish sympathizer.[94]

In interpreting this statement, it is probably wise to differentiate between Poppaea's actual religious sympathies and Josephus's particular portrayal of her. Concerning the former, Smallwood is probably right: there is little evidence that she worshipped the God of the Jews to any significant extent, even if she was prepared to intervene in support of certain Jewish causes. But what does Josephus mean by θεοσεβής? He tends to use the word in its basic adjectival sense, so that there is no convincing reason to follow Feldman in taking the word as a substantive. Josephus is saying that Poppaea was "pious," not that she was a "worshipper of God" in any technical sense. Further, while the adjective appears in *Antiquities* to describe the piety primarily of Jews,[95] the fact that on one occasion it is used of Gentile piety toward their own gods (*Ag. Ap.* 2.140) means that we cannot rule out a generic piety in this case. Josephus may be saying nothing more than that she was a religious woman (so Smallwood 1981, 278–79, n. 79). But on the other hand, the only appearance of the word with reference to Gentile piety is in a statement that Josephus attributes to Apion; Josephus himself uses it only of piety shown to the Jewish God by Jews. The use of the word in an emphatic way (the clause is an interjection) in an account where Poppaea intervenes in order to preserve the sanctity of the temple certainly leaves the passage open to a more Judeo-centered interpretation. Whatever she may have been in reality, Josephus presents her

94. Smallwood (1959; 1976, 278–79, n. 79).

95. *Ant.* 7.130, 153; 9.260 [var. εὐσεβής];12.284; 14.308.

as piously supportive of the Jewish temple and thus—the implication would seem to be—of the Jewish God as well.[96]

§154 Life *112–13*

> *About this time there came to me from the region of Trachonitis two nobles, subjects of the king, bringing their horses, arms, and money which they had smuggled out of their country. The Jews would have compelled them to be circumcised as a condition of residence among them. I, however, would not allow any compulsion to be put upon them, declaring that every one should worship God in accordance with the dictates of his own conscience and not under constraint, and that these men, having fled to us for refuge, ought not to be made to regret that they had done so.*

Category: CONVERSION

The only passage from Josephus's *Life* that bears on our investigation is this account of two noblemen from Trachonitus who came to him in Sepphoris and put themselves under his command. Josephus himself had come to Sepphoris in the course of his ongoing struggle with John of Gischala and others for control of Galilee. His subsequent statement, that they had "fled to us for refuge," is odd, on the face of it. As part of the territory of Agrippa II, Trachonitus had remained loyal to the Romans; thus there is no readily apparent reason why they would be safer in Galilee, at the center of a rebellion, than they would have been at home. Mason suggests that they had really "opted to join the revolt," adding that this, however, was for "their own nationalistic reasons" and not necessarily in support of the Judean revolt itself (Mason 2001, 75). He is certainly correct that these nobles were not simply "refugees"; since they brought with them "horses, arms, and money," they evidently wanted to participate in the revolt, not simply to seek refuge. But would "their own nationalistic" purposes really have been served by going over to the Judeans? In order to make sense of Josephus's statement, it would be necessary to supplement Mason's scenario with the suggestion that their revolutionary leanings had made things unsafe for them at home. One is tempted to speculate that it was a measure of sympathy for Jews and Judaism that had resulted both in their need to leave their own territory and in their subsequent siding with the Jews. But if this had been the case, one would have expected Josephus to make mention of it. Thus, the narrative remains opaque to their real motivations.

What is important for our purposes, however, is the reception they received when they arrived. The Jewish population—Josephus here just calls them "the Jews"; in the second part of the story he speaks of "the crowd" (τὸν ὄχλον; *Life* 149)—tried to force circumcision on them, arguing that if they wanted to find

96. For similarly cautious views, see Barclay (1996, 308); Matthews (2001, 33–36).

refuge among them, they should adopt the customs of their hosts. Josephus objected to this position, arguing instead "that every one should worship God [τὸν θεὸν εὐσεβεῖν] in accordance with their own choosing [κατὰ τὴν ἑαυτοῦ προαίρεσιν] and not under constraint." While Josephus's arguments were initially persuasive, the sentiment reasserted itself later, and he had to smuggle the noblemen out of the country to save their lives (*Life* 149–54).

Several things are of interest here. One is the attempt at forced conversion, something that we have seen already as part of the social policy of the Hasmoneans. The issue is similar: if Gentiles wanted to live among the Jews (παρ' αὐτοῖς appears in both *Life* 113 and 149) or, in the case of the Hasmoneans, under Jewish rule, they needed to accept circumcision. The attitude seems to have been tied to the land rather than something that could have been readily transported to the Diaspora. A second item of interest is the assumption that circumcision carries with it both a "passing over into [Jewish] customs" (μεταβῆναι εἰς τὰ ἔθη; *Life* 149) and the "worship of God" *(Life* 113). Thus, while political allegiance was naturally to the fore in a revolutionary context, it did not stand alone. Cultural observance, religious worship, and political allegiance are inextricably bound together in this story.

A third item of interest is Josephus's own position. Cohen has pointed to this passage to argue that Josephus was categorically opposed to forced conversion, and thus that he was at least implicitly critical of the policy of the Hasmoneans (Cohen 1987a, 422–23). In our examination of the pertinent passages, however, we found no critique of the policy whatsoever; indeed, Josephus consistently portrays the Idumeans as full and legitimate converts to Judaism, and thus as kinfolk and even "Jews." What, then, are we to make of the position that he takes in this incident?

The issue is not easily resolved, but perhaps the answer lies in the recognition of the difference in context.[97] For one thing, Josephus found himself in a much trickier and more precarious position than that enjoyed by the Hasmoneans. While they were in full control of an expanding kingdom, he was supposedly co-commander of a revolution but hard pressed even to control his territory, let alone defend it against the Romans. Further, and perhaps more importantly, in Josephus's case the only alternative to conversion seems to have been death: the noblemen "ought not to live if they refused" to adopt Jewish customs (*Life* 149). This is in contrast to Hasmonean policy, where the alternative was less severe: expulsion from their land (*Ant.* 13.257, 318). Presumably Josephus believed nevertheless that conversion should be freely chosen; but this preference should not be pushed to imply that he must therefore have disapproved of Hasmonean policy.

97. For a somewhat similar reading of the passage, see Mason (2001, 75).

§155 Against Apion *1.162*

> *Now, Pythagoras, that ancient sage of Samos, who for wisdom and piety is ranked above all the philosophers, evidently not only knew of our institutions, but was even in those distant ages an ardent admirer of them.*

Category: SYMPATHIZATION

Against Apion begins with a lengthy introduction, in which Josephus sets out the need for the work and some of its fundamental bases (*Ag. Ap.* 1.1–59), and a section in which he deals with the silence of Greek historians on Jewish history (*Ag. Ap.* 1.60–68). This reference to Pythagoras, whom he a little later refers to as "that great man" (*Ag. Ap.* 1.165), appears in the next section of the work (*Ag. Ap.* 1.69–218), in which Josephus is describing references to Jews and Judaism by pagan authors. With Pythagoras, he begins to deal with Greek authors in particular. Here he depends for his information on the historian and biographer Hermippus of Smyrna, who, Josephus tells us, says that in certain of Pythagoras' precepts "he was imitating and appropriating the doctrines of Jews and Thracians" (*Ag. Ap.* 1.165). It is difficult to identify what Jewish doctrines might be linked to the "precepts" in question,[98] and in any case they have little to do with the religious and ethical distinctives of the Jews. So it is interesting to see how Josephus turns Hermippus' passing comment into a statement of more general emulation: Pythagoras was a "zealot" (ζηλωτής) for our ways (τὰ παρ' ἡμῖν).

§156 Against Apion *1.166*

> *In ancient times various cities were acquainted with the existence of our nation, and to some of these many of our customs have now found their way, and here and there been thought worthy of imitation.*

Category: SYMPATHIZATION

This statement is also found in the section in which Josephus is enumerating references to Jews and Judaism by Greek authors. The striking thing about the statement is that the material he adduces contains virtually no indication of imitation whatsoever. He begins with Theophrastus (Aristotle's successor), Herodotus of Halicarnassus, and the poet Cheorilus of Samos (*Ag. Ap.* 1.167–75), but these references are (at best) simply allusions to Jews and Judaism.[99] His next statement begins by acknowledging this ("not only did the

98. Pythagoras instructed one of his students "not to pass a certain spot, on which an ass had collapsed, to abstain from thirst-producing water, and to avoid all calumny" (*Ag. Ap.* 1.164).

99. There are no explicit references to Jews or Judaism in these texts. Josephus' inferences are probably valid in the first two instances but not in the third; see Thackeray's notes *ad loc.*

Greeks know the Jews") but goes on to refer to admiration ("but they admired any of their number whom they happened to meet"; *Ag. Ap.* 1.176). The passages that he subsequently adduces contain a few suggestions of admiration[100] but none whatsoever of imitation. However, this gap between the content of his sources and the conclusions that he wishes to draw from them is revealing. Josephus is firmly committed to the belief that foreign cities not only admired Jewish customs (τῶν ἐθῶν) but also "thought them worthy of emulation [ζήλου]" and adopted them as their own.

§157 Against Apion *1.225*

> *These frivilous and utterly senseless specimens of humanity, accustomed from the first to erroneous ideas about the gods, were incapable of imitating the solemnity of our theology, and the sight of our numerous admirers filled them with envy.*

Category: SYMPATHIZATION

In the next section of the work (*Ag. Ap.* 1.219–2.144) Josephus responds to various criticisms and calumnies leveled against Jews and Judaism by Gentile authors. He begins with the Egyptians, who, he says, were the originators of these libels. One source of the animosity was the original "domination of our ancestors over their country" (*Ag. Ap.* 1.224). Another was "the profound contrast between the two cults," since the "national custom" of the Egyptians was "to regard animals as gods." This leads into the statement cited above, where Josephus introduces a third reason for the anti-Jewish attitudes of the Egyptians, namely, their envy at seeing Jewish ideas "being zealously emulated by many" (ζηλουμένους ὑπὸ πολλῶν). Their envy is intensified by their own inability to "imitate" (μιμήσασθαι) Jewish ideas about God (θεολογίας) themselves. Again one notes the gratuitous way in which Josephus introduces the theme of Gentile sympathizing into his argument.

§158 Against Apion *2.45*

> *His successor, Ptolemy surnamed Philadelphus, not only surrendered all prisoners of our race within his realm, but was liberal in his presents of money. The highest compliment, however, which he paid us lay in his keen desire to know our laws and to read the books of our sacred scriptures.*

Category: SYMPATHIZATION

100. Clearchus, one of Aristotle's students, was impressed with a certain Jew who "not only spoke Greek but had the soul of a Greek" (*Ag. Ap.* 1.180); while Clearchus says that he learned something from this Jew, his description of him (Greek in language and soul) leaves us little reason to believe that what he learned was distinctively Jewish. Hecataeus is said to have admired Jews for their tenacious commitment to their laws (*Ag. Ap.* 1. 190–93), but this is quite distinct from imitation.

Continuing with his response to anti-Jewish polemic, Josephus turns to Apion at the start of book 2, arguing (among other things) that all of Alexander's successors in Egypt have treated their Jewish subjects with respect and honor. Although there is historical evidence for this general claim (Schürer 1986, 3:114), the two passages of interest to us here (see the following entry as well) tell us more about Josephus's assumptions than about historical realities. In *Ag. Ap.* 2.45–47 he deals with Ptolemy II Philadelphus, essentially by providing a concise summary of the narrative related in the *Letter of Aristeas*. As we have seen, Josephus is quite capable of producing a lengthy rehearsal of the *Aristeas* narrative (*Ant.* 12.11–118). What is of interest in this passage is the way in which he sums it up when he wants to be brief. The story has to do with the king's liberal benefaction and his "keen desire"[101] to read Israel's scriptures and to know the law. His main point has to do with Ptolemy's support for the value and status of the Jewish community in Alexandria. He argues that such royal support is demonstrated by the *Aristeas* narrative, whose central theme as he summarizes it is the king's desire "to learn our laws and our ancestral philosophy" (τὴν πάτριον ἡμῶν φιλοσοφίαν; *Ag. Ap.* 2.47).

§159 Against Apion *2.48*

> *Apion has further ignored the extreme kindness shown to us successively by nearly all the kings of his Macedonian ancestors. Thus, Ptolemy III surnamed Euergetes, after his conquest of the whole of Syria, instead of sacrificing to the gods of Egypt in thanksgiving for his success, came to Jerusalem, and there, after our manner, offered numerous sacrifices to God, and dedicated votive gifts appropriate to such a victory.*

Category: SYMPATHIZATION

Here Josephus continues to chronicle Ptolemaic support for the Jews. While there is some evidence of such support on the part of Ptolemy III—inscriptional evidence suggesting that he granted the right of asylum to a Jewish community (προσευχή)[102]—there is no corroborating evidence for this account of worship in Jerusalem. The event itself is certainly within the realm of possibility; victorious kings did this sort of thing. But Josephus's particular rendition tells us more about Josephus than about Ptolemy. Even if Ptolemy gave thanks for his victory by offering sacrifice in the Jewish manner to the deity worshipped at the Jerusalem temple, this would by no means have been an exclusive affair; no doubt he would have also sacrificed "to the gods of Egypt in thanksgiving for his success" when he got home. Nor would he have acknowledged the deity worshipped at the temple simply as "God" (τῷ θεῷ), with all of the monotheistic overtones of this term in Jewish usage. As is often the case,

101. Literally, the king became "one who eagerly desired" (ἐπιθυμητής).

102. See the discussion in Schürer (1986, 3:46–47).

Josephus has put the maximal interpretation on normal royal practice; in his account Ptolemy III is a Jewish sympathizer.

§160 Against Apion *2.123*

> *From the Greeks we are severed more by our geographical position than by our institutions, with the result that we neither hate nor envy them. On the contrary, many of them have agreed to adopt our laws; of whom some have remained faithful, while others, lacking the necessary endurance, have again seceded.*

Category: CONVERSION

At this point in Book II Josephus picks up Apion's spurious charge that Jews swear "to show no goodwill to a single alien [ἀλλοφύλῳ], above all to Greeks" (*Ag. Ap.* 2.121). By way of response, he returns to the theme of Gentile attraction to Jewish ways (cf. *Ag. Ap.* 1.162–66). While he does not say so explicitly, the argument seems to be that the adoption of Jewish laws by Greeks demonstrates a willingness on the part of Jews to share their customs with others and thus a readiness "to show goodwill" to any "alien" who finds Jewish customs appealing.

It is true that elsewhere in *Against Apion* Josephus can use similar language of Gentiles who clearly are not proselytes. That is, there are texts that speak of Gentiles who adopt Jewish laws and customs but in a piecemeal or less than complete way (e.g., *Ag. Ap.* 1.166; 2.279–82). Thus it might be possible to interpret this passage as a reference to sympathizers rather than converts. But two things suggest that converts are in view. One is the language in which he describes these Gentiles: they have agreed εἰς τοὺς ἡμετέρους νόμους εἰσελθεῖν ("to enter into our laws"). Josephus does not use "proselyte" at all in his writings, but, etymologically at least, εἰσελθεῖν is a close equivalent.[103] In any case, to speak of Gentiles "entering into [the Jewish] laws" seems to suggest a more intimate association than is indicated elsewhere by language of admiration or imitation. This is confirmed, secondly, by what he goes on to say about Gentile apostates—those who, after adopting Jewish laws, have not "remained faithful" but "have again seceded" (*Ag. Ap.* 2.123). He introduces such persons in order to make the point that not one of them has said anything about the oath to which Apion makes scurrilous reference. Especially in view of the distinction that Josephus makes later between true converts and casual admirers (*Ag. Ap.* 2.209–10), his argument seems to rest on the assumption that only a convert would have been privy to such an in-group oath (if there were one).

Two aspects of this brief argument are worthy of further notice. One is the implication that Jewish and Greek "institutions" (or customs; ἐπιτηδεύμασιν) are comparable. While the idea of a fundamental convergence between Jewish

103. προσήλυτος, of course, is formed from προσέρχομαι. Cf. Philo, who uses "proselyte" but prefers formations from ἐπέρχομαι.

law and Greek ethos is more pronounced elsewhere (e.g., Philo, *Letter of Aristeas*), it is interesting to see it cropping up in Josephus as well. The other, as has already been mentioned, is the reference to apostates: Gentiles who had first become proselytes and then, "lacking the necessary endurance," had withdrawn (ἀπέστησαν). It is only because it serves his argument that Josephus introduces such figures; typically, he emphasizes the traffic that moves in the positive direction. Still, the reverse flow must have happened more frequently than is indicated in the material. Josephus's statement draws back a curtain on what must have been a more common phenomenon.

§161 Against Apion *2.163*

> *But the question, who was the most successful legislator, and who attained to the truest conception of God, may be answered by contrasting the laws themselves with those of others.*

Category: ETHICAL MONOTHEISM

After responding directly to the accusations and calumnies of Apion and his ilk (*Ag. Ap.* 1.219–2.144), Josephus turns from the negative to the positive, setting out to provide "a brief account of our constitution [τοῦ πολιτεύματος] as a whole and of its details" (*Ag. Ap.* 2.145). He will argue that the constitution prescribed by the law is "excellently designed to promote piety [εὐσέβειαν], friendly relations with each other, and humanity [φιλανθρωπίαν] towards the world at large, besides justice, hardihood, and contempt of death" (*Ag. Ap.* 2.146). What is important about this description of the law is not only the use of terms drawn from Hellenistic moral discourse but also the assumption conveyed by this usage and cropping up from time to time in the subsequent argument that Gentiles, or at least the best and wisest among them, are already in a position to recognize and value the excellent qualities of the law. In other words, the law embodies virtues that are universal in character and accessible to all.

He begins by arguing for the superiority of Moses as a lawgiver. First, he claims that Moses is "the most ancient of all legislators in the records of the whole world" (*Ag. Ap.* 2.154). While he will subsequently argue that Moses was also the source of what was beneficial in the work of subsequent legislators, here Josephus's point is simply that of antiquity and priority. In addition, he puts to Moses's credit the fact that even though, through the brilliance of his leadership in the exodus, "[h]e succeeded in making the whole people dependent upon himself," he chose not to "assume absolute and despotic power" (*Ag. Ap.* 2.158) but instead to secure the future well-being of his people by providing them with good laws. This leads to his main argument, having to do with the superiority of the laws themselves, which, he claims, demonstrates not only that Moses was "the most successful legislator" of all but also that he "attained to the truest conception of God" (*Ag. Ap.* 2.163).

This last statement, thrown in almost gratuitously, is what is of particular interest here. Josephus claims that a comparison of the various bodies of legislation will demonstrate that Moses is the legislator who arrived at the "most right belief concerning God" (τῆς δικαιοτάτης περὶ θεοῦ πίστεως). Since he uses the same construction ("this belief concerning God") a little later (*Ag. Ap.* 2.169) in a context where it is equivalent to ways of "thinking about the nature of God" (περὶ τῆς τοῦ θεοῦ φύσεως πεφρονηκότες; *Ag. Ap.* 2.168), Thackeray's translation—"the truest conception of God"—is on the mark.[104] The statement is interesting because it assumes the existence of a more basic or universal standpoint from which Moses's conception of God can be compared with that of other legislators. Knowledge of God is something that can, in some measure, be attained apart from the Jewish law, even if the law demonstrates the superiority of Moses in this regard. While the argument is perhaps not incompatible with the notion that Moses himself was the source of this universal standpoint, the fit is nevertheless awkward. The statement seems to assume that other legislators have attained some "conception of God" on their own, even if it is inferior to that of Moses.

§162 Against Apion *2.168*

> *That the wisest of the Greeks learned to adopt these conceptions of God from principles which Moses supplied them, I am not not concerned to urge; but they have borne abundant witness to the excellence of these doctrines, and to their consequence with the nature and majesty of God. In fact, Pythagoras, Anaxagoras, Plato, the Stoics who succeeded him, and indeed nearly all the philosophers appear to have held similar views concerning the nature of God.*

Category: SYMPATHIZATION, ETHICAL MONOTHEISM

Here Josephus notes in passing a second explanation as to the origin of the similarities between Jewish law and Greek philosophy, one that makes a stronger claim for Moses and Judaism. He could argue, he says, that, in their conceptions of God at least, Greek thinkers had not only come later than Moses (*Ag. Ap.* 2.154) but had actually been instructed by him. But he does not feel it necessary to insist on the point: "I am not not concerned to urge [this]." He is content to argue on the basis of similarity rather than influence. The law, he asserts, inculcates a form of ethical monotheism already known to and valued by the best of the Greek philosophers: "Nearly all the [Greek] philosophers appear to have held similar views concerning the nature of God." That is, like Moses, they believed that God was all-knowing, "One, uncreated and immutable to all eternity; in beauty surpassing all mortal thought, made known to us by His power,

104. In *Ag. Ap.* 2.224 and 255 Josephus uses a similar construction with δόξα instead of πίστις: τὴν περὶ θεοῦ δόξαν.

although the nature of His real being passes knowledge" (*Ag. Ap.* 2.167). Moreover, says Josephus, they have "borne abundant witness to the excellence" of Moses's teaching and to its "consonance with the nature and majesty of God." This last statement puts the philosophers in the guise not of Moses's disciples but of autonomous thinkers who have their own independent understanding of God, on the basis of which they can judge the excellence of Moses's own conceptions.

§163 Against Apion *2.209–10*

> *The consideration given by our legislator to the equitable treatment of aliens also merits attention. It will be seen that he took the best of all possible measures at once to secure our own customs from corruption, and to throw them open ungrudgingly to any who elect to share them. To all who desire to come and live under the same laws with us, he gives a gracious welcome, holding that it is not family ties alone which constitute relationship, but agreement in the principles of conduct. On the other hand, it was not his pleasure that casual visitors should be admitted to the intimacies of our daily life.*

Category: SYMPATHIZATION, CONVERSION

As part of his positive description of the law and its virtues, Josephus touches on Mosaic legislation concerning the treatment of aliens (ἀλλοφύλους; *Ag. Ap.* 2.209). His main point has to do with Jewish readiness to accept as full members of the community "all who desire to come and live under the same laws." But the passage is also of interest because of the sharp distinction he makes between these full converts and "casual visitors" (literally, "those coming in in a secondary way"; τοὺς ἐκ παρέργου προσιόντας).

This sharp distinction stands in contrast with Josephus's usual tendencies. Elsewhere he tends to treat sympathizers and converts as part of a single phenomenon—those who have adopted Jewish customs to a lesser or greater extent—with full conversion just the end point of a spectrum the whole of which he views positively (e.g., *J.W.* 7.45; *Ant.* 20.34–53). In the case of Izates, for example, while it was circumcision that would make him "genuinely a Jew," before he took this step he had already moved through several stages of increasing levels of Jewish observance. In such cases, the most significant line is drawn between this group of pious Gentiles on the one hand and those who are caught up in the folly of pagan religion on the other. In *Ag. Ap.* 2.209–10, however, we encounter a more fundamental line of division between sympathizers and converts: on the one side there are those who choose to share the "customs" (τὰ οἰκεῖα) of the Jews and to "live under the same laws," thereby becoming part of the same "household relationship" (τὴν οἰκειότητα). On the other side are "casual visitors," whom Moses would not allow to mingle with the insiders. It is not clear how Gentile sympathizers such as we have already met in *Against Apion*—the "numerous admirers" (*Ag. Ap.* 1.225) or those who have imitated "many of our customs (*Ag. Ap.* 1.166)—would fit into this sharply bifurcated map of humanity.

Another distinctive aspect of this passage is the choice of vocabulary. Elsewhere when speaking of Gentiles who have adopted Jewish customs but without necessarily becoming converts, he has used ἔθη or θρησκείαι. Here he uses words drawn from the context of household or family: τὰ οἰκεῖα; τὴν οἰκειότητα. Similarly, while here he speaks of Gentiles coming to "share" (μετέχειν) Jewish customs, elsewhere he uses different verbs.[105] This distinctive vocabulary serves to signal Josephus's distinctive focus: here he is concerned with the distinction between converts and sympathizers. Still, this is simply another aspect of the different emphasis found in this passage and not an explanation of it.

In part, we can account for the difference by recognizing that Josephus's account is constrained by the scripture he is describing. While incorporating the resident alien into Jewish life to a significant extent, the Mosaic legislation nevertheless makes a sharp distinction between resident aliens and native-born Israelites. In his description of it, Josephus understandably follows suit. But further, the passage also reveals that the distinction continues to be a reality in the world Josephus inhabits. Even though he tends to approve of Gentile sympathizers and to see them according to a continuous spectrum rather than a set of sharply defined categories, he is nevertheless aware that only at a certain point in the spectrum does a Gentile become "genuinely a Jew."

His primary point, however, has to do with those Gentiles who have reached this point in the spectrum. In contrast to the "casual visitors," converts are described here as those who have "come to live with us under the same laws" (ὑπὸ τοὺς αὐτοὺς ἡμῖν νόμους ζῆν ὑπελθόντες). By virtue of sharing the practices of the household (τὰ οἰκεία), they have entered into a family relationship (τὴν οἰκειότητα) with the rest. Josephus alludes to the fact that the Jewish family has traditionally been determined on the basis of race; but, he says, the family relationship (τὴν οἰκειότητα) that he is describing is one that is determined not simply by race (οὐ τῷ γένει μόνον) but "by the choice of a way of life" (τῇ προαιρέσι τοῦ βίου). Seen from the angle of conversion, then, Judaism is not so much an ethnic entity that one enters through birth (though it continues to be so) as it is a kind of philosophic way of life that one enters through choice.

§164 Against Apion *2.224*

Plato himself admits that it is hazardous to divulge the truth about God to the ignorant mob.

Category: ETHICAL MONOTHEISM

105. E.g., τιμᾶν (*Ant.* 3.217); ζηλοῦν (*Ant.* 20.41); μιμεῖσθαι (*Ag. Ap.* 1.225). μετέχειν appears in *Ag. Ap.* 2.261 as well; see §166 below.

In this section of his discourse Josephus is continuing his comparison of the Jewish law with legislative systems devised by Plato and other philosophers. Here his point is that unlike these other systems, which are often held to be impossibly idealistic, the Jewish law is actually observed faithfully by the common people as a whole. It is in this context that he cites Plato himself, who chose to withhold "the truth about God" (τὴν ἀληθῆ περὶ θεοῦ δόξαν) from the "ignorant mob" (cf. Plato *Tim.* 28C). The pertinent aspect of this comment is the assumption that Plato has knowledge of "the truth about God." Of course, given what Josephus has had to say already about Moses as the teacher of the Greeks (see *Ag. Ap.* 2.168; §162, the assumption here could be that Plato derived this truth from Moses himself. But Josephus does not say so; furthermore, earlier in this immediate argument he has made another statement implying that non-Jews might have independent knowledge about God.

The statement is hypothetical, but it is no less significant on that account. Imagine, says Josephus, that the Jewish nation was unknown to the Greek world but that someone described to a Greek audience "a people who held such sublime ideas about God and had for ages continued steadily faithful to such laws as ours" (*Ag. Ap.* 2.221). The reaction of the audience would be astonishment, says Josephus, precisely because Greek philosophers have not been successful in making their sublime legislative programs acceptable to the masses. This leads to the comparison with Plato that we have already observed, but what is important here is the assumption that both the imaginary orator and his audience already had the requisite knowledge to recognize "sublime ideas about God" when they heard them. In other words, the argument assumes that Greeks had enough independent knowledge of God to make a judgment on the virtues and authenticity of the Jewish law.

§165 Against Apion *2.255–57*

> *The genuine exponents of Greek philosophy were well aware of all that I have said, nor were they ignorant of the worthless shifts to which the allegorists have resort. That was why they rightly despised them and agreed with us in forming a true and befitting conception of God. From this standpoint Plato declares that no poet ought to be admitted to the republic, and dismisses even Homer in laudatory terms, after crowning and anointing him with unguents, in order to prevent him from obscuring by his fables the correct doctrine about God. In two points, in particular, Plato followed the example of our legislator. He prescribed as the primary duty of the citizens a study of their laws, which they must all learn word for word by heart. Again, he took precautions to prevent foreigners from mixing with them at random, and to keep the state pure and confined to law-abiding citizens.*

Category: SYMPATHIZATION, ETHICAL MONOTHEISM

This passage follows a lengthy section in which Josephus ridicules the gods of Greek mythology (*Ag. Ap.* 2.236–54), denouncing the poets for their part in popularizing such notions and thus in providing a flawed foundation for Greek legislative systems. Such views were not universal, however. Josephus points to the "genuine exponents of Greek philosophy," Plato included, who "agreed" (συνεφώνησαν) with the Jews in that they held the same "true and befitting conception of God." While agreement does not necessarily imply dependence, Josephus immediately goes on to say that at two points in particular Plato "followed the example of"—literally, "imitated" (μεμίμηται)—"our legislator."

For present purposes the specific points of "imitation" do not require any closer examination (the second will come into the discussion of the next entry below). What is of interest here is the reappearance of a pattern of argumentation that we have already observed. As we have seen, in *Ag. Ap.* 2.168 (§162) Josephus claimed that he could make the case, if he so chose, that the best of the Greek philosophers had learned important things from Moses; but he would not press the point, he said, since for his present argument it was sufficient to note the similarities between them. In the passage under discussion here, we again see a readiness to assert dependence even though the main thrust of his argument depends on the lesser claim of similarity.

On the one hand, Josephus is prepared to claim not only that statements made by Greek philosophers were similar to the teaching of Moses but also that Moses was their teacher: they "imitated" him, depending on him for their best and most characteristic conceptions. But on the other, Josephus does not insist on the point. He makes no attempt to demonstrate that any "imitation" had actually taken place, being content simply with a brief presentation of (putative) similarities. Perhaps he is assuming that the existence of similarities between Moses and Plato can be combined with the temporal priority of Moses (cf. *Ag. Ap.* 2.154) to demonstrate the dependence of the one on the other. If so, he is expecting a lot of his readers; only the most cooperative and docile reader would be convinced that any deliberate imitation had taken place. But his argument does not rest on the point. Even if he himself believed it to be true, it was not necessary for him to convince his readers that Plato and the others actually borrowed from Moses; it was enough that they agreed with the Jews in their critique of Greek polytheism.

§166 Against Apion *2.260–61*

> *They might perhaps be justly reproached for discourtesy, because they accorded to no one the rights either of citizenship or of residence among them. We, on the contrary, while we have no desire to emulate the customs of others, yet gladly welcome any who wish to share our own. That, I think, may be taken as a proof both of humanity and magnanimity.*

Category: SYMPATHIZATION, CONVERSION

This passage appears shortly after the one just considered, as Josephus continues to discuss similarities between Moses and Plato. At this point in his discussion Josephus is comparing the Lacedaemonians and the Jews with respect to their policies towards foreigners. The reference to the welcome that Jews extended towards foreigners is somewhat unexpected, however, in that the preceding argument has to do with the opposite. Josephus has been pointing out ways in which "Plato followed the example of our legislator," one of which is the fact that both took precautions "to prevent foreigners from mixing with them at random, and to keep the state pure and confined to law-abiding citizens" (*Ag. Ap*. 2.257). At this point, Josephus is treating such separatism as a virtue, citing Plato as an ally in this regard. This leads him to take up the criticism of Apollonius Molon, who had condemned Jews for their separatism but who, Josephus asserts, failed to recognize that Philo, along with "Greeks of the highest reputation," (*Ag. Ap*. 2.259), had held similar views. The fact that Apollonius's home city of Alabanda claimed ancestry from the Spartans (Calder and Sherwin-White 2003) perhaps explains why Josephus then presents the Lacedaemonias as taking such separatism to an extreme. It is at this point that he switches rhetorical gears, arguing that, in contrast to the Spartans, the Jews should be commended for their readiness to give a glad welcome to any foreigners who wish to share Jewish customs.

Josephus's language here is vague: "we do not think it proper [ἀξιοῦμεν] to be zealous for the things of others [τὰ τῶν ἄλλων], yet gladly welcome any who wish to share [μετέχειν] our own." Concerning the extent of such sharing, he could be thinking of any point along the whole spectrum that leads from admiration to conversion. In fact, since in speaking of the Lacedaemonians he refers both to citizenship (analogous to conversion) and to residence (analogous to sympathizing), the whole spectrum is probably in view here. Still, it is not without significance that in the only other place where Josephus uses μετέχειν with reference to Gentile attraction to Judaism, he is speaking of full converts rather than "casual visitors" (see §163 above). Thus it is probably correct to say that when Josephus shifts from the Lacedaemonians to the Jews, he has converts primarily in view.

The most significant aspect of the passage, however, is its unexpected character. Moving along a path of free association, Josephus's thoughts are drawn from the main theme of exclusion and separation to his more typical theme of attraction and inclusion. Thus he ends up by making an assertion—we gladly welcome foreigners—that completely undermines the argument that he set out to establish—Jewish separatism is consistent with Greek ideals. The oddness of the rhetorical sequence only serves to reveal the underlying tendencies of Josephus's thought. Whether he is thinking of sympathizers or converts here, he takes it as fundamental that Judaism attracts Gentiles and that Jews are happy to welcome them. While separatism might be justifiable in Greek terms, it is this inclusiveness that corresponds to the higher Greek ideals of "humanity and magnanimity."

§167 Against Apion *2.279–84*

> *An infinity of time has passed since Moses, if one compares the age in which he lived with those of other legislators; yet it will be found that throughout the whole of that period not merely have our laws stood the test of our own use, but they have to an ever increasing extent excited the emulation of the world at large. Our earliest imitators were the Greek philosophers, who, though ostensibly observing the laws of their own countries, yet in their conduct and philosophy were Moses's disciples, holding similar views about God, and advocating the simple life and friendly communion between man and man. But that is not all. The masses have long since shown a keen desire to adopt our religious observances; and there is not one city, Greek or barbarian, nor a single nation, to which our custom of abstaining from work on the seventh day has not spread, and where the fasts and the lighting of lamps and many of our prohibitions in the matter of food are not observed. Moreover, they attempt to imitate our unanimity, our liberal charities, our devoted labour in the crafts, our endurance under persecution on behalf of our laws. The greatest miracle of all is that our Law holds out no seductive bait of sensual pleasure, but has exercised this influence through its own inherent merits; and, as God permeates the universe, so the Law has found its way among all mankind.*

Category: SYMPATHIZATION

This oft-cited passage[106] is probably the most unreserved—even exuberant—acclamation of Gentile sympathizing in the whole Josephan corpus. It is significant not only for what it says but also for where it is placed. It represents the grand conclusion to the section in which Josephus describes the law as an ideal constitution (*Ag. Ap*. 2.145–286). While his main theme concerns "the excellence of our laws" (*Ag. Ap*. 2.286), one of the primary evidences for its excellence is the degree to which it has been admired, imitated, and adopted.

Of particular interest is his reference to "the Greek philosophers." In this grand conclusion, as he presents his catalog of all those who have "shown a keen desire to adopt our religious observances," he gives pride of place to these philosophers, who were "our earliest imitators" (*Ag. Ap*. 2.281–86). We have observed how, at several points in the argument up to this point, Josephus has introduced the theme of imitation only to back away from it (*Ag. Ap*. 2. 168, 255–57). By the time he arrives at the end of his argument, however, Josephus seems to have abandoned his reticence. While his decision not to press the point has freed him from the necessity of demonstrating it, it is nevertheless the position that he ultimately wants to claim for himself: to the extent that ethical monotheism can be found among "the wisest of the Greeks," it is because

106. E.g., Barclay (1996, 365); Feldman (1993, *passim*); McKnight (1991, 41). Even Cohen, who wants to downplay this aspect of Josephus, recognizes the positive character of this passage (Cohen [1987a, 426]).

they "learned to adopt these conceptions of God from principles with which Moses supplied them" (*Ag. Ap.* 2.168).

To claim it, of course, is not to demonstrate it. While a skeptical reader might be prepared to grant some similarities between Torah piety and such ethical monotheism as can be found among the Greek philosophers, it would take much more credulity to accept his claim that the philosophers actually admired and imitated the law. Likewise it would be difficult to demonstrate that in the areas of unanimity, liberality, labor, or steadfastness under persecution, Gentiles were emulating Jewish models. For similar reasons, the claims would be difficult to refute. But other claims rest on firmer foundations. Josephus's references to specifically Jewish customs—Sabbath observance, for example—together with the more general claim that Gentile sympathizers can be found throughout the civilized world, would not carry any weight if there were not some correspondence with the lived reality of Josephus and his intended readers. Of course, his language is dramatic and hyperbolic: the law has made its way through the whole of humanity (διὰ πάντων ἀνθρώπων) just as God pervades the whole cosmos.[107] Nevertheless, the passage tells us something not only about Josephus's assumptions and biases but also about what was accepted as true in his wider social context.

While the passage makes reference to a range of ways in which Gentiles imitated Jews and adopted their ways, there is no reference to full conversion. None of the examples have to do with Gentiles who embrace the law fully and thus are admitted as full members of the community (cf. *Ag. Ap.* 2.209–10). Rather, they have to do with the adoption of this law or that custom, a piecemeal pattern of sympathizing rather than thoroughgoing proselytism. This is borne out as well by the language that Josephus uses—for example, that of zealous emulation or of imitation.[108] This may suggest that Josephus places more emphasis on sympathizing and adherence than on conversion, though it is also true that, since Gentile sympathizers were more commonly encountered than proselytes, it served his argument here to emphasize the former.

One other aspect of the passage is worthy of note. The law has permeated the world, Josephus says, simply because of its inherent attractiveness. The statement should not be taken in a one-sided way, of course. Josephus's world also contains advocates for the law such as Eleazar and Ananias (in the Izates narrative), not to mention Josephus himself. Still, he explains the popularity of the law among "the masses" throughout the world (*Ag. Ap.* 2.282) as the result

107. Also, "the world at large" (τοῖς ἄλλοις ἅπασιν ἀνθρώποις); "the masses" (πλήθεσιν); "not one city" (ἔστιν οὐ πόλις); "all mankind" (διὰ πάντων ἀνθρώπων); and, a little further on (2.286), "multitude of admirers" (τοῦ πλήθους τῶν ζηλούντων).

108. Zeal: *Ag. Ap.* 2.280, 282, 286; cf. *Ant.* 20.41; *Ag. Ap.* 1.162, 166; imitation: *Ag. Ap.* 2.283; cf. 1.165; 2.225, 283.

of the virtues clearly evident in the law itself and the communities that it has created rather than of any deliberate initiative on the part of the Jews.

§168 Against Apion *2.293–95*

> *I would therefore boldly maintain that we have introduced to the rest of the world a very large number of very beautiful ideas. What greater beauty than inviolable piety? What higher justice than obedience to the laws? What more beneficial than to be in harmony with one another, to be a prey neither to disunion in adversity, nor to arrogance and faction in prosperity; in war to despise death, in peace to devote oneself to crafts or agriculture; and to be convinced that everything in the whole universe is under the eye and direction of God? Had these precepts been either committed to writing or more consistently observed by others before us, we should have owed them a debt of gratitude as their disciples. If, however, it is seen that no one observes them better than ourselves, and if we have shown that we were the first to discover them, then the Apions and Molons and all who delight in lies and abuse may be left to their own confusion.*

Category: SYMPATHIZATION

This stirring paean to Jewish virtue stands at the end of Josephus's final peroration, thus bringing *Against Apion* to a close. The main thrust of the passage is to ascribe to the Jews a special accomplishment vis-à-vis the rest of the nations: they are both the source and the primary model of these "very numerous and beautiful things" (πλείστων ἅμα καὶ καλλίστων). But although the passage only alludes to the existence of Gentile sympathizers, since it concludes a work that has been at pains to emphasize their significance, it is appropriate to mention it here as well.

For not only have the Jews discovered these virtues—piety, justice, faithfulness to the laws, harmonious relations, and, above all, a life lived under divine providence—they have been the ones to introduce (εἰσηγητάς) these things to "the others" (τοῖς ἄλλοις). If these things had been introduced by others, then it would have been the Jews who were the "disciples" (μαθηταί). But since they were the originators, it is the others—so it is implied—who have become the "disciples" of the Jews, at least to the extent that they have been willing to accept and assimilate the beautiful gifts that the Jews have introduced to the world.

Concluding Observations

Josephus's writings provide us with a substantial collection of texts dealing with sympathization and a smaller but still significant set of texts dealing with conversion, together with a handful of texts reflecting his apparent belief that some Gentiles were capable of arriving at a form of ethical monotheism on their own. The texts are of interest at two levels. First, they provide us with evidence pertaining to social and religious realities in the first-century Mediterranean world. To be sure, this evidence is mediated to us by someone who was by no means an impartial observer and a simple recorder of facts. At each point it is necessary to take account both of Josephus's own biases and interests, and of the value of his sources. Still, as a measure of what he assumes his readers will know and accept, his work provides us with a window into the world inhabited by both. Second, the texts surveyed here provide us with evidence for Josephus's own viewpoint and beliefs.

There is little more that needs to be said at this point about the first level of interest; we will return to this in Part 2. But a few comments are in order about Josephus himself. As we observed at the start of this chapter, in his study of sympathization and conversion in Josephus's writings, Cohen has attempted to minimize the significance of this material in several ways: (1) by treating reverence shown by foreign monarchs and dignitaries as simply the way such figures were expected to behave; (2) by characterizing all of the references in the *Jewish War* and *Antiquities*, except for the Adiabene narrative, as "cool" towards Gentile sympathizers and converts; (3) by treating the Adiabene narrative as a source that Josephus has incorporated without reworking; and (4) by accounting for the more positive attitude in *Against Apion* on the basis of a change in Josephus's circumstances, together with his use of sources. As we have noted along the way, these conclusions are not borne out by the material.[109]

First, while it was common for monarchs in antiquity to honor foreign temples as a means of political policy, Josephus typically puts an additional interpretation on such actions. Darius, Xerxes, Alexander, Antiochus VII, and other monarchs are presented as displaying particular piety towards the God of Israel, and of a kind that Josephus by no means restricts to the royal elite. Josephus makes no fundamental distinction between foreign potentates and Gentiles in general. He approves of it when Gentile kings worship at the temple and venerate the God of Israel not because this is the sign of a good king (though it is) but because this is a good thing for any Gentile to do.

Second, in all of his writings Josephus assumes that it is a good thing for Gentiles to adopt Jewish ways and observances, and he takes evident pride in the fact that they do so in great numbers. Further, there is no evidence that Josephus disapproved of it when such adoption went as far as full conversion. True, he recounts instances where converts got into difficulties (e.g., Fulvia). But nowhere does he suggest that conversion was therefore inappropriate or something to be avoided. In one instance, he expresses opposition to forced conversion (*Life* 112–13). But even if the statement is given full weight, he nevertheless in the same context speaks in favor of people worshipping God (which in the context means conversion) when they can do so as a matter of free choice.

109. Since I have learned so much from Shaye Cohen's work over the years, I am somewhat dismayed to find myself using him as a foil for my own interpretation of Josephus. But such is scholarship; I think he is wrong here, but usefully so.

Elsewhere, his description of the Idumeans contains no hint of disapproval over the degree of coercion in their original acceptance of Jewish customs.

Third, the way in which the Adiabene narrative both echoes the programmatic themes set out in the introduction to the work and stands in continuity with Josephus's positive attitude towards Gentile sympathizers throughout the work means that it cannot be set to one side. The story of Izates is a parade example of the lesson that he wants his readers to draw from his *Antiquities* as a whole—namely, that God will reward those who seek God's will and live in accordance with God's laws. Josephus's own attitudes are fully on display in this prototypical account of a Gentile sympathizer and convert.

Fourth, the significance of *Against Apion* lies not only in its own enthusiasm towards Gentile sympathizers but also in its links with *Antiquities*. In the introduction to the later work, Josephus links it tightly to its predecessor. The goal of *Antiquities*—to demonstrate to its readers "the extreme antiquity of our race" (*Ag. Ap.* 1.1)—and that of *Against Apion*—"to instruct all who desire to know the truth concerning the antiquity of our race" (*Ag. Ap.* 1.3)—are identical. In responding to those "detractors" whose "calumnies" served to "discredit the statements in my history concerning our antiquity," Josephus was attending to some unfinished business so that he might thereby bring his initial intentions to completion. In the closing words of *Against Apion*, he presents the willingness of the Jews to accept converts as a sign of their "humanity and magnanimity." Thus we are justified in taking the unambiguous enthusiasm of *Against Apion* as a key to the interpretation of the references to Gentile sympathizers and converts in *Antiquities*, even though the impact of those references, scattered through a much larger and more complex work, is more diffuse.

At the same time, however, this does not mean that we can go all the way with Mason in arguing that Josephus wrote with the definite purpose of encouraging readers to emulate Izates. One small but telling detail is the way in which Josephus eliminated the "missionizing" element from his account of Solomon's prayer of dedication (*Ant.* 8.117–18).

With respect to Izates himself, while the story provided Josephus with plenty of opportunity to exhort his readers to emulate the king, either in his initial adoption of Jewish ways or in his subsequent conversion, Josephus studiously avoids doing so. In *Against Apion*, while he is immensely proud of the fact that "the masses have long since shown a keen desire to adopt our religious observances" and that "there is not one city, Greek or barbarian, nor a single nation" to which Jewish customs have not spread (*Ag. Ap.* 2.282), he makes no direct or implied appeal to his readers to join the ranks of Gentile sympathizers or converts. He is evidently proud that such people exist, and in considerable numbers; but he gives us no reason to believe that increasing the numbers was a primary goal of his work. His purpose in introducing the theme is to convince his readers of the "excellence of our lawgiver and of the revelation concerning God which he has transmitted to us" (*Ag. Ap.* 2.279). Despite what

Manetho, Apion, and the others might have said, Josephus argues, Judaism is a noble and distinguished form of piety, conforming to the highest ideals of the Greek world itself.

Fifth, while most of the material in Josephus has to do with sympathization and conversion, apparently Josephus also believed that certain non-Jews had been able to attain a knowledge of the one God independently and on their own. This is certainly implied by his statements that Claudius, Vespasian, and Titus, in engaging in their own religious observances and activity, were worshipping or praying to "God" (*J.W.* 2.214; 3.444; 5.519). It is also implied in the way in which he picks up and amplifies Aristeas's statement that Jews and Greeks worship the same God but by different names (*Ant.* 12.22). And even in his discourse on the law in *Ag. Ap.* 2.145–286, while he explicitly asserts that the best Greek philosophers were dependent on Moses, his arguments often implicitly assume that they had independent knowledge of the one God and the life of piety and virtue which this God requires. Josephus was no philosopher himself, and so there is no reason to attempt to resolve any ambiguities or inconsistencies between these two strands in his work. Still, even if he placed more personal weight on the theme of imitation and dependence, his work bears witness to the alternative idea that there were non-Jews who had arrived independently at "a true and befitting conception of God" (*Ag. Ap.* 2.255).

Finally, while it has not come up explicitly in any of the passages, a brief comment is in order about eschatological participation. Although Josephus's distaste for eschatological enthusiasm is clearly apparent in his disdain for end-time prophets and messianic pretenders, this does not mean that he had abandoned eschatological expectations in a categorical way. A case can be made that he too harbored nationalistic expectations that were thoroughly rooted in biblical prophecy.[110] This is particularly apparent in two passages.

In his account of Balaam and Balak (*Ant.* 4.112–30) Josephus recounts Balaam's prophecies, including those concerning a wonderful future for Israel on the far side of hardship and distress. After observing that some of these have already come to pass, he adds cryptically: "And from all these prophecies having received the fulfilment which he predicted one may infer what the future has in store" (*Ant.* 4.125). In other words, Josephus understands Balaam's prophecy as having to do with a course of events stretching through Israel's past and into the future. There can be little doubt that among the things that "the future has in store" is the full experience of the kind of national blessing promised by the seer. In this connection, a comment made by Balaam in his final admonition to Balak is of particular interest: "Yet misfortunes may well befall them of little moment and for a little while, whereby they will appear to be

110. See especially Bilde (1998); also Bilde (1988, 147–48, 187); Rajak (1998, 233); Sterling (1992, 236, 292–93).

abased, though only thereafter to flourish once more, to the terror of those who inflicted these injuries upon them" (*Ant.* 4.128). It takes little imagination to imagine what kind of abasement, taking place in "times within my memory," Josephus might have had in mind.

The other passage of interest is found in Josephus's account of Daniel 2 (*Ant.* 10.195–210), where the king has a dream concerning a statue made of four different types of material. Daniel interprets the statue as referring to four successive empires, the fourth of which Josephus clearly understands to be that of Rome. What is of interest here is the enigmatic way in which he speaks of the "stone" that appears at the end of the dream. The stone, which shatters the statue and grows into a mountain filling the whole earth, is said by Daniel to represent God's own kingdom, which will supplant the others and last forever. Josephus rushes past this part of the story, saying that his job is "to write of what is past and done and not of what is to be" (*Ant.* 10.210). But as this statement indicates, he continues to believe that Daniel has indeed described "what is [yet] to be." For not only has "Daniel also revealed to the king the meaning of the stone," but anyone "who wishes to learn about the hidden things that are to come" has only to "take the trouble to read the Book of Daniel" (*Ant.* 10.210). Thus there is a place for a kind of national eschatology in Josephus's view of history. Given his enthusiasm for Gentile sympathizers, one can imagine him being open to the idea that Gentiles would participate in the "things that are to come." But there is no hint of this in the pertinent passages.

Chapter 7

Greco-Roman Literature

Introduction

The texts of interest here, stemming from some fourteen authors, primarily consist of secondary references to sympathizers, proselytes, and related phenomena. Of course, we would be most fortunate if we had at our disposal texts written by Gentiles who themselves had become sympathizers or proselytes and that thus would provide primary evidence for the phenomena. But the closest we get to this are those authors who seem to display admiration of the Jews or who portray them in a sympathetic light.[1] To include these, however, would take us well beyond the bounds that we have set for this study. We will make an exception, however, in the case of Varro, for, with his monotheistic tendencies and his willingness to identify Jupiter with the God of the Jews, he provides a striking Gentile counterpart to the views of certain Jewish authors that we have described as ethical monotheism.

Texts and Commentary

Varro

§169 Varro Antiquitates rerum humanarum et divinarum

> *Yet Varro, one of themselves—to a more learned man they cannot point—thought the God of the Jews to be the same as Jupiter, thinking that it makes no difference by which*

1. E.g., Hecataeus (in Diodorus Siculus *Bibliotheca Historica* 40.3.1–8), Strabo (*Geog.* 16.2.34–46), Varro (in Augustine *City of God* 4.31).

name he is called, so long as the same thing is understood. I believe that he did it being terrified by his sublimity. Since the Romans habitually worship nothing superior to Jupiter, a fact attested well and openly by their Capitol, and they consider him the king of all the gods, and as he perceived that the Jews worship the highest God, he could not but identify him with Jupiter. (Augustine *De Consensu Evangelistarum* 1.22.30)

Text: Condemi (1965)
Translation: Stern (1974, §72b)
Date: 40s B.C.E.
Provenance: Rome
Original Language: Latin
Bibliography: Boyancé (1955); Feldman (1993, 149–51); Kaster (2003, 1582); Lehmann (1997); Rawson (1985); Stern (1974, 1:207–12).
Category: ETHICAL MONOTHEISM

It is a pity that more of Varro's work has not survived, for it represents the first major attempt on the part of a Latin writer to rework Roman tradition in order to place it in a more cosmopolitan intellectual framework. Born in 116 B.C.E., Marcus Terentius Varro was part of the first wave of Roman intellectuals who went to study philosophy in Greece (with Antiochus of Ascalon, in his case) as part of their education. Retiring from public life after the assassination of Julius Caesar,[2] he eventually produced some seventy-five works comprising six hundred volumes. While his reach was broad—social commentary, Latin language and literature, farming and agriculture, Roman history and religion, and philosophy—his most important work was undoubtedly *Antiquitates rerum humanarum et divinarum*, a forty-one-book treatment of Roman history (*res humanarum*) and religion (*res divinarum*). For our knowledge of this work we are dependent largely on Augustine, who made extensive use of its second part in book 4 of his *City of God*, where he asks whether the past success of the Roman empire can be attributed to the Roman gods. From Augustine's description, it appears that Varro treated Roman religion in sixteen books—an introduction, followed by discussions of religious officials, sacred places, festivals, rites, and gods, in three books each. Augustine's refers primarily to the last of these sections.[3]

We have access to this work only through the perceptions and presentation of Augustine, who, while he admires Varro to a significant extent,[4] nevertheless uses him for his own purposes. This needs to be borne in mind as we look at the passages of interest here, where he describes and paraphrases Varro instead of quoting him. Still, the nature of Augustine's purposes and the public arena

2. He had supported Pompey, was given amnesty by Caesar, but was proscribed by Mark Antony.

3. See Rawson (1985, 312).

4. For example, he calls him a "highly intelligent and learned writer" (*City of God* 4.31).

in which he sought to carry them out surely meant that his presentation of Varro needed to conform to what his Roman readers already knew of him.

Taken by itself, the passage cited above, in which Varro is cited as identifying the God of the Jews with Jupiter, the king of the Roman gods,[5] need not signify anything more than an attempt to locate a foreign religion on a Roman religious map by correlating a foreign god with a member of the Roman pantheon. Varro says that Jews worship the "highest god" (*summum deum*), a phrase that probably reflects the Jewish formulation "the Most High God."[6] If this is so, the fact that Varro is apparently willing to take this formulation at face value and thus to align the Jewish God with no less a deity than Jupiter suggests a certain degree of respect for Judaism and generosity of spirit. Nevertheless, from a Roman perspective, to describe the God of the Jews as "the highest god" is to speak the language of polytheism. Thus this correlation from the Gentile side is much less significant for our purposes than is the willingness on the part of the author of *Aristeas* to make the correlation from the Jewish side.[7] It was much more momentous for a Jewish monotheist to acknowledge that a worshiper of Zeus or Jupiter might be worshiping the same god by a different name than it was for a Roman polytheist to fit the Jewish god into the Roman pantheon.[8]

The passage becomes more significant, however, when seen in connection with other passages referred to by Augustine in book 4 of the *City of God*. In *City of God* 4.9 we find another reference in which Jupiter is equated with (it appears) the God of the Jews: "Varro believes that he [Jupiter] is worshipped even by those who worship one God only, without an image, though he is called by another name." Since Varro elsewhere praises the Jews for their imageless worship,[9] it is probable that the Jewish God is in view here. If so, Varro in this passage explicitly recognizes the monotheistic character of Judaism: they

5. Augustine repeats the theme elsewhere in *De Consensu Evangelistarum* (i.e., 1.23.31; 1.27.42; see Stern [1974, §§72c, 72d]).

6. See Schäfer (1997, 37–38). On "the Most High God" in Jewish usage, see §178, together with the discussion prior to §212, below.

7. *Let. Aris.* 16; the Gentile characters in the *Letter of Aristeas* also refer to the God held in common by Jews and Gentiles as "the Most High God" (e.g., *Let. Aris.* 19, 37).

8. Feldman correctly observes the absence of any monotheistic implications to Varro's statement but is too quick to draw a parallel with *Let. Aris.* 16 (Feldman 1993, 150).

9. "He [Varro] also says that for more than one hundred and seventy years the ancient Romans worshipped the gods without an image. 'If this usage had continued to our own day,' he says, 'our worship of the gods would be more devout.' And in support of his opinion he adduces, among other things, the testimony of the Jewish race. And he ends with the forthright statement that those who first set up images of the gods for the people diminished reverence in their cities as they added to error, for he wisely judges that gods in the shape of senseless images might easily inspire contempt" (*City of God* 4.31 [Green LCL]).

"worship one God only" (*unum Deum solum colunt*). Further, Augustine presents Varro as having monotheistic tendencies of his own. According to *City of God* 4.31, while Varro retained the Roman pantheon out of respect for tradition, his basic belief was that "the only ones who have discovered what God really is are those who have adopted the view that he is the soul which governs the world by a movement that accords with reason." In other words, Varro was partial to the monotheistic view of the Stoics.[10]

When we put these passages together, then, Varro appears as something closer to a Gentile counterpart to the Jewish view expressed in the *Letter of Aristeas*. If we can rely on Augustine's presentation of him, Varro was at bottom a monotheist who was prepared to equate the God of the Greek philosophers (particularly the Stoics) with the God of the Jews. Although he admires the imageless worship of the Jews, there is no indication that he adopted any Jewish observances or associated himself in any direct way with the Jewish community. In other words, he should not be classed with Jewish sympathizers. Instead, his value for our study is that he seems to represent a real example of the kind of ethical monotheist envisaged by the Jewish material that we have examined. The example of Varro demonstrates that the pious Gentiles whom we have encountered in the *Letter of Aristeas* or Aristobulus or Philo—dedicated to virtue and ready to recognize Jews as fellow travelers on the monotheistic way—are not simply the fanciful projection of Jewish authors but instead are reflections of a flesh-and-blood reality.

Horace

Quintus Horatius Flaccus was born in 65 B.C.E. into an upwardly mobile family in Venusia. Sent by his father to study in Rome and Greece, Horace joined the army of Brutus in Athens and suffered an initial reversal in fortune with Brutus's defeat in 42. Returning to Rome, he managed to land a position as a treasury scribe and began to gain a reputation as a poet and writer. His status was secured when in 38 he was introduced to Gaius Maecenus, Octavian's trusted administrator, whose patronage he enjoyed until Maecenus's death in 8 B.C.E.

Horace refers to the Jews on three occasions in his *Satires*.[11] Little sympathy for Jews or Judaism is on display here; in one passage he speaks dismissively of Jewish belief in divine intervention, contrasting such credulity with his own hard-headed realism (*Sat.* 1.5.100–03). Jews appear in his pages simply because he finds them to be useful means towards his satirical ends. But their very usefulness demonstrates the extent to which the Jewish community had become a visible and recognizable element in Roman society.

10. Varro attempted "integrer à la religion romaine la religion du dieu cosmique" (Boyancé 1955, 83). On monotheism and polytheism in Varro, see also Lehmann (1997, 226–42).

11. There is also a reference to "Herod's rich palm-groves" in his *Epistles* (2.2.183–89).

§170 Horace Satires *1.4.139–43*

> *This is one of those lesser frailties I spoke of, and if you should make no allowance for it, then would a big band of poets come to my aid—for we are the big majority—and we, like the Jews, will compel you to make one of our throng.*

Text and translation: LCL (Fairclough 1929)
Date: *Circa* 38 B.C.E.[12]
Provenance: Rome
Original Language: Latin
Bibliography: Barclay (1996, 295–96); Goodman (1994, 74); Nolland (1979); Rudd (1966); Schäfer (1997, 107–8); Shackleton Bailey (1982); Stern (1974, 1:324–26); Syndikus (2003); Wander (1998, 163–65).
Category: CONVERSION

Satires 1.4 is Horace's defense of the satirical genre, in response to those who would charge that "you like to give pain . . . and you do so with spiteful intent" (*Sat.* 1.4.78–79). Horace responds that he is simply following the wise pedagogy of his father, who, to teach him how to avoid various vices and follies, would illustrate them by pointing to specific individuals. As a result of this training, he declares, "I am free from vices which bring disaster," adding (a comment to which we will return) that he is nevertheless "subject to lesser frailties such as you would excuse" (*Sat.* 1.4.129–31). Also as a result of his training, he continues, he is in the habit of observing the conduct of those around him, passing judgment on it in order to learn positive lessons from their negative behavior. If he then commits his observations to writing, he does so only for his friends, not for the general public (*Sat.* 1.4.70–77). In any case, he concludes, his writing of satires is one of the "lesser frailties" to which he has already made reference and which, he argues, his critics should be prepared to condone.

The passage under discussion here, then, forms the conclusion to the whole satire. Thus it is not a throwaway line but a carefully crafted grand finale. If his critics are not willing to make allowance for this "lesser frailty" of his, he will call in "a big band of poets" (*multa poetarum*) who will do with force (*cogemus*) what he has tried to do on his own with persuasion. It is in the context of this statement that he draws the much-discussed comparison between the group of poets and the Jews.

12. Since there is no reference in the satire to Maecenas, it is probable that it was written prior to Horace's acceptance by Maecenas as a favored client in 38 B.C.E. See the biographical sketch above.

But what is the point of the comparison? Fairclough's translation—"we, like the Jews, will compel you to make one of our throng"—reflects a widespread interpretation that the passage refers to assertive proselytism on the part of the Jews. In a note to the translation, Fairclough himself speaks of "the eagerness of the Jews to proselytize," referring the reader to Matthew 23:15. Feldman reads the passage in a similar way: Horace here "refers to the zeal of Jewish missionary activity as if it were proverbial."[13]

But this translation of the statement is open to question. The final clause reads: *ac veluti te Iudaei cogemus in hanc concedere turbam*. The first part of the clause is clear: "and we, like the Jews, will compel/force you." The remainder of the clause consists of a prepositional phrase, "in this (disorderly) throng," and a complementary infinitive (*concedere*). The verb has the basic sense "to give ground, withdraw, retire"; by extension it can be used of argumentative or permissive ground: "to concede, to yield a point, to consent to, to allow." Thus it could be rendered "to go over to the other side" (e.g., of a debate), which seems to have provided Fairclough with the germ of his translation; in effect, "we will compel you to go over to the other side, into this [i.e., our] group." Even on its own, this seems to put a forced construction on a verb that ordinarily has nothing to do with joining a group (and why a turbulent, disorderly group [*turba*]?). But as Nolland (1979) has pointed out, this usage of the verb cannot be taken on its own, since it has already appeared earlier in the sentence, where it has nothing whatsoever to do with joining a group. The first part of the sentence reads: "This is one of those lesser frailties I spoke of, and if you should make no allowance for it" (*cui si concedere nolis*). Here *concedere* has the ordinary extended sense of sense of granting a concession or making an allowance. Is it likely that Horace would use the same word in quite a difference sense a few lines later in the same sentence? This is especially unlikely in the case of the climactic final sentence of the whole satire. Following Nolland, I think that *concedere* has the same sense in both instances and that the prepositional phrase needs to be construed with the main verb (*cogemus*) rather than the infinitive. The sentence then should read: "This is one of those lesser frailties I spoke of, and if you should make no allowance for it, then . . . we [I and a big band of poets], like the Jews, will, in our turbulent mob, compel you to make allowances."

In this construal of the sentence, the point of comparison is an aggressive defense of a group's right to engage in practices that set them apart from the rest of society, not an aggressive program to turn outsiders into group members. This both makes better sense of the sentence (including the choice of *turba*) and comports well with what we know of Jewish activity in the Diaspora generally. Thus while the passage provides important evidence for the degree to which the Jewish community was established as a self-confident minority

13. Feldman (1993, 1:299). See also Segal (1990, 85–86); Stern (1974, 1:232).

in Roman society, it should not be taken as providing evidence for Jewish proselytizing activity.[14]

§171 Horace Satires *1.9.63–72*

> *I begin to twitch his cloak and squeeze his arms—they were quite unfeeling—nodding and winking hard for him to save me. The cruel joker laughed, pretending not to understand. I grew hot with anger. "Surely you said there was something you wanted to tell me in private." "I mind it well, but I'll tell you at a better time. Today is the thirtieth Sabbath. Would you affront the circumcised Jews?" "I have no scruples," say I. "But I have. I'm a somewhat weaker brother, one of the many. You will pardon me; I'll talk another day."*

Date: c. 30 B.C.E.
Bibliography: Barclay (1996, 295–96); Rudd (1966); Schäfer (1997, 107–8); Shackleton Bailey (1982); Stern (1974, 1:324–26); Syndikus (2003); Wander (1998, 163–65).
Category: SYMPATHIZATION

The ninth satire is an amusing narrative of an encounter between Horace and an annoyingly persistent acquaintance ("a man I knew only by name"; *Sat.* 1.9.3) who wanted Horace to provide him with an introduction to Maecenus. So persistent was he that he was even prepared to miss a scheduled court appearance, and thus to lose a lawsuit, in order to take advantage of his encounter with Horace. Eventually the pair ran into Aristius Fuscus, a friend of Horace "who knew the fellow right well" (*Sat.* 1.9.61–62). The dialog cited above took place between Horace and Fuscus. Horace appealed to his friend for rescue, suggesting a private conversation. Fuscus, presumably enjoying the sight of Horace's discomfort,[15] begged off on the grounds that it was "the thirtieth sabbath" and that he did not want to offend (*oppedere*) the "circumcised Jews." When Horace responded that he had no religious scruples (*nulla mihi religio est*), Fuscus replied that he, like many others, was a little weaker (*paulo infirmior*) and that the conversation would have to wait.

What Horace had in mind with the reference to the "thirtieth sabbath" is not clear. Perhaps it is a confused reference to the new moon, which was celebrated in a somewhat similar manner. Perhaps it is simply an impressive-sounding invention.[16] The more important question, however, is what the passage tells us about the adoption of Jewish observances by non-Jews. In his response

14. For similar readings of the passage, see (in addition to Nolland), Barclay (1996, 295–96); McKnight (1991, 64); Schäfer (1997, 107–08).

15. Horace calls him a "rascal" (*improbus*).

16. For discussion of the various interpretations that have been suggested, see Stern (1974, 1:326) and Feldman (1989–1990).

to Horace, Fuscus seems to imply that Jews would take offense at the sight of two Gentiles conducting business on the Sabbath. Taken at face value, then, the passage might suggest that Jews were aggressively imposing their observances on others. Feldman has gone so far as to say that the passage provides evidence for the "zeal" in which Jews sought "to convert others to their religion."[17] But exaggeration is one of the tools of the satirist; the face value of the passage should probably be subjected to a considerable discount. It is unlikely that any Roman Gentile would feel compelled to refrain from certain activity on the Sabbath simply to avoid offending Jews. All that need be assumed for Horace's satire to be effective is a general recognition that many non-Jews observed the Sabbath and that the Jewish community looked on this with favor. Still, the positive side of this is not to be overlooked. Even with the discount, the passage indicates that higher-echelon Roman citizens were adopting aspects of Jewish Sabbath observance in sufficient numbers for Horace's intended readers to get the humor.

Ovid

§172 The Art of Love *1.75–76*

Nor let Adonis bewailed of Venus escape you, nor the seventh day that the Syrian Jew holds sacred.

§173 The Art of Love *1.413–16*

You may begin on the day on which woeful Allia flows stained with the blood of Latian wounds, or on that day, less fit for business, whereon returns the seventh-day feast that the Syrian of Palestine observes.

§174 The Remedies for Love *218–20*

Hope not for rain, nor let foreign sabbaths stay you, nor Allia well-known for its ill-luck.

Text and translation: LCL (Mozley and Goold 1979)
Date: 1 B.C.E. (*The Art of Love*); 1 or 2 C.E. (*The Remedies for Love*)
Provenance: Rome
Original Language: Latin
Bibliography: Barclay (1996, 296–97); Hinds (2003); Hollis (1977); Stern (1974, 1:347–49); Syme (1978)
Category: SYMPATHIZATION

The Roman poet Ovid (43 B.C.E.–17 C.E.) was both a master of elegiac verse and a keen observer of Roman life and mores. The passages of interest here

17. Feldman (1993, 510, n. 103). Feldman sees Horace's comment that Fuscus had left him "under the knife" as a punning allusion to circumcision.

come from two works written around the turn of the Common Era. In the first (*The Art of Love*) Ovid provides lessons in how to succeed in love; in the second (*The Remedies for Love*) he sews up the other side of the market by offering advice in how to avoid or get out of an undesirable love affair. According to Ovid himself, the first of these works was somehow a factor in his banishment from Rome by Augustus in 8 C.E., though the primary factor appears to have been some indiscretion—presumably some actual practice of the "art of love" that offended the emperor.

In *The Art of Love*, Ovid addresses himself first to men (books 1 and 2) and then to women (book 3). In book 1 he analyzes the "art of love" according to three aspects: how to find someone to love, how to win her once you have found her, and how to make love last. The first text cited above appears in his discussion of the first of these aspects (*Art* 1.41–268). While he recognizes that some have gone far afield in order to find a lover, he says that there is no need to go outside Rome ("Here is all the beauty of the world"; *Art* 1.56), as long as you know where to look. He recommends the theater in particular: "They come to see, they come that they may be seen; to chastity that place is fatal" (*Art* 1.99–100)! Before getting to this piece of advice, however, he provides a list of other places that should not be overlooked: the portico of Pompey, especially in the heat of summer; the portico of Octavia (the sister of Augustus) and the adjacent theater of her son Marcellus; the colonnade named after Livia (the wife of Augustus); and the temple of Apollos (built by Augustus in 36 B.C.E.) (*Art* 1.67–74). Then he adds to his list the text cited above, referring to the festival of Adonis and "the seventh day that the Syrian Jew holds sacred." Although these items appear to represent a shift from places to times, in view of the fact that he continues his discourse by listing additional places (the temple of Isis; the law-courts; the theaters), it is probable that he has particular places in view here as well. In other words, Ovid is advising his male readers that on the Jewish Sabbath one will be able to find gatherings of potentially desirable women.

Unfortunately, Ovid does not tell us anything more. Hollis has suggested that Ovid has synagogues in mind (Hollis 1977, 47); given the emphasis on specific places in this section of the poem, he is probably right. But is he right in his further suggestion that the women in question would be Gentile visitors and adherents, rather than Jews? This is certainly possible, especially since the section begins with the observation that there is no need to go searching for foreign women when there are so many beautiful women here at home (*Art* 1.51–66). What makes it perhaps even probable is the absence of any reference to the kind of obstacles that normally would hinder sexual relations between Gentile men and Jewish women. If so—if Ovid is advising his readers that available non-Jewish women can be found congregating around the synagogue on the Sabbath—the passage provides evidence of how common and widespread the phenomenon had become in Rome. Still, since there is no explicit indication that these objects of potential affection were Gentile, the text needs to be used with caution.

The second passage comes from a section in *The Art of Love*, where Ovid has turned from the matter of finding a potential lover to that of winning her affections. After giving advice on how to gain the support and use the influence of the woman's maidservant, he goes on to talk about appropriate and inappropriate times for making advances. Just as there are times when sailors and farmers need to be cautious, so there are times when it is not "safe to angle for young girls" (*Art* 1.403). In particular, Ovid warns against days on which a present would be expected ("let that be a black day whereon a present must be given"; *Art* 1.418)—the girl's birthday, days of special celebration at the Circus when peddlers tend to press their wares on unsuspecting lovers, and so on. In contrast to these dangerous days, Ovid suggests that suitors choose the anniversary of a particularly bitter defeat (at the river Allia),[18] a day when the shops would be closed and no gift would be expected, or "the seventh day feast that the Syrian of Palestine observes [*culta Palaestino septima festa Syro*]." Given the similarity between this phrase and the reference in *Art* 1.76 to "the seventh day that the Syrian Jew holds sacred (*cultaque Iudaeo septima sacra Syro*)," there can be no doubt that when Ovid speaks of the "Syrian of Palestine" he has Jews in mind and thus that the Jewish Sabbath is in view in this second passage as well. Ovid is saying, then, that the Jewish Sabbath is a day especially suitable for lovers who want to avoid unwanted financial pressures, since on that day the shops tend not to be open. Because there is no reason to believe that the majority of Roman shopkeepers would be Jewish, the passage seems to reflect a situation where the Jewish practice of abstaining from work on the seventh day has made considerable inroads into Roman society.[19]

Such a situation seems to be reflected as well in the third passage from Ovid. This appears in *The Remedies for Love*, a sequel to *The Art of Love* in which the poet offers healing to those who had been wounded by the advice he had given in the previous work.[20] In this section of the work, Ovid is advising his love-wounded readers to avoid leisure ("so does Venus delight in leisure"; *Remedies* 143) by immersing themselves in public affairs, military activity, agriculture, hunting, or travel—all of which will help "you unlearn your love" (*Remedies* 211). If you have decided to go away, says Ovid, do not let yourself be held back by the weather, by "foreign sabbaths" (*peregrina sabbata*), or even by the evil omens associated with the commemoration of the defeat at the river Allia. Again we find the combination of Sabbath and Allia, though here in a context having to do with travel rather than commerce. And again the implication seems to be that Sabbath observance—here apparently involving restrictions on one's ability to travel on the Sabbath—has spread to the Roman

18. At the hands of the Gauls, on July 18, 390 B.C.E.

19. See Hollis (1977, 108) Barclay (1996, 296–97).

20. "Learn healing from him through whom ye learnt to love: one hand alike will wound and succour" (*Remedies* 43–44).

populace to such an extent that Ovid expects the practice to have been adopted by at least some of his readers. This takes the matter one step beyond the first two passages. All three passages are striking for the matter-of-fact way in which Ovid speaks of the spread of Jewish observance into Roman society; there is no hint of condemnation or even of condescending satire. But in this passage he goes further, as he assumes that such adoption of Jewish observance is not simply a fact of Roman life but will actually be found among his literate—and thus upper-class—circle of readers.

§175 Ptolemy History of King Herod

> *Jews and Idumaeans differ, as Ptolemy states in the first book of the History of King Herod. Jews are those who are so by origin and nature. The Idumaeans, on the other hand, were not originally Jews, but Phoenicians and Syrians; having been subjugated by the Jews and having been forced to undergo circumcision, so as to be counted among the Jewish nation and keep the same customs, they were called Jews.*

Text: Nickau (1966)
Translation: Stern (1974, 1:146)
Date: Early first century C.E.?
Provenance: Uncertain
Original Language: Greek
Bibliography: Cohen (1999, 60, 113); Schürer (1973, 1:27–28); Stern (1974, 1:355–56).
Category: CONVERSION

We have already had occasion to observe that there is a certain ambivalence in Josephus's characterization of the Idumeans and their relationship with the Jews (above, §§139, 140). On the one hand, he considers them in his own day as the "kinfolk" of the Jews and as full and willing converts to Judaism. On the other, he describes their original conversion as something imposed on them by the Hasmoneans. This ambivalence is reflected in the combination of the passage cited here (which speaks of coercion) and of the passages from Strabo cited below (which do not). In our previous discussion, we noted that while scholars have often emphasized the coercive element, more recent interpreters have argued instead that there must have been a significant degree of willingness on the part of the Idumeans (and Itureans) to accept a Jewish way of life. The two are not mutually exclusive, of course; a policy of forced conversion on the Hasmonean side might have been willingly accepted by nations who saw benefit in a politico-religious alliance with a newly powerful neighbor. Thus the conclusion that was drawn in the previous discussion was that we should see this as an instance of full and willing conversion, without necessarily denying an element of coercion. While there is no need to discuss the whole issue again here, we can supplement the earlier discussion by looking more closely at these additional texts.

The passage under discussion here is found in a work entitled *De adfinium vocabulorum differentia* ("concerning the distinction between related names"), attributed to a certain Ammonius. Nothing much can be said with certainty about either Ammonius or Ptolemy, who according to Ammonius was the author of a work *Concerning Herod the King*. Schürer takes the position that this was Ptolemy of Ascalon, an early first-century grammarian.[21] But since he is not known to have written on any topic other than grammar, this ascription is open to question (Stern 1974, 1:355).

Whatever the origin of this work, two things are of particular interest. One is that Ptolemy considers the conversion of the Idumeans to have been forced. They were "subjugated" or "conquered" (κρατηθέντες) by the Jews and "compelled [ἀναγκασθέντες] to be circumcised and to be counted among the nation [συντελεῖν εἰς τὸ ἔθνος] and to keep the same customs." Ptolemy thus adds his voice to that of Josephus in seeing an element of coercion in the conversion of the Idumeans. The second thing to note is that having taken on these obligations—circumcision, the observance of Jewish customs, the responsibility to pay taxes[22]—the Idumeans "were called Jews" (ἐκλήθησαν Ἰουδαῖοι). To be sure, Ptolemy makes a distinction between the Jews proper, "who are so by origin and nature," and the Idumeans, who "were not originally [ἀρχῆθεν] Jews." No doubt it is this distinction that has led to the inclusion of the passage from Ptolemy in a work dealing with "distinctions between related names." Nevertheless, whatever they were originally, and even though they are still known as Idumeans, by virtue of their circumcision and adoption of Jewish customs and responsibilities they can also properly be called Jews.

§176 Strabo Historical Notes

> *This man was a kindly person and very serviceable to the Jews, for he acquired additional territory for them, and brought over to them a portion of the Ituraean nation, whom he joined to them by the bond of circumcision.* (cited in Josephus *Antiquities* 13.319)

§177 Strabo Geography *16.2.34*

> *As for Judaea, its western extremities towards Casius are occupied by the Idumaeans and by the lake. The Idumaeans are Nabataeans, but owing to a sedition they were banished from there, joined the Judaeans, and shared in the same customs with them.*

Text and translation: *Historical Notes:* LCL (Thackeray, Marcus, and Feldman 1926–65); *Geography*: LCL (Jones 1930).

21. Schürer (1973, 1:27–28); also Sacks (2003).

22. The construction συντελεῖν εἰς τὸ has the sense of belonging to a particular class of citizens for taxation purposes; see LSJ on συντελέω.

Date: Early first century C.E.
Provenance: Rome or Pontus
Original Language: Greek
Bibliography: Dueck (2000); Purcell (2003); Stern (1974, 1:261–315).
Category: CONVERSION

A native of Amaseia in Pontus (born c. 64 B.C.E.), Strabo is best known for his *Geography*, a seventeen-volume survey of the Mediterranean world, beginning in Iberia and moving in a clockwise direction around to north Africa. At least some of the work was completed no earlier than 18 C.E., though whether the whole work dates to this period or whether the bulk of the work was completed earlier (3–7 C.E.), with some later revision, is a matter of some dispute.[23] But he wrote his *Geography* only after having completed a substantial survey of Roman history from 146 B.C.E. (where Polybius's history came to an end) down to his own day.[24] While *Geography* is extant, his historical work survives only in excerpts, primarily in Josephus.[25]

Strabo seems to have been well disposed towards Jews and Judaism; his description of Moses and the origins of the Jewish people, in particular, is strikingly laudatory.[26] Our interest, however, is directed at two passages in which he refers to the incorporation of neighboring groups—specifically, Itureans and Idumeans—into the Jewish people. As was observed in our discussion of the previous entry, these passages have already come into view in our earlier discussion of parallel passages in Josephus (§§139, 140), the second of which is the source of the quotation. We noted in these earlier discussions that while an element of coercion should probably not be eliminated, the emphasis should be placed on the willingness of the Itureans and Idumeans to adopt a Jewish way of life. An important factor leading to this conclusion is the absence of any element of coercion in Strabo's statements.

23. See the thorough discussion in Dueck (2000, 145–51), who argues for the later date. The difficulty with the later date is that the work would then have been carried out when Strabo was some eighty years of age.

24. Presumably this was the work *Historical Notes* to which Strabo refers in *Geog.* 1.1.23. If so, this work began with four books dealing generally with the writing of history, including a discussion of historians writing on Alexander, and then went on to treat Roman history in forty-three books. Dueck has argued, however, that *Historical Notes* is to be identified solely with the four-book section, a separate work written after the main history. For our purposes, this issue, together with that concerning the date of *Geography*, can be safely left to one side.

25. There are twelve excerpts in Josephus, three in Plutarch's *Lives*, and one in Tertullian (Dueck 2000, 70).

26. *Geog.* 16.2.35–36. His praise is tempered, however, by his subsequent statement that Moses was succeeded first by superstitious people, who introduced strange customs ("abstinence from flesh . . . circumcisions and excisions"), and then by tyrants (*Geog.* 16.2.37).

The "kindly person" who is the subject of the statement preserved by Josephus is Aristobulus I. Strabo's description of Aristobulus (derived from Timagenes, one of his sources) thus stands in contrast with Josephus's harsh portrait of him (presumably influenced by his source Nicolaus of Damascus). Strabo attributes two accomplishments to Aristobulus: he extended the boundaries of Judea, and he incorporated some of the Iturean people into the Jewish domain. The first statement—"he acquired [προσεκτήσατο] additional territory"—might be taken to imply an element of coercion in the second. Such a reading seems to have influenced Marcus's translation: he "brought over" part of the Iturean nation. The word, however, is ᾠκειώσατο: he brought them into the family; he made them kinsfolk. This idea of incorporation into the Jewish family is continued in the latter part of the statement: through circumcision (which, after all, is the sign of full membership in the Jewish people), he caused the Itureans to be "joined" (συνάψας) to the Jewish household. To be sure, this incorporation of the Itureans was part of the territorial expansion of Judea under the Hasmoneans. Nevertheless nothing in Strabo's statement requires us to see it as something that was imposed against the will of the Itureans or that worked to their detriment.

The statement about the Idumeans in *Geog.* 16.2.34 is even less open to the idea of coercion. Here the Idumeans are the active party. After they were banished by the Nabateans, they "joined"—went over to, crossed to the side of (προσεχώρησαν)—"the Judaeans and shared"—became partners (ἐκοινώνησαν) —"in the same customs [νομίμων] with them." Again, the picture is of willing incorporation into the Jewish people, this time with the outside group taking the initiative.

§178 Valerius Maximus Memorable Doings and Sayings *1.3.3*

> *Cn. Cornelius Hispalus, Foreign Praetor, in the Consulship of M. Popillius Laenas and L. Calpurnius, ordered the astrologers by edict to leave Rome and Italy within ten days. For they spread profitable darkness with their lies over frivolous and foolish minds by fallacious interpretation of the stars. The same Hispalus made the Jews go home, who had tried to infect Roman manners with the cult of Jupiter Sabazius.* (Paris)

> *Therefore Cornelius Hispalus expelled the astrologers from the city, ordering them to leave Italy within ten days, lest they tout foreign knowledge. The same Hispalus banished the Jews too from the city (they had tried to pass on their religion to the Romans) and threw out their private altars from public places.* (Nepotianus)

Text and translation: LCL (Shackleton Bailey 2000)
Date: c. 30 C.E.
Provenance: Rome
Original Language: Latin
Bibliography: Cumont (1906); Dickson (2003, 24–26); Feldman (1993, 301, 559); Goodman (1994, 82–83); Gruen (2002,

15–19); Lane (1979); Stern (1974, 1:357–60); Schäfer (1997, 51); Schürer (1986, 3:73–75); Smallwood (1981, 128–30); Stern (1974, 1:357–60); Wander (1998, 163–65).

Category: SYMPATHIZATION, CONVERSION

Valerius Maximus is known only by his work *Memorable Doings and Sayings*, which itself contains very little by way of personal information. The work is dedicated to (Tiberius) Caesar, and several other details suggest a date in the latter part of Tiberius's reign. Valerius makes mention of a sea voyage to Asia with his patron Sextus Pompeius and others (2.6.8), probably when Pompeius was on his way to assume the governorship (c. 25 C.E.). The "conspirator" who is fiercely denounced in one passage (9.11.ext.4) is probably to be identified with Sejanus (executed in 31 C.E.).

The work itself consists of a collection of vignettes drawn from a variety of sources (Cicero and Livy prominent among them) to form a kind of handy source book of edifying examples. The majority of the examples deal with Roman subjects and tend to uphold traditional Roman religion and practice, though with due reverence for the emperors as the new guarantors of Roman tradition. Each of the nine books in the work is divided into chapters; each chapter contains examples dealing with a particular theme. Book 1 begins with chapters on "religion," on "those who feigned religion," and on foreign "superstitions." The passage to be discussed here forms part of chapter 3.

Unfortunately, our passage also is located in the middle of a significant lacuna in the extant manuscripts of the work, a gap that stretches from the latter part of chapter 1 to the start of chapter 4. For our knowledge of this missing material we are dependent on two epitomes, one by Julius Paris (perhaps fourth c.) and the other by Januarius Nepotianus (perhaps fifth c.), preserved in later manuscripts. As is illustrated by the passages cited here, there are some not insubstantial differences between the versions provided by the two epitomists. Thus while the account is potentially of great value in that it represents the earliest evidence we have for a Jewish community in Rome, its value has to be marked down somewhat with each successive stage in its transmission (Valerius's source, Valerius himself, his epitomizers).

In the scholarly discussion of the passage, it is the unique features of the epitomes—especially Paris's reference to the "cult of Jupiter Sabazius," but also the detail of the "private altars" of the Jews in Nepotianus—that have attracted the most attention. But interpretation of the passages should begin with what they have in common. According to both Paris and Nepotianus, the theme of chapter 3 had to do with Roman resistance to the incursion of foreign "superstitions." Both epitomes begin with the same three examples: the abolition of the Bacchanalian mysteries, which ceased to be tolerated "when they passed into pernicious madness" (Paris); the senate's rejection of Lutatius Cerco's attempt to consult foreign auspices at the time of the first Punic war; and

Cornelius Hispalus's expulsion of both the astrologers (*Chaldaeos*) and the Jews from Rome. Paris adds a fourth: the senate's decree during the consulship of Aemelius Paullus that the temples of Isis and Sarapis be demolished.

According to both Paris and Nepotianus, what was objectionable about the Jews in Rome was not simply their presence in the city but also the fact that they had tried (*conati erant* appears in both) to spread their religious observances among the Romans. According to Nepotianus, they "had tried to pass on [*tradere*] their religion [*sacra sua*] to the Romans"; in Paris's version, they "had tried to infect [*inficere*] Roman manners [*mores*]" with their cult. One should probably not overstress the element of Jewish initiative here. What is being objected to in the chapter as a whole is the spread of foreign religion among the Roman populace, not necessarily the degree to which this was the result of deliberate propagation on the part of non-Roman adherents. Still, the fact that both epitomes refer to Jewish initiative suggests that this element was present in Valerius's original work and thus, probably, in his source. Thus Valerius preserves evidence that by 139 B.C.E.,[27] a Jewish community was not only well established in Rome but was also attracting positive interest from outsiders. At least from the perspective of those who were critical of this development, the Jews were actively encouraging the spread of their religious observances among the Roman population.

Moving beyond the ground held in common by the two epitomizers, we come first to the curious statement in Paris that the Jews were spreading "the cult of Jupiter Sabazius" (*Sabazii Iovis culta*). Originally Sabazios was the god of a cult native to Phrygia and Thrace, but the cult spread throughout the Greco-Roman world as Sabazios came to be identified with Zeus and Jupiter. Since *Sabazios* could easily be confused with *Sabaoth* (Lord of hosts) or with Sabbath, it is possible that Paris's account (which is usually the more reliable of the two) simply reflects an instance of this confusion on the part of Valerius or his source. In other words, a confused awareness that the Jews worshiped the "most high God" and observed the Sabbath (or worshiped the Lord Sabaoth) led to the statement that the cult of the Jews was that of "Jupiter Sabazius." Cumont, however, has used this passage as an important element in his argument that there was a strong syncretistic Jewish element in the Sabazios cult, Jews having

27. For the date and the identification of Hispalus, see the note in Shackleton Bailey (2000, 46, n. 4). This puts the date intriguingly close to the arrival in Rome of the delegation from Simon the Hasmonaean, a delegation that was received favorably by the Romans (1 Macc 14:24; 15:15–24). The contrast between the two reports reflects Rome's ability to make a distinction between a treaty with a foreign state and the activity of *peregrini* in their own city. Smallwood (1981, 128–30) has attempted to link the two events, arguing that the positive reception of the delegation from Jerusalem emboldened the Jewish community in Rome, leading them to step up their proselytizing initiatives. The argument, while plausible, nevertheless outruns the evidence.

linked their Lord Sabaoth with Sabazios, a link that helped to spread the cult through the Mediterranean world (Cumont 1906). We will look at Cumont's theory in more detail below.[28] The statement in Paris's epitome, however, provides little support for this grand construction. The fact that the detail is absent from Nepotianus raises doubt as to its originality. And even if it should have been present originally in Valerius (or in his source), it is much more probable that the term is to be understood as the result of confusion than with reference to a syncretistic phenomenon for which there is very little other evidence.[29]

The reference in Nepotianus to the "private altars" of the Jews is probably also to be seen as a confused outside observation, made by someone who was aware that Jews met together for worship and who assumed that, like all other oriental cults, their worship involved sacrifice (so Smallwood 1981, 130). Indeed, if this reference reflects Valerius's own account, it reinforces the conclusion that the account as a whole presented quite a confused picture of Jewish religious life.

Seneca

Two passages in the writings of the younger Seneca are of interest here—one from his *Moral Letters* and the other, preserved only in a quotation by Augustine in *City of God*, from a lost work entitled *On Superstition*. Both passages reflect the spread of Jewish customs among non-Jews in Rome in the first century C.E.; thus they reinforce the impression that has emerged from our examination of other Roman authors discussed to this point. But in contrast to these authors, with Seneca we encounter a strikingly negative tone; for the first time the popularity of Jewish observance is met with resentment and even animosity.

Seneca's achievements were the combined result of birth (into a wealthy and influential Spanish-Italian family from Corduba, sometime between 4 and 1 B.C.E.), natural brilliance (both as an orator and as a philosopher), and opportunity (especially such as came his way when his former pupil Nero came to imperial power in 54 C.E.). Only two aspects of his life are of significance here. One is his early philosophical training—first under Attalus, a Stoic teacher; and later under Fabianus and Sotion, followers of the Roman philosopher Sextius, who combined Stoicism with elements of Pythagoreanism (especially vegetarianism). The other is his increasing retirement from public life in

28. See the discussion in ch. 9 below (between §211 and §212).

29. Lane (1979) has argued that that Valerius Maximus had originally mentioned three expulsions—Chaldeans, Sabazius-worshippers, and Jews—but that Paris had conflated the last two in a confused way. The argument is not capable of demonstration, but the article is valuable more generally for its critique of Cumont's hypothesis. See also Barclay (1996, 285); Schäfer (1997, 51).

the early 60s, as Nero's rule became more erratic. Both works that concern us here were produced in this period, which was brought to an end by his forced suicide in 65.

§179 Seneca Moral Letters *108.22*

> *I was imbued with this teaching, and began to abstain from animal food; at the end of a year the habit was as pleasant as it was easy. . . . Do you ask how I came to abandon the practice? It was this way: The days of my youth coincided with the early part of the reign of Tiberius Caesar. Some foreign rites were at that time being inaugurated, and abstinence from certain kinds of animal food was set down as a proof of interest in this strange cult. So at the request of my father, who did not fear prosecution, but who detested philosophy, I returned to my previous habits.*

Text and translation: LCL (Gummere 1953)
Date: 62–65 C.E.
Provenance: Rome
Original Language: Latin
Bibliography: Barclay (1996, 299); Cohen (1999, 61–62); Feldman (1993, 303); Griffin (1976); Reynolds, Griffin, and Fantham (2003); Stern (1974, 1:433–34); Wander (1998, 162–63)
Category: SYMPATHIZATION

In his *Moral Letters*, addressed to his friend Lucilius, Seneca used the epistolary form as a vehicle for addressing an array of philosophical issues. The topic in this letter is the proper approach to the study of philosophy. In the course of a discussion concerning the need to combine eager receptivity with a disciplined, gradual pattern of learning, Seneca pointed to his own experience with Attalus, noting how the polished oratory of a master teacher is especially effective with one whose "mind is young" (*Let.* 108.16). In particular, Seneca was impressed by Attalus's ascetic teaching; often, he declared, he left the lecture hall with a fervent desire to live as "a poor man" and "to limit my food and drink" (*Let.* 108.14). Although he felt it necessary, Seneca said, to abandon some of his youthful resolutions as he grew older and took up public life, he nevertheless continued to observe many of his earlier ascetic habits, abstaining from rich food (he mentions oysters and mushrooms), wine, perfume, and the bath. And even when he "ceased to practise abstinence," he continued to observe "a limit, which is indeed next door to abstinence" (*Let.* 108.16).

It is in the context of this theme—youthful abstinence giving way to more moderate adult restraint—that Seneca recounts his experiment with vegetarianism. His teacher Sotion introduced him to the vegetarianism of Sextius, who thought that the consumption of meat was both unnecessary and cruel, and of Pythagoras, whose abstinence was based on a belief in the transmigration of souls. "Imbued with this teaching," Seneca too became a vegetarian. But not for long. This period of his life coincided, he said, with the emergence in Rome of "some foreign rites" (*alienigena sacra*) that were characterized by "abstinence from certain kinds of animal foods." Under pressure from his father, he abandoned this practice. While Seneca's account is somewhat elliptical, the reference to "prosecution" (*calumnia*) seems to suggest that any who were suspected of having adopted these "foreign rites" could become the victims of malicious accusation. Seneca's father may not have feared this as a real threat in his son's case, but the way in which Seneca mentions it seems to imply that it was at least a potential danger.

This took place, Seneca tells us, in the "early part of the reign of Tiberius Caesar." This temporal reference immediately calls to mind the events of 19 C.E., when Tiberius took steps to banish both Jewish and Egyptian cults from Rome,[30] an event described by Josephus, Suetonius, and Dio Cassius, each of whom understood Tiberius's action as prompted by the phenomenon of conversion to Judaism.[31] In Dio's words: "As the Jews flocked to Rome in great numbers and were converting [μεθιστάντων]) many of the natives [ἐπιχωρίων] to their ways, he [Tiberius] banished most of them" (*Hist.* 57.18.5). Seneca of course could not be mistaken for a convert to Judaism. Indeed, as we will see presently, he speaks disparagingly both of Judaism itself and of its attractiveness to non-Jews. But what his narrative tells us is that Tiberius's measures affected not only those who had become full converts but also any who had adopted Jewish observances in a less thoroughgoing way. Seneca's vegetarianism could have been interpreted as a way of abstaining from not just meat in general but pork in particular. For this reason, even though he found this diet otherwise appealing and beneficial, he was prepared to give it up and thus to avert any suspicion of sympathy for such "foreign rites."

§180 Seneca On Superstition *(Augustine* City of God *6.11)*

> *Meanwhile the customs of this accursed race have gained such influence that they are now received throughout all the world. The vanquished have given laws to the victors.*

Text and translation: Augustine *City of God*: LCL (Green 1963)
Date: 62–65 C.E.
Provenance: Rome
Original Language: Latin
Bibliography: Griffin (1976); Reynolds, Griffin, and Fantham (2003); Schäfer (1997, 111–13); Stern (1974, 1:431–32).
Category: SYMPATHIZATION, CONVERSION

Seneca's lost work *On Superstition* is known to us primarily through Augustine's references to it in his *City of God*. From Augustine's discourse in the preceding

30. See Barclay (1996, 299); Cohen (1999, 61–62); Feldman (1993, 303).

31. See above, Josephus *Ant.* 18.82 (§146); and below, Tacitus *Ann.* 2.85.4 (§186); Suetonius *Tiberius* 36.1 (§189); and Dio Cassius *Hist.* 57.18.5.

section (*City of God* 6.10) it is apparent that in this work Seneca carried out a typically Stoic critique of various popular religious cults with their "irrational" practices and bizarre deities. Apparently this lost work also contained a discussion of Jewish religion, for Augustine goes on to describe Seneca's criticism of Judaism. In some ways, his criticism of the Jews was more muted than in the case of the other oriental religions, for he was prepared to recognize that, in contrast to many others, the Jews were "aware of the origin and meaning of their rites." Still, says Augustine, Seneca "also censures the sacred institutions of the Jews, especially the sabbath," which he saw as a literal waste of time. This comment is reminiscent of his criticism elsewhere of those who light lamps on the Sabbath, as if the gods were in need of light (*Let.* 95.47).

But his harshest criticism is evoked by the spread of Jewish custom among non-Jews. The "manner of living" (*consuetudo*) of this "most villainous race" (*sceleratissimae gentis*) has been "received throughout all the world" (*per omnes terras recepta*). With the next statement—Seneca's complaint that "the vanquished have given their laws [*leges*] to their victors"—it is clear that he is particularly piqued with the spread of Jewish observance among the Romans in particular. While Seneca took great pride in the fact that it was Roman policy to draw conquered states into the life of the empire—to convert *hostes* into *socii*, as Griffin puts it (Griffin 1976, 223)—he was clearly annoyed at the extent to which the process was reversed in this case. Although the Romans were the victors (writing before the war with Rome, Seneca is of course thinking of Pompey), they were adopting the way of life (*consuetudo*) and even the laws (*leges*) of the vanquished.

It is not possible to say whether Seneca was referring here to full converts or simply to those who had adopted Jewish observances in a less thoroughgoing way. Given the passage that was discussed in the previous entry, it is apparent that he was aware of the latter possibility. But probably he was upset by the whole phenomenon, converts and sympathizers alike.[32]

On the question of Jewish initiative, his language is somewhat ambiguous. On the one hand, he speaks in the passive: Jewish custom has been "received" throughout the world. On the other, he uses the active: the Jews "have given" (*dederunt*) their laws to the Romans. What tilts the balance in the direction of the latter is the matter of culpability. Clearly, he holds the Jews responsible for this deplorable state of affairs. His bitterness is directed at those who "have given" rather than at those who have "received." While his language should not be pressed too far,[33] Seneca clearly thinks of the Jews in some sense as active participants in the process.

32. See Schäfer (1997, 112).

33. Stern overstates things when he speaks of this passage as having been written "at the height of the Jewish proselytizing movement" (Stern 1974, 1:429)

§181 Petronius Satyricon *102*

> *"Eumolpus, as a man of learning, is sure to have some ink. Let us use this medicine to dye ourselves, hair, nails, everything. Then we will stand by you with pleasure like Aethiopian slaves, without undergoing any tortures, and our change of colour will take in our enemies." "Oh! yes", said Giton, "and please circumcise us to so that we look like Jews, and bore our ears to imitate Arabians, and chalk our faces till Gaul takes us for her own sons; as if this colour alone could alter our shape, and it were not needed that many things act in unison to make a good lie on all accounts."*

Text and translation: LCL (Heseltine and Warmington 1969)
Date: 54–68 C.E. (i.e., during Nero's reign)
Provenance: Rome
Original Language: Latin
Bibliography: Harrison (2003); Schäfer (1997, 77–78); Stern (1974, 1:441–44)
Category: CONVERSION

This passage from Petronius's *Satyricon* has to do with assuming a disguise and not with any sincere adoption of Jewish identity and, thus, is not of great significance for our study. Still, since it describes (albeit sarcastically) a situation in which Gentiles contemplate being circumcised in order to appear as Jews (*ut Iudaei videamur*), it deserves a brief mention.

At this point in the story Encolpius, the narrator, and Giton, his traveling companion and sometime lover, have just discovered that the ship on which they have taken refuge is under the command of an enemy. After considering various stratagems, Encolpius comes up with the idea of dying their skin black in order to disguise themselves as Ethiopian slaves. Replying that much more than a change in skin color would be necessary to pass as Ethiopians, Giton reinforces his point by referring to other distinctive ethnic characteristics—the white skin of the Gauls, the bored ears of the Arabian and the circumcision of the Jews. The force of Giton's statement is that while one could not pass oneself off as a Jew without circumcision, it would take more than circumcision to do it convincingly.

Still, the statement demonstrates that Petronius considered circumcision to be the primary defining mark of the Jews—an opinion that appears more categorically in one of his poems[34]—and thus as essential for any Gentile who would want to appear Jewish. In this sense it bears on the discussion at least indirectly.

34. Poem 24: "The Jew may worship his pig-god and clamour in the ears of high heaven, but unless he also cuts back with a knife the region of his groin, and unless he unlooses by art the knotted head, he shall go forth from the holy city cast forth from the people, and transgress the sabbath by breaking the law of fasting." Schäfer (1997, 78) suggests that the passage refers to a "godfearer," who is not regarded as a full Jew until he undergoes

Plutarch

While Plutarch spent most of his life (c. 50–120 C.E.) in his home town of Chaeronea (in central Greece) and was a priest at Delphi for his final thirty years, he was neither a stranger to Rome nor unappreciative of things Roman. As with many of his contemporaries, he was a man of dual loyalties. Fervently committed to the religious and philosophical heritage of his homeland, he also sought to render it accessible to the wider Roman world of his own day.

In spite of the voluminous nature of Plutarch's writings, his extant works contain only two passages that bear directly on our investigation. The first is in his treatise *On Superstition*, probably written when he was a young man, and the second is a passing comment in his *Life of Cicero*, dating from the latter part of his life.

§182 Plutarch On Superstition *3 (166A)*

> *"Greeks from barbarians finding evil ways!"*
> *because of superstition, such as smearing with mud, wallowing in filth, keeping of the Sabbath [Babbitt: immersions], casting oneself with face to the ground, dis graceful besieging of the gods, and uncouth prostrations.*

Translation: Stern (1974, 1:549), a slight revision of LCL (Babbitt 1928)
Date: Last third of the first century C.E.?
Provenance: Greece
Original Language: Greek
Bibliography: Defradas, Hani, and Klaerr (1985); Feldman (1993, passim); Moellering (1963); Schäfer (1997, 88–89); Smith (1975); Stern (1974, 1:545–76); Wander (1998, 171)
Category: SYMPATHIZATION

In his treatise *On Superstition* Plutarch seeks to establish the reprehensible character of "superstition" (δεισιδαιμονία) by comparing and contrasting it with atheism. He argues that they both stem from the same fault—"ignorance and blindness in regard to the gods" (1, 164E). For those of softer minds, such ignorance leads to the fearful belief that the gods are responsible for human misfortune and suffering, which in turn leads to various "superstitious" attempts to placate the gods and turn aside their malevolence. Those of tougher minds,

---

circumcision. But this is unlikely. Not only is the person introduced at the outset as a Jew (*Iudaeus*) but he is also described as having been "cast forth from the people," something that could be said of a native-born Jew who remained uncircumcised (cf. Gen 17:14) but not of a Gentile. See Cohen (1999, 40–41); Feldman (1993, 156); Stern (1974, 1:444).

however, look to their own behavior as the source of their troubles and deny the existence of the gods altogether. Of the two, Plutarch finds superstition the more objectionable. Those who have a superstitious fear of the gods inevitably become fearful of everything—"earth and sea, air and sky, darkness and light, sound and silence, and a dream" (2, 165E). Atheism has at least this much to be said for it: it eliminates such irrational fear. The deficiency of atheism is simply its indifference to the positive good that comes with a healthy belief in the gods. Arguing by analogy, Plutarch says that he would prefer it if someone "should say about me that I have never been born at all" than if they attributed all sorts of malevolent qualities to him (10, 169–70).[35]

In the process of drawing out this comparison, Plutarch describes many examples of "superstitious" behavior. Included in his examples are two references to Sabbath observance. The second of these refers to religious observance carried out by Jews exclusively. As an example of the "many ills" that "are made to result fatally by men's superstition" (8, 168F), he describes an incident in which Jews sat passively "while the enemy were planting ladders against the walls and capturing the defenses," offering no resistance simply because the assault took place on the Sabbath.[36] In the earlier example, however, the (presumably) Jewish practice of Sabbath observance is one of a number of superstitious practices that Greeks have taken over from barbarians. Citing a line from Euripides' *The Trojan Woman* ("Greeks from barbarians finding evil ways"), Plutarch lists Sabbath observance (σαββατισμούς) as one of the "evil ways" that Greeks have taken over from barbarians "because of superstition" (τῇ δεισιδαιμονίᾳ; 3, 166A). While the origin of the practice is not specified here, both the term itself[37] and the presence later in the work of an explicit reference to Jewish Sabbath observance make it certain that Jewish Sabbath-keeping is in view here.

35. Elsewhere in his writings Plutarch does prescribe some form of appropriate fear for the gods (for references, see Smith 1975, 3). This, together with other anomalous features of *On Superstition* (e.g., the absence of any reference to demons), has led some to argue that Plutarch was not its author (so Smith 1975, 3–5). While these differences are not lightly to be set aside, they can probably be accounted for by an appeal to the constraints imposed by the genre of the work and by the possibility that it was written very early in Plutarch's career (so Moellering 1963, 17–21).

36. Plutarch does not tell us who "the enemy" was. The closest parallel to the account is the description of the capture of Jerusalem by Ptolemy I Soter, recounted by Josephus (depending on Agartharchides) in *Against Apion* (1.208–12). Other suggestions include Pompey, Antony, and Titus; see Babbitt (1928, 481); Moellering (1963, 19–20); and Schäfer (1997, 88).

37. σαββατισμός is related closely to σαββατίζω, "to keep the sabbath." Richard Bentley's emendation βαπτισμούς (immersions) has been adopted by Babbitt (1928, 460), who has been followed by some scholars (e.g., Smith 1975, 15). On the basis of the manuscript evidence, however, σαββατισμούς is to be preferred (see Defradas, Hani, and Klaerr 1985, 251).

We can infer from the allusive way in which Plutarch refers to the phenomenon that, in his estimation of things, his readers were well familiar with examples of Greeks who had adopted the practice of Sabbath observance. Of course, he refers to it in highly critical terms: the practice of Sabbath observance is seen, along with "smearing with mud" and "disgraceful besieging of the gods," as one of the ways in which Greeks have been led away from proper worship into the disgrace of superstition. It goes without saying that the people who were attracted to such "superstitions" would have had put a much more positive complexion on their behavior.

In this connection it is to be observed that Plutarch himself is not uniformly disdainful of Jewish religious practice. A later work contains an account of a symposium in which the dinner guests discussed several aspects of Jewish identity—specifically, the reasons for their abstaining from pork and the nature of the Jewish god (*Quaestiones Convivales* 4.4.4–4.6.2 [669C–672B]). The participants in the discussion display an open curiosity towards Jews and Judaism, treating Jewish practice with sincere interest and even sympathy.

In any case, what is of primary interest here is not the extent to which Plutarch was disdainful towards Judaism, but the evidence he provides that some of his contemporaries found Judaism sufficiently attractive that they were prepared to risk the disdain of the educated elite in order adopt some of its practices.

§183 Plutarch Cicero *7.4–5*

> *Nevertheless, many witty sayings of his in connection with this trial are on record. For instance, "verres" is the Roman word for a castrated porker; when, accordingly, a freedman named Caecilius, who was suspected of Jewish practices, wanted to thrust aside the Sicilian accusers and denounce Verres himself, Cicero said: "What has a Jew to do with a Verres?"*

Text and translation: LCL (Perrin 1919)
Date: Early second century C.E.
Provenance: Greece
Original Language: Greek
Bibliography: Barclay (1996, 288); Cohen (1999, 175–97); Feldman (1993, passim); Schürer (1986, 3:701–4); Stern (1974, 1:566)
Category: SYMPATHIZATION, CONVERSION

This passage appears in Plutarch's *Life of Cicero* as he is discussing Cicero's prosecution of Verres, who was accused by the Sicilians of engaging in corruption during his term as praetor of Sicily (73–71 B.C.E.). According to Plutarch's account, the praetors of Rome, who supported Verres, delayed the trial until the last possible day, giving Cicero no time to deliver his prepared speeches. Nevertheless, says Plutarch, Cicero was still able to find the opportunity for a few witticisms. This one was a play on Verres's name, which was also the word for a boar or pig. When a certain Caecilius, who was known for his Jewish sympathies, attempted to intervene in the proceedings, Cicero asked what business a Jew had with a pig.

The historicity of the account is open to serious doubt. To be sure, one Quintus Caecilius Niger served as quaestor in Sicily under Verres, and Cicero himself refers to Caecilius's attempt to take over the prosecution of Verres from the Sicilians (with the actual intent of freeing Verres from the charges). But Cicero's own account of the trial makes no mention of Caecilius's Jewish sympathies. This, together with the unlikelihood that a freedman could have risen so high in the Roman civil service, has led some scholars to suspect that the anecdote is apocryphal, originating instead as the result of some confusion between this Caecilius and Caecilius of Calacte, an orator from the Augustan period who was both a freedman and probably of Jewish origin.[38]

Still, whether the anecdote originated in the first century B.C.E. or, as is more likely, sometime a century or so later, it nevertheless reveals something of Roman attitudes in this period, as refracted through the sensibilities of a Greek writer early in the second century C.E. As has been noted by Cohen, Plutarch's version of the story contains the only appearance of ἰουδαΐζειν outside of Jewish and Christian sources.[39] According to Plutarch, Caecilius was ἔνοχος τῷ ἰουδαΐζειν. Perrin's rendering—"suspected of Jewish practices"—is an overtranslation. While ἔνοχος can have the sense "liable to" or "guilty of" when used in a legal setting, the basic sense of the term is simply "bound by," "subject to" or "given to." Cohen (1990, 180, n. 26) has shown that Plutarch uses the term elsewhere with reference to people who are subject to various conditions or influences; for example, Julius Caesar was "subject to epileptic fits" (*Life of Caesar* 17.2) and, in a more pertinent example, women in the area of Alexander's birthplace were "given to the Orphic rites and the orgies of Dionysus" (*Life of Alexander* 2.5). So Caecilius was not "suspected" of Judaizing; he was given to it or was subject to its influence.

How thoroughgoing was the influence? As we have already seen on the basis of a comparison with other -ιζειν formulations, ἰουδαΐζειν can be used with reference to a range of accommodation to or sympathy with the Jewish community. The example of Metilius was seen to be particularly instructive. Since Josephus says of him that he was prepared "to Judaize as far as circumcision" (*J.W.* 2.454; §112), ἰουδαΐζειν could extend as far as full conversion, though the word is to be taken in this sense only if the context requires it. Metilius would have been "Judaizing" even if his adoption of Jewish ways or sympathies did not go as far as circumcision.

38. For a detailed argument against authenticity, with full references to the relevant source material, see Schürer (1986, 3:701–04); see also Stern (1974, 1:566).

39. Cohen (1999, 180); the Jewish sources (LXX Esther 8:17; Josephus *J.W.* 2. 454 and 2.463) are discussed elsewhere in this work.

What then of Caecilius? The fact that he was also called a Jew (Ἰουδαίῳ) might be taken as an indication that he had become a full proselyte. But such a conclusion would be hasty. For one thing, while Greeks and Romans tended to recognize that circumcision was the decisive mark of the proselyte from the Jewish perspective, from their own perspective the decisiveness of circumcision may not have loomed as large. Viewing things from outside, they were probably inclined to think that anyone who adopted Jewish ways and associated with the Jewish community had "become a Jew." But in addition to this, since exaggeration was quite acceptable in the service of humorous satire, all that was required for Cicero's *bon mot* to be effective was that Caecilius be known to have Jewish sympathies. So while full conversion cannot be eliminated categorically, it is more likely that, from the perspective of the account, Caecilius had simply adopted some Jewish ways.[40]

§184 Epictetus Discourses *2.9.19–21*

> *Why, then, do you call yourself a Stoic, why do you deceive the multitude, why do you act the part of a Jew, when you are a Greek? Do you not see in what sense men are severally called Jew, Syrian, or Egyptian? For example, whenever we see a man halting between two faiths, we are in the habit of saying, "He is not a Jew, he is only acting the part." But when he adopts the attitude of mind of the man who has been baptized and has made his choice, then he both is a Jew in fact and is also called one. So we also are counterfeit "baptists," ostensibly Jews, but in reality something else, not in sympathy with our own reason, far from applying the principles which we profess, yet priding ourselves upon them as being men who know them.*

Text and translation: LCL (Oldfather 1928)
Date: c. 105–13 C.E.
Provenance: Greece
Original Language: Greek
Bibliography: Cohen (1999, passim); Feldman (1993, 33, 346–47); Long (2002); McEleney (1973–1974, 332); Nolland (1981, 179–82); Schäfer (1997, 97–98); Stern (1974, 1:541–44); Wander (1998, 166–68); Xenakis (1969)
Category: SYMPATHIZATION, CONVERSION

Epictetus, an influential teacher in the Stoic tradition, left no writings of his own but is known to us through classroom notes taken down "word for word" by Arrian,[41] his student and subsequently a historian of note. Epictetus was

40. Of course, if the account does not go back to Cicero but developed instead as the result of a confusion between two Caeciliuses, the original Caecilius was a Jew by birth and in actuality. But even if this was the case originally, the story as Plutarch received it assumed that Caecilius was a "Judaizing" Gentile.

41. So Arrian says in his prefatory greeting to Lucius Gellius in the *Discourses*. See further below.

born to a slave mother in the Phrygian city of Hierapolis, sometime around 50 C.E. At some point he was acquired by Epaphroditus, Nero's freedman and trusted secretary, and it was while he was in Epaphroditus's service that he studied under Musonius Rufus, Rome's most influential Stoic teacher of the period. Later he became an influential Roman teacher in his own right, though he moved his school to Nicopolis in Greece after Domitian expelled the philosophers from Rome in 89 C.E. Arrian was one of his students in Nicopolis, probably in the period 105–13 C.E. (Long 2002, 38).

While Arrian's hand can be seen in the overall shaping and arranging of the material, the *Discourses* evidently preserve the actual voice of Epictetus in dialog with his students during the period in which Arrian was his pupil.[42] Of the original eight books of these *Discourses*, four have survived. Although he was thoroughly Stoic in his own commitments and viewpoints—or perhaps because of this—Epictetus had an independent cast of mind and was not averse to criticizing Stoicism and other Stoic teachers (e.g., *Discourses* 1.4.6; 2.19.22). A recurring theme in his *Discourses* is the contrast between philosophy simply as an intellectual exercise and philosophy as an ethical way of life. He is sharply critical of those who lightly call themselves philosophers but continue to "eat in the same fashion, drink in the same fashion, give way to anger and irritation" (*Discourses* 3.15.10)—that is, to continue in a self-indulgent style of life totally at odds with the philosophical teaching they espouse. It is in the context of one discussion of this theme that we find the passage under discussion here.

In the ninth discourse in book 2, Epictetus contrasts the difficulty that is involved in living up to the "profession" (ἐπαγγελία) of a human being, with the much greater difficulty in living up to the "profession" of a philosopher. By "profession" he means the task or calling that any entity (e.g., a flute, a lyre) or living being (e.g., a horse, a carpenter) is expected to carry out by virtue of its essential character or identity. Part of the calling of a human being, he argues, involves rationality; we fail to live up to our calling when we live simply on a sensual level, like sheep, or when we give vent to our anger, like wild beasts. One of the goals of philosophy, he continues, is to teach us to live up to our calling: "The philosophers admonish us not to be satisfied with merely learning, but to add thereto practice also, and then training" (2.9.13). With this reference to philosophers, Epictetus turns to the case of people who call themselves philosophers but who have not even lived up to the calling of being human. These are people who can give a learned discourse about things good, evil, and indifferent, but who react in a base and beastly way when confronted with things that are indifferent and thus should not matter to a true philosopher. Such pseudo-philosophers have a lot of food stored away in the pantry, but they have not even started to digest it and make it their own (2.9.18).

42. For one thing, the koine Greek of the *Discourses* stands in contrast to the Attic style in Arrian's own writings. For a discussion of Arrian's role, see Long (2000, 38–43).

It is here that Epictetus uses the example of the vacillating "half-Jew" to illustrate his point. He compares the person professing to be a Stoic with the Greek who is "playing the part" (ὑποκρίνῃ) of a Jew. Like other ethnic groups—here he mentions Syrians and Egyptians—Jews have their own defining characteristics.[43] But there are those, he says, who are ambiguous, halfway in between, trying to have it both ways (ἐπαμφοτερίζοντα). Such a person "is not really a Jew, but is just playing the part" (οὐκ ἔστιν Ἰουδαῖος, ἀλλ᾽ ὑποκρίνεται). It is important to note that this comparison with the "play-acting Jew" is not simply Epictetus's own analogy; rather, he introduces it as a commonplace saying:[44] "Whenever [ὅταν] we see someone half-way in between, we are in the habit [εἰώθαμεν] of saying, 'He is not a Jew, but is just playing the part.'" The phenomenon of Gentile attraction to Judaism had become sufficiently widespread that the saying could be used as a way of describing any situation where a person was hesitating between two options or commitments. The fact that Epictetus had taught both in Rome and in Greece suggests that the phenomenon was commonly known in both places.

Epictetus does not specify what is involved in the in-between state. Presumably, as Cohen has suggested, these people had adopted some subset of Jewish practices that served to identify them with the Jewish community even though they stopped short of full incorporation.

Epictetus goes on to contrast this "play-acting Jew" with one who decides to leave the in-between state and to become a full Jew. To do so, such a person ceases to hesitate and "adopts" (ἀναλάβῃ) the "attitude of mind" or the "experienced condition" (πάθος) of "the one who has been immersed" (τοῦ βεβαμμένου) and who has "made his choice" (ᾑρημένου). A puzzling feature of the passage is that immersion, rather than circumcision, is seen as the definitive marker for the convert to Judaism. In an older line of interpretation it was suggested that perhaps he was confusing Judaism with (Jewish) Christianity, for which baptism was the decisive rite of initiation.[45] But this has generally been abandoned. Since Epictetus speaks elsewhere both of Jews (*Discourses* 1.11.12–13; 1.22.4) and of Christians,[46] it is quite unlikely that he would confuse the two. In a different line of approach, McEleney (1973–1974) has seized on the passage as evidence for the existence of "uncircumcised proselytes." That is, his argument is that the Gentile in view in this passage became "a Jew in fact" and in name without having to be circumcised. But this thesis has been widely rejected[47] and should also be dismissed here. The most probable interpretation

43. In fact, Epictetus makes reference to such ethnographical distinctions elsewhere; *Discourses* 1.11.12–13; 1.22.4.

44. See also Feldman (1993, 346–47); Nolland (1981, 181).

45. See Oldfather (1928, 1:272–73); the suggestion is also entertained by Long (2002, 110, n. 8).

46. Assuming, as is likely, that this is what he means by "Galileans" (*Discourses* 4.7.6).

47. See especially Nolland (1981); Cohen (1999, 152).

is that Epictetus has decided, in view of his own rhetorical purposes, to use the part for the whole.

There are two aspects to this interpretation. One is that Epictetus's statement reflects a situation in which ritual immersion was part of the process by which a Gentile became a proselyte. The difficulty with this part of the interpretation is that the statement itself would be the earliest explicit reference to the practice. Still, there are good reasons for believing that the immersion was already a common practice. For one thing, it arises logically from the ritual immersions that formed a normal part of Jewish purity practice. Proselytes would eventually need to undergo the ritual in any event, and it is easy to see how the first instance of this could take on initiatory significance. Further, the evidence from rabbinic literature indicates that proselyte baptism was taken for granted within rabbinic Judaism in the Tannaitic period.[48] Thus it is likely that Epictetus's statement about immersion reflected one aspect of the process by which proselytes were incorporated into Judaism.[49]

But why no reference to circumcision? Perhaps the answer is to be found in the fact that Epictetus wants to use the situation as an analogy, to refer to philosophers who fail to practice what they preach. After completing the analogy, Epictetus returns to his main point. There are many who profess to be philosophers who nevertheless are not able to apply "the principles which [they] profess"[50] to their own lives. Such philosophers, he says, are like the "play-acting Jews"; they are not really immersed (παραβαπτισταί) even though they pretend that they have been. Given Hellenistic distaste for the practice of circumcision, one could understand why Epictetus might choose a more innocuous practice for the analogy. His hearers might have been more ready to consider the admonition "not to be satisfied with merely learning, but to add thereto practice also" (*Discourses* 2.9.13) if this second step were represented figuratively by immersion rather than by circumcision.[51]

However this aspect of the text is to be understood, the most significant aspect of the passage is that once they have taken this decisive second step and have fully adopted the Jewish frame of mind and way of life, the convert is seen, by Gentile outsiders at least, as fully a Jew, in fact as well as in name.

48. As Cohen has observed (1999, 222–23), the practice is simply assumed in the Tosefta. Tannaitic rabbis debate aspects of the practice (*b. Yeb.* 46a), and the ritual is described in a *baraita* in *b. Yeb.* 47a–b.

49. See Feldman (1993, 33); Goodman (1994, 81); Nolland (1981, 179–82); Cohen (1999, 222); Schäfer (1997, 97–98).

50. Epictetus includes himself in the criticism: "which we profess."

51. This reading is similar to that of Nolland (1981, 179–82), who argues that immersion was more readily generalized. The argument can be strengthened, however, by taking into account the negative connotations of circumcision.

Tacitus

Tacitus is known primarily for his histories of the early imperial period (*Histories* and *Annals*, as they have come to be known), but his work as a historian was both preceded and made possible by a successful public career that took him into the upper levels of Roman political life in the Flavian period. Born into an equestrian family in Gaul sometime very early in Nero's reign, he first gained attention as an orator in Rome, which led to a series of appointments and public offices under Vespasian ("my political career owed its beginning to Vespasian"; *Hist.* 1.1), Titus (during whose rule he was elected as quaestor) and Domitian (who appointed him as praetor and as a member of the *Quindecimviri sacri faciundis*, an elite college of priests). His public career reached its pinnacle when he attainted the consulship in 97 C.E. The next year saw the start of his career as a writer, with the publication of a laudatory biography of his father-in-law Julius Agricola. While he devoted much of his remaining time to his writing projects (he died early in Hadrian's reign), he continued to play a part in public life, including a term as proconsul of the province of Asia in 112.

It was not coincidental that his career as a writer began shortly after the death of Domitian. A prominent Roman politician could not have survived the terrible tyranny of Domitian's last years without some measure of compromise and even complicity, and Tacitus's views both of political power and of the historian's role were shaped in decisive ways by his experience of tyranny close-up. In *Agricola*, Tacitus set out to provide his father-in-law with the kind of eulogy that had not been possible at the time of his death (93), when to praise someone for their accomplishments as an effective senator, a successful general, and a man of honor was a potentially subversive and thus dangerous thing to do. Themes that can be seen in Tacitus's subsequent historical works—the evils of tyranny; the importance of frank speech; the decline of the traditional Roman *mores* that had served as a bulwark against tyranny—are already on view in his first work.

Tacitus's *Histories* was completed sometime around 109 or 110 C.E. The account begins with the tumultuous events of 69 and traces the story down to the death of Domitian in 96. Unfortunately, however, only the first four-and-a-half books (out of a total of twelve or fourteen) have survived. The extant portion reaches only to the events of 70 C.E., breaking off in the middle of Civilis's revolt in Germany, Titus's seige of Jerusalem not yet having reached its conclusion. At the outset of this work (*Hist.* 1.1), Tacitus announced his intention to follow it up with a history of the subsequent emperors Nerva and Trajan. Somewhere along the way, however, he changed his mind. Perhaps several years of Trajan's rule led him to revise his opinion that he was now living in "an age in which we may feel what we wish and may say what we feel" (*Hist.* 1.1). In any case, his subsequent work, the *Annals*, treated the period from the accession of Tiberius to the death of Nero. Again, only a portion of his work has survived.

Passages of interest to us here appear in both the *Histories* and the *Annals*, part of a larger set of passages in which he refers to Jews and Judaism. One of Tacitus's themes is the decline of morality and of respect for traditional Roman ways among the populace. It is in this context that Tacitus's well-known disparagement of Jews and Judaism needs to be seen. He is not anti-Jewish in a thoroughgoing way. Concerning the outbreak of the Jewish revolt, for example, he places much more blame on venal Roman governors than he does on the Jews themselves, and he displays some grudging respect for the Jews as combatants (as he does elsewhere for the Britons and Germans). But it is another matter when Jews take up residence in Rome, especially when they begin to infect good Romans with their strange and decidedly un-Roman ways.

Text and translation: LCL (Moore and Jackson 1931)
Date: c. 109–10 C.E. (*Histories*); 114–20 (*Annals*)
Provenance: Rome
Original Language: Latin
Bibliography: Barclay (1996, 298–301, 314–16); Chilver and Townend (1985); Cohen (1999, passim); Feldman (1993, passim); Goodyear (1981); Mellor (1993); Schäfer (1997, 31–33, 109, 191–92); Stern (1974, 2:1–93); Syme (1958); Wander (1998, 175–76)

§185 Tacitus Histories *5.5.1–2*

> *Whatever their origin, these rites are maintained by their antiquity: the other customs of the Jews are base and abominable, and owe their persistence to their depravity. For the worst rascals among other peoples, renouncing their ancestral religions, always kept sending tribute and contributing to Jerusalem, thereby increasing the wealth of the Jews; again, the Jews are extremely loyal toward one another, and always ready to show compassion, but toward every other people they feel only hate and enmity. They sit apart at meals, and they sleep apart, and although as a race, they are prone to lust, they abstain from intercourse with foreign women; yet among themselves nothing is unlawful. They adopted circumcision to distinguish themselves from other peoples by this difference. Those who are converted to their ways follow the same practice, and the earliest lesson they receive is to despise the gods, to disown their country, and to regard their parents, children and brothers as of little account.*

Category: SYMPATHIZATION, CONVERSION

At the start of book 5, Tacitus begins to relate Titus's siege of Jerusalem. But before describing "the last days of a famous city," it is only "proper," he says, that he first say something about its origin. What follows is "the most detailed account of the history and religion of the Jewish people extant in classical Latin literature" (Stern 1974, 2:1), an account that is striking as much for its sloppiness as for its length. As Mellor has pointed out, Tacitus could easily have avoided some of his factual errors (e.g., Jewish ass-worship) if he had consulted the work of Josephus; Tacitus must have been aware of his work, since Josephus also belonged to the circle of Flavian clients in Rome (Mellor 1993, 21, 32). One might attempt to mitigate the charge of sloppiness by pointing to the objective historical guise that Tacitus adopts: he proceeds, in good ethnographical fashion, by describing various explanations of Jewish origins that have been held by others. But the last of these—the story, well-known in Alexandrian circles, that the Jews had been expelled by the Egyptians because they had been disfigured by a plague—is quite clearly the option that he prefers, as can be seen from the fact that it is much longer than any of the others and that he slides imperceptibly from historical description to contemporary denunciation. The charge of sloppiness remains.

The shift from objective reporting to partisan critique is apparent at least by 5.4. Here Tacitus turns to the "new religious practices" that Moses introduced in order "to establish his influence over this people." Before providing a list of these practices (which include the worship of an ass, abstaining from pork, fasting, unleavened bread, and observance of the Sabbath), Tacitus provides a more general characterization. They are "quite opposed to those of all other religions," for "the Jews regard as profane all that we hold sacred" and "permit all that we abhor."

These observances have a certain legitimacy, Tacitus continues, because of their antiquity. But at 5.5 (the passage cited above) he differentiates these from "the other customs of the Jews," presumably of more recent origin, which are "base and abominable" and rooted in "depravity." The passage is somewhat confused in that he begins not with a Jewish custom per se but with a complaint about "tribute and contributions" that were sent to Jerusalem by non-Jews—disreputable people (*pessimus quisque*) who had renounced their own ancestral religions (*spretis religionibus patriis*). But taken together with the rest of the passage, what seems to have aroused Tacitus's ire here is the perceived anti-social separatism of the Jews on the one hand, coupled with the readiness of many non-Jews, on the other, to join them in their perverse inversion of the values adhered to by everyone else. Jews are "extremely loyal" to each other but hate everyone else; they eat separately, sleep separately, marry only those of their own group; they have adopted circumcision precisely as a means of maintaining this hateful distinction between them and the rest of the world. But what is worse, from Tacitus's perspective, is that many non-Jews have been prepared to cross this line of distinction and join them. The fact that his description of Jewish separatism is sandwiched in between two denunciations of such Gentile behavior witnesses to the animosity with which he views the phenomenon.

In the second of these denunciations, converts are clearly in view. Although Moore's rendering of *transgressi* as "those who are converted" is perhaps stronger than the normal sense of the verb (from *transgredior*: to go across, to pass over to another side or party), it is justified by the context. These persons have accepted circumcision; while the "same practice" (*idem*) that they have come to follow probably refers not just to circumcision but to the whole attitude of separation that circumcision represents, circumcision is nevertheless part of it. Further, they have "despised" their own gods, which implies that they have accepted the exclusive worship of the Jewish God. And they have become fully incorporated into the Jewish people, having learned "to disown their country and to regard their parents, children and brothers as of little account." What we have here is an extremely jaundiced, outside view of the three elements that constitute conversion to Judaism in this period.

Conversion is not as clearly in view in the denunciation with which this section begins. Here the only practice that these non-Jews adopt is the sending of gifts to the temple in Jerusalem, something that was open to Gentiles as Gentiles and that need not imply any significant level of attachment to Jewish ways. Nevertheless, Tacitus seems to make no distinction between this group and those in view in the second denunciation. Further, he does present this devotion to the Jerusalem temple as involving a renunciation of their own "ancestral religions." Thus even if there are finer distinctions that might have been apparent from the Jewish side, Tacitus seems to treat all of these despicable defectors alike; that is, he thinks of them as what we would call "converts."

One other aspect of this passage deserves attention, which has to do with a certain balance of initiative. On the one hand, the fact that these Gentiles are instructed (*imbuuntur*) in certain things suggests a measure of initiative on the part of the Jewish community. These Gentiles do not simply imitate Jews or adopt their ways; rather, they receive instruction, presumably from the Jews themselves. But on the other hand, the primary initiative seems to lie with the non-Jews. They are those who have "gone over" (*transgressi*) to Jewish ways; they "use" or follow (*usurpant*) the same customs. The language perhaps is not to be pressed too far. Still, if Jews were engaged in aggressive proselytizing activity, one would expect that Tacitus would have pounced on the fact, holding it up as further evidence of Jewish opposition to everything that a traditional Roman held dear. The picture that emerges is more one where the primary initiative lay with Gentiles. Jews may have been willing to instruct those who sought them out, but the seeking was the first step.

§186 Tacitus Annals *2.85.4*

> *Another debate dealt with the proscription of the Egyptian and Jewish rites, and a senatorial edict directed that four thousand descendants of enfranchised slaves, tainted with that superstition and suitable in point of age, were to be shipped to Sardinia and there employed in suppressing brigandage: "if they succumbed to the pestilential climate, it was a cheap loss." The rest had orders to leave Italy, unless they had renounced their impious ceremonial by a given date.*

Additional bibliography: Abel (1968); Dickson (2003, 26–31); Feldman (1993, 302–3); Smallwood (1981, 201–10); Williams (1989)
Category: CONVERSION

As we have seen, (§146 above), Josephus, Tacitus, Suetonius, and Dio Cassius each recount an expulsion of Jews from Rome during the reign of Tiberius. There we gave consideration to the event itself; here we will focus our attention on the details and characteristics of Tacitus's account.

Since Tacitus organized his *Annals* according to the succession of annual consuls, his account (alone of the four) provides us with a date: "in the consulate of Marcus Silanus and Lucius Norbanus" (*Annals* 2.59.1), that is, 19 C.E. Tacitus also is the only one to attribute the action not simply to Tiberius but also to a senatorial edict (*patrum consultum*), which, if true, indicates that the expulsion was the result of considered deliberation rather than imperial whim. He is also alone in saying that Jews were banished from the whole of Italy rather than just from Rome. In this detail he is probably not to be followed; since Josephus wants to impress upon his readers the unfairness of the edict, it is not likely that he would have spoken only of Rome if the edict referred to the whole of Italy.[52] Another unique detail is his description of the conscripts as being "of the freedman class" (*libertini generis*). Presumably this expression was meant to include descendants of freed slaves; it is quite unlikely that there would have been four thousand recently freed Jewish slaves in Rome.

In each of the other passages, there are explicit references to Gentile converts. Dio is the most categorical, identifying proselytism as the reason for the expulsion: "As the Jews flocked to Rome in great numbers and were converting [μεθιστάντων] many of the natives to their ways, he [Tiberius] banished most of them" (*Hist.* 57.18.5). Something similar appears in Josephus's account, though here the expulsion is attributed, oddly, to a single case in which a would-be convert is defrauded by a group of Jewish con artists posing as teachers of the law. Suetonius we will consider in a moment. But what of Tacitus?

Tacitus does not refer to non-Jews in any explicit way, and if it were not for the other accounts we would probably not suspect that converts were implicated. But given the existence of this other evidence, two aspects of his account are suggestive. First, he speaks of the conscripts as having been "tainted [*infecta*] with that superstition." This would be an odd way to speak of those who had been born Jewish and who were simply following ancestral custom. *Inficio* in its most basic sense means "to dip into" and by extension "to dye" or "stain." By further extension it is used in a negative and figurative sense to refer to a taint or a corruption. Thus the language seems to refer more to persons who were drawn into this "superstition" than to the native-born. Similar things can be said of the escape clause, which only Tacitus reports: those who "had renounced

52. See Goodyear (1981, 442); Smallwood (1981, 204).

their impious ceremonial" (*profanos ritus exuissent*) by a given time would not be expelled. Again the language seems to be more appropriate as a reference to Gentiles who at some point previous had adopted this "impious ceremonial" than to those who had been born into it. In view of the magnitude of the consequences—conscription or expulsion—if Gentiles are included, it is much more plausible to think of people who had fully identified with the Jewish community than simply of those who had adopted a few Jewish observances.

If this reading is accepted,[53] it also implies a certain lack of precision on Tacitus's part. The terms in question (*infecta, exuissent*) seem to be used in a comprehensive way, which, if construed strictly, would suggest that those who were conscripted or expelled were all Gentile converts. But since there are other signs of imprecision in the passage,[54] it is best to conclude that Tacitus is speaking loosely of a Jewish group that also included Gentile converts. If so, the choice of language suggests that in his view the offensive thing about this superstition was its tendency to spread and thus to "infect" the Roman populace at large.

§187 Tacitus Annals *13.32*

> *Pomponia Graecina, a woman of high family, married to Aulus Plautius—whose ovation after the British campaign I recorded earlier,—and now arraigned for alien superstition, was left to the jurisdiction of her husband. Following the ancient custom, he held the inquiry, which was to determine the fate and fame of his wife, before a family council, and announced her innocent.*

Category: SYMPATHIZATION, CONVERSION

The case of Pomponia Graecina requires only brief comment. Since Tacitus orders his *Annals* according to the annual succession of consuls, this incident can be dated with precision. It took place when Nero was consul for the second time, along with Lucius Piso—that is, 57 C.E. Although "little occurred that deserves remembrance" in this year, Tacitus does describe this case in which a certain elite woman was accused (*rea*) of alien superstition (*superstitionis externae*). The case was referred to the jurisdiction of her husband, who convened a family council and cleared her of the charge. While nothing further is said about the identity or character of the "superstition," some have suggested that it might have been Judaism or, less likely, Christianity.[55] While some support for the possibility of Judaism might be sought in Tacitus's use of *superstitio* elsewhere with reference

53. For a similar reading, see Goodyear (1981, 2:441); Schäfer (1997, 109); Stern (1974, 2:73).

54. E.g., strictly speaking *ea superstitione* should include the Egyptian rites as well, though it is clear that by this point in the sentence Tacitus is dealing with Jews exclusively.

55. So, with hesitation, Barclay (1996, 307); Schäfer (1997, 191–92); Stern (1974, 2:88).

to Judaism (*Ann.* 2.85), and perhaps in the interest shown towards Judaism by Nero's wife Poppaea,[56] the issue is very uncertain. Little weight should be placed on the passage.

SUETONIUS

Like his older contemporary Tacitus, Suetonius (Gaius Suetonius Tranquillus) combined a literary career with public service at the highest levels. He was born into an equestrian family sometime around 70 C.E., perhaps in Italy but more likely in the Numidian city of Hippo: the fact that the city of Hippo honored him with an inscription (found in 1952) detailing his public career is best explained on the supposition that he was a native son. From this inscription we know that he occupied several significant positions in the Roman civil service, culminating in that of the *ab epistulis*, a position that gave him responsibility for overseeing the correspondence of the emperor (Hadrian). His rise to such positions of influence was no doubt due in part to the support of important patrons—first Pliny the Younger and then Septicius Clarus. Patronage was a two-sided affair, however; the end of Suetonius's public career coincided with Hadrian's dismissal of Septicius Clarus from his position as praetorian prefect (reportedly because of some impropriety involving Hadrian's wife Sabrina).[57]

While Suetonius wrote on a wide variety of topics, he is best known for his biographies of the emperors from Julius to Domitian (*Lives of the Caesars*), not only because this is the only one of his works to have been preserved (almost) in its entirety,[58] but also because it was probably the capstone of his literary career (Bradley 1998, 6). Because of its straightforward and unadorned style and of its lack of attention to the broader sweep of imperial history, *Lives of the Caesars* has often been compared in unfavorable terms to the historical work of a Sallust or a Tacitus. Suetonius displays little interest in chronology, for example, dealing with his subjects more on the basis of themes or topics than of a connected narrative. More recently, however, it has been recognized that Suetonius needs to be judged not as a historian but as a biographer. Implicit in *Lives of the Caesars* is a well-defined picture of how emperors ought to rule and comport themselves, and the purpose of the work is to evaluate each of these emperors in turn according to this norm. Both the content and the structure of each biography have been determined by this overarching purpose.

Four passages are of interest to us, all from the *Lives of the Caesars*.[59]

56. Josephus *Ant.* 20.195; *Life* 13–16; see the introduction to ch. 6 and §153 above.

57. For biographical details, see especially Bradley (1998) and Wallace-Hadrill (1995).

58. It is missing only the early chapters of the first biography, *The Deified Julius*. Also surviving are portions of *Lives of Illustrious Men*.

59. In *Tiberius* 32, Suetonius describes an incident involving the emperor Tiberius and a certain Rhodian grammarian named Diogenes. Tiberius wanted to hear Diogenes lecture

Text and translation: LCL (Rolfe and Bradley 1997; 1998)
Date: c. 117–27 C.E.
Provenance: Rome
Original Language: Latin
Bibliography: Baldwin (1983); Barclay (1996, 310–13); Bradley (1998); Cohen (1999, 42–43); Dickson (2003, 26–31); Feldman (1993, 302–3); Goodman (1994, 122–23); Schäfer (1997, 113–16); Smallwood (1981, 371–85); Stern (1974, 2:110–11); L. Thompson (1982); Wallace-Hadrill (1995); Wander (1998, 172–75)

§188 Suetonius The Deified Augustus *93*

He treated with great respect such foreign rites as were ancient and well established, but held the rest in contempt. . . . But on the other hand he not only omitted to make a slight detour to visit Apis, when he was travelling through Egypt, but highly commended his grandson Gaius for not offering prayers at Jerusalem as he passed by Judaea.

Category: SYMPATHIZATION

This passage, which presents Augustus as commending his grandson Gaius for choosing not to worship (*non supplicasset*) at the Jerusalem temple, provides us with a negative counterpart to many texts already discussed. Indeed, it provides a negative counterpart to other texts dealing with Augustus himself. As we have seen, Josephus and Philo took great pride in recounting benefactions given to the Jerusalem temple by Augustus and other members of his household.[60] The contrast tells us as much about the predispositions of the respective authors as it does about the complexity of imperial religious policy.

While Suetonius is not as acerbic as Juvenal or Tacitus in his comments about the intrusion of foreign customs into Roman society, nevertheless one of the traits of a model emperor, in his view, was a commitment to "the preservation of traditional social norms" (Bradley 1998, 18). With respect to this trait, as with most others, Augustus comes close to the ideal. A case in point is Suetonius's treatment of Augustus's religious dispositions (*The Deified Augustus* 90–93), which contains the passage cited above. On the one hand, in keeping with the high value that Romans placed on long-standing tradition, Augustus

---

on a particular day, but Diogenes refused, since he lectured only on the seventh day. It is possible that Diogenes' practice bore some relation to the Jewish Sabbath (Feldman 1993, 345), but the reference is vague. Even if there was a Sabbath connection, it is just as possible that Diogenes was Jewish as that he was a Gentile sympathizer. Thus the passage will not be included here.

60. See above, on Josephus *J.W.* 5.562–64; *Ant.* 16.14; Philo *Embassy* 157, 291, 294–97, 309–10, 317–19.

is commended for the respect that he displayed towards "such foreign rites as were ancient and well established." As an example, Suetonius cites an instance in which Augustus, while hearing a case involving priests of the cult of Ceres—a mystery into which he himself had been initiated—heard part of the case *in camera* in order to preserve the integrity of the mystery. On the other hand, however, when it came to presumably upstart and dubious cults such as Sarapis or Judaism, Suetonius commends Augustus for his studious disregard. The incident concerning Gaius Caesar took place during his journey to the east as Augustus's emissary (1 B.C.E.–2 C.E.).

While this text has to do with the non-occurrence of foreign worship at Jerusalem, it is nevertheless important for our purposes in several ways. First, it demonstrates that such veneration was common practice for Roman officials. The implication of Suetonius's comment is that Gaius's behavior was somehow out of the ordinary; it was to be expected that representatives of the emperor, traveling through Judea, would pay their respects at the temple as a matter of course. Second, even if this was common practice, Suetonius disapproved of it in the case of Judaism and was pleased when it did not take place. Third, such veneration is to be understood as an expression of Roman values and public policy rather than—as many Jewish writers wanted to see it—as an endorsement of the unique characteristics of Judaism as seen from within. While from the perspective of a comparative religionist the cults of Apis and Ceres might have more in common with each other than either of them did with Judaism, Rome's attitude towards each of them had more to do with the political status of Greece, Egypt, and Judea than with the inherent characteristics or qualities of each religion.

§189 Suetonius Tiberius *36.1*

> *He abolished foreign cults, especially the Egyptian and the Jewish rites, compelling all who were addicted to such superstitions to burn their religious vestments and all their paraphernalia. Those of the Jews who were of military age he assigned to provinces of less healthy climate, ostensibly to serve in the army; the others of that same race or of similar beliefs he banished from the city, on pain of slavery for life if they did not obey.*

Category: CONVERSION

This is Suetonius's version of the expulsion of the Jews from Rome under Tiberius.[61] In accordance with his preconceived picture of what an ideal emperor should look like, he divides the life of Tiberius into three phases. Tiberius "at first played a most unassuming part, almost humbler than that of a private citizen" (*Tib.* 26). Gradually he began to take a more active role ("little by little he

61. For other accounts, see §§144 and 183.

unmasked the ruler"; 33), though at first all his actions and interventions were aimed at the common good. Eventually, however, the death of his sons and his departure from Rome led to a disregard for his duties and to a life of vice and sensuality.

The passage under discussion here appears in the second phase of Tiberius's rule. Suetonius presents the abolishment of foreign cults as one of the positive accomplishments of his reign, along with his edicts against luxury (34), the introduction of measures designed to tighten certain legal loopholes (35), and initiatives taken to suppress banditry and lawlessness (37). Suetonius's account overlaps to a significant extent with that of Tacitus, with whom he may have shared a common source.[62] Again the initiative is directed against both Jewish and Egyptian rites, though Suetonius goes on to add a detail about the astrologers. Again there is the distinction between those of military age who were conscripted for military duty and the others who were banished. Suetonius makes no reference, however, to the legal status of the conscripts (cf. Tacitus's *libertini generis*) or to the role of the senate (cf. Tacitus's *patrum consultum*), and he speaks more vaguely of "provinces of less healthy climate" (both Josephus and Tacitus specify Sardinia). In place of Tacitus's indication that people could avoid expulsion by renouncing Jewish observances, Suetonius refers to the penalty of lifetime slavery for those who tried to evade the expulsion order. Perhaps the edict included both a carrot and a stick.

What is most significant for our purposes, however, is Suetonius's description of those who were expelled: "The others of that same race (*gentis eiusdem*) or of similar beliefs (*similia sectantes*) he banished from the city." Here Suetonius is more precise than Tacitus. Those who were expelled fell into two groups—those who were ethnically Jewish and those who had adopted Jewish beliefs (literally, those eagerly following [from *sector*] similar things). Given the severity of the consequences, it is probable that we are to think of wholesale adoption—that is, full incorporation into the Jewish community—rather than a more casual association or imitation of Jewish ways. Thus while Suetonius does not go as far as Dio Cassius or Josephus, each of whom in his own way suggests that the expulsion was a reaction to the spread of Jewish practices among the Roman populace, he nevertheless makes it clearer than Tacitus does that Gentile converts were included in the expulsion order.

§190 Suetonius Domitian *12.2*

Besides other taxes, that on Jews was levied with the utmost rigour, and those were prosecuted who without publicly acknowledging that faith yet lived as Jews, as well as those who concealed their origin and did not pay the tribute levied upon their people. I recall

62. There are similarities of language (especially *ea superstitione*); see Stern (1974, 2:113).

> *being present in my youth when the person of a man ninety years old was examined before the procurator and a very crowded court, to see whether he was circumcised.*

Category: SYMPATHIZATION, CONVERSION

Suetonius leaves his readers in no doubt whatsoever as to his assessment of Domitian. As soon as his father Vespasian came to power and Domitian assumed his first public office (that of city praetor), "he exercised all the tyranny of his high position so lawlessly that it was even then apparent what sort of man he was going to be" (*Domitian* 1.3). The passage under discussion here appears in a section in which Suetonius is describing the kinds of legalized robbery that the emperor practiced in order to pay for his lavish expenditures. The first part of the section deals with his confiscation of private property on the basis either of trumped-up charges or, in the case of an estate, of a flimsy claim that the deceased had designated the emperor as his heir. Then Suetonius turns to the matter of taxation, with the *fiscus Iudaicus* receiving the bulk of his attention.

The *fiscus Iudaicus*, as it had come to be known by Domitian's time (Smallwood 1981, 372–73), was first levied by Vespasian at the end of the war "on all Jews, wheresoever resident" (Josephus, *J.W.* 7.218). The amount, an annual levy of two *drachmae*, was equal to what adult male Jews had contributed to the Jerusalem temple prior to its destruction. Since Vespasian extended it to include children, women, and slaves, it represented a substantial sum. But according to Suetonius, Domitian began to collect this tax with excessive harshness (*acerbissime*). Specifically, he applied the tax to two groups of people who, presumably, had previously been exempt. The identity of the second group mentioned is clear: "those who concealed their origin and did not pay the tribute levied upon their people" were native-born Jews who were no longer identifying themselves as such. That is, they had become "apostates."[63] But the identity of the first group is not as readily apparent.

These people "lived a Jewish life" (*Iudaicam viverent vitam*) but *inprofessi*—"without acknowledging it openly." Almost all commentators see this group as consisting of Gentiles who had either become proselytes[64] or who had adopted Jewish customs to some lesser degree.[65] A few scholars, however, have objected to this identification, pointing to the fact that Domitian is on record as having condemned certain Gentile Judaizers on a charge of atheism (including his relatives Flavius Clemens and Flavia Domitilla; see the next entry). If he considered the adoption of Jewish practices as a crime against the state, how could he then turn around and give it legitimacy by implying that as long as such persons paid the Jewish tax they had discharged their obligations to the state?[66]

63. On Jewish apostates, including those referred to here, see S. Wilson (2004, 23–65).
64. See Cohen (1999, 42–43); Schäfer (1997, 115); Stern 1974, 2:130).
65. See Feldman (1993, 347); Smallwood (1981, 377).
66. See L. Thompson (1982); Goodman (1994, 122–23).

While there is a certain logic to the argument, it requires a very forced reading of Suetonius. Goodman, for example, understands the first group as "ethnic Jews who had given up public identification with their religion either by hiding their continued Jewish practices or by pretending that their customs had nothing to do with their Jewish ethnic origins, which they dissimulated" (Goodman 1994, 123). But such a reading leaves the first group virtually indistinguishable from the second; in either of Goodman's scenarios, such persons could readily be classified as "those who concealed their origin." With respect to the logic of Domitian's policies, his condemnation of Flavius Clemens and Flavia Domitilla took place near the end of his reign and should thus be seen as part of an attempt to hold onto power through terror rather than as the reflection of a consistent policy on Judaizing practices. There is no problem seeing his treatment of Clemens and Domitilla as an aberration and the "harsh" application of the *fiscus Iudaicus* as his basic policy. Thus there can be little doubt that the group in question—those "who lived a Jewish life"—consisted of people whose ethnic origin was not Jewish.

But how fully had they adopted a "Jewish life"? In other words, are we dealing here with converts or with adherents and sympathizers? Before addressing the question directly, one should note the unlikelihood that converts would have been exempt in principle from the tax prior to Domitian. Since it originally applied to all who had previously paid the temple tax—a group that would have included converts—the tax would have applied to converts from the beginning. The question, then, is whether Domitian's initiative was directed against converts who had somehow been able to stay off the tax rolls or whether it was extending the reach of the tax to include those who associated with the Jewish community without having become full converts.

The matter would be settled if we could be sure that Suetonius's example—concerning the physical examination of a ninety-year-old man to determine whether he had been circumcised—was meant to relate to both cases. If so—which would mean that the question as to who was liable to the tax was one that could be categorically settled on the basis of circumcision—then the first group must be seen as Gentile converts who had somehow been able to escape paying the tax. The fact that these converts had lived as Jews without "acknowledging it openly" would then be understood as meaning that they had been sufficiently discreet about their conversion so as to keep their names off the tax lists (Schäfer 1997, 114–15). In this reading, Domitian's initiative is to be seen simply as a more rigorous collection of the tax from those (i.e., ethnic Jews and Gentile converts) who had been officially subject to the tax from the beginning.

But it is not necessary that Suetonius's example refer to both aspects of Domitian's new tax initiatives. The example immediately follows his comment "about those who concealed their origin," and it seems to make more sense in this immediate context: it is easier to imagine an old man being examined to determine if he had been born Jewish than to determine whether he had become a crypto-proselyte. With respect to the passage as a whole, it is just as possible to understand Domitian's initiatives as having the effect of extending the tax so that it also applied to those whose association with the Jewish community was less formal than in the case of full converts. First, one can question the likelihood that there would have been many Gentiles converts who avoided paying the *fiscus Iudaicus*. Conversion, which signaled full incorporation into the Jewish community, would not have been an inconspicuous affair. Roman tax-collectors in particular would not have been oblivious to it. Nor is it likely that Jews would have taken kindly to those who wanted to be have it both ways: to be part of the Jewish community but to use their non-Jewish origin to escape an unpleasant feature of common Jewish existence. Indeed, since converts had probably been subject to the tax from the beginning, it is logical to imagine that it would have been just one of the obligations that a Gentile would have expected to assume on becoming a convert. Following on from this, given the significance of circumcision for Jewish identity, any Gentile who underwent the rite and who was thus formally incorporated into the Jewish community would thereby have been making an "open acknowledgment" of his allegiance. Thus it is quite plausible to understand Suetonius as describing a group of Gentiles who "lived a Jewish life"—that is, they had abandoned the Roman gods and adopted Jewish observances—but without having made the kind of "open acknowledgment" of their allegiance that would have transformed them from sympathizers and adherents into full converts. The fact that Domitian took other measures against certain members of the Roman elite who had "drifted into Jewish ways" (see the next entry) lends further support to this reading.

Thus, while the question cannot be resolved conclusively, it seems likely that the group of those affected by Domitian's "harsher" collection of the *fiscus Iudaicus* included Gentile sympathizers and adherents.

§191 Suetonius Domitian *15.1*

> *Finally he put to death his own cousin Flavius Clemens, suddenly and on a very slight suspicion, almost before the end of his consulship. . . . And it was by this deed in particular that he hastened his own destruction.*

Category: SYMPATHIZATION

Suetonius gives us no reason to believe that the "very slight suspicion" that led to the death of Flavius Clemens had anything to do with Jewish sympathies. The passage is of interest here, however, because of the version of the incident provided for us by Dio Cassius:

> And the same year Domitian slew, along with many others, Flavius Clemens the consul, although he was a cousin and had to wife Flavia Domitilla, who was also a relative of the emperor. The charge brought against them both was that of atheism, a charge on which many others who drifted into Jewish ways were condemned.

> Some of these were put to death, and the rest were at least deprived of their property. Domitilla was merely banished to Pandateria.[67]

Flavius Clemens and Flavia Domitilla were members of the Roman elite. Not only were they both related to Domitian but also the emperor had designated Flavius's sons as his own heirs, renaming them Vespasian and Domitian (Suetonius *Domitian* 15.1). In Suetonius's account, Domitian's action against Flavius was the culmination of his reign of terror and the deed by which the emperor "hastened his own destruction." Given the status of Flavius's sons, it is readily apparent that Domitian was motivated much more by a desire for self-preservation—the fear that Flavius might be tempted to hasten their accession to the imperium—than by a concern to prevent the Roman elite from adopting Jewish ways. If Dio's account is trustworthy, Domitian was using Jewish sympathy simply as a pretext for the accomplishment of other purposes.

The only possible reason for questioning Dio's account is the version of the story that appears in Eusebius (*H. E.* 3.18.3), which says that Domitilla was banished because of her "testimony to Christ." Dio is closer to the events than Eusebius, however, and his version is also consistent with the detail he relates that Nerva reversed Domitian's policy of allowing Romans "to accuse other people of *maiestas* or Jewish life" (*Hist.* 68.1.2). While one needs to allow for the possibility that Christianity was still seen as a form of Judaism, there is no pressing reason to disallow Dio's account.

Dio presents the case of Clemens and Domitilla as one of a larger number of instances in which Domitian used a charge of "atheism" as a way of eliminating enemies and confiscating wealth. Dio's understanding of the charge, presumably based on his sources, is that the persons so charged had "drifted into Jewish ways" (ἐς τὰ τῶν Ἰουδαίων ἤθη ἐξοκέλλοντες). The verb ἐξοκέλλω is used of a ship running aground or, more generally, of being adrift. Dio's description, then, suggests not the kind of decisive transition that would be characteristic of full conversion but a range of associations with Judaism that would stop short of full conversion.[68] In Clemens's own case, it would have been virtually impossible for a convert to fulfill the religious duties that would have fallen to a consul. Nevertheless, Dio's version of the event suggests that Clemens, Domitilla, and "many others" were attracted to Judaism and had adopted "Jewish ways" to a sufficient extent that it could have been used against them.

Two aspects of these accounts are of particular interest. One has to do with social strata. In his status as consul, as cousin of the emperor, and as father of the emperor's designated heirs, Clemens, with his family, was part of the Roman elite. Dio's account, then, suggests that sympathy for Judaism had penetrated to

67. *Hist.* 67.14.1–2 (early third century C.E.).

68. Contra G. Moore (1927, 349), who describes them as "probably proselytes to Judaism."

the highest levels. The other thing to note has to do with the capriciousness of the evidence. We have this evidence for Roman adoption of Jewish ways not because of its direct significance but because Domitian happened to use it as a convenient tool for his own purposes. In other words, we do not need to suppose that attraction to Judaism was any more widespread during the latter part of Domitian's rule than it was before or after. It may have been, of course, but we cannot argue this simply because this evidence has been preserved.

§192 Juvenal Satires *14.96–106*

> *Some happen to have been dealt a father who respects the sabbath. They worship nothing but the clouds and spirit of the sky. They think there is no difference between pork, which their fathers abstained from, and human flesh. In time, they get rid of their foreskins. And with their habit of despising the laws of Rome, they study, observe, and revere the Judaic code, as handed down by Moses in his mystic scroll, which tells them not to show the way to anyone except a fellow worshipper and if asked, to take only the circumcised to the fountain. But it's their fathers who are to blame, taking every seventh day as a day of laziness and separate from ordinary life.*

Text and translation: LCL (Braund 1940)
Date: c. 130 C.E.
Provenance: Rome
Original Language: Latin
Bibliography: W. Anderson (1982); Bernays (1985); Courtney (1980); Feldman (1993, 347–48); Highet (1954); Schäfer (1997, 79–81); Stern (1974, 2:94–107); Wander (1998, 168–70)
Category: SYMPATHIZATION, CONVERSION

Except for the bit of information contained in three epigrams addressed to him by Martial, nothing is known about Juvenal (Decimus Iunius Iuvenalis) apart from what can be deduced from his five books of *Satires*. An older form of scholarship, operating on the assumption that the primary characters in each satire spoke unambiguously for their author, attempted to patch together a biographical profile on the basis of scattered comments (e.g., Highet 1954). More recently, however, especially since the work of W. Anderson (1982), it has been recognized that the satiric persona must be understood as a function of the genre rather than simply as Juvenal's alter ego. In some cases there may even be elements of irony, the reader being expected in the end to recognize the "moral flaws" of the primary speakers and to assess their satiric utterances accordingly (Braund 1940, 24). This recognition calls for a more cautious approach, which has a bearing not only on the quest for Juvenal's biography but also on our interpretation of the *Satires* themselves.

What is known about Juvenal can be summarized briefly. Martial's references to him, which can be dated to 92 and 101–02 C.E., describe him as an accomplished orator (*Epigrams* 7.91.1) who was fully engaged with public affairs in Rome (*Epigrams* 12.18.1–6). The absence of any reference to a patron in his own work suggests that he was a member of the Roman elite. References to datable events indicate that the *Satires* were written in the early decades of the second century C.E.; book 5, which contains *Satire* 14, originated sometime after 127 C.E. (Braund 1940, 23).

Juvenal addresses two issues in *Satire* 14—the negative influence that parents can have on their children through their own bad example (14.1–106) and the vice of avarice (14.107–331). The two are linked to a certain extent: Juvenal introduces the theme of avarice by saying that in contrast to the instances just discussed, in which the negative influence was the inadvertent result of parental practice, the inordinate love of money was a fault that many parents deliberately attempted to instill in their offspring. But the idea of parental influence eventually falls away, and the latter part of the satire (from 14.255) addresses avarice directly and on its own terms.

Juvenal wastes no time getting into his theme. There are many disreputable practices, he declares to Fuscinus (the addressee of the satire), that "fix a lasting stain" on people's character but that "are actually demonstrated and passed on . . . by their parents" (14.1–3), who thus bear the primary responsibility. Whether it is gambling, gluttony, cruelty to slaves, or sexual license, "bad examples in the home corrupt us more speedily and quickly" because they are impressed on young minds with the "powerful authority" that parents possess (14.31–33). Parents thus have the responsibility to set good examples (14.38–58) so that a son might be "an asset to his fatherland, capable of farming, capable of action in war and peace alike" (14.71–72). At this point Juvenal gives two more extended examples. One concerns a wealthy individual, a certain Caetronius (one of Claudius's freedmen) who spent extravagant amounts of money to construct luxurious villas and whose son then went on to squander what was left of the family fortune by erecting even more opulent houses (14.86–95). The second example is the passage under discussion here, having to do with Sabbath-observing fathers, whose sons take things several steps further by becoming circumcised and committing themselves exclusively to the "Judaic code, as handed down by Moses."

In this satire there is little ambiguity concerning the voice of the satirist. While it may be going too far to say that "this is more a sermon than a satire" (Highet 1954, 148), it is nevertheless Juvenal's own concerns and attitudes that are on display here. Several things are of interest in his choice of this particular example as an illustration of his theme.

The first is the choice itself. Unlike several of his other satires, such as the well-known tirade against foreigners in *Satire* 3[69] or the denunciation of people's folly in praying for things that are not beneficial (*Satire* 10), where the

69. "The Syrian Orontes has for a long time now been polluting the Tiber"; "There's no room for any Roman here in Rome" (*Satires* 3.58–59, 119).

example of Judaism might have readily suggested itself, here the example is gratuitous and not related in any intrinsic way with the theme. This suggests that Juvenal, who here is concerned with the production of good citizens for the "fatherland" (14.70), sees attraction to Judaism not only as something that his readers will readily recognize but also as posing a significant threat to the *mos maiorus* of Rome. Elsewhere Juvenal makes clear his dislike of Jewish customs (*Satires* 6.159–60) and his objection to their conspicuous presence in Rome (*Satires* 3.10–18, 290–96; 6.542–47). This passage demonstrates that for him the threat posed by Judaism is not simply its intrusive presence in Rome but in addition the adoption of Jewish ways by many Romans for themselves. Further, since Juvenal is concerned here with the case of fathers, who are in principle expected to produce good citizens, it appears that these Jewish sympathizers come from the Roman upper classes.

A second point of interest in the passage is the striking way in which several stages of attachment to Judaism are demarcated (Feldman 1993, 347). What Juvenal sees as an insidious process begins simply enough, with a father adopting Sabbath observance (*metuentem sabbata*; 14.96) and abstaining from pork. Their children take this one step further, worshipping "nothing except the clouds and spirit of the sky." Juvenal's description here reflects both the imageless character of Jewish worship and perhaps the use of "heaven" by the Jews as a way of referring to their deity (Courtney 1980, 97). Subsequently (*mox*), the same children go so far as to "get rid of their foreskins," which seems to be the final step in a process of abandoning the laws of Rome and committing themselves exclusively to the "Judaic code" (*Iudaicum ius*). Juvenal thus recognizes several degrees of attachment to Jewish ways—which, of course, is the point of the example; disreputable practices are worthy of double condemnation because they become more entrenched and even worse in the second generation. He is aware, then, that before the final stage demarcated by circumcision, Romans were adopting a variety of Jewish practices (Sabbath observance, abstinence from pork, exclusive worship of the Jewish God, study of Jewish scriptures) to a lesser or greater degree.

Thirdly, Juvenal twice uses *metuo* (to fear) with reference to the practices of these non-Jews: the father "fears the sabbath" (*metuentes sabbata*); the sons "study, observe and fear the Judaic code" (*Iudaicum ediscunt et servant ac metuunt ius*). This usage has occasioned considerable scholarly discussion, to which we will return. Since the work of Bernays (1885), it has often been suggested that Juvenal provides evidence here for the existence of a class of "God-fearers,"[70] but this is unlikely.[71] The most pertinent consideration here is that the object of the verb is not "God"; what is being "feared" or revered here are

70. Also Schäfer (1997, 79–81); Stern (1974, 2:103–06).

71. See Courtney (1980, 571); Feldman (1993, 347–48).

aspects of Jewish practice—the Sabbath, the law. While the question of *metuentes deum* (as a Latin equivalent for φοβούμενοι τὸν θεόν) needs to remain open for now, it is quite unlikely that Juvenal's use of *metuo* with quite different objects provides us with any pertinent evidence. Still, looking at the usage more generally, the verb needs to be included in any list of vocabulary items that pertain to the phenomenon.

Concerning those who take the final step, while circumcision in Juvenal's perception represented the ultimate stage, the point at which adoption of Jewish ways was full and complete, it needs to be seen as part of a larger constellation of identifying markers. Three elements are discernible: abandonment of pagan worship and the exclusive worship of Israel's God ("they worship nothing except the clouds and spirit of the sky"); full adherence to the law of Moses and the way of life that it prescribes (Sabbath observance, dietary regulations, "despising the laws of Rome"); and social incorporation into the Jewish community (signaled by the exaggerated statements concerning "fellow worshippers" and association with "only the circumcised").[72]

Finally, it is perhaps instructive to note the absence of any Jewish initiative. The fathers seem to have adopted Sabbath observance and dietary restrictions on their own; the only influence on the sons was the bad example of their fathers. Against this it might be argued that this absence may simply have been determined by Juvenal's rhetorical purpose; the point of the illustration, after all, is the negative influence that parents can have on their children. The presence of the Jewish community, while muted, is nevertheless assumed: converts associate only with "a fellow worshipper" or with "only the circumcised." Their role in the process may simply have been disregarded to make the point. This argument is not to be dismissed completely. The Jewish community could well have had its own "negative influence" on these fathers and sons. Still, for this to be a pertinent illustration of the theme, Juvenal and his intended readers must have shared the impression that such Jewish sympathizers were acting on their own initiative and out of their own desires, not that they had succumbed to pressures or blandishments from the Jewish community.

72. On these three aspects see Cohen (1999, 156–57).

CHAPTER 8

EARLY CHRISTIAN LITERATURE

Introduction

What eventually came to be known as Christianity originated as a distinct group within the Jewish world but very quickly began to admit non-Jews into its membership. This development was controversial (e.g., Acts 15; Gal 2), the controversy having to do not so much with whether Gentiles should be included but with the terms and conditions of their inclusion. Not surprisingly, given the Jewish character of the movement, the Christian debate proceeded, to a significant extent, along lines already present within the Jewish world itself. Some, for example, insisted on a form of proselytism, taking the position that "it is necessary for them to be circumcised and ordered to keep the law of Moses" (Acts 15:5). Others, however, took the position that while Jewish believers should continue to "keep the law of Moses," God had also chosen "a people for his name" from among the Gentiles (Acts 15:14), who were fully acceptable to God as Gentiles. Still others saw the inclusion of Gentiles within the community of Jesus's disciples as having been made possible by the resurrection of the Messiah and the inauguration of his universal rule (Matt 28:18–20). Indeed, most early Christian material that deals with the relative place of Jews and Gentiles within the movement will display some affinity with the Jewish patterns of universalism under investigation here.

Yet while such material has a bearing on our investigation, it would be imprudent to include it. The task of disentangling the Jewish patterns from the strands of distinctively Christian tradition would require a thoroughgoing analysis of early Christianity that would extend the work unreasonably without adding much to its substance. Likewise, we will exclude texts that reflect an attraction to Judaism and Jewish practices on the part of Gentile Christians.[1]

At the same time, however, there are early Christian texts that pertain more directly to our investigation, in that they deal with non-Christian Gentiles who stand in some relationship with Judaism and the Jewish community itself. Given our temporal parameters, all of the passages of interest here and in subsequent chapters are found in the New Testament.[2]

Texts and Commentary

Matthew

§193 Matthew 23:15

Woe to you, scribes and Pharisees, hypocrites! For you cross sea and land to make a single convert, and you make the new convert twice as much a child of hell as yourselves.

Text: Nestle-Aland 27th ed.
Translation: NRSV
Date: Circa 80 C.E.
Provenance: Syria
Original Language: Greek
Bibliography: Davies and Allison (1997, 3:288–89); Dickson (2003, 39–46); Garland (1979, 129–31); Goodman (1994, 69–74); Gundry (1982, 461); Hagner (1995, 668–69); McKnight (1991, 106–8); Schnabel (2004, 163–65); Wander (1998, 218–21); Will and Orrieux (1992, 115–36)
Category: CONVERSION

1. E.g. *Barn* 3.6, which speaks of Christian Judaizers as being "converts to their law" (probably ἐπήλυτοι, though some manuscripts read προσήλυτοι); also *Did.* 8.1–2; Ignatius *Phld.* 6.1; Justin *Dial.* 47. For a thorough study of Gentile Christian attraction to Judaism, see Murray (2004). Also to be excluded is Paul's statement that there was a time when he was "preaching circumcision" (Gal 5:11). In the context of Galatians, to "preach circumcision" means to encourage Gentiles to accept circumcision as the only means of entry into the family of Abraham. While it is likely that Paul is referring here to his pre-Christian activity (which would mean that the text is pertinent to our investigation), the issue is by no means clear and beyond dispute; for a full discussion, see Donaldson (1997, 278–84).

2. Later passages dealing with sympathizers include Justin *Dial.* 8, 80, 122–23; Irenaeus *Heresies* 3.21.1; Origen *Celsus* 5.11; *Acts of Pilate* 2.2–4. For later Christian references to proselytes, see Justin *Dial.* 8.3; 23.2; 80.1; 122–23; Irenaeus, *Against Heresies* 3.21.1; Origen *Celsus* 5.41; *Acts of Pilate* 2.2–4; Epiphanius *Of Measures and Weights* 15.

This little verse has had an influence all out of proportion to its size. In keeping with a tendency among Christian scholars of an earlier generation to view Judaism through the window of the New Testament, this verse has provided apparent justification for the idea that in this period Judaism "possessed a missionary impulse of such vigour and attained so large a measure of success" that it can properly be described as a missionary religion.[3] Nor is this description restricted to Christian scholars; for Feldman, Matt 23:15 is "the most striking passage indicating the zeal with which the Jews pursued their missionary activities" (Feldman 1993, 298). More recently, however, this reading of the verse has been hotly disputed, with Goodman going so far as to assert that the verse has nothing to do with Gentile converts at all, let alone a full-blown Gentile mission.[4]

The verse forms one of a series of seven woes addressed by Jesus to the "scribes and Pharisees" (23:13–36). These woes in turn form the central section of a longer discourse in which Jesus denounces these Jewish leaders in the harshest of terms. While the saying is attributed to Jesus, it is doubtful that we can recover an authentic Jesus saying with any degree of confidence. For one thing, the saying is unique to Matthew, having no parallel whatsoever in any of the other Gospels.[5] For another, the attitude displayed by the saying, as by the discourse as a whole, is characteristically Matthean. From their first appearance (3:7) to the last (23:29), the "scribes and Pharisees" are presented in unrelentingly negative terms, consistently denounced for their "hypocrisy," false leadership and opposition to Jesus. Thus the verse is best interpreted with respect to the context of Matthew's Gospel, probably in the early 80s C.E., rather than in the context of Jesus's own activity.

Matthew's Gospel is generally understood as written in and for a Christian community that was living in an urban center somewhere in Roman Syria (cf. 4:24; Antioch?). The community consisted originally of Jewish believers in Jesus but had begun to incorporate Gentiles into its group (28:18–20). It continued to adhere to the law of Moses, though as reinterpreted by Jesus, its authoritative teacher. And it was engaged in conflict and hostility with the Pharisees, who were attempting to provide leadership for the Jewish community in the period after the war with Rome (66–70 C.E.).[6]

3. The quotation comes from Harnack (1908, 9). See also G. Moore (1927–1930, 1:323–24); Garland (1979, 129–31); Schürer (1986, 160); Boccaccini (1991, 252).

4. Goodman (1994, 69–74). Other significant critics of this reading of Matt 23:15 are McKnight (1991) and Will and Orrieux (1992).

5. Likewise, the discourse as a whole is unique to Matthew, though some of its building blocks have been drawn from Matthew's two major sources, Mark (12:37–40) and Q (Luke 11:39–51). I use "Matthew" (also "Luke" and "John" below) as a matter of convenience, without implying thereby any opinion about the identity of the actual author.

6. The literature on Matthew's life setting is immense. For a thorough and judicious treatment, see Davies and Allison (1988, 1:1–147)

Taken at face value, the verse seems to reflect a belief that "scribes and Pharisees" engaged in a deliberate effort to make Gentile converts (ποιῆσαι προσήλυτον), being prepared to travel considerable distances (περιάγετε τὴν θάλασσαν καὶ τὴν ξηράν) in the process. As mentioned above, the verse has been used as evidence for a thoroughgoing Jewish mission; it has also been interpreted as having nothing to do with Gentile converts at all. These readings are extreme, and the significance of the verse is probably to be found somewhere in between.

Goodman has argued that the verse had to do with attempts on the part of Pharisees not to make Gentile converts but to convince other Jews to adopt their interpretation of the law of Moses. Matthew's vehemence is to be understood as arising from the fact that Pharisees were interfering with their own attempts to win Jewish converts. Goodman argues that first-century uses of προσήλυτος with reference to Gentile converts are rare[7] and that the related verb προσέρχομαι is often used generically, in Matthew and elsewhere, to describe the approach of a believer to something sacred. He concludes that "*proselytos* in the first century had both a technical and a non-technical sense, and that in the latter sense it could quite easily be applied to Jews" (Goodman 1994, 73). The problem with the argument, however, is that he is not able to adduce a single instance in which προσήλυτος has this generic sense. As he acknowledges, the first-century occurrences of the term[8] all refer to Gentile converts to Judaism. In addition, even if one should dispute the presence of a full technical meaning for the term in the Septuagint, the fact remains that as a rendering of גר, προσήλυτος was from the beginning linked inextricably with non-Jews. There can be no doubt whatsoever that Matt 23:15 has to be understood as having to do with Gentiles.

Will and Orrieux (1992), who have also objected strenuously to the idea of a Jewish proselytizing mission, also interpret the verse as having to do with a conflict between Jewish Christian communities and post-war Pharisaic Judaism. They, however, understand the conflict—more plausibly—as having to do with Gentile sympathizers. In their reading, the Pharisaic leadership was not primarily interested in making converts. Rather, as they sent out envoys[9] to carry out a process of consolidation—reorganizing communities, regulating the liturgical calendar, imposing their discipline, and collecting funds—they encountered a specific problem, namely, a vigorous Jewish Christian mission among Gentile "God-fearers." In response, they attempted to thwart the Christian mission, not so much by attempting to turn godfearers into proselytes (though there may

7. For example, it is not found in Josephus at all; Philo prefers ἔπηλυς and related terms.

8. Philo *QE* 2.2; Acts 2:11; 6:5; 13:43; inscriptions (§§202–08 below). Josephus uses προσέρχομαι of Fulvia (*Ant.* 18.82).

9. "[L]es *sheliahim/apostoloi*" (Will and Orrieux 1992, 119).

have been isolated instances of this), but by dissuading these Gentiles from leaving the synagogue and joining the church. Matthew has seized on these isolated instances and has formulated the Christian riposte in such a way as to suggest that proselytism was the main purpose of the enterprise (Will and Orrieux 1992, 119–22).

Several aspects of this reading are persuasive. Instead of understanding the verse in a global sense—that is, "the Jews" engaged in a worldwide "mission"—it is better to look for a meaning that arises from the specific circumstances of Matthew's community. Further, the suggestion of a link with the institution of traveling Jewish emissaries[10] makes better sense of "you cross land and sea" than does the suggestion that it metaphorically indicates a willingness "to go to great lengths" (J. J. Collins 2000, 263). In addition, it is more plausible to understand the Pharisaic activity as having to do with Gentiles who were already associated with the synagogue than with any sort of direct proselytizing activity to the wider Gentile world. We have plenteous evidence for the former but very little for the latter.

But there seems to be no good reason to follow Will and Orrieux in their attempt to minimize the possibility that Matthew's Pharisaic opponents were interested in convincing Gentile sympathizers to become full converts. For one thing, while Matthew does not shy away from accusing his Jewish opponents of persecuting Christians,[11] there is no hint of persecution in 23:15. In other words, the activity that draws Matthew's criticism here does not seem in the first instance to have been directed at Christians. Matthew presents the "scribes and Pharisees" as being interested in "proselytes" for their own sake, not simply to keep them out of the clutches of the Christians. For another, the example of Eleazar, the second Jewish advisor to King Izates of Adiabene, demonstrates that there were Jews who were both "extremely strict when it came to the ancestral laws" (Josephus *Ant.* 20.43) and extremely concerned to convince Gentile sympathizers to become full converts. To be sure, Matt 23:15 is not to be overinterpreted; it cannot be taken as a generalized description about Pharisees as a whole. Still, the verse provides localized evidence that some "scribes and Pharisees" were perceived as actively encouraging sympathizers to become full converts.[12]

Luke-Acts

Luke-Acts contains references both to proselytes and to sympathizers. While the material pertaining to the latter is not limited to Luke's references to those who

10. On which see, e.g., Schürer (1986, 3: 124–25); Rengstorf (1964, 416–19).

11. E.g., 5:11–12; 10:17; 23:29–36.

12. This reading of the verse is similar to those of J. J. Collins (2000, 263); Cohen (1987b, 56–57); Davies and Allison (1997, 3:288–89); Hagner (1995, 669); McKnight (1991, 106–07); Schnabel (2004, 163–65); Wander (1998, 220).

"feared" or "worshipped God" (οἱ φοβούμενοι/σεβόμενοι τὸν θεόν), these references have featured prominently in the long-standing discussion of Gentile sympathizers. Already in 1933 Lake could speak of "a long and complicated discussion of which the outcome is not clear as yet and perhaps never will be" (Lake 1933, 84). Before looking at individual passages, it will be important to sketch the salient features of this larger discussion.

Much of the discussion takes as its point of departure a viewpoint first articulated by Bernays (1885), according to which Luke's phrases are understood to be technical terms for a definite class of Gentiles who had adopted significant aspects of Jewish belief and practice and who were granted some form of official recognition and status by the synagogue community. Bernays's contribution was to link the Acts passages with Juvenal's well-known account (§192 above) of the father who "fears the sabbath" (and whose son progresses to full conversion; *Satires* 14.96–106). This opened the door to an approach in which a wide variety of material dealing with Judaizing Gentiles was homogenized into a single category for which Acts supplied the technical term—that is, God-fearers (with variants, especially θεοσεβής and *metuens*). This approach made its way into standard reference works,[13] which has been both a measure and a source of its enduring influence.

This approach, however, has been called into question along at least two lines. One is terminological. Lake (1933, 84–86) and later Feldman (1950; also 1993, 342) pointed out that the terms found in Acts are often used with respect to Jews, especially in the LXX, where φοβεῖσθαι τὸν θεόν is the normal rendering of ירא יהוה (to fear YHWH). Thus it cannot simply be assumed without further contextual information that when the term appears in extra-biblical Greek literature it refers to a class of Gentiles. Since Feldman's work, the term "sympathizer" has come into common use as an alternative to "God-fearer" when speaking of Gentiles.

This observation has been brought to bear on the Acts material in two different ways. On the one hand, there are those who see the terms as having a more or less technical sense in Acts, even if this sense was not necessarily shared more widely. In other words, these were Luke's own particular terms for Gentile sympathizers. Kraabel (1981), who (as we will see in more detail) has argued that Luke has largely invented the category for his own theological purposes, is an extreme case in point. On the other hand, there are others—especially Lake (1933) and Wilcox (1981)—who argue that the terms have no technical sense in Acts at all. In other words, Luke used the terms to describe various persons and groups as "pious" and not as nomenclature (whether already existing or of

13. Especially through the work of Karl Georg Kuhn, who wrote both the entry on "προσήλυτος" in the *Theologische Wörterbuch zum Neuen Testament* (ET: Kuhn 1968) and, with Hartmut Stegemann, the article on "Proselyten" in *Realencyclopädia der klassischen Altertumswissenschaft* (Kuhn and Stegemann 1962).

his own creation) for a specific category of person or group.[14] One aspect of this argument is the plurality of terms: not only does Luke make a curious switch from φοβούμενοι to σεβόμενοι in Acts 13, but he uses other terms to describe pious Gentiles as well (εὐσεβής, δίκαιος).

The other line of questioning has to do not with terminology but with social reality (though, of course, the two overlap considerably). Kraabel, mentioned in the previous paragraph, has argued that Luke's narrative bears little relationship to social reality at all. Basing his argument on what he sees as the lack of archaeological evidence for "a kind of Gentile 'penumbra' around the Diaspora synagogue communities" (Kraabel 1981, 117), he concludes that Luke has largely invented the idea for his own theological purposes. Specifically, by portraying the movement of Christianity into the Gentile world as a smooth, step-by-step process from synagogue to "God-fearers" to Gentiles, Luke was attempting to present the Christian movement as the legitimate continuation of the history, scripture, and tradition of Israel.[15]

Few scholars have been prepared to go this far. But many have questioned whether it is possible to speak of a well-defined category of Gentiles taking their place in the synagogue community alongside Jews and proselytes. In Lake's view, we should think not of "a specific group with a definite place in organized Judaism" but of a "vague class" of Gentiles (Lake 1933, 88). Siegert (1973) has attempted to retain a place for the older view by arguing for a distinction between "God-fearers"—those who made an exclusive commitment to Israel's God and were devoted adherents of the synagogue—and "sympathizers"—those who simply demonstrated some interest in the Jews and their ways. More often, however, scholars have tended to emphasize the complexity of the situation, postulating varying levels of attachment (Cohen 1989) or sets of overlapping patterns (Wander 1998).

The "God-fearer" debate took what seemed to be a decisive turn in 1987 with the publication of an inscription found in Aphrodisias (Reynolds and Tannenbaum 1987). The inscription contains two lists of names, apparently donors to some civic project, perhaps a soup kitchen. One (face a) bears the heading "Below (are) listed the (members of the) decany of the serious students (φιλομαθῶν), also known as those who continually praise [God?] (τῶν κὲ παν–τευλογ[-ων]."[16] While most of the names to follow are identifiably Jewish (e.g.,

14. The phrase "those who fear [God]" is used of pious Israelites in Luke 1:50.

15. Kraabel continued to develop and refine this argument in several subsequent publications (Kraabel 1982; 1986; 1994).

16. Reynolds and Tannenbaum (1987, 41) render this as "the (members) of the decany of the students/disciples/sages of the law, also known as those who fervently/continually praise God." While this translation, with its explicitly Jewish overtones (law, God) is probably justified (also van der Horst 1990, 171), the more neutral translation given above is closer to the inscription itself.

Samuel, Joseph, Judas), three are identified as "proselyte" and two, with clearly Gentile names, as "god-worshipper" (θεοσεβ[ής]). A second list (face b), which seems to refer to additional contributors to the project who were not part of the group designated as the "decany," contains two sets of names. The first, whose heading is lost, contains recognizably Jewish names; the second, beginning with the heading "and those who are God-fearers" (καὶ ὅσοι θεοσεβῖς), contains Gentile names, the first nine of whom are also identified as "councillor" (βουλ[ευτής]).

When the inscription first came to scholarly attention, some took it as decisive confirmation "that θεοσεβεῖς could be a formal designation for a group distinct from both proselytes and native Jews, but still enrolled in the membership of a synagogue."[17] But while the significance of the inscription is not to be doubted, it by no means puts an end to the debate. For one thing, its later date (probably third-century C.E.) means that it does not necessarily tell us anything about first-century usage.[18] For another, as Murphy-O'Connor (1992) has persuasively argued, information from the inscription itself serves to undermine the conclusions that have been drawn from it. For θεοσεβής is used to refer to two quite different groups of people. Those who are designated as "god-worshippers" on the first list (face a) fit the traditional definition of a "God-fearer" in that (in Reynolds's and Tannenbaum's rendering) they study the law and fervently praise God. But the second list (face b) contains those who, by virtue of their role as civic officials ("councillors"), would have had to participate in pagan worship and thus would have had only a low-level attachment to Judaism and the synagogue.[19] The term, then, is ambiguous, being used "in two consciously differentiated senses in the same document" (Murphy-O'Connor 1992, 424). Thus, while the inscription provides additional evidence for the phenomenon of Gentile sympathizers and while it indicates that such Gentiles could be described as θεοσεβεῖς, it also demonstrates that this term continued to be used in a vague and non-technical sense, its specific meaning being determined by its particular usage in each new context. With respect to Acts, then, we are thrown back on the text itself and a passage-by-passage examination of the way in which Luke uses these terms in specific contexts.

17. Meeks (1983, 208, n. 175). Feldman (1993, 367), too, concluded that the inscription "establishes once and for all that there was a special class" known as "god-fearers." See also Rajak (1992, 20–21); Segal (1990, 94–95).

18. Both Meeks and Feldman (see previous note) qualify their statements by noting that the inscription provides evidence only for its own time and place.

19. See also Fredriksen (1991, 542–43). Kraabel (1994, 81) appeals to Murphy-O'Connor to argue that the term functions merely as "a gracious compliment to their moral character without implying that they belonged in any sense to the local synagogue," but he fails to do justice to the use of "God-fearer" in the first list.

Before turning to the passages, however, a few preliminary comments are in order about Luke-Acts. As the prefaces (Luke 1:1–4; Acts 1:1–2) indicate, Luke and Acts are to be seen as two parts of a single work, written by an author who was familiar with Hellenistic literary conventions and who was addressing himself to a higher level of readership than was the case, say, with the Gospel of Mark, one of his sources. The narrative begins with a scene in the Jerusalem temple (Luke 1:5–23), prior to the birth of Jesus, and ends with Paul's arrival in Rome (Acts 28:16–31). These geographical framing scenes signal the scope of the work: Luke wants to tell the story of the Christian movement as it progressed from its Jewish origins in Galilee and Judea into the heart of the Roman world. Various aspects of his narrative indicate that Luke wanted to present this progression as logical, orderly, and divinely intended, and thus to make the case for his intended readers that the emerging Gentile church was the legitimate continuation of the biblical story that began with the call of Abraham and the formation of Israel as a people (e.g., Acts 13:16–49). Luke-Acts can then be appropriately described as a piece of apologetic history (Sterling 1992). While the work was probably intended primarily for Christian readers as an aid to their task of theological self-identification rather than for Gentile outsiders, the distinction does not need to be over-emphasized, in that one of the factors that needed to be addressed in the process of self-identification was the way in which this new movement would have been perceived by outsiders.

As can be seen already from the references to Kraabel's work, the question of Luke's reliability as a historian has been hotly debated. Here we will not engage this issue in any detailed way. For our purposes there is little to be gained by worrying about the accuracy of Luke's reports concerning events in the middle of the first century. He apparently assumed that his readers in the latter part of the century would find his account to be plausible. Thus at the very least we can assume a certain measure of verisimilitude between his narrative world and the real world in which he and his readers found themselves (J. J. Collins 1985a, 183).

As we will see, Gentile sympathizers (and to a lesser extent, proselytes) play an important part in Luke's apology for the Gentile church, in that in city after city they provide the link by which the Christian message moves out from the synagogue into the wider Gentile world. The fact that Luke is a (probably Gentile) Christian writer reminds us of a third dimension of the discussion about "God-fearers." In addition to the phenomenon itself (Gentiles attracted to the synagogue and/or adopting some of the practices and beliefs of the Jews) and to the terms that might have been used to describe such Gentiles (worshippers/fearers of God, etc.), there is also the matter of differing perspectives. The same phenomenon was no doubt perceived differently by the Jewish community, the Gentile sympathizers themselves, and various outside observers. We will need to keep Luke's own angle of perception in mind as we examine these passages. The passages will first be examined individually, and then we will draw some conclusions about the work as a whole.

Text: Nestle-Aland 27th ed.
Translation: NRSV (adapted in some cases)
Date: Circa 80–90 C.E.
Provenance: Unknown, though probably some significant city in the Roman world (Caesarea, Antioch, Rome?)
Original Language: Greek
Bibliography: Barrett (1994, 1998); Bernays (1885); Feldman (1950; 1993, 343–82); Finn (1985); Haenchen (1971); Kraabel (1981; 1982); Kraabel and MacLennan (1986); Kuhn (1968); Kuhn and Stegemann (1962); Lake (1933); Levinskaya (1996, 120–26); McKnight (1991, 108–13); Overman (1988); Reynolds and Tannenbaum (1987); Siegert (1973); Sterling (1992); Wander (1998); Wilcox (1981); S. Wilson (1973)

§194 Luke 7:2–5

> *A centurion there had a slave whom he valued highly, and who was ill and close to death. When he heard about Jesus, he sent some Jewish elders to him, asking him to come and heal his slave. When they came to Jesus, they appealed to him earnestly, saying, "He is worthy of having you do this for him, for he loves our people, and it is he who built our synagogue for us."*

Category: SYMPATHIZATION

Variants of this story, in which Jesus heals the slave of a prominent resident of Capernaum, are also found in the Gospels of Matthew (8:5–13) and John (5:46b–54). In Matthew and Luke, the slave owner is identified as a centurion, and his identity as a non-Jew is an emphatic part of the story.[20] Only in Luke, however, does the centurion approach Jesus through the agency of Jewish elders, and only in Luke is he described as one who "loves our people" (ἀγαπᾷ τὸ ἔθνος ἡμῶν) and who has demonstrated this affection by means of a significant benefaction—the building of a synagogue. While nothing explicit is said about the centurion's own religious disposition, the facts that the Jewish community saw him as "worthy" (ἄξιός) and that his worthiness was based precisely on the building of a synagogue indicate that Luke's portrait contains religious coloring. It is interesting to note that the qualities and credentials of the centurion are recognized and proclaimed by the Jewish community itself (in the persons of its elders).

Luke is fond of constructing parallels between his Gospel and Acts (e.g., the trials of Jesus and of Paul), and there can be little doubt that the account of

20. The story concludes with Jesus words: "Not even in Israel have I found such faith" (Luke 7:9; also Matt 8:10). In John, the slaveowner is a royal official (βασιλικός), presumably of Herod Antipas; his ethnic identity is not specified.

this sympathetic centurion in Luke 7 is meant to foreshadow the more elaborate account of the pious centurion Cornelius in Acts 10 and 11 (Siegert 1973, 132). By means of such a linkage Luke seems to suggests that Peter's breakthrough with the Gentile Cornelius was anticipated and legitimized by Jesus's earlier encounter. This is the only such instance, however, in the Gospel of Luke. The rest of Luke's pious Gentiles appear in Acts.

§195 Acts 2:9–11

> *Parthians, Medes, Elamites, and residents of Mesopotamia, Judea and Cappadocia, Pontus and Asia, Phrygia and Pamphylia, Egypt and the parts of Libya belonging to Cyrene, and visitors from Rome, both Jews and proselytes, Cretans and Arabs—in our own languages we hear them speaking about God's deeds of power.*

Category: CONVERSION

This demographic list is contained within a speech uttered by a crowd of people "from every nation under heaven" (2:5) who were present in Jerusalem for the feast of Pentecost. In the speech they express their reaction to a miracle of glossolalia in which the Christian disciples "were filled with the Holy Spirit and began to speak in other languages, as the Spirit gave them ability" (2:4). The passage contains a number of puzzles and problems (Barrett 1994, 106–26), some of which have a bearing on the reference to "both Jews and proselytes" (Ἰουδαῖοί τε καὶ προσήλυτοι) in v. 11.

One issue concerns the identity of the group that is described as comprising "both Jews and proselytes." The nearest possible antecedent is "the visiting Romans," but this produces an odd result. Why single out Rome when visitors from other areas in the list (e.g., Asia, Egypt) were just as likely to have included proselytes? For this reason, a number of scholars have suggested that the phrase should be taken as referring to the whole preceding list.[21] In other words, the whole crowd of pilgrims consisted of "both Jews and proselytes." While such an interpretation makes better narrative sense and is also just as possible grammatically,[22] it is hampered by the subsequent reference to "Cretans and Arabs" (v. 11). One would have expected a phrase descriptive of the list as a whole to appear at the end of the list. In the text as it stands,[23] then, it is probably advisable to take

21. E.g., Kuhn (1968, 742); McEleney (1973–74: 323); McKnight (1991: 108); S. Wilson (1973, 123).

22. The preceding list falls into three groups, each headed by a noun in the nominative masculine plural (Πάρθοι, οἱ κατοικοῦντες, οἱ ἐπιδημοῦντες Ῥωμαῖοι).

23. Kuhn (1968, 742) suggests, without providing any justification, that the reference to Cretans and Arabs is a later addition. While it is quite possible that Luke has here made use of an already-existing list in which the phrase under discussion stood at the end (S. Wilson 1973, 123, 127), the list in its final form seems to require that the phrase be understood in a more restricted way.

the phrase in the narrower sense. The crowd of pilgrims included "visiting Romans, both Jews and proselytes." Perhaps Rome has been singled out because of the importance of Rome in the structure of the Acts narrative.

A second issue has to do with the way in which this crowd of pilgrims is introduced in v. 5. In most textual witnesses, this crowd is described as "Jews, devout men from every nation under heaven." Ἰουδαῖοι, however, is missing from some early manuscripts (א it^{ph} vg^{ms}) and there is considerable variation in word order in the manuscripts. While it is probable that "Jews" is original, the fact that Peter goes on to address the crowd as "men, Israelites" (v. 22) means that the matter does not need to be decided here. The "proselytes" in v. 11 are part of a crowd that is addressed as "Israelites" and (probably) "Jews."

This brings us to the main point—the meaning of προσήλυτοι in v. 11. How did Luke understand the term? One thing to note is that the term is introduced without comment or explanation. Luke seems to assume that the meaning of the word would be clearly evident to his readers. Since Luke and his readers were familiar with the Septuagint and since προσήλυτος first appears in the Septuagint, we can take it for granted that the term has to do with Gentiles who have become incorporated into the Jewish community in significant measure. But is "proselyte" to be understood in the older sense of "sojourner," or does it here carry the later sense of "convert"? The question can be answered more clearly in the case of Nicolaus, the next passage to be discussed. Since Nicolaus has already become a Christian believer by the time he appears in the narrative, and since Cornelius represented, for Luke, the first Gentile to be accepted into the Christian movement (Acts 10), Nicolaus the "proselyte from Antioch" must be seen as someone who at the time of his conversion to Christianity was no longer a Gentile; that is, he had already become a full convert to Judaism. The same logic probably applies to the identification of the proselytes who were present at Peter's Pentecost sermon, though here we find no explicit indication that any of them actually became Christian believers. Still, given the evidence of Nicolaus, it can be concluded that Luke understands the proselytes of 2:11 to be full converts to Judaism.

This is the framework in which we are probably to interpret the apparent tension between v. 11—where "proselytes" are differentiated from "Jews"—and the other verses, in which the crowd is described as consisting of "Jews" (v. 5) or "Israelites" (v. 22). It is not impossible that in these latter verses Luke was simply ignoring the presence of "proselytes" and focusing solely on the Jews. But it is simpler to see the tension as a reflection of the two-sided character of the convert's status. On the one hand, they have become members of the covenant people and heirs of the promises (cf. v. 39) and thus can be addressed in the same breath and with the same terms as Jews. But on the other, they can be differentiated from those who by birth and ethnic origin are "Jews" (v. 11). Thus there is no need to dismiss them from view.

§196 Acts 6:5

> *What they said pleased the whole community, and they chose Stephen, a man full of faith and the Holy Spirit, together with Philip, Prochorus, Nicanor, Timon, Parmenas, and Nicolaus, a proselyte, an Antiochine.*

Category: CONVERSION

Here "proselyte" appears in another list, this time a list of seven men whose appointment was part of an attempt to resolve a dispute between two groups in the Jerusalem church—the "Hebrews" and the "Hellenists" (6:1–4). Since the narrative has not yet reached the point where Gentiles begin to be admitted into the church, both the Hellenists and the Hebrews need to be seen as Jewish groups. While the seven are not explicitly defined as Hellenists and while the precise difference between Hebrews and Hellenists is not made clear in the passage, the fact that each of the seven bears a Greek name suggests that we should see them as part of the latter group.

One of the seven is identified as "Nicolaus, a proselyte, an Antiochine" (προσήλυτον Ἀντιοχέα). As in 2:11, "proselyte" is introduced without elaboration or explanation, which suggests that Luke and his readers shared an environment in which the Septuagint provided the basic meaning of the term.[24] In this instance, however, it is clear that "proselyte" refers to a Gentile who has become a full convert to Judaism. In Luke's account of Christian origins it is only with the conversion of Cornelius that Gentiles were first admitted into the church. Thus while the designation of Nicolaus as a "proselyte" served to differentiate him from the other six on the list, he nevertheless also needs to be differentiated from those "uncircumcised" (Acts 11:3) "Gentiles" (10:27) such as Cornelius. In other words, Nicolaus had become a full convert to Judaism before he entered the Christian movement.

§197 Acts 10:1–33

> *In Caesarea there was a man named Cornelius, a centurion of the Italian Cohort, as it was called. [2]He was a devout man who feared God with all his household; he gave alms generously to the people and prayed constantly to God.. . . [21]So Peter went down to the men and said, "I am the one you are looking for; what is the reason for your coming?" [22]They answered, "Cornelius, a centurion, an upright and God-fearing man, who is well spoken of by the whole Jewish nation, was directed by a holy angel to send for you to come to his house and to hear what you have to say."*

Category: SYMPATHIZATION

24. See the discussion on Acts 2:11 above.

In Acts, the progression of the Christian message into the Gentile world begins[25] with an encounter between the apostle Peter and the Roman centurion Cornelius, which results in the conversion of the latter. The initiative for the encounter did not lie with either one, however, but was taken directly by God, who visited both Cornelius (10:3–6) and Peter (10:9–16) with visions. Cornelius is instructed by "an angel of God" to send for Simon Peter; Peter, for his part, is instructed that he needs to set aside his Jewish dispositions ("it is unlawful for a Jew to associate with or to visit a Gentile" [10:27]) and to recognize that "God shows no partiality" (10:34). For our purposes, however, Cornelius is of interest not for his Christian conversion but for his prior association with Judaism and the Jewish God.

Cornelius's piety is first attested by Luke himself, who describes him as "devout [εὐσεβής] and fearing God [φοβούμενος τὸν θεόν] with all his household, giving many alms to the people and praying constantly to God" (10:2). This is the first instance in Acts of the participial phrase "fearing God," and it is important to note that here it is purely adjectival. That is, it simply describes an aspect of Cornelius's piety; it does not identify him as a member of a specific class or category.[26] It is also to be noted that the Jewish character of Cornelius's piety is assumed rather than stressed. It is not until v. 22 that his relationship with "the nation of the Jews" is referred to explicitly. In retrospect it is clear that "the people" (τῷ λαῷ) to whom he gave alms must have been the Jewish people and thus that he himself must have perceived the "God" to whom he prayed as the God worshipped by the Jews. But this is not made clear at the outset. There is one additional detail to note in Luke's introduction of Cornelius: he was joined in his piety by his whole household. As the narrative proceeds, this group expands: the soldier whom he sends to fetch Peter is also "devout" (10:7); when Peter arrives at Cornelius's house, he is received eagerly not only by Cornelius himself and (presumably) his household but also by his "relatives and close friends" (10:24). If Cornelius is meant to be seen as a model sympathizer,[27] the model is not an isolated "fearer of God" but one who is part of a larger company.

But Luke as narrator is not the only one to attest to Cornelius's piety. The angel who appears to him in a vision makes reference to his "prayers" and

25. See §195 and §196 for earlier references in Acts to proselytes. Acts 8:26–39 deals with the conversion of an "Ethiopian eunuch" who "had come to Jerusalem to worship" (8:27). Certain features of the account are more descriptive of a Gentile than a Jew (e.g., v. 27), and it is quite likely that Luke's source material presented him as such. But Luke does not identify him as a Gentile, and his presentation of Cornelius as the first Gentile convert suggests that he does not intend his readers to make such an idenification either. For an analysis of the narrative, see Barrett (1994, 419–36).

26. Also observed by Lake (1933, 86); Wilcox (1981, 104).

27. See Kraabel (1981, 114); Wander (1998, 195–96).

"alms," informing him that they have been received by God (10:4). Later, his emissaries describe him to Peter as "a man righteous [δίκαιος] and fearing God [φοβούμενος τὸν θεόν], well spoken of by the whole Jewish nation" (10:22). Here again the participial construction is adjectival rather than substantive.

Cornelius plays an important part in the overall progress of Luke's narrative. Peter's encounter with Cornelius precipitates a significant debate in the Jerusalem church as to the place of Gentiles in the movement (11:1–18). The positive resolution of the debate ("Then God has given even to the Gentiles the repentance that leads to life" [11:18]) opens the door to the development of a Gentile mission in Antioch (11:19–21) and eventually to the Roman world as a whole.

This adds significance to the details of Cornelius's profile as it is sketched by Luke. Despite his piety, Cornelius is clearly a Gentile; this is indicated clearly by the reactions first of Peter (10:28) and then of the Jerusalem church (11:1).[28] His religious disposition can be described as a combination of qualities and activities on the one hand (pious, righteous, fearing God, praying, giving alms) and association with the Jewish community on the other ("well spoken of by the whole Jewish nation" [10:22]).[29] But the emphasis falls on the former; Judaism is not mentioned explicitly until 10:22 and, as Wander (1998, 186) has observed, in contrast to subsequent accounts in Acts the synagogue does not appear in the Cornelius story at all. Still, an association with the Jewish community is implied by 10:22, and this verse is of further significance because of its assumption that "the whole Jewish nation" approved of and were proud of people like Cornelius. While this may tell us more in the first instance about Luke than about first-century Judaism, Luke at least feels that his readers will find such an attitude to be plausible. Further, the way in which Luke takes the Jewish character of Cornelius's piety for granted suggests also that, in his opinion, his readers would have been quite familiar with Cornelius as a religious type.

One other observation is in order. Since Peter's declaration that "God shows no partiality" (10:34) stands at the introduction to his proclamation of the Christian message, it is probably not to be taken as the expression of a specifically Jewish sentiment.[30] Still, the statement is addressed to Cornelius, which means that Peter's subsequent comment—"in every nation the one who fears him [God] and does what is right is acceptable to him" (v. 35)—can be seen as a kind of generalization of Cornelius's example. Here, in contrast to the previous occurrences, the participle is used substantively: ὁ φοβούμενος—the one who fears God. To be sure, the statement does not necessarily exclude Jews.

28. As noted by Levinskaya (1996, 121); Wander (1998, 189); Wilcox (1981, 104).

29. This distinction derives from Wander (1998, 188), who differentiates *Qualifikationsbezeichnungen* (qualification designations) and *Affinitätsbezeichnungen* (affinity designations).

30. For a contrasting reading, see Siegert (1973, 132).

Still, the thrust of the passage has to do with Gentiles and their standing before God, which creates in the mind of Luke's readers a certain association between the substantive use of the participle and Gentile subjects.

§198 Acts 13:16–50

> [16]*So Paul stood up and with a gesture began to speak: "Men, Israelites and those who fear God, listen.* [17]*The God of this people Israel chose our ancestors.. . .* [26]*"Men, brothers, sons of the race of Abraham and those among you who fear God, to us the message of this salvation has been sent." . . .* [43]*When the meeting of the synagogue broke up, many of the Jews and of the devout proselytes followed Paul and Barnabas, who spoke to them and urged them to continue in the grace of God.. . .* [50]*But the Jews incited the devout women of high standing and the leading men of the city, and stirred up persecution against Paul and Barnabas, and drove them out of their region.*

Category: SYMPATHIZATION, CONVERSION

This passage recounts the visit of Paul and Barnabas to the synagogue in Pisidian Antioch. In the course of his sermon, which takes up much of the passage, Paul addresses the assembled congregation directly on two occasions: "Men, Israelites and those who fear God" (ἄνδρες Ἰσραηλῖται καὶ οἱ φοβούμενοι τὸν θεόν; v. 16); "Men, brothers, sons of the race of Abraham and those among you who fear God" (ἄνδρες ἀδελφοί, υἱοὶ γένους Ἀβρααμ καὶ οἱ ἐν ὑμῖν φοβούμενοι τὸν θεόν; v. 26). While these two terms of direct address are parallel in form and thus need to be interpreted together, the identification of the group being addressed is complicated by Luke's statement after the sermon that "many of the Jews and of the devout proselytes" (πολλοὶ τῶν Ἰουδαίων καὶ τῶν σεβομένων προσηλύτων) responded positively to the message (v. 43). It is hard to imagine this as anything other than an alternative way of referring to the same group. But how we are to correlate "those who fear God" and "the devout proselytes" is anything but clear. The conclusion of the narrative makes reference to a separate group, "the devout women [τὰς σεβομένας] of high standing" (v. 50).

In contrast to its appearance in the Cornelius account, where φοβούμενος was purely adjectival, in v. 16 it is used substantively: οἱ φοβούμενοι τὸν θεόν—"those who fear God." Most commonly the term is understood to refer to a part of the audience distinct from the "Israelites." That is, Paul is addressing himself to a single congregation ("men") comprising two groups: "Israelites" and "those who fear God." Lake (1933, 86) and Wilcox (1981, 107) have pointed out, however, that two groups are not necessarily in view. The two terms may be synonymous ways of describing a single group. Some slight support for this reading might be found in the fact that Paul goes on to speak of "our fathers" (v. 17), which might be taken to indicate that a totally Jewish audience is in view.

But Paul's second direct address to the same group almost certainly implies a bifurcated group: the fact that "those who fear God" are said to be "among you" seems clearly to indicate that this group is distinct from those who are addressed as "sons of the race of Israel."[31] Wilcox (1981, 107) has argued that this group is not necessarily Gentile: Paul might have been addressing (perhaps sarcastically) a sub-set of more devout Jews. But this is a strained reading of the text. The second group stands in contrast to the "sons of the race of Israel"—or, in v. 16, to the "Israelites"—and thus seems to be Gentile in character. Further, since the only previous occurrences of the participle φοβούμενος have been with reference to Cornelius, either as an individual or as an example of a more general type ("in every nation the one who fears him . . . is acceptable to him" [10:35]), Luke's readers will naturally hear echoes of the Cornelius account when they read of "those who fear God" in chapter 13. The fact that the participle is used substantively in the generalizing conclusion that Peter draws from his encounter with Cornelius ("the one who fears [ὁ φοβούμενος] him [God]" [10:35]) serves to amplify the echoes.

What are we to make, then, of the third description of the audience: "many of the Jews and of the devout proselytes" (v. 43)? The parallel structure of the three terms seems to suggest that "those who fear God" (vv. 16, 26) and "the devout proselytes" (v. 43) are synonymous terms. But how can a term that Luke first used to describe Cornelius be the equivalent of "proselyte"? Not surprisingly, there have been a variety of attempts to resolve this tension. Some have attempted to emend the text, either seeing προσηλύτων as a later gloss[32] or conjecturing that a καί has fallen out between σεβομένων and προσηλύτων.[33] But such desperate measures have little to commend them. Others, attempting to arrive at a global solution, have taken the position that the terms are synonymous throughout Acts. Taking one tack, Bertholet (1896) argued that all of the constructions with σέβομαι and φοβέομαι referred to full converts (proselytes). Taking another, Overman (1988) has argued that Luke used "proselyte" in its "original" LXX sense of "sojourner," so that all of the terms under discussion referred to Gentiles as pious sympathizers or "God-fearers."

Of course, either of these arguments for synonymity can appeal to the apparently synonymous use of the terms here in chapter 13. In addition, one

31. Two early mss (p45 B) omit καί in v. 26 ("men, brothers, sons of the race of Abraham, those among you who fear God"). If "among you" were not present, this variant reading would lend itself to an interpretation in which all four terms are taken to be synonymous. But as it stands, this variant reading also seems to present "those who fear God" as distinct from the group identified as "you."

32. So that the verse reads "many of the Jews and of the worshippers," with τῶν σεβομένων taken to be a technical term for Gentile "worshippers." Haenchen (1971, 413) takes this position; Kuhn (1968, 743) is open to it.

33. Barrett (1994, 654) mentions the possibility but rejects it. This possibility would require the loss not only of καί but also, since the other terms would then have the article, of τῶν as well ("the Jews and the devout ones and *the* proselytes").

can observe that nowhere in Acts do we find any scene or situation that involves both converts and sympathizers. We find Jews and proselytes (2:11; 13:43) or Jews and "fearers/worshippers of God" (10:2, 22; 13:16, 26; 16:14; 17:4, 17; 18:4), but nowhere do we find any grouping of Jews, Gentile sympathizers (such as Cornelius), and proselytes (such as Nicolaus; 6:5). As is suggested by these references to Cornelius and Nicolaus, however, Luke seems to know the difference between a sympathizer and a full convert. Clearly, Cornelius, despite his "fear of God," is not a convert; the criticism directed at Peter for associating with an uncircumcised (11:2) Gentile (11:18) says as much. Likewise, while Luke does not provide a precise indication of what is involved in becoming a "proselyte," he is aware of the position that "unless [Gentiles] are circumcised according to the custom of Moses, [they] cannot be saved" (15:1), which implies that he is aware of what is involved in conversion to Judaism. In all likelihood, he understood the "proselyte" Nicolaus (6:5) to be just such a full convert, especially since he presents Cornelius a few chapters later as the first breakthrough into the non-Jewish world.

What then do we do with the shift in chapter 13 from "those who fear God" (vv. 16, 26) to "the pious proselytes" (v. 43)? Perhaps we have to understand it, if not precisely as a case of Lukan carelessness (Kuhn 1968, 743), then as an indication that the distinction between sympathizers and "God-fearers" was of no programmatic interest to Luke, at least at this point in his narrative. While he probably assumed that any of the synagogue congregations that he describes consisted of Jews, sympathizers, and converts, for his purposes all that mattered was that the latter two groups represented Gentiles who had learned to "fear" or "reverence" God through their attachment to the synagogue and thus that they functioned as the primary means by which the gospel made its transition from the Jewish world to the Gentile.

This leaves the conclusion to the story, in which "the Jews" enlisted the help of "the devout women [τὰς σεβομένας γυναῖκας] of high standing and the leading men of the city" (v. 50) to drive Paul and Barnabas out of town. Once again the participle is used attributively. And once again (as in v. 43) the participle is σεβόμενος. In fact, this is a decisive shift: up to 13:26 Luke uses φοβέομαι; after, σεβόμενοι. While there is no clear indication why he shifts from one to the other, it coincides with two other shifts: from "Saul" to "Paul" (13:9) and from "Barnabas and Saul" (to 13:17) to "Paul and Barnabas" (13:43; cf. 13:13: "Paul and his companions").[34]

34. It is also in this passage that Paul and Barnabas say to "the Jews" that since they by their opposition demonstrated that they were "unworthy of eternal life," they were "now turning to the Gentiles" (13:46). This is not as decisive a shift as it might appear to be, however, in that as he moves on to other cities Paul continues to begin in the synagogue and repeats this "turning to the Gentiles" speech on two other occasions (18:6; 28:25–28).

Since it is "the Jews" who take the initiative here, it is clear that the "devout women of high standing"[35] are Gentile. Further, there can be little doubt that their "devotion" is connected with the Jewish community; nowhere else does Luke describe Gentiles as "fearing" or "revering" God apart from some connection with Jews and Judaism.[36] But were they full converts (e.g., Haenchen 1971, 414) or merely sympathizers (e.g., Levinskaya 1996, 122–23)? Luke does not say. In particular, σεβομένας does not provide us with an answer either way. On the one hand, though it is linked with "proselytes" in v. 43, an adjective does not acquire meaning simply by having been used to modify a noun; all v. 43 tells us is that these proselytes were "devout" or "worshipping." On the other hand, σεβομένας can be taken as an indication that these women were sympathizers only if we already know that Luke uses the term in a technical sense—which is precisely the point under discussion. Luke leaves the matter ambiguous, which probably should be taken to mean that the differentiation is one that he is not interested in making.

§199 Acts 16:13–14

> *On the sabbath day we went outside the gate by the river, where we supposed there was a place of prayer; and we sat down and spoke to the women who had gathered there. A certain woman named Lydia, a dealer in purple cloth, of the city of Thyatira, a worshipper of God, was listening to us. The Lord opened her heart to listen eagerly to what was said by Paul.*

Category: SYMPATHIZATION

This event takes place in Philippi, to which Paul, now accompanied by Silas and Timothy, has traveled from Asia. On the Sabbath he and his companions go to a "place of prayer" (προσευχήν). That Luke uses this term in place of his usual "synagogue" may suggest that this was not a designated building, though the question cannot easily be decided.[37] Here they encounter a woman who, among other designations, is described as "a worshipper of God." Since there is no definite article (σεβομένη τὸν θεόν), it is not impossible that it should be read attributively: "a certain woman named Lydia,. . . attending the service, listened" (Lake 1933:87). This translation is awkward, however. Since the other elements of the description are nouns (especially, "a dealer in purple cloth," also

35. Some mss (א* E Byz) add καί: "the devout women *and* those [women] of high standing." The reading is unlikely, but even if it were original it would not affect our discussion in any substantial way.

36. Contra Wilcox (1981, 110), who says that nothing in the text requires us to see a synagogue connection here.

37. προσευχην is commonly used to refer to Jewish meeting places (Schürer 1979, 2:439–40). On this passage, see Barrett (1998, 781–82)

anarthrous), it is probable that the phrase is to be taken as an indefinite substantive: "a worshipper of God."

Lydia is almost certainly a Gentile (Wilcox 1981, 111), even if she is not specifically designated as such. For one thing she has a Gentile name. For another, all of the others whom Paul encounters in Philippi appear to be Gentile. Since Paul encounters her at a house of prayer on the Sabbath, there can be little doubt that her piety was connected with the Jewish community and directed towards the Jewish God. Thus Luke seems to assume that the term "worshipper of God" refers to a non-Jew worshipping God in a Jewish context. Again, however, he gives us no indication as to Lydia's specific status. She may have been a full convert; she may simply have been an adherent and sympathizer. Admittedly, here as in the previous case, the fact that the "worshipper of God" is a woman means that the distinction is less easily made. Still, Luke does not seem to be interested in the distinction. It is enough that she was a Gentile and that she was an important part of the process by which Paul was able to establish a Gentile church.[38]

§200 Acts 17:4

> *Some of them were persuaded and joined Paul and Silas, as did a great many of the devout Greeks and not a few of the leading women.*

Category: SYMPATHIZATION

This statement is part of yet another scene set in a Jewish synagogue, this time in Thessalonica. Since the setting has been described as a "synagogue of the Jews" (v. 1), the first-mentioned group who were persuaded by Paul's preaching ("some of them") is to be seen as a group of Jews. But these Jews were joined by others. According to the most probable reading, two other groups found Paul persuasive: "a great many of the devout Greeks" (τῶν τε σεβομένων Ἑλλήνων πλῆθος πολύ) and "not a few of the leading women."[39] Since all of them were present in the synagogue, we are probably justified in thinking that the women are also to be seen as σεβόμεναι. Here the participle is used attributively; the Greeks are not "[God-]worshippers" but are simply "devout" or "worshipping." Once again it is not clear whether these Gentiles are to be seen as full converts or as adherents and sympathizers. Perhaps the term "Greeks" suggests that the

38. Wander attaches greater programmatic significance to Lydia, seeing her as having been deliberately paired with Cornelius as two model "God-fearers" (Wander 1998, 195–96). But while Luke does tend to pair male and female figures (e.g., Simeon and Anna in Luke 2), the story of Lydia is much less fully developed than that of Cornelius.

39. A few manuscripts insert a καί, so that the verse reads "a great many of the worshippers/devout ones and of Greeks." The reading, however, is not strongly attested (p^{74} A D) and is probably not to be accepted.

latter is more probable (Levinskaya 1996, 124). But even so, it appears that this distinction is of little interest to Luke. He provides no indication of their status other than that they were Gentiles who were worshipping the Jewish God at the synagogue. While this group is of evident importance for Luke, the fact that he uses yet another term to describe it—"the devout Greeks"—indicates that they are not to be taken as technical terms.

§201 Acts 17:11–12

> *These Jews were more receptive than those in Thessalonica, for they welcomed the message very eagerly and examined the scriptures every day to see whether these things were so. Many of them therefore believed, also not a few Greek women of high standing and men.*

Category: SYMPATHIZATION

Paul, Silas, and Timothy, after leaving Thessalonica, went to Beroea, where again they proclaimed their message in the Jewish synagogue. According to Luke there was a positive response not only from "many" of Paul's Jewish hearers but also (καί)[40] from a substantial number ("not a few" [cf. 17:4]) of non-Jews. What is of interest here is not their positive response to Paul but the prior fact that they formed part of the audience that heard him speak.

Several aspects of Luke's presentation should be noted. One is his matter-of-fact narration. As in the previous passage (17:4), he gives his readers no prior indication that there were Greeks in the audience. He simply takes it for granted that a synagogue gathering would include non-Jews. Further, these Greeks were not just casual bystanders; they were present "every day," which seems to suggest that they stood in some sort of ongoing association with the synagogue community. A third point to note is the absence of any further descriptors; in other words, they are not described as "devout," "pious," "God-fearing," or the like. To be sure, Luke does draw the social status of the women to our attention. But it is the presence of Gentiles in the synagogue community, rather than any particular terms of status or identity, that appears to be significant for him.

§202 Acts 17:16–17

> *While Paul was waiting for them in Athens, he was deeply distressed to see that the city was full of idols. So he argued in the synagogue with the Jews and the devout persons, and also in the market-place every day with those who happened to be there.*

Category: SYMPATHIZATION

40. The NRSV translation, "including not a few Greek women" assumes that the non-Jews formed part of the "many." This, however, does not render it precisely. Luke's use of "not a few," which stands as a structural counterpart to "many," and of καί serve to indicate two distinct groups: "many of [the Jews] and not a few of the Greeks."

Luke begins his account of Paul's preaching in Athens with a description of his distress over the prevalence of idols, which sets the stage for his famous Areopagus sermon (17:22–31). Tucked into this account, however, is a brief reference to a more typical scene—Paul in the synagogue, arguing with a mixed groups of Jews and Gentiles (τοῖς Ἰουδαίοις καὶ τοῖς σεβομένοις). To be sure, some have argued that τοῖς σεβομένοις could be rendered "the worshippers," and thus does not necessarily refer to a group distinct from "the Jews."[41] But the argument fails to convince. Twice within the previous fifteen verses Paul has visited a synagogue, and on both occasions not only have non-Jews been present (17:4, 12) but Luke has taken their presence for granted. Further, in the three previous appearances of σεβόμενος in the narrative (13:43, 50; 16:14) the term was used to describe pious Gentiles associated with Jewish worship; while the first two of these were simply descriptive, in the most recent reference the participle was used substantively (one who worshipped God). Thus it is scarcely to be doubted that once again Luke presents us with a scene in which Paul encounters a mixed group of Jews and Gentiles in a synagogue, this time in Athens. And once again he seems to assume that this is a perfectly normal state of affairs.

Beyond this, however, there is not much more that can be said about either the characteristics of these devout Gentiles or about Luke's description of them. While they seem to be associated with the synagogue community in some ongoing way and while their piety is directed toward the Jewish God, Luke has nothing further to say about the nature of either their piety or their status in the synagogue. In particular, there is no reason to think that οἱ σεβόμενοι functions here as a technical term.[42] Since the participle has already appeared in the narrative in a purely attributive sense—"devout proselytes" (13:43); "devout [Greek] women" (13:50)—the reader has already been given enough information to make sense of the participle in 17:17: these are "devout ones," like the proselytes or Gentile women already encountered in the narrative. Of course, this does not preclude the possibility of a more widespread use of the term. Still, since the term seems to refer to the whole company of Gentiles who were present alongside "the Jews," and since this company presumably included both proselytes (cf. 13:43) and those who were more loosely associated with the synagogue community, the passage here does not necessarily support the thesis that οἱ σεβόμενοι was a technical term for a well-defined group.

§203 Acts 18:4–7

> *Every sabbath he would argue in the synagogue and would try to convince Jews and Greeks. When Silas and Timothy arrived from Macedonia, Paul was occupied with*

41. Lake (1933, 87); Wilcox (1981, 112–13).

42. Levinskaya (1996, 124) goes too far when she says that in 17:17 "σεβόμενοι has the same meaning as the full formula," i.e., as σεβόμενοι τὸν θεόν. Luke's usage gives us very little reason to suppose that there was such a "formula."

proclaiming the word, testifying to the Jews that the Messiah was Jesus. When they opposed and reviled him, in protest he shook the dust from his clothes and said to them, "Your blood be on your own heads! I am innocent. From now on I will go to the Gentiles." Then he left the synagogue and went to the house of a man named Titius Justus, a worshipper of God; his house was next door to the synagogue.

Category: SYMPATHIZATION

The final set of pertinent references in Acts appears in the account of Paul's sojourn in Corinth. The account follows a pattern that has become quite familiar: Paul begins his preaching activity in the synagogue; the synagogue congregation contains non-Jews (here "Greeks" [Ἕλληνας]) as well as Jews; the existence of such a mixed audience in the synagogue is simply taken for granted; Paul is opposed by "the Jews"; but the group of those who respond positively to his message contains both Jews (here, e.g., Crispus; v. 8) and Gentiles (Titius Justus). While Titius Justus is not explicitly identified as a Gentile, this seems to be the clear implication of the immediately preceding statement in which Paul says that he is now going "to the Gentiles."[43]

Titius Justus is further described as "a worshipper of God" (σεβομένη τὸν θεόν). The phrase has appeared once previously as part of the description of Lydia in 16:14. Here there is no possibility that the participle can be read adjectivally;[44] it is a substantive—indefinite, to be sure, but a substantive nonetheless: "Titius Justus, a worshipper of God." Luke understands this term to refer to a Gentile who is associated in an ongoing way with the synagogue community. Again, however, he provides no further information about the nature or intensity of this association or the way in which it might have been perceived by either Titius Justus himself or the Jewish community.

This completes the survey of pertinent references in Luke-Acts. A few concluding observations are in order. (1) Luke seems to know the difference between a full convert to Judaism and a pious sympathizer such as Cornelius. He recognizes the kind of Jewish perspective that would produce both the criticism of Peter for associating freely with "uncircumcised" (11:3) "Gentiles" (11:18) and the idea that Gentiles could be admitted to full fellowship with Jews if they were "circumcised according to the custom of Moses" (15:1). (2) Luke seems to assume that "proselyte" refers to full conversion. For prior to the Cornelius

43. Wilcox (1981, 113–15) takes advantage of the textual uncertainty surrounding the name Titius Justus to raise questions about his ethnic identification. But while he is right to question conclusions that have been drawn from the further description of Titius Justus as "a worshipper of God," there can be very little doubt that Luke expects his readers to perceive him as a Gentile.

44. Cf. Lake's suggestion for 16:14: "a certain woman named Lydia,. . . attending the service, listened" (Lake 1933, 87).

account, which clearly represents for him the decisive breakthrough into the Gentile world, Luke tells us that Nicolaus, "a proselyte from Antioch" (6:5), was already a member of the church. (3) Luke took it for granted that in a typical synagogue one would encounter a body of non-Jews associated with the synagogue community in some ongoing way. While this configuration has an evident part to play in Luke's own literary and theological agenda, since he seems to assume that his readers would also take it for granted, it cannot be dismissed as simply his own invention. (4) This body contains both full converts ("devout proselytes" [13:43]) and those whose association and identification with the Jewish community was less complete (e.g., Cornelius). (5) Once the decisive breakthrough has been accomplished through the conversion and acceptance of Cornelius, Luke does not seem to be interested in differentiating converts from sympathizers. While we need to assume that both were present in most instances (see the previous point), for the purposes of his own literary and theological agenda, they constitute a single group. (6) Luke uses a variety of terms to refer to this group and its members. One way of categorizing them is to differentiate between qualities (e.g., piety) and attachment to the Jewish community (e.g., presence in the synagogue, benefaction). Another is to differentiate between attributive terms—pious (10:2), fearing God (10:2, 22), righteous (10:22), worshipping (13:43. 50; 17:4)—and substantives—the one who fears God (10:35); those who fear God (13:16. 26); a worshipper of God (16:14; 18:7); the worshipping ones (17:17). (7) With respect to the disputed constructions "those who fear God" (οἱ φοβούμενοι τὸν θεόν) and "those who worship God" (οἱ σεβόμενοι τὸν θεόν), no evidence can be drawn from Luke's usage to support the idea that these were technical terms for a well-defined category of Gentile adherents. For one thing, the sheer multiplicity of terms tells against the idea. For another, the group described by these terms included a range of affinity levels. For still another, it is important to note that these substantive forms appear only after the participle has been used in a purely attributive way. The substantives, then, might simply be understood as anaphoric—that is, as deriving their meaning solely from the earlier attributive usage. (8) The previous point notwithstanding, one cannot exclude the possibility that these terms already carried a Gentile connotation for Luke and his intended readers. In fact, the lack of any tight and specific connection between the initial attributive use and subsequent substantive use makes this likely. But even so, the connotation would be of a general phenomenon rather than a specific, well-defined category.

§204 John 12:20

Now among those who went up to worship at the festival were some Greeks.

Text: Nestle-Aland 27th ed.
Translation: NRSV
Date: Circa 90 C.E.

Provenance: Asia (?)
Original Language: Greek
Category: SYMPATHIZATION, CONVERSION

The final Christian text to be considered is found in the Gospel of John. The festival in question is Passover, specifically the Passover season during which Jesus was arrested, tried, and crucified. At this point in the narrative, Jesus has just made his triumphal entry into Jerusalem (12:19), after which "some Greeks," who were "among those who had gone up to worship at the festival," came to one of Jesus's disciples because they wanted to see Jesus. The incident is of great significance for the author of the Gospel. Prior to this we have consistently been told that Jesus's "hour has not yet come" (2:4; 7:30; 8:20; cf. 7:6, 8). Yet the arrival of these Greeks prompts Jesus to say that his "hour"—the time of his death, which is also his glorification—has arrived (12:23).

For our purposes, however, the text can be dealt with briefly. While some have taken the position that "Greeks" here and in 7:35 refers not to Gentiles but to Diaspora Jews,[45] it is generally accepted that John has non-Jews in view. These Gentiles have "come up" to Jerusalem to worship. They are part of a larger company ("among those who went up") composed primarily of Jews, and thus are connected in some way with the Jewish community. Further, the purpose of their journey was to participate in some way in the celebration of Passover. But whether they are to be seen as full converts (Brown 1966, 466) or simply as pious sympathizers[46] cannot be determined.

45. Robinson (1959–1960); Malina and Rohrbaugh (1998, 211).

46. Schnackenburg (1980, 2:381) calls them "God-fearers," but also suggests that they might be "full proselytes."

Chapter 9

Inscriptions

With the recent publication of the inscriptions from Aphrodisias (Reynolds and Tannenbaum 1987) and from the Akeldama tombs in Jerusalem (Avni and Greenhut 1996), there are now eighteen known inscriptions which refer explicitly to proselytes:[1] seven from Rome;[2] six from Jerusalem;[3] and single inscriptions from Venosa (in Italy),[4] Cyrene (Lüderitz 1983, 26, no. 12), Caesarea Maritima (Lifshitz 1961, 115, no. 2), Aphrodisias (Reynolds and Tannenbaum 1987, 5–7), and Dura Europos (Naveh 1978, 127, no. 88). The latter two are synagogue inscriptions; all the others are epitaphs. Since in the Aphrodisias inscription three persons are so identified, the inscriptional evidence for proselytes now totals twenty individuals.[5]

1. For lists of these, with some commentary, see Figueras (1990) and Levinskaya (1996, 25–26). For convenience we will treat these inscriptions first and then deal with those pertaining to sympathization.

2. *CIJ* 21, 68, 202, 222, 256, 462, 523 = *JIWE* 2: 489, 491, 392, 224, 218, 62, 577.

3. For sources and documentation, see the discussion below.

4. *CIJ* 576 = *JIWE* 1:52.

5. Of course, it is possible—even probable—that other proselytes are included among the two thousand or so known Jewish inscriptions (for the figure, see van der Horst [1991, 15]). Kraemer (1989) suggests that the term "Jew" might indicate various forms of Gentile adherence to Judaism, including proselytism. Applebaum (1979, 154) observes that the name "Sarah" was sometimes assumed by proselytes and suggests that several such inscriptions in Cyrene might indicate proselytes. Such suggestions, while intriguing, are too uncertain to warrant inclusion here.

Many of these inscriptions date from the third century C.E. or later and so fall outside the scope of this collection. Seven of them, however—the six from Jerusalem and one from Cyrene—are early enough to be included here.

§205 Corpus inscriptionum judaicarum *1390*

Maria the proselyte ha-doleqet

מריה הגרית הדולקת

Text and translation: Figueras (1990, 196, no. 2); also *CIJ* II 1390.
Date: First century B.C.E. to first century C.E.
Provenance: Jerusalem
Original Language: Hebrew
Bibliography: Bagatti (1971, 237–39); Donaldson (2000); Figueras (1990, 196); Sukenik (1931, 18–20)
Category: CONVERSION

This inscription was found in the latter part of the nineteenth century at a gravesite on a hill north of the Mount of Olives.[6] While the inscription itself is fully legible,[7] there is uncertainty surrounding the proper interpretation of the third word. *Ha-doleqet* (הדולקת) is a participial form of the verb דלק, which appears in Biblical and Mishnaic Hebrew with the meanings "to burn" (both transitive and intransitive)[8] and "to pursue hotly" (e.g., Gen 31:36; 1 Sam 17:53).

Two interpretations have been suggested, one literal, the other figurative (Figueras 1990, 196)—and both problematical. The figurative interpretation sees the participle as descriptive of Maria's fervor as a proselyte—"the fervent proselyte," in Figueras's rendering. Frey argues instead for a literal rendering, taking it as a reference to the actual lighting of lamps and fires (*CIJ* 1390). In particular, he suggests that prior to her conversion Maria had the task of lighting lamps and fires on the Sabbath, a task that was forbidden to Jews on this day (cf. *m. Sabb.* 7.2; 16.6, 8). This earned her the epithet "lamplighter" (Frey's term is "allumeuse"), which continued to be used of her even after her conversion.

While the figurative interpretation ("the fervent proselyte") is semantically possible, it is improbable on two counts. First, if the intention had been to indicate the quality of Maria's piety, there would have been any number of appropriate, less obscure terms to choose from. Second, as will be documented below, laudatory descriptions of the deceased are completely absent from ossuary

6. See *CIJ* 1390; according to Frey the hill is named *Viri Galilaei*.

7. See the reproduction in Bagatti (1971, 238).

8. Figueras mentions only the intransitive (1990, 196), but it appears in Obad 1:18 in a transitive sense; for the intransitive, see Ps 7:13; Prov 26:23. The Hiphil is also found with the meanings "to kindle" (Ezek 24:10; *m. Sabb.* 2.1) and "to inflame" (Isa 5:11; cf. Deut 28:22).

inscriptions found in the Jerusalem area.[9] This makes it highly unlikely that the term under discussion here is descriptive of Maria's piety. But Frey's alternative suggestion—that it refers to an occupation ("lamplighter")—is equally improbable, since this would require a causative form of the verb (*hiphil*). On the basis of the other Jerusalem inscriptions it seems safe to conclude that the term was used for purposes of identification, but its precise meaning remains elusive.

Whatever the uncertainty surrounding the final word in this inscription, however, the first two words (מריה הגרית) clearly indicate that the ossuary contained the remains of Maria, a proselyte.[10]

§206 Corpus inscriptionum judaicarum *1385*

[Ossuary] of Judah, of Laganion, proselyte

ΙΟΥΔΑΤΟΣ ΛΑΓΑΝΙΟΝΟΣ ΠΡΟΣΗΛΥΤΟΥ

Text and translation: Figueras (1990, 197, no. 5); also *CIJ* 1385.
Date: First century B.C.E. to first century C.E.
Provenance: Jerusalem
Original Language: Greek
Bibliography: Donaldson (2000); Figueras (1990, 197–98); Sukenik (1931, 18–20)
Category: CONVERSION

Carefully chiseled onto the end of an ossuary now located in the archaeological museum at St. Anne's Church in Jerusalem, this inscription also presents problems of interpretation. The ossuary was clearly that of a man named Judah. But what of Laganion? Was Laganion Judah's father, the genitive form being used (as was often the case) to indicate paternity?[11] If so, who was the proselyte—Judah (a name commonly assumed by a proselyte; Ilan 1991–1992: 154–55) or Laganion?[12] Or is Laganion, which is not well attested as a personal name, to be seen instead as a place name, the geographical origin of Judah the proselyte?

9. Such descriptions are more frequently found in later inscriptions at Beth She' arim (e.g., "Sarah the pious" [*CIJ* 1045]; "Joseph the pious" [*CIJ* 1052, 1056]) and Rome (e.g., "Iolia Marcella, a worthy woman" [*CIJ* 34]; "Asterias, father of the synagogue, pious, irreproachable" [*CIJ* 93]).

10. The spelling (גרית), found here and in §170 below, is unusual; the normal feminine form of the Hebrew term is גיורת (see *m. Keth.* 4.3).

11. With respect to the first genitive (ΙΟΥΔΑΤΟΣ), this was a common way of indicating the occupant of a tomb or ossuary; see van der Horst (1991, 41).

12. Figueras leaves the issue open (1990, 197). While he says that Sukenik identifies the proselyte as Judah, Sukenik seems to lean in the other direction ("Judas, dem Sohne des Laganion des Proselyten"; 1931, 18).

Several considerations lead to the probable conclusion that the proselyte was Laganion, who was the father of the deceased person Judah. To begin with, it is unlikely that the term is geographical. In other proselyte inscriptions, geographical indicators appear as the final element, following the name and the designation "proselyte." For example, one of the Dominus Flevit inscriptions reads: "Judah the proselyte from Tyre."[13] This seems to indicate that Laganion is the name of a person rather than of a place, and thus that he is the father of Judah. But evidence from the other proselyte inscriptions makes it unlikely that it was Judah who was the proselyte. First, in each of the other nineteen inscriptions, the term "proselyte" follows immediately after the name of the convert. Second, in none of the other inscriptions is the name of the proselyte's father given.[14] Indeed, it would be out of place, since proselytes are those who, according to Philo, "have left . . . their country, their kinsfolk and their friends for the sake of virtue and religion" (*Spec. Laws* 1.52). An identity based on paternity is thus one of the things left behind in conversion. In fact, a comparison with Jewish ossuary inscriptions in general, where the name of the father is the most common identifying mark in addition to the name of the deceased itself, suggests that "proselyte" functions as a kind of substitute patronymic.[15] Taken together, these considerations suggest strongly that the proselyte was the father Laganion, who subsequently gave his son the common Jewish name Judah.

The next three inscriptions come from a massive cemetery discovered in 1953 on the grounds of Dominus Flevit,[16] the Franciscan chapel halfway up the Mount of Olives directly across from the Haram esh-Sharif or Temple Mount. Excavations revealed a total of more than 500 separate chambers, grouped into some 75 identifiable tombs or sepulchers, containing 122 ossuaries and 7 sarcophagi. Forty-three of the ossuaries contained inscriptions, and three of these identified the occupants as proselytes. One of these inscriptions was in Hebrew, the other two in Greek.

§207 Dominus Flevit 13

Judah the proselyte from Tyre

ΙΟΥΔΑΝ ΠΡΟΣΗΛΥΤΟ[ ] ΤΥΡΑ /

13. See the next entry. The other probable instance is also from Dominus Flevit: "Diogenes the proselyte, from Zena" (§208 below). Figueras suggests that Zena is the father, but this is unlikely.

14. Figueras has suggested that the father's name appears in one of the inscriptions at Dominus Flevit (§208 below). But this is unlikely, for similar reasons.

15. Donaldson (2000, 382–83); see also the next entry.

16. "The Lord wept," from Luke 19:39–44. Finds from the excavation are on display at a museum in the Franciscan Monastery of the Flagellation, in the old city.

Text and translation: Bagatti and Milik (1958, 84, no. 13); Figueras (1990, 197)
Date: First century B.C.E. to first century C.E.
Provenance: Jerusalem
Original Language: Greek
Bibliography: Bagatti and Milik (1958, 6–7); Donaldson (2000); Figueras (1990, 197)
Category: CONVERSION

The ossuary of Judah was one of twenty five ossuaries in another large tomb (sixteen chambers); fourteen of the twenty five were inscribed. Bagatti and Milik interpreted the N (following ΙΟΥΔΑ) as an abbreviation of ΝΕΟΤΕΡΟΥ (the younger) and ΤΥΡΑ as "cheesemaker" (cf. τυρός [cheese]). But there is other epigraphic evidence for the form ΙΟΥΔΑΝ, and ΤΥΡΑ is clearly a reference to the city of Tyre (Figueras 1990, 197).

§208 Dominus Flevit 21

Diogenes the proselyte, (of?) Zena

ΔΙΟΓΕΝΗΣ ΠΡΟΣΗΛΥΤΟΣ ΖΗΝΑ

Text and translation: Bagatti and Milik (1958, 89, no. 21); Figueras (1990, 197)
Date: First century B.C.E. to first century C.E.
Provenance: Jerusalem
Original Language: Greek
Bibliography: Bagatti and Milik (1958, 12–14); Donaldson (2000); Figueras (1990, 197)

Diogenes is the only one of the Jerusalem proselytes to bear a pagan name. His ossuary was found in a smaller tomb (eight chambers) which contained two sarcophagi and twenty two ossuaries; only three of the ossuaries were inscribed. One of the other inscriptions was found in the same chamber, this one referring to Menahem, a priest. Figueras takes Zena to be the name of the father, but this is unlikely. Not only is there little evidence for such a name, but, as was observed above in the case of Laganion, fathers' names tend not to appear in proselyte inscriptions, probably because "proselyte" functioned as a kind of substitute patronymic for those who could not trace their Jewish identity through the normal route of paternity. It is more probable that "Zena" is a place name; thus, "Diogenes the proselyte from Zena."

§209 Dominus Flevit 31

Salome the proselyte

שלום הגרית

Text and translation: Bagatti and Milik (1958, 95, no. 31); Figueras (1990, 196)
Date: First century B.C.E. to first century C.E.
Provenance: Jerusalem
Original Language: Hebrew
Bibliography: Donaldson (2000); Figueras (1990, 196)

Salome's ossuary was found in the tomb of the family of Agra, a large tomb with twelve separate chambers, containing a total of twenty seven ossuaries, eleven of which were inscribed.[17] The inscription is straightforward, except for the unusual spelling, הגרית ([female] proselyte), found also in the first inscription listed above.

§210 Akeldama 19

Ariston
Ariston of Apamea
Judah the proselyte

ΑΡΙΣΤΩΝ
ארסטון אפמי
יהודה הגיור

Text and translation: Avni and Greenhut (1996, 66 [Inscription 19, Ossuary 31])
Date: Mid-first century C.E.
Provenance: Jerusalem
Original Language: Greek, Hebrew
Bibliography: Avni, Greenhut, and Ilan (1994); Ilan (1991–1992)

During repairs to the road from Abu Tur to Silwan in the summer of 1989, three burial caves were discovered near the junction of the Kidron and Hinnom Valleys, not far from the Akeldama monastery.[18] Evidence indicates that the caves were in use from the first century B.C.E. through to the destruction of Jerusalem.[19] A total of forty ossuaries and one sarcophagus were found in the caves, twenty three of them with inscriptions. The inscribed reference to Judah the proselyte appears on an ossuary found in an ossuary repository in Cave 3.

With its elaborately carved walls and pivoting stone doors, Cave 3 is one of the more elegant tombs to have been discovered in and around Jerusalem. Since the name Ariston appears on three ossuaries—the one under discussion

17. For a description of the tomb, see Bagatti and Milik (1958, 18–19).

18. The site traditionally associated with "Field of Blood" (Akeldama), linked in different ways in Matt 27:3–10 and Acts 1:18–19 with the death of Judas.

19. The tombs were also reused in the later Roman and Byzantine periods.

here and two others belonging to his children[20]—it is probable that this is a family tomb, belonging to a well-to-do family of Syrian origin (Apamea). Intriguingly, there is a reference in the Mishnah to a certain Ariston of Apamea (*m. Hal.* 4.11); the context concerns the legitimacy of firstfruits being brought from the Diaspora to Jerusalem. The name and circumstances are similar enough to suggest that the same person is in view in both references.[21]

The inscription on Ossuary 31, scratched in a rough hand on the back, contains three lines: "Ariston," in Greek (ΑΡΙΣΤΩΝ); "Ariston of Apamea," in Hebrew (ארסטון אפמי); and "Judah the proselyte," in Hebrew (יהודה הגיור).[22] Since it is common for ossuaries to contain the bones of more than one individual,[23] the simplest interpretation of the presence of two names (Ariston and Judah) is that this ossuary is another example of the phenomenon. Ilan, however, observing that Judah is a name often adopted by proselytes and that double occupancy is rare at Akeldama, has suggested that Ariston himself was the proselyte, having adopted the Hebrew name Judah when he converted to Judaism (Ilan 1991–1992, 154–55; 1996, 66).

While this is possible,[24] several pieces of evidence tend to make it unlikely. First, the fact that "Ariston" appears on the ossuaries of two of his own children—in both Greek and Hebrew—indicates that this is the name by which he was known and remembered; if Judah was his Jewish name, it was little used. Secondly, Ariston does appear as a Jewish name in the period (Ilan 1996, 66); the name does not necessarily suggest a Gentile. Thirdly, from the appearance of the inscription, it is possible that "Judah the proselyte" was inscribed by a different hand, which would suggest a later burial. Thus it is probable that Ossuary 31 contained the remains of two individuals—Ariston, a wealthy immigrant to Jerusalem from Syria; and another, originally Gentile, member of the family who had become a proselyte to Judaism and had taken the name Judah upon conversion.

20. Ariston appears on two other ossuaries—as the father of Selampsin (inscriptions sixteen and seventeen, ossuary twenty eight), and as the father of Shalom (ossuary thirty five, inscriptions twenty two and twenty three).

21. For a detailed argument see Ilan (1991–1992: 150–54); see also Avni, Greenhut, and Ilan (1994, 215).

22. While recognizably Hebrew (the definite article ה), the inscription is closer in spelling to the Aramaic (גיורא) than to the Hebrew (גר).

23. Ossuary 34 bears an inscription (21) referring to four members of one family. There are additional examples at Beth She'arim (#23, 36, 42, 60, 61); see Schwabe and Lifshitz (1974).

24. There is at least one example of an inscription with two names for one person, one a birth name and the other the name taken on conversion: an inscription from Rome (*CIJ* 523) refers to a certain Beturia Paucla, "who lived eighty-six years and six months, a proselyte for sixteen years, Sara by name." But in contrast to the Akeldama inscription, this more detailed text makes it completely clear that a single individual is in view.

§211 Cyrene 12

Joses of Crispus, 4 years
Quintus of Quintus, 15 years
Luka of Gaius, 58 years
Sarra the proselyte, 18 years

ΙΩΣΗΣ ΚΡΙΣΠΟΥ L δ
ΚΟΙΝΤΟΣ ΚΟΙΝΤΟΥ L ιε
ΛΥΚΑ ΓΑΙΟΥ L νη
ΣΑΡΡΑ ΠΡΟΣΣΗΛΥΤΟΣ L ιε

Text and translation: Lüderitz (1983, 26, no. 12); Figueras (1990, 200)
Date: Prior to 117 C.E.
Provenance: Cyrene
Original Language: Greek
Bibliography: Applebaum (1979); Barclay (1996, 232–42); Lüderitz (1983, 26–27); Vattier de Bourville (1855)
Category: CONVERSION

This inscription was found near a necropolis at Cyrene, during a short visit to the site by Vattier de Bourville in 1848. Literary and inscriptional evidence suggests that by the first century C.E. there was a sizable and prosperous Jewish community in Cyrene (Applebaum 1979, 175–90). Tensions existed between the Jewish community and the rest of the city, however, culminating eventually in the tumultuous uprising during the reign of Trajan (in 115–17). The uprising was disastrous for the Jewish population, resulting in the disappearance of any form of organized Jewish existence in the city for at least a century.[25] One implication of this is that 117 C.E. serves as a *terminus ad quem* for Jewish epigraphical remains, the Sarah inscription included.

Few inferences are possible about Sarah's family situation or her relationships with the other persons mentioned on the tombstone. Lüderitz suggests that she was a slave or perhaps an adopted daughter (Lüderitz 1983, 27). Since she was of marriageable age,[26] however, perhaps she had become a proselyte in marriage.

Taken as a whole, these epigraphs provide concrete illustration of the ambiguous status experienced by proselytes. On the one hand, these inscriptions were all found in Jewish burial sites, indicating the extent to which these converts had been incorporated into the community. On the other hand, they were

25. Applebaum indicates the existence of some—albeit scanty—evidence from the third century.

26. According to Lüdertiz (1983, 55), the demotic L was used in Cyrenaikan inscriptions to denote "years."

nevertheless differentiated from their neighbors in burial by the fact that their non-Jewish origins followed them to the grave.

As I have argued in more detail elsewhere (Donaldson 2000), it is probably an overstatement to say that "the proselyte felt obligated (was obligated?) to call attention to" his or her anomalous status (Cohen 1989, 29–30). At least in the cases surveyed here, the inscriptional material did not serve to "call attention to" anything other than the identity of the deceased. Unlike later epitaphs from Beth She'arim and Rome, which are replete with various supplementary material (e.g., words of praise, terms of endearment, expressions of sorrow, or words of encouragement addressed directly to the deceased), the whole corpus of Jerusalem ossuary inscriptions, together with those from Cyrene, contain nothing but basic identifying information.[27] The only material in addition to the name of the deceased are such elements as would serve the basic purpose of identification—usually the name of the father, but also names of other family members, occupation, place of origin, or status. For a convert, the usual Jewish means of identification—that is, a patronymic—was not appropriate. In such cases, the convert's status as a proselyte served as the identifying marker of first resort, a kind of substitute patronymic, making clear which Miriam or Judah was being referred to. This is seen most clearly in cases such as those of Sarah or of Salome, where "proselyte" is the only additional element. But this is no less true in the case of the others listed here whose inscriptions contain additional identifying elements. Thus the term appears not as the result of any sense of obligation resting on proselytes as a distinct category. The only obligation operative is to identify the deceased clearly, and this obligation fell equally on proselytes and native-born Jews alike.

Still, there is a fundamental difference, starkly reflected in the inscriptional form: the basic means of identification in Jewish society—the father's name—was not available to proselytes. While "proselyte" appears on these epitaphs simply as a means of identification, it nevertheless points to an irreducible difference in identity between the proselyte and the native-born Jew. The proselyte may be fully incorporated into the family and the society, but on the basis of a different and ineradicable badge of membership.

Epigraphical evidence has also played an important part in discussions concerning the phenomenon of Gentile sympathizers and "God-fearers." Indeed, as we

27. For a more thorough study, drawing on the corpus of inscriptions in *CIJ* along with the more recently discovered inscriptions from Dominus Flevit (Bagatti and Milik 1958) and the Akeldama tombs (Avni and Greenhut 1996), see Donaldson (2000). These inscriptions contain only three brief examples of epithetical material: "Alas" (*CIJ* 1222); "Peace" (*CIJ* 1226); "Do not open" (*CIJ* 1359). The inscriptions from Cyrene (see Lüderitz 1983, 25–29) tend also to include a reference to the age of the deceased, which is typical for Roman Africa (van der Horst 1991, 74).

have seen, the discovery and publication of the synagogue inscription from Aphrodisias (Reynolds and Tannenbaum 1987) has opened up a new phase in the scholarly discussion. In light of the evidence from Aphrodisias, it can no longer be doubted that the term could be used to describe Gentiles who were not proselytes but who nevertheless stood in some sort of relationship to the synagogue. At the same time, however, the ambiguity of the evidence from the Aphrodisias inscription itself means that the debate has by no means been settled.[28] Many of the inscriptions, however, including the one from Aphrodisias, date from the third century C.E. or later and thus fall outside the temporal limits of this study. Fortunately, they have been collected and thoroughly discussed in a recent publication by Levinskaya,[29] to which reference can be made for inscriptions not discussed here. Still, before we take up the discussion of those that can be dated with some certainty before 150 C.E., it is appropriate to begin with a more inclusive survey.

The inscriptions that might have some bearing on the phenomenon of Gentile sympathizers fall into several overlapping categories. First, there are inscriptions in which the adjective θεοσεβής (pious, worshipping God) or an equivalent is applied to individuals. Since the term itself could be used generically—that is, with reference to any type of piety—for an inscription to be pertinent, there must be some possibility that it refers (1) to a Gentile whose piety (2) was directed towards the God of the Jews. The set of pertinent texts includes nineteen that contain θεοσεβής itself; this total includes two Latin epitaphs in which the term is simply transcribed into Latin characters.[30] The term appears three times in the Aphrodisias inscription, bringing the total number of occurrences to twenty-one. In addition, several Latin epitaphs in which the deceased is described as *metuens* (fearing) have been interpreted by some as evidence for Gentile sympathizers; one of them, in which an apparently Gentile woman is described as a "fearer of the Jewish religion" *(religioni Iudaicae metuenti)*,[31] clearly belongs to this category. Finally, an inscription from Panticapaeum in the Bosporus Kingdom (*CIRB* 71), which recorded the synagogue manumission of a slave, contains a phrase (θεὸν σέβων) that may be a variant of θεοσέβων. Since the inscription dates from the late-first or early-second century C.E.—the only one in this group earlier than 150 C.E.—it will be discussed in detail below.

28. For a discussion of the inscription, see the introduction to Luke-Acts in ch. 8 above.

29. See Levinskaya (1996). Many of the texts are also discussed in Figueras (1990), Schürer (1986, 3:165–68) and Trebilco (1991).

30. I.e., *theosebes* (*JIWE* 2.207); *teuseues* (*JIWE* 1.113).

31. "Aurelius Soter and Aurelius Stephanus for Aurelia Soteria, their very devout mother, a fearer of the Jewish religion, her sons set up (this monument)" (*JIWE* 1.9). If the whole family were Jewish, one would not expect the mother's religious commitments to be singled out in this way. For other inscriptions containing *metuens*, see Levinskaya (1996, 69).

Of these twenty-one inscriptions, nine are epitaphs, including the three in Latin (from Italy);[32] eight or nine commemorate synagogue benefactions, including six from Sardis and the famous Aphrodisias inscription, which its publishers suggest was located at the entrance to the synagogue but which commemorated the construction of a separate building "for the relief of suffering in the community";[33] one formalizes a manumission that took place in a synagogue in the Bosporus Kingdom (though the inscription was not found *in situ*);[34] and two are inscribed on theater benches in Miletus.[35] Fourteen of the twenty-one come from western Asia Minor (including the islands), six from Italy and one from the Bosporus.

Second, the synagogue manumission inscription mentioned above (*CIRB* 71) belongs to a set of sixteen manumission inscriptions from the Bosporus Kingdom on the north shore of the Black Sea, dating from the first to mid-second century C.E.[36] Nine of these, including *CIRB* 71, make explicit reference to a Jewish synagogue.[37] Three others invoke the "Most High God" (*CIRB* 1123, 1124, 1125); since one of the three (*CIRB* 1123) also mentions the prayerhouse (προσευχή), a relationship with Judaism is probable. Two others (*CIRB* 74 and 1021) contain nothing that might indicate Jewish association, and so can be left out of account here.[38]

32. The Greek epitaphs are as follows: *CIJ* 500 (Italy, date undetermined); *JIWE* 2.392 (Rome, 3rd century C.E.); *CIJ* 731e (Rhodes, date undetermined); Paton and Hicks (1891, # 278) (Cos, date undetermined); *JIWE* 1.12 (Italy, 2nd to 4th century C.E.); Pfuhl and Möbius (1977, 1979, #1697) (Asia Minor; 3rd century C.E.).

33. The Sardis inscriptions can be found in Trebilco (1991, 158 and 252, n. 60); the official publication has not yet appeared (Kroll, forthcoming). They date from the 4th (or perhaps the 3rd) century C.E. For Aphrodisias, see Reynolds and Tannenbaum (1987). Other inscriptions: *CIJ* 754 (Deliler, near Philadelphia in Asia; 3rd century C.E.); *CIG* 2924 (Tralles, in Asia; 3rd century C.E.).

34. *CIRB* 71; since the inscription was not found *in situ* (see Gibson [1999, 124]), there is no evidence that would identify the synagogue as the original location of the inscription.

35. One of these (τοπος Ειουδεων των και θεοσεβιον; *CIJ* 748) has been frequently discussed since it was first published by Deissmann in 1927. A second (θε[οσ]εβιον) has been recently published by Rehm and Herrmann (1997–98, #940g). Dating is uncertain, but probably from the 3rd (or perhaps 2nd) century C.E.

36. For full studies, see Gibson (1999) and Levinskaya (1996, 105–16, 227–46)

37. Four of these (*CIRB* 70, 71, 73 and *SEG* 43.510) are more or less intact. Each of them mentions the prayerhouse (προσευχή) twice, once as the location of the manumission itself and the other in a phrase that will require further discussion; each of them also makes reference to the "community of the Jews" (τῆς συναγωγῆς τῶν Ἰουδαίων). Of the incomplete inscriptions, three of them clearly contain either προσευχή (*CIRB* 73, 1127) or Ἰουδαίων (*CIRB* 1124). In two others (*CIRB* 72, 985) one or more of the terms can be plausibly reconstructed).

38. Gibson's list of sixteen contains two further texts that are very fragmentary; they are *CIRB* 69 and an inscription published by Boltunova (1971, no. 1).

Third, there is a mixed collection of inscriptions in which—at least according to some interpreters—Gentiles invoke the Jewish God. This collection comprises inscriptions of three types: inscriptions that (like the three Bosoprus manumission inscriptions mentioned above) invoke or otherwise refer to "the Most High God" (ὁ Θεὸς ὁ ὕψιστος, or variations thereof), inscriptions referring to Sabazios, and inscriptions found on Gentile altars with Biblical-sounding language for God. In the course of scholarly discussion, a range of approaches has been taken to these inscriptions. Some have been inclined to see Jewish influence or association in the whole collection, even in the absence of any other Jewish evidence. Particularly influential has been Cumont's theory that the Jews of Asia Minor were markedly syncretistic, and as such contributed to the emergence of Gentile associations that fused the worship of Yahweh ("the Most High God") with the local deity Sabazios.[39] Others have been just as inclined to see extensive Jewish influence in these inscriptions but without any element of syncretism, interpreting the texts instead as reflecting the result of a Jewish mission whose purpose was to create God-fearers (so, e.g., Bickerman [1980]; Levinskaya [1996, 83–103]). At the other extreme, Kraabel (1969) has denied any Jewish influence whatsoever. Several positions have been marked out between these extremes. Mitchell has argued for the existence of a pagan Theos Hypsistos cult with which some Jews associated because of its monotheistic emphases (Mitchell 1999). Trebilco (1991, 127–44) has argued, against Kraabel, that Jewish influence is not to be ruled out but should be ascribed only where there is corroborating evidence of one kind or another. Such an approach is well advised and will be adopted here.

"The Most High" (ὁ ὕψιστος) or "the Most High God" (ὁ Θεὸς ὁ ὕψιστος) appears frequently in the LXX and other Jewish literature written in Greek (Trebilco 1991, 129–31). The phrase is thus completely at home in Judaism. At the same time, however, variations of the phrase are frequently found with reference to Zeus and other pagan deities.[40] While Levinskaya has questioned Trebilco's conclusion that the term was widely "used of pagan deities throughout the Roman Empire" (Trebilco 1991, 128), the evidence that she herself cites demonstrates that, in addition to Zeus, the term was connected to Helios, Apollo, Attis, Isis, an unnamed god in Samothrace, and an unnamed goddess in Lydia (Levinskaya 1996, 92–93). The question, then, has to do with those instances in which the term appears without any further specification of the deity being addressed. While Trebilco's argument may need to be fine-tuned in

39. Cumont (1897; 1906), followed by Nilsson (1956; 1967), Hengel (1974, 1:263), and others. See §178 above.

40. For documentation, see Trebilco (1991, 128–29), Levinskaya (1996, 84–85) and Mitchell (1993, 2:43–51).

response to some of Levinskaya's criticisms,[41] the main point remains sound: since the term is current in non-Jewish usage, one should not posit Jewish influence unless there are supplementary reasons for doing so.

Proceeding on this basis, one can identify a number of pertinent "Theos Hypsistos" inscriptions[42] in addition to the three manumission inscriptions from the Bosporus kingdom (*CIRB* 1123, 1125, 1126). One is a dedication found in the vicinity of Acmonia and published by Drew-Bear (1976). Since there is evidence that the Jews of Acmonia used the term with reference to Yahweh (*CIJ* 769), Trebilco detects Jewish influence;[43] but in view of the opening dedication "To Good Fortune" (Ἀγαθῇ Τύχ[ῃ]), he is of the opinion that Aurelia Tatis and her husband Onesimus, who together erected the monument, were Gentiles. The inscription, unfortunately, has not been dated. The other pertinent inscriptions, some fifteen in total,[44] originate in the Bosporus region. Since one of them dates to the mid-first century, they will be discussed below.

The worship of Sabazios originated in Phrygia and Thrace, but as the god came to be identified syncretistically with Zeus and then Jupiter, the cult became popular throughout the Mediterranean world. The hypothesis that there was a strong Jewish element in the cult was first developed by Cumont (1906). While the hypothesis has been widely influential,[45] it has more recently been subjected to severe criticism. Cumont's construction was erected primarily on the foundation of the passage from Valerius Maximus discussed above (§178), which contains the report of an expulsion of Jews from Rome in 139 B.C.E. by Cornelius Hispalus, the *praetor peregrinus*, because the Jews were attempting "to infect the Roman customs with the cult of Jupiter Sabazius."[46] Pointing to the similarity between *Sabazios* and *Sabaoth*, Cumont argued that Jews had linked their own God with Sabazios, a connection taken up into the cult.[47]

41. For example, Trebilco (1991, 128), depending on A. B. Cook, states that Theos Hypsistos was used with reference to the Syrian Baal. Levinskaya (1996, 88) points out, however, that this was simply an inference on Cook's part; the inscriptions in question did not refer to Baal explicitly, but were found in an area where Baal Shamin was the primary deity.

42. Of course, this does not include inscriptions produced by Jews; Trebilco lists ten of these (Trebilco 1991, 133–37).

43. Interestingly enough, Drew-Bear does not.

44. The inscriptions are very fragmentary. Schürer identified twenty-one of them, but subsequent reconstruction has reduced the total to fifteen (see Levinskaya 1996, 111): *CIRB* 1260, 1260a, 1261, 1277, 1278, 1279, 1280, 1281, 1282, 1283, 1284, 1285, 1286, 1287, 1289.

45. For bibliography, see Trebilco (1991, 244, n. 64) and Schürer (1986, 3:74).

46. Valerius Maximus, *Memorable Doings and Sayings* 1.3.3.

47. For a similar argument, albeit with the assumption that the Jews in question were missionaries rather than syncretists, see Bickerman (1980, 329–32).

As we have seen (§178), any connection between the Jews and Jupiter Sabazios is much more probably the result of confusion on the part of Valerius or of his epitomizer than of any syncretistic phenomenon in Roman antiquity. In other words, no Sabazios inscriptions should be included here.

In addition to the Theos Hypsistos inscriptions, however, there are two further inscriptions found on Gentile altars that seem to address the God of the Jews. Both are to be dated within our time frame and thus will be discussed below.

Fourth and finally, in addition to the synagogue benefactions in which θεοσεβής appears explicitly, there is an inscription from Acmonia (Phrygia) that provides evidence of another Gentile benefactor.[48] The inscription honors several individuals for their efforts in repairing the synagogue. While the individuals are Jewish, the inscription mentions in passing that the synagogue had been built originally by Julia Severa, a prominent Gentile woman known from other sources. Since she lived in the latter part of the first century C.E., the inscription will be discussed in detail below.

We begin, then, with *CIRB* 71, the one possible "God-fearer" inscription that predates 150 C.E., together with the other synagogue manumission inscriptions from the Bosporus.

§212 Corpus inscriptionum regni Bosporani *71*

Since the translation of this inscription is a matter of some dispute, I will provide the full Greek text along with two English renderings.

> - - - - - - - - - - - ΚΑ-
> κου ἀφίημι ἐπὶ τῆς προσευ-
> χῆς Ἐλπία[—]α[-]τῆς θρεπτ[—]
> ὅπως ἐστὶν ἀπαρενόχλητος
> καὶ ἀνεπίληπτος ἀπὸ παντος
> κληρονόμου χωρὶς τοῦ προσ-
> καρτερεῖν τῇ προσευχῇ ἐπι-
> τροπευούσης τῆς συναγω-
> γῆς τῶν Ἰουδαίων καὶ θεὸν
> σέβων

I release in the prayerhouse my slave Elpis in order that she is undisturbed and unassailable by any heir, except for service to the prayerhouse, as a guardian, the synagogue of the Jews and god-fearers (Gibson 1999, 161)

I free in the prayer-house Elpias, my household slave, so that he will be undisturbed and unassailable by any of my heirs, on condition that he works for the prayer-house under the guardianship of the Jewish community, and honours God (Levinskaya 1996, 74).

48. *CIJ* 766 = *MAMA* VI 264 = Lifshitz (1967, #33).

Text and translation: Gibson (1999, 161) and Levinskaya (1996, 74)
Date: Late first- or early second-century C.E.
Provenance: Panticapaeum, in the Bosporus kingdom
Original Language: Greek
Bibliography: Bellen (1965–1966); Gibson (1999, 139–44); Harrill (1995, 177); Levinskaya (1996, 74–77, 105–16); Trebilco (1991, 155–56)
Category: SYMPATHIZATION

Before we look at the manumission inscriptions as a group, it is necessary to treat *CIRB* 71 as a special case, since it contains a phrase that some have translated as "the synagogue of the Jews and God-fearers." The inscription is difficult and has been interpreted in two quite distinct ways, represented quite nicely by two recent and detailed discussions of the text (Gibson 1999; Levinskaya 1996). The key part of the phrase (καὶ θεὸν σέβων) is clear enough on its own; taking σέβων as the nominative masculine singular form of the present participle, it reads "and fearing God." The difficulty comes in relating it to the inscription as a whole.

Levinskaya sees the phrase in question as a second injunction placed on the manumitted slave, thus depending grammatically on χωρίς and standing in parallel with τοῦ προσκαρτερεῖν τῇ προσευχῇ; literally: "except to continue with the prayer-house . . . and fearing God." She takes the participle σέβων as dependent on Elpias, having reconstructed line 3 as Ἐλπίαν ἐμαυτῆς τῆς θρεπτόν; that is, Elpias is the male slave of a female owner.

This reading, however, is difficult in several respects. First, while the inscription itself seems to have been lost,[49] original observers of the inscription report that the letter following θρεπτ had a quadrilateral shape, suggesting θρεπτήν rather than θρεπτόν. This would mean that the slave was female (Elpis), thus eliminating the possibility of a masculine antecedent for σέβων.[50] Further, the awkward shift from an infinitive (τοῦ προσκαρτερεῖν) to a participial form (σέβων) and the distance separating σέβων from χωρίς pose additional problems for this reading. Nevertheless, to support her reading, Levinskaya appeals to the form of the other Bosporus manumission inscriptions, in which there are usually two injunctions laid on the freed slave—normally, "except for προσκαρτερήσεως (perseverance) and θωπεία (flattery) with respect to the prayer-house." Levinskaya takes θωπεία in the sense of "piety,"

49. Current analysis is carried out on the basis of photographs and comments from earlier observers of the actual inscription.

50. Several interpreters (Nadel, Lifshitz) have suggested some variation of Ἐλπίαν τῆς θρεπτῆς, that is, "Elpias, son of the female slave" (see Gibson 1999, 141–42). But the absence of the mother's name, together with the fact that slave parentage is rarely found on inscriptions, makes this suggestion doubly unlikely.

and argues that "fearing God" in *CIRB* 71 should be taken as the equivalent of this second injunction in the other inscriptions. The terms will come up for discussion in the next section, but anticipating the results of that discussion, it can be said that "piety" is an unlikely rendering of the word. But further, an appeal to form actually works against Levinskaya's reading. For, as Gibson has demonstrated in her study of the form of the Bosporus manumission inscriptions, the section dealing with oversight ("under the guardianship of the synagogue of the Jews") is always a discrete entity, following the section dealing with ongoing obligations (Gibson 1999, 126–27). It is unlikely that the obligation section would be fragmented, with the oversight section intruding into its midst (see also Bellen [1965–1966: 173]).

The alternative, proposed originally by Bellen (1965–1966) and defended in detail by Gibson, involves the emendation of καὶ θεὸν σέβων to καὶ θεοσεβῶν, so that the final lines of the inscription read, "the synagogue of the Jews and God-fearers serving as guardians." Since there is no doubt about the wording of the inscription at this point, essential to the proposal is the suggestion that there was an error on the part of the stonemason. While such a suggestion necessarily has to bear the burden of proof, there are several things in its favor. In particular, the resultant reading is much simpler in grammatical terms, and it preserves the formal structure apparent in the other manumission inscriptions from the Bosporus region. Since irregularities in grammar and spelling are frequently encountered in epigraphs and since θεοσεβής is a relatively rare term, it is certainly not implausible to imagine a stonemason replacing this unfamiliar term with something more immediately recognizable (i.e., θεὸν σέβων).

Paradoxically, however, if this reading is adopted so that the inscription makes explicit reference to God-fearers, it serves to undermine the widely accepted argument that the other inscriptions concerning synagogue manumission provide evidence for God-fearers. To these inscriptions we now turn.

The inscription discussed in the previous section (*CIRB* 71) is one of nine inscriptions from the Bosporus kingdom in which the manumission of a slave is associated in some way with a Jewish community (συναγωγή) and its prayer-house (προσευχή). Except for the possible reference to God-fearers in *CIRB* 71, these inscriptions display a similar form and thus need to be discussed as a group. Five of the inscriptions are fragmentary; little is to be gained by reproducing them here.[51] In addition to *CIRB* 71 (discussed in the previous section), the complete inscriptions follow.

§213 Corpus inscriptionum regni Bosporani *70*

> *In the reign of King Tiberius Julius Rhescuporis, loyal to the emperor and a friend to the Romans, pious, in the year 377, on the 12th of the month of Peritios, I, Chreste, former wife of Drusus, in the prayerhouse* [ἐπὶ τῆς πρ(ο)σευχῆς] *set my slave*

51. *CIRB* 72, 985, 1124, 1127, 1128. For texts, see Gibson (1999, 161–70).

Heraklas free once and for all according to my vow, [to be] unassailable and undisturbed by any heir, to go wherever he should want without restraint just as I vowed, except for submissiveness and service [θωπείας τε καὶ προσκαρτερήσεω(ς)] *to the prayerhouse, and joining in assent are my heirs Herakleides and Helikonias, and also serving as joint guardian is the community of the Jews* [συνεπ(ιτ)ροπευούσης δὲ καὶ τῆς συναγωγῆς τῶν Ἰουδαίων].

§214 Corpus inscriptionum regni Bosporani *73*

In the reign of King . . . , loyal to the emperor and a friend to the Romans, pious, in the year . . . , in the month of Artemisios, I set my slaves free in the prayerhouse [(ἐν τῇ π)ροσευχῇ] *according to my vow once and for all, male slaves (?) . . . and Hermes, [to be] unassailable and undisturbed by me and every heir . . . upon the condition of* paramonē *for [the duration of] my life . . . popular with my mother . . . and everything just as . . . and with my death . . . they have done everything, and after the death, they are to go unhindered without any dispute just as I have vowed, wherever in the world they should want, except for submissiveness and service* [θωπείας τε καὶ προς(καρτ)ερήσεως] *to the prayerhouse, and also serving as joint guardian is the community of the Jews* [συνεπιτροπε(υούσης δὲ) καὶ τῆς συναγωγῆς τῶν Ἰουδαίων].

§215 Supplementum epigraphicum graecum 43.510

In the reign of Kong Cotys, in the year 348, on the 1st of the month of Xandikos, Psycharion and his sons Sogos and Anos. Karsandanos and Karagos and Metroteimos are released in the prayerhouse [τῇ προσευχῇ], *to be unassailable [and] without restraint except for submissiveness and service* [προσκαρτερήσεως καὶ θωπίας] *to the prayerhouse and that they are released with the synagogue as a joint guardian* [συνεπιτροπε(υ)ούσης τῆς συναγω(γῆς) τῶν Ἰουδαίων].

Text and translation: Gibson (1999, 160, 162, 172)
Date: 80/81 C.E. *(CIRB* 70); late first- or early second-century C.E. (*CIRB* 73); 51 C.E. (*SEB* 43.510)
Provenance: Panticapaeum (*CIRB* 70, 71, 72, 73), Phanagoria *(CIRB* 985) and Gorgippia *(CIRB* 1124, 1127), in the Bosporus kingdom
Original Language: Greek
Bibliography: Bellen (1965–1966); Gibson (1999, 139–44); Goodenough (1956–1957); Harrill (1995, 177); Levinskaya (1996, 74–77, 105–16); Trebilco (1991, 155–56)
Category: SYMPATHIZATION, CONVERSION

Ever since Schürer's influential early study of the Bosporus inscriptions (Schürer 1897), it has been common to interpret the synagogue manumissions as having to do with slaves who were Gentile and whose manumission had a religious dimension. More specifically, it has been suggested that manumission was conditional on the slave continuing to attend the synagogue as a God-fearing adherent, or even that manumission was part of the process by which a slave became a proselyte.[52] Support for such a suggestion has been offered along two lines.

First, while there is no indication in any of these inscriptions as to the ethnic identity of the slave (or, for that matter, that of the slaveowner), it has been inferred from the Biblical injunctions concerning slavery that the slaves in question must have been Gentile. Biblical texts containing legislation on slavery (Exod 21:2–11; Lev 25:39–55; Deut 15:12–18), while not completely consistent, nevertheless make a clear distinction between Israelite and Gentile slaves. For one thing, in each passage a limit is set to the term of slavery for an Israelite—either six years or, in the case of Leviticus, until the next jubilee. Further, on being set free Israelite slaves are to receive material recompense (Lev 25:41; Deut 15:14), which suggests that their situation is more that of a hired servant than of a slave. In fact, the passage from Leviticus states this explicitly; referring to those who might seek to sell themselves into slavery because of indebtedness, the text commands: "you shall not make them serve as slaves; they shall remain with you as hired or bound laborers" (Lev 25:39–40). Thus, it is argued, Jewish slaves would have been set free according to these particularly Jewish patterns; the slaves in these inscriptions, which reflect characteristically Hellenistic patterns of manumission, therefore must have been Gentile.[53] Levinskaya takes this one step further, to argue that the slaveowner was Gentile as well; more specifically, she argues that these slaveowners were God-fearers themselves,[54] who "showed their sympathy by following the Jewish example and manumitting their slaves in Jewish synagogues on condition that the freedmen would be attached to the synagogues" (Levinskaya 1996, 113).

Second, it has been argued that the ongoing obligations laid on the former slave with respect to the prayerhouse, expressed by the terms θωπεία and προσκαρτέρησις, are specifically religious in nature. Neither term, of course, denotes religious activity in any explicit way; προσκαρτέρησις refers to persistence or perseverance of any sort, while θωπεία usually has the negative sense of flattery or fawning. Still, the facts that the "perseverance" is to be carried out with respect to the Jewish prayerhouse and that the guarantor of the manumission is the Jewish community have led many interpreters to the plausible conclusion that the freed slave was obligated to maintain a religious association

52. See Gibson (1999, 137–40). Among those arguing for proselyte status are Nadel (1966) and Dan'shin (1996). Levinskaya (1996, 105–16) and Trebilco (1991, 155–56) see the manumitted slave as a God-fearer; Levinskaya also sees the slave owner as a God-fearer. For Bellen (1965–1966), the slave is a God-fearer on the way to proselytism. Others assume an ongoing religious connection with the synagogue, but without further specification (e.g., Westermann [1955, 126]; Rajak [1985, 259]).

53. E.g., Goodenough (1956–57, 221); Westermann (1955, 125).

54. Worshippers of the "Most High God"; see the discussion in the next section.

with the Jewish synagogue. This conclusion was apparently strengthened by the discovery in 1928 of *CIRB* 71. As we have seen, this manumission inscription contains a phrase (καὶ θεὸν σέβων) that could be interpreted as referring to the piety of the freed slave. Since the phrase could also be interpreted as a substitute for θωπεία (which does not appear; προσκαρτέρησις appears alone), the inscription convinced a number of interpreters that θωπεία and θεὸν σέβων are synonymous, so that θωπεία in these inscriptions should be given the positive sense of piety or reverence.[55]

Both lines of argument, however, are open to serious question. First, more recent study of slavery within Judaism has tended to demonstrate that Diaspora Jews differed little from their Gentile counterparts in their slaveholding and manumission practices.[56] One cannot simply infer from the Hellenistic form of the manumission inscriptions that the slaves were non-Jews[57] (or, for that matter, that the slaveowners were Gentile).

Secondly, with regard to the ongoing obligations, Gibson has argued persuasively that these can be more readily understood as having to do with material service than with religious observance (Gibson 1999, 144–50). The basis of her argument is the *paramonē* clause that appears frequently in Hellenistic manumission inscriptions (especially those from Delphi). In these inscriptions the slave is set free by his or her owner but on condition that the slave "remain with" the owner for a period of time, usually until the owner's death. The *paramonē* condition is expressed by some form of the verb παραμένω, (to remain with), hence its name. While the term is vague in and of itself, the obligation to which it refers is apparently both very specific and of great significance: failure to comply means that freedom is revoked. Fortunately, the term occasionally receives further definition. In *SGDI* 1721, to take one especially pertinent example, the slave Sosikrates "is to remain with [παραμεινάτω] Krato doing all that is asked for as long as Krato lives." In other words, as this example makes explicit, the *paramonē* condition obliges the slave to continue in service to his or her master until death, at which point the slave's freedom comes fully into force. While some have expressed surprise at this apparent logical tension between freedom and continuing servitude, the situation is not unlike the more general Hellenistic and Roman practice of *donatio mortis causa* ("gifts in contemplation of death"), in which the ownership of goods or property is legally

55. See Levinskaya (1996, 75, 232), as well as the discussion in Gibson (1999, 139–40).

56. See Gibson (1999, 56–94); she refers to studies by Dale B. Martin, E. E. Urbach, and Benjamin Wright.

57. Harrill suggests that the slave was Jewish and furthermore that the costs of manumission were borne by the synagogue itself (Harrill 1995, 172–78). While the first suggestion is possible, there is nothing in the inscriptional evidence to support the conclusion that the manumission was paid for out of community funds.

transferred to the beneficiary while the donor is still living, but the donor retains usufruct until his or her death (see Yaron 1960).

Gibson argues that προσκαρτερέω functions as the Bosporan equivalent of παραμένω, so that in these Bosporus inscriptions the phrase χωρὶς τοῦ προσκαρτερεῖν τῇ προσευχῇ (or its equivalents) is a *paramonē* clause, by means of which the emancipated slave is obligated to give ongoing service of some material kind to the synagogue. In support of this argument she points first to the similarity in terminology; προσκαρτερέω (to continue with) is virtually synonymous with παραμένω (to remain with). She is also able to adduce an additional Bosporan manumission inscription (*CIRB* 1127) which, while badly preserved, nevertheless contains a clause concerning the prayerhouse, but with a form of προσμένω (προσμέ[νου]σα) in place of the expected προσκερτερέω. While προσμένω is not quite παραμένω, it is close enough to provide support for the argument. Further, while it might be objected that the Bosporus inscriptions differ from the usual *paramonē* conditions not only in terminology but also in the beneficiary of the service (the synagogue, not the slaveowner), Gibson is able to show that service to a religious community is also attested in *paramonē* conditions.[58] Thus the proposed situation wherein a slaveowner becomes a synagogue benefactor by means of manumission is not without parallel in the wider Hellenistic environment.

What then of θωπεία? While the term usually has a negative connotation (captured in the English rendering, "flattery"), such a sense is unlikely here. For in this instance the term refers to an attitude or behavior that is actually required of the freed slave, which means that a negative sense would be out of place. As we have seen, some have argued that the term here should be rendered "piety." But the fact that in the inscriptions the term is closely linked with προσκαρτέρησις (most frequently with τε καί) suggests that the two terms be understood together rather than as expressing two quite distinct sets of obligations.[59] The question, then, is whether θωπεία can be understood as referring to an attitude or a pattern of behavior that might be seen as appropriate for slaves who were given freedom on the condition that they continue to provide material service to the synagogue. Gibson argues that the term is sufficiently associated with slavery—specifically, to describe the kind of attitude and behavior that

58. Gibson 1999: 147. She cites two inscriptions from Beroea, one of which contains the clause "He will serve me throughout the time of my life, staying with the goddess on the festival days." As Gibson observes, this double obligation (to serve both the master and the religious community) is paralleled in one of the Bosporus inscriptions (*CIRB* 73), which contains both a *paramonē* clause (apparently) and the formula under discussion ("except for θωπείας and προσκαρτερήσεως towards the prayerhouse").

59. This argument is directed at those who take θωπεία as indicating religious piety but προσκαρτέρησις as referring to material service; see Gibson (1999, 144–45). Of course, the argument carries no weight against those who see both terms as indicative of religious piety.

characterize slaves in their relationship with their masters (e.g., Philo *Good Person* 99–100)—that one can understand how it could be enjoined on slaves in this set of circumstances. It refers to an attitude of dutiful subservience with which the slave is expected to carry out his or her ongoing obligation to the prayerhouse; "the freed slave is to work in an appropriately servile, respectful, and perhaps even flattering manner" (Gibson 1999, 149).

Of course, if the slave were Gentile, there is nothing inherently implausible to the suggestion that he or she might have developed some religious attachment to Judaism, either before or after manumission. But it is unlikely that the Bosporus inscriptions provide evidence that such attachment was an explicit condition of the manumission itself.

In addition to these manumission inscriptions in which the freed slave continues in a relationship with the synagogue, there are five others from the Bosporus region characterized by an opening dedication "to the most high god, almighty, blessed [Θεῷ ὑψίστῳ παντοκράτορι εὐλογητῷ]."

§216 Corpus inscriptionum regni Bosporani *1123*

To the most high god, almighty, blessed, in the reign of King Mithridates, loving . . . and patriotic, in the year 338, in the month of Dios, Pothos son of Strabo dedicated in the prayerhouse [προσευχῇ] *according to a vow his slave whose name is Chrusa, on the condition that she be inviolable and unmolested by any heir under Zeus, Ge, and Helios.*

§217 Corpus inscriptionum regni Bosporani *1125*

To the most high god, almighty, blessed, in the reign of King Tiberius Julius Sauromates, loyal to the emperor and a friend to the Romans, pious, Teimotheos, son of Numphagoros Makarius, along with his sister Helidos, wife of Nanobalamurus, according to the vow of our father, Numphagorus Makarius, we set free our slave Dorea . . .

§218 Corpus inscriptionum regni Bosporani *1126*

To the most high god, almighty, blessed, in the reign of king Rhescuporis, loyal to the emperor and a friend to the Romans, pious, in the year 64, in the month of Daisios, I, Neokles, son of Athenodoros, under Zeus, Ge, and Helios, set free my slaves (?) . . . joining in assent is my father, Athenodoros, son of Athenaius, on the condition that they be inviolable and unmolested by any heir of mine. And they are to go wherever they should want on account of the order by me, their master.

Text and translation: Gibson (1999, 110)
Date: 41 C.E. *(CIRB* 1123); late first- or early second-century C.E. (*CIRB* 1125, 1126)
Provenance: Gorgippia, in the Bosporus kingdom
Original Language: Greek
Bibliography: Gibson (1999, 109–23); Goodenough (1956–1957, 222–24); Schürer (1986, 3:37); Trebilco (1991, 136).
Category: SYMPATHIZATION

As was indicated above, since the term "the most high god" was current in both Jewish and pagan usage, we should be cautious in attributing Jewish influence or provenance without additional evidence. In the case of these inscriptions, however, such additional evidence is clearly present: the supplementary adjectives—almighty (παντοκράτωρ), blessed (εὐλογητός)—which are found most frequently in Jewish literature (Schürer 1897); the reference in one of the inscriptions *(CIRB* 1123) to the "prayerhouse" as the locus of the manumission; the existence of other manumission inscriptions from the Bosporus kingdom that display clear connections with the synagogue (see above). But the significance of this evidence is complicated by the reference in two of the three inscriptions to the pagan gods Zeus, Ge, and Helios.

While almost all interpreters see these inscriptions as Jewish in some sense, there is a range of scholarly opinion on their precise relationship with the Jewish community.[60] At one end of the range, Gibson appeals to the patently formulaic character of the phrase, as well as to the presence of other pagan formulae in epitaphs that are certainly Jewish, to argue that the inscriptions could well have been produced by Jews.[61] At the other end are scholars, generally of an earlier era (e.g., Schürer 1897), who found it unthinkable that a Jew could have used such a pagan phrase but were nevertheless prepared to concede some Jewish influence. In between are those who take the position that the inscriptions were produced by Gentile God-fearers (e.g., Levinskaya 1996, 113).

The evidence is ambiguous, making it difficult to come to any firm conclusion. Still, these inscriptions differ from the other synagogue manumission inscriptions in ways that might be significant. Both the absence of any ongoing relationship between the slave and the synagogue and the invocation of these pagan deities give these inscriptions a more Gentile character. If a decision is to be made, it is more likely that these inscriptions were the work of Gentile sympathizers than of Jewish synagogue members.

In addition to these synagogue manumission inscriptions, there is a set of some fifteen additional inscriptions from the Bosporus kingdom that address the Most High God. They come from the region of Tanais, at the extreme northeast end of the Black Sea. While many of them are fragmentary and all of them are later than our period, the issues that they raise are of sufficient importance that it is worth discussing the earliest of them, which, dated to 155 C.E. is just slightly outside our temporal limits.

§219 Corpus inscriptionum regni Bosporani *1260*

> *With good fortune. To the Most High God, who listens, the vow. In the reign of the king Tiberius Iulius Eupaator, the friend of the Emperor and the friend of the Romans,*

60. See Gibson (1999, 122, n. 34) for a description with full bibliography.

61. Gibson (1999, 119–23); also Goodenough (1956–57, 222–24); Trebilco (1991, 136).

pious, in the year 452, in the month . . . . The association [σύνοδος] *under the presidency of the priest Phannes the son of Stratoneikos and the convenor . . . . Iulianos and other members of the association* [θιασῶται] . . . [here follows a list of names] . . . . *Phannes the son of Stratoneikos, the priest, in fulfilment of the vow restored this stele at his own expense.*

Text and Translation: Levinskaya (1996, 243)
Date: 155 C.E.
Provenance: Tanais, Bosporan kingdom
Original Language: Greek
Bibliography: Goodenough (1956–1957); Levinskaya (1996, 111–4, 242–43); Schürer (1897); Trebilco (1991, 139)
Category: SYMPATHIZATION

Each of the inscriptions from Tanais contains a list of the members of a voluntary association (σύνοδος, θίασος[62]), with various ones further designated according to role: priest, convenor (συναγωγός), promoter of goodness (φιλάγαθος), supervisor of youth (νιανισκάρχης), director of the gymnasium (γυμνασιάρχης). Each of them is addressed to the Most High God. In addition, two of them (*CIRB* 1281, 1283) have apparently been erected by new members (εἰσποιητοι ἀδελφοί: "adopted brothers") who are further described as "worshipping the Most High God" (σεβόμενοι θεὸν ὕψιστον).

The inscriptions contain a curious juxtaposition of Jewish and non-Jewish elements. Schürer (1897), the first to study them in detail, while convinced of the Jewish character of "Most High God" (on the basis of Jewish use of the phrase in other Bosporan inscriptions), nevertheless felt that both the reference to priests and the presence of an eagle on several of the inscriptions militated against a Jewish provenance. He concluded that it was neither Jewish nor pagan, but somewhere in between (Schürer 1897, 225). Even Goodenough, who was convinced that neither of these features would be necessarily out of place in a Jewish environment, nevertheless "hesitate[s] to conclude definitely that the groups were made up of native Jews" (Goodenough 1956–1957, 232), preferring to describe them as "converts" (though not necessarily circumcised). Levinskaya (1996, 105–6) links these inscriptions with the synagogue manumission inscriptions, using both as the foundation for her theory of a widespread, cohesive organization of Gentile God-fearers in the Bosporan kingdom as a whole.

As has been argued above, it is unlikely that the manumission inscriptions provide any firm evidence for Gentile God-fearers apart from the passing reference to θεὸν σέβων in *CIRB* 71. Levinskaya's reconstruction, then, has probably been attempted on too large a scale. Nevertheless, these inscriptions from

62. While θίασος itself does not appear, the members are designated as θιασῶται; σύνοδος has been reconstructed by the editor of the inscription.

Tanais seem to provide evidence for Gentile associations that had adopted some form of reverence for the Jewish God. On the one hand, these associations seem not to be Jewish: the terms by which they are designated are Hellenistic (σύνοδος, θίασος) rather than Jewish (προσευχή, συναγωγή); the lists of names contain none that are clearly Jewish (Levinskaya 1996, 112–13); it would not be necessary for a Jewish person to be adopted into membership (εἰσποιητοι ἀδελφοί). But on the other hand, the use of "Most High God" in a geographical area where the term had definite Jewish associations, together with the language of "worshiping" (σεβόμενοι) God, seems to indicate a definite Jewish coloring to the group. It is likely that these inscriptions were set up by Gentile associations exhibiting some degree of devotion toward the God of the Jews.

If this is the case, one might wonder what Jews would have thought of the presence in these associations of officers designated as priests.[63] A similar question is raised by two further inscriptions that seem to dedicate Gentile altars to the God of Israel.

§220 Altar (Pergamon)

> θεὸς κύριος ὁ ὢν εἰς ἀεί
> Ζώπυρος τῷ κυρίωι τὸν βωμόν καὶ τὴν φωιτοθόρον μετὰ τοῦ φλογούχου
>
> *God Lord who is forever.*
> *Zopyros (dedicated) to the Lord this altar and the lamp-stand with the lantern.*

Text: Nilsson (1956); Bickerman (1980).
Translation: Bickerman (1980)
Date: Second century C.E.
Provenance: Pergamon
Original Language: Greek
Bibliography: Bickerman (1980); Delling (1964); van der Horst (1994, 69–70); Nilsson (1956); Siegert (1973, 142); Trebilco (1991, 163)
Category: SYMPATHIZATION

63. Goodenough does not seem to be aware of the implications here. On the one hand, he is quite right to point out that Jews are often identified as priests in inscriptions (Goodenough 1956–57, 226). Thus the term in and of itself does not indicate a Gentile provenance. But if one concludes—as he does—that the groups were probably made up of Gentile "converts" rather than native-born Jews, then the term takes on quite a different valence. A Gentile could become a proselyte; but he could not become a priest in the Jewish sense of the term. In this case, one can no longer appeal to the designation of Jewish persons as priests to argue that "there is nothing in the inscriptions alien to what we know of the practices of loyal Jews of the period" (Goodenough 1956–57, 233). The idea of a Gentile "convert" who was also a priest would have strained the categories of most loyal Jews of whom we have any evidence.

This inscription was found during the German excavation at Pergamon in the early twentieth century but was first published by Nilsson only in 1956. The dating is uncertain; perhaps it is too late to be properly included here.[64] Commentators are agreed on the Jewish character of the inscription. The combination of θεός and κύριος; the use of κύριος by itself in the second line to refer to the deity;[65] the designation of God as "the one who is forever"[66]—all are too distinctly Jewish to have emerged from a purely Gentile milieu. But what of the altar? Since Jewish sacrifice was restricted to the temple in Jerusalem, if it was an altar that Zopyros was dedicating, it is hard to imagine that he was Jewish.

While most commentators have been inclined to see Zopyros as a Gentile sympathizer of some sort, Trebilco (1991, 163) has attempted to argue that he was Jewish by translating βωμός differently. Since the term in its basic meaning denotes a base or a raised stand, he argues that βωμός referred to the base of the lantern-stand rather than to an altar. But while the translation is possible, it seems unlikely. First, the term would then be redundant. Why would it be necessary to mention both the lantern-stand and its own base or raised stand? But more significantly, the most common use of βωμός was to denote an altar, not only in Hellenistic usage[67] but also in Jewish usage. For example, in the LXX, all forty-five occurrences of the term refer to an altar (usually a pagan altar, but on occasion the altar in Jerusalem). Likewise, both Josephus and Philo use the term exclusively of Jewish altars (in Jerusalem, and others in Biblical history). Why would a Jewish person choose to use a term with such associations when other, less ambiguous terms were readily available? Of course, one could argue that the original setting would have eliminated ambiguity: if the only thing present was a lantern and lantern-stand, no one would have taken the term to refer to an altar. Still, on balance, it seems more probable that the inscription originally stood on an altar erected by a Gentile in honor of the God of Israel.

This is probably all that can be said with any level of confidence. Nilsson (1956; 1967) has used the inscription as evidence to support his theory of a widespread syncretistic movement in which Sabazios was fused with Yahweh; but as we have noted, such theories are ill-founded and have generally been abandoned. Bickerman (1980) has pressed the inscription into the service of a different theory. He has argued that for some Jews at least, the prohibition of

64. Much of the documentation from the original excavation was destroyed in World War II. Nilsson does not venture any opinion about the date. Bickerman (1980, 341), on the basis of lettering, dates it "to the advanced period of the Roman Empire, say second century."

65. For Hellenistic Jewish usage, see Delling (1964, 74–75).

66. Nilsson (1956, 169) pointed to Exod 3:14 (Εγώ εἰμι ὁ ὤν). Delling (1964, 78) rightly observed that in this verse the emphasis is on God's existence rather than eternal nature; he suggested more general parallels to such phrases as ὁ ζῶν εἰς τὸν αἰῶνα (e.g., Sir 18:1; Dan 12:7).

67. See the entry in Liddell and Scott.

sacrifice apart from the Jerusalem temple applied only to Jews, which meant that Gentile altars were not objectionable simply because they were located elsewhere. He sees Zopyros, then, as a God-fearer who has been encouraged by his Jewish tutors to worship God in a manner appropriate to him as a Gentile, that is, by offering sacrifice to the God of Israel. But none of the evidence that he adduces in support of his theory demonstrates that Jews would have approved of, let alone encouraged, the erection of Gentile altars to Israel's God. While the question of Jewish attitudes towards such altars is an interesting one, all the inscription can tell us, if it has been interpreted properly, is that such altars existed.

§221 Altar (Belkis, Pamphylia)

θεῷ ἀψευδ[εῖ καὶ]
ἀχειροποιήτῳ
εὐχήν

For the truthful god who is not made with hands (in fulfilment of) a vow.

Text: Brixhe and Hodot (1988, 124–26; #42)
Translation: van der Horst (1994)
Date: First or second century C.E.
Provenance: Belkis (Pamphylia)
Original Language: Greek
Bibliography: Cohen (1999, 144); van der Horst (1994); Levinskaya (1996, 81–82)
Category: SYMPATHIZATION

This inscription, only recently published, is similar in many respects to the Pergamon inscription just discussed. Once again, we have to do with an inscription that, on the one hand, appears on an altar and that, on the other, uses language with strong Jewish echoes.

Before looking at the Jewish evidence, however, it needs to be noted that the language of the inscription also appears in connection with Sarapis. In an inscription from Pisidia, also published by Brixhe and Hodot (1988, #46), Sarapis is described as ἀψευδής. Further, Clement of Alexandria says of the Egyptian Sarapis that his adherents "even dare to call him the one not made with hands" (ἀχειροποίητον; *Protrepticos* 4.48.1). In both cases, however, the deity is explicitly named. There is nothing to indicate that the adjectives by themselves would carry any connotations of Sarapis worship.

Strong Jewish associations are present, however, in the case of ἀχειροποιήτῳ (not made with hands). To be sure, as van der Horst (1994, 66) has observed, ἀχειροποίητος appears only in Christian usage (Mark 14:58; 2 Cor 5:1; Col 2:11; Clement and other later writers). Both the early date and the locus of the inscription (i.e., an altar) make a Christian identification highly unlikely. But in all probability the early Christian writers formed the term under the influence of the LXX, where its positive counterpart—χειροποίητος (made with hands)—appears fifteen times, always as a rendering of אליל (idol). Christian use of ἀχειροποίητος, then, as a way of referring to things pertaining to the true God, has as its background the Jewish use of χειροποίητος as a technical term for idolatry. The force of the Christian evidence is to suggest that a parallel development has gone on with respect to the language of the inscription. That is, θεὸς ἀχειροποίητος may have been formed under the influence of the LXX as the semantic opposite of the LXX's χειροποίητος—the true God, not a hand-made idol. If so, the term would indicate that the altar had been erected in devotion to the God of Israel.

The other adjective—ἀψευδής—is less distinctive. It rarely appears as a divine epithet in either pagan or Jewish usage (see van der Horst 1994, 65). Still, its presence does nothing to weaken the Jewish associations of ἀχειροποίητος. In the LXX ἀληθινός (true) is often applied to God.[68] Perhaps the synonym ἀψευδής was chosen for stylistic reasons (i.e., two adjectives starting with α-).

While certainty is not possible, the language of this inscription has a strong Jewish ring to it. It is likely that it represents a second instance where a Gentile has erected an altar as a means of expressing some level of devotion towards the God of Israel.

§222 Corpus inscriptionum judaicarum *II 766 or* Monumenta Asiae Minoris Antiqua *VI 264 (Julia Severa)*

This building was erected by Julia Severa; P(ublius) Tyrronios Klados, the head for life of the synagogue, and Lucius, son of Lucius, head of the synagogue, and Publius Zotikos, archon, restored it with their own funds and with money which had been deposited, and they donated the (painted) murals for the walls and the ceiling, and they reinforced the windows and made all the rest of the ornamentation, and the synagogue honoured them with a gilded shield on account of their virtuous disposition, goodwill and zeal for the synagogue.

Text: *CIJ* 766 = *MAMA* VI 264 = Lifshitz (1967, #33)
Translation: Trebilco (1991, 58–59)
Date: Late first century C.E.
Provenance: Acmonia (Phrygia)
Original Language: Greek
Bibliography: Cohen (1999, 147); Feldman (1993, 310); Goodman (1994, 54–55); Mitchell (1993, 2:8–9); Rajak (1999); Ramsay

68. For θεὸς ἀληθινός, see Isa 65:16; 3 Macc 6:18. God is described as ἀληθινός in Exod 34:6; Num 14:18; Ps 85 [86]:15; 3 Macc 2:11; God's deeds or words are ἀληθινός in Deut 32:4; Ps 18 [19]:9; LXX Dan 3:27, 31.

(1897, 637–51); Schürer (1986, 3:30–31); Trebilco (1991, 58–60)

Category: SYMPATHIZATION, CONVERSION

This inscription evidently stood originally in a synagogue in Acmonia (Phrygia). While the synagogue has not survived, there is considerable evidence of Jewish life and presence in the city.[69] Our interest in this inscription has to do primarily with the figure of Julia Severa, though a comment will need to be made about Publius Tyrronios Klados as well. In the inscription itself, Julia Severa is mentioned only in passing; although she is remembered as the founding benefactor, the purpose of the inscription is to honor three subsequent donors (of whom Publius Tyrronios Klados was one) who restored and decorated the synagogue. What has made Julia Severa the focus of scholarly investigation of this inscription, however, is the fact that she is well-known from other inscriptional and numismatic evidence as a wealthy, almost certainly Gentile, woman who played an influential role in the civic and religious affairs of the city.

First, Julia Severa is named on many coins issued in honor of Nero, Agrippina, and Poppaea, her name appearing alongside (and after) that of Servenius Capito. The names are usually introduced by ἐπί, that is, "in the time of." Sometimes αρχ is added, an abbreviation normally indicating ἄρχων or "magistrate."[70] Once, on a coin of Agrippina, we find επι αρχ το γ (the third magistracy), indicating that they had held office for at least three years prior to 58 or 59 C.E. Taken together with the fact that the Poppaea coins did not appear until 63 C.E., this indicates that Julia Severa and Servinius Capito were in office together for at least seven years. In addition, her name appears in a similar construction in an inscription honoring Nicias Lucius as gymnasiarch, this time with Tyrronius Rapon as her partner and this time with her name first.[71] Since Nicias Lucius was gymnasiarch for two game periods of four years each (πενταετηρικούς), Julia Severa's term of office must have lasted for at least eight years. In a further inscription (Ramsay 1897, 647), she is designated as high priestess (ἀρχιερείᾳ), probably of the Imperial cult, and president of the games (ἀγωνοθέτιδι).

On the assumption that "it seems hardly in accordance with ancient custom to associate a man and a women so markedly as is done in [these inscriptions] unless they were married" (Ramsay 1897, 639, n. 2), Ramsay argues that Julia Severa was married first to Servinius Capito and then, after his supposed

69. For the evidence, see Schürer (1986, 3:31) and Mitchell (1993, 2:35). The only possible surviving evidence of the synagogue is in the form of two marble capitals decorated with a menorah and a Torah scroll (Trebilco 1991, 60).

70. Ramsay (1897, 639) suggests that in this case it might mean ἀρχιερεύς (high priest). This suggestion arises from his assumption that the two must have been married (as high priests often were). See further below.

71. Ramsay (1897, 637, #530) = *CIG* 3858.

death in 63 C.E., to Tyrronius Rapon. The argument might have been more plausible if there had been only one co-magistrate. But an assumption that requires us to postulate such a complex sequence of events—a death, a remarriage and a further election of the wife and her new husband as magistrates—is best abandoned. Julia Severa was in all likelihood a well-to-do benefactor and civic leader in her own right, taking her place in civic and religious affairs with members of other leading Acmonian families.[72]

In a recent article, Rajak has suggested the possibility that a second person honored in the inscription can be identified as a Gentile sympathizer—the benefactor Publius Tyrronios Klados (Rajak 1999, 169). Not only does he bear a full Roman name, but the name itself also links him with a distinguished family: as we have seen, another Tyrronios held office alongside Julia herself. Rajak suggests that there is a "good chance, therefore, that in this man we have another pagan notable with an interest in the synagogue."

The problem with this suggestion is the fact that Klados has been appointed *archisunagogos* for life. Rajak suggests that the office might have been an honorary one—having more to do with benefaction than with being in charge of synagogue activity—and thus one that a Gentile might hold. But this does not seem likely. Her second suggestion is more probable, namely, that Klados was a (Jewish) freedman of the Tyrronios family who had taken the name on emancipation. This suggestion has the advantage of providing an explanation for Julia's involvement: she had a patronal interest in the affairs of a freedman who belonged to a family with which she had significant association.

For our purposes, the important question is Julia's relationship not to her co-magistrates nor to her freedmen but to the synagogue and the Jewish community. How are we to understand the combination of synagogue benefaction and pagan high priesthood? On this question there has been a whole spectrum of scholarly opinion. Ramsay takes it as "obvious" that she was Jewish,[73] evidently counting her synagogue benefaction as much more indicative of her ethnic and religious identity than her role as high priestess in the imperial cult. Indeed, remarking on the "strange forms [into which] the Jewish customs had degenerated," he takes her to be representative of a supposed syncretistic form of Judaism prevalent in Asia Minor (Ramsay 1897, 651). Most subsequent scholars, however, have seen Julia Severa as Gentile. Feldman, finding it difficult to combine the two, arranges them sequentially: it was later, after she had converted to Judaism (or at least had become a sympathizer), that she built the

72. For other evidence of the Servenius and Severus families, see Ramsay (1897, 647–49).

73. Ramsay (1897, 650). Surprisingly, he makes no attempt to connect the Publius Tyrronius Klados, mentioned in the inscription as ruler-for-life of the synagogue (ὁ διὰ βίου ἀρχισυνάγωγος), with the Tyrronius Rapon who was Julia's co-magistrate.

synagogue (Feldman (1993, 576, n. 120). More commonly she is seen as a sympathizer in a less exclusive, but still religious, sense—that is, as one who admired aspects of Jewish communal and religious life, but without giving exclusive loyalty to the God of Israel.[74] At the other end of the spectrum are those who downplay the religious element and understand Julia Severa's benefaction less as an act of religious devotion and more as one of patronage designed to win the support of a significant civic subgroup. In Kraabel's words, "It is preferable to attribute what she did to philanthropy and a benevolent attitude toward her Jewish neighbors, even though this is a less 'religious' explanation of her actions."[75]

There can be little doubt that Julia Severa's construction of the synagogue needs to be understood primarily in the context of patron–client relationships and the politics of benefaction. No less than her sponsorship of the games, the donation to the Jewish community was designed to enhance her honor and to help assure her place in civic affairs. Nevertheless, it would not be wise to eliminate the religious element entirely. After all, what she funded was a synagogue, with all its religious associations and significance, not a colonnade or plaza. The Jewish community in Acmonia shows every evidence of having been characterized by a lively and conventional Jewish piety (Trebilco 1991, 58–84). It is hard to imagine a woman of such prominence making a donation of such substance to a community of such religious character without having had some appreciation of Judaism in its religious aspects.

Looking at the relationship from the Jewish side, it is striking that the community was willing to accept benefaction from a Gentile who was so closely identified with pagan religion. Of course, we do not have any clear access to their intentions in so doing, but their willingness should not be taken as evidence for any syncretistic blurring of the lines separating the monotheistic worship of the synagogue from the various civic and imperial cults with which Julia Severa would have been associated. Apparently they were prepared to honor a Gentile who demonstrated support and appreciation for the Jewish community in such a public way without either expecting that she demonstrate exclusive loyalty to the God of Israel or feeling that their own identity was somehow compromised or threatened in the process.

74. See, e.g., Hengel and Schwemer (1997, 68–69).
75. Kraabel (1982, 456). See also Cohen (1999, 147).

Part II

Patterns of Universalism

Chapter 10

Sympathization

With this chapter we turn from commentary to synthesis, attempting to draw conclusions about the patterns of universalism that have been apparent in the texts discussed in Part I. In this chapter we are interested in Gentile sympathization and the ways in which Jews assessed and thought about the phenomenon. More specifically, we are interested in whether some Jews thought it possible for such Gentiles to be acceptable to God (to be "righteous," to have a share in the age to come, and so on) and, if so, what level of attachment to Judaism or degree of sympathization was thought to be necessary or sufficient.

In order to answer this question, however, we have found it necessary to cast our net more widely and to include all passages that describe or refer to such activity (acknowledgement of Israel's God, worship at the temple, adoption of some Jewish customs, attendance at synagogue, exclusive worship of Israel's God, and so on), even if Jewish attitudes are not explicitly indicated. At the same time, we have set some limits. We have not included passages that display nothing more than simple admiration for Judaism, nor have we included those papyri in which the name of Israel's God is invoked (along with many others) in magical incantations, invocations and the like. While the line between sympathization and syncretism is not easy to draw precisely, little would have been gained by including this material here.[1]

1. In some instances it is not possible to determine whether the material stemmed from a Gentile or from a highly Hellenized Jew; see, e.g., the prayer addressed to both Horus and the God of Israel that is an Aramaic reworking of Ps 20:2–6 (Feldman 1993, 573, n. 68). For other examples and discussion, see Cohen (1999, 142); Georgi (1986, 102).

The material under discussion in this chapter is striking in its diversity. While we cannot subject it to a full analysis, we can at least note some of the categories that might bear more careful examination. First, while most of the material comes from Jewish sources, some of it originates with outsiders (Greco-Roman, Christian). Further, at a very general level, we have encountered a great variety of genres: biblical translation (LXX), paraphrase (e.g., Josephus *Antiquities* I-XI), and commentary (e.g., Philo); histories of various kinds (e.g., 2 Maccabees, Josephus, Luke-Acts, Tacitus); biographies (the Gospel of Luke, Plutarch, Suetonius); apologetic tractates (Josephus *Against Apion*); historical "novels" (e.g., *3 Maccabees, Letter of Aristeas*); romances (e.g., *Joseph and Aseneth*); prayers and liturgical texts (*11QPsalms*[a], *4QPrayer of Nabonidus, 4QWords of the Luminaries*); apocalypses (*2 Baruch*); and inscriptions.

Related to the matter of genre, but not correlated to it precisely, is the degree to which the material is presented as ostensibly factual at one end of the spectrum or as patently fictional at the other. Of course, there are distinctions to be made all the way down the line. With inscriptions (e.g., Julia Severa) and with reports of events in which the author was directly involved—for example, the cessation of the sacrifice for the emperor (Josephus *J.W.* 2.409–17) and Philo's account of the annual festival on Pharos (*Moses* 2.41–43)—very little intervenes between the report and the event. But more often the ostensibly factual reports are clearly dependent on sources (e.g., Luke-Acts, Josephus in many instances) or are laden with interpretation (as when royal benefaction for the temple is seen as a sign of piety rather than of *Realpolitik*),[2] in which case we need to reckon with the effect of these intervening layers. And with Josephus's account of the origins of the Septuagint (*Ant.* 12.11–118), in which he takes as sober history an account (*Letter of Aristeas*) that is patently romantic,[3] and the version of the Maccabean revolt presented in 2 Maccabees, in which divine intervention again and again is the decisive factor, we have clearly moved a significant distance toward that portion of the spectrum occupied by such clearly imaginative works as 3 Maccabees, *Joseph and Aseneth*, and the *Letter of Aristeas*. Still, the whole spectrum of material is valuable for our purposes, both for what it assumes its intended readers would take for granted and for what it tells us about the attitudes of the various authors.

The material can also be arrayed along an axis ranging from the general to the specific. Some of the passages discussed above deal with very specific instances involving particular individuals: Heliodorus's comeuppance in the Jerusalem temple (2 Macc 3:33–39), the story of Izates and his mother Helena (*Ant.* 20.34–53), Agrippa's visit to Judea (*Ant.* 16.14), Cicero's reply to Caecilius (Plutarch *Cicero*

2. We have seen many examples: e.g., 2 Macc 3:1–3; Josephus *Ant.* 11.120–32; 13.242–44; Philo *Embassy* 309–10.

3. See also his account of Alexander's visit to Jerusalem; *Ant.* 11.331–36.

7.4–5), and so on. But we also encounter highly generalized statements. Some of these describe sympathization as a universal phenomenon: the temple was "honored throughout the whole world" (2 Macc 3:12); "almost every other people . . . value and honor our laws" (Philo *Moses* 2.17); "not one city, Greek or barbarian, nor a single nation . . ." (Josephus *Ag. Ap.* 2.282); "the customs of this accursed race . . . are now received throughout all the world" (Seneca *On Superstition*). Others assume that the phenomenon is widely known and generally recognized. This is especially true of the Greek and Roman authors (Horace, Ovid, Plutarch, Epictetus), on which more below.

With respect to Gentile sympathization itself, we encounter it in a variety of forms. Occasionally our sources speak generally of Jewish customs or observances[4] or describe Gentiles as engaged in the practice of "Judaizing."[5] Typically, however, we encounter more specific activities or dispositions: honoring the temple or bestowing it with gifts;[6] participating in specific acts of veneration at the temple (prayer, worship, sacrifice);[7] attending synagogue services or associating with the synagogue;[8] recognizing the truth and value of the law;[9] adopting specific Jewish customs and observances, especially the Sabbath[10] and abstinence from pork;[11] and honoring God, making vows to God, acknowledging the God of the Jews as the supreme deity, or even worshipping this God exclusively.[12] As we have noted, Cohen has attempted to discern two distinct types of Judaizing or sympathization—support for the Jews as a political entity on the one hand and association with the Jews and Judaism as a culture on the other. But there is little evidence in the material surveyed here for such a clear distinction. To be sure, different aspects of Judaism can be highlighted. Sometimes Judaism is presented as an exclusive, monotheistic form of worship in which one can participate; sometimes it appears as a social entity with its

4. E.g., Josephus *J.W.* 2.560; *Ant.* 20.17; *Ag. Ap.* 1.166; 2.282; Seneca *On Superstition.*

5. LXX Esth 8:17; Josephus *J.W.* 2.454; 2.463; Plutarch *Cicero* 7.5.

6. E.g., 2 Macc 3:12; 5:16; 9:11–18; 4 Macc 4:11–12; *2 Bar.* 68:5–6; Philo *Embassy* 157, 291–320; 4QDibHam 1–2 IV, 2–13; Josephus *J.W.* 2.340–41; 2.409–17; 4.181; 5.562–64; *Ant.* 12.11–118; 13.78, 242–44; 14.110; *Ag. Ap.* 2.48.

7. E.g., 2 Macc 3:33–39; 9:11–18; 13:23; 3 Macc 1:9; Josephus *J.W.* 4.275; 5.15–18; *Ant.* 3.318–19; 8.116–17; 11.87, 331–36; 16.14; 18.122; *Ag. Ap.* 2.48; John 12:20.

8. Ovid *Remedies for Love* 218–20; various passages in Luke-Acts; several inscriptions (CIRB 71; MAMA VI 264 [Julia Severa]).

9. E.g., *Let. Aris.* 4–7, 176–78; Philo *Moses* 2.17–43; Josephus *Ant.* 3.214–17; *Ag. Ap.* 2.45.

10. E.g., Philo *Moses* 2.21; Josephus *Ag. Ap.* 2.282; Horace *Satires* 1.9.63–72; Ovid *Art of Love* 1.75–76, 413–16; *Remedies for Love* 218–20; Plutarch *On Superstition* 3 (166A).

11. Seneca *Moral Letters* 108.22; Plutarch *Cicero* 7.4–5; Juvenal *Satires* 14.96–106.

12. E.g., 2 Macc 3:33–39; LXX Esth 16:15–16; *Jos. Asen.* 3:3–4; 4.7; 18:1, 11; 20:7; 21:6;11QPs[a] XXIV, 8–9; 4QPrNab ar; Philo *Embassy* 245; Josephus *J.W.* 2.201; *Ant.* 11.3–5, 103, 120–32, 331–36; 13.69–71; 18.286–309; CIRB 1260; altar inscriptions (§§217, 218).

own particular culture into which one can be incorporated.[13] Sometimes it is a way of life prescribed by the Torah, something akin to a philosophy that can be followed and "imitated";[14] alternatively, the law is sometimes presented as the constitution of a political entity that one can support or of which one can even become a citizen.[15] But these appear as aspects of a single phenomenon rather than distinct types of sympathization.

We also encounter considerable variety in the identity and social class of the sympathizers. Perhaps the most frequently encountered "sympathizer" is a foreign king or sovereign,[16] usually (but not always) one whose domain included the land of Israel.[17] In the same category are court officials, royal emissaries, members of the family, and so on.[18] Many of these references need to be seen as narrative wishful thinking[19] or, as we have seen, as the imputation of pious motives for what was in reality an act of normal diplomatic practice. Still, the example of Helena and Izates indicates that this was not always the case. Other passages make reference to common people in distinction from rulers, such as Philo's reference to "ordinary citizens and rulers alike" (*Moses* 2.43) or that of Josephus to "the masses" (πλήθεσιν; *Ag. Ap.* 2.282). More particular groups are sometimes singled out: philosophers;[20] women;[21] Greeks;[22] Romans;[23] or, more generally, the "nations."[24] We also have encountered a variety of individuals: the soldier Metilius (Josephus *J.W.* 2.454); the governor Petronius;[25] the freedman Caecilius (Plutarch *Cicero* 7.4–5); Philocrates, the pious addressee of the *Letter of Aristeas* (1–8); and so on. In addition, as we have already observed, our

13. *Joseph and Aseneth*; Philo *Spec. Laws* 1.52; Josephus *J.W.* 7.45.

14. On Judaism as a philosophy, see, e.g., Philo *Embassy* 245; Josephus *Ag. Ap.* 2.47, 279–84. On imitation, see Aristobulus (frag. 4; P.E. 13.12.6–7); Josephus *Ag. Ap.* 1.166; 1.225; 2.163; 2.255–57; 2.260–61; 2.279–84.

15. Philo *Spec. Laws* 1.52; Josephus *Ant.* 1.1–15.

16. 2 Macc 3:1–3; 5:16; 9:11–18; 13:23; LXX Esth 16:15–16; 3 Macc 1:9; 6:33; *Let. Aris.* 176–178; *Jos. Asen.* 21:6; 4QPrNab ar; Philo *Embassy* 157; Josephus *J.W.* 5.562–64; *Ant.* 11.3–5, 103, 120–32, 331–36; 12.11–118; 13.69–71, 78, 242–44; 20.34–53; *Ag. Ap.* 2.45, 48. Suetonius *Augustus* 93.

17. Exceptions include Ptolemy II Philadelphus in the *Letter of Aristeas* and the royal family of Adiabene (Josephus *Ant.* 20.34–53).

18. 2 Macc 3:33–39; *Jos. Asen.* 3:3–4; 4:7. 20:7; Philo *Embassy* 291–320; Josephus *J.W.* 2.201, 340–41; *Ant.*16.14; 18.122, 286–309; 20. 195.

19. E.g., the various figures in 2 Maccabees; Ptolemy in the *Letter of Aristeas*; Alexander in Josephus *Ant.* 11.331–36.

20. Josephus *Ag. Ap.* 2.260–62, 279–84; *Letter of Aristeas* 201, 235.

21. Josephus *J.W.* 2.559–61; Acts 13:50; 17:12.

22. Josephus *J.W.* 7.45; *Ant.* 3.214–17; Plutarch *On Superstition* 3 (166A).

23. Josephus *J.W.* 4.181; Valerius Maximus (§175).

24. *2 Bar* 68:5–6; 11QPs[a]; 4QDibHam 1–2 IV, 2–13; Philo *Moses* 2.25.

25. Philo *Embassy* 245; Josephus *Ant.* 18.286–309.

sources do not refrain from hyperbolic references to the "whole inhabited world from end to end."[26]

Also to be noted are indications of degree—that is to say, statements indicating that sympathization with Judaism is something that Gentiles could engage in to a lesser or greater extent, with full conversion as the ultimate stage or level. This is readily apparent in the story of Helena and Izates, where the king's circumcision culminates a process of increasing adoption of Jewish ways (Josephus *Ant.* 20.34–53). A spectrum of sympathization, culminating in conversion, is also implied by the desperate promises of Metilius "to Judaize as far as circumcision" (Josephus *J.W.* 2.454) and of Antiochus not only to shower benefactions on the Jews but "in addition to all this . . . [to] become a Jew" (2 Macc 9:17). Juvenal provides us with a scathingly critical account of a family that moves through this full spectrum within two generations (*Satires* 14.96–106), and Epictetus speaks more generally of a similar process (*Discourses* 2.9.19–21). Closely related to these passages are several in which attention is paid to the distinction between sympathization and full conversion—especially the debate between Izates's advisors Ananias and Eleazar, and Josephus's distinction between "casual visitors" and members of the household (*Ag. Ap.* 2.209–10). On several occasions we find reference to the ambiguous status of Gentile sympathizers or to the partial character of their identification with Judaism: Josephus describes Gentile sympathizers in Antioch as being "in some measure incorporated" into the Jewish community there (*J.W.* 7.45) and, more generally, of Gentiles who constituted an "ambiguous" and "mixed" element in the cities of Syria (*J.W.* 2.462–63); the passage from Epictetus describes a situation of someone "halfway in between" two worlds. Also to be mentioned here are texts in which it is said or implied that sympathization with Judaism was combined with ongoing non-Jewish religious practice: the foreigners settlers in LXX 4 Kgdms 17:34, who "fear" the God of the land but follow their own "regulations"; Petronius, who had acquired some "glimmers" of Jewish "philosophy and piety" (Philo *Embassy* 245); Julia Severa, who both served as priestess of a local cult and provided generous benefaction to the Jewish community (§222); Gentiles who constructed their own altars in honor of the Jewish God (§§220, 221); and Bosporus slave owners responsible for manumission documents that invoke both the God of Israel and pagan deities (§§216, 218).

Finally, we need to make some observations about vocabulary and terminology. Again we encounter considerable variety. We begin at the most basic level, the ways in which "Gentiles" or non-Jews are designated.[27] "Nations" is

26. This is Philo's phrase (*Moses* 2.20).

27. For convenience the material in this paragraph deals with texts discussed in the whole of Part I, not simply those dealing with sympathization. There is no need to subdivide the material according to our analytical categories.

found frequently, of course, often modified by "all."[28] "All" appears in other formulations, either alone[29] or in combination (e.g., "all [other] human beings";[30] "all flesh" [*T. Jud.* 24:4]; "all peoples" [*1 En.* 10:21; *T. Jud.* 25:5; 11QPs[a] (11Q5) XXIV, 9]; "whole world" [2 Macc 3:12]; "whole earth" [*1 En.* 91:14]). "Man" appears in various phrases: "race of men" (Philo *Mos.* 2.27); "seed of man" (Sir 10:19); "sons of men" (*T. Zeb.* 9:8). Assorted other terms appear: the "others";[31] "the rest" (*Let. Aris.* 140); "the sons of earth" (*1 En.* 105:1); the "inhabited world";[32] various terms for "alien" or "foreigner";[33] "strangers";[34] "mortals."[35]

With respect to sympathization itself, while some terms and vocabulary sets reoccur, for the most part the description tends to vary from author to author and from context to context.[36] Clearly defined or widely accepted terminology seems to be lacking; there is little evidence for technical terms or standardized language. Still, some patterns are apparent and worthy of notice, especially in Greek texts. The term that perhaps spans the broadest cultural distance is Ἰουδαΐζειν (to Judaize), found in Jewish, Christian and pagan sources.[37] Nouns and verbs from the root τιμ- (honor) are also frequent in Jewish literature,[38] as are forms of ζηλ- (zeal, eagerness, eager emulation).[39] The vocabulary of piety (ευσεβ-) is also used by a number of authors.[40] The verb προσκυνεῖν (to

28. "All the nations": e.g., *T. Zeb.* 9:8; *2 Bar.* 72:5; *Ps. Sol.* 17:34; 4QDibHam (4Q504) 1–2 IV, 8. "Nations": e.g., Tob 13:11; 14:6; *2 Bar.* 68:5; 72:2; *Jos. Asen.*15:7; *T. Levi* 18:9; *T. Jud.* 24:6; *T. Naph.* 8:3; *2 En.* 48:7; Josephus *Ant.* 11.285.

29. 2 Macc 3:34; Philo *Moses* 2.43.

30. 4 Macc 4:12; Josephus *J.W.* 5.17; *Ant.* 11.87; *Ag. Ap.* 2.284; Philo *Embassy* 210; *1 En.* 10:21.

31. *1 En.* 50:2; Philo *Mos.* 2.17; 2.25; Josephus *Ag. Ap.* 2.163, 293.

32. Philo *Mos.* 2.20; Josephus *J.W.* 4.262, 324; *T. Ab.* 10:12; *T. Levi* 18:3.

33. Josephus *J.W.* 2.409; 4.275; 5.18, 563; *Ag. Ap.* 2.121, 209; Philo *QG* 3.62.

34. Josephus *J.W.* 5.15; *Ant.* 3.214.

35. *Sib. Or.* 3:195, 601; 4:162; 5:331.

36. If we were extending this study into the rabbinic material, we would need to look at references to the "fearers of heaven" (יראי שמים; e.g., *Pesiqta Rabbati* 42.1; 43.4; *y. Megilla* 1.11 III; *Deuteronomy Rabbah* 2.24) and to the "resident alien" (גר תושב; e.g., *Mekilta* Bahodesh 7 [to Exod 20:10]; Kaspa 3 [to Exod 23:12]; *y. Yebamot* 8.1).

37. LXX Esther 8:17; Josephus *J.W.* 2.454, 463; Gal 2:14; Plutarch *Cicero* 7.4–5. Cf. Suetonius' description of someone having "lived a Jewish life" (*Iudaicam viverent vitam;* Domitian 12.2).

38. E.g., 2 Macc 3:2, 12; Philo *Moses* 2.15–20; *Embassy* 291; Josephus *J.W.* 4.262; 5.563; *Ant.* 3.217; 11.120, 336); cf. *2 Bar.* 68.5–6; 11QPs[a] XXIV, 9; 4QPrNab ar 5; 4 Q DibHam 1–2 IV, 11.

39. Josephus *Ant.* 20.41; *Ag. Ap.* 1.162, 166, 225; 2.257, 280, 282, 286; Philo *Moses* 2.31, 43.

40. E.g., 2 Macc 3:1; *Let. Aris.* 2, 4; Philo *Embassy* 245, 319; Josephus *Ant.* 11.120; 13.69, 242; Acts 10:2; 13:50.

worship) also appears in more than one source.[41] The adjective "righteous," which is used by R. Joshua later in *t. Sanh.* 13.2, appears also in Acts 10:22. Finally because of their importance in the "God-fearer" debate, special mention should be made of the verbs φοβεῖν (to fear)[42] and σέβειν (to reverence).[43]

To this point, these summarizing comments have been primarily descriptive; I have simply drawn attention to some things that become apparent when we look at the surface level of these texts and writings, taken together as a group rather than individually. But our primary concern here is with what these texts can tell us about Jewish attitudes and beliefs in the period under consideration. We need to reckon with variety and diversity in this area as well. Each text should be seen on its own terms and as providing evidence in the first instance for its own author, context, and intended readership. We need to be wary of broad assertions and generalized conclusions. Thus to a certain extent our goal has already been accomplished, in that we have already drawn conclusions for most of the individual passages, writings, and authors. Still, none of these texts existed in a hermetically sealed environment. As long as one proceeds with caution, it is not inappropriate to expect that they might point beyond themselves and reveal something about larger realities.

First, there can be little doubt about the phenomenon itself: Gentile sympathizers existed throughout the areas represented by these texts and in sufficient numbers that the phenomenon was widely recognized not only by Jews themselves but also by outsiders.[44]

To be sure, it is not my purpose here to attempt anything like a thick or localized description of the phenomenon.[45] It is enough to be able to say in more general terms that it existed. Of course, not much weight can be placed on material that clearly is describing imaginative or ideal worlds rather than immediate realities (e.g., 2 Maccabees, *Letter of Aristeas*), or on hyperbolic assertions (Jewish customs have won the attention "of the whole inhabited world"; Philo *Moses* 2.20), or on gullible historiography (e.g., Josephus's face-value

41. E.g, Josephus *J.W.* 4.262; *Ant* 11.87; Philo *Embassy* 310.

42. The foreign settlers "fear" the God of the land (LXX 4 Kgdms 17:34); in Acts the participle is used both attributively (10:2, 22) and substantively (10:35; 13:16, 26); Juvenal uses the Latin equivalent *metuo* on two occasions in *Satires* 14.96–106.

43. Josephus uses σέβειν τὸν θεόν twice (*Ant.* 11.87; 20.34); the participle, used substantively (σεβομένων τὸν θεόν), appears in *Ant.*14.110; the adjective θεοσεβής is found in *Ant.* 20.195. Luke uses the participle both attributively (Acts 13:43, 50; 17:4) and substantively (16:14; 17:17; 18:7). σέβειν τὸν θεόν seems to appear on one inscription (CIRB 71).

44. This is widely recognized by scholars; Kraabel's claim to the contrary has received little support. See, e.g., Cohen (1999, 140–62); J. J. Collins (2000, 265–72); Feldman (1986; 1993); Hengel and Schwemer (1997, 61–76); Schürer (1986, 3:161–71); Segal (1990, 93–96); Wander (1998).

45. Such as Barclay has carried out for Diaspora Judaism more generally (Barclay 1996).

acceptance of the story in the *Letter of Aristeas*). But other texts are tied more tightly to social realities. As we have noted, we can have considerable confidence in information arising from inscriptions (due account being taken of transcriptional or interpretive problems) or from first-person accounts. There is no reason to doubt that Julia Severa built a synagogue in Acmonia or that Philo participated in an annual festival on the island of Pharos in which non-Jews were typically present.

Further, statements about current realities that are more general in character—even if ornamented with hyperbole—tell us something about actual shared perceptions of reality. Take, for example, Josephus's comment that "the masses have long since shown a keen desire to adopt our religious observances." Since he makes the statement not for its own sake but in support of a more general *apologia* for the virtues of the Jewish law, it is hard to imagine him adducing such an argument if neither he nor his intended readers were aware of at least *some* Gentiles who exhibited at least *some* desire to adopt at least *some* Jewish observances. Similarly, while questions can be raised about specific aspects of Luke's narrative in Acts, he seems to take it for granted that his readers will be fully familiar with the social realities portrayed in his synagogue scenes. A principle of verisimilitude can be invoked in many of these cases, especially when the theme of Gentile sympathization is introduced in the service of some other rhetorical agenda.

Finally, the evidence from Jewish sources receives decisive confirmation from material originating with outside observers who had no vested interest in the phenomenon. Since he found the situation lamentable, for example, Seneca would have had no reason to invent the complaint that Jewish customs "are now received throughout the world" (§180). Cicero's pun as reported by Plutarch (*Cicero* 7.4–5) depends for its force on a general recognition that Caecilius, who was "given to Jewish practices," was a typical member of a larger group. Epictetus's description of a Gentile sympathizer—"He is not a Jew, he is only acting the part" (*Discourses* 2.9.19–21)—is presented as a common saying, which in turn indicates that the situation described was common as well. The phenomenon was sufficiently widespread and well established that general awareness of it could be taken for granted.

Moving a step closer to the question of Jewish attitudes, it is appropriate to look briefly at Israel's scriptures and to note the various threads of biblical material that at least had the potential to suggest or support the idea of a positive relationship between Gentiles and Israel's God. To be sure, we need to guard against prejudging the matter. Many of the references to Gentile sympathizers in the post-biblical period do not tell us much about the attitude of the Jewish community towards them, and we should not rush to fill the gap by appealing to "universalistic" themes accessible to all Jews through their scriptures. Still, such themes are present, which means that even if this is not the place for a full study,[46] it will nevertheless be helpful to cast a cursory glance in this direction.

The canon strikes a universal note right at the outset. While much of Genesis consists of narratives concerning Israel's patriarchs (Gen 12–50), these are preceded by primordial accounts of the creation of the world and the origins of human culture (Gen 1–11). These accounts serve to place Israel's story within a larger framework, so that the God who eventually calls Abraham to be the progenitor of a special nation is first encountered as the creator of the cosmos and the providential overseer of every nation. Of particular note is the role played by the two most prominent human figures in this section—Adam and Noah. Both of them, along with their families, stand in a relationship with God that includes blessing, commandment, judgment, and promise. Since both of them evidently represent all of their descendants in some way (Gen 2:24; 3:20; 9:1–17), these passages suggest that these relationships are somehow paradigmatic for humankind as a whole. Israel's story is thus set within the universal story of God's dealings with the whole human race, rather than over against it. And while the angle of vision is inevitably narrowed in the patriarchal narratives, the universal framework is glimpsed at several points, especially in the recurring promise that Abraham and his family would be a source of blessing for "all the families of the earth" (Gen 12:3; also 22:18; 26:4).

In the rest of the Pentateuch, the inclusion of the nations within the divine scheme of things appears primarily in the legislation concerning the גרים, the "sojourners" who lived in the land of Israel as resident aliens and who were included in significant ways in the cult and culture of Israel. Since this material contributed in significant ways to the development of the proselyte concept, we will look at it in more detail in the next chapter. But in its original context in the Torah, where there is no real concept of conversion, this material provides another example of Gentiles relating to the God of Israel as Gentiles.

The historical books contain a smattering of universalistic material. Solomon's prayer at the inauguration of the Jerusalem temple (1 Kgs 8:23–53) is particularly striking. Solomon envisages a series of occasions in which people might appeal to God at the temple. In one of them, the petitioners are non-Israelites:

> Likewise when a foreigner [נכרי], who is not of your people Israel, comes from a distant land because of your name—for they shall hear of your great name, your mighty hand, and your outstretched arm—when a foreigner comes and prays toward this house, then hear in heaven your dwelling place, and do according to all that the foreigner calls to you, so that all the peoples of the earth [כל עמי הארץ] may know your name and fear you, as do your people Israel, and so that they may know that your name has been invoked on this house that I have built. (1 Kgs 8:41–43)

46. See, e.g., Bockmuehl (2000, 88–97); Goldenberg (1998); Kraus (1996, 16–44); Martin-Achard (1962); Schnabel (2004, 55–91); Senior and Stuhlmueller (1983).

Equally generous in its outlook is the story of Naaman (2 Kgs 5), even if the temple plays no part in the events. After his leprosy is healed, Naaman declares, "Now I know that there is no God in all the earth except in Israel" and "[I] will no longer offer burnt offering or sacrifice to any god except the LORD" (2 Kgs 5:15, 17). His declaration of devotion to the God of Israel is diminished only slightly by his request to be forgiven for those times when, accompanying his master to worship, he would find it necessary to "bow down in the house of Rimmon" (2 Kgs 5:18). One can also mention the story of Ruth the Moabitess, who is incorporated into Israel through marriage to Boaz, thus becoming the great-grandmother of David.

In the Psalms, the nations are frequently invited to join Israel in praising the LORD. Psalm 96 is typical:

> Ascribe to the LORD, O families of the peoples [מִשְׁפְּחוֹת עַמִּים],
> ascribe to the LORD glory and strength.
> Ascribe to the LORD the glory due his name;
> bring an offering, and come into his courts.
> Worship the LORD in holy splendor;
> tremble before him, all the earth. (Ps 96:8–9)

Or again: "Praise the LORD, all you nations [כָּל־גּוֹיִם]; extol him all you peoples" (Ps 117:1). The assumption here and elsewhere (e.g., Pss 47; 148) is that Israel's God is the God of all the nations and that it is appropriate for all nations to offer their own praise and worship to this universal deity.

In the prophetic corpus, a universal outlook appears primarily in the future tense, as prophets looked forward to a time when the nations would recognize Israel's God and seek to worship this God in Zion. This material will come up for discussion in chapter 13. Of course, such an emphasis on the future is not incompatible with an openness to Gentile worship in the present. One of the characteristics of eschatological expectation is that it looks to the future for the establishment of a state of affairs that would exist in the present if people would behave as they should. But in addition, one can mention the book of Jonah, in which we read of God's concern in the present for "Nineveh, that great city, in which there are more than a hundred and twenty thousand persons who do not know their right hand from their left" (Jonah 4:11)[47] and of their readiness to "turn from their evil ways" and to "cry mightily to God" (Jonah 3:8).

Of course, in the scriptural fabric as a whole such universalistic threads are woven together with contrasting material, in which the emphasis is placed on the wickedness of the Gentiles, the need for Israel to remain separate from the

47. We will not pause to wonder about the kind of universalism reflected by the attention given to animals in the story—i.e., their participation in the public display of repentance, even to the point of being covered in sackcloth, and God's expression of concern for them (Jonah 3:7–8; 4:11)!

nations around them, and the certainty of divine punishment. The purpose of this brief discussion is not to sketch the whole woven pattern but simply to draw attention to this particular thread, thus to make the point that Israel's scriptures contained raw material for the idea that Gentiles might be able to recognize the God of Israel as their God as well and to worship this God in appropriate ways as Gentiles.

Turning to the question of Jewish attitudes more directly, we need to ask whether our material reflects any sense of a clearly defined class or category (or of classes and categories) or whether we are dealing instead with a blurry and ill-defined penumbra. Certainly, we can speak of a clear and generally recognized line of demarcation at one end of the phenomenon. Jewish, Christian, and Greco-Roman writers alike are aware of the difference between what we are calling Gentile sympathizers and those who take the necessary steps (usually involving circumcision) to become full converts.[48] But it is much more difficult to identify any line of demarcation at the other end, some set of minimum requirements that a Gentile would need to fulfil in order to belong to a specific class existing somewhere between pagan outsiders and full converts. The absence of any technical terminology is one indicator. True, there are indications that certain word groups were commonly used with reference to the phenomenon. But σεβ- language can be used to describe both Poppaea (θεοσεβής), whose level of adherence to Judaism must have been minimal at best, and Izates (τὸ θεῖον σέβειν), who lacked only circumcision,[49] and piety (εὐσέβεια) can be ascribed alike to Augustus, Cornelius, and Izates;[50] all this indicates that the language was not used with any precision. While it was readily apparent to observers both inside and out that there were different degrees of sympathization, there seems to have been little interest in more precise definition. In particular, we do not encounter any recognition of distinct categories (other than that of full conversion), nor do we see any concerted attempt to define a minimum level of sympathization such as would serve to create a distinct category or recognized class.

To put this observation within a larger framework, we find little indication of a compelling need in this period to think about the religious status of Gentile sympathizers. In much of the literature that we have examined, Gentile sympathizers

48. Josephus brings the distinction into clear focus on a couple of occasions (*Ant.* 20.34–53; *Ag. Ap.* 2.209–10). Luke recognizes that, despite his piety, the uncircumcised Cornelius (Acts 10–11) is in a different category than the proselyte Nicolaus (Acts 6:5). Likewise Epictetus (*Discourses* 2.9.19–21) and Juvenal (*Satires* 14.96–106) recognize the distinction between a Gentile who is "only acting the part" and one who "has made his choice" and thus "both is a Jew and is also called one," to use Epictetus' language.

49. Poppaea: Josephus *Ant.* 20.195; Izates: *Ant.* 20.41.

50. Augustus: Philo *Embassy* 319; Cornelius: Acts 10:2 (εὐσεβής); Izates: Josephus *Ant.*, 20.44.

come into view not so much for their own sake as for their usefulness in other rhetorical agendas. In an idealized historical narrative such as 2 Maccabees, the transformation of a Holofernes (or an Antiochus IV) from an adversary into a worshipper of Israel's God and a witness to God's power serves to vindicate Israel's own self-understanding and to move the intended readers to follow the models of Jewish faithfulness on which the narrative turns. In the apologetic work of a Philo or a Josephus, the eagerness displayed by "the masses" for the laws and practices of Judaism is recounted primarily to demonstrate the inherent virtue of the Jewish law and the honorable character of those whose law it is. The debate between R. Eliezer and R. Joshua as to whether there are any Gentiles who can be described as righteous and who will therefore have a place in the age to come[51] does not seem to have been a pressing one in our period.

This does not mean that the question was not posed at all. We have encountered at least one explicit debate on the question, that between Izates' advisors Ananias and Eleazar. Eleazar takes a position somewhat akin to that of his namesake, Rabbi Eliezer. For him, sympathization is just a station on the road to full conversion. Gentiles who start down the road but fail to press on to its end are, in some ways, worse off than when they began. Before, they might have claimed innocence. But through association with the Jewish community they inevitably become aware of the full array of God's commands, which they then ignore at their peril. For Eleazar, the law in its entirety is incumbent on humanity in its entirety; Gentiles need to assume the full law in order to be pleasing to God. Ananias, however, took the position that while conversion was admirable, Izates was able to "worship God" in an acceptable way without being circumcised. Although the text is somewhat ambiguous and open to differing interpretations, it seems unlikely that Ananias was suggesting the possibility of Izates becoming a convert in every respect but circumcision. Instead, it is better to understand him as saying that it was sufficient for Izates as a Gentile to worship God exclusively and to adopt some suitable set of Jewish observances. We might wish that he had been more forthcoming on what observances were essential, but Ananias's position was soon eclipsed by that of Eleazar and thus disappears from the narrative.

51. *T. Sanh.* 13.2. No indication is given in this passage as to the criteria for righteousness. It is possible that such criteria are to be found in the Noahide commandments (purportedly given by God to Noah and thus to the whole Gentile world; *t. 'Abod. Zar.* 8.4–8; *Mekilta* Baḥodesh 1 [to Exod 19:2]; Baḥodesh 5 [to Exod 20:2]; *Sifre Deut.* 322; 343). The first explicit connection between "righteous Gentiles" and the Noahide commandments is not found until Maimonides (see Schoeps 1963, 13; Gaston 1987, 23), but it seems plausible that R. Joshua and those of like mind would have held the opinion that any of Noah's offspring who adhered to these commandments would have done all that God had required of them and thus were "righteous" (see Bockmuehl 2000, 158; Novak 1984; E. P. Sanders 1985, 216; Segal 1993, 178; but cf. Goldenberg 1998, 88–89, 161, n. 47).

But the most important aspect of the material under discussion in this chapter is not the relative absence of explicitly positive statements such as that attributed to Ananias in *Ant.* 20.41 but the almost complete absence of the attitude exhibited by Eleazar. The phenomenon of Gentile sympathization is rarely seen in negative light.[52] In this chapter we have seen some instances where it is presented in a neutral way,[53] but more typically the attitude is positive. In passage after passage, the assumption seems to be that those Gentiles who acknowledge God, who worship at the temple, or who adopt Jewish ways are doing something commendable. There is little indication that these practices are seen simply as a good start or as defective in any way. Rather, such Gentiles seem to be presented as fulfilling what might legitimately be expected of them as Gentiles and thus as standing in an appropriate relationship with Israel's God. To be sure, this literature takes a sufficiently strong stand against polytheism and "idolatry" that syncretistic worship would certainly be seen as defective and thus out of bounds. But the impression is given that Gentiles who engaged in monotheistic worship, who recognized the divine origin of Israel's law, and who adopted a Jewish way of life to a certain extent were thereby fulfilling everything that God expected of them as Gentiles. Of course, we might wish for more precision, particularly in the latter area. What aspects of a Jewish way of life were important? To what extent did they need to be adopted? While one can discern the profile of a "righteous Gentile" in general terms, detailed portraits are lacking. The literature under review shows little interest in pressing the question, though in chapter 12 we will trace attempts to come at the question from a different angle.

Finally, we can make some brief and preliminary observations concerning Jewish initiative. Our most extensive discussion of this issue took place in conjunction with Josephus's literary agenda, and in particular the debate between Cohen and Mason as to Josephus's purposes.[54] There I tended to agree with Mason that Josephus was addressing himself to a readership that included Gentile sympathizers and that one of his purposes was to reinforce their admiration for Judaism and the law; but I also expressed doubt that adding to their number was a primary purpose. The balance between Gentile attraction and Jewish initiative that needs to be struck in the case of Josephus seems to obtain elsewhere as well. On the one hand, the fact that Gentiles are interested in Judaism and Jewish ways is frequently taken for granted. The penumbra of Gentile sympathizers is something assumed rather than something that needs

52. Subsequent chapters contain comments on others who shared Eleazar's opinion that proselytism was the only acceptable option for Gentiles (ch. 11) and on those who saw Gentiles as categorically excluded from divine favor (ch. 14). But such opinions rarely come into view in passages describing the phenomenon of sympathization itself.

53. E.g., many of the occurrences in Josephus' *Jewish War*.

54. See the introductory section in ch. 6 above.

to be created or encouraged. The innate attractiveness of the law is its best advocate (*Ag. Ap.* 2.279–84); in Juvenal's satire about the father and son (§192), progressive Judaization appears to be solely the result of their own desires and initiatives. Yet on the other hand, particular instances of Jewish initiative do appear. The activity of Ananias and Eleazar, Izates' advisors, provides us with the most explicit example. But we have also noted a variety of other indications: Josephus's statement that the Jews in Antioch had incorporated Gentiles into their community to a certain extent (*J. W.* 7.45); the psalmist's hope that as God instructs him in the law, "many may hear of [God's] deeds and nations may honour [God's] glory" (11QPs[a] XXIV, 8–9); Seneca's lament that the vanquished Jews have "given" their laws to their victors (§180); Valerius Maximus's statement (found in both epitomes) to the effect that the Jews had "tried to pass on their religion to the Romans" (§178). But further pertinent material will come to view in subsequent chapters, and we will need to return to the issue.

Chapter 11

Conversion

Viewed from one angle, the material under discussion in this chapter represents a decisive and categorical step beyond sympathization. As long as he remained uncircumcised, Izates was not "genuinely a Jew" (Josephus *Ant.* 20.38); he was a "casual visitor" rather than a member of the household, to use another phrase from Josephus (*Ag. Ap.* 2.209–10). Yet as Juvenal's lament indicates (*Satires* 14.96–106) and as the example of Izates demonstrates, conversion was often the end result of a process that moved through several stages of sympathization. From another angle of view, then, conversion appears as sympathization taken to its highest level. If there is a spectrum of sympathizers (though the image is a little too linear for what was much more complex in reality),[1] converts stand at the high-intensity end of the spectrum. While Metilius was not a typical convert, his promise that he would "Judaize as far as circumcision" (§136; Josephus *J.W.* 2.454) conforms to a typical pattern.

This being so, it is not surprising that some observations from the previous chapter carry over into this one. Again we encounter a diversity of voices (Jewish, Greco-Roman, Christian) and a variety of genres. Indeed, many of the authors and writings discussed in chapter 10 have reappeared here. Again there is little reason to doubt the reality of the phenomenon. Proselyte inscriptions found in Jewish burial plots (§§205, 207–10), the remains of Queen Helena's family tomb in Jerusalem, gratuitous references by Greek and Roman authors

1. As an alternative, Wander (1998, 229) suggests a set of overlapping (not concentric) circles, along the lines of the five rings in the Olympic logo.

who assume that the phenomenon will be readily recognized by their readers (§§183, 185, 192)—all testify that conversion was a widespread social reality.

As in the previous chapter, conversion accounts appear in imaginative narrative fiction as well. In chapter 10 we observed that sympathization appears frequently as a plot element in a story of vindication: the truth of Jewish belief and the power of Israel's God is demonstrated and affirmed when an Alexander (Josephus *Ant.* 11.331–36) or a Heliodorus (2 Macc 3) or a Ptolemy (*Let. Aris.*) recognizes it and displays appropriate levels of honor and veneration. Although such recognition rarely reaches the level of full conversion, there are a few such instances. Achior's conversion, which came about when he "saw all that the God of Israel had done" in the defeat of Holofernes (Jdt 14:10)—is an exemplary case in point. Antiochus's deathbed offer to become a Jew (2 Macc 9:17) functions in a similar way, though in this case the author's purpose is better served by having the offer soundly rejected. The story of Helena and Izates, however, is more typical of material under discussion in this chapter. While their conversion serves to underscore Josephus's primary thesis concerning God's power and faithfulness, in this case the point is not restricted to Israel: "God thus demonstrated that those who fix their eyes on him and trust in him alone"—whether native-born Jew or Gentile—"do not lose the reward of their piety" (*Ant.* 20.48; cf. 1.14). Here the conversion and incorporation of outsiders is presented as part of Israel's social reality, significant for its own sake.

Before we turn to the vocabulary of conversion directly, it is appropriate to look at the biblical material dealing with the גר, the resident alien, material that provided both terminological and conceptual raw material for the later phenomenon. There are ninety-two occurrences of גר in the MT, sixty-eight of which are found in the Pentateuch. The term, often rendered as "sojourner" or "resident alien," designates a foreigner who lives in the midst of another people and culture. Occasionally the term is used of Israelites—for example, Abraham (Gen 23:4) or the people in Egypt (Gen 15:13; Exod 22:21; Deut 23:7). Most frequently, however, it is used of non-Israelites, people not born into the people of Israel but who nevertheless live in the land and have been incorporated to some extent into the life of the people.

Two emphases are apparent in this collection of texts. Both serve to differentiate the גר from the תושב, a term used of foreigners who are more transient or who are in the land as temporary laborers.[2] One emphasis is the concern that resident aliens be treated with generosity and compassion.[3] Resident aliens are

2. While תושב is often paired with גר (Gen 23:4; Lev 25:23, 35, 47; Num 35:15; 1 Chr 29:15; Ps 39:12), it never appears in texts in which either of these two emphases is apparent.

3. For a contrary interpretation, see Bennett (2002). While his argument—that the Deuteronomy legislation served to institutionalize oppressive treatment of all those forced to live without an adult male protector—is no doubt valid in part, it does not negate the relative benevolence of these provisions.

frequently listed with widows and orphans as those deserving of special consideration and assistance. For example, one of the curses in Deuteronomy 27 is directed at "anyone who deprives the resident alien, the orphan and the widow of justice" (v. 19).[4] In other texts they are included with the poor.[5] On several occasions a rationale is given: "You shall not wrong or oppress a resident alien, for you were aliens in the land of Egypt" (Exod 22:21; also Exod 23:9; Deut 10:18–19).

The second emphasis has to do with the incorporation of the resident alien into the legal and cultic life of Israel. This is the key difference between the גר and the תושב. On a number of occasions we encounter general declarations that there is to be "one law for the alien and for the citizen" (Lev 24:22; also Exod 12:49; Num 9:14; 15:16, 29–30) or that "the alien who resides with you shall be to you as the citizen among you" (Lev 19:34; also Exod 12:48–49; Num 15:15). Resident aliens are explicitly included with the native-born in prescriptions concerning a variety of legal and cultic matters: the Festival of Weeks (Deut 16:11, 14), the Day of Atonement (Lev 16:29), Passover (Num 9:14), the Sabbath (Exod 20:10; Deut 5:14), sacrifices (Lev 17:8–9; 22:18; Num 15:14), purity (Num 19:10), cities of refuge (Num 35:15; Josh 20:9), dietary regulations (Lev 17:10–15), and other assorted matters (Lev 18:26; 20:2; 24:16; Num 15:26; Deut 24:14). In none of these texts is any distinction made between the resident alien and the citizen (apart from the two categories themselves). To be sure, there are a few other texts in the Torah where a distinction is made between the alien and the native born. Exodus 12:48 declares that resident aliens can participate in the Passover only if circumcised; Deuteronomy 14:21 prohibits the eating of anything that dies of itself but allows such meat to be given to resident aliens or foreigners. In each case, however, there are parallel texts in which no such distinction is made and resident aliens are treated on the same terms as citizens (Passover [Num 9:14]; meat of an animal that dies naturally [Lev 17:15]). The overall tendency, then, is for thoroughgoing inclusion of resident aliens in the life of Israel. The capstone, perhaps, is the explicit inclusion of resident aliens in the event by which the covenant community was formally established: "You stand assembled today," Moses says to "the leaders of your tribes, your elders, and your officials, all the men of Israel, your children, your women, and the aliens who are in your camp,. . . to enter into the covenant of the Lord your God, sworn by an oath, which the Lord your God is making with you today" (Deut 29:10–12).

Despite this tendency towards inclusion and incorporation, however, the fundamental distinction between the resident alien (גר) and the citizen (אזרח) remains fully intact in the Hebrew scriptures (Cohen 1999, 120–23). Israelite

4. Also Deut 14:29; 16:11, 14; 24:17–21; 26:11–13.

5. Lev 19:10; 23:22; Deut 24:14; Ezek 22:29. See also Exod 23:12; Lev 19:33–34; Ps 94:6; 146:9; Jer 7:6; 22:3; Ezek 22:7; Zech 7:10.

identity was rooted in a combination of birth and land. The only means of entrance into Israel was through birth. A foreigner (נכרי) could become a resident in the land, but such a resident alien could not become a native-born Israelite. The geographical and cultural boundary was somewhat permeable, but the genealogical boundary was not. The only gap in the boundary was through marriage (e.g., Num 31:17–18; Deut 21:10–14; Ruth), but even here it was only over the course of several generations that the descendants of a resident alien and a native-born Israelite would "be admitted to the assembly of the Lord" (Deut 23:8), that is, considered a native-born Israelite.[6]

It was only with the arrival of the Greeks that it became possible to conceive of Gentiles stepping over this boundary and becoming full members of the Jewish community. Still, if the form of this new conception owed a lot to the Greeks, its substance was provided in significant ways by the biblical material dealing with the resident alien. Indeed, since the Septuagint rendered גר as προσήλυτος ("proselyte"), the biblical model provided one of the primary terms used to designate the convert.[7]

For the only terms used with something approaching a technical sense in our period are the Hebrew and Greek forms of "proselyte" (גר, προσήλυτος), even if the terms are relatively rare outside the Hebrew scriptures and its Greek translation. The Greek term appears twice in the Apocrypha (Tobit 1:8; Sirach 10:22), six times in Philo,[8] four times in the New Testament (Matt 23:15; Acts 2:11; 6:5; 13:43), and four times in inscriptions (§§206–8, 211). The Hebrew is found five times in Qumran material[9] and three times in inscriptions (§§205, 209, 210). In every instance the term is used without elaboration or identification, indicating that its meaning was taken as readily apparent. Of course, in scriptural usage the

6. If indeed Deut 23 is to be interpreted as referring to intermarriage. In one strand of Jewish tradition, Deut 23 was seen as having to do with entrance into the Temple (Lam 1:10; 4QFlor I, 6; 4QMMT 8 III, 9–10; 1QSa II, 3–10). Rabbinic tradition, however, related it to marriage. On the issue of intermarriage generally, see Cohen (1999, 241–307). Deut 23:8 concerns Edomites and Egyptians but should probably not be restricted to them. The same passage, however, excludes an Ammonite or a Moabite, "even to the tenth generation" (Deut 23:3). On the significance of this for the account of the conversion of Achior the Ammonite in Jdt 14:10, see §23 above.

7. And other vocabulary as well, especially verbs associated with the status or experience of the proselyte: παροικέω (Exod 12:48; 20:10; Ezek 47:22); προσγίνομαι (Lev 18:26; 20:2; Num 15:14–16); προσέρχομαι (Lev 19:33; Num 9:14); προσκείμαι (Lev 16:29; 17:8, 10, 12; 22:18; Num 15:16, 26, 29; 19:10; Josh 20:9); προσπορεύομαι (Lev 19:34; Josh 8:35); προστίθημι (Isa 14:1).

8. *Dreams* 2.273; *Spec. Laws* 1.51, 308; three times in *QE* 2.2. In addition the term appears twice in *Cherubim* (108, 119), but with reference to Israel, not to Gentile converts.

9. CD VI, 21; XIV, 6; 4QpNah (4Q169) 3–4 II, 7–9; 11QT[a] (11Q19) XL, 5–6; 4QFlor(4Q 174) I, 1–7.

term refers to the earlier concept of the sojourner or resident alien; thus one cannot simply assume that where it appears elsewhere it refers to a full convert in the later sense. Still, the older sense of the term seemed to be required in only one instance (Sir 10:22). The fact that all of these instances appear in sources where knowledge of Israel's scriptures could be taken for granted does not detract from the sense that the terms were used in a technical way.

Nevertheless, as this list indicates, the term is relatively rare. It is completely absent from Josephus and from the pseudepigraphal literature. Philo uses προσήλυτος only when it appears in the scriptural passage under discussion. Elsewhere he uses a set of closely related terms (ἐπηλύτης, ἐπήλυτος ἔπηλυς)[10] that had wider currency in the Greek world. When he uses προσήλυτος under the influence of his scriptural text, either he defines the term (*Spec. Laws* 1.51) or he quickly shifts to one of these other terms (*Spec. Laws* 1.308; *QE* 2.2).

There are other words and phrases, however, that are used by more than one author and thus may reflect an established vocabulary of conversion. Although Josephus avoids προσήλυτος, he does use the related verb προσέρχομαι with reference to conversion (*Ant.* 18.82), and the term also appears in Philo (*Spec. Laws* 1.51) and in several pertinent Septuagint texts (LXX Lev 19:33; Num 9:14). In addition to προσέρχομαι, there are several other verbs compounded with προς, each conveying the sense of joining or attachment. προσκείμαι (to attach oneself), which is frequently linked with προσήλυτος in the LXX, where it often renders גור,[11] appears in Tob 1:8 and *Jos. Asen.* 16:14. προστίθημι, which in the passive has the sense "to be added to, to join," is used in the LXX in proselyte contexts to render the niphal form of לוה (to be attached, to join)[12] and is used in a similar way in Jdt 14:10, Philo *Spec. Laws* 1.51, and Josephus *Ant.* 13.319. The Hebrew equivalent appears in 4QpNah (4Q169) 3–4 II, 7–9 ("the גר attached [נלום] to them"). Also to be mentioned is προσχωρέω (to go over to, cross to the side of, join), used by Strabo with reference to the Idumeans in *Geog.* 16.2.34. Somewhat similar is Tacitus's use of *transgredior* (to go across, to pass over to another side or party) in his contemptuous description of converts (*Histories* 5.5.1–2).

Also to be mentioned is a set of verbs compounded with μετα, a preposition that adds the sense of transfer or change. Included in this set are μεταβάλλω, "to turn about, change, alter";[13] μεταλλάσσω, "to change, alter" (Philo *Virtues* 108); μετατίθημι, "to change one's mind or opinion [mid.]" (Josephus *Ant.* 20.38); and μεταλαμβάνω, "to take in exchange, substitute" (Josephus *Ant.* 20.139).

10. For a list of passages, see above, ch. 5, n. 77.

11. LXX Lev 16:29; 17:8, 10, 12; 22:18; Num 15:16, 26, 29; 19:10; Josh 20:9.

12. LXX Isa 14:1; Esth 8:17.

13. Philo *Spec. Laws* 1.51; *Virtues* 177, 217; *Rewards* 152.

Not unexpectedly, we encounter several formulations with Ἰουδαῖος or related words. On a number of occasions, a Gentile convert is described as becoming or being a Jew.[14] In addition, Ἰουδαΐζειν is used with respect to converts but only with some further specification of the degree of Judaization.[15]

Finally, on several occasions proselytes are described as having taken refuge under God's wings. The formulation is first used in Ruth 2:12, where Boaz tells Ruth that because of her faithfulness to Naomi she will be rewarded by the God of Israel, "under whose wings you have taken refuge." The phrase, which is common in rabbinic literature,[16] appears with reference to converts in *2 Bar.* 41:4. An interesting variation is found in *Joseph and Aseneth*, where the phrase is used of Aseneth herself: "in you many nations will take refuge with the Lord God, the Most High, and under your wings many peoples trusting in the Lord God will be sheltered" (*Jos. Asen.* 15:7). Aseneth plays a mediating role; nations will find divine refuge by taking shelter under her wings.

In the previous chapter it was argued that sympathization could progress along three axes—monotheistic worship, association with the Jewish community, and adoption of practices prescribed by the Jewish law. While these axes are not independent—optional packages of sympathization, as it were—they nevertheless highlight different conceptions of Judaism: as a form of worship in which an outsider might participate, as an ethnic group with which one might associate, or as a way of life set out in the Torah, conceived alternatively as a kind of philosophy that one might practice or as a political constitution that others might adopt. Although one should refrain from imposing a rigid schema on the evidence, from the material under discussion in this chapter it is apparent that conversion was widely understood as consisting of a full adoption of all three.

This appears explicitly in the account of Achior's conversion. The story of Judith pivots on two points: whether Nebuchadnezzar or the God of Israel was the supreme deity (Jdt 6:2) and whether the people of Israel would faithfully observe the law (Jdt 11:11–15). In the context of this story, then, to say that Achior "believed firmly in God . . . was circumcised and joined the house of Israel" (Jdt 14:10) is to say that he committed himself to exclusive monotheism, that he undertook to live according to the law code of which circumcision was a defining mark, and that he was therefore incorporated into the people of Israel. With respect to the circumcision of converts, we have seen clear indication that it was seen not as a stand-alone requirement but as an indication of the person's willingness to adhere to the whole law. The same three elements are also apparent to Tacitus *(Hist* 5.5.1–2). Converts "follow the same practice"

14. E.g., Bel and the Serpent 28; 2 Macc 9:17; Josephus *Ant.* 20.38; Epictetus *Discourses* 2.9.19–21.

15. LXX Esther 8:17; Theodotus (§37); Josephus J.W. 2.454.

16. In the form "under the wings of the Shekinah"; e.g., *Sifre Deut.* 32 (on Deut 6:5); *b. Yeb.* 48b; see also Goodman (1994, 145); Chesnutt (1995, 168).

(the whole Jewish way of life), "despise the gods" (because of their devotion to the God of the Jerusalem temple), and participate in the social exclusivism of the Jewish people, "disown[ing] their country" and family in the process.[17] In Josephus's account, Polemo's circumcision was not simply a one-off operation that made it possible for him to marry Berenice; it carried with it the obligation to adhere "to the Jewish way of life" (Josephus *Ant.* 20.146). More generally, there is no evidence that Josephus contemplated distinct categories of conversion. In some cases, political support or allegiance might be to the fore (e.g., the Idumeans or, in a different way, Metilius); in others, marriage or, more generally, becoming part of an ethnic group; in others still, religious beliefs and observance (Izates). But Josephus makes no fundamental differentiation among them; for example, he can use similar language—most commonly "the customs of the Jews"[18]—to describe each of them. Just as Judaism itself was a single entity despite its ethnic, political, and religious complexity, so conversion was a transfer into a single entity, even if the characteristics of the transfer varied from case to case.

At the same time, we have observed considerable variation in emphasis. In Diaspora literature, circumcision and other ethnos-specific aspects of the Torah are downplayed. In addition to those passages in which circumcision is mentioned, Josephus can describe the distinction between the convert and the outsider by using the language of social incorporation. This appears most clearly in *Ag. Ap.* 2.209–10, where he differentiates "casual visitors" from those who have "come to live under the same laws with us" and who thus enter into a family relationship. Similarly, he describes the Jewish community in Antioch as attracting Greeks to their religious ceremonies, whom "they had in some measure incorporated with themselves" (*J.W.* 7.45). The phenomenon is particularly apparent in the writings of Philo, who, to cite just one instance, ignores circumcision entirely in his presentation of Abraham as the first convert, choosing instead to focus on monotheism and virtue (*Virtues* 212–19). The conversion of Aseneth involves not only the renunciation of all other gods, but also an odd event involving bread, wine, oil, and a honeycomb. While some have interpreted this as an otherwise unknown initiatory rite, it is more likely to be seen as simply an idiosyncratic detail of the narrative. Indeed, there is very little evidence of an established process of initiation such as is found later in rabbinic literature (*b. Yeb* 47a–b). Cohen argues persuasively that the rabbinic ritual, involving acceptance of the commandments, circumcision, and immersion, was precisely an attempt on the part of the Tannaim to bring order

17. For Juvenal, circumcision is the ultimate indication that a person has abandoned "the laws of Rome" and has adopted "the Judaic code" (*Satires* 14.96–106). Also Paul: "every man who lets himself be circumcised . . . is obliged to obey the entire law" (Gal 5:3).

18. Political: *Ant.* 13.397; 15.254; marital: *Ant.* 16.225; religious: *Ant.* 3.318–19; *Ag. Ap.* 1.166; 2.209–10; 2.260–61.

to "what until then had been an entirely personal and chaotic process."[19] Nevertheless, one is on safe ground to say that conversion involved exclusive worship of the God of Israel, adherence to the Torah, and incorporation into the Jewish community. Further, given the wide recognition that circumcision was an essential part of conversion (for males),[20] it is highly unlikely that there were "uncircumcised proselytes."

The element of social incorporation requires further comment, not only because it has been especially prominent in this material but also because it raises the question of status. On the negative side of it, conversion is often described as entailing a separation from one's native culture and an alienation from one's kinfolk. The theme is highlighted in the story of *Joseph and Aseneth* (e.g., 11:4–5; 12:12–13), albeit unevenly, and is stressed by Philo (see, e.g., *Spec. Laws* 1.51–52; 4.176–78). Corresponding to this is a positive emphasis on the incorporation of the convert into a new culture and set of social relations. Again this theme is to the fore in Philo,[21] but it is also present in Josephus's description of the Idumeans as kinfolk[22] and of converts generally as members of the same household (*Ag. Ap.* 2.209–10).[23] Such an emphasis on incorporation might seem to imply equality of status, and this is made explicit by Philo. Converts are equal in rank to the native-born, with equal access to all the privileges prescribed by Moses (*Spec. Laws* 1.51–52). They are fellow citizens (*Embassy* 211) who are to be loved "not only as friends and kinsfolk but as themselves" (*Virtues* 103)

Of course, the fact that Philo feels that native-born Jews need to be exhorted to honor the incomers (*Spec. Laws* 1.52) suggests that equality of status was harder to achieve in practice than in theory. As was noted in the discussion of inscriptions, there was an irreducible and ineradicable difference between the proselyte and the native-born. Further, in Qumran material this difference was not negated even in theory, as proselytes were relegated to a definitely inferior status.[24]

19. Cohen 1999, 234. There is no explicit reference to proselyte immersion in our period (J. J. Collins 2000, 106). Still, the three requirements are taken sufficiently for granted in the Tannaitic period that it is hard to imagine immersion as a later innovation (McKnight 1991, 78; Schiffman 1985, 19). On proselytism in the Tannaitic period generally, see Bamberger (1968 [1939]); Braude (1940); Cohen (1999), especially chs. 7–10; Hayes (2002); G. Moore (1927–1930, 1:323–53); Porton (1988).

20. E.g., LXX Esth 8:17; Jdt 14:10; Theodotus (§37); Josephus *Ant.* 20.38; cf. Acts 11:3.

21. See the discussion above of *Spec. Laws* 1.51–52, 308–09; 4.176–178; *Virtues* 102–04, 175–82, 212–19.

22. E.g., J.W. 4.265, 278. See §§118 and 119 above..

23. See also *Jos. Asen.* 8:9 and Theodotus (above §37).

24. At Qumran, it was entirely a matter of theory; it is unlikely that there were any actual proselytes. On the question of status more generally, see §§81 and 83 above.

With respect to proselytism as a Jewish "pattern of universalism," Jews in both Judea and the Diaspora believed that it was possible for Gentiles to join the Jewish community as converts, that conversion was a positive thing and converts were to be welcomed, and that converts enjoyed the same relationship with God as did native-born Israelites. Only rarely do we encounter categorical rejections of the possibility.[25] Within this general consensus, however, some variations appear. We have already considered the matter of status, noting a range of opinion from theoretical equality at one end (Philo) to categorical inferiority at the other (Qumran). There is also a difference of opinion on the necessity of conversion. Eleazar of Galilee held that anything short of conversion left one "guilty of the greatest offence against the law and thereby against God" (Josephus *Ant.* 20.44). The opinion that apart from conversion Gentiles stood condemned by the law was shared by the author of *2 Baruch*.[26] Izates' other adviser, however, took the opinion that while circumcision was preferable, one could "worship God" in an appropriate and acceptable manner without undergoing full conversion. The position taken by Ananias was probably widespread. It was evidently held by Josephus and seems to be assumed in those writings that deal positively with both sympathization and conversion. In any case, the relative absence of the stringent view attributed to Eleazar is significant in itself. Concerning the possibility of conversion, an interesting variation shows up in a couple of passages where conversion is dependent not only on the desire of the would-be convert but also on God's willingness. In *Joseph and Aseneth*, Aseneth's desire for conversion will come to fruition only if her prayer of repentance is heard in heaven and granted by God.[27] Although her request is granted, that of Antiochus was not and he was forced to "[give] up all hope for himself" (2 Macc 9:17–18). But while few would be prepared to deny God's prerogative in the matter, the general assumption seems to be that God is willing to accept converts and that human willingness is the decisive factor.

Finally, what about the question of mission? As we have seen, there is little question that many Jews looked on conversion with approval and were pleased when it did occur. Philo's parallel treatment of conversion and apostasy at prominent points in his Exposition indicates that he was as eager to encourage the one as he was to discourage the other.[28] Further, we have seen individual instances where Jews took the initiative to encourage potential converts and to instruct them in Jewish ways. Again, Ananias and Eleazar provide us with prominent examples, but there are others as well. Tacitus speaks of converts

25. See below, ch. 14, n. 3.

26. Feldman suggests that if we had more evidence we would find others who shared Eleazar's opinion "that to become a God-fearer was not enough" (Feldman 1993, 333).

27. See 8.9; 11.3–14, 16–18; chs.12 and 13; and 15.3.

28. See §§90, 97, 98, 100 above.

being given lessons in Jewish practices (*Histories* 5.5.2). Josephus attributes Tiberius's expulsion of Jews from Rome to the aggressive activity of Jewish teachers (*Ant.* 18.81–84); even if this is an oversimplification of the situation and even if the teachers were unscrupulous, the account indicates that it was common for interested outsiders to seek tutelage from Jewish teachers.

But the evidence seems to suggest that Jewish initiative was a response to a prior interest in Judaism on the part of Gentiles. Tacitus's account reflects a certain balance of initiative: first Gentiles "go over" to the Jews and then they receive instruction. On the one hand, there is little evidence of an active mission designed to create interest where it did not already exist; on the other, many Jews were eager to instruct and encourage those who were attracted to Judaism and who took the initiative to seek them out. It is probable that such interested Gentiles formed part of the audience addressed by Philo, Josephus, and other authors of apologetic literature. Matthew's famous reference to the worldwide proselytizing activity of the Pharisees (Matt 23:15) is probably to be understood in the same way. In most of this literature, Gentiles are understood to be motivated primarily by the inherent attraction of Judaism itself. Occasionally other motivations are indicated: fear (LXX Esth 8:17; *J.W.* 2.454); a desire for marriage with a Jew;[29] even coercion.[30] But the dominant assumption throughout the literature surveyed in this chapter is that Gentiles were attracted to Judaism—for its monotheistic worship, the distinctive way of life prescribed in its law, and its inclusive community—and that Jews were eager to welcome them and provide them with appropriate instruction and encouragement.

29. Josephus *Ant.* 16.225; 20.139; 20.145–46; Theodotus (§37).

30. Josephus *Ant.* 13.257–58, 318–19, 397; 15.254–55; *Life* 112–13; Ptolemy (§175).

CHAPTER 12

ETHICAL MONOTHEISM

The material of interest in this chapter provides evidence for a third pattern of universalism, one in which Jews consider it possible for Gentiles to acquire accurate and adequate knowledge of the one true God, or to relate to this God in appropriate ways, without any knowledge of Judaism or association with the Jewish community. The material reflects several different ways of correlating this belief with Jewish identity and commitments, correlations that are not free of internal tension. Nevertheless, we have evidence here for what might be described as "generous monotheism"—an outlook characterized by a positive attitude toward outsiders who claim to worship the one true creator God and defined in terms of its contrast with the "exclusive monotheism" of religious groups that would reject all monotheistic belief outside of their own.[1]

In the most fully developed version of this outlook, the law of Moses is understood to represent a particular—and usually the best—articulation of a monotheistic ethic that in principle is accessible to humans generally.[2] This enterprise involves two conceptual moves. One is the adoption of a natural theology—the idea that human beings should be able to perceive something about God and God's requirements by rational reflection on the created order. For the author of *On Jonah* a knowledge of God and of God's commandments should

1. Cf. Wolfson's categories of "positive" and "negative" monotheism, discussed by Goldenberg (1998, 41).

2. On this two-pronged enterprise, see, e.g., J. J. Collins (2000); Gruen (2002, e.g. 227); Kuhn (1968, 731); Schürer (1986, 3:153–55).

be as readily apparent from a consideration of the natural world as is the existence of an architect from consideration of a building (217). While this might suggest that such knowledge is available to the rank and file generally, more commonly it is seen as the province of the philosophers. For Aristobulus, it is in the philosophical schools (Judaism included) that one finds an authentic concern for "holy opinions concerning God" and "the things that are truly good" (piety, justice, temperance, and the other virtues).[3] This concept of a natural law was developed most thoroughly by Philo, who believed that it is "the disciples of the most excellent philosophy" who are able "to know the highest, the most ancient Cause of all things and reject the delusion of created gods" (*Virtues* 65).

The other half of this enterprise is the attempt to align the law of Moses with this natural law and its exposition in the work of the philosophers. Sometimes Jewish authors are content to equate the Jewish law with Greek philosophy. In the passage just cited, Philo also says that what the disciples of the philosophers gain from their teaching "the Jews gain from their laws"; Josephus claims that "nearly all the philosophers appear to have held similar views concerning the nature of God" (i.e., as those of Moses; *Ag. Ap.* 2.168). Aristeas's declaration that Jews and Greeks worship the same God though known by different names (*Let. Aris.* 16) moves in the same direction. More often, however, these authors are concerned to present Judaism as superior, as having "surpassed" (*Let. Aris.* 235) the philosophers in their knowledge of God and practice of virtue. For Philo, Moses was "an oracle higher than Zeno" (*Good Person* 160). For Josephus, Moses had both the best conception of God and the best *politeia* (*Ant.* 1.15–26; *Ag. Ap.* 2.163).[4] Taking this line of thinking one step further, Moses is sometimes presented as the teacher of the philosophers or the source of their ideas. Says Josephus: "our earliest imitators were the Greek philosophers, who . . . were Moses's disciples."[5] Since this might seem to suggest that anything true or good in Greek philosophy was simply borrowed from Judaism, it stands in some tension with the assertion that "knowledge of the truth" can be attained independently, through the investigation of nature (Philo *Good Person* 74). If they were aware of the tension, however, our authors were prepared to live with it. In any case, it should not be allowed to overshadow the clear evidence for the belief that Greek philosophy and the Jewish law represented independent paths to the same destination, even if one were inferior to or less effective than the other.

3. Frag. 4; Eusebius *P.E.* 13.12.8.

4. Aristobulus is a little less assertive: "It is agreed by all the philosophers that it is necessary to hold holy opinions concerning God, a point our philosophical school makes particularly well" (frag. 4; Eusebius *P.E.* 13.12.8).

5. *Ag. Ap.* 2.281. Also Philo (e.g., *Good Person* 29, 43, 57, 68); Aristobulus (frag. 2, Eusebius *P.E.* 8.10.4; frag. 3, *P.E.* 13.12.1; frag. 3, *P.E.* 13.12.4).

This attempt to align the law of Moses with all that is good in Greek philosophy was made difficult, of course, by the emphasis in the law on regulations that serve to mark out the Jewish nation as ethnically distinct—food laws, purity regulations, circumcision, festivals, and the like. One approach to the problem is to search for rational explanations for these commandments (*Let. Aris.* 130–71; Aristobulus frags. 1, 5), to interpret them allegorically (Aristobulus frag. 2; Philo), and so on. Another approach is simply to ignore these troublesome aspects of the law and to characterize the law as a system of monotheistic worship and virtuous living. Philo, for example, can carry on an interpretation of Genesis 17 without once mentioning the command that Abraham and his descendents be circumcised (*Virtues* 212–19). Such a characterization of the law—in which those aspects that would resonate with sympathetic Gentiles are emphasized and those that are more particularistic in nature are simply ignored—is also found in literature that pays little explicit attention to Hellenistic philosophy. In *Sibylline Oracles* 3, for example, the Gentiles are expected to obey the law but what this means is monotheistic worship (548–50, 624–29, 733, 740, 763) and a set of commonly recognized ethical precepts (630, 764–66). In the *Testament of Joseph*, the offer made by the wife of Pentephris to live according to the law boils down to a willingness to worship God, to practice self-control, and to abstain from sexual immorality. For the author of *On Jonah*, obedience to the law involves a recognition of God and a moral life (concern for justice, care for the poor, sexual morality, moderation, honesty; 111–40).

In other literature, the law of Moses itself is downplayed. *Sibylline Oracles* 4, for example, displays a similar concern for a universal piety characterized by monotheistic worship and moral uprightness (a life free of murder, dishonesty, sexual immorality, and homosexual relations; 25–34) but without any attempt to link this with the law of Moses, even if the world projected by the work is explicitly Jewish. Similarly *2 Enoch* understands the whole human race as subject to a set of God's "commandments" (2:2, 34:1)—again a combination of monotheism and ethics—but makes no mention whatsoever of the law of Moses. Analogous patterns are present in *Pseudo-Phocylides* and the *Testament of Abraham*. In these works, a Jewish frame of reference is readily apparent, but in place of ethnic particularity and a distinctively Jewish law we find a universal standard of righteousness that is equally binding on all of humankind.[6]

While most of the material under discussion in this chapter had to do with a correlation between Jewish law and Hellenistic virtue, we also encountered several passages where the emphasis fell more on worship and the nature of God. Each of these passages is striking in its own way. Two authors made the bold claim that Zeus was just a different name for the same God as was worshipped by the Jews. Such a statement appears explicitly in the *Letter of Aristeas*

6. Georgi (1986, 121) speaks of history and covenant as being "absorbed by nature."

(16), where even though it is attributed to a Gentile it clearly comes with the endorsement of the (Jewish) author. Aristobulus says essentially the same thing in a comment on his revision of a poem by Aratus (frag. 4, Eusebius *P.E.* 13.12.6–7). In addition, on several occasions Josephus speaks offhandedly about Roman leaders offering thanks to "God" when in actuality they were engaging in their own religious observances (*J.W.* 2.214; 3.444), which seems to imply that non-Jews were able to worship God in an appropriate manner through their own patterns of worship. While such endorsement of non-Jewish religion is rare,[7] it is found in an almost scandalous form in Artapanus (§36), who credits Moses with the creation and organization of Egyptian religion, including its worship of many gods.

Although there can be little doubt that such a strain of generous ethical monotheism was present within the Judaism of our period, several questions arise about how it is to be understood. One has to do with the role of scripture and the degree to which it was a factor in the development of the phenomenon. This question requires only brief comment. Certainly many of the universalistic themes that were outlined at the beginning of chapter 10 would be consistent with the pattern of thought under discussion here. In particular, there are definite affinities with aspects of Wisdom literature—in Proverbs, for example, where there seems to be little concern to connect Wisdom with either the story of Israel or the giving of the law.[8] But the impetus for this pattern of thought seems to have arisen primarily from forces at work in the Hellenistic environment of the Jewish Diaspora rather than from anything in Israel's scriptures themselves.

Second, we can ask to what extent the idea of ethical monotheism functioned simply as a conceptual device to reassure Jews about the rationality and legitimacy of their own beliefs. Did our authors take an interest in such ethical monotheists as an experienced reality and for their own sake, or were they of interest simply as a hypothetical construction or for their apologetic utility?

Certainly there are some passages in which ethical monotheism is just a hypothetical concept. In *Wisdom of Solomon*, for example, despite a veneer of generous universalism, this material seems to be present only for purposes of theodicy—that is, to justify God's punishment of those outside Israel, who had the ability to recognize the truth but failed to use it. Further, while the Ninevites come to acknowledge God in a spectacular way in *On Jonah*, they do so not on the basis of their own resources or insight but only when confronted with the truth as it was presented by the Jewish prophet Jonah. For the author of *Sibylline Oracles* 3, while Gentiles should recognize the ways of God in the

7. For a full study see Goldenberg (1998).

8. See also Bockmuehl's discussion of places in Israel's scripture where the existence of a universal standard of behavior seems to be assumed; e.g., Gen 6:5, 11–13; 20:3–4, 9; 2 Sam 13:12; Isa 1:2–3; Amos 6:12 (Bockmuehl 2000, 88–97).

present, it is only in the eschatological future that this will happen, and then in response to the divine vindication of the Jews (*Sib. Or.* 3:710–23).

Other texts, however, present us with actual cases. Ptolemy and his philosophers seem to qualify as ethical monotheists even prior to their encounter with the glories of Judaism and its law (*Letter of Aristeas*).[9] For Aristobulus the philosophers really do grasp "holy opinions about God" together with "piety and justice and temperance and the rest of the things that are truly good" (frag. 4; Eusebius *P.E.* 13.12.8). In the world as seen by the author of *2 Enoch*, there really do seem to be non-Jews among the community of the righteous. Philo is particularly explicit; while the group of those "who practise wisdom, either in Grecian or barbarian lands" (*Spec Laws* 2.44) is not large, they can be found in each city in the civilized world (2.47), including areas outside the Hellenistic world (*Good Person* 72–74). To be sure, these ethical monotheists function as part of an inwardly directed apologetic enterprise; the payoff in the *Letter of Aristeas*, for example, is precisely that such noble Gentiles recognize the superior virtues of Judaism when they are presented with an opportunity to see it. But even so, the apologetic depends for its effectiveness on the assumption that such Gentiles do exist. Further, especially in the case of Philo, it is difficult to contain this material entirely within a Jewish horizon; Philo wants to locate his discourse in the midst of the open marketplace (*Spec. Laws* 1.320–23) and to make his claims about ethical monotheists in the hearing of interested outsiders. The example of Varro demonstrates that there were some sympathetic outsiders who were prepared to reinforce such claims from the other side.

The third set of questions to be considered here concerns the relationship between this pattern of universalism and those explored in the previous two chapters. With respect to sympathization, we have observed on several occasions the assumption that true ethical monotheists, if they had an opportunity to encounter Judaism, would recognize that the law of Moses represented an equally valid—and probably superior—route to the same destination. This is the clear implication of the *Letter of Aristeas*, where the king and the philosophers fall over each other in their attempt to heap praises on the law and those who were explaining it to them. Further, while Philo's discourse is more complex, we have seen reasons to believe that he would expect such virtuous outsiders to respond in the same way.[10] In other words, the assumption seems to be that such ethical monotheists would sympathize with Judaism to some appropriate degree if they had a chance to see Judaism as it truly was. Still, there is little indication in the material surveyed here that such ethical monotheism was only a way station on the path to sympathization and that

9. Of course, in the *Letter of Aristeas* we are dealing with fictional characterization. But for our purposes this is just as "real" as some flesh-and-blood example. It is the conception that counts.

10. See the concluding observations in ch. 5 above.

only if Gentiles recognized Judaism as ethical monotheism *par excellence* would their form of piety and practice be legitimate and acceptable to God. Ethical monotheists are not simple latent sympathizers. In the case of ethical monotheism, the law functions as a means towards a transcending end, one that can be attained independently of the Mosaic law. In the case of sympathization, the law is an end in itself but contains within it a smaller set of requirements for the Gentiles. Thus in one, there is universal territory existing beyond or alongside the law of Moses; in the other, there is specifically Gentile territory existing within the law.[11]

Of course, our authors do not draw the distinction quite so neatly. Philo and others want to equate the "law" of Moses, suitably defined and focused, with the "law" perceived by the philosophers. The result is a kind of leveling or homogenization—at least at the rhetorical level—between adherents of the two "laws." In an earlier discussion of the phenomenon, I used the term "natural law 'proselytes'" to describe such ethical monotheists (Donaldson 1997, 60–65). The term should probably be abandoned, even with "proselytes" in quotation marks. Proselytism involved more than monotheism and ethics in general; it required incorporation into the Jewish community and practice of the Jewish law in particular. But the term highlights the ambiguities and tensions that emerge when the law of Moses is aligned in this way with Hellenistic ideals. If Gentiles could agree with Philo that the special laws (circumcision, for example) really symbolize universal virtues, why would they need to observe these laws in all their literal specificity in order to be full and equal members of Philo's community? How is one to correlate—and to differentiate—the law as universal monotheistic ethic and the law as ethnic identifier? Several scholars have noted the similarity between the specific patterns of belief and behavior expected of these ethical monotheists and the requirements contained in the Noahide decrees.[12] To the extent that the Noahide tradition can be seen as a form of natural law (Novak 1984), perhaps the best explanation of the tension (as I argued earlier) is that Philo and other Diaspora authors operated on the basis of a distinction (between proselytes and ethical monotheists) for which they did not yet have adequate categories or terminology.[13]

11. Cf. Bockmuehl's distinction between between "positive law" (laws about Gentiles contained in the Torah) and "natural law" (universally valid laws that can be discerned without the specific divine revelation in the Torah) (2000, 87).

12. See esp. J. J. Collins (2000, 170–71).

13. It is perhaps a failure to recognize such a distinction that accounts for this startling statement (E. P. Sanders 1976, 39): "What is remarkable is that there is no clear evidence at all from Hellenistic Judaism that the salvation of Gentiles who did not convert was seen as possible. . . . [I]t would seem that, in this sense, Hellenistic Judaism was more consistently exclusivistic than Palestinian Judaism."

Chapter 13

Participation in Eschatological Salvation

A distinctive feature of Judaism in our period is its variety of end-time expectations and the important place they occupy in Jewish thought and self-understanding. Each of the patterns of universalism explored to this point has had eschatological implications, though we have not treated these thematically. By virtue of their incorporation into the people of Israel, for example, proselytes would have an equal share with their new co-religionists in the blessings of the age to come. Likewise, to the extent that sympathizers and ethical monotheists were seen as doing all that God required of them as Gentiles in the present, it would be expected that they would participate, in ways appropriate for Gentiles, in the future. But in this chapter our attention is drawn to an additional set of texts in which the decisive factor, as far as the fate of the Gentiles is concerned, is located in the future rather than in the present. These texts contain various expectations that in the end times, when the lines are clearly drawn, when evil has been eradicated and righteousness established, when God's promises to Israel have been fully realized, and when Israel's status has been vindicated and its claims about God verified—then the Gentiles, or at least some portion of them, would recognize the truth, acknowledge their folly, worship God in some appropriate way, and thus be granted their own share in the blessings of the end time.

Positive expectations concerning the place of Gentiles in the eschatological future are deeply rooted in Israel's scriptures, which makes this perhaps the earliest and most fundamental pattern of Jewish universalism. The most common scenario centers on Zion and the restoration of Jerusalem and involves a grand reversal of Israel's fortunes. "In days to come" (Isa 2:2) God will act to vindicate the righteous within Israel and to fulfill the prophetic promises. Israel's enemies will be overturned;[1] sinners within Israel will be punished;[2] Jerusalem and the temple will be purified and glorified;[3] God's rule will be fully established, either directly[4] or through a restored Davidic king;[5] and Israelites who had been dispersed in exile will return to the land,[6] where all will enjoy peace, plenty, and the presence of the Lord.[7]

Gentiles are not always treated positively in this tradition of eschatological restoration. Sometimes nothing but punishment is foreseen and no redemption is anticipated on the far side of judgment.[8] More often Gentiles are present in a secondary or subservient way—simply as mute witnesses of Israel's vindication or docile facilitators of Israel's return to the land.[9] But there is a more positive version of the scenario, one in which Gentiles are included in the redemption and participate in the blessings. They will be summoned to Jerusalem "from the coastlands far away" (Isa 66:19) in order to see the glory of the Lord. They stream to Zion to learn God's ways and to be instructed in God's paths (Isa 2:2–4 / Mic 4:1–3). "Full of the knowledge of the Lord," they will search out the "root of Jesse" and his glorious dwelling (Isa 9:9–10). "Many peoples and strong nations shall come to seek the Lord of hosts in Jerusalem" (Zech 8:22), where they will participate in a joyous end-time banquet on the "mountain of the Lord of hosts" (Isa 25:6) and where they will offer gifts (Isa 18:7; 60:5–6; Hag 2:21–22) and sacrifices to God in a temple that "shall be called a house of prayer for all peoples" (Isa 56:7). Although most of this material has to do with the restoration of Jerusalem (or Zion or the temple), which serves as the focus and location of Gentile participation in end-time blessings, mention should also be made of Isa 19:18–25, which anticipates a day when "there will be an altar to the Lord in the center of the land of Egypt" (v. 19) and when Egypt and Assyria will stand alongside Israel as "[God's] people [עמי]" and "the work of [God's] hands" (v. 25). Here the idea of an eschatological pilgrimage of the Gentiles to Jerusalem, which is dominant in most of the other passages, is absent.

This last passage leads us to the question of the status accorded these Gentiles in the end times. In this passage, even though Egypt and Assyria seem

1. E.g., Isa 24:23; 29:8; Jer 30: 11, 16; Ezek 17:11–21; Joel 3:9–21.

2. E.g., Isa 1:24–31.

3. E.g., Isa 2:2–4 / Mic 4:1–3; Isa 60:1–22; Jer 31:23, 38–40; Ezek 17:22–24; 40:1–48:35; Zech 8:1–23; 14:10–11, 20–21.

4. E.g., Isa 24:23; 52:7; Ezek 20:33; 34:11–16; 43:7; Mic 4:6–7; Zech 14:8–11.

5. E.g., Ezek 17:22–24; 34:23–31; Mic 5:2–4.

6. E.g., Isa 35; Jer 31:1–25; Ezek 20:33–44; Zech 8:7–8, 20–23.

7. E.g., Isa 25:6–10a; 30:23; 35:5–6; 61:6; Jer 31:12; Joel 2:26; Amos 9:13–15.

8. E.g., Jer 30–31; Ezek 17, 34.

9. E.g., Isa 18:7; 60:1–22; 66:18–21; Hag 2:21–22.

to take an equal place alongside Israel, it is clear that they are not incorporated into Israel and thus do not lose their separate identity. Other passages are less clear but nevertheless seem to suggest that Gentiles continue to be Gentiles (e.g., Isa 25:6–10; Zech 8:20–23), doing no more than what is allowed to Gentiles even in the present (e.g., to worship at the temple, to acknowledge the God of Israel). Some of the other passages, however, might lean more in the direction of full incorporation. In Isa 2:2–4, for example, the nations stream to Zion to learn God's ways, "for out of Zion shall go forth instruction [תורה]." If the nations are gathering to Jerusalem in order to learn Torah, the passage might be read as implying that in the eschatological future Gentiles are to become full Torah observers—that is, proselytes. Of course, as we have seen, the full-blown concept of proselytism was a later development, which means that it is anachronistic to ask whether this was the intention of the text in its original time and place. But at a later time it might be interpreted in this way. Likewise the statement in Isa 66:21—that when the nations gather to Jerusalem to worship God, bringing the exiles with them, God "will take some of them as priests and as Levites"—might be read as saying that Gentiles will be so thoroughly incorporated into the people of Israel that they will serve as priests and Levites.[10] We do not need to explore this question further with respect to Israel's scriptures, but we will return to it with respect to the material under discussion in this chapter.

Contrary to an opinion that was common in an earlier generation of scholarship,[11] there is no reason to believe that by the later Second Temple period traditional expectations of an eschatological pilgrimage of the nations to Zion had attenuated and Jewish attitudes concerning the place of Gentiles in Israel's end-time restoration had become much more negative. As we have seen, there is considerable evidence, both from Judea and from the Diaspora, for the Jewish belief that, when God should act in a final way to vindicate Israel and to establish the anticipated era of righteousness and peace, Gentiles would abandon their own sinful ways, turn to the God of Israel, and thus be granted a share in the blessings of the end time.[12]

10. See Kraus (1996, 23–24); Schnabel (2004, 84–86). The syntax is ambiguous, however; the antecedent of "them" (i.e. those selected to be priests and Levites) could just as easily—and perhaps more plausibly—be the "kindred" who are brought as an offering to the Lord, i.e., the returning Jewish exiles.

11. E.g., Davies (1948, 61–62); Jeremias (1958, 61–62); Munck (1959, 258–59).

12. Evidence for such an expectation is not plentiful in Tannaitic material, but it is present nonetheless. In *t. Ber.* 6.2, R. Simeon b. Eleazar cites Zeph 3:9 in support of the opinion that the Gentiles are destined to turn to God. Similarly, in *Mekilta* Shirata 8 (on Exod 15:11) we read that not only did the nations of the world join with Israel in praising God for the overthrow of the Egyptians, but also "in the future the nations of the world will renounce their idols." This future expectation is justified on the basis of several prophetic texts (Isa 2:20–21; 20:18; Jer 16:19–20). For instances in later midrash, see, e.g., *Gen. Rab.* 26.2; 98.9; *Num. Rab.* 1.3.

As we should have come to expect by now, however, we have encountered significant variety and diversity. In one set of passages, the pattern of an eschatological pilgrimage to Jerusalem is fully on display. We encounter it in *1 Enoch* 90, where it appears in the vernacular of apocalyptic literature. After the reestablishment of righteousness within Israel and the defeat of Israel's enemies, Jerusalem is gloriously refurbished, the exiles are delivered and reunited with their compatriots, and the Gentiles who have survived the judgment come to Jerusalem to join the grand gathering, where they are transformed into the purity of the primordial era (*1 En.* 90:30–38). We also encounter the full pattern in the last of the three eschatological oracles in *Sibylline Oracles* 3. Presented with definitive evidence that Israel and the temple are under God's protection, "all islands and cities" renounce their idols, "ponder the Law of the Most High God," and journey with "incense and gifts to the house of the great God" (*Sib. Or.* 3:719, 772). With respect to *Psalms of Solomon* 17, while questions remain as to the essential disposition of the passage, this psalm probably provides us with another example. The psalmist expects that nations will come "from the ends of the earth" to Jerusalem "to see his glory," bringing Jewish exiles with them "as gifts" to the Lord (*Ps. Sol.* 17:31). Although the scenario is less detailed in *4 Ezra* 13 and *2 Baruch* 72, in both passages it appears that when the nations gather to experience divine mercy, it is to "Mount Zion" (*4 Ezra* 13:35) or to "the holy land" (*2 Bar.* 71:1) that they are summoned.

In a second set of passages, while the idea of an eschatological pilgrimage to Zion is absent, we nevertheless encounter the same rationale—namely, that the end-time vindication of Israel or restoration of Jerusalem precipitates a change of heart on the part of Gentiles or somehow makes it possible for Gentiles to share in the blessings. In the Apocalypse of Weeks, after the vindication of the remnant and the purification of the temple, the Gentiles "look to the path of eternal righteousness" (*1 En.* 91:14). In the *Testaments of the Twelve Patriarchs* it is the purification of the priesthood (*T. Levi* 18:2–4) or the return from exile (*T. Jud.* 23:5) or the salvation of Israel (*T. Naph.* 8:2; *T. Benj.* 11:2) that makes possible the enlightenment and salvation of the Gentiles. In *4 Ezra* 6:25–26, after the salvation of Israel, "the heart of the earth's inhabitants shall be changed and converted to a different spirit." While the author of *Sibylline Oracles* 5 devotes more attention to the future glorification of Israel and the temple than to its effect on outsiders, nevertheless it is because they are able to "see the glory of the eternal God" that Gentiles sing praises to God's glory (*Sib. Or.* 5:420–28). The same logic is present in Philo as well: when the Jews experience "national prosperity," then "each nation [will] abandon its peculiar ways, and, throwing overboard their ancestral customs, turn to honouring our laws alone" (*Moses* 2:44).

The passages mentioned to this point conform to the pattern already present in Israel's scriptures. To these one other passage can be added. While *Sibylline Oracles* 5 is unique in its expectation of a temporary end-time temple located in Egypt (*Sib. Or.* 5:484–503), this idea is nevertheless based on an (equally unusual) expectation found in the prophet Isaiah (Isa 19:18–25). In addition to these passages, however, we have encountered a few that go beyond or fall outside the biblical pattern. *Second Baruch* 72 conforms to eschatological pilgrimage traditions in some respects, but it provides a unique twist: those who will be granted life in the days of the messiah are precisely those nations that have neither known nor oppressed Israel; all the others will be destroyed. The *Testament of Benjamin* displays too much Christian reworking to justify full inclusion in our study; nevertheless we can note that here the end-time change of disposition on the part of the Gentiles requires an additional act of God on their behalf: God will "liberate every captive of the sons of men from Beliar" and "will turn all nations to being zealous for him" (*T. Benj.* 9:8). The material surveyed in this chapter, then, represents both a continuation of the biblical pattern and a development of that pattern in new forms and different directions. This observation is further illustrated when we ask about the status of the Gentiles in this material.

While there has been considerable scholarly interest in the positive place of Gentiles in Jewish end-time scenarios, less attention has been paid to the precise status of these second-order participants in eschatological redemption.[13] Are they fully incorporated into Israel, end-time proselytes, as it were? Or do they continue to exist as non-Jews, taking their place as Gentiles alongside Israel in some way? Or are these basic identities somehow to be transformed in a more fundamental way, along with other categories of the created order?

As we have observed, the biblical material is ambiguous. Although the question would not have presented itself to the biblical authors, nevertheless some scriptural passages might be taken to suggest that Gentiles become full Torah-observers in the end times (e.g., Isa 2:2–4), while others leave open the possibility that Gentile identity would be preserved (e.g., Isa 25:6–10; Zech 8:20–23). By our period, however, when the concept of proselytism had developed, the question could emerge with more immediacy. When Gentiles are invited to share with Israel in the blessings of the age to come, are they to be fully incorporated into the people of Israel as "end-time proselytes," or do they continue in their separate existence outside Israel, worshipping God as Gentiles? In the material itself, however, there is little evidence that the question was addressed in any direct or explicit way. As with the biblical material that preceded it, we encounter both a certain ambiguity and a sense that the focus of attention lies elsewhere.

13. Sometimes they are loosely described as undergoing a "conversion" (McKnight 1991, 47; also Volz 1934, 356) or said to experience "salvation by incorporation into Israel" (Gaston 1987, 27), but without any consideration of alternatives. Similarly it is sometimes said that they continue to be Gentiles, though with equal imprecision (e.g., E. P. Sanders 1985, 94). The question has been brought more clearly into focus, however, by Fredriksen (1991), Kraus (1996), and others (see Donaldson 1990; 1997, 69–74).

On the one hand, there are a few passages that seem to imply full incorporation, though none say so explicitly or categorically. The Septuagint version of Isa 54:15 speaks of end-time pilgrims as "proselytes"; while this implies that the idea is possible, the use of the term is dictated more by peculiarities in the MT Hebrew than by any interest in the idea itself. In describing Gentiles in the end times as people "upon whom my name is called," LXX Amos 9:11–12 describes them in terms usually reserved for Israel, but such associative terminology does not by itself imply identity. More explicit references to the law as being observed by Gentiles in the end times are found in the *Testament of the Twelve Patriarchs* (*T. Levi* 18:9; cf. 14:4; *T. Naph.* 3:2), in the *Sibyllines* (*Sib. Or.* 3:719, 757–58; *Sib. Or.* 5:265) and in Philo (*Moses* 2.43–44). In each case, however, the "law" of Moses has been aligned with a natural law that Gentiles are able to recognize on their own. If the law of Moses and Gentile wisdom represent two routes to the same ethical-monotheistic end, the expectation that Gentiles might ultimately attain to this end does not necessarily imply that they will be incorporated into Israel. Some have interpreted *1 En.* 90:30–38 as presenting a different type of incorporation, one in which the categories of "Israel" and "Gentile" are transcended entirely, so that the righteous of the end-times recreate the unified humanity that was intended at the beginning. This interpretation, however, is unlikely; more probably the distinction is expected to continue into the future.

One the other hand, there are a few passages—but only a few—that seem explicitly to envisage the continued existence of Gentiles as Gentiles. *Psalms of Solomon* 17 makes a clear distinction between Israel and the nations (e.g., v. 28), which means that if it is to be interpreted in a positive way, the "nations" to whom the messiah shows compassion (v. 34) retain their identity as Gentiles. Certainly those Egyptians who "erect a sanctuary of the true God" in Egypt (*Sib. Or.* 5:493) continue to exist as non-Jews, though this passage is a unique case.

Most of the passages, however, are ambiguous. Since the Epistle of Enoch (*1 En.* 91–105) places a great deal of stress on the "paths of righteousness," which are explicitly equated with "the commandments of the Most High,"[14] one could argue that the Gentiles who are to receive "instruction" in the end times (*1 En.* 105:1) will be instructed in the full law of Moses. But while this is a plausible inference, it is not made explicit in the passage itself. On the other side of the ledger, in the foregoing discussion I have tended to argue that Gentiles maintain their identity in many of these passages (e.g., Tob 14:5–7; *1 En.* 90:30–38; *2 Bar.* 72). But again this is a case that needs to be argued. While the question may be of interest to us as interpreters, it does not seem to have been of pressing interest to Jews in antiquity. Another form of ambiguity is found in a few passages that combine a positive expectation for the whole of humankind with a decreased emphasis on Israel as a distinct, covenanted entity (*1 En.* 10:21–11:2; 48:4–5; 50:2–5).

14. *1 Enoch* 99:10; also 91:4, 18, 19; 94:1, 3, 4.

Thus within the Judaism of this period there certainly was a widespread expectation that Gentiles would turn to God in the end times and thus share in the blessings of the coming age. For the most part, this future blessing of the Gentiles is dependent on the vindication and restoration of Israel; the expectation seems to be that the blessings poured out by God on Israel spill over to benefit at least some of the Gentile world as well. In this respect the material develops patterns that were already sketched out in Israel's scriptures, though the developments go beyond the biblical patterns in some ways and adapt them to new patterns of thought. Perhaps it was precisely because the focus of these patterns was on Israel—the vindication of Israel's place among the nations of the world and the consummation of Jewish expectations of what the world should be like—that the status of the Gentiles was not addressed directly. The primary function of this material had to do with Israel's expectations and self-understanding. Still, it would be a mistake to discount the significance of the Gentiles in this material; their presence in the pattern is more than simply decoration. In this strand of Jewish thinking, the inclusion of the Gentiles in the final consummation was an essential part of Israel's expectations and self-understanding.

CHAPTER 14

CONCLUSION

The primary conclusion to be drawn from this study concerns the existence of what we have called patterns of universalism. To be sure, we have had to guard against the temptation to generalize. Jewish opinions varied through time, place, and cultural context. Each text has to be treated primarily as providing evidence for its own time and place. Nevertheless, we have been able to apply a form of what in the study of the historical Jesus is called a criterion of multiple attestation: where a similar viewpoint is attested in multiple sources—especially if those sources differ in form and provenance—it is appropriate to conclude that the viewpoint represents a possibility that is present—at least in latent form—in the tradition.[1] That is, we are justified to think that it was an inherent option, something that could exist between and beyond the points on the graph for which we have evidence.

Even when we apply this criterion, however, we need to recognize that the actual viewpoints reflected in the textual evidence tend to be more variable, and the boundaries between different groups of them tend to be fuzzier than the more sharply defined categories we might construct in order to analyze them. But while a map is different than the terrain it depicts, maps nevertheless are useful things. It is much easier to find one's way through difficult or unfamiliar terrain if one has a well-conceived map. Thus the attempt to identify discrete patterns of universalism is not a misguided exercise in oversimplification.

We have identified four such patterns. The first, emerging from our study of Gentile sympathizers, is the idea, apparently held by many Jews, that

1. See Fredriksen (1991, 534) for a similar approach.

Gentiles who acknowledged the divine origin of the Mosaic law and the Jerusalem temple, who worshipped the God of Israel, and who adopted Jewish ways and observances to some appropriate extent would have fulfilled their religious obligations as Gentiles and thus would be acceptable to God. As we have seen, it is difficult to find any precise indication of the degree to which Jewish observances would need to be adopted. Nor do we find any clear articulation of a rationale that might be used to determine this—for example, the idea that what was required of Gentiles was precisely that portion of the Torah that pertained to Gentiles. Further, while many Jewish communities seem to have attracted a penumbra of Gentile sympathizers, there is little evidence that these adherents—or a defined subset of them—constituted a particular class or possessed a recognized status within the Jewish community. In a related matter, while a rich variety of terms was used to describe such Gentiles, there is little evidence for a well-established technical terminology. It is not inappropriate to refer to this pattern of universalism with such terms as "righteous Gentiles" or "God-fearing Gentiles," since such language does appear. But in doing so we should not suppose nor imply that the terms had a technical currency in antiquity. The pattern or category might have been recognized and the language might have been used, but any categorical use of such language is our own. Nevertheless, the primary point is that such a pattern did exist.

The second pattern of universalism is conversion. This pattern was made possible by the development of the idea that birth need not be the sole means of entrance into the Jewish community; Jewish identity came to be understood as something that could also be acquired by outsiders. The biblical conception of the sojourner provided the raw materials for this pattern, and Hellenism—an ethnos-based culture that could be adopted by non-Greeks—provided the prototype and stimulus. Thus non-Jews who abandoned the gods of the Gentiles and devoted themselves completely to monotheistic worship, who identified fully with the Jewish community, and who committed themselves to the way of life prescribed by the law were accepted as (at least in principle) full and equal members of the Jewish people. While circumcision was widely recognized as the required mark of conversion, we saw little evidence that this was part of a well-established initiation rite, such as is found in rabbinic tradition with its threefold requirement of circumcision, immersion, and sacrifice. Rather than thinking of conversion with respect to initiation rites and formal status, it is probably more fruitful to think of it as an incorporation into the Jewish community that is effected by significant levels of commitment along the three axes just mentioned (monotheism, identification with the Jewish community, and Torah observance). These three axes reflect three ways in which "Judaism" was perceived and construed: as a form of worship and cultic observance, as an ethnic group with its own land and history, or as a way of life prescribed by the Torah, sometimes thought of as a kind of philosophy and sometimes as a form of political constitution.

The third pattern of universalism, which we have called "ethical monotheism," downplays the second of these construals (Judaism as a social and ethnic entity) and conceives of the other two (monotheism and an ordered, ethical way of life) as virtues that non-Jews could recognize on their own and even to some extent achieve. Here the Torah is perceived as a particular formulation of a natural law that is written into the fabric of the universe. Thus the Torah on the one hand and human reason or philosophical teaching on the other are seen as two paths to the same transcendent goal. Without a doubt this conception had an internal apologetic impetus and function—to provide the Torah with a rational base and framework for those Jews who recognized the value of Greek philosophy and who felt the force of criticisms directed at Judaism by learned outsiders. Nevertheless, the conception was directed outward as well and at least some Jews thought of ethical monotheism as a real possibility.

The final pattern focuses not on Gentile attitudes and activity in the present but on the possibility that a substantial number of Gentiles would turn to worship God in the eschatological future. This expectation, deeply rooted in Israel's scriptures, did not exist in isolation but was always one aspect of a larger eschatological scenario centered on Israel itself. Often a kind of cause-and-effect process seems to be envisaged: as a consequence of Israel's end-time vindication and the visible establishment of God's glory in Jerusalem, the nations finally recognize the validity of Israel's self-understanding, abandon their futile ways of worship, and devote themselves to Israel's God. Even where such a causal sequence is not explicit, the general understanding is that any future blessing of the Gentiles is a by-product of Israel's vindication and redemption. Nevertheless, the theme does not function simply as embroidery on material whose sole purpose was to reassure Israel about the validity of its own self-understanding. There was a very real expectation that Gentiles would come to join them as very real participants in the blessings of the end times. Or perhaps a better way to put it is that, within this tradition at least, Israel's self-understanding required that the final establishment of God's glory should be universal and that the nations as well should be included in God's purposes.

Of course, as has been mentioned, things are often fuzzier on the ground than on the map. The distinctions are not always as sharply drawn in the material itself as we are inclined to make them in our analysis of it. Josephus, for example, frequently describes Gentile attraction to Judaism as a single, undifferentiated phenomenon without drawing distinctions between sympathization and conversion, even though he makes it clear elsewhere that he is fully aware of the difference. Philo is equally ambiguous at times, so concerned is he to align Moses and Plato that it is sometimes difficult to differentiate adherents of the former from disciples of the latter. In the case of the eschatological pattern, it is often left unclear whether those Gentiles who participate in the blessings of the end times do so as converts or as righteous Gentiles. In other words, the degree to which they are incorporated into Israel itself is ambiguous. Despite the fuzziness, however, we can conclude that these four patterns were present on the ground and that this fourfold map provides us with a helpful guide to the terrain.

Turning to a consideration of the interrelationships between these four categories, we have seen that most of the pertinent material operates at a primary level, with little second-order discussion or debate about the religious status of Gentiles. Nevertheless, on the basis both of such second-order discourse as is present and of inferences that can be drawn in other cases, we are able to say something about how advocates of one pattern might have thought of the others. The situation is clearest in the case of those texts in which full conversion is seen as the only positive option for Gentiles. One example is provided by Izates' advisor Eleazar, who counseled the king that the only way to please God was to follow the injunctions of the law in their entirety. For Eleazar, the only hope that Gentiles might have of sharing in the blessings of the future age is to become converts to Israel in the present age. All other options, by implication, are eliminated. A similar viewpoint is found in a more extreme form in *4 Ezra* and *2 Baruch*. While these works hold out the possibility of conversion (*4 Ezra* 3:31b–36; *2 Bar.* 41:4), the possibility remains little more than hypothetical. The dominant thrust in both writings is that God is justified in condemning the Gentiles because, while they knew God's requirements and had a real opportunity to repent, "they scorned his Law, and denied his covenants; they have been unfaithful to his statutes and have not performed his works" (*4 Ezra* 7:24).[2] The (slight) possibility of conversion serves only to demonstrate the culpability of the vast majority of Gentiles. While Eleazar is somewhat more optimistic about the possibility of conversion, the difference in outlook is just a matter of degree.[3]

Ananias, Izates' other advisor, together with Josephus himself, seems to take the position that while it would be possible for a Gentile to worship God

2. Also *4 Ezra* 7:72–74; 8:55–61; 9:9–12.

3. A similar concern to establish the culpability of Gentiles, and thus the justice of divine punishment, is present in Pseudo-Philo's *Biblical Antiquities* and the *Apocalypse of Abraham*, though neither presents even the hypothetical possibility of conversion. For Pseudo-Philo, while the law was given as "a light to the world" (*L.A.B.* 11:1), the only function of this light is to silence any Gentiles who might protest their condemnation (*L.A.B.* 11:1–2). The *Apocalypse of Abraham* describes God as waiting for the Gentiles to "come to me" (31:6), even though the waiting is futile; it also sees the ultimate fate of the Gentiles as the result of divine predetermination ("prepared . . . for revenge and perdition at the end of the age" [*Apoc. Ab.* 22:4]), a theme also present in the *Testament of Moses* (1:11–13). The extreme position on the negative end of the spectrum, however, is occupied by *Jubilees*. For the author of this work, the only way to please God is to keep the Torah in its entirety. Since the Torah contains the injunction requiring circumcision on the eighth day, Gentiles are excluded from the outset (*Jub.* 15:26). The author feels no need to explain or to justify this exclusion; in his viewpoint it seems to be axiomatic.

in an acceptable manner as a Gentile, proselytism was a better option, even the ideal. Presumably this would be the case for many others, though much of the material we examined seemed to be content with the phenomenon of Gentile sympathization as it was, without seeing it as a lesser good or as simply a step to something better. Looking at sympathization from another angle, the *Letter of Aristeas* seems to operate on the assumption that while there may indeed be true ethical monotheists among the Gentiles, when such people encounter Judaism (at least Judaism as it is portrayed by the high priest Eleazar!) they will acknowledge its excellence and worship the God who stands behind it. In other words, ethical monotheists will inevitably become sympathizers, given the opportunity. Similar tendencies are present in Philo, though he seems to lean in the direction of proselytism as the ideal, even if the goal of the law is located far beyond mere external conformity to the law's provisions. Looking at sympathization from yet another angle, Philo provides us with one example of an author who is prepared to see a connection between sympathization in the present and eschatological pilgrimage expectations for the future. In *Moses* 2.17–44 there is a kind of a *qal waḥomer* or *a minori ad maius* logic at work: if Gentiles are attracted to Judaism in the present when "our nation has not prospered for many a year" (*Moses* 2.43), how much more will such attraction take place in the future, when Israel's glory is fully restored?

While the identification and documentation of these patterns has been our primary goal, we have also paid attention to some related questions pertaining to Judaism more generally.[4] There is no need to revisit these questions in detail here; it will be sufficient to summarize the conclusions drawn in the preceding four chapters and to make just a few additional comments. One of the questions has come up already in this chapter—whether there was a recognized class of synagogue adherents or "God-fearers." Another has had to do with image and reality—whether and to what extent the literary depiction of Gentiles in these patterns of universalism corresponded to some social reality. We have observed that while this depiction undeniably served internal needs—rationalizing and reinforcing the Jews' own social construction of reality—there can also be little doubt both that Gentiles were attracted to Judaism in considerable numbers and that the positive or hopeful depiction of Gentiles in Jewish literature often reflected an interest in Gentiles for their own sake.

We have also paid attention to related questions, having to do with the intended function of this literature, especially literature that displays an apologetic character. Were these writings directed outwards to a readership that would at least include Gentiles? Was this literature written as part of an attempt to increase the numbers of Gentile adherents or converts? Or was it intended primarily for internal consumption? We have seen that these questions probably

4. For an introduction to these questions of interest, see ch. 1 above.

should not be posed in either-or terms. While this literature was probably written in the first instance for the Jewish community itself, this community included a penumbra of adherents and converts for whom the literature would be of special interest.

A fourth question has had to do with the possibility of a Jewish mission. Did Jews in this period engage in—and see themselves as engaged in—an active mission to attract Gentile sympathizers, turn sympathizers into proselytes, and so on? We have seen that care needs to be taken with the question itself, since too often it is constructed on the basis of an unexamined notion of "mission," usually imported from Christian missionary movements of a much later period. Still, the question can be posed in a less freighted way, asking about the Jewish role in the process by which a Gentile became a synagogue adherent or convert and about the degree to which Jews took the initiative in inviting Gentiles to take these steps. Again we have found it advisable to answer the question in a nuanced way. The evidence seems to suggest that the primary initiative was taken by the Gentiles themselves; in other words, it was a matter of Gentile attraction to Judaism rather than of active recruitment on the part of Jews. Nevertheless, there is substantial evidence indicating that Jews took pride in the phenomenon and were ready to welcome such Gentiles as sought them out. In addition, there are indications that individual Jews took initiative to encourage and to provide instruction for such inquirers, even in the form of substantial literary works (e.g., *Against Apion*). Further, there is some evidence that Jews saw either the law itself, or themselves as custodians of the law, as God's light in the world.[5] The fact that this speaks more of passive visibility than of active promotion only serves to underline the point being made here. With respect to the geographical spread of the evidence, while there certainly was local variation and while the evidence tends to be more plentiful for certain localities, especially Alexandria and Rome, there is no reason to treat these as exceptional cases.[6]

This leads to a final question, that of unity and diversity. We have repeatedly encountered diversity, not only in the patterns of universalism themselves but also in various other related matters. With respect to our primary area of investigation, there simply was no unified view whatsoever on the religious status of non-Jews, either now or in the future. The range of diversity is striking.

5. E.g., Wisdom 18:4: "through whom the imperishable light of the law was to be given to the world"; *T. Levi* 14:4: "the light of the Law which was granted to you for the enlightenment of every man"; *Sib. Or.* 3:195: "guides in life for all mortals"; Rom 2:19–20: "a guide to the blind, a light to those who are in darkness, . . . having in the law the embodiment of knowledge and truth." Also pertinent here are Philo's assertions that Israel offers prayers and sacrifice on behalf of the whole human race or serves as priest for the rest of the world or exists as the "first fruits" of humanity (see ch. 5, "Concluding Observations"). See also *Sib. Or.* 5:238–41, 328–32.

6. McKnight (1991, 74) has suggested that Rome be seen as an exceptional case.

Nevertheless, there are elements of unity as well. Not only is it the case that these various patterns of universalism are rooted in and arise out of the same ethnic and religious tradition, but we also find expressions of similar patterns emerging in quite different geographical and cultural contexts. If we can find proselytes in Adiabene and in Rome, Gentile sympathizers in 2 Maccabees and the *Letter of Aristeas*, and eschatological pilgrimage traditions in *1 Enoch* and in Philo, we need to reckon with a considerable level of interaction and interconnection. In other words, we are dealing with a phenomenon for which the singular (Judaism) continues to be more appropriate than the plural (Judaisms). Still, the diversity to which the plural draws our attention is amply demonstrated by the range of Jewish attitudes towards the non-Jewish other and the patterns of universalism that are readily apparent.

I began this work with a criticism of the common tendency to differentiate Judaism and Christianity on the basis of the supposed particularism of the former and universalism of the latter. It should be apparent from the intervening pages that the Judaism within which Christianity came to birth was just as universalistic in its own way as was its upstart offspring. Even more, while Christianity may have taken its universalistic heritage and developed it in ways unforeseen, in the process becoming a worldwide religion into which "all the nations" have been drawn, there are still some things that it may be able to learn from its parent. In a world of globalized relationships and pluralistic cultures, the "religious other" has become a more immediate fact of human life—at levels ranging from the interpersonal to the geopolitical—than at any point in the past. In such a world it is imperative that persons of faith learn how to create theological space for the other even as they remain true to their own identity and vision. (I speak as a Christian, but the point is of more general applicability.) I am not suggesting that Second-Temple Judaism provides us with any sort of final word on the matter. Still, by providing us with several models of how universalism might be envisaged, it broadens our perspective, increases our conceptual resources, and renews our hope for a day in which "all the deeds of wickedness will vanish from the whole earth . . . and all humankind will look to the path of eternal righteousness" (*1 En.* 91.14).

Works Cited

Abel, Ernest L. 1968. "Were the Jews Banished from Rome in 19 A.D.?" *Revue des études juives* 127: 383–86.

Allegro, John M. 1969. *Qumran Cave 4. I (4Q158–4Q186)*. DJD V. Oxford: Clarendon.

Andersen, Francis I. 1983. "2 Enoch." Pages 91–221 in *Old Testament Pseudepigrapha*. Vol. 1. Edited by James H. Charlesworth. Garden City, N.Y.: Doubleday.

Andersen, Francis I., and David Noel Freedman. 1989. *Amos: A New Translation with Introduction and Commentary*. AB 24A. New York: Doubleday.

Anderson, H. 1985a. "3 Maccabees." Pages 509–29 in *Old Testament Pseudepigrapha*. Vol. 2. Edited by James H. Charlesworth. Garden City, N.Y.: Doubleday

———. 1985b. "4 Maccabees." Pages 531–64 in *Old Testament Pseudepigrapha*. Vol. 2. Edited by James H. Charlesworth. Garden City, N.Y.: Doubleday

Anderson, William Scovil. 1982. *Essays on Roman Satire*. Princeton, N.J.: Princeton University Press.

Applebaum, Shim'on. 1979. *Jews and Greeks in Ancient Cyrene*. Studies in Judaism in Late Antiquity 28. Leiden: E. J. Brill.

Avni, Gideon, Zvi Greenhut, and Tal Ilan. 1994. "Three New Burial Caves of the Second Temple Period in Aceldama (Kidron Valley)." Pages 206–18 in *Ancient Jerusalem Revealed*. Edited by Hillel Geva. Jerusalem: Israel Exploration Society.

Avni, Gideon, and Zvi Greenhut. 1996. *The Akeldama Tombs: Three Burial Caves in the Kidron Valley, Jerusalem*. Jerusalem: Israel Antiquities Authority.

Babbitt, Frank Cole, ed. and trans. 1928. *Plutarch: Moralia*. Vol. II. Loeb Classical Library. Cambridge, Mass.: Harvard University Press.

Bagatti, Bellarmino. 1971. *The Church from the Circumcision: History and Archaeology of the Judeo-Christians*. Jerusalem: Franciscan Printing Press.

Bagatti, Bellarmino, and J. T. Milik. 1958. *La Necropoli del Periodo Romano*. Vol. 1 of *Gli Scavi del Dominus Flevit*. Jerusalem: Franciscan Press.

Baillet, M. 1982. *Qumran grotte 4.III (4Q482–4Q520)*. DJD VII. Oxford: Clarendon.

Balch, David L. 1998. "Attitudes Toward Foreigners in 2 Maccabees, Eupolemus, Esther, Aristeas, and Luke-Acts." Pages 22–42 in *The Early Church in Its Context: Essays in Honor of Everett Ferguson*. Edited by Abraham J. Malherbe, Frederick W. Norris, and James W. Thompson. Leiden: E. J. Brill.

Baldwin, Barry. 1983. *Suetonius*. Amsterdam: Hakkert.

Baltzer, Klaus. 2001. *Deutero-Isaiah: A Commentary on Isaiah 40–55*. Hermeneia. Minneapolis: Fortress.

Bamberger, B. J. 1968. *Proselytism in the Talmudic Period.* Cincinnati: Hebrew Union College Press, 1939. Repr. New York: Ktav.

Barclay, John M. G. 1996. *Jews in the Mediterranean Diaspora: From Alexander to Trajan (323 BCE–117 CE).* Edinburgh: T. & T. Clark.

———. 1998. "Josephus v. Apion: Analysis of an Argument." Pages 194–221 in *Understanding Josephus: Seven Perspectives.* Edited by Steve Mason. Journal for the Study of the Pseudepigrapha 32. Sheffield: Sheffield Academic Press.

Barrett, C. K. 1994, 1998. *A Critical and Exegetical Commentary on the Acts of the Apostles.* 2 vols. International Critical Commentary. Edinburgh: T. & T. Clark.

Bartlett, John R. 1985. *Jews in the Hellenistic World: Josephus, Aristeas, The Sybilline Oracles, Eupolemus.* Vol. 1, pt. 1. Cambridge Commentaries on Writings of the Jewish and Christian World, 200 BC to AD 200. Cambridge: Cambridge University Press.

Batiffol, P. 1889–1890. "Le livre de la priére d'Aseneth." Pages 1–115 in *Studia patristica: études d'ancienne littérature chrétienne.* 2 vols. Paris: Leroux.

Baumgarten, Joseph M. 1972. "The Exclusion of 'Netinim' and Proselytes in 4QFlor." *Revue de Qumran* 8: 87–96.

———. 1982. "Exclusions from the Temple: Proselyte and Agrippa I." *Journal of Jewish Studies* 33: 215–25.

Becker, Jürgen. 1970. *Untersuchungen zur Entstehungsgeschichte der Testamente der Zwölf Patriarchen.* Arbeiten zur Geschichte des antiken Judentums und des Urchristentums. Leiden: E. J. Brill.

Beckwith, R. T. 1984. "The Solar Calendar of Joseph and Asenath: A Suggestion." *Journal for the Study of Judaism* 15: 90–111.

Beentjes, Pancratius Cornelis. 1997. *The Book of Ben Sira in Hebrew: A Text Edition of All Extant Hebrew Manuscripts and a Synopsis of All Parallel Hebrew Ben Sira Texts.* Supplements to Vetus Testamentum 68. Leiden: E. J. Brill.

Belkin, S. 1940. *Philo and the Oral Law.* Cambridge, Mass.: Harvard University Press.

Bellen, Heinz. 1965–1966. "Συναγωγή τῶν Ιουδαίων καὶ Θεοσεβῶν: Die Aussage einer bosporanischen Freilassungsinschrift (*CIRB* 71) zum Problem der 'Gottfürchtigen.'" *Jahrbuch für Antike und Christentum* 8/9: 171–76.

Bennett, Harold V. 2002. *Injustice Made Legal: Deuteronomic Law and the Plight of Widows, Strangers, and Orphans in Ancient Israel.* Grand Rapids: Eerdmans.

Berg, Sandra Beth. 1979. *The Book of Esther: Motifs, Themes, and Structure.* Missoula, Mont.: Scholars Press.

Bernays, Jakob. 1885. "Die Gottesfürchtigung bei Juvenal." Pages 71–80 in *Gesammelte Abhandlungen.* Edited by Hermann Usener. New York: G. Olms.

Bertholet, Alfred. 1896. *Die Stellung der Israeliten und der Juden zu den Fremden.* Freiburg and Leipzig: Mohr.

Bickerman, Elias J. 1933. "Ein jüdischer Festbrief vom Jahre 124 v. Chr. (II Macc. 1.1–9)." *Zeitschrift für die neutestamentliche Wissenschaft* 32: 233–54.

———. 1944. "The Colophon of the Greek Book of Esther." *Journal of Biblical Literature* 63: 39–62.

———. 1980. *Studies in Jewish and Christian History: Part Two.* Arbeiten zur Geschichte des antiken Judentums und des Urchristentums 9. Leiden: E. J. Brill.

Bilde, Per. 1988. *Flavius Josephus Between Jerusalem and Rome: His Life, His Works and Their Importance*. Journal for the Study of the Pseudepigrapha: Supplement Series 2. Sheffield: JSOT Press.

———. 1998. "Josephus and Jewish Apocalypticism." Pages 35–61 in *Understanding Josephus: Seven Perspectives*. Edited by Steve Mason. Journal for the Study of the Pseudepigrapha: Supplement Series 32. Sheffield: Sheffield Academic Press.

Birnbaum, Ellen. 1996. *The Place of Judaism in Philo's Thought: Israel, Jews and Proselytes*. Atlanta: Scholars Press.

Black, Matthew. 1970. *Apocalypsis Henochi Graece*. Pseudepigrapha Veteris Testamenti Graece 3. Leiden: E. J. Brill.

———. 1985. *The Books of Enoch or 1 Enoch: A New English Edition with Commentary and Textual Notes*. Studia in Veteris Testamenti pseudepigraphica 7. Leiden: E. J. Brill.

———. 1992. "The Messianism of the Parables of Enoch: Their Date and Contribution to Christological Origins." Pages 145–68 in *The Messiah: Developments in Earliest Judaism and Christianity*. Edited by James H. Charlesworth. Minneapolis: Fortress.

Blenkinsopp, Joseph. 2002. *Isaiah 40–55: A New Translation with Introduction and Commentary*. Anchor Bible 19A. New York: Doubleday.

Blidstein, G. 1974. "4QFlorilegium and Rabbinic Sources on Bastard and Proselyte." *Revue de Qumran* 8: 431–35.

Boccaccini, Gabriele. 1991. *Middle Judaism: Jewish Thought, 300 B.C.E. to 200 C.E.* Minneapolis: Fortress.

Bockmuehl, Markus. 2000. *Jewish Law in Gentile Churches: Halakhah and the Beginning of Christian Public Ethics*. Edinburgh: T. & T. Clark.

Bogaert, Pierre. 1969. *Apocalypse de Baruch: introduction, traduction du Syriaque et commentaire*. Paris: Editions du Cerf.

Bohak, Gideon. 1996. *Joseph and Aseneth and the Jewish Temple in Heliopolis*. Early Judaism and Its Literature 10. Atlanta: Scholars Press.

Borgen, Peder. 1984 "Philo of Alexandria: A Critical and Synthetical Survey of Research Since World War II." Pages 98–154 in *Aufstieg und Niedergang der Römischen Welt*. Vol. II/21.1. Edited by Wolfgang Haase. Berlin: De Gruyter.

———. 1996. "Militant and Peaceful Proselytism and Christian Mission." Pages 45–69 in *Early Christianity and Hellenistic Judaism*. Edinburgh: T. & T. Clark.

———. 1997. *Philo of Alexandria: An Exegete for His Time*. Novum Testamentum Supplements 86. Leiden: E. J. Brill.

Box, G. H. 1913. "4 Ezra." Pages 542–624 in *The Apocrypha and Pseudepigrapha of the Old Testament*. Vol. 2. Edited by R. H. Charles. Oxford: Clarendon Press.

Boyancé, Pierre. 1955. "Sur la théologie de Varron." *Revue des études anciennes* 57: 57–84.

Bradley, K. R. 1998. "Introduction." Pages 1–34 in *Suetonius*. Translated by John Carew Rolfe. Loeb Classical Library 38. Cambridge, Mass.: Harvard University Press.

Braude, W. E. 1940. *Jewish Proselyting in the First Five Centuries of the Common Era*. Providence, R.I.: Brown University Press.

Braund, Susanna Morton, ed. and trans. 1940. *Juvenal and Persius*. Loeb Classical Library. Cambridge, Mass.: Harvard University Press.

Breitenstein, Urs. 1976. *Beobachtungen zu Sprache, Stil und Gedankengut des vierten Makkabäerbuchs*. Basel: Schwabe.

Brixhe, Claude, and René Hodot. 1988. *L'Asie mineure du nord au sud: inscriptions inédites*. Etudes d'archéologie classique 6. Nancy: Presses universitaires de Nancy.

Brooke, George J. 1985. *Exegesis at Qumran: 4QFlorilegium in Its Jewish Context.* Journal for the Study of the Old Testament: Supplement Series 29. Sheffield: JSOT Press.

Brooke, George J. et al. 1996. *Qumran Cave 4. XVII: Parabiblical Texts, Part 3.* DJD XXII. Oxford: Clarendon.

Brown, Raymond E. 1966; 1970. *The Gospel According to John.* 2 vols. AB 29. Garden City, N.Y.: Doubleday.

Bruce, F. F. 1979. "Prophetic Interpretation in the Septuagint." *Bulletin of the International Organization for Septuagint and Cognate Studies* 12: 17–26.

Bunge, Jochen Gabriel. 1971. *Untersuchungen zum zweiten Makkabäerbuch: Quellenkritische, literarische, chronologische und historische Untersuchungen zum zweiten Makkabäerbuch als Quelle syrisch-palästinensischer Geschichte im 2. Jh. v. Chr.* Bonn: Rheinische Friedrich-Wilhelms-Universität.

Burchard, Christoph. 1965. *Untersuchungen zu Joseph und Aseneth: Überlieferung, Ortsbestimmung.* Wissenschaftliche Untersuchungen zum Neuen Testament 8. Tübingen: J. C. B. Mohr (Paul Siebeck).

———. 1996. *Gesammelte Studien zu Joseph und Aseneth.* Studia in Veteris Testamenti pseudepigraphica 13. New York: E. J. Brill.

———. 1985. "Joseph and Aseneth." Pages 177–247 in *Old Testament Pseudepigrapha.* Vol. 2. Edited by James H. Charlesworth. Garden City, N.Y.: Doubleday.

Calder, William Moir, and Susan Mary Sherwin-White. 2003. "Alabanda." Page 49 in *The Oxford Classical Dictionary.* 3d ed., rev. Edited by Simon Hornblower and Antony Spawforth. Oxford: Oxford University Press.

Cancik, Hubert, Hermann Lichtenberger, and Peter Schäfer, eds. 1996. *Geschichte-Tradition-Reflexion: Festschrift für Martin Hengel zum 70. Geburtstag.* Tübingen: J. C. B. Mohr (Paul Siebeck).

Carleton Paget, James. 1996. "Jewish Proselytism at the Time of Christian Origins: Chimera or Reality?" *Journal for the Study of the New Testament* 62: 65–103.

Cazelles, Henri. 1951. "Le personnage d'Acior dans le livre de Judith." *Recherches de science religieuse* 39: 125–37.

Charles, R. H. 1908. *The Greek Versions of the Testaments of the Twelve Patriarchs. Edited from Nine MSS. Together with the Variants of the Armenian and Slavonic Versions and Some Hebrew Fragments.* Oxford: Clarendon Press.

———. 1913a. *The Apocrypha and Pseudepigrapha of the Old Testament.* 2 vols. Oxford: Clarendon Press.

———. 1913b. "1 Enoch." Pages 163–281 in *The Apocrypha and Pseudepigrapha of the Old Testament.* Vol. 2. Edited by R. H. Charles. Oxford: Clarendon Press.

———. 1913c. "The Testaments of the XII Patriarchs." Pages 282–367 in *The Apocrypha and Pseudepigrapha of the Old Testament.* Vol. 2. Edited by R. H. Charles. Oxford: Clarendon Press.

———. 1913d. "2 Baruch." Pages 470–526 in *The Apocrypha and Pseudepigrapha of the Old Testament.* Vol. 2. Edited by R. H. Charles. Oxford: Clarendon Press.

———. 1917. *The Book of Enoch or 1 Enoch.* Oxford: Clarendon Press.

Chesnutt, Randall D. 1995. *From Death to Life: Conversion in Joseph and Aseneth.* Journal for the Study of the Pseudepigrapha: Supplement Series 16. Sheffield: Sheffield Academic Press.

Chilver, G. E. F., and G. B. Townend. 1985. *A Historical Commentary on Tacitus' Histories IV and V.* Oxford: Clarendon Press.

Christiansen, Ellen Juhl. 1995. *The Covenant in Judaism and Paul: A Study of Ritual Boundaries as Identity Markers*. Arbeiten zur Geschichte des antiken Judentums und des Urchristentums 27. Leiden: E. J. Brill.

Clines, David J. A. 1984. *The Esther Scroll: The Story of the Story*. Journal for the Study of the Old Testament: Supplement Series 30. Sheffield: JSOT Press.

Cohen, Shaye J. D. 1979. *Josephus in Galilee and Rome: His Vita and Development as a Historian*. Leiden: E. J. Brill.

———. 1987a. "Respect for Judaism by Gentiles According to Josephus." *Harvard Theological Review* 80: 409–30.

———. 1987b. *From the Maccabees to the Mishnah*. Philadelphia: Westminster.

———. 1989. "Crossing the Boundary and Becoming a Jew." *Harvard Theological Review* 82: 11–33.

———. 1990. "The Rabbinic Conversion Ceremony." *Journal of Jewish Studies* 41: 177–203.

———. 1992. "Was Judaism in Antiquity a Missionary Religion?" Pages 14–23 in *Jewish Assimilation, Acculturation and Accommodation: Past Traditions, Current Issues and Future Prospects*. Edited by Menachem Mor. Studies in Jewish Civilization 2. Lanham, Md.: University Press of America.

———. 1999. *The Beginnings of Jewishness: Boundaries, Varieties, Uncertainties*. Berkeley: University of California Press.

Collins, Adela Yarbro. 1985. "Aristobulus." Pages 831–42 in *Old Testament Pseudepigrapha*. Vol. 2. Edited by James H. Charlesworth. Garden City, N.Y.: Doubleday.

Collins, John J. 1974. *The Sibylline Oracles of Egyptian Judaism*. Society of Biblical Literature Dissertation Series 13. Missoula, Mont.: Scholars Press.

———. 1980. "The Epic of Theodotus and the Hellenism of the Hasmonaeans." *Harvard Theological Review* 73: 91–104.

———. 1983. "Sibylline Oracles." Pages 317–472 in *Old Testament Pseudepigrapha*. Vol. 1. Edited by James H. Charlesworth. Garden City, N.Y.: Doubleday, 1983.

———. 1985a. "A Symbol of Otherness: Circumcision and Salvation in the First Century." Pages 163–86 in *"To See Ourselves as Others See Us": Christians, Jews and "Others" in Late Antiquity*. Edited by J. Neusner and E. S. Frerichs. Chico, Calif.: Scholars Press.

———. 1985b. "Artapanus." Pages 889–903 in *Old Testament Pseudepigrapha*. Vol. 2. Edited by James H. Charlesworth. Garden City, N.Y.: Doubleday.

———. 1992. "'The King Has Become a Jew': The Perspective on the Gentile World in Bel and the Snake." Pages 335–45 in *Diaspora Jews and Judaism: Essays in Honor of, and in Dialogue with, A. Thomas Kraabel*. Edited by J. Andrew Overman and Robert S. MacLennan. Atlanta: Scholars Press.

———. 1993. *Daniel: A Commentary on the Book of Daniel*. Hermeneia. Minneapolis: Fortress.

———. 1995. *The Scepter and the Star: The Messiahs of the Dead Sea Scrolls and Other Ancient Literature*. The AB Reference Library. New York: Doubleday.

———. 1997. *Jewish Wisdom in the Hellenistic Age*. The Old Testament Library. Louisville, Ky.: Westminister John Knox Press.

———. 1998. *The Apocalyptic Imagination: An Introduction to Jewish Apocalyptic Literature*. 2d ed. Grand Rapids: Eerdmans.

———. 2000. *Between Athens and Jerusalem: Jewish Identity in the Hellenistic Diaspora*. 2d ed. Grand Rapids: Eerdmans.

Colson, F. H., G. H. Whitaker, and Ralph Marcus. 1929–62. *Philo*. 12 vols. Loeb Classical Library Cambridge, Mass.: Harvard University Press.

Condemi, Augusta Germana. 1965. *M. Terenti Varronis. Antiquitates Rerum Divinarum Librorum I–II, Fragmenta*. Bologna: Zanichelli.

Courtney, E. 1980. *A Commentary on the Satires of Juvenal*. London: Athlone Press.

Craven, Toni. 1983. *Artistry and Faith in the Book of Judith*. Chico, Calif.: Scholars Press.

Cross, Frank Moore. 1984. "Fragments of a Prayer of Nabonidus." *Israel Exploration Journal* 34: 260–64.

Cumont, Franz. 1897. *Hypsistos*. Bruxelles: Polleunis et Ceuterick.

———. 1906. "Les mystères de Sabazius et le Judaïsme." *Comptes rendus de l'académie des inscriptions et belles-Letters*.

Dan'shin, D. I. 1996. "The Jewish Community of Phanagoria." *Ancient Civilizations from Scythia to Siberia* 3: 133–50.

Davies, Philip R. 1983. *The Damascus Covenant: An Interpretation of the "Damascus Document."* Sheffield: JSOT Press.

———. 1994. "The 'Damascus Sect' and Judaism." Pages 70–84 in *Pursuing the Text: Studies in Honor of Ben Zion Wacholder on the Occasion of His Seventieth Birthday*. Edited by John C. Reeves and John Kampen. Journal for the Study of the Old Testament: Supplement Series 184. Sheffield: Sheffield Academic Press.

Davies, W. D. 1948. *Paul and Rabbinic Judaism*. London: SPCK.

Davies, W. D., and Dale C. Allison. 1988, 1991, 1997. *A Critical and Exegetical Commentary on the Gospel According to Saint Matthew*. 3 vols. ICC. Edinburgh: T. & T. Clark.

Davila, James R. 2000. *Liturgical Works*. Commentaries on the Dead Sea Scrolls 6. Grand Rapids: Eerdmans.

Day, Linda. 1995. *Three Faces of a Queen: Characterization in the Books of Esther*. Journal for the Study of the Old Testament: Supplement Series 186. Sheffield: Sheffield Academic Press.

Dedering, S., ed. 1973. "Apocalypse of Baruch." Pages 1–50 in *The Old Testament in Syriac according to the Peshitta Version*. Part IV, fascicle 3. Leiden: E. J. Brill.

Defradas, Jean, Jean Hani, and Robert Klaerr, ed. and trans. 1985. *Plutarch: Œvres morales: Tome II*. Paris: Les Belles Lettres.

Deines, Roland. 1994. "Die Abwehr der Fremden in den Texten aus Qumran: Zum Verständnis der Fremdenfeindlichkeit in der Qumrangemeinde." Pages 59–91 in *Die Heiden: Juden, Christen und das Problem des Fremden*. Edited by Reinhard Feldmeier and Ulrich Heckel. Wissenschaftliche Untersuchungen zum Neuen Testament 70. Tübingen: J. C. B. Mohr (Paul Siebeck).

Delcor, M. 1962. "Un roman d'amour d'origine Therapeute: Le livre de Joseph et Asénath." *Bulletin de littérature ecclésiastique* 63: 3–27.

———. 1973. *Le Testament d'Abraham*. Studia in Veteris Testamenti pseudepigrapha 2. Leiden: E. J. Brill.

Delia, Diana. 1991. *Alexandrian Citizenship During the Roman Principate*. American Classical Studies 23. Atlanta: Scholars Press.

Delling, G. 1964. "Die Alterinschrift eines Gottesfürchtigen in Pergamon." *Novum Testamentum* 7: 73–80.

Deselaers, Paul. 1982. *Das Buch Tobit: Studien zu seiner Entstehung, Komposition und Theologie*. Orbis Biblicus et Orientalis 43. Freiburg: Universitätsverlag; Göttingen: Vandenhoeck & Ruprecht.

Dexinger, Ferdinand. 1977. *Henochs Zehnwochenapokalypse und offene Probleme der Apokalyptikforschung*. Studia post-Biblica 29. Leiden: E. J. Brill.

Di Lella, Alexander A. 1966. *The Hebrew Text of Sirach: A Text-Critical and Historical Study*. The Hague: Mouton.

———. 1979. "The Deuteronomic Background of the Farewell Discourse in Tob 14:3–11." *Catholic Biblical Quarterly* 41: 380–89.

Dickson, John P. 2003. *Mission-Commitment in Ancient Judaism and in the Pauline Communities: The Shape, Extent and Background of Early Christian Mission*. Wissenschaftliche Untersuchungen zum Neuen Testament/2 159. Tübingen: J. C. B. Mohr (Paul Siebeck).

Dimant, Devorah. 1986. "4QFlorilegium and the Idea of Community as Temple." Pages 165–89 in *Hellenica et Judaica: Hommage à Valentin Nikiprowetzky*. Edited by A. Caquot, M. Hadas-Lebel, and J. Riaud. Leuven: Peeters.

Donaldson, Terence L. 1990. "Proselytes or 'Righteous Gentiles'? The Status of Gentiles in Eschatological Pilgrimage Patterns of Thought." *Journal for the Study of the Pseudepigrapa* 7: 3–27.

———. 1997. *Paul and the Gentiles: Remapping the Apostle's Convictional World*. Minneapolis: Fortress.

———. 2000. "Jerusalem Ossuary Inscriptions and the Status of Jewish Proselytes." Pages 372–88 in *Text and Artifact in the Religions of Mediterranean Antiquity: Essays in Honour of Peter Richardson*. Edited by Stephen G. Wilson and Michel Desjardins. Études sur le christianisme et le judaïsme 9. Waterloo, Ont.: Wilfrid Laurier University Press.

Doran, Robert. 1981. *Temple Propaganda: The Purpose and Character of 2 Maccabees*. Catholic Biblical Quarterly Monograph Series 12. Washington, D.C.: Catholic Biblical Association of America.

Drew-Bear, Thomas. 1976. "Local Cults in Graeco-Roman Phrygia." *Greek, Roman and Byzantine Studies* 17: 247–68.

Droge, Arthur J. 1996. "Josephus Between Greeks and Romans." Pages 115–42 in *Josephus's Contra Apionem: Studies in Its Character and Context with a Latin Concordance to the Portion Missing in Greek*. Edited by Louis H. Feldman and John R. Levison. Arbeiten zur Geschichte des antiken Judentums und des Urchristentums 34. Leiden: E. J. Brill.

Dueck, Daniela. 2000. *Strabo of Amasia: A Greek Man of Letters in Augustan Rome*. London; New York: Routledge.

Dupont-Sommer, André. 1959. *Les écrits esséniens découverts près de la Mer Morte*. Paris: Payot.

———. 1963. "Le commentaire de Nahum découvert près de la Mer Morte (4QpNah): Traduction et notes." *Semitica* 13: 55–88.

Enslin, Morton S., and Solomon Zeitlin. 1972. *The Book of Judith*. Jewish Apocryphal Literature 7. Leiden: E. J. Brill.

Fairclough, H. Rushton. 1929. *Horace: Satires, Epistles and Ars poetica*. Loeb Classical Library Cambridge, Mass.: Harvard University Press.

Falk, Daniel K. 1998. *Daily, Sabbath and Festival Prayers in the Dead Sea Scrolls*. Studies on the Texts of the Desert of Judah 27. Leiden: E. J. Brill.

Fallon, F. 1985. "Theodotus." Pages 785–93 in *Old Testament Pseudepigrapha*. Vol. 2. Edited by James H. Charlesworth. Garden City, N.Y.: Doubleday.

Feldman, Louis H. 1950. "Jewish 'Sympathizers' in Classical Literature and Inscriptions." *Transactions of the American Philological Association* 81: 200–08.

———. 1984. "Flavius Josephus Revisited: The Man, His Writings and His Significance." Pages 763–862 in *Geschichte und Kultur Roms im Spiegel der neueren Forschung*. Vol. II/21.2. of *Aufstieg und Niedergang der Römischen Welt.* Edited by Wolfgang Haase. Berlin: De Gruyter.

———. 1986. "The Omnipresence of the God-Fearers." *Biblical Archaeology Review* 12(5): 58–63.

———. 1989–1990. "The Enigma of Horace's Thirtieth Sabbath." *Scripta Classica Israelica* 10: 87–112.

———. 1992. "Was Judaism a Missionary Religion in Ancient Times?" Pages 24–37 in *Jewish Assimilation, Acculturation and Accommodation: Past Traditions, Current Issues and Future Prospects*. Edited by Menachem Mor. Studies in Jewish Civilization 2. Lanham, Md.: University Press of America.

———. 1993. *Jew and Gentile in the Ancient World: Attitudes and Interactions from Alexander to Justinian*. Princeton, N.J.: Princeton University Press.

———. 1998. *Josephus's Interpretation of the Bible*. Berkeley: University of California Press.

Feldman, Louis H., and John R. Levison eds. 1996. *Josephus's Contra Apionem: Studies in Its Character and Context with a Latin Concordance to the Portion Missing in Greek*. Arbeiten zur Geschichte des antiken Judentums und des Urchristentums 34. Leiden: E. J. Brill.

Feldman, Louis H., and Steve Mason. 2000. *Flavius Josephus: Translation and Commentary*. Leiden: E. J. Brill.

Figueras, Pau. 1990. "Epigraphic Evidence for Proselytism in Ancient Judaism." *Immanuel* 24/25: 194–206.

Finn, Thomas M. 1985. "The God-Fearers Reconsidered." *Catholic Biblical Quarterly* 47: 75–84.

Fitzmyer, Joseph A. 1981. *The Gospel According to Luke I–IX*. 2 vols. Anchor Bible 28. Garden City, N.Y.: Doubleday.

———. 1995. "Tobit." Pages 1–76 in *Qumran Cave 4.XIV*. Edited by Magen Broshi et al. Discoveries in the Judaean Desert 19. Oxford: Clarendon Press.

———. 2003. *Tobit*. Commentaries on Early Jewish Literature. Berlin: Walter de Gruyter.

Flint, Peter W. 1997. *The Dead Sea Psalms Scrolls and the Book of Psalms*. Studies on the Texts of the Desert of Judah 17. Leiden: E. J. Brill.

Fox, Michael V. 1991. *Character and Ideology in the Book of Esther*. Columbia: University of South Carolina Press.

Fredriksen, Paula. 1991. "Judaism, the Circumcision of Gentiles and Apocalyptic Hope: Another Look at Galatians 1 and 2." *Journal of Theological Studies* 42: 532–64.

Freudenthal, Jacob. 1874. *Alexander Polyhistor und die von ihm erhaltenen Reste jüdischer und samaritanischer Geschichtswerke*. Breslau: Grass.

García Martínez, Florentino. 1992. "Prayer of Nabonidus." Pages 116–36 in *Qumran and Apocalyptic: Studies on the Aramaic Texts from Qumran*. Studies on the Texts of the Desert of Judah 9. Leiden: E. J. Brill.

García Martínez, Florentino, and Eibert J. C. Tigchelaar, eds. 1997, 1998. *The Dead Sea Scrolls: Study Edition*. 2 vols. Leiden: E. J. Brill.

García Martínez, Florentino, Eibert J. C. Tigchelaar, and A. S. van der Woude. 1998. *Qumran Cave 11. II: 11Q2–18, 11Q20–31*. Discoveries in the Judaean Desert 23. Oxford: Clarendon.

Garland, David E. 1979. *The Intention of Matthew 23*. Novum Testamentum Supplements 52. Leiden: E. J. Brill.

Gaston, Lloyd. 1987. *Paul and the Torah*. Vancouver: University of British Columbia Press.

Gärtner, Bertil. 1965. *The Temple and the Community in Qumran and the New Testament*. Society for New Testament Studies Monograph Series 1. Cambridge: Cambridge University Press.

Geffcken, Johannes. 1902. *Die Oracula Sibyllina*. Griechischen christlichen Schriftsteller der ersten drei Jahrhunderte 8. Leipzig: J. C. Hinrichs.

Georgi, Dieter. 1986. *The Opponents of Paul in Second Corinthians*. Philadelphia: Fortress.

Gibson, E. Leigh. 1999. *The Jewish Manumission Inscriptions of the Bosporus Kingdom*. Texts and Studies in Ancient Judaism 75. Tübingen: J. C. B. Mohr (Paul Siebeck).

Gilbert, Gary. 1991. "The Making of a Jew: 'God-Fearer' or Convert in the Story of Izates." *Union Seminary Quarterly Review* 44: 299–313.

Goldenberg, Robert. 1998. *The Nations that Know Thee Not: Ancient Jewish Attitudes Towards Other Religions*. Sheffield: JSOT Press.

Goldingay, John. 1989. *Daniel*. Word Biblical Commentary. Dallas, Tex.: Word Books.

Goldstein, Jonathan A. 1983. *II Maccabees*. Anchor Bible 41A. Garden City, N.Y.: Doubleday.

———. 1991. "The Message of *Aristeas to Philokrates*." Pages 1–23 in *Eretz Israel, Israel, and the Jewish Diaspora: Mutual Relations*. Vol. 1 of the proceedings of the first annual Symposium of the Philip M. and Ethel Klutznick Chair in Jewish Civilization, Sunday–Monday, October 9–10, 1988. Edited by Menahem Mor. Studies in Jewish Civilization 1. Lanham, Md.: University Press of America.

Goodenough, Erwin R. 1933. "Philo's Exposition of the Law." *Harvard Theological Review* 27: 109–25.

———. 1956–1957. "The Bosporus Inscriptions to the Most High God." *Jewish Quarterly Review* 47: 221–44.

———. 1962. *An Introduction to Philo Judaeus*. Oxford: Basil Blackwell.

Goodman, Martin. 1992. "Jewish Proselytizing in the First Century." Pages 53–78 in *The Jews Among Pagans and Christians in the Roman Empire*. Edited by Judith Lieu, John North, and Tessa Rajak. London: Routledge.

———. 1994. *Mission and Conversion: Proselytizing in the Religious History of the Roman Empire*. Oxford: Clarendon Press.

Goodyear, Francis Richard David. 1981. *The Annals of Tacitus, Books 1–6*. Vol. 2. Cambridge: Cambridge University Press.

Grabbe, Lester L. 1992. *Judaism from Cyrus to Hadrian*. 2 vols. Minneapolis: Fortress.

Gray, G. B. 1913. "The Psalms of Solomon." Pages 625–52 in *The Apocrypha and Pseudepigrapha of the Old Testament*. Vol. 2. Edited by R. H. Charles. Oxford: Clarendon Press.

Gray, John. 1963. *I & II Kings: A Commentary*. Old Testament Library. Philadelphia: Westminster.

Green, W. M., ed. and trans. 1963. *Augustine: City of God*. Vol. II. Books 4–7. Loeb Classical Library. Cambridge, Mass.: Harvard University Press.

Griffin, Miriam T. 1976. *Seneca: A Philosopher in Politics*. Oxford: Clarendon Press.

Gruen, Erich S. 1998. *Heritage and Hellenism: The Reinvention of Jewish Tradition*. Berkeley: University of California Press.

———. 2002. *Diaspora Jews Amidst Greeks and Romans*. Cambridge, Mass.: Harvard University Press.

Gummere, Richard M., ed. and trans. 1953. *Seneca*. Vol. VI. Epistles 93–124. Loeb Classical Library. Cambridge, Mass.: Harvard University Press.

Gundry, Robert H. 1982. *Matthew: A Commentary on His Literary and Theological Art*. Grand Rapids: Eerdmans.

Haag, Ernst. 1963. *Studien zum Buche Judith: Seine theologische Bedeutung und literarische Eigenart*. Trier: Paulinus.

Hadas, Moses. 1951. *Aristeas to Philocrates (Letter of Aristeas)*. New York: Harper.

———. 1953. *The Third and Fourth Books of Maccabees*. New York: Ktav.

Haenchen, Ernst. 1971. *The Acts of the Apostles: A Commentary*. Oxford: Blackwell.

Hagner, Donald A. 1993, 1995. *Matthew*. 2 vols. Word Biblical Commentary. Dallas, Tex.: Word Books.

Hann, Robert R. 1982. *The Manuscript History of the Psalms of Solomon*. Chico, Calif.: Society of Biblical Literature.

———. 1985. "Christos Kurios in Ps Sol 17.32: 'The Lord's Anointed' Reconsidered." *New Testament Studies*.

———. 1988. "The Community of the Pious: The Social Setting of the Psalms of Solomon." *Studies in Religion/Sciences religieuses* 17: 169–89.

Hanson, K. C., and Douglas E. Oakman. 1998. *Palestine in the Time of Jesus: Social Structures and Social Conflicts*. Minneapolis: Fortress.

Harnack, Adolf von. 1908. *The Mission and Expansion of Christianity in the First Three Centuries*. London: Williams and Norgate.

Harrill, J. Albert. 1995. *The Manumission of Slaves in Early Christianity*. Hermeneutische Untersuchungen zur Theologie. Tübingen: J. C. B. Mohr (Paul Siebeck).

Harrison, Stephen J. 2003. "Petronius Arbiter." Pages 1149–50 in *The Oxford Classical Dictionary*. 3d ed., rev. Edited by Simon Hornblower and Antony Spawforth. Oxford: Oxford University Press.

Hayes, Christine. 2002. *Gentile Impurities and Jewish Identities: Intermarriage and Conversion from the Bible to the Talmud*. Oxford: Oxford University Press.

Hempel, Charlotte. 1998. *The Laws of the Damascus Document: Sources, Tradition and Redaction*. Studies on the Texts of the Desert of Judah 29. Leiden: E. J. Brill.

———. 2000. *The Damascus Texts*. Vol. 1 of *Companion to the Qumran Scrolls*. Sheffield: Sheffield Academic Press.

Hengel, Martin. 1974. *Judaism and Hellenism: Studies in Their Encounter in Palestine During the Early Hellenistic Period*. Philadelphia: Fortress.

Hengel, Martin, and Anna Maria Schwemer. 1997. *Paul Between Damascus and Antioch: The Unknown Years*. Louisville: Westminster John Knox.

Henten, J. W. van. 1997. *The Maccabean Martyrs as Saviours of the Jewish People: A Study of 2 and 4 Maccabees*. Supplements to the Journal for the Study of Judaism 57. Leiden: E. J. Brill.

Heseltine, M., and W. H. D. Rouse, ed. and trans.; E. H. Warmington, rev. 1969. *Petronius: Satyricon*. Loeb Classical Library. Cambridge, Mass.: Harvard University Press.

Highet, Gilbert. 1954. *Juvenal the Satirist: A Study*. Oxford: Clarendon Press.

Hinds, Stephen E. 2003. "Ovid." Pages 1084–87 in *The Oxford Classical Dictionary*. 3d ed., rev. Edited by Simon Hornblower and Antony Spawforth. Oxford: Oxford University Press.

Hobbs, T. R. 1985. *2 Kings*. Word Biblical Commentary. Waco, Tex.: Word Books.

Holladay, Carl R. 1983. *Historians*. Vol. 1 of *Fragments from Hellenistic Jewish Authors*. Chico, Calif.: Scholars Press.

———. 1989. *Poets*. Vol 2. of *Fragments from Hellenistic Jewish Authors*. Altanta, Ga.: Scholars Press.

———. 1995. *Aristobulus*. Vol 3. of *Fragments from Hellenistic Jewish Authors*. Altanta, Ga.: Scholars Press.

———. 1996. *Orphica*. Vol 4. of *Fragments from Hellenistic Jewish Authors*. Altanta, Ga.: Scholars Press.

Hollander, Harm W., and M. de Jonge. 1985. *The Testaments of the Twelve Patriarchs: A Commentary*. Studia in Veteris Testamenti pseudepigraphica 8. Leiden: E. J. Brill.

Hollis, A. S. 1977. *Ovid, Ars Amatoria, Book I*. Oxford: Clarendon Press.

Holm-Nielsen, Svend. 1977. *Die Psalmen Salomos*. Jüdische Schriften aus hellenistisch-römischer Zeit IV/2. Gütersloher: Gerd Mohr.

Hooker, Morna D. 1967. *The Son of Man in Mark: A Study of the Background of the Term "Son of Man" and Its Use in St. Mark's Gospel*. Montreal: McGill University Press.

Horgan, Maurya P. 1979. *Pesharim: Qumran Interpretations of Biblical Books*. Catholic Biblical Quarterly Monograph Series 8. Washington, D.C.: Catholic Biblical Association.

van der Horst, Pieter W. 1978. *The Sentences of Pseudo-Phocylides*. Studia in Veteris Testamenti pseudepigraphica 4. Leiden: E. J. Brill.

———. 1985. "Pseudo-Phocylides." Pages 565–82 in *Old Testament Pseudepigrapha*. Vol. 2. Edited by James H. Charlesworth. Garden City, N.Y.: Doubleday.

———. 1988. "Pseudo-Phocylides Revisited." *Journal for the Study of the Pseudepigrapha* 3: 3–30.

———. 1990. "Jews and Christians in Aphrodisias in the Light of Their Relations in Other Cities of Asia Minor." Pages 166–81 in *Essays on the Jewish World of Early Christianity*. Göttingen: Vanderhoeck und Ruprecht.

———. 1991. *Ancient Jewish Epitaphs: An Introductory Survey of a Millennium of Jewish Funerary Epigraphy (300 BCE – 700 CE)*. Kampen: Kok Pharos.

———. 1994. "A New Altar of a Godfearer?" Pages 65–72 in *Hellenism - Judaism - Christianity: Essays on Their Interaction*. Kampen: Kok.

Hultgård, Anders. 1977. *L'eschatologie des Testaments des Douze Patriarches*. Vols. 6–7 of *Historia religionum*. Uppsala: Almqvist & Wiksell.

Humphrey, Edith McEwan. 1995. *The Ladies and the Cities: Transformation and Apocalyptic Identity in Joseph and Aseneth, 4 Ezra, the Apocalypse and the Shepherd of Hermas*. Journal for the Study of the Pseudepigrapha: Supplement Series 17. Sheffield: Sheffield Academic Press.

———. 2000. *Joseph and Aseneth*. Guides to Apocrypha and Pseudepigrapha. Sheffield: Sheffield Academic Press.

Ilan, Tal. 1991–1992. "New Ossuary Inscriptions from Jerusalem." *Scripta Classica Israelica* 11: 149–59.

———.1996. "The Ossuary and Sarcophagus Inscriptions." Pages 57–72 in *The Akeldama Tombs: Three Burial Caves in the Kidron Valley, Jerusalem*. Edited by Gideon Avni and Zvi Greenhut. Jerusalem: Israel Antiquities Authority.

Isaac, E. 1983. "1 Enoch." Pages 5–89 in *Old Testament Pseudepigrapha*. Vol. 1. Edited by James H. Charlesworth. Garden City, N.Y.: Doubleday.

James, M. R. 1892. *The Testament of Abraham: The Greek Text Now First Edited with an Introduction and Notes*. Cambridge: Cambridge University Press.

Jellicoe, Sidney. 1974. *Studies in the Septuagint: Origins, Recensions, and Interpretations: Selected Essays, with a Prolegomenon*. Library of Biblical Studies. New York: Ktav.

Jeremias, Joachim. 1958. *Jesus' Promise to the Nations*. Studies in Biblical Theology. London: SCM Press.

Jervell, Jacob. 1969. "Ein Interpolator Interpretiert: Zu der christlichen Bearbeitung der Testamente der Zwölf Patriarchen." Pages 30–61 in *Studien zu den Testamenten der Zwölf Patriarchen*. Edited by Walther Eltester. Berlin: A. Töpelmann.

Jones, Horace L., ed. and trans. 1930. *Strabo: Geography*. Vol. VII. Books 15–16. Loeb Classical Library. Cambridge, Mass.: Harvard University Press.

Jonge, Marinus de, ed. 1975a. *Studies on the Testaments of the Twelve Patriarchs: Text and Interpretation*. Studia in Veteris Testamenti pseudepigraphica 3. Leiden: E. J. Brill.

———. 1975b. *The Testaments of the Twelve Patriarchs: A Study of Their Text, Composition and Origin*. Assen: Van Gorcum.

———. 1978. *The Testaments of the Twelve Patriarchs: A Critical Edition of the Greek Text*. Leiden: E. J. Brill.

Kampen, John. 1996. "4QMMT and New Testament Studies." Pages 129–44 in *Reading 4QMMT: New Perspectives on Qumran Law and History*. Edited by John Kampen and Moshe J. Bernstein. Atlanta: Scholars Press.

Kasher, Aryeh. 1985. *The Jews in Hellenistic and Roman Egypt: The Struggle for Equal Rights*. Texte und Studien zum antiken Judentum 7. Tübingen: J. C. B. Mohr (Paul Siebeck).

———. 1988. *Jews, Idumaeans, and Ancient Arabs: Relations of the Jews in Eretz-Israel with the Nations of the Frontier and the Desert During the Hellenistic and Roman Era (332 BCE–70 CE)*. Texte und Studien zum antiken Judentum 18. Tübingen: J.C.B. Mohr (Paul Siebeck).

———. 1996. "Polemic and Apologetic: Methods of Writing in *Contra Apionem*." Pages 143–86 in *Josephus's Contra Apionem: Studies in Its Character and Context with a Latin Concordance to the Portion Missing in Greek*. Edited by Louis H. Feldman and John R. Levison. Arbeiten zur Geschichte des antiken Judentums und des Urchristentums 34. Leiden: E. J. Brill.

Kaster, Robert A. 2003. "Varro." Page 1582 in *The Oxford Classical Dictionary*. 3d ed., rev. Edited by Simon Hornblower and Antony Spawforth. Oxford: Oxford University Press.

Kee, Howard Clark. 1978. "Ethical Dimensions of the Testaments of the XII as a Clue to Provenance." *New Testament Studies* 24: 259–70.

———. 1983a. "The Socio-Cultural Setting of Joseph and Aseneth." *New Testament Studies* 29: 394–413.

———. 1983b. "Testaments of the Twelve Patriarchs." Pages 775–828 in *Old Testament Pseudepigrapha*. Vol. 1. Edited by James H. Charlesworth. Garden City, N.Y.: Doubleday.

Klauck, Hans-Josef. 1989. *4 Makkabäerbuch. Jüdische Schriften aus hellenistisch-römischer Zeit* 6. Gütersloh: Gütersloher Verlagshaus G. Mohn.

Klausner, Joseph. 1955. *The Messianic Idea in Israel from Its Beginning to the Completion of the Mishnah*. New York: Macmillan.

Klijn, A. F. J. 1983a. *Der lateinische Text der Apokalypse des Esra*. Texte und Untersuchungen zur Geschichte der altchristlichen Literatur 76. Berlin: Akademie-Verlag.

———. 1983b. "2 Baruch." Pages 615–52 in *Old Testament Pseudepigrapha*. Vol. 1. Edited by James H. Charlesworth. Garden City, N.Y.: Doubleday.

Knibb, Michael A. 1978. *The Ethiopic Book of Enoch: A New Edition in the Light of the Aramaic Dead Sea Fragments*. Oxford: Clarendon Press.

Kolarcik, Michael. 1991. *The Ambiguity of Death in the Book of Wisdom 1–6: A Study of Literary Structure and Interpretation.* Analecta biblica 127. Rome: Editrice Pontificio Istituto Biblico.

Kraabel, A. Thomas. 1969. "῞Υψιστος and the Synagogue at Sardis." *Greek, Roman and Byzantine Studies* 10: 81–93.

———. 1981. "The Disappearance of the 'God-Fearers'." *Numen* 28: 113–26.

———. 1982. "The Roman Diaspora: Six Questionable Assumptions." *Journal of Jewish Studies* 33: 445–64.

———. 1994. "Immigrants, Exiles, Expatriates, and Missionaries." Pages 71–88 in *Religious Propaganda in the New Testament World: Essays in Honor of Dieter Georgi.* Edited by Lukas Bormann, Kelly Del Tredici, and Angela Standhartinger. Leiden: E. J. Brill.

Kraabel, A. Thomas, and Robert S. MacLennan. 1986. "The God-Fearers—A Literary and Theological Invention." *Biblical Archaeology Review* 12: 46–53.

Kraemer, Ross Shepard. 1998. *When Aseneth Met Joseph: A Late Antique Tale of the Biblical Patriarch and His Egyptian Wife, Reconsidered.* Oxford: Oxford University Press.

Kraus, Wolfgang. 1996. *Das Volk Gottes: Zur Grundlegung der Ekklesiologie bei Paulus.* Wissenschaftliche Untersuchungen zum neuen Testament 85. Tübingen: J. C. B. Mohr (Paul Siebeck).

Kugler, Robert A. 2001. *The Testaments of the Twelve Patriarchs.* Guides to Apocrypha and Pseudepigrapha. Sheffield: Sheffield Academic Press.

Kuhn, Karl Georg. 1968. "προσήλυτος." Pages 727–44 in *TDNT*, Vol. VI.

Kuhn, K. G., and H. Stegemann. 1962. "Proselyten." Pages 1248–83 in Pauly-Wissowa *Sup 9.*

Lake, Kirsopp. 1933. "Proselytes and God-Fearers." Pages 74–96 in *The Beginnings of Christianity.* Part I: *The Acts of the Apostles.* Vol. 5. Edited by Kirsopp Lake and F. J. Foakes-Jackson. London: Macmillan.

Lanchester, H. C. O. 1913. "Sibylline Oracles." Pages 368–406 in *The Apocrypha and Pseudepigrapha of the Old Testament.* Vol. 2. Edited by R. H. Charles. Oxford: Clarendon Press.

Lane, Eugene N. 1979. "Sabazius and the Jews in Valerius Maximus: A Re-Examination." *Journal of Roman Studies* 69: 35–38.

Laqueur, Richard Albrecht. 1920. *Der jüdische Historiker Flavius Josephus: Ein biographischer Versuch auf neuer quellenkritischer Grundlage.* Giessen: Münchow'sche Verlangsbuchhandlung.

Lehmann, Yves. 1997. *Varron: Théologien et philosophe romain.* Collection Latomus 237. Bruxelles: Latomus.

Leonhardt, Jutta. 2001. *Jewish Worship in Philo of Alexandria.* Texte und Studien zum antiken Judentum 84. Tübingen: J. C. B. Mohr (Paul Siebeck).

Levine, Amy-Jill. 1992. "Diaspora as Metaphor: Bodies and Boundaries in the Book of Tobit." Pages 105–17 in *Diaspora Jews and Judaism: Essays in Honor of, and in Dialogue with, A. Thomas Kraabel.* Edited by Robert S. MacLennan and J. Andrew Overman. Atlanta: Scholars Press.

———. 1995. "Sacrifice and Salvation: Otherness and Domestication in the Book of Judith." Pages 208–23 in *A Feminist Companion to Esther, Judith and Susanna.* The Feminist Companion to the Bible. Sheffield: Sheffield Academic Press.

Levinskaya, Irina. 1996. *The Book of Acts in Its Diaspora Setting.* Vol. 5 of *The Book of Acts in its First Century Setting.* Edited by Bruce W. Winter. Grand Rapids: Eerdmans.

Lewy, Hans. 1936. *The Pseudo-Philonic De Jona.* Studies and Documents 7. London: Christophers.

Lifshitz, Baruch. 1961. “Inscriptions grecques de Césaré en Palestine (Caesarea Palaestinae).” *Revue biblique* 68: 115–26.

———. 1967. *Donateurs et fondateurs dans les synagogues juives répertoire des dédicaces grecques relatives à la construction et à la réfection des synagogues*. Paris: J. Gabalda.

Long, A. A. 2002. *Epictetus: A Stoic and Socratic Guide to Life*. Oxford: Oxford University Press.

Longenecker, Bruce W. 1991. *Eschatology and the Covenant*. Journal for the Study of the New Testament: Supplement Series 57. Sheffield: JSOT Press.

———.1995. *2 Esdras*. Sheffield: Sheffield Academic Press.

Ludlow, Jared W. 2002. *Abraham Meets Death: Narrative Humor in the Testament of Abraham*. Journal for the Study of the Pseudepigrapha: Supplement Series 41. London: Sheffield Academic Press.

Lüderitz, Gert. 1983. *Corpus jüdischer Zeugnisse aus der Cyrenaika mit einem Anhang von Joyce M. Reynolds*. Wiesbaden: Dr. Ludwig Reichert Verlag.

MacMullen, Ramsay. 1984. *Christianizing the Roman Empire (A.D. 100–400)*. New Haven: Yale University Press.

Maier, Johann. 1985. *The Temple Scroll: An Introduction, Translation and Commentary*. Journal for the Study of the Old Testament: Supplement Series 34. Sheffield: JSOT Press.

Malina, Bruce J., and Richard L. Rohrbaugh. 1998. *Social-Science Commentary on the Gospel of John*. Minneapolis: Fortress.

Marcus, Ralph. 1952. “The *Sebomenoi* in Josephus.” *Jewish Social Studies* 14: 247–50.

Martin-Achard, R. 1962. *A Light to the Nations*. London: Oliver and Boyd.

Mason, Steve. 1991. *Flavius Josephus on the Pharisees: A Composition-Critical Study*. Studia post-Biblica 39. Leiden: E. J. Brill.

———. 1996. “The *Contra Apionem* in Social and Literary Context: An Invitation to Judean Philosophy.” Pages 187–228 in *Josephus's Contra Apionem: Studies in Its Character and Context with a Latin Concordance to the Portion Missing in Greek*. Edited by Louis H. Feldman and John R. Levison. Arbeiten zur Geschichte des antiken Judentums und des Urchristentums 34. Leiden: E. J. Brill.

———. 1998. “‘Should Any Wish to Enquire Further’ (*Ant.* 1.25): The Aim and Audience of Josephus's *Judean Antiquities/Life*.” Pages 64–103 in *Understanding Josephus: Seven Perspectives*. Edited by Steve Mason. Journal for the Study of the Pseudepigrapha: Supplement Series 32. Sheffield: Sheffield Academic Press.

———. 2001. *Life of Josephus*. Vol. 9 of *Flavius Josephus: Translation and Commentary*. Edited by Steve Mason and Louis H. Feldman. Leiden: E. J. Brill.

———. 2003. *Josephus and the New Testament*. Peabody, Mass.: Hendrickson Publishers.

Mason, Steve, ed. 1998. *Understanding Josephus: Seven Perspectives*. Journal for the Study of the Pseudepigrapha: Supplement Series 32. Sheffield: Sheffield Academic Press.

Matthews, Shelly. 2001. *First Converts: Rich Pagan Women and the Rhetoric of Mission in Early Judaism and Christianity*. Stanford, Calif.: Stanford University Press.

McEleney, Neil J. 1973–1974. “Conversion, Circumcision and the Law.” *New Testament Studies* 20: 319–41.

McKnight, Scot. 1989. “*De Vita Mosis* 1.147: Lion Proselytes in Philo?” *The Studia Philonica Annual* 1: 58–62.

———. 1991. *A Light Among the Gentiles: Jewish Missionary Activity in the Second Temple Period*. Minneapolis: Fortress.

Meeks, Wayne A. 1983. *The First Urban Christians: The Social World of the Apostle Paul*. New Haven: Yale University Press.

Mellor, Ronald. 1993. *Tacitus*. New York: Routledge.

Mendelson, Alan. 1988. *Philo's Jewish Identity*. Brown Judaic Studies 161. Atlanta: Scholars Press.

Metzger, Bruce Manning. 1957. *An Introduction to the Apocrypha*. New York: Oxford University Press.

———. 1983. "The Fourth Book of Ezra." Pages 517–59 in *Old Testament Pseudepigrapha*. Vol. 1. Edited by James H. Charlesworth. Garden City, N.Y.: Doubleday.

Milik, J. T. 1956. "Prière de Nabonide et autres écrits d'un cycle de Daniel: Fragments araméens de Qumrân." *Revue biblique* 63: 407–11.

———. 1976. *The Books of Enoch: Aramaic Fragments of Qumrân Cave 4*. Oxford: Clarendon Press.

Mitchell, Stephen. 1993. *Anatolia: Land, Men, and Gods in Asia Minor*. Oxford: Clarendon Press; Oxford University Press.

———. 1999. "The Cult of Theios Hypsistos Between Pagans, Jews and Christians." Pages 81–148 in *Pagan Monotheism in Late Antiquity*. Edited by Polymnia Athanassiadi and Michael Frede. Oxford: Clarendon Press.

Modrzejewski, Joseph. 1995. *The Jews of Egypt from Rameses II to Emperor Hadrian*. Edinburgh: T. & T. Clark.

Moellering, Howard Armin. 1963. *Plutarch on Superstition: Plutarch's De Superstitione, Its Place in the Changing Meaning of Deisidaimonia and in the Context of His Theological Writings*. Boston: Christopher Pub. House.

Montgomery, James A. 1951. *A Critical and Exegetical Commentary on the Books of Kings*. International Critical Commentary. Edinburgh: T. & T. Clark.

Moore, Carey A. 1971. *Esther*. Anchor Bible 7B. Garden City, N.Y.: Doubleday.

———. 1977. *Daniel, Esther, and Jeremiah: The Additions*. Anchor Bible 44. Garden City, N.Y.: Doubleday.

———. 1985. *Judith: A New Translation with Introduction and Commentary*. Anchor Bible 40B. Garden City, N.Y.: Doubleday.

———. 1996. *Tobit: A New Translation with Introduction and Commentary*. Anchor Bible 40A. New York: Doubleday.

Moore, Clifford H. and John Jackson, ed. and trans. 1931. *Tacitus*. Vol. III. Histories 4–5. Annals 1–3. Loeb Classical Library. Cambridge, Mass.: Harvard University Press.

Moore, George Foot. 1927–1930. *Judaism in the First Centuries of the Christian Era*. 3 vols. Cambridge, Mass.: Harvard University Press.

Morris, Jenny. 1987. "The Jewish Philosopher Philo." Pages 809–89 in *The History of the Jewish People in the Age of Jesus Christ*. Vol. 3.2. Edited by Emil Schürer et al. Edinburgh: T. & T. Clark.

Mozley, J. H., and G. P. Goold. 1979. *Ovid: The Art of Love and Other Poems*. Revised by G. P. Goold. Loeb Classical Library. Cambridge, Mass.: Harvard University Press.

Munck, Johannes. 1959. *Paul and the Salvation of Mankind*. London: SCM.

Munoa, Phillip B. 1998. *Four Powers in Heaven: The Interpretation of Daniel 7 in the Testament of Abraham*. Journal for the Study of the Pseudepigrapha: Supplement Series 28. Sheffield: Sheffield Academic Press.

Murphy, Frederick J. 1985. *The Structure and Meaning of Second Baruch*. Society of Biblical Literature Dissertation Series 78. Atlanta: Scholars Press.

Murphy-O'Connor, Jerome. 1992. "Lots of God-Fearers? Theosebeis in the Aphrodisias Inscription." *Revue biblique* 99: 418–24.

Murray, Michele. 2004. *Playing a Jewish Game: Gentile Christian Judaizing in the First and Second Centuries CE*. Études sur le christianisme et le judaïsme 13. Waterloo, Ont.: Wilfrid Laurier University Press.

Myers, Jacob M. 1974. *I and II Esdras*. Anchor Bible 42. Garden City, N.Y.: Doubleday.

Nadel, Benjamin. 1966. "On the Cult of the Nameless 'Most High God' in Tanais in the Third Century C.E. [article and title originally in Russian]." *Listy Filologicke* 89: 13–24.

Naveh, Joseph. 1978. *On Stone and Mosaic: The Aramaic and Hebrew Inscriptions from Ancient Synagogues* [article and title originally in Hebrew]. Tel Aviv: Ha-Hevrah le-hakirat erets Yisrael ve-atikotenah.

Nickau, Klaus. 1966. *Ammonii, Qui Dicitur Liber De Adfinium Vocabulerum Differentia*. Lipsiae: Teubner.

Nickelsburg, George W. E. 1976. *Studies on the Testament of Abraham*. Missoula, Mont.: Scholars Press.

———. 1985. "Revealed Wisdom as a Criterion for Inclusion and Exclusion: From Jewish Sectarianism to Early Christianity." Pages 73–91 in *"To See Ourselves as Others See Us": Christians, Jews, "Others" in Late Antiquity*. Edited by Jacob Neusner and Ernest S. Frerichs. Chico, Calif.: Scholars Press.

———. 2001. *1 Enoch: A Commentary on the Book of 1 Enoch: Chapters 1–36; 81–108*. Hermeneia. Minneapolis: Fortress.

———. 2005. *Jewish Literature Between the Bible and the Mishnah: A Historical and Literary Introduction*. Minneapolis: Fortress.

Niehoff, Maren. 2001. *Philo on Jewish Identity and Culture*. Texte und Studien zum antiken Judentum 86. Tübingen: J. C. B. Mohr (Paul Siebeck).

Nikiprowetzky, Valentin. 1970. *La troisième Sibylle*. Paris: Mouton.

Nilsson, Martin P. 1956. "Zwei Altäre aus Pergamon." *Eranos* 54: 167–73.

———. 1967. *A History of Greek Religion*. Oxford: Clarendon Press.

Nolland, John. 1979. "Proselytes or Politics in Horace Satires I, 4, 138–143?" *Vigiliae christianae* 33: 347–55.

———. 1981. "Uncircumcised Proselytes?" *Journal for the Study of Judaism* 12: 173–94.

North, John. 1992. "The Development of Religious Pluralism." Pages 174–93 in *The Jews Among Pagans and Christians in the Roman Empire*. Edited by Judith Lieu, John North, and Tessa Rajak. London: Routledge.

Novak, David. 1984. *The Image of the Non-Jew in Judaism: An Historical and Constructive Study of the Noahide Laws*. Toronto Studies in Theology. New York & Toronto: Edwin Mellen Press.

Nowell, Irene. 1987. "Tobit: Attitude Toward the Nations." *The Bible Today* 25: 283–88.

Oldfather, W. A, ed. and trans. 1925. *Epictetus*. Vol. I. Discourses Books 1–2. Loeb Classical Library. Cambridge, Mass.: Harvard University Press.

Overman, J. Andrew. 1988. "The God-Fearers: Some Neglected Features." *Journal for the Study of the New Testament* 32: 17–26.

Paton, W. R., and E. L. Hicks. 1891. *The Inscriptions of Cos*. Oxford: Clarendon Press.

Paul, Shalom M. 1991. *Amos: A Commentary on the Book of Amos*. Hermeneia. Minneapolis: Fortress.

Pelletier, André. 1962. *Lettre d'Aristée à Philocrate*. Sér. annexe de textes non-chrétiens 89. Paris: Éditions du Cerf.

Perrin, Bernadotte, ed. and trans. 1919. *Plutarch: Parallel Lives*. Vol. VII. Loeb Classical Library. Cambridge, Mass.: Harvard University Press.

Pervo, Richard I. 1991. "Aseneth and Her Sisters: Women in Jewish Narrative and in the Greek Novels." Pages 145–60 in *"Women Like This": New Perspectives on Jewish Women in the Greco-Roman World*. Edited by Amy-Jill Levine. Atlanta: Scholars Press.

Petit, Françoise. 1978. *Quaestiones in Genesim et in Exodum: Fragmenta Graeca*. Paris: Éditions du Cerf.

Pfuhl, Ernst, and Hans Möbius. 1977. *Die ostgriechischen Grabreliefs*. Mainz am Rhein: Von Zabern.

Philonenko, Marc. 1960. *Les interpolations chrétiennes des Testaments des Douze Patriarches et les manuscrits de Qoumrân*. Cahiers de la Revue d'histoire et de philosophie religieuses 35. Paris: Presses universitaires de France.

———. 1968. *Joseph et Asenath: Introduction, texte critique, traduction, et notes*. Studia post-Biblica 13. Leiden: E. J. Brill.

Porton, Gary. 1988. *Goyim: Gentiles and Israelites in Mishnah-Tosefta*. Atlanta: Scholars Press.

Puech, Emile. 1996. "La prière de Nabonide (4Q242)." Pages 208–27 in *Targumic and Cognate Studies: Essays in Honour of Martin McNamara*. Edited by Kevin J. Cathcart and Michael Maher. Journal for the Study of the Old Testament: Supplement Series 230. Sheffield: Sheffield Academic Press.

Purcell, Nicholas. 2003. "Strabo." Page 1447 in *The Oxford Classical Dictionary*. 3d ed., rev. Edited by Simon Hornblower and Antony Spawforth. Oxford: Oxford University Press.

Rahlfs, A., ed. 1979. *Septuaginta*. 2 vols. Stuttgart: Deutsche Bibelgesellschaft.

Rajak, Tessa. 1981. "Roman Intervention in a Seleucid Siege of Jerusalem?" *Greek, Roman, and Byzantine Studies* 22: 65–81.

———. 1983. *Josephus, the Historian and His Society*. London: Duckworth.

———. 1985. "Jewish Rights in the Greek Cities Under Roman Rule: A New Approach." Pages 19–35 in *Studies in Judaism and Its Greco-Roman Context*. Edited by William Scott Green. Approaches to Ancient Judaism 5. Atlanta: Scholars Press.

———. 1992. "The Jewish Community and Its Boundaries." Pages 9–28 in *The Jews Among Pagans and Christians in the Roman Empire*. Edited by Judith Lieu, John North, and Tessa Rajak. London: Routledge.

———. 1998. "The *Against Apion* and the Continuities in Josephus's Political Thought." Pages 222–46 in *Understanding Josephus: Seven Perspectives*. Edited by Steve Mason. Journal for the Study of the Pseudepigrapha: Supplement Series 32. Sheffield: Sheffield Academic Press.

———. 1999. "The Synagogue Within the Greco-Roman City." Pages 161–73 in *Jews, Christians and Polytheists in the Ancient Synagogue: Cultural Interaction in the Greco-Roman Period*. Edited by Steven Fine. London: Routledge.

Rambo, Lewis R. 1993. *Understanding Religious Conversion*. New Haven: Yale University Press.

Ramsay, William Mitchell. 1895, 1897. *The Cities and Bishoprics of Phrygia: Being an Essay of the Local History of Phrygia from the Earliest Times to the Turkish Conquest*. 2 vols. Oxford: Clarendon Press.

Rawson, Elizabeth. 1985. *Intellectual Life in the Late Roman Republic*. Baltimore, Md.: Johns Hopkins University Press.

Reese, James M. 1970. *Hellenistic Influence on the Book of Wisdom and Its Consequences*. Analecta biblica 41. Rome: Biblical Institute Press.

Rehm, Albert, and Peter Herrmann. 1997–98. *Inschriften von Milet*. Berlin; New York: W. de Gruyter.

Rengstorf, Karl Heinrich 1964. "Απόστολος." *TDNT* 1:407–45.

Reynolds, Joyce M., and Robert Tannenbaum. 1987. *Jews and God-Fearers at Aphrodisias: Greek Inscriptions with Commentary*. Cambridge: Cambridge University Press.

Reynolds, Leighton Durham, Miriam T. Griffin, and Elaine Fantham. 2003. "Annaeus Seneca (2), Lucius." Pages 96–98 in *The Oxford Classical Dictionary*. 3d ed., rev. Edited by Simon Hornblower and Antony Spawforth. Oxford: Oxford University Press.

Richardson, Peter. 1996. *Herod: King of the Jews and Friend of the Romans*. Columbia: University of South Carolina Press.

Robinson, John A. T. 1959–1960. "The Destination and Purpose of St. John's Gospel." *New Testament Studies* 6: 117–31.

Roitman, Adolfo D. 1992. "Achior in the Book of Judith: His Role and Significance." Pages 31–45 in *No One Spoke Ill of Her: Essays on Judith*. Edited by James C. VanderKam. Early Judaism and Its Literature 2. Atlanta: Scholars Press.

Rolfe, J. C., and K. R. Bradley, ed. and trans. 1997–98. *Suetonius. The Lives of the Caesars*. 2 vols. Loeb Classical Library. Cambridge, Mass.: Harvard University Press.

Rowland, Christopher. 1982. *The Open Heaven: A Study of Apocalyptic in Judaism and Early Christianity*. New York: Crossroad.

———. 2002. *Christian Origins: An Account of the Setting and Character of the Most Important Messianic Sect of Judaism*. London: SPCK.

Rudd, Niall. 1966. *The 'Satires' of Horace: A Study*. London: Cambridge University Press.

Runesson, Anders. 1999. "Particularistic Judaism and Universalistic Christianity? Some Critical Remarks on Terminology and Theology." *Studia Theologica* 53: 55–75.

Russell, D. S. 1964. *The Method & Message of Jewish Apocalyptic, 200 BC–AD 100*. Old Testament Library. Philadelphia: Westminster.

Ryle, Herbert Edward, and M. R. James. 1891. *Psalmoi Solomontos = Psalms of the Pharisees, Commonly Called The Psalms of Solomon: The Text Newly Revised from All the Mss.* Cambridge: Cambridge University Press.

Sacks, Kenneth S. 2003. "Ptolemaeus (7)." Page 1271 in *The Oxford Classical Dictionary*. 3d ed., rev. Edited by Simon Hornblower and Antony Spawforth. Oxford: Oxford University Press.

Sanders, E. P. 1976. "The Covenant as a Soteriological Category and the Nature of Salvation in Palestinian and Hellenistic Judaism." Pages 11–44 in *Jews, Greeks and Christians: Religious Cultures in Late Antiquity*. Edited by R. Hamerton-Kelly and R. Scroggs. Leiden: E. J. Brill.

———. 1977. *Paul and Palestinian Judaism*. Philadelphia: Fortress.

———. 1983. "Testament of Abraham." Pages 871–902 in *Old Testament Pseudepigrapha*. Vol. 1. Edited by James H. Charlesworth. Garden City, N.Y.: Doubleday.

———. 1985. *Jesus and Judaism*. Philadelphia: Fortress.

Sanders, James A. 1965. *The Psalms Scroll of Qumran Cave 11 (11QPsa)*. Discoveries in the Judaean Desert 4. Oxford: Clarendon.

———. 1967. *The Dead Sea Psalms Scroll*. Ithaca, N.Y.: Cornell University Press.

Sandmel, Samuel. 1979. *Philo of Alexandria: An Introduction*. New York: Oxford University Press.

Sayler, Gwendolyn B. 1984. *Have the Promises Failed? A Literary Analysis of 2 Baruch*. Society of Biblical Literature Dissertation Series 72. Chico, Calif: Scholars Press.

Schäfer, Peter. 1997. *Judeophobia: Attitudes Toward the Jews in the Ancient World*. Cambridge, Mass.: Harvard University Press.

Schiffman, Lawrence H. 1985. *Who Was a Jew?* Hoboken, N. J.: Ktav.

———. 1987. "The Conversion of the Royal House of Adaibene in Josephus and Rabbinic Sources." Pages 293–312 in *Josephus, Judaism and Christianity*. Edited by Louis H. Feldman and Gohei Hata. Detroit: Wayne State University Press.

———. 1997. "Non-Jews in the Dead Sea Scrolls." Pages 153–71 in *The Quest for Context and Meaning: Studies in Biblical Intertextuality in Honor of James A. Sanders*. Edited by Craig A. Evans and Shemarayahu Talmon. Leiden: E. J. Brill.

Schmidt, Francis. 1976. "The Two Recensions of the Testament of Abraham: In Which Direction Did the Transformation Take Place?" Pages 65–83 in *Studies on the Testament of Abraham*. Edited by George W. E. Nickelsburg. Missoula, Mont.: Scholars Press.

———. 1986. *Le testament grec d'Abraham*. Texte und Studien zum antiken Judentum 11. Tübingen: J. C. B. Mohr (Paul Siebeck).

Schnabel, Eckhard J. 2004. *Early Christian Mission*. 2 vols. Downers Grove, Ill.: InterVarsity Press.

Schnackenburg, Rudolf. 1980. *The Gospel According to St. John*. Vol. 2. New York: Crossroad.

Schoeps, H. J. 1963. *The Jewish-Christian Argument*. New York: Holt, Reinhart and Winston.

Schreckenberg, Heinz. 1968. *Bibliographie zu Flavius Josephus*. Leiden: E. J. Brill.

———. 1979. *Bibliographie zu Flavius Josephus: Supplementband mit Gesamtregister*. Arbeiten zur Literatur und Geschichte des hellenistischen Judentums 14. Leiden: E. J. Brill.

Schreiner, Josef. 1981. *Das 4. Buch Esra*. Jüdische Schriften aus hellenistisch-römischer Zeit 4. Gütersloh: Gütersloher Verlagshaus G. Mohn.

Schüpphaus, Joachim. 1977. *Die Psalmen Salomos: Ein Zeugnis Jerusalemer Theologie und Frömmigkeit in der Mitte des vorchristlichen Jahrhunderts*. Arbeiten zur Literatur und Geschichte des hellenistischen Judentums 7. Leiden: E. J. Brill.

Schürer, Emil. 1897. "Die Juden im bosporanischen Reich und die Genossenschaften der σεβόμενοι θεὸν ὕψιστον Ebendaselbst." *Sitzungsberichte der königlich preussischen Akademie der Wissenschaft zu Berlin* 12/13: 200–25.

———. 1973, 1979, 1986, 1987. *The History of the Jewish People in the Age of Jesus Christ (175 B.C.–A.D. 135)*. 3 volumes in 4. Revised by Matthew Black, Martin Goodman, Fergus Millar, and Geza Vermes. Edinburgh: T. & T. Clark.

Schwabe, Moshe, and Baruch Lifshitz. 1974. *Beth She'arim, Vol. 2: The Greek Inscriptions*. Jerusalem: Massada Press.

Schwartz, Daniel R. 1992. "On Sacrifice by Gentiles in the Temple of Jerusalem." Pages 102–16 in *Studies in the Jewish Background of Christianity*. Tübingen: J. C. B. Mohr (Paul Siebeck).

———. 1996. "God, Gentiles, and the Jewish Law: On Acts 15 and Josephus's Adiabene Narrative." Pages 263–82 in *Geschichte—Tradition—Reflexion: Festschrift für Martin Hengel zum 70. Geburtstag*. Edited by Hubert Cancik, Hermann Lichtenberger, and Peter Schäfer. Tübingen: J. C. B. Mohr (Paul Siebeck).

———. 1998. "The Other in 1 and 2 Maccabees." Pages 30–37 in *Tolerance and Intolerance in Early Judaism and Christianity*. Edited by Graham N. Stanton and Guy G. Strousma. Cambridge: Cambridge University Press.

Schwartz, Seth. 1990. *Josephus and Judaean Politics*. Columbia Studies in the Classical Tradition 18. Leiden: E. J. Brill.

Scott, James M. 1995. "Philo and the Restoration of Israel." Pages 553–75 in *Society of Biblical Literature Seminar Papers*. Edited by Eugene H. Lovering. Atlanta: Scholars Press.

Segal, Alan F. 1990. *Paul the Convert: The Apostolate and Apostasy of Saul the Pharisee*. New Haven: Yale University Press.

———. 1991–1992. “Universalism in Judaism and Christianity.” *Bulletin of the Canadian Society of Biblical Studies* 51: 20–35.

———. 1993. “Conversion and Universalism: Opposites That Attract.” Pages 162–89 in *Origins and Method: Towards a New Understanding of Judaism and Christianity*. Edited by Bradley H. McLean. Journal for the Study of the New Testament: Supplement Series 86. Sheffield: Sheffield Academic Press.

Senior, Donald, and Carroll Stuhlmueller. 1983. *The Biblical Foundations for Mission*. Maryknoll, N.Y.: Orbis Books.

Shackleton Bailey, D. R. 1982. *Profile of Horace*. Cambridge, Mass.: Harvard University Press.

Shackleton Bailey, D. R., ed. and trans. 2000. *Valerius Maximus: Memorable Doings and Sayings*. Loeb Classical Library. Cambridge, Mass.: Harvard University Press.

Shutt, R. J. H. 1985. “Letter of Aristeas.” Pages 7–34 in *Old Testament Pseudepigrapha*. Vol. 2. Edited by James H. Charlesworth. Garden City, N.Y.: Doubleday.

Siegert, Folker. 1973. “Gottesfürchtige und Sympathisanten.” *Journal for the Study of Judaism* 4: 109–64.

———. 1980. *Drei hellenistisch-jüdische Predigten. I. Übersetzung aus dem armenischen und sprachliche Erläuterungen*. Wissenschaftliche Untersuchungen zum neuen Testament 20. Tübingen: J. C. B. Mohr (Paul Siebeck).

———. 1992. *Drei hellenistisch-jüdische Predigten. II. Kommentar*. Wissenschaftliche Untersuchungen zum neuen Testament 61. Tübingen: J. C. B. Mohr (Paul Siebeck).

———. 1994. “Die Heiden in der Pseudo-Philonischen Predigt De Jona.” Pages 52–58 in *Die Heiden: Juden, Christen und das Problem des Fremden*. Edited by Reinhard Feldmeier and Ulrich Heckel. Wissenschaftliche Untersuchungen zum neuen Testament 70. Tübingen: J. C. B. Mohr (Paul Siebeck).

Siegert, Folker, and Jacques de Roulet, trans. 1999. *Prédications synagogales / Pseudo-Philon*. Sources chrétiennes 435. Paris: Cerf.

Skehan, Patrick W., and Alexander A. Di Lella. 1987. *The Wisdom of Ben Sira: A New Translation with Notes*. Anchor Bible 39. New York: Doubleday.

Slingerland, H. Dixon. 1977. *The Testaments of the Twelve Patriarchs: A Critical History of Research*. Missoula, Mont.: Scholars Press.

———. 1986. “The Nature of Nomos (Law) Within the *Testaments of the Twelve Patriarchs*.” *Journal of Biblical Literature* 105: 39–48.

Sly, Dorothy. 1996. *Philo's Alexandria*. London; New York: Routledge.

Smallwood, E. Mary. 1959. “The Alleged Jewish Sympathies of Poppaea Sabina.” *Journal of Theological Studies* 10: 329–35.

———. 1981. *The Jews Under Roman Rule from Pompey to Diocletian*. Studies in Judaism in Late Antiquity 20. Leiden: Brill.

Smith, Morton. 1975. “De Superstitione (Moralia 164E–171F).” Pages 1–35 in *Plutarch's Theological Writings and Early Christian Literature*. Edited by Hans Dieter Betz. Studia ad corpus Hellenisticum Novi Testamenti 3. Leiden: E. J. Brill.

———. 1996. “The Gentiles in Judaism 125 BCE–66 CE.” Pages 263–319 in *Studies in the Cult of Yahweh*, vol 1. Edited by Shaye J. D. Cohen. Leiden: E. J. Brill.

Soll, William. 1989. “Misfortune and Exile in Tobit: The Juncture of a Fairy Tale Source and Deuteronomic Theology.” *Catholic Biblical Quarterly* 51: 209–31.

Spencer, Richard A. 1999. “The Book of Tobit in Recent Research.” *Currents in Research: Biblical Studies* 7: 147–80.

Spilsbury, Paul. 1998a. *The Image of the Jew in Flavius Josephus's Paraphrase of the Bible*. Texte und Studien zum antiken Judentum 69. Tübingen: J. C. B. Mohr (Paul Siebeck).

———. 1998b. "God and Israel in Josephus: A Patron-Client Relationship." Pages 172–91 in *Understanding Josephus: Seven Perspectives*. Edited by Steve Mason. Journal for the Study of the Pseudepigrapha: Supplement Series 32. Sheffield: Sheffield Academic Press.

Standhartinger, Angela. 1994. "'Um zu Sehen die Töchter des Landes': Die Perspective Dinas in der jüdisch-hellenistischen Discussion um Gen 34." Pages 89–116 in *Religious Propaganda in the New Testament World: Essays in Honor of Dieter Georgi*. Edited by Lukas Bormann, Kelly Del Tredici, and Angela Standhartinger. Leiden: E. J. Brill.

Steinmann, Jean. 1953. *Lecture de Judith*. Paris: Lecoffre.

Sterling, Gregory E. 1992. *Historiography and Self-Definition: Josephos, Luke-Acts, and Apologetic Historiography*. Supplements to Novum Testamentum 64. Leiden New York: E. J. Brill.

Stern, Menaham. 1974. *Greek and Latin Authors on Jews and Judaism*. 3 Vols. Jerusalem: Israel Academy of Sciences and Humanities.

Stone, Michael E. 1972. *The Testament of Abraham: The Greek Recensions*. New York: Society of Biblical Literature.

———. 1977. "New Evidence for the Armenian Version of the Testaments of the Twelve Patriarchs." *Revue biblique* 84: 94–107.

———. 1990. *Fourth Ezra: A Commentary on the Book of Fourth Ezra*. Hermeneia. Minneapolis: Fortress.

Sukenik, E. L. 1931. *Jüdische Gräber Jerusalems um Christi Geburt*. Jerusalem: N.p.

Suter, David Winston. 1979. *Tradition and Composition in the Parables of Enoch*. Society of Biblical Literature Dissertation Series 47. Missoula, Mont.: Scholars Press.

Syme, Ronald. 1958. *Tacitus*. Oxford: Clarendon Press.

———. 1978. *History in Ovid*. Oxford: Clarendon Press; Oxford University Press.

Syndikus, Hans Peter. 2003. "Horace." Pages 724–27 in *The Oxford Classical Dictionary*. 3d ed., rev. Edited by Simon Hornblower and Antony Spawforth. Oxford: Oxford University Press.

Tcherikover, Victor. 1956. "Jewish Apologetic Literature Reconsidered." *Eos* 48: 169–93.

———. 1959. *Hellenistic Civilization and the Jews*. Philadelphia: Jewish Publication Society of America.

———. 1961. "The Third Book of Maccabees as a Historical Source of Augustus' Time." *Scripta Hierosolymitana* 7: 1–26.

———. 1974 [1958]. "The Ideology of the Letter of Aristeas." Pages 181–207 in *Studies in the Septuagint: Origins, Recensions, and Interpretations: Selected Essays, with a Prolegomenon*. Edited by Sidney Jellicoe. Library of Biblical Studies. New York: Ktav.

Thackeray, Henry St. John. 1914. "The Letter of Aristeas." Pages 551–606 in *An Introduction to the Old Testament in Greek*. Edited by Henry Barclay Swete and Henry St. John. Thackeray. Cambridge: Cambridge University Press.

———. 1929. *Josephus, the Man and the Historian*. New York: Jewish Institute of Religion Press.

Thackeray, Henry St. John, Ralph Marcus, and Louis H. Feldman. 1926–65. *Josephus*. Loeb Classical Library. Cambridge, Mass.: Harvard University Press.

Thompson, Alden Lloyd. 1977. *Responsibility for Evil in the Theodicy of IV Ezra: A Study Illustrating the Significance of Form and Structure for the Meaning of the Book*. Missoula, Mont.: Scholars Press.

Thompson, L. A. 1982. "Domitian and the Jewish Tax." *Historia* 31: 329–42.

Tiller, Patrick A. 1993. *A Commentary on the Animal Apocalypse of 1 Enoch*. Early Judaism and its Literature 4. Atlanta: Scholars Press.

Trafton, J. L. 1994. "The *Psalms of Solomon* in Recent Research." *Journal for the Study of the Pseudepigrapha* 12: 3–19.

Trebilco, Paul R. 1991. *Jewish Communities in Asia Minor*. Society for New Testament Studies Monograph Series 69. Cambridge: Cambridge University Press.

Vaillant, André. 1976. *Le livre des Secrets d'Hènoch*. Paris: Institut d'Études slaves.

VanderKam, James C. 1984. *Enoch and the Growth of an Apocalyptic Tradition*. Catholic Biblical Quarterly Monograph Series 16. Washington, D.C.: Catholic Biblical Association.

———. 1995. *Enoch, a Man for All Generations*. Columbia: University of South Carolina Press.

VanderKam, James C., ed. 1992. *No One Spoke Ill of Her: Essays on Judith*. Early Judaism and Its Literature. Atlanta: Scholars Press.

Vattier de Bourville, M. J. 1855. "Rapport adressé à M. le ministre de l'instruction publique et des cultes." *Archives des missions scientifiques et littéraires, 1850*, 1855, 580–86.

Vermes, Geza. 1981. *The Dead Sea Scrolls: Qumran in Perspective*. Philadephia: Fortress.

———. 1999. *An Introduction to the Complete Dead Sea Scrolls*. Minneapolis: Fortress.

Viteau, J. 1911. *Les Psaumes de Salomon: introduction, texte grec et traduction*. Paris: Letouzey et Ané.

Volz, Paul. 1934. *Die Eschatologie der jüdischen Gemeinde im neutestamentlichen Zeitalter*. Tübingen: J. C. B. Mohr (Paul Siebeck).

Wallace-Hadrill, Andrew. 1995. *Suetonius*. Bristol Classical Paperbacks. London: Bristol Classical Press.

Walter, Nikolaus. 1964. *Der Thoraausleger Aristobulos: Untersuchungen zu seinen Fragmenten und zu pseudepigraphischen Resten der jüdisch hellenistischen Literatur*. Texte und Untersuchungen zur Geschichte der altchristlichen Literatur. Berlin: Akademie-Verlag.

Wander, Bernd. 1998. *Gottesfürchtige und Sympathisanten: Studien zum heidnischen Umfeld von Diasporasynagogen*. Wissenschaftliche Untersuchungen zum neuen Testament 104. Tübingen: J. C. B. Mohr (Paul Siebeck).

Westermann, William L. 1955. *The Slave Systems of Greek and Roman Antiquity*. Philadelphia: American Philosphical Society.

White, Sidnie Ann. 1992. "In the Steps of Jael and Deborah: Judith as Heroine." Pages 5–16 in *No One Spoke Ill of Her Essays on Judith*. Edited by James C. VanderKam. Early Judaism and its Literature. Atlanta: Scholars Press.

Wilcox, M. 1981. "The God-Fearers in Acts: A Reconsideration." *Journal for the Study of the New Testament* 13: 102–22.

Will, Edouard and Claude Orrieux. 1992. *"Prosélytisme juif?" historie d'une erreur*. Paris: Les Belles Lettres.

Williams, Margaret H. 1989. "The Expulsion of the Jews from Rome in A.D. 19." *Latomus* 48: 765–84.

Williamson, G. A. and E. Mary Smallwood. 1981. *Josephus: The Jewish War*. The Penguin Classics. Harmondsworth: Penguin.

Wills, Lawrence M. 1990. *The Jew in the Court of the Foreign King: Ancient Jewish Court Legends*. Harvard Dissertations in Religion. Minneapolis: Fortress.

———. 1995. *The Jewish Novel in the Ancient World*. Ithaca: Cornell University Press.

Wilson, Gerald Henry. 1985. *The Editing of the Hebrew Psalter*. Society of Biblical Literature Dissertation Series 76. Chico, Calif.: Scholars Press.

Wilson, Stephen G. 1973. *The Gentiles and the Gentile Mission in Luke-Acts*. Society for New Testament Studies Monograph Series 23. Cambridge: Cambridge University Press.

———. 2004. *Leaving the Fold: Apostates and Defectors in Antiquity*. Minneapolis: Fortress.

Winninge, Mikael. 1995. *Sinners and Righteous: A Comparative Study of the Psalms of Solomon and Paul's Letters*. Coniectanea biblica 26. Stockholm: Almqvist & Wiksell.

Winston, David. 1979. *The Wisdom of Solomon: A New Translation with Introduction and Commentary*. Anchor Bible 43. Garden City, N.Y.: Doubleday.

Wise, Michael O. 1990. "The Eschatological Vision of the Temple Scroll." *Journal of Near Eastern Studies* 49: 155–72.

———. 1991. "4Q Florilegium and the Temple of Adam." *Revue de Qumran* 15: 103–32.

Wolfson, Harry A. 1948. *Philo: Foundations of Religious Philosophy in Judaism, Christianity, and Islam*. Cambridge, Mass.: Harvard University Press.

van der Woude, A. S. 1978. "Bemerkungen zum Gebet des Nabonid." Pages 121–29 in *Qumrân: Sa piété, sa théologie et son milieu*. Edited by M. Delcor. Bibliotheca ephemeridum theologicarum lovaniensium 46. Paris & Gembloux: Duculot; Leuven: Leuven University Press.

Wright, R. B. 1985. "Psalms of Solomon." Pages 639–70 in *Old Testament Pseudepigrapha*. Vol. 2. Edited by James H. Charlesworth. Garden City, N.Y.: Doubleday.

Xenakis, Iason. 1969. *Epictetus. Philosopher-Therapist*. The Hague: Martinus Nijhoff.

Yadin, Yigael. 1959. "A Midrash on 2 Sam. vii and Ps. i–ii (4Q Florilegium)." *Israel Exploration Journal* 9: 95–98.

———. 1983. *The Temple Scroll*. Jerusalem: Israel Exploration Society.

Yaron, Reuben. 1960. *Gifts in Contemplation of Death in Jewish and Roman Law*. Oxford: Clarendon Press.

Young, Douglas. 1961. *Theognis, Ps.-Pythagoras, Ps.-Phocylides, Chares, Anonymi Aulodia, Fragmentum Teliambicum*. Leipzig: B. G. Teubner.

Zeitlin, Solomon. 1965–1966. "Did Agrippa Write a Letter to Gaius Caligula?" *Jewish Quarterly Review* 56: 22–31.

Ziegler, Joseph. 1965. *Sapientia Iesu Filii Sirach*. Göttingen: Vandenhoeck & Ruprecht.

———. 1999. *Susanna, Daniel, Bel et Draco*. Septuaginta Vetus Testamentum Graecum. Göttingen: Vandenhoeck & Ruprecht.

Zimmerman, Frank. 1958. *The Book of Tobit: An English Translation with Introduction and Commentary*. New York: Harper & Brothers.

Zuntz, G. 1974. "Aristeas Studies II: Aristeas on the Translation of the Torah." Pages 208–25 in *Studies in the Septuagint: Origins, Recensions, and Interpretations: Selected Essays, with a Prolegomenon*. Edited by Sidney Jellicoe. Library of Biblical Studies. New York: Ktav.

INDICES

1. Principal Texts According to Category

Each of the principal texts discussed in the book has been assigned to one or more of the following four categories: sympathization, conversion, ethical monotheism, and eschatological participation. Inclusion in one or other of these categories means that the text is pertinent to the discussion of the corresponding "pattern of universalism." It does not necessarily imply that the text provides positive evidence for the pattern, though in most cases I believe that it does. For each text I indicate the entry number (e.g., §1) and the page on which the discussion begins. Although the principal texts in each chapter have been discussed in more or less chronological order, they are listed in this index and the next one according to the order found in standard sources (e.g., NRSV for the Apocrypha, Charlesworth for the Pseudepigrapha).

SYMPATHIZATION

Qumran

Philo

Josephus

Greco-Roman Literature

Conversion

Greco-Roman Literature

Early Christian Literature

Inscriptions

Ethical Monotheism

Apocrypha

Pseudepigrapha

Eschatological Participation

2. Ancient Sources

In this index the principal texts can be identified by the bold font used for the text itself, the number of the section in which the text is discussed (e.g., **§1**), and the corresponding page numbers. Normal font is used for other page references to these texts or for other texts. Since Part 1 is organized into relatively short sections according to primary sources, little would be gained by indexing every reference within a particular section either to the principal text itself, in whole or in part, or to the primary source from which it is drawn. Such internal references have not been included in this index. In other words, taking Tobit as an example, the index includes the principal texts from Tobit (1:8 [§13], 13:11–14 [§14], and 14:5–7 [§15]) and any references to Tobit that appear elsewhere in the book (i.e., anywhere except the section in Chapter 2 dealing with Tobit [39–45]), but no further references within this section. In Chapters 5 (Philo) and 6 (Josephus) a similar practice will be followed in the Texts and Commentary portion; references within a passage under discussion and references to other sections of the same treatise (e.g., *Moses*) or work (e.g., *Against Apion*) will not be indexed, though references to other treatises or works will be. All references in the Introduction and Concluding Observations of these chapters will be indexed.

Israel's Scriptures (Hebrew)

Septuagint

Apocrypha

Pseudepigrapha

Qumran

Philo

Josephus

Greco-Roman Literature

New Testament

Early Christian Literature

Inscriptions

Rabbinic literature

3. Modern Authors